INVESTMENT MANAGEMENT

SECURITY ANALYSIS AND PORTFOLIO MANAGEMENT

INVESTMENT MANAGEMENT

SECURITY ANALYSIS AND PORTFOLIO MANAGEMENT

M. Madana Mohan

Ph. D, M. Phil MBA., M.Com.., B.Ed., BLISc. IRPM., PDGCA.

Principal

VISHWA VISHWANI SCHOOL OF BUSINESS

Thumkunta, Shamirpet Road,

Hyderabad – 500 078, (Telangana).

Y. Siva Reddy

MBA., Ph.D

Associate Professor

VISHWA VISHWANI SCHOOL OF BUSINESS

Thumkunta, Shamirpet Road,

Hyderabad – 500 078, (Telangana).

BSP BS Publications™

An Imprint of **BSP Books Pvt. Ltd.**

4-4-309/316, Giriraj Lane,

Sultan Bazar, Hyderabad - 500 095

Investment Management: Security Analysis and Portfolio Management
***by* M. Madana Mohan and Y. Siva Reddy**

Disclaimer: The author and publishers have taken due care to provide authentic, reliable and up-to-date information related to the subject. However, neither the author nor the publisher shall be responsible for any liability for any damage caused because of the use of this book. The respective users must check the accuracy from other sources too.

Published by:

BSP BS Publications™
An Imprint of **BSP Books Pvt. Ltd.**

4-4-309/316, Giriraj Lane,
Sultan Bazar, Hyderabad - 500 095
Phone: 040 - 23445688
e-mail: info@bspbooks.net
www.bspbooks.net

ISBN: 978-93-49562-57-8 (Hardback)

Preface

This book is designed to be an essential resource for finance specialization students across various programs, including B. Com, BBA, BBM, PGDM, M. Com, and MBA. It is organized into 17 comprehensive chapters that explore critical topics in investment management, including a dedicated focus on financial derivatives.

Recognizing the academic needs of students, we have incorporated a variety of practical elements, including problems and solutions based on different university question papers. This approach not only aids in understanding theoretical concepts but also enhances problem-solving skills relevant to real-world scenarios.

To facilitate a thorough understanding of the material, each chapter concludes with a diverse range of assessment tools, including multiple-choice questions, fill-in-the-blanks, short answer questions, essay-type questions, exercise problems with detailed answers, and simple case analyses. This structure is intended to reinforce learning and prepare students for examinations and practical applications in the field of investment management.

We hope this book serves as a valuable companion in your academic journey, equipping you with the knowledge and skills necessary for success in the dynamic world of finance.

We are very thankful to BSP Books Pvt. Ltd., for bringing out this book.

Finally, we would like to express our deep sense of gratitude the Principal Director-Vishwa Vishwani Institutions, **Sri Shrinivas Acharya T**, President **Sri GSS Venkateshwar Rao**, Director Admissions- **Sri Shree Rama Krishna Chinnam**, Vice President & Director- **Prof. Dr. Mohan S Rao**, Director, BS CS **- Dr. P. Chakravarthy** and Director -IMBA, **Prof. Mir Irfan UL Haque.**

We sincerely hope that both students and faculty members find this book highly beneficial. We welcome feedback and suggestions from all readers to help us enhance future editions.

- Authors

Contents

CHAPTER 1

Investment Management

NATURE AND SCOPE OF INVESTMENT

Investment involves making of a sacrifice in the present with the hope of deriving future benefits. Two most important features of an investment are current sacrifice and future benefit. Investment is the sacrifice of certain present values for the uncertain future reward. It involves numerous decision such as type, mix, amount, timing, grade etc., of investment the decision making has to be continues as well as investment may be defined as an activity that commits funds in any financial/physical form in the present with an expectation of receiving additional return in the future. The expectation brings with it a probability that the quantum of return may vary from a minimum to a maximum. This possibility of variation in the actual return is known as investment risk. Thus, every investment involves a return and risk.

Investment as the process of, "sacrificing something now for the prospect of gaining something later". So, the definition implies that we have four dimensions to an investment-time, today be sacrifice and prospective gain. The word investment has many interpretations as it means different things to different persons. For a person who has lent money to another, it may be an investment for a return. Similarly, if a person purchases share of a company, bullion or real estates for the purpose of price appreciation, it is also an investment for him and an insurance plan or a pension plan is an investment to its purchaser. It is clear that investment is a commitment of funds for an earning additional income. In other words, investment is considered the scarifies of certain value of money in anticipation of a reward.

MEANING OF INVESTMENT

The term 'investing" could be associated with the different activities, but the common target in these activities is to "employ" the money (funds) during the time period seeking to enhance the investor's wealth.

Funds to be invested come from assets already owned, borrowed money and savings. By foregoing consumption today and investing their savings, investors expect to enhance their future consumption possibilities by increasing their wealth. Some information presented in some chapters of this material developed for the investments course could be familiar for those who have studied other courses in finance, particularly corporate finance. Corporate finance typically covers such issues as capital structure, short -term and long-term financing, project analysis, current asset management. Capital structure addresses the question of what type of long-term financing is the best for the company under current and forecasted market conditions; project analysis is concerned with the determining whether a project should be undertaken. Current assets and current liabilities management addresses how to manage the day-by-day cash flows of the firm. Corporate finance is also concerned with how to allocate the profit of the firm among shareholders (through the dividend payments), the government (through tax payments) and the firm itself (through retained earnings). But one of the most important questions for the company is financing. Modern firms raise money by issuing stocks and bonds. These securities are traded in the financial markets and the investors have possibility to buy or to sell securities issued by the companies. Thus, the investors and companies, searching for financing, realize their interest in the same place in financial markets.

Corporate finance area of studies and practice involves the interaction between firms and financial markets and Investments area of studies and practice involves the interaction between investors and financial markets. Investments field also differ from the corporate finance in using the relevant methods for research and decision making. Investment problems in many cases allow for a quantitative analysis and modeling approach and the qualitative methods together with quantitative methods are more often used analyzing corporate finance problems. The other very important difference is, that investment analysis for decision making can be based on the large data sets available from the financial markets, such as stock returns, thus, the mathematical statistics methods can be used.

INVESTMENT DEFINITIONS

(i) "An investment is a commitment of funds made in the expectation of some positive rate of returns. If the investment is properly undertaken, the returns will commensurate with the risk the investor assumes".

(ii) "The Purchase by an individual or institutional investor of a financial or real asset that produces a return in proportion to the risk assumed over some future investment period".

(iii) "Investment means conversion of cash or money into monetary asset or a claim on future money for a return. Purchase of asset like shares and securities can either for investment or speculate or both Investments are long term in nature".

In the financial sense, investment is the commitment of a person's funds to derive future income in the form of interest, dividend, premiums, pension's benefits or appreciation in the value of their capital. Purchasing of shares, debentures, post offices savings certificates, insurance policies are all investments in the financial sense. Such investments generate financial assets.

Investing in various types of assets is an interesting activity that attracts people from all walks of life irrespective of their occupation, economic status, education and family background. When a person has more money than he requires for current consumption, he would be coined as a potential investor. The investor who is having extra cash could invest it in securities or in any other assets like or gold or real estate or could simply deposit it in his bank account. The companies that have extra income may like to invest their money in the extension of the existing firm or undertake new venture. All of these activities in a broader sense mean investment. Investment has many meaning and facets. However, investment can be interpreted broadly from three angles –

(i) Economic,

(ii) Layman,

(iii) Financial.

(i) **Economic Investment** includes the commitment of the fund for net addition to the capital stock of the economy. The net additions to the capital stock means an increase in building equipment's or inventories over the amount of equivalent goods that existed, say, one year ago at the same time.

(ii) **Layman uses** of the term investment as any commitment of funds for a future benefit not necessarily in terms of return. For example, a commitment of money to buy a new car is certainly an investment from an individual point of view. In the Economic sense, investment means the net addition to the economy's capital stock which consists of goods and services that are used in the production of other goods services that are used in the production of other goods and services. Investment in this sense includes the information of new productive capital in the form of new construction, plant and machinery; inventories etc., such investment generates Real assets.

(iii) **Financial investment** is the commitment of funds for a future return, thus investment may be understood as an activity that commits funds in any financial or physical form in the presence of an expectation of receiving additional return in future. In the present context of portfolio management, the investment is considered to be financial investment, which imply employment of funds with the objective of realizing additional income or growth in value of investment at a future date. Investing encompasses very conservative position as well as speculation the field of investment involves the study of investment process.

Investment is concerned with the management of an investors' wealth which is the sum of current income and the present value of all future incomes. In this text investment refers to financial assets. Financial investments are commitments of funds to derive income in form of interest, dividend premium, pension benefits or appreciation in the value of initial investment. Hence the purchase of shares, debentures post office savings certificates and insurance policies all are financial investments. Such investment generates financial assets. These activities are undertaken by anyone who desires a return, and is willing to accept the risk from the financial instruments

A genuine investor is interested in a good rate of return, earned on a rather consistent basis for a relatively long period of time. The speculator, on the other hand, seeks opportunities promising very large returns, earned rather quickly. In this process, he assumes a risk that is disproportionate to the anticipated return. Thus, from the discussion we cannot infer that there exists a demarcation between stocks and speculative stocks. The same stock can be purchased as a speculation or as investment, depending on the motive of the purchaser. For example, the decision of the professor to invest in the stock of Reliance industries is considered as a genuine investment because he seems to be interested in a regular dividend income and prospects of long-term capital appreciation. However, if another person buys the same stock with the anticipation that the share price is likely to rise, his decision will be characterized as speculation.

But at the same time both Corporate Finance and Investments are built upon a common set of financial principles, such as the present value, the future value, the cost of capital). And very often investment and financing analysis for decision making use the same tools, but the interpretation of the results from this analysis for the investor and for the financier would be different. For example, when issuing the securities and selling them in the market the company perform valuation looking for the higher price and for the lower cost of capital, but the investor using valuation search for attractive securities with the lower price and the higher possible required rate of return on his/ her investments.

Together with the investment the term ***speculates***

Ion is frequently used. Speculation can be described as investment too, but it is related with the short) term investment horizons and usually involves purchasing the salable securities with the hope that its price will increase rapidly, providing a quick profit. Speculators try to buy low and to sell high, their primary concern is with anticipating and profiting from market fluctuations. But as the fluctuations in the financial markets are and become more and more unpredictable speculations are treated as the investments of highest risk. In contrast, an investment is based upon the analysis and its main goal is to promise safety of principle sum invested and to earn the satisfactory risk. There are *two types of investors:*

(i) Individual investors;

(ii) Institutional investors.

(i) **Individual Investors** are individuals who are investing on their own. Sometimes individual investors are called retail *investors*.

(ii) **Institutional Investors** are entities such as investment companies, commercial banks, insurance companies, pension funds and other financial institutions.

In recent years the process of institutionalization of investors can be observed. As the main reasons for this can be mentioned the fact, that institutional investors can achieve economies of scale, demographic pressure on social security, the changing role of banks. One of important preconditions for successful investing both for individual and institutional investors is the favorable investment environment.

DIRECT INVESTING VS. INDIRECT INVESTING

Investors can use direct or indirect type of investing. ***Direct investing*** is realized using Financial markets and ***Indirect Investing*** involves financial intermediaries. The primary difference between these two types of investing is that applying direct investing investors buy and sell financial assets and manage individual investment portfolio themselves. Consequently, investing directly through financial markets investors take all the risk and their successful investing depends on their understanding of financial markets, its fluctuations and on their abilities to analyze and to evaluate the investments and to manage their investment portfolio.

Contrary, using indirect type of investing investors are buying or selling financial instruments of financial intermediaries (financial institutions) which invest large pools of funds in the financial markets and hold portfolios. Indirect investing relieves investors from making decisions about their portfolio. As shareholders with the ownership interest in the portfolios managed by financial institutions (investment companies, pension funds, insurance companies, commercial banks) the investors are entitled to their share of dividends, interest and capital gains generated and pay their share of the institution's expenses and portfolio management fee. The risk for investor using indirect investing is related more with the credibility of chosen institution and the professionalism of portfolio managers. In general, indirect investing is more related with the financial institutions which are primarily in the business of investing in and managing a portfolio of securities (various types of investment funds or investment companies, private pension funds). By pooling the funds of thousands of investors, those companies can offer them a variety of services, in addition to diversification, including professional management of their financial assets and liquidity.

Investors can "employ" their funds by performing direct transactions, bypassing both financial institutions and financial markets (for example, direct lending). But such transactions are very risky, if a large amount of money is transferred only to one's hands, following the well-known American proverb **"don't put all your eggs in one basket"** That turns to the necessity to diversify your investments. From the other side, direct transactions in the businesses are strictly limited by laws avoiding possibility of money laundering.

TYPES OF INVESTING AND ALTERNATIVES FOR FINANCING

Types of investing in the economy	Alternatives for financing in the economy
Direct investing (through financial markets)	Raising equity capital or borrowing in financial markets
Indirect investing (through financial institutions)	Borrowing from financial institutions
Direct transactions	Direct borrowing, partnership contracts

Companies can obtain necessary funds directly from the general public (those who have excess money to invest) by the use of the financial market, issuing and selling their securities. Alternatively, they can obtain funds indirectly from the general public by using financial intermediaries. And the intermediaries acquire funds by allowing the general public to maintain such investments as savings accounts, Certificates of deposit accounts and other similar vehicles.

Investment Environment can be defined as the existing investment vehicles in the market available for investor and the places for transactions with these investment vehicles. Thus, further in this subchapter the main types of investment vehicles and the types of financial markets will be presented and described.

Investment Vehicles: The financial investments that mean the object will be financial assets and the marketable securities in particular. But even if further in this course only the investments in financial assets are discussed, for deeper understanding the specifics of financial assets comparison of some important characteristics of investment in this type of assets with the investment in physical assets is presented.

Investment in financial assets differs from investment in physical assets in those important aspects:

- **Financial Assets** are divisible, whereas most physical assets are not. An asset is *divisible* if investor can buy or sell small portion of it. In case of financial assets, it means, that investor, for example, can buy or sell a small fraction of the whole company as investment object buying or selling a number of common stocks.
- **Marketability (or Liquidity)** is a characteristic of financial assets that is not shared by physical assets, which usually have low liquidity. Marketability (or liquidity) reflects the feasibility of converting of the asset into cash quickly and without affecting its price significantly. Most of financial assets are easy to buy or to sell in the financial markets.
- The planned **Holding Period** of financial assets can be much shorter than the holding period of most physical assets. ***The holding period for investments** is* defined as the time between signing a purchasing order for asset and selling the asset. Investors acquiring physical asset usually plan to hold it for a long period, but investing in financial assets, such as securities, even for some months or a year can be reasonable. Holding period for investing in financial assets vary in very wide interval and depends on the investor's goals and investment strategy.
- **Information** about financial assets is often more abundant and less costly to obtain, than information about physical assets. ***Information availability*** shows the real possibility of the investors to receive the necessary information which could influence their investment decisions and investment results. Since a big portion of information important for investors in such financial assets as stocks, bonds are publicly available, the impact of many disclosed factors having influence on value of these securities can be included in the analysis and the decisions made by investors. Even if we analyze only financial investment there is a big variety of financial investment vehicles. The ongoing processes of globalization and integration open wider possibilities for the investors to invest into new investment vehicles which were unavailable for them some time ago because of the weak domestic financial systems and limited technologies for investment in global investment environment.

The most important characteristics of investment vehicles on which bases the overall variety of investment vehicles can be assorted are the return on investment and the risk which is defined as the uncertainty about the actual return that will be earned on an investment. Each type of investment vehicles could be characterized by certain level of profitability and risk because of the specifics of these financial instruments. Though all different types of investment vehicles can be compared using characteristics of risk and return and the riskiest as well as less risky investment vehicles can be defined. However, the risk and return on investment are close related and only using both important characteristics we can really understand the differences in investment vehicles.

The main types of financial investment vehicles are:

(i) Short term investment vehicles; Fixed) income securities;

(ii) Common stock;

(iii) Speculative investment vehicles;

(iv) Other investment tools.

Short - Term Investment Vehicles are all those which have a maturity of one year or less. Short term investment vehicles often are defined as money) market instruments, because they are traded in the money market which presents the financial market for short term (up to one year of maturity) marketable financial assets. The risk as well as the return on investments of short-term investment vehicles usually is lower than for other types of investments. The main *short-term investment vehicles* are:

(i) Certificates of deposit;

(ii) Treasury bills;

(iii) Commercial paper;

(iv) Bankers' acceptances;

(v) Repurchase agreements.

Certificate of Deposit is debt instrument issued by bank that indicates a specified sum of money has been deposited at the issuing depository institution. Certificate of deposit bears a maturity date and specified interest rate and can be issued in any denomination. Most certificates of deposit cannot be traded and they incur penalties for early withdrawal. For large money) market investors financial institutions allow their large) denomination certificates of deposits to be traded as negotiable certificates of deposits.

Treasury Bills (also called T-bills) are securities representing financial obligations of the government. T-bills have maturities of less than one year. They have the unique feature of being issued at a discount from their nominal value and the difference between nominal value and discount price is the only sum which is paid at the maturity for these short-term securities because the interest is not paid in cash, only accrued. The other important feature of T) bills is that they are treated as risk) free securities ignoring inflation and default of a government, which was rare in developed countries, the T) bill will pay the fixed stated yield with certainty. But, of course, the yield on T) bills changes over time influenced by changes in overall macroeconomic situation. T-bills are issued on an auction basis. The issuer accepts competitive bids and allocates bills to those offering the highest prices. Non-competitive bid is an offer to purchase the bills at a price that equals the average of the competitive bids. Bills can be traded before the maturity, while their market price is subject to change with changes in the rate of interest. But because of the early maturity dates of T) bills large interest changes are needed to move T) bills prices very far. Bills are thus regarded as high liquid assets.

Commercial Paper is a name for short-term unsecured promissory notes issued by corporation. Commercial paper is a means of short) term borrowing by large corporations. Large, well) established corporations have found that borrowing directly from investors through commercial paper is cheaper than relying solely on bank loans. Commercial paper is issued either directly from the firm to the investor or through an intermediary. Commercial paper, like T-bills is issued at a discount. The most common maturity range of commercial paper is 30 to 60 days or less. Commercial paper is riskier than T-bills, because there is a larger risk that a corporation will default. Also, commercial paper is not easily bought and sold after it is issued, because the issues are relatively small compared with T-bills and hence their market is not liquid.

Bankers Acceptances are the vehicles created to facilitate commercial trade transactions. These vehicles are called bankers acceptances because a bank accepts the responsibility to repay a loan to the holder of the vehicle in case the debtor fails to perform. Bankers acceptances are short-term fixed-income securities that are created by non) financial firm whose payment is guaranteed by a bank. This short-term loan contract typically has a higher interest rate than similar short –term securities to compensate for the default risk. Since bankers' acceptances are not standardized, there is no active trading of these securities.

Repurchase Agreement (often referred to as a repo) is the sale of security with a commitment by the seller to buy the security back from the purchaser at a specified price at a designated future date. Basically, a repo is a collectivized short) term loan, where collateral is a security. The collateral in a repo may be a Treasury security, other money) market security. The difference between the purchase price and the sale price is the interest cost of the loan, from which repo rate can be calculated. Because of concern about default risk, the length of maturity of repo is usually very short. If the agreement is for a loan of funds for one day, it is called overnight repo; if the term of the agreement is for more than one day, it is called a term repo. A reverse repo is the opposite of a repo. In this transaction a corporation buys the securities with an agreement to sell them at a specified price and time. Using repos helps to increase the liquidity in the money market.

Fixed-Income Securities are those which return is fixed, up to some redemption date or indefinitely. The fixed amounts may be stated in money terms or indexed to some measure of the price level. This type of financial investments is presented by two different groups of securities:

(i) Long-term debt securities

(ii) Preferred stocks.

(i) Long-Term Debt Securities can be described as long) term debt instruments representing the issuer's contractual obligation. Long- term securities have maturity longer than 1 year. The buyer (investor) of these securities is landing money to the issuer, who undertake obligation periodically to pay interest on this loan and repay the principal at a stated maturity date.

Long-term debt securities are traded in the capital markets. From the investor's point of view these securities can be treated as a "safe" asset. But in reality, the safety of investment in fixed –income securities are strongly related with the default risk of an issuer. The major representatives of long-term debt securities are *bonds*, but today there are a big variety of different kinds of bonds, which differ not only by the different issuers (governments, municipals, companies, agencies, etc.), but by different schemes of interest payments which is a result of bringing financial innovations to the long-term debt securities market.

As demand for borrowing the funds from the capital markets is growing the long-term debt securities today are prevailing in the global markets. And it is really become the challenge for investor to pick long-term debt securities relevant to his/ her investment expectations, including the safety of investment. We examine the different kinds of long) term debt securities and together with the other aspects in decision making investing in bonds.

(ii) **Preferred Stocks** are equity security, which has infinitive life and pay dividends. But preferred stock is attributed to the type of fixed) income securities, because the dividend for preferred stock is fixed in amount and known in advance. Though, this security provides for the investor the flow of income very similar to that of the bond. The main difference between preferred stocks and bonds is that for preferred stock the flows are forever, if the stock is not callable.

The preferred stockholders are paid after the debt securities holders but before the common stock holders in terms of priorities in payments of income and in case of liquidation of the company. If the issuer fails to pay the dividend in any year, the unpaid dividends will have to be paid if the issue is cumulative.

If preferred stock is issued as noncumulative, dividends for the years with losses do not have to be paid. Usually same rights to vote in general meetings for preferred stockholders are suspended. Because of having the features attributed for both equity and fixed) income securities preferred stocks are known as hybrid security. A most preferred stock is issued as non-cumulative and callable. In recent years the preferred stocks with option of convertibility to common stock are proliferating.

The Common Stock is the other type of investment vehicles which is one of most popular among investors with long) term horizon of their investments. Common stock represents the ownership interest of corporations or the equity of the stock holders. Holders of common stock are entitled to attend and vote at a general meeting of shareholders, to receive declared dividends and to receive their share of the residual assets, if any, if the corporation is bankrupt. The issuers of the common stock are the companies which seek to receive funds in the market and though are "going public". The issuing common stocks and selling them in the market enables the company to raise additional equity capital more easily when using other alternative sources. Thus, many companies are issuing their common stocks which are traded in financial markets and investors have wide possibilities for choosing this type of securities for the investment.

SPECULATIVE INVESTMENT VEHICLES

The term "speculation" could be defined as investments with a high risk and high investment return.

Using these investment vehicles speculators try to buy low and to sell high, their primary concern is with anticipating and profiting from the expected market fluctuations. The only gain from such investments is the positive difference between selling and purchasing prices. Using short-term investment strategies investors can use for speculations other investment vehicles, such as common stock, but here we try to accentuate the specific types of investments which are more risky than other investment vehicles because of their nature related with more uncertainty about the changes influencing their price in the future. ***Speculative investment vehicles*** could be presented by these different vehicles:

(i) Options;
(ii) Futures;
(iii) Commodities, traded on the exchange (coffee, grain metals, other Commodities);

(i) Options are the Derivative Financial Instruments. An options contract gives the owner of the contract the right, but not the obligation, to buy or to sell a financial asset at a specified price from or to another party. The buyer of the contract must pay a fee (option price) for the seller. There is a big uncertainty about if the buyer of the option will take the advantage of it and what option price would be relevant, as it depends not only on demand and supply in the options market, but on the changes in the other market where the financial asset included in the option contract are traded. Though, the option is a risky financial instrument for those investors who use it for speculations instead of hedging.

(ii) Futures are the other type of derivatives. A future contract is an agreement between two parties than they agree tom transact with the respect to some financial asset at a predetermined price at a specified future date. One party agree to buy the financial asset, the other agrees to sell the financial asset. It is very important, that in futures contract case both parties are obligated to perform and neither party charges the fee.

There are two types of people who deal with options (and futures) contracts: speculators and hedgers. Speculators buy and sell futures for the sole purpose of making a profit by closing out their positions at a price that is better than the initial price. Such people neither produce nor use the asset in the ordinary course of business. In contrary, hedgers buy and sell futures to offset an otherwise risky position in the market. Transactions using derivatives instruments are not limited to financial assets. There are derivatives, involving different commodities (coffee, grain, precious metals, and other commodities). But in this course the target is on derivatives where underlying asset is a financial asset.

OTHER INVESTMENT TOOLS

- Various types of investment funds;
- Investment life insurance;
- Pension funds;
- Hedge funds.

Investment companies/Investment funds. They receive money from investors with the common objective of pooling the funds and then investing them in securities according to a stated set of investment objectives. Two types of funds:

- Open-end Funds (Mutual Funds),
- Closed-end Funds (Trusts).
- ***Open - End Funds*** have no pre-determined amount of stocks outstanding and they can buy back or issue new shares at any point. Price of the share is not determined by demand, but by an estimate of the current market value of the fund's net assets per share (NAV) and a commission.

- ***Closed - End Funds*** arc publicly traded investment companies that have issued a specified number of shares and can only issue additional shares through a new public issue. Pricing of closed-end funds is different from the pricing of open-end funds: the market price can differ from the NAV.
- ***Insurance Companies*** are in the business of assuming the risks of adverse events (such as fires, accidents, etc.) In exchange for a flow of insurance premiums.
- Insurance companies are investing the accumulated funds in securities (treasury bonds, corporate stocks and bonds), real estate. Three types of Insurance Companies: life insurance; non-life insurance (also known as property) casualty insurance and re-insurance. During recent years *investment life insurance* became very popular investment alternative for individual investors, because this hybrid investment product allows to buy the life insurance policy together with possibility to invest accumulated life insurance payments or lump sum for a long-time selecting investment program relevant to investor 's future expectations.
- ***Pension Funds*** are an asset pools that accumulates over an employee's working years and pays retirement benefits during the employee's nonworking years. Pension funds are investing the funds according to a stated set of investment objectives in securities (treasury bonds, corporate stocks and bonds), real estate.
- ***Hedge funds*** are unregulated private investment partnerships, limited to institutions and high) net) worth individuals, which seek to exploit various market opportunities and thereby to earn larger returns than are ordinarily available. They require a substantial initial investment from investors and usually have some restrictions on how quickly investor can withdraw their funds. Hedge funds take concentrated speculative positions and can be very risky. It could be noted that originally, the term "hedge" made some sense when applied to these funds.They would by combining different types of investments, including derivatives, try to hedge risk while seeking higher return. But today the word "hedge' is misapplied to these funds because they generally take an aggressive strategy investing in stock, bond and other financial markets around the world and their level of risk is high. Investment generally involves commitment of funds in two types of assets:
    - Real assets
    - Financial assets

Real assets: Investment in this sense includes the information of new productive capital in the form of new construction, plant and machinery; inventories etc., such investment generate Real assets. Real assets are tangible material things like building, automobiles, land, gold etc.

Financial assets: In the financial sense, investment is the commitment of a person's funds to derive future income in the form of interest, dividend, premiums, pension's benefits or appreciation in the value of their capital. Purchasing of shares, debentures, post offices savings certificates, insurance policies are all investments in the financial sense. Such investments generate financial assets.

FINAICIAL ASSETS		REAL ASSETS
Marketable Assets ➢ Shares ➢ Bonds ➢ MF Schemes ➢ UTI Units ➢ Govt. Securities **Non-Marketable Assets** ➢ Bank Deposits ➢ PF &LIC Schemes ➢ Pension Schemes ➢ PO Deposits	**SAVER** ↕ **INVESTOR**	**Real Estate** ➢ House ➢ Land ➢ Buildings ➢ Flats **Bullion** ➢ Gold ➢ Silver ➢ Diamond **Art Instruments** ➢ Paintings ➢ Sculptures **Consumer Durables**

In the Economic sense, investment means the net addition to the economy's capital stock which consists of goods and services that are used in the production of other goods services that are used in the production of other goods and services. Financial assets are piece of paper representing an indirect claim to real assets held by someone else. These pieces of paper represent debt or equity commitment in the form of IOUs or stock certificates. Investments in financial assets consist of:

- Securities (i.e. security forms of) invest
- Non-securities investment

The term 'securities' used in the broadest sense, consists of those papers which are quoted and are transferable. Under section 2 (h) of the Securities Contract (Regulation) Act, 1956 (SCRA) 'securities' include:

1. Shares, Scrip's, stocks, bonds, debentures, debenture stock other marketable securities of a like nature in or of any incorporated company or other body corporate.
2. Government securities.
3. Such other instruments as may be declared by the central
4. Government as securities

OBJECTIVES OF INVESTMENTS

The main investment objectives are increasing the rate of return and reducing the risk. Other objectives like safety, Liquidity and hedge against inflation can considered as subsidiary objectives. Return- Investors always expects a good rate of return from their investments. Rate of return could be defined as the income the investor receives during the holding period stated as a percentage of the purchasing price at the beginning of the holding period.

Return: Investors wish to earn a return on their money. Cash has an opportunity cost. By holding cash, you forego the opportunity to earn a return on that cash. Furthermore, in an inflationary environment, the purchasing power of cash diminishes, with high rates of inflation bringing a relatively rapid decline in purchasing power. In investments it is critical to distinguish between an expected return (the anticipated return for some future period) and a realized return (the actual return over some past period). Investors invest for the future for the returns they expect to earn but when the investing period is over, they are left with their realized returns. What investors actually earn from their holdings may turn out to be more or less than what they expected to earn when they initiated the investment. This point is the essence of the investments process; Investors must always consider the risk involved in investing.

Return = End period value – Beginning period value + Dividend/Beginning Period Value × 100

Return = Sale Price value – Purchasing price value + Dividend Yield/Purchasing Price value × 100

Return = Capital Gains or Price changes or Capital appreciation + Dividend Yield.

Risk: Risk is inherent in any investment. Risk may relate to loss of capital, delay in repayment of capital, nonpayment of return or variability of returns. The risk of an investment is determined by the investments, maturity period, repayment capacity, nature of return commitment and so on. Risk and expected return of an investment are related. Theoretically, the higher the risk, higher is the expected returned. The higher return is a compensation expected by investors for their willingness to bear the higher risk.

Risk of holding securities is related with probability of actual return becoming less than the expected return. The word risk is synonymous with the phrase variability of return. Investment' risk is just as important as measuring its expected rate of return because minimizing risk and maximizing the rate of return are interested objectives in the investment management. An investment whose rate of return varies widely from period to period is risky than whose return that does not change much.

Safety: The safety of investment is identified with the certainty of return of capital without loss of time or money. Safety is another feature that an investor desires from investments. Every investor expects to get back the initial capital on maturity without loss and without delay. The selected investment avenue should be under the legal regulatory frame work. If it is not under the legal frame work, it is difficult to represent the grievances, if any approval of the law itself adds a flour of safety. Even though approved by law, the safety of the principal differs from one mode of investment to another.

Liquidity: An investment that is easily saleable without loss of money or time is said to be liquid. A well-developed secondary market for security increases the liquidity of the investment. An investor tends to prefer maximization of expected return, minimization of risk, safety of funds and liquidity of investment. Marketability of the investment provides liquidity to the investment. The liquidity depends upon the marketing and trading facility

Hedge against inflation since there is inflation in almost all the economy, the rate of return should ensure a cover against the inflation. The return rate should be higher than the rate of inflation; otherwise the investor will have loss in real terms. Growth stocks would appreciate in their values overtime and provide a protection against inflation. The return thus earned should assure thus should the safety of the principal amount, regular flow of income and be hedge against inflation.

Tax Planning in Practice, many investors are taxpaying individuals. As the income tax rates vary from 10% to 30% with a surcharge, the tax liability of those with higher income brackets is somewhat heavy. The interest earned by the investor from his investment is a taxable income and in certain cases tax is to be deducted at source of interest income (TDS). An Investor generally prefers liquidity for his investment along with safety of his funds, a good return with minimum stock.

SECURITIES

Security forms of investments include Equity shares, preference shares, debentures, government bonds, Units of UTI and other Mutual Funds, and equity shares and bonds of Public Sector Undertakings (PSUs). Non-security forms of investments include all those investments, which are not quoted in any stock market and are not freely marketable. viz., bank deposits, corporate deposits, post office deposits, National Savings and other small savings certificates and schemes, provident funds, and insurance policies. Another popular investment in physical assets such as Gold, Silver, Diamonds, Real estate, Antiques etc. Indian investors have always considered the physical assets to be very attractive investments. There are a large number of investment avenues for savers in India. Some of them are marketable and liquid, while others are non-marketable, some of them are highly risky while some others are almost risk less. The investor has to choose proper avenues from among them, depending on his specific need, risk preference, and return expectation. Investment avenues can be broadly Classification of securities under the following heads:

CLASSIFICATION OF SECURITIES

Joint stock companies in the private sector issue corporate securities. These include equity shares, preference shares, and debentures. Equity shares have variable dividend and hence belong to the high-risk high return category; preference shares and debentures have fixed returns with lower risk.

Equity Shares: By investing in shares; investors basically buy the ownership right to that company. When the company makes profits, shareholders receive their share of the profits in the form of dividends. In addition, when a company performs well and the future expectation from the company is very high, the price of the company's shares goes up in the market. This allows shareholders to sell shares at profit, leading to capital gains. Investors can invest in shares either through primary market offerings or in the secondary market. Equity shares can be classified in different ways but we will be using the terminology of Investors. It should be noted that the line of demarcation between the classes are not clear and such classification are not mutually exclusive.

Growth Stocks: Growth stocks are companies whose earnings per share is grows faster than the economy and at a rate higher than that of an average firm in the same industry. Often, the earnings are ploughed back with a view to use them for financing growth. They invest in research and development and diversify with an aggressive marketing policy. They are evidenced by high and strong EPS. Examples are ITC, Dr. Reddy's Bajaj Auto, Statham Computers and Infosys Technologies act... The high growth stocks are often called **"GLAMOUR STOCK' or HIGH FLYERS'.**

Income Stocks: A company that pays a large dividend relative to the market price is called an income stock. They are also called defensive stocks. Drug, food and public utility industry shares are regarded as income stocks. Prices of income stocks are not as volatile as growth stocks.

Cyclical Stocks: Cyclical stocks are companies whose earnings fluctuate with the business cycle. Cyclical stocks generally belong to infrastructure or capital goods industries such as general engineering, auto, cement, paper, construction etc. Their share prices also rise and fall in tandem with the trade cycles.

Discount Stocks: Discount stocks are those that are quoted or valued below their face values. These are the shares of sick units.

Under Valued Stock: Under-valued shares are those, which have all the potential to become growth stocks, have very good fundamentals and good future, but somehow the market is yet to price the shares correctly.

Turn Around Stocks: Turn around stocks are those that are not really doing well in the sense that the market price is well below the intrinsic value mainly because the company is going through a bad patch but is on the way to recovery with signs of turning around the corner in the near future. Examples- EID – Parry in 80's, Tata Tea (Tata Finlay), SPIC, Mukand Iron and steel etc.

Preference Shares: Preference shares refer to a form of shares that lie in between pure equity and debt. They have the characteristic of ownership rights while retaining the privilege of a consistent return on investment. The claims of these holders carry higher priority than that of ordinary shareholders but lower than that of debt holders. These are issued to the general public only after a public issue of ordinary shares.

Debentures and Bonds: These are essentially long-term debt instruments. Many types of debentures and bonds have been structured to suit investors with different time needs. Though having a higher risk as compared to bank fixed deposits, bonds, and debentures do offer higher returns. Debenture investment requires scanning the market and choosing specific securities that will cater to the investment objectives of the investors.

Depository Receipts (GDRs/ADRs): Global Depositary Receipts are instruments in the form of a depositary receipt or certificate created by the overseas depositary bank outside India and issued to non-resident investors against ordinary shares or Foreign Currency Convertible Bonds (FCCBs) of an issuing company. A GDR issued in America is an American Depositary Receipt (ADR). Among the Indian companies, Reliance Industries Limited was the first company to raise funds through a GDR issue. Besides GDRs, ADR are also popular in the capital market. As investors seek to diversify their equity holdings, the option of ADRs and GDRs are very lucrative. While investing in such securities, investors have to identify the capitalization and risk characteristics of the instrument and the company's performance in its home country (underlying asset).

Warrants: A warrant is a certificate giving its holder the right to purchase securities at a stipulated price within a specified time limit or perpetually. Sometimes a warrant is offered with debt securities as an inducement to buy the shares at a later date. The warrant acts as a value addition because the holder of the warrant has the right but not the obligation of investing in the equity at the indicated rate. It can be defined as a long-term call option issued by a company on its shares.

A warrant holder is not entitled to any dividends; neither does he have a voting right. But the exercise price of a warrant gets adjusted for the stock dividends or stock splits. On the expiry date, the holder exercises an option to buy the shares at the predetermined price. This enables the investor to decide whether or not to buy the shares or liquidate the debt from the company. If the market price is higher than the exercise price, it will be profitable for the investor to exercise the warrant. On the other hand, if the market price falls below the exercise price, the warrant holder would prefer to liquidate the debt of the firm.

Derivatives: The introduction of derivative products has been one of the most significant developments in the Indian capital market. Derivatives are helpful risk-management tools that an investor has to look at for reducing the risk inherent in as investment portfolio. The first derivative product that has been offered in the Indian market is the index future. Besides index futures, other derivative instruments such as index options, stock options, have been introduced in the market. Stock futures are traded in the market regularly and in terms of turnover, have exceeded that of other derivative instruments. The liquidity in the futures market is concentrated in very few shares. Theoretically the difference between the futures and spot price should reflect the cost of carrying the position to the future of essentially the interest. Therefore, when futures are trading at a premium, it is an indication that participants are bullish of the underlying security and vice versa. Derivative trading is a speculative activity. However, investors have to utilize the derivative market since the opportunity of reducing the risk in price movements is possible through investments in derivative products.

Deposits: Among non-corporate investments, the most popular are deposits with banks such as savings accounts and fixed deposits. Savings deposits carry low interest rates whereas fixed deposits carry higher interest rates, varying with the period of maturity, Interest is payable quarterly or half-yearly or annually. Fixed deposits may also be recurring deposits wherein savings are deposited at regular intervals. Some banks have reinvestment plans whereby savings are re - deposited at regular intervals or reinvested as the interest gets accrued. The principal and accumulated interests in such investment plans are paid on maturity.

Savings Bank Account with Commercial Banks: A safe, liquid, and convenient investment option, a savings bank account is an ideal investment avenue for setting aside funds for emergencies or unexpected expenses. Investors may prefer to keep an average balance equal to three months of their living expenses. A bank fixed deposit is recommended for those looking for preservation of capital along with current income in the short-term. However, over the long-term the returns may not keep pace with inflation.

Company Fixed Deposits: Many companies have come up with fixed deposit schemes to mobilize money for their needs. The company fixed deposit market is a risky market and ought to be looked at with caution. RBI has issued various regulations to monitor the company fixed deposit market. However, credit rating services are available to rate the risk of company fixed deposit schemes.

The maturity period varies from three to five years. Fixed deposits in companies have a high risk since they are unsecured, but they promise higher returns than bank deposits. Fixed deposit in non-banking financial companies (NBFCs) is another investment avenue open to savers. NBFCs include leasing companies, hire purchase companies, investment companies, chit funds, and so on. Deposits in NBFCs carry higher returns with higher risk compared to bank deposits.

Post Office Deposits and Certificates: The investment avenues provided by post offices are non-marketable. However, most of the savings schemes in post offices enjoy tax concessions. Post offices accept savings deposits as well as fixed deposits from the public. There is also a recurring deposit scheme that is an instrument of regular monthly savings. National Savings Certificates (NSC) is also marketed by post office to investors. The interest on the amount invested is compounded half-yearly and is payable along with the principal at the time of maturity, which is six years from the date of issue. There are a variety of post office savings certificates that cater to specific savings and investment requirements of investors and is a risk free, high yielding investment opportunity. Interest on these instruments is exempt from income tax. Some of these deposits are also exempt from wealth tax.

Life Insurance Policies: Insurance companies offer many investment schemes to investors. These schemes promote savings and additionally provide insurance cover. LIC is the largest life insurance company in India. Some of its schemes include life policies, convertible whole life assurance policies, endowment assurance policies, Jevon Saatchi, Money Back Plan, Jevon Dara, and Marriage Endowment Plan. Insurance policies, while catering to the risk compensation to be faced in the future by investors, also have the advantage of earning a reasonable interest on their investment insurance premiums. Life insurance policies are also eligible for exemption from income tax.

Provident Fund Scheme: Provident fund schemes are deposit schemes, applicable to employees in the public and private sectors. There are three kinds of provident funds applicable to different sectors of employment, namely, Statutory Provident Fund, Recognized Provident Fund, and Unrecognized Provident Fund. In addition to these, there is a voluntary provident fund scheme that is open to any investor, employed or not. This is known as the Public Provident Fund (PPF). Any member of the public can join the PPF, which is operated by the State Bank of India.

Equity Linked Savings Schemes (ELSSs): Investing in ELSSs gets investors a tax rebate of the amount invested. ELSSs are basically growth mutual funds with a lock-in period of three years. ELSSs have a risk higher than PPF and NSCs, but have the potential of giving higher returns.

Pension Plan: Certain notified retirement/pension funds entitle investors to a tax rebate. UTI, LIC, and ICICI are some financial institutions that offer retirement plans to investors.

Government and Semi-Government Securities: Government and semi-government bodies such as the public sector undertakings borrow money from the public through the issue of government securities and public sector bonds. These are less risky avenues of investment because of the credibility of the government and government undertakings. The government issues securities in the money market and in the capital market.

Money market instruments are traded in the Wholesale Debt Market (WDM) trades and retail segments. Instruments traded in the money market are short-term instruments such as treasury bills and repos. The government also introduced the privatizations programmer in many corporate enterprises and these securities are traded in the secondary market. These are the semi-government securities. PSU stocks have performed well during the years 2003-04 in the capital market.

Mutual Fund Schemes: The Unit Trust of India is the first mutual fund in the country. A number of commercial banks and financial institutions have also set up mutual funds. Mutual funds have been set up in the private sector also. These mutual funds offer various investment schemes to investors. The number of mutual funds that have cropped up in recent years is quite large and though, on an average, the mutual fund industry has not been showing good returns, select funds have performed consistently, assuring the investor better returns and lower risk options.

Real Assets: Investments in real assets are also made when the expected returns are very attractive. Real estate, gold, silver, currency, and other investments such as art are also treated as investments since the expectation from holding of such assets is associated with higher returns.

Real Estate: Buying property is an equally strenuous investment decision. Real estate investment is often linked with the future development plans of the location. It is important to check the value while deciding to purchase a movable/immovable property other than buildings. Besides making a personal assessment from the market, the assistance of government-approved values may also be sought. A valuation report indication the value of the each of the major assets and also the basis and manner of valuation can be obtained from an approved value against the payment of a fee. In case of a plantation, a valuation report may also be obtained from recognized private values.

Bullion Investment: The bullion market offers investment opportunity in the form of gold, silver, and other metals. Specific categories of metals are traded in the metals exchange. The bullion market presents an opportunity for an investor by offering returns and end value in future. It has been observed that on several occasions, when the stock market failed, the gold market provided a return on investments. The changing pattern of prices in the bullion market also makes this market risky for investors. Gold and Silver prices are not consistent and keep changing according to the changing local/global demands in the market. The fluctuation prices, however, have been compensated by real returns for many investors who have followed a buy and hold strategy in the bullion market.

TYPES OF GOALS RELATED TO INVESTORS APPROACH

Near- Term High Priority Goals: These are goals, which have a high emotional priority to the investor, and he wishes to achieve these goals within a few years at the most. For example: a new house. As a result; investment vehicles for these goals tend to be either in the forms equivalent to "cash or as fixed income 'instruments with maturity dates in correspondence with the goal dates. Because of the high emotional, importance these goals have, investor, especially the one with moderate means will not go for any other form of investment which involves more risk especially where, his goal is just in sight.

Long-Term High Priority Goals: For most people, this goal is an indication of: their need for financial independence at a point some, years ahead in the future. Egg: Financial independence at the time of retirement or starting a fund for the higher education of a three-year-old child. Normally, we find that either because of personal preference or because the discounted present value is larger in relation to their resources, the time of realization for such goals is set around 60 years of age for people of moderate means. Because of the long-term nature of such goals, there is not a tendency to adopt more aggressive investment approaches except perhaps, in the last 5 to 10 years before retirement. Even then, investors usually prefer a diversified approach using different classes of assets.

Low Priority Goals: These goals are much lower down in the scale of priority and are not particularly painful achieved. For people with moderate to substantial wealth, these could range from a world tour to donating funds for charity. As a result, investors often invest in speculative kinds of investment either for the fun of it or just to tryout some particular aspect of the investment process.

Entrepreneurial or Money-making goals: These goals pertain to individuals who want to maximize wealth and who are not satisfied by the conventional saving and investing approach. These investors usually put all the spare money they have into stocks preferably of the company in which they are working/owing and leave it there until it reaches some level which either the individual believes is enough or is scared of losing what has been built-up over the years. Even then the process of diversification and building up a conventional portfolio usually takes him a long time involving a series of opportunities and sales spread over many years.

INVESTMENT PROCESS

An organized view the investment process involves analyzing the basic nature of investment decisions and organizing the activities in the decision process. A share market needs both investment and speculative activities. Speculative activity adds to the market liquidity. A wider distribution of shareholders makes it necessary for a market to exist. Investment process is governed by the two important facets of investment they are risk and return.

Therefore, we first consider these two basic parameters that are of critical importance to all investors and the tradeoff that exists between expected return and risk. Given the foundation for making investment decisions the tradeoff between expected return and risk- we next consider the decision process in investments as it is typically practiced today. Although numerous separate decisions must be made, for organizational purposes, this decision process has traditionally been divided into a two-step process: security analysis and portfolio management. Security analysis involves the valuation of securities, whereas portfolio management involves the management of an investor's investment selections as a portfolio (package of assets), with its own unique characteristics. The investment process involves a series of activities leading to the purchase of securities or other investment alternatives. The investment process can be dividing into five stages

These parts of the process are summarized and we will return to this figure to emphasize the steps in the process as we move through the book. The book is built around the same structure. It begins with a chapter that provides an overview of investment management as a business. The first major section is on understanding client needs and preferences, where we look at not only how to think about risk in investing but also at how to measure an investor's willingness to take risk. The second section looks at the asset allocation decision, while the third section examines different approaches to selecting assets. The fourth section takes a brief look at the execution decision, and the fifth section develops different approaches to evaluating performance.

The investment process involves a series of activities leading to purchase of securities of other investment alternatives. The investment process can be divided into five stages. They are:

1. Framing of investment policy or knowledge about investments
2. Investment Analysis
3. Portfolio Selection
4. Portfolio construction
5. Portfolio Evaluation (Appraisal)
6. Portfolio Revision

1. **Framing of investment policy or knowledge about investments:** The government or the investor before proceeding into the investment formulates the policy for the system functioning. The essential ingredients of the policy are the investible funds, objective and knowledge about investment alternatives and market.
2. **Investment Analysis:** After formulating the investment policy, the securities to be bought have to be scrutinized through the market industry and company analysis
3. **Portfolio Selection:** The valuation helps the investor to determine the return and risk expected from an investment in the common stock. The intrinsic value of the share is measured through the book value of the share and price earnings ratio. Simple discounting models also be adopted to value the shares. The stock market analysis has developed many advanced models to value the shares. The real worth of the share is compared with the market price and then investment decisions are made.
4. **Portfolio Construction**: A portfolio is a combination of securities. The portfolio is constructed in such a manner to meet the investor goals and objectives. The investor should decide how best it meets the goals with the securities available. The investor tries to attain maximum return with minimum risk. Towards this end, he diversifies his portfolio and allocates funds among the securities. The main objective of diversification is the reduction of risk in the loss of capital and income. A diversified portfolio is comparatively less risky than holding a single portfolio.

4.1 Debt and equality diversification: Debt instrument provides assured return with limited capital appreciation. Common stock provides income and capital gain but with the flavor of uncertainty. Both debt instruments and equity are combined to complement each other.

4.2 Industry diversification: The growth of industry and their reaction to government policies differ from each other. Banking industry shares may provide regular returns but with limited capital appreciation. The IT stock yields high return and capital appreciation. The IT stock yields high return and capital appreciation. The IT stock yields high return and capital appreciation but their growth potential after the Terrorists on WTC building at New York is not predictable.

4.3 Company diversification: When securities from different companies are purchased, the risk is reduced. Technical analyst suggests the investors to buy securities based on the price movement. Fundamental analyst suggests the selection of financially sound and investor friendly companies.

4.4 Selection: Based on the diversification level, industry and company analyses the securities have to be selected. Funds are allocated for the selected securities and allocation of funds will help the managers to construct sound portfolio management process.

5. Portfolio Evaluation: The portfolio has to be managed efficiently. The efficient management calls for evaluation of the portfolio. This process consists of portfolio appraisal and revision.

5.1 Appraisal: The return and risk performance of the security may vary from time to time. The variability in returns of the securities is measured and compared. The developments in the economy, industry and relevant companies from which the stocks are brought have to be appraised. The appraisal may predict the loss and steps can be taken to avoid such losses.

6. Portfolio Revision: Revision depends on results of the appraisal. The low yielding securities with high risk are replaced with high yielding securities with low risk factor. To keep the return at a particular level necessitated the investor to revise the components of the portfolio periodically.

Various types of securities are traded in the market. According to the securities Contracts Regulation Act, Securities include shares, scripts, stocks, bonds, debentures or other marketable securities of any incorporated company or other body corporate, or government. Securities are classified on the basis of return and the source of issue. Based on the income, they may be classified as fixed or variable income securities. Sources of issue may be government, semi government and corporate. Corporate houses generally raise funds through fixed or variable income securities. Sources of issue may be government, semi government and corporate. Corporate houses, generally raise funds through fixed and variable income securities like equity shares, preference shares and debentures.

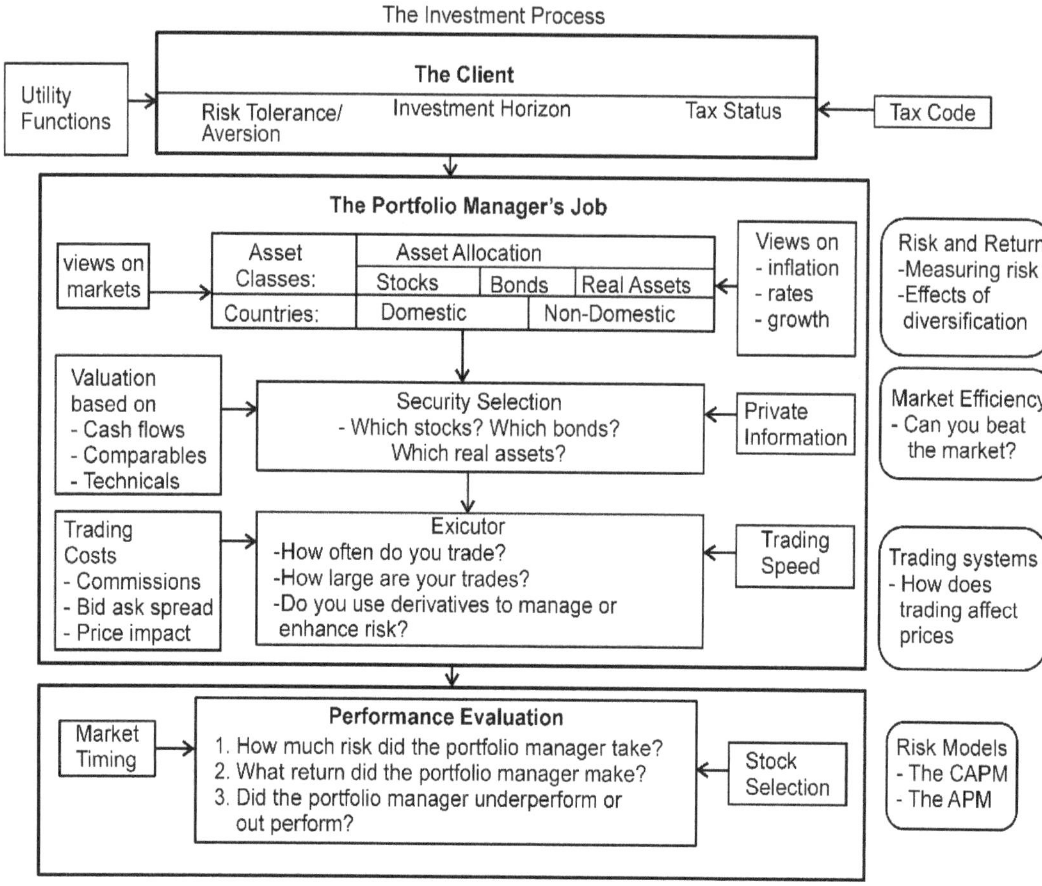

Figure 1.1 Investment management process.

SPECULATOR

An investor has a longer planning horizon. His holding period is usually at least one year. A speculator has a relatively short planning horizon. His holding may be a few days to a few months. Risks disposition an investor is normally not willing to assume more than moderate risk. Rarely does he assume high risk. A speculator is ordinarily willing to assume high risk Return expectation an investor usually seeks a modest rate of return, which is commensurate with the limited risk assumed by him. Return expectation. An investor usually seeks a modest rate of return, which is commensurate with the limited risk assumed by him. A speculator looks for a high rate of return in exchange for the high risk borne by him. Basis of decisions and investor attaches greater significance to fundamental factors and attempts a careful evaluation of the prospects of the firm. A speculator relies more on hearsay, technical charts and market psychology. Leverage Typically an investor uses his own funds and eschews borrowed funds. Leverage Typically an investor uses his own funds and eschews borrowed funds. A speculator normally resorts to borrowings, which can be very substantial, to supplement his personal resources.

ROLE OF SPECULATOR

- The speculator seeks opportunities promising very large returns earned quickly and is the prepared to take higher risk.
- The speculator is interested in getting abnormal return i.e., extremely high rate of return than the normal return in the short-run.
- Speculator investments are made for short-term trade gains through buying and selling investments.
- The speculator is more interested in the market action and its price movement.
- The speculator would like to assure greater risk than the investors. The negative short-term fluctuations affect the speculators in worse manner then the investors.

Speculation means taking up the business risk in the hope of getting short term gain. Speculation essentially involves buying selling activities with the expectation of getting profit from the price fluctuations. The speculator is more interested in the action and its price movement. The investor constantly evaluates the worth of security whereas the speculator evaluates the price movement. He is not worked about the fundamental factors like his counterpart, the investor. Difference between Investor and Speculator

	Investor	Speculator
Time	Plans for a longer time horizon. His holding period may be from one year to few years.	Plans for a very short period. Holding period varies from few days to months
Risk	Assumes moderate risk	Willing to undertake high risk.
Return	Likes to have moderate of return associated with limited risk.	Like to have high return for assuming high risk.
Decision	Considers fundamental factors and evaluates the performance of the company regularly.	Considers inside information, here says and market behavior
Funds	Uses his own funds and avoids borrowed funds	Uses borrowed funds to supplement these personal resources.

Basis	Investment	Speculation
Type of contract	Creditor	Ownership
Basis of acquisition	Usually by outright purchase	Often- on-margin
Length of commitment	Comparatively long term	For a short time only
For a short time only	Earnings of enterprise	Change in market price
Quantity of Risk	Small	Large
Stability of income	Very stable	Uncertain and erratic
Psychological attitude of Participants	Daring and careless reasons for purchase Scientific analysis of intrinsic worth Hunches, tips, “inside dope”, etc.	Cautious and conservative

INVESTMENT VS SPECULATION

Investment and speculation are somewhat different and yet similar because speculation requires an investment and investment are at somewhat speculative. Probably the best way to make a distinction between investment and speculation is considering the role of expectation. Investments are usually made with the expectation that a certain stream of income or a certain price that has existed will not change in the future. Whereas speculation is usually based on the expectation that some change will occur in future, there by resulting a return. Thus, an expected change is the basis for speculation but not for investment.

An investment also can be distinguished from speculation by the time horizon of the investor and often by the risk return characteristic of investment. A true investor is interested in a good and consistent rate of return for a long period of time. In contrast, the speculator seeks opportunities promising very large return earned within a short period of time due to changing environment. Speculation involves a higher level of risk and a more uncertain expectation of returns, which is not necessarily the case with investment.

The identification of these distinctions of these distinctions helps to define the role of the investor and the speculator in the market. The investor can be said to be interested in a good rate of return of a consistent basis over a relatively longer duration. For this purpose, the investor computes the real worth of the security before investing in it. The speculator seeks very large returns from the market quickly. For a speculator, market expectations and price movements are the main factors influencing a buy or sell decision.

Speculation, thus, is riskier than investment in any stock exchange; there are two main categories of speculators called the bulls and bears. A bull buys shares in the expectation of selling them at a higher price. When there is a bullish tendency in the market, share prices tend to go up since the demand for the shares is high. A bear sells shares in the expectation of a fall in price with the intention of buying the shares at a lower price at a future date. These bearish tendencies result in a fall in the price of shares. A share market needs both investment and speculative activities. Speculative activity adds to the market liquidity. A wider distribution of shareholders makes it necessary for a market to exist.

GAMBLING

Gambling is the wagering of money or something of material value on an event with an uncertain outcome with the primary intent of winning additional money and/or material goods. Gambling thus requires three elements be present: consideration, chance and prize. Typically, the outcome of the wager is evident within a short period. Betting (wagering) that must result either in a gain or a loss. Gambling is neither risk taking in the sense of speculation (assumption of substantial short-term risk) nor investing (acquiring property or assets for securing long-term capital gains).

Investment has also to be distinguished from gambling. Typical examples of gambling are horse races, card games, lotteries etc., Gambling involves taking high risks not only for high return but also for thrill and excitement. Gambling is unplanned and nonscientific, without knowledge of the nature of the risk involved. It is surrounded by uncertainty and is based on tips and rumors. In gambling artificial and unnecessary risks are created for increasing the returns.

Investment is an attempt of careful planning, evaluation and allocation of funds to various investments outlets which offer safety of principal with moderate and continuous return over a long period of time. It also differs from insurance which may reduce or eliminate the risk of loss but offers no legitimate chance of gain Gambling, defined as 'the act of betting on an uncertain outcome'. Investing means committing money in order to earn a financial return. The definitions seem to indicate a higher element of chance or randomness in gambling, while investing appears to be more rational.

INVESTMENT AND GAMBLING

Investment has also to be distinguished from gambling. Typical examples of gambling are horse races, card games, lotteries etc., Gambling involves taking high risks not only for high return but also for thrill and excitement. Gambling is unplanned and nonscientific, without knowledge of the nature of the risk involved. It is surrounded by uncertainty and is based on tips and rumors. In gambling artificial and unnecessary risks are created for increasing the returns. Investment is an attempt of careful planning, evaluation and allocation of funds to various investments outlets which offer safety of principal with moderate and continuous return over a long period of time.

DIVERSIFICATION

Diversification means the existence or the development of a very wide variety of financial institutions, markets, instruments, services and practices in the financial system. It also refers to the presence of opportunities for investors to minimize the risk for a given rate of return or they can maximize the return for a given risk.

SOURCES OF INVESTMENT INFORMATION

Security analysis calls for collection of vast information relating to industry, company and market. The market for securities can be regarded as perfect when demand and supply forces determine the prices of securities. Availability of money and flow of information into market largely affect the demand and supply forces determine the prices of securities. Availability of money and flow of information into market largely affect the demand and supply forces. Besides the market price, the investors are interested in knowing the intrinsic value of shares. Intrinsic value of shares means the value of net assets available per equity share of the company. Intrinsic value always revolves around the market price. When the intrinsic value is less than the market price, it is advisable to sell the shares. The sources and types of information are→

1. World affairs
2. Domestic Economic and Political Factors.
3. Industry information
4. Company information
5. Security market information
6. Security Price quotations
7. Data on related markets
8. Data on mutual funds
9. Data on new Issue market
10. Financial information

World Affairs: International Factors such as international political developments, wars, foreign markets etc., influence domestic income, output, employment and investment for domestic market. Besides, financial journals like Economic Times, Financial Express and Business Line etc., report on world economic affairs.

Domestic Economic and Political Factors: Domestic economic and political factors relate to gross domestic products (GDP), agricultural output, monsoon, money supply, inflation, government policies, taxation etc., besides the leading newspapers, financial dailies like economic times, financial express, and business line. Etc.

Industry Information: Industry information is quite essential for investment decision-making. It includes market demand, installed capacity, capacity utilization competitor's activities and their share in the market, market leaders, prospects of the industry, and requirements of foreign buyers, inputs and capital goods in foreign countries.

Company Information: Company information relates to the corporate data, annual reports, stock Exchange publications, Department of company affair's circulars, press releases on corporate affairs by government industry, chamber, and financial papers fortnightly journals of capital markets, Dalai Street, business India furnish information about the companies listed on recognized stock exchanges. They also publish the results of equity and market research. Weekly reviews and monthly reviews of Bombay stock Exchange provide useful information required for security analysis

Security Market Information: Investment management needs information about security market. The credit rating of companies, market analysis, market reports, equity research reports, trade and settlement data, listing and delisting records, book closures, BETA factors etc., are called security market information.

Security Price Quotations: Generally, technical analysis is based on security price quotations. These include price indices, price and volume data, breadth, daily volatility etc. Each stock exchange publishes daily prices and also low and closing quotations of securities traded in it. It is also publishing volume of trade for securities.

Data on Related Markets: Government securities market, money market and Forex market are closely related to security market. Publications of RBI, DFHI, Indian banks association's securities trading corporation, banks, NSE give data on such related markets. RBI publications, foreign exchange Dealers Associations and foreign banks particularly report on Forex market.

Data on Mutual Fund: Various schemes of mutual funds and their performance, net asset value (NAV) and repurchase prices are useful in analyzing various investments avenues available to modern investors. Daily financial papers, investment weekly and Investors' guide publish data on mutual funds. They contain information on current mutual fund schemes, NAV of each scheme, repurchase price, redemption rate of close-ended funds, daily purchase and sale prices for open-ended funds. Most of the mutual funds are quoted on the stock exchanges. In addition, capital market Dalai Street Business India also gives information on mutual funds.

Data on New Issue Market: New issue market is primary market for securities. IN this market, companies issue securities to the investors directly for raising long-term capital. Reports of the merchant bankers and SEBI have firsthand information on the various new issues floated in the market. They get draft prospectus for vetting. A magazine called Prime Publication publishes all information relating to the new issues that are the pipeline. Merchant bankers, underwriters and brokers in the new issue market analyze the performance of the issuing companies. Cable operators' financial journals, etc., give write ups on forthcoming issues. Reserve bank of India Department of Company Affairs publishes periodically data on new issues in the primary market.

Financial Information: The balance sheet analysis done by stock market is based on the financial data furnished by financial statements of a company. The term financial statements refer to the balance sheet, or other statements of financial position of a company and the income and expenditure statement or the profit and loss statement. I addition, the profit allocations statement reconciles the balance in this account at the end of the period with that the beginning. Thus, financial statements contain a summary of the accounts of a company over a period of one year i.e., one financial year (from 1st April to 31 March). The balance sheets show the assets, liabilities and capital at the end of the year. The financial statements of a company help financial analysts to know the financial soundness of the company and its management. Financial statements help the investors in ascertaining whether it is profitable to invest in securities of a particular company.

INVESTMENT PLANNING

Investors like to invest through the instinct and want to gain profit from the market by investing. However, while financial institutions are undoubtedly a part of the process of investing. As investors, it is not surprising that we focus so much of our energy and efforts on investment philosophies and strategies, and so little on the investment process. It is far more interesting to read about how Peter Lynch picks stocks and what makes Warren Buffett a valuable investor, than it is to talk about the steps involved in creating a portfolio or in executing trades. Though it does not get sufficient attention, understanding the investment process is critical for every investor for several reasons:

1. Investment planning centrally depends upon the portfolio of the investor; as a result, the primary step of the investment process is to make a portfolio. By emphasizing the sequence, it provides for an orderly way in which an investor can create his or her own portfolio or a portfolio for someone else.
2. The investment process provides a structure that allows investors to see the source of different investment strategies and philosophies. By so doing, it allows investors to take the hundreds of strategies that they see described in the common press and in investment newsletters and to trace them to their common roots.
3. The investment process emphasizes the different components that are needed for an investment strategy but strategies that look good on paper never work for those who use them.

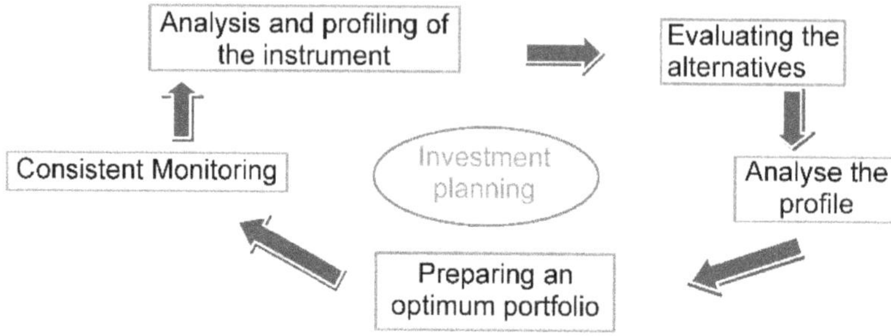

Steps involved in investment planning

Investment is not only prediction it has its own reasons behind every up and down in the market. So, it is having its own theory to move in particular directions. To get in to the market investors must go through the following process.

- **Analysis and profiling of the instrument**: The first step is performing a Need Analysis check. The requirements and expectations of the investor should be met by the instrument. During the profiling investor should consider their age, their profession, the number of dependents, and their income. By doing this check, the risk profile of the investor should be designed.
- **Evaluating the alternatives**: The next step would be revaluating the needs. Other investment instruments and options should be analyzed. The risk-return profile of investment products is evaluated in this step. Every investment product varies according to its return potential and riskiness. Investment products giving a high rate of return are generally risky and volatile. The products giving a lower rate of return usually are less risky.
- **Analyze the Profile**: The next step would be analyses the risk-return profile of the investor on to the investment portfolio. The investment instruments are matched with the risk-return profile of the investor. All the investment alternatives that offer expected rate of return are evaluate for consideration.
- **Preparing an Optimum Portfolio**: Then according to the risk appetite and return pattern an optimum portfolio is designed for the investor. The basket of investment instrument selected in the previous step are given due weightage and appropriate amount of money is invested in each of the investment avenue so as to get maximum return with minimum possible risk.
- **Consistent Monitoring**: Finally, a continuous watch on the portfolio is extremely important. Fundamental analysis of the investment products done in the previous stages would only help in selecting the right product but the right time of entry or exit from a particular stream is evaluated by doing a technical analysis.

Factors to be considered in Investment Decision

The main investment objectives are increasing the rate of return and reducing the risk. Other objectives like safety, Liquidity and hedge against inflation can considered as subsidiary objectives. Return- Investors always expects a good rate of return from their investments.

Rate of return could be defined as the income the investor receives during the holding period stated as a percentage of the purchasing price at the beginning of the holding period. The objectives of investment can be understood in terms of as return, risk, safety, liquidity Hedge against inflation etc.

SUMMARY

1. Investment environment can be defined as the existing investment vehicles in the market available for investor and the places for transactions with these investment vehicles.
2. The most important characteristics of investment vehicles on which bases the overall variety of investment vehicles can be assorted are the return on investment and the risk which is defined as the uncertainty about the actual return that will be earned on an investment. Each type of investment vehicles could be characterized by certain level of profitability and risk because of the specifics of these financial instruments. The main types of financial investment vehicles are: short- term investment vehicles; fixed-income securities; common stock; speculative investment vehicles; other investment tools.
3. Financial market, in which only short-term financial instruments are traded, is Money market, and financial market in which only long-term financial instruments are traded is Capital market.
4. The investment management process describes how an investor should go about making decisions. Investment management process can be disclosed by five-step procedure, which includes following stages (1) Framing of investment policy or knowledge about investments (2) Investment Analysis (3) Portfolio Selection (4) Portfolio construction (5) Portfolio Evaluation (Appraisal) (6) Portfolio Revision.
5. Investment policy includes setting of investment objectives regarding the investment return requirement and risk tolerance of the investor. The other constrains which investment policy should include and which could influence the investment management are any liquidity needs, projected investment horizon and preferences of the investor.
6. Investment portfolio is the set of investment vehicles, formed by the investor seeking to realize its' defined investment objectives. Selectivity, timing and diversification are the most important issues in the investment portfolio formation. Selectivity refers to micro forecasting and focuses on forecasting price movements of individual assets. Timing involves macro forecasting of price movements of particular type of financial asset relative to fixed-income securities in general. Diversification involves forming the investor's portfolio for decreasing or limiting risk of investment.

FILL IN THE BLANKS AND TRUE OR FALSE

1. Return can be in the form of: - (Dividends, Interests, Capital appreciation)
2. An investor with a higher tolerance of risk should tilt his portfolio in favor of________. (Stocks)
3. Investment decisions can be viewed as an integrated process to which security analysis makes its unique contribution. (True)

4. Risk can be referred as the ________ in the return with respect to the expected return. (Volatility)
5. A security represents evidence of :-(A property right)
6. Investments could be made in retail government securities through ☹Primary dealers)
7. The security analysis process will achieve: - (True picture of a company, Normal earning power, Projection of future profitability)
8. The return to the bond investor can be measured in terms of: - Current yield, Yield to maturity, Realized yield
9. The security market is the market for: - (Correct Answer Equity, Debt, Derivatives)
10. In a typical stock market cycle which are the types of trends? (Trends upward, Trend downward, Sideway trend)
11. What is the objective of Portfolio management? (To Minimize risk and maximize return)
12. Current liabilities include all liabilities due in the next ________ and provisions. (12 months)
13. S&P NSE 50 index is known as ________. (NIFTY)
14. ________ measures the profitability of equity funds invested in the firms. (Return on equity)
15. Risk can be referred as the ________ in the return with respect to the expected return. (Volatility)
16. A firm uses a combination of equity and debt for financing its assets. (True)
17. Risk on a portfolio of assets is always same as the risk on individual asset. (False)
18. Debt is less risky source of finance than equity. (False)
19. Post office monthly schemes have a 10-year tenor. (False)
20. With the introduction of on-line trading by NSE and BSE, the role of regional stock exchanges have diminished. (True)
21. How would you rate a portfolio with 90% investment in stocks? (Highly aggressive)
22. ________ absorbs the excess demand or supply generated by hedgers and assume the risk of price fluctuations. (Speculators).
23. Investing in this avenue enable you participate in the equity market indirectly: (Mutual Funds)
24. What is the objective of an income fund? (To provide regular and steady income)
25. What is a technical approach to investment? (A reflection of the idea that prices move in trends which are determined by various factors)
26. Financial assets can be classified as: (Marketable and non-marketable) (Marketable and non-marketable)

27. Active investment managers: (Do not believe that markets are efficient, puts efforts to search mispriced securities in the market, are relatively active traders in securities to acquire abnormal returns).
28. Risk on a portfolio of assets is always same as the risk on individual asset. (False)
29. Question Risk can be referred as the ________ in the return with respect to the expected return. (Volatility).
30. What is the objective of Portfolio management? (To Minimize risk and maximize return)
31. Investors in high tax bracket would benefit by investing in equity schemes. (False)
32. ________ Deal in futures to offset a pre-existing risk. (Hedger)
33. The return to the bond investor can be measured in terms of: - (Current yield, Yield to maturity, Realized yield)
34. Certificate of Deposits offers high rate of interest than Treasury Bills. (True)
35. A security analysis is done: - (For decision making for investments)
36. Secured Premium Notes are ________. (Debentures)
37. Banks issue Guarantees on behalf of their clients. (TRUE)
38. Kian Visas Petra are issued through ________. (Post Offices)
39. The return which the company pays on borrowed funds is termed as......... (Interest)
40. Assets and liabilities in the Balance Sheet are shown at ________ prices (Historical)
41. The classification of return on Investment are .... (Return on Asset, Return on Capital Employed)

SHORT ANSWER QUESTIONS

1. Define Investment.
2. What is Investment management?
3. What is the Investment process?
4. Define direct investing.
5. What are the financial institutions?
6. What are financial intermediaries?
7. Define financial investments.
8. Explain financial markets.
9. Define indirect investing.
10. What are Institutional investors?
11. What is Investment environment?
12. What are Investment vehicles?
13. What are Investment funds?
14. Define Hedge funds.

15. What is Investment portfolio?
16. What are Real investments?
17. What are financial Investments?
18. Define Speculation.
19. Who are Individual investors?
20. Who are Institutional investors
21. Differentiate Direct investing vs. Indirect investing
22. What is Investment environment?
23. What is Holding period?
24. What are Treasury bills?
25. What is Commercial paper?
26. What is Fixed-income securities?
27. What are Preferred stocks?
28. Define common stock.
29. Define Futures.
30. What are financial assets?
31. What are real assets
32. What is Return?
33. What is Risk?
34. Define Liquidity.
35. Define Securities.
36. What is Portfolio construction?
37. Define Security analysis.
38. Define Equity shares.
39. Define Income stocks.
40. What are cyclical stocks?
41. Define Preference shares.
42. Define Debentures and bonds.
43. Define Depository receipts.
44. What is mean by Warrants?
45. Define Derivatives.
46. What are Mutual fund schemes?
47. Define Bullion investment.
48. What is mean by Evaluation of portfolio?
49. Who is Speculator?

50. Who is Investor?
51. What is mean Gambling?
52. Define Diversification.
53. Define new issue market.
54. Define Investment planning.

ESSAY TYPE QUESTIONS

1. What is Investment and investment process describe briefly the different steps involved in investment decisions?
2. Define investment. What are the characteristics of investment and also explain the criteria for evaluating the investment?
3. What is an investment? Explain the scope, importance and features of investment programmers.
4. How investment differs from gambling
5. Explain the concept of liquidity, return and risk related to investment decisions.
6. Explain various approaches to investment decisions.
7. Distinguish between Financial and Real assets.
8. Distinguish investment and speculation.
9. Explain the difference between direct and indirect investing.
10. How could you describe the investment environment?
11. Comment the differences between investment in financial and physical assets using following characteristics: a) Divisibility b) Liquidity c) Holding period d) Information ability.
12. Why preferred stock is called hybrid financial security?
13. Why Treasury bills considered being a risk-free investment?
14. What factors might an individual investor take into account in determining his/ her investment policy?
15. Think about your investment possibilities for 3 years holding period in real investment environment.
    (i) What could be your investment objectives?
    (ii) What amount of funds you could invest for 3 years period?
    (iii) What investment vehicles could you use for investment? (What types of investment vehicles are available in your investment environment?)
    (iv) What type (-is) of investment vehicles would be relevant to you? Why?
    (v) What factors would be critical for your investment decision making in this particular investment environment?

CASE STUDIES

CASE STUDY 1

Mr. Rajesh is an electrical engineer having a fairly long experience of working in various types of industries in India. For quite some time he has been planning to set up his own enterprise. He has been looking for suitable investment opportunities and has been collecting information from various sources. However, he has been skeptical in deciding on any specific idea because of the following reasons.

Any investment in an industrial enterprise will require an expenditure of substantially high amount of funds. Given the fact that he will set up his own business for the first time and has limited funds for investment, such a decision will be crucial for his own financial well - being. Any investment in an industrial enterprise will be irreversible once taken. Hence a wrong decision taken cannot be subsequently changed in order to stop the losses from taking place. In his search for information he has come across a wide range of ideas for new venture, each having its own merits and demerits. Though each idea looked to be attractive to him initially, he is in a state of confusion. In spite of the above problems in decision-making, he is eager to set up his own venture and wants to make the right investment before it gets too late i.e. before other potential competitors exploit the opportunity.

Give Suitable advice to Mr. Rajesh, which will help him in identifying suitable investment opportunities.

CASE STUDY 2

1. Consider two situations, a young man 'X' in early twenties and another young man 'Y' in late thirties. X and Y earn same amount of money. Mr. Y has a family, a house, a car and all the encumbrances related with the marital status. Both of them like to invest in securities. What would be their constraints and objectives of investment?

CHAPTER 1A

Time Value of Money

Time Value of Money (TVM) means that the value of a sum of money received today is more than its value received after some times. Conversely, the sum of money received. In feature is less valuable than it is today. In other words, the present worth of a rupee received today has more value, Individuals, as rational human beings would naturally prefer current receipts to future receipts. The time value of money can also be referred to as time preference for money. This, then, constitutes the rational of considering time value of money in financial decision making. The main reason for time preference for money is to be funds in the re investment opportunities for funds which are received early. The funds so invested will earn a rate of return which will not be possible in case they are received later. The time preference for money is, therefore, expressed generally in terms of a rate of return or more popularly as a discount rate. The expected rate of return as also the time value of money will vary from individual to Individual depending on perception, among other things.

Time Value of Money (TVM) is an important concept in financial management. It can be used to compare investment alternatives and to solve problems involving loans, mortgages, leases, savings, and annuities TVM is based on the concept that a dollar that you have today is worth more than the promise or expectation that you will receive a dollar in the future. Money that you hold today is worth more because you can invest it and earn interest. After all, you should receive some compensation for foregoing spending. For instance, you can invest your dollar for one year at a 6% annual interest rate and accumulate Rs.1.06 at the end of the year. You can say that the future value of the dollar is Rs.1.06 given a 6% interest rate and a one-year period. It follows that the present value of the Rs.1.06 you expect to receive in one year is only Rs.1.

A key concept of TVM is that a single sum of money or a series of equal, evenly-spaced payments or receipts promised in the future can be converted to an equivalent value today. Conversely, you can determine the value to which a single sum or a series of future payments will grow to at some future date.

It has been explained previously that maximization of shareholders' wealth is the basic objective of the finance manager of a firm. This requires him to take appropriate decisions on financing, investment and dividends. While taking these decisions the finance manager must keep the "Time factor" in mind.

For example:

(i) When interest on funds rose will have to be paid;

(ii) When return on investment will be received;

(iii) Whether it will be received on a consistent basis or otherwise etc.

All this requires that the finance manager knows about the various valuation concepts, viz., Compound Value Concept, Annuity Concept, Present Value Concept etc. All these concepts are basically based on this fact that the money has a time value.

The **time value of money** (TVM) or the **present discounted value** is one of the basic concepts of finance. We know that if we deposit money in a bank account we will receive interest. Because of this, we prefer to receive money today rather than the same amount in the future. Money, we receive today is more valuable to us than money received in the future by the amount of interest we can earn with the money. This is referred to as the time value or cash value of money. It is the change in purchasing power of money over time. It also takes into account default risk and inflation. 100 monetary units today is a sure thing and can be enjoyed now. In 5 years, that money could be worthless or not returned to the investor. To adjust for this time value, we use two simple formulae. The present value formula is used to discount future money streams: that is, to convert future amounts to their equivalent present-day amounts. The future value formula is used to convert today's money into the equivalent amount at some time in the future (i.e., to compound money...either a lump sum or streams of payments).

Meaning of Time Value of Money: 'Money has time value' - i.e., the value of money changes over period of time. The value of a rupee received today is different from the value of a rupee to be received after a year. A rupee today has more value than a rupee after a year.

Factors contributing to the Time Value of Money:

Money has a time value because of the following reasons:

- Individuals general y prefer current consumption to future consumption,
- An investor can profitably employ a rupee received today to give him a higher value to be received tomorrow or after a certain period,
- In an inflationary economy the money received today has more purchasing power than money to be received in future.
- **'A bird in hand is worth two in the bush':** This statement implies that people consider a rupee today worth more than a rupee in the future, say, after a year. This is because of the uncertainty connected with the future.

Thus, the fundamental principle behind the concept of time value of money is that a sum of money received today is worth more than if the same is received after some time. For example, if an individual is given an alternative either to receive Rs. 10,000 now or after six months; he will prefer Rs. 10,000 now. This may be because he may be in a position to purchase more goods with this money than what he is going to get for the same amount after six months. Time value of money or time preference for money is one of the central ideas in finance. It becomes important and sometime vital consideration in decision "Taking". This will be clear with the following examples.

This principle allows for the valuation of a likely stream of income in the future, in such a way that annual incomes are discounted and then added together, thus providing a lump-sum "present value" of the entire income stream; all of the standard calculations for time value of money derive from the most basic algebraic expression for the present value of a future sum, "discounted" to the present by an amount equal to the time value of money. For example, the future value sum *FV* to be received in one year is discounted at the rate of interest r to give the present value sum *PV*:

$$PV = \frac{FV}{(1+r)}$$

Some standard calculations based on the time value of money are:

- **Present value**: The current worth of a future sum of money or stream of cash flows, given a specified rate of return. Future cash flows are "discounted" at the *discount rate;* the higher the discount rate, the lower the present value of the future cash flows. Determining the appropriate discount rate is the key to valuing future cash flows properly, whether they be earnings or obligations.[2]
- **Present value of an annuity**: An annuity is a series of equal payments or receipts that occur at evenly spaced intervals. Leases and rental payments are examples. The payments or receipts occur at the end of each period for an ordinary annuity while they occur at the beginning of each period for an annuity due.

  Present value of a perpetuity is an infinite and constant stream of identical cash flows.

Future value: The value of an asset or cash at a specified date in the future, based on the value of that asset in the present.

Future value of an annuity (FVA): The future value of a stream of payments (annuity), assuming the payments are invested at a given rate of interest.

CALCULATIONS

There are several basic equations that represent the equalities listed above. The solutions may be found using (in most cases) the formulas, a financial calculator or a spreadsheet. The formulas are programmed into most financial calculators and several spreadsheet functions (such as PV, FV, RATE, NPER, and PMT).[6]

For any of the equations below, the formula may also be rearranged to determine one of the other unknowns. In the case of the standard annuity formula, however, there is no closed-form algebraic solution for the interest rate (although financial calculators and spreadsheet programs can readily determine solutions through rapid trial and error algorithms).

These equations are frequently combined for particular uses. For example, bonds can be readily priced using these equations. A typical coupon bond is composed of two types of payments: a stream of coupon payments similar to an annuity, and a lump-sum return of capital at the end of the bond's maturity - that is, a future payment. The two formulas can be combined to determine the present value of the bond.

An important note is that the interest rate *i* is the interest rate for the relevant period. For an annuity that makes one payment per year, *i* will be the annual interest rate. For an income or payment stream with a different payment schedule, the interest rate must be converted into the relevant periodic interest rate. For example, a monthly rate for a mortgage with monthly payments requires that the interest rate be divided by 12 (see the example below). See compound interest for details on converting between different periodic interest rates.

The rate of return in the calculations can be either the variable solved for, or a predefined variable that measures a discount rate, interest, inflation, rate of return, cost of equity, cost of debt or any number of other analogous concepts. The choice of the appropriate rate is critical to the exercise, and the use of an incorrect discount rate will make the results meaningless.

For calculations involving annuities, you must decide whether the payments are made at the end of each period (known as an ordinary annuity), or at the beginning of each period (known as an annuity due). If you are using a financial calculator or a spreadsheet, you can usually set it for either calculation. The following formulas are for an ordinary annuity. If you want the answer for the Present Value of an annuity due simply multiply the PV of an ordinary annuity by $(1 + i)$.

Formula

The following formula use these common variables:

- *PV* is the value at time=0 (present value)
- *FV* is the value at time=n (future value)
- *A* is the value of the individual payments in each compounding period
- *n* is the number of periods (not necessarily an integer)
- *i* is the interest rate at which the amount compounds each period
- *g* is the growing rate of payments over each time period

FUTURE VALUE OF A PRESENT SUM

The future value (FV) formula is similar and uses the same variables.

$$FV = PV.(1+i)^n$$

PRESENT VALUE OF A FUTURE SUM

The present value formula is the core formula for the time value of money; each of the other formulae is derived from this formula. For example, the annuity formula is the sum of a series of present value calculations.

The present value (PV) formula has four variables, each of which can be solved for:

$$PV = \frac{FV}{(1+i)^n}$$

The cumulative present value of future cash flows can be calculated by summing the contributions of FV_t, the value of cash flow at time t

$$PV = \sum_{t=1}^{n} \frac{FV_t}{(1+i)^t}$$

Note that this series can be summed for a given value of n, or when n is ∞. This is a very general formula, which leads to several important special cases given below.

PRESENT VALUE OF AN ANNUITY FOR N PAYMENT PERIODS

In this case the cash flow values remain the same throughout the n periods. The present value of an annuity (PVA) formula has four variables, each of which can be solved for:

$$PV(A) = \frac{A}{i} \cdot \left[1 - \frac{1}{(1+i)^n}\right]$$

To get the PV of an annuity due, multiply the above equation by $(1 + i)$.

PRESENT VALUE OF A GROWING ANNUITY

In this case each cash flow grows by a factor of (1+g). Similar to the formula for an annuity, the present value of a growing annuity (PVGA) uses the same variables with the addition of g as the rate of growth of the annuity (A is the annuity payment in the first period). This is a calculation that is rarely provided for on financial calculators.

Where $i \neq g$:

$$PV = \frac{A}{(i-g)} \left[1 - \left(\frac{1+g}{1+i}\right)^n\right]$$

Where $i = g$:

$$PV = \frac{A \times n}{1+i}$$

To get the PV of a growing annuity due, multiply the above equation by $(1 + i)$.

PRESENT VALUE OF A PERPETUITY

A perpetuity is payments of a set amount of money that occur on a routine basis and continues forever. When $n \rightarrow \infty$, the PV of a perpetuity (a perpetual annuity) formula becomes simple division.

$$PV(P) = \frac{A}{i}$$

Present Value of Int Factor Annuity

$$A = P(1 + r/n)^{nt}$$

Example:

Investment P = Rs.1000

Interest i – 6.90% Compounded Qtrly (4 Times in Year)

Tenure Years $n = 5$

$$= 1000 \times (1 + .069/4)^{(5 \text{ yrs} \times 4 \text{ qtrs in a year})} = 1000 \times (1 + 0.069/4)^{20} \approx 1407.84$$

PRESENT VALUE OF A GROWING PERPETUITY

When the perpetual annuity payment grows at a fixed rate (g) the value is theoretically determined according to the following formula. In practice, there are few securities with precise characteristics, and the application of this valuation approach is subject to various qualifications and modifications. Most importantly, it is rare to find a growing perpetual annuity with fixed rates of growth and true perpetual cash flow generation. Despite these qualifications, the general approach may be used in valuations of real estate, equities, and other assets.

This is the well-known Gordon Growth model used for stock valuation.

FUTURE VALUE OF AN ANNUITY

Find	Given	Formula
Future value (F)	Present value (P)	$F = P.(1+i)^n$
Present value (P)	Future value (F)	$P = F.(1+i)^{-n}$
Repeating payment (A)	Future value (F)	$A = F.\frac{i}{(1+i)n - 1}$
Repeating payment (A)	Present value (P)	$A = P.\frac{i(1+i)^n}{(1+i)^n - 1}$
Future value (F)	Repeating payment (A)	$F = A.\frac{(1+i)^n - 1}{i}$
Present value (P)	Repeating payment (A)	$P = A.\frac{(1+i)^n - 1}{i(1+i)^n}$
Future value (F)	Gradient payment (G)	$F = G.\frac{(1+i)^n - in - 1}{i^2}$
Find	**Given**	**Formula**

Table *Contd....*

Present value (P)	Gradient payment (G)	$P = G.\frac{(1+i)^n - in - 1}{i^2(1+i)^n}$
Fixed payment (A)	Gradient payment (G)	$A = G.\left[\frac{1}{i} - \frac{n}{(1+i)^n - 1}\right]$
Future value (F)	Exponentially increasing payment (D) Increasing percentage (g)	$F = D.\frac{(1+g)^n - (1+i)^n}{g-i}$ (for $i \neq g$) $F = D\frac{n(1+i)^n}{1+g}$ (for $i = g$)
Present value (P)	Exponentially increasing payment (D) Increasing percentage (g)	$P = D.\frac{\left(\frac{1+g}{1+i}\right)^n - 1}{g-i}$ (for $i \neq g$) $P = D.\frac{n}{1+g}$ (for $i = g$)

The future value of an annuity (FVA) formula has four variables, each of which can be solved for:

$$FV(A) = A.\frac{(1+i)^n - 1}{i}$$

To get the FV of an annuity due, multiply the above equation by $(1 + i)$.

FUTURE VALUE OF A GROWING ANNUITY [EDIT]

The future value of a growing annuity (FVA) formula has five variables, each of which can be solved for:

Where $i \neq g$:

$$FV(A)A.\frac{(1+i)^n - (1+g)^n}{i-g}$$

Where $i = g$:

$$FV(A) = A.n(1+i)^{n-1}$$

FORMULA TABLE [EDIT]

The following table summarizes the different formulas commonly used in calculating the time value of money.[8]

Notes:

A is a fixed payment amount, every period

G is a steadily increasing payment amount that starts at *G* and increases by *G* for each subsequent period.

D is an exponentially or geometrically increasing payment amount, which starts at D and increases by a factor of (1+g) each subsequent period

DERIVATIONS

ANNUITY DERIVATION

The formula for the present value of a regular stream of future payments (an annuity) is derived from a sum of the formula for future value of a single future payment, as below, where *C* is the payment amount and *n* the period.

A single payment C at future time *m* has the following future value at future time *n*:

$$FV = C(1+i)^{n-m}$$

Summing over all payments from time 1 to time n, then reversing t

$$FVA = \sum_{m=1}^{n} C(1+i)^{n-m} = \sum_{k=0}^{n-1} C(1+i)^{k}$$

Note that this is a geometric series, with the initial value being $a = C$, the multiplicative factor being $1 + i$, with n terms. Applying the formula for geometric series, we get

$$FVA = \frac{C\left(1-(1+i)^{n}\right)}{1-(1+i)} = \frac{C\left(1-(1+i)^{n}\right)}{-i}$$

The present value of the annuity (PVA) is obtained by simply dividing by $(1+i)^n$:

$$PVA = \frac{FVA}{(1+i)^{n}} = \frac{C}{i}\left(1-\frac{1}{(1+i)^{n}}\right)$$

Another simple and intuitive way to derive the future value of an annuity is to consider an endowment, whose interest is paid as the annuity, and whose principal remains constant. The principal of this hypothetical endowment can be computed as that whose interest equals the annuity payment amount:

$$\text{Principal} \times i = C$$

$$\text{Principal} = C/i + \text{goal}$$

Note that no money enters or leaves the combined system of endowment principal + accumulated annuity payments, and thus the future value of this system can be computed simply via the future value formula:

$$FV = PV(1+i)^n$$

Initially, before any payments, the present value of the system is just the endowment principal $(PV = C/i)$. At the end, the future value is the endowment principal (which is the same) plus the future value of the total annuity payments $(FV = C/i + FVA)$. Plugging this back into the equation:

$$\frac{C}{i} + FVA = \frac{C}{i}(1+i)^n$$

$$FVA = \frac{C}{i}\left[(1+i)^n - 1\right]$$

PERPETUITY DERIVATION

Without showing the formal derivation here, the perpetuity formula is derived from the annuity formula. Specifically, the term:

$$\left(1 - \frac{1}{(1+i)^n}\right)$$

can be seen to approach the value of 1 as *n* grows larger. At infinity, it is equal to 1, leaving $\frac{C}{i}$ as the only term remaining.

EXAMPLES

Example 1: Present value

One hundred euros to be paid 1 year from now, where the expected rate of return is 5% per year, is worth in today's money:

$$P = F \times (P/F) = F \times \frac{1}{(1+i)^n} = \frac{100}{1.05} = 95.24$$

So the present value of €100 one year from now at 5% is €95.24.

Example 2: Present value of an annuity — solving for the payment amount

Consider a 10-year mortgage where the principal amount *P* is Rs.200,000 and the annual interest rate is 6%.

The number of monthly payments is

$$n = 10 \text{ years} \times 12 \text{ months per year} = 120 \text{ months}$$

and the monthly interest rate is

$$i = \frac{6\% \text{ per year}}{12 \text{ months per year}} = 0.5\% \text{ per month}$$

The annuity formula for (*A*/*P*) calculates the monthly payment:

$$A = P \times (A/P) = P \times \frac{i(1+i)^n}{(1+i)^n - 1} = \$200{,}000 \times \frac{0.005(1.005)^{120}}{(1.005)^{120} - 1}$$

$$\approx \$200{,}000 \times 0.01110205 \approx \$2{,}220.41 \text{ per month}$$

This is considering an interest rate compounding monthly. If the interest were only to compound yearly at 6%, the monthly payment would be significantly different.

AN APPROXIMATE SOLUTION

For those who only want a rough idea of the mortgage payment there is a much less intimidating approximate formula here. For the numbers given above we simply compute an approximate annual repayment of 200,000*(1/n + (2/3)*i) where n=10 yrs, i=0.06. So 200,000*(1/10 + (2/3)*0.06) = 200,000*(0.1+0.04) = 200,000*0.14 = Rs.28,000 per year, roughly, via mental arithmetic alone. Note, as this is an approximation we may ignore the subtleties of monthly compounding. Now Rs.28,000 per year is about 28,000/12 = Rs.2,333 per month, which approximates the true answer to within about 5% but has required only mental arithmetic.

Example 3: Solving for the period needed to double money

Consider a deposit of £100 placed at 10% (annual). How many years are needed for the value of the deposit to double to £200?

Using the algebraic identity that if:

$$x = b^y$$

then

$$y = \frac{\log(x)}{\log(b)}$$

The present value formula can be rearranged such that:

$$y = \frac{\log\left(\frac{FV}{PV}\right)}{\log(1+i)} = \frac{\log\left(\frac{200}{100}\right)}{\log(1.10)} = 7.27(\text{years})$$

This same method can be used to determine the length of time needed to increase a deposit to any particular sum, as long as the interest rate is known. For the period of time needed to double an investment, the Rule of 72 is a useful short-cut that gives a reasonable approximation of the period needed.

Example 4: What return is needed to double money?

Similarly, the present value formula can be rearranged to determine what rate of return is needed to accumulate a given amount from an investment. For example, £100 is invested today and £200 return is expected in five years; what rate of return (interest rate) does this represent?

The present value formula restated in terms of the interest rate is:

$$i=\left(\frac{FV}{PV}\right)^{\frac{1}{n}}-1=\left(\frac{200}{100}\right)^{\frac{1}{5}}-1=2^{0.20}-1=0.15=15\%$$

Example 5: Calculate the value of a regular savings deposit in the future.

To calculate the future value of a stream of savings deposit in the future requires two steps, or, alternatively, combining the two steps into one large formula. First, calculate the present value of a stream of deposits of Rs.1,000 every year for 20 years earning 7% interest:

$$PVA=A.\frac{1-\frac{1}{(1+i)^{n}}}{i}=1000.\frac{1-\frac{1}{(1+.07)^{20}}}{.07}=1000.\frac{1-0.258}{.07}=1000\times 10.594\approx \$10.594$$

This does not sound like very much, but remember - this is *future money* discounted back to its value *today*; it is understandably lower. To calculate the future value (at the end of the twenty-year period):

$$FV = PV\,(1+i)^{n} = \$10,594\times(1+.07)^{20} \approx \$10,594\times 3.87 = \$40,995$$

These steps can be combined into a single formula:

$$FV=A.\frac{1-\frac{1}{(1+i)^{n}}}{i}.(1+i)^{n}=A.\frac{(1+i)^{n}-1}{i}$$

Example 6: Price/earnings (P/E) ratio

It is often mentioned that perpetuities, or securities with an indefinitely long maturity, are rare or unrealistic, and particularly those with a growing payment. In fact, many types of assets have characteristics that are similar to perpetuities. Examples might include income-oriented real estate, preferred shares, and even most forms of publicly traded stocks. Frequently, the terminology may be slightly different, but are based on the fundamentals of time value of money calculations. The application of this methodology is subject to various qualifications or modifications, such as the Gordon growth model.

For example, stocks are commonly noted as trading at a certain P/E ratio. The P/E ratio is easily recognized as a variation on the perpetuity or growing perpetuity formulae - save that the P/E ratio is usually cited as the *inverse* of the "rate" in the perpetuity formula.

If we substitute for the time being: the *price* of the stock for the present value; the earnings per share of the stock for the cash annuity; and, the discount rate of the stock for the interest rate, we can see that:

$$\frac{P}{E}=\frac{1}{i}=\frac{PV}{A}$$

And in fact, the P/E ratio is analogous to the inverse of the interest rate (or discount rate).

$$\frac{1}{P/E}=i$$

Of course, stocks may have increasing earnings. The formulation above does not allow for growth in earnings, but to incorporate growth, the formula can be restated as follows:

$$\frac{P}{E}=\frac{1}{(i-g)}$$

If we wish to determine the implied rate of growth (if we are given the discount rate), we may solve for *g*:

$$g=i-\frac{E}{P}$$

CONTINUOUS COMPOUNDING

Rates are sometimes converted into the continuous compound interest rate equivalent because the continuous equivalent is more convenient (for example, more easily differentiated). Each of the formulæ above may be restated in their continuous equivalents. For example, the present value at time 0 of a future payment at time **t** can be restated in the following way, where **e** is the base of the natural logarithm and **r** is the continuously compounded rate:

$$PV = FV\,.\,e^{-rt}$$

This can be generalized to discount rates that vary over time: instead of a constant discount rate *r*, one uses a function of time *r*(*t*). In that case the discount factor, and thus the present value, of a cash flow at time *T* is given by the integral of the continuously compounded rate *r*(*t*):

$$PV = FV.\exp\left(-\int_0^T r(t)\,dt\right)$$

Indeed, a key reason for using continuous compounding is to simplify the analysis of varying discount rates and to allow one to use the tools of calculus. Further, for interest accrued and capitalized overnight (hence compounded daily), continuous compounding is a close approximation for the actual daily compounding. More sophisticated analysis includes the use of differential equations, as detailed below.

Examples [edit]

Using continuous compounding yields the following formulas for various instruments:

Annuity

$$PV = \frac{A\left(1 - e^{-rt}\right)}{e^{r} - 1}$$

Perpetuity

$$PV = \frac{A}{e^{r} - 1}$$

Growing annuity

$$PV = \frac{Ae^{-g}\left(1 - e^{-(r-g)t}\right)}{e^{(r-g)} - 1}$$

Growing perpetuity

$$PV = \frac{Ae^{-g}}{e^{(r-g)} - 1}$$

Annuity with continuous payments

$$PV = \frac{1 - e^{(-rt)}}{r}$$

These formulas assume that payment A is made in the first payment period and annuity ends at time t.

DIFFERENTIAL EQUATIONS

Ordinary and partial differential equations (ODEs and PDEs) – equations involving derivatives and one (respectively, multiple) variables are ubiquitous in more advanced treatments of financial mathematics. While time value of money can be understood without using the framework of differential equations, the added sophistication sheds additional light on time value, and provides a simple introduction before considering more complicated and less familiar situations. This exposition follows.

The fundamental change that the differential equation perspective brings is that, rather than computing a *number* (the present value *now*), one computes a *function* (the present value now or at any point in *future*). This function may then be analyzed – how does its value change over time – or compared with other functions.

Formally, the statement that "value decreases over time" is given by defining the linear differential operator ***L*** as:

$$L := -\partial_t + r(t)$$

This states that values decrease (−) over time (∂_t) at the discount rate ($r(t)$). Applied to a function it yields:

$$Lf = -\partial_t f(t) + r(t)f(t)$$

For an instrument whose payment stream is described by $f(t)$, the value $V(t)$ satisfies the inhomogeneous first-order ODE $LV = f$ ("inhomogeneous" is because one has f rather than 0, and "first-order" is because one has first derivatives but no higher derivatives) – this encodes the fact that when any cash flow occurs, the value of the instrument changes by the value of the cash flow (if you receive a £10 coupon, the remaining value decreases by exactly £10).

The standard technique tool in the analysis of ODEs is Green's functions, from which other solutions can be built. In terms of time value of money, the Green's function (for the time value ODE) is the value of a bond paying £1 at a single point in time u – the value of any other stream of cash flows can then be obtained by taking combinations of this basic cash flow. In mathematical terms, this instantaneous cash flow is modeled as a Dirac delta function $\delta_u(t) := \delta(t-u)$.

The Green's function for the value at time t of a £1 cash flow at time u is

$$b(t;u) := H(u-t).\exp\left(-\int_t^u r(v)dv\right)$$

where H is the Heaviside step function – the notation ";u" is to emphasize that u is a *parameter* (fixed in any instance—the time when the cash flow will occur), while t is a *variable* (time). In other words, future cash flows are exponentially discounted (exp) by the sum (integral, $\int$) of the future discount rates ($\int_t^u$ for future, $r(v)$ for discount rates), while past cash flows are worth 0 ($H(u-t) = 1$ if $t < u$, 0 if $t > u$), because they have already occurred. Note that the value *at* the moment of a cash flow is not well-defined – there is a discontinuity at that point, and one can use a convention (assume cash flows have already occurred, or not already occurred), or simply not define the value at that point.

In case the discount rate is constant, $r(v \equiv r)$ this simplifies to

$$b(t;u) = H(u-t).e^{-(u-t)r} = \begin{cases} e^{-(u-t)r} & t<u \\ 0 & t>u \end{cases}$$

Where (u – t) is "time remaining until cash flow".

Thus for a stream of cash flows $f(u)$ ending by time T (which can be set to $T = +\infty$ for no time horizon) the value at time t, $V(t; T)$ is given by combining the values of these individual cash flows:

$$V(t;T) = \int_t^T f(u)b(t;u)du.$$

This formalizes time value of money to future values of cash flows with varying discount rates, and is the basis of many formulas in financial mathematics, such as the Black–Scholes formula with varying interest rates.

VALUATION CONCEPTS OR TECHNIQUES

The Time value of money implies

- That a person will have to pay in future more for a rupee received today; and
- A person may accept less today for a rupee to be received in future.

The above statements relate to two different concepts they are

(i) Compound Value Concept

(ii) Discounting or Present Value Concept.

COMPOUND VALUE CONCEPT

Illustration 1: In this concept the interest earned on the initial principal becomes a part of the principal at the end of a compounding period.

Solution

Amount at the end of 1st year wil be: 1,100

[000x 11 = 1,100]

Amount at the end of 2nd year wil be: 1,210

[1100 x 11% = 1,210]

Amount at the end of 3rd year will be: 1,331

[1210 x 11% = 1,331]

This compounding process will continue for an indefinite time period.

Compounding of Interest Over 'N' years: The compounding of interest can be calculated by the following equation. $A = P(1 + i)^n$ In which

A = Amount at the end of period 'n'

P = Principal at the beginning of the period.

i = Interest rate.

n = Number of years.

By taking illustration 2.1 we get $A = P(1 + i)^n$

$$\mathbf{A = 1000(1 + .10)^3 \quad = A = 1,331}$$

Computation by this formula can also become very time consuming if the number of years become large, say 10, 20 or more. In such cases to save upon the computational efforts, **Compound Value table*** can be used. The table gives the compound value of Re. 1, after n years for a wide range of combination of 'I' and 'n' For instance, in the above illustration Table gives the compound value of Re. 1 at 10% p.a. at the end of 3 years as 1.331. Hence, the compound value of Rs. 1,000 will amount to:

$$1000 \text{ x } 1.331 = \text{Rs. } 1331$$

Multiple Compounding Periods:

Interest can be compounded, even more than once in a year. For calculating the multiple compounded value, above logic can be extended. For instance, in case of Semi-annual compounding, interest is paid twice a year but at half the annual rate. Similarly in case of quarterly compounding, interest rate effectively is $1/4^{th}$ of the annual rate and there are four quarter years.

Formula

$$\mathbf{A = (P + i/m)\ m \times n}$$

Where

A = Amount after a period.

P = Amount in the beginning of the period.

i = Interest rate

M = Number of times per year compounding is made.

n = Number of years for which compounding is to be done.

Illustration 2: Calculate the compounded value when Rs. 1,000 is invested for 3 years and the interest on it is compounded at 10% p.a. semi-annually.

Solution:

$$A = P\left(1 + \frac{i}{m}\right) m \times n$$

$$A = 1{,}000\left(1 + \frac{10}{2}\right) 2 \times 3$$

$$A = \text{Rs. } 1{,}340$$

Alternatively, we can look to Table. The compound value of Re. 1, at 5% interest at the end of 6 years is Rs. 1.340. Hence, the value of Rs. 1,000 will be:

$$1{,}000 \times 1.340 = \text{Rs. } 1{,}340$$

Future Value of Series of Cash Flows:

So far we have considered only the future value of a single payment made at time zero. The transactions in real life are not limited to one. An investor investing money in installments may wish to know the value of his saving after n years.

Illustration 3: Mrs. Mohan invests Rs. 500, Rs. 1,000, Rs. 1,500, Rs. 2,000 and Rs. 2,500 at the end of each year. Calculate the compound value at the end of 5 years compounded annually when interest is charged at 5% p.a.

Statement of the Compound Value

End of the Year	Amount deposited	No. of years Compounded	Compounded interest factor from table 3	Future Value (2x4)
1	2	3	4	5
1	Rs. 500	4	1.216	Rs. 608.00
2	1,000	3	1.158	1158.00
3	1,500	2	1.103	1,654.50
4	2,000	1	1.050	2,100.00
5	2,500	0	1.000	2,500.00
		Amount at the end of 5th Year ==	Rs. **8,020.50**	

It may be noted here that we are making use of the Compound interest formula for each payment separately. For instance, Rs. 500 put in at the end of the first year compounds for four years, and has a future value of Rs. 608 at 5% interest [Rs. 500 (1 + 0.05)4]. Similarly, Rs. 1,000 deposited at the end of 2 year compounds for 3 years and amounts to Rs. 1,158 [Rs. 1000 $(1 + 0.05)^3$] and so on.

0 1 2 3 4 5
Rs. 500 Rs. 1,000 Rs. 1,500 Rs.2,000 Rs. 2,500.00
L-----------------------------2,100.00
I--1,654.50
L---1,158.00
L---608.00

Rs. 8,020.50

Figure 1.1(A) Graphic Illustration of Compounding Values.

COMPOUND SUM OF AN ANNUITY

An annuity is a stream of equal *annual cash flows. Annuities involve calculations* based upon the regular periodic contribution or receipt of a fixed sum of money.

Illustration 4: Mr Ramesh deposits Rs. 2,000 at the end of every year for 5 years in his saving account paying 5% interest compounded annually. Determine how much sum of money he wil have at the end of the 5th year.

Statement of the Compound Value

End of the Year	Amount deposited	No. of years Compounded	Compounded interest factor from table 3	Future Value (2x4)
1	2	3	4	5
1	Rs. 2,000	4	1.216	2,432
2	Rs. 2,000	3	1.158	2,316
3	Rs. 2,000	2	1.103	2,206
4	Rs. 2,000	1	1.050	2,100
5	Rs. 2,000	0	1.000	2,000
		Amount at the end of 5th Year ==		Rs. 11,054

Taking out the common factor Rs. 2,000

= Rs. 2,000 (1.216 + 1.158 + 1.103 + 1.050 +1.000)

= Rs. 2,000 (5.527)

= Rs. 11,054

From the above, it follows that in order to find the sum of the annuity; the annual amount must be multiplied by the sum of the appropriate compound interest factors. Such calculations are available for a wide range of i and n. They are given in Table. To find the answer to the annuity question of illustration 2.4 we are required to look for the 5% column and the row for the fifth year and multiply the factor by annuity amount of Rs. 2000. From the table we find that the sum of annuity of Re. 1 deposited at the end of each year for 5 years is 5.526 (IF). Thus, when multiplied by Rs. 2,000 annuity (A).

We find the total sum as Rs. 11,052.

Symbolically, Sn = IF x A

Where,

A - is the value of annuity?

IF - represents the appropriate factor for the sum of the annuity of Re. 1

Sn - represents the compound sum of an annuity.

Annuity tables are great innovations in the field of investment banking as they guide the depositors and investors as to what sum an amount (X) paid for number of years, n, will accumulate to at a stated rate of compound interest.

Illustration 5: Find the compound value of annuity, when three equal yearly payments of Rs. 2,000 are deposited into an account that yields 7% compound interest.

Solution: The Annuity Table gives the compound value as 3.215 when Re. 1 is paid every year for 3 years at 7%. Thus, the compounded value of annuity of Rs. 2,000 is:

Sn = IF x A

Sn = 3.215x2000

Sn = 6,430

2. Discounting or present value concept

The concept of present value is the exact opposite of that of compound value. In case of compounding we calculate the future value of a sum of money or series of payments, while in case of present value concept, we estimate the present worth of a future payment/ installment or series of payments adjusted for the time value of money. The basis of present value approach is that opportunity cost exists for money lying idle. That is to say, that interest can be earned on the money. This return is termed as 'discounting rate'. Given a rate of interest, the present value of future rupee will always be lower. The technique for finding the present value is termed as 'discounting'.

Present value after 'n' years:

Formula:

$$PV = \frac{A}{(1+I)n}$$

Where:

PV = principal amount the investor is willing to forego at present.

i = Interest rate.

A = Amount at the end of the period n.

n = Number of years.

With this formula, we can directly calculate the amount; any depositor would be willing to sacrifice at present, with a time preference rate or discount rate of x %.

Example : If Mr. X, depositor, expects to get Rs. 100 after one year at the rate of rate of 10 % the amount he will have to forego at present can be calculated as follows:

$$PV = A \ / (1 + i)^n$$

$$PV = 100 / (1 + .10) = \text{Rs. } 90.90$$

Similarly, the present value of an amount of inflow at the end of 'n' years can be computed.

Present Value of a Series of Cash Flows:

In a business situation, it is very natural that returns received by a firm are spread over a number of years. An investment made now may fetch returns for a period after some time. Every businessman will like to know whether it is worthwhile to invest or forego a certain sum now, in anticipation of returns he expects to earn over a number of years. In order to take this decision he will need to equate the total anticipated future returns, to the present sum he is going to sacrifice. To estimate the present value of future series of returns, the present value of each expected inflow will be calculated. The present value of series of cash flows can be represented by the following

Formula:

$$PV = \frac{C1}{(1+i)^1} + \frac{C2}{(1+i)^2} + \frac{C3}{(1+i)^3} + \frac{Cn}{(1+i)^n}$$

Where,

PV = sum of individual present values of each cash flow; C1, C2, C3.........

Cn = Cash flows after period 1, 2, 3...........n

i = Discounting rate.

However, a project may involve a series of cash inflows and outflows. The computation of the present value of inflows by the above equation is a tedious problem. Hence, present value Table is used (i.e. Table 1A.1)

Illustration 6: Given the time value of money as 10% (i.e. the discounting factor), You are required to find out the present value of future cash inflows that will be received over next four years.

Year	Cash Flows (Rs.)
1	1,000
2	2,000
3	3,000
4	4,000

Solution:

Present Value of Cash Flows

End of the Year	Cashflows	Present Value Factor at 10%	Present value
1	2	3	4=(2x3)
1	2,000	0.909	909
2	3,000	0.826	1,652
3	4,000	0.751	2,253
4	5,000	0.683	2,732
		Present value of series of Cash flows	Rs. 7,546

Present value of an Annuity: In the above case there was a mixed stream of cash inflows. An individual or depositor may receive only constant returns over a number of years. This implies that the cash flows are equal in amount. To find out the present value of annuity either we can find the present value of each cash flow or use the annuity table. The annuity table gives the present value of an annuity Re. 1 for interest rate over number of years 'n'.

Illustration 7: Calculate the present value of annuity of Rs. 500 received annually for four years, when discounting factor is 10%.

Solution:

Present Value of Cash Flows Rs.500

End of the Year	Cash Flows	Present Value Factor at 10%	Present value
1	2	3	4=(2x3)
1	500	0.909	454.50
2	500	0.826	413.50
3	500	0.751	375.50
4	500	0.683	341.50
	Present value of annuity of Rs. **500**		Rs. 1,585.00

This basically means add up the Present Value Factors and multiply with Rs. 500

i.e., 3.170 x 500 = Rs. 1,585

Illustration 8: Find out the present value of an annuity of Rs. 5,000 over 3 years when discounted at 5%.

Solution:

PVAn = A x ADF = 5000 x 2.773 = 13,865

Where PVAn = Present value of an annuity having a duration of 'n' periods

A = Value of single installment

ADF = Annuity Discount Factor

PRESENT VALUE OF A PERPETUAL ANNUITY:

A person may like to find out the present value of his investment, in case he is going to get a constant return year after year. An annuity of this kind which goes on for ever is called 'perpetuity'. The present value of a perpetual annuity can be ascertained by simply dividing A' by interest or discount rate 'I', symbolical y represented as A/i.

Illustration 9: Mr. Bharat, principal wishes to institute a scholarship of Rs. 5,000 for an outstanding student every year. He wants to know the present value of investment which would yield Rs. 5,000 in perpetuity, discounted at 10%.

Solution

P = A = 5000 = 50,000

I .10

Illustration 10: Mr. Madan intends to have a return of Rs. 10,000 p.a. for perpetuity. Incase the discount rate is 20%, calculate the present value of this perpetuity.

Solution:

P = A = 10000 = 50,000

I .20

This means that Mr. Madan should invest Rs. 50,000 at 20% to get an annual return of Rs. 10,000 for perpetuity.

Illustration 11: What is the present value of Rs.100 received at the end of the first year and Rs.50 received at the end of the second year and each year after that forever? The discount rate is 10%

Solution

$$P = 100(P/F, 0.1, 1) + 50(P/A, 0.1, inf)\ (P/F, 0.1, 1) = 545.45$$

The P/A factor for infinity is 1/i. The factor moves the uniform series back to a single payment one period before the first payment

Illustration 12: What present expenditure would be justified by the prospect of saving of Rs.500 every quarter of the year for 10 years? Assume interest is at 16% compounded quarterly

Solution

Use a period of 3 months. The interest per 3 months is 0.16/4 = 0.04.

P = 500(P/A, 0.04, 40) = 9896.39. This is what you should be willing to pay. This illustrates the situation of a compounding period other than one year. The 9896.39 is an investment that saves expenditures in the future. The value of P is the investment that makes the net present worth equal to zero.

Illustration 13: A person making small loans offers to lend Rs.200 with the borrower required to pay Rs.14.44 at the end of each week for 16 weeks to extinguish the debt. By appropriate use of your interest tables, find the approximate interest rate per week. What is the nominal interest rate per annum? What is the effective interest rate per annum?

Solution

The solution is the interest rate at which the net present worth is zero.

At 1%, P = 200 + 14.44(P/A, 0.01, 16) = 12.53.

At 2%, P = 200 + 14.44(P/A, 0.02, 16) = 3.94.

Interpolating: i = 0.01 + 0.01[12.53/(12.53 + 3.94)]= 0.01760 or 1.76%.

The effective rate is = (1.0176)52 1 = 2.4774 1 = 1.4774 or 148%/year

Illustration 14: A man arranges to repay a 5 percent Rs.1000 loan in 10 equal annual installments. After his sixth payment, he borrows another Rs.1000, also at 5 percent, with the following understanding: he is to pay nothing for the next two years and then repay the balance of the first loan plus the entire second loan in eight equal annual installments starting at the end of the third year. What will this annual payment be?

Solution

Annual payment on loan = 1000(A/P, 0.05, 10) = 129.50.

Find the value of A that makes the present worth of the cash flow equal to zero.

PW = 1000 129.50(P/A, 0.05, 6) + 1000(P/F, 0.05, 6) A(P/A, 0.05, 8)(P/F, 0.05, 8) = 0

or

A = [1000 129.50(P/A, 0.05, 6) + 1000(P/F, 0.05, 6)] / [(P/A, 0.05, 8)(P/F, 0.05,8)]

A = [1000 129.50(5.076) + 1000(0.7462)] / [6.463 ¥ 0.6768]

A = [342.66 + 746.2] / [4.372] = 249.1

Illustration 15: Mr. Smith has received an income contract which provides for 25 decreasing payments to him, starting with Rs.1000 at the end of the first year and decreasing by Rs.20 each year thereafter. Thus his last receipt, at the end of the 25th year, will be Rs.520. Using interest at 10 percent, compute the uniform annual equivalent of these 25 payments.

Solution

Find the uniform annual equivalent: A = 1000 - 20(A/G, 0.1, 25) = 850.840

Illustration 16: You are now 25 years old and have just been sold an insurance policy with Rs.10,000 protection on your life. The cost is Rs.170 per year. If you live to age 65, the insurance company will pay you Rs.20,000. Assuming you live to age 65, what portion of the annual cost can be called an investment and what portion of the cost purchased protection? Your minimum acceptable rate of return is 10%. Assume payments are at the end of the year.

Solution

Find out how much you would have to invest to save 20,000 in 40 years at 10% interest. A = 20000(A/F, 0.1, 40) = 45.19. Then you are paying 170 45.19 = 124.81 per year for protection.

Illustration 17: A Rs.1000 bond pays 5% simple interest at the end of each year. The bond matures in 20 years at which time the full Rs.1000 is paid to the bond holder. If the current interest rate is 10%, what amount should one pay for the bond?

Solution

The cash flows associated with the problem are the bond investment at time 0, returns of Rs.50 at the end of each year and Rs.1000 at the end of 20 years. The investment should equal the present worth of the receipts computed at 10% interest.

PW = 50(P/A, 0.1, 20) + 1000(P/F, 0.1, 20)

= 50(8.5135) + 1000(0.1486)

= 425.68 + 148.64 = 574.32

Illustration 18: A bank pays 10% annual interest compounded quarterly. What is the effective annual interest rate?

Solution:

The interest rate per quarter is 0.1/4 = 0.025 per quarter. The effective rate is the annual rate that yields the same annual return as when the interest is compounded quarterly. 1 + i_eff = (1 + 0.025)4 . Therefore, i_eff = 10.38%.

Illustration 19: You borrow Rs.2000 from the Credit Union. The interest rate is 12% annually (nominal). You pay back the bank in 24 equal installments starting one month from the date you borrow the money.

a. What is your monthly payment? b. How much of your first payment is interest

Solution

Since the loan is paid monthly, the interest rate is 0.12/12 = 0.01 per month.

a. The monthly payment is: A = 2000(A/P, 0.01, 24) = 211.16.

b. The interest in any period is the money still owed times the interest rate. In the first period the money owed is 2000 so the interest in the first payment is

2000(0.01) = Rs.20.

Illustration 20: You are 20 years old and just got married. Your spouse and you agree that you want to retire at age 60 with Rs.1,000,000. How much do you have to put away each year if you earn 10% on your investments.

Solution

1. Assuming end of year payments, your annual deposit is:

   A = 1,000,000*(A/F, 0.1, 40) = 1,000,00*.002259 = Rs.2,259.

   Without interest this corresponds to less than Rs.200 per month.

Illustration 21: At age 5 you were left Rs.10,000 from the fortune of a favorite aunt. Your parents put the money in a trust fund earning 10% interest. You are now 25 years old and may draw from the trust fund. How much do you have?

Solution

After 20 years deposited at 10% interest, the money will grow to:

F = 10000*(F/P, 0.1, 20) = 10000*6.7275 =Rs.67,274

Illustration 22: You finally have a job after 4 years of college. To escape the high rent of the Austin area you buy a house for Rs.100,000. You finance the full amount with a 30 year mortgage. The interest rate is 9% a year, and your payments are monthly. What are the total of all payments if you make all payments as scheduled

Solution

First calculate the monthly payment. Note that since payments are monthly, interest is charged every month. This is the same as compounding once a month. Since the periods are expressed in months, the interest must be expressed per month. The interest per month is 0.09/12 or 0.0075, 0.75% per month.

$$A = 100000(A/P, 0.0075, 360) = 100000*0.008046 = 804.62$$

The sum of all payments is:

Total Payments 804.62*360 = 289,663

The principal paid is Rs.100,000. The remaining Rs.189,663 is interest. It costs a lot of money to borrow so much for so long

Illustration 23: You can afford Rs.300 a month to purchase a car. If the interest rate is 6% a year and the loan is for 60 months, how much can you finance?

A loan is money received now in return for payments in the future. Since the payments are a uniform series. The equivalent of a uniform series moved to one period before the series begins is found with the P/A factor. Again, we use a monthly interest rate since the payments are monthly.

$$P = 300(P/A, 0.005, 60) = 300*51.725 = \text{Rs.}15{,}517$$

This assumes that the first payment occurs one month after the loan is taken out.

Illustration 24: You win the lottery and the government promises to pay you Rs.1,000,000 in ten years. Your minimum acceptable rate of return on investments is 10%. What is the prize worth to you now?

Solution

Money that is to be received in the future has a smaller equivalent value at the present. We discount the future amount with the P/F factor.

$$P = 1{,}000{,}000(P/F, 0.1, 10) = 1{,}000{,}000*0.385543 = \text{Rs.}385{,}543$$

Illustration 25: You are a freshman in college and you just paid Rs.1000 for tuition and fees for the University. Assuming the cost goes up by Rs.100 per semester for the remaining 7 semesters of your education, how much must you have in the bank right now to cover the remaining charges? Assume your investments earn 3% every six months.

Solution

Here the interest rate is 3% every six months. Since the payments are every six months we identify a 6-month interval as one period. The payments start one period (six months) from now with a payment of Rs.1,100. The first Rs.1,000 is already gone. Two periods from now, the payment will increase by Rs.100, three periods by Rs.200, and so-on for the remaining 7 periods.

The cash flow is a uniform series of Rs.1,100, plus a uniform gradient of Rs.100. You must have in the bank the equivalent of the cash flow computed with an interest rate of 3% per period.

P = 1100(P/A, 0.03, 7) + 100(P/G, 0.03, 7)

= 1100*6.230283 + 100*17.9547

P = Rs.8,648.78

Illustration 26: You are a parent. Your daughter starts college in 18 years. If you put away Rs.100 each month for 18 years, how much will you have when she is ready to begin college? The CD's you invest in return 6% per year compounded monthly.

Solution

We must find the future equivalent of the monthly payment. Since the account is compounded monthly, the cash flow is expressed in month. The monthly interest rate is 0.5%, The savings will grow to:

F = 100(F/A, 0.005, 216) = 100*387.35 = Rs.38,735.

Since F/A factor for 216 is probably not in the tables, you would use the formula for the factor to compute the value.

Illustration 27: If Rs.1000 is invested now, Rs.1500 two years from now, and Rs.800 four years from now at an interest rate of 8% compounded annually, what will be the total amount in 10 years?

Solution

The three different single payments can be considered individually and the results added. Note that the F/P factor moves money from one point in time to a later point in time. The N value in the factors is the number of periods moved.

F = 1000(F/P, 0.08, 10) + 1500(F/P, 0.08, 8) + 800(F/P, 0.08, 6) = 1000*2.158 + 1500*1.850 +800*1.568 = Rs.6,187

Illustration 28: What is the amount of 10 equal annual deposits that can provide five annual withdrawals, when a first withdrawal of Rs.1,000 is made at the end of year 11, and subsequent withdrawals increase at the rate of 6% per year over the previous year's if the interest rate is 8%, compounded annually?

Solution

Withdrawals are A11=Rs.1000, A12 = Rs.1000*(1.06), A13 = Rs.1000*(1.06) ^2, A14 = Rs.1000*(1.06) ^3, A15 = Rs.1000 *(1.06) ^4. (The ^ indicates exponentiation.)

This is geometric series starting at Rs.1000 and growing at a 6% rate. Use the geometric series factor to find the equivalent worth at period 10, using i=8% and g = 6%.

P = 1000(P/A, 0.06, 0.08, 5) = Rs.4,461.

Assuming that the uniform deposits are made at the end of the year, the deposits must grow to this value. Use the A/F factor to compute the deposit.

A = 4461 (A/F,0.08,10) = 4461*0.069 = Rs.307.9. This is the annual deposit.

MULTIPLE CHOICE QUESTIONS

1. The time value of money concept can be defined as:
   a. The time in your life when you receive an inheritance.
   b. The relationship between money spent versus money received.
   c. The relationship between a dollar to be received in the future and a dollar today.
   d. The relationship of interest rate stated and amount paid.
   e. None of the above.

2. A firm borrows Rs.1,000 at 8 percent simple interest with all payments due at the end of four years. What amount must be repaid?
   a. Rs.1,150. b. Rs.1,660.
   c. Rs.1,470. d. Rs.1,320.
   e. None of the above.

3. If you have a choice to earn simple interest on Rs.10,000 for three years at 8% or compound interest at 7.5% for three years which one will pay more and by how much?
   a. Simple interest by Rs.50. b. Compound interest by Rs.52.
   c. Compound interest by Rs.23. d. Simple interest by Rs.30.
   e. None of the above.

4. You deposit Rs.1,000 into a bank account. If the bank pays 4 percent simple inter-est, how much will you accumulate in your account after 10 years?
   a. Rs.1,400. b. Rs.1,450.
   c. Rs.1,500. d. Rs.1,560.
   e. None of the above.

5. You deposit Rs.1,000 into a bank account. If the bank pays 4 percent compound interest, how much will you accumulate in your account after 10 years?
   a. Rs.1,380. b. Rs.1,250.
   c. Rs.1,480. d. Rs.1,580.
   e. None of the above.

6. A credit Union recently advertised an investment certificate that pays 1.75% in the first year, 2.25% in the second year, 2.75% in the third year, 3.25% in the fourth year and 5.25% in the fifth and final year. If you invest Rs.10,000 in this investment certificate and hold it to maturity, how much will you have at the end of five years?

   a. Rs.17,561.94. b. Rs.15,205.85.

   c. Rs.13,890.20. d. Rs.11,616.94.

   e. None of the above.

7. Suppose someone invests Rs.1,000 today for a five-year term and receives 10 percent annual compound interest. How much would the investor have after five years

   a. Rs.1,550.42. b. Rs.1,610.51.

   c. Rs.1,770.25. d. Rs.1,980.78.

   e. None of the above.

8. You have deposited Rs.1,500 in an account that promises to pay 8% compounded quarterly for the next five years. How much will you have in the account at the end?

   a. Rs.1,598.33. b. Rs.2,020.92.

   c. Rs.2,228.58. d. Rs.3,303.00

   e. None of the above.

9. An investor estimates that she needs Rs.1 million to live comfortably when she re-tires in 40 years. How much does she have to invest today, assuming a 10 percent interest rate on the investment?

   a. Rs.22,094.93. b. Rs.22,660.85.

   c. Rs.23,770.62. d. Rs.24,980.33.

   e. None of the above

10. An investment of Rs.500 today will grow to Rs.1,500 at the end of 10 years. What is the effective annual interest rate at which compounding takes place?

    a. 10.512%. b. 12.850%.

    c. 13.225% d. 11.612%

    e. None of the above.

11. You are considering a one-year investment. If you put up Rs.1,250, you would get back Rs.1,350. What rate is this investment paying?

    a. 6%. b. 7%.

    c. 8% d. 10%.

    e. None of the above.

12. You have just graduated and need money to buy a new car. Your rich Uncle Henry will lend you the money so long as you agree to pay him back within four years, and you offer to pay him the rate of interest that he would otherwise get by putting his money in a savings account. Based on your earnings and living expenses, you think you will be able to pay him Rs.5,000 in one year, and then Rs.8,000 each year for the next three years. If Uncle Henry would otherwise earn 6% per year on his savings, how much can you borrow from him?

    a. Rs.21,550.94.
    b. Rs.22,660.85.
    c. Rs.23,770.62.
    d. Rs.24,980.65.
    e. None of the above.

13. Suppose you are examining an asset that promises to pay Rs.500 at the end of each yea for the next three years. The cash flows from this asset are in the form of a three-year, Rs.500 annuity. If you wanted to earn 10 percent on your money, how much would you offer for this annuity?

    a. Rs.1,243.50.
    b. Rs.1,876.55.
    c. Rs.1,465.98.
    d. Rs.1,455.25.
    e. None of the above.

14. An annuity pays Rs.3,000 per year at year end and earns an annual return of 12 percent per year for 30 years. What is the present value of this annuity?

    a. Rs.18,165.55.
    b. Rs.19,865.20.
    c. Rs.21,554.76.
    d. Rs.24,165.55.
    e. None of the above.

15. A court settlement awarded an accident victim four payments of Rs.50,000 to be paid at the end of each of the next four years. Which of the following amounts is closest to the current value of these payments? The appropriate discount rate is an effective annual rate of 4%.

    a. Rs.181,530.
    b. Rs.210,095.
    c. Rs.170,495.
    d. Rs.199,020.
    e. None of the above.

16. You discover that you are the lucky winner of the Rs.30 million prize. You can take your prize money in 30 payments of Rs.1 million per year (starting today). If the interest rate is 8%, what is the present value of these payments?

    a. Rs.10.50 million.
    b. Rs.12.16 million.
    c. Rs.13.25 million.
    d. Rs.14.35 million.
    e. None of the above.

17. Ellen just turned 35 years old, and she has decided it is time to plan seriously for her retirement. On each birthday, beginning in one year and ending when she turns 65, she will save Rs.10,000 in an RRSP account. If the account earns 10% per year, how much will Ellen have saved at age 65?

    a. Rs.1,950 million.
    b. Rs.1,764 million.
    c. Rs.1,645 million.
    d. Rs.1,350 million.
    e. None of the above.

18. A person plans to retire in 10 years and, through annual savings, wants to build her wealth to Rs.100,000 by that time. Money can be invested to yield interest of 14 percent per year. How much will she have to set aside at the end of each of the next 10 years in order to achieve her objective?

    a. Rs.2,866.22.
    b. Rs.3,225.67.
    c. Rs.4,879.44.
    d. Rs.5,171.35.
    e. None of the above.

19. Suppose you plan to contribute Rs.2,000 every year into a Registered Retirement Savings Plan (RRSP) paying 8 percent. If you retire in 30 years, how much will you have?

    a. Rs.240,879.40.
    b. Rs.226,567.60
    c. Rs.308,376.66.
    d. Rs.206,560.00.
    e. None of the above.

20. How much must be saved annually, beginning one year from now, in order to accumulate Rs.50,000 over the next 10 years, earning 9% annually?

    a. Rs.3,291.
    b. Rs.3,587.
    c. Rs.4,500.
    d. Rs.4,587.
    e. None of the above.

21. A bank will pay you Rs.100 a year for your lifetime if you deposit Rs.2,500 in the bank today. If you plan to live forever, what interest rate is the bank paying?

    a. 4%.
    b. 6%.
    c. 7%.
    d. 11%.
    e. None of the above.

22. If the interest is 7 percent, what is the value of an investment that offers you Rs.100 a year in perpetuity with the payment at the beginning of each year.

    a. Rs.1,428.57.
    b. Rs.1,628.57.
    c. Rs.1,728.57.
    d. Rs.1,528.57.
    e. None of the above.

23. Aunt Clarisse has promised to leave you Rs.60 a year starting next year and have it increase at 4% a year thereafter. The payments are expected to go on indefinitely. How much has Aunt Clarisse left you if your opportunity cost is 9%.

    a. Rs.693.33. b. Rs.1,300.00.
    c. Rs.1,200.00. d. Rs.660.67.
    e. None of the above.

24. You own an oil pipeline which will generate a Rs.2 million cash return over the coming year. The pipeline's operating costs are negligible, and it is expected to last for a very long time. Unfortunately, the volume of oil shipped is declining, and cash flows are expected to decline by 4 percent per year. The discount rate is 10 percent.

    What is the present value (PV) of the pipeline's cash flows if its cash flows are assumed to last forever?

    a. Rs.17.45 million. b. Rs.14.29 million.
    c. Rs.18.78 million. d. Rs.15.64 million.
    e. None of the above.

25. You planned to donate money to your university to fund an annual Rs.30,000 graduation party. Before accepting the money, however, the president of the student association has asked that you increase the donation to account for the effect of inflation on the cost of the party in future years. Although Rs.30,000 is adequate for next year's party, the president estimates that the party's cost will rise by 4% per year thereafter. To satisfy the president's request, how much do you need to donate now if the interest rate is 8% per year?

    a. Rs.750,000. b. Rs.864,000.
    c. Rs.710,000. d. Rs.650,000.
    e. None of the above.

26. You have just been offered a job at Rs.50,000 a year. You anticipate your salary increasing by 5 percent a year until retirement in 40 years. Given an interest rate of 8 percent, what is the present value of your lifetime salary?

    a. Rs.1,126,666.67. b. Rs.3,245,890.30.
    c. Rs.4,356,675.76. d. Rs.1,453,983.95.
    e. None of the above.

27. A sports team in an effort to solve the sadary cap problem has offered a player a contract of Rs.1 million dollars a year for the next season with the payments growing at 7% per year for the next 25 years. The player believes the discount rate for such payments is 13%. What is the value today of taking this contract?

    a. Rs.12,405,955.40. b. Rs.16,666,666.67.
    c. Rs.884,956.09. d. Rs.5,824,965.76.
    e. None of the above.

28. Lenny Loanshark charges 1 percent per week on his loans. Assume there are exectly 52 weeks in a year. What is the effective annual rate?

    a. 22.55%.
    b. 38.98%.
    c. 67.77%.
    d. 77.20%.
    e. None of the above.

29. If you take out a 4-year Rs.8,000 car loan that calls for monthly payments at an annual percentage rate (APR) of 10 percent, compounded monthly, what is your monthly payment?

    a. Rs.170.05
    b. Rs.180.20.
    c. Rs.240.40.
    d. Rs.202.90.
    e. None of the above.

30. Charles Carr borrowed Rs.3,500 to consolidate his debts. Since Charles had an excellent credit rating, he was able to borrow at a 12% effective annual rate. Charles is required to make monthly payments. Charles will make equal payments for the next 36 months. Which one of the following values is closest to his monthly payments?

    a. Rs.121.34.
    b. Rs.122.55.
    c. Rs.115.24.
    d. Rs.118.98.
    e. None of the above.

31. As a lender, you know you want to actually earn 18% effective annual rate on a particular loan. You want to quote a rate that features monthly compounding. What rate would you quote?

    a. 15.42%.
    b. 14.52%.
    c. 17.38%.
    d. 16.68%.
    e. None of the above.

32. What effective annual interest rate (EAR) is being earned on a deposit of Rs.5,000 made ten years ago today if the deposit is worth Rs.9,948.94 today? The deposit pays interest semi-annually.

    a. 3.56%.
    b. 6.76%.
    c. 7.00%.
    d. 8.00%.
    e. None of the above.

33. If the compound period is greater than one:

    a. The effective annual interest rate is always equal to the annual percentage rate.
    b. The effective annual interest rate is always less than the annual percentage rate.
    c. The effective annual interest rate is always greater than the annual percentage rate.
    d. The effective annual interest rate is never greater than the annual percentage rate.
    e. None of the above.

34. Investing Rs.2,000 at a continuously compounded rate of 15 percent for 2 years is equivalent to an annually compounded rate of14.28%.

    a. 16.18%. b. 17.45%.

    c. 18.36%. d. None of the above.

    The following situation concerns questions 35-36. A firm borrows Rs.1,000 at 8 percent compounded continuously with all payments due at the end of three years.

35. What is the equivalent effective annual interest rate?

    a. 9.42%. b. 8.33%.

    c. 7.33%. d. 6.88%.

    e. None of the above.

36. What is the amount due at the end of three years?

    a. Rs.1,371.35. b. Rs.1,271.29.

    c. Rs.1, 165.24. d. Rs.1, 051.48.

    e. None of the above.

37. If T-bill rates are presently 6.0 percent and the expected rate of inflation is 2.0 percent, the real rate of return is expected to be

    a. 5.45%. b. 6.20%.

    c. 4.23%. d. 3.92%.

    e. None of the above

38. An engineer in 1950 was earning Rs.6,000 a year. Today, in 2006, she earns Rs.60,000 a year. However, on average, goods today cost 8.2 times what they did in 1950. What is her real income today in terms of constant 1950 dollars?

    a. Rs.8,405.22. b. Rs.7,317.07.

    c. Rs.6,456.96. d. Rs.9,046.45.

    e. No.ne of the above

SHORT ANSWER QUESTIONS

1. Time Value of Money
2. Face Value
3. Present Value
4. Compounding interest
5. Define annuity
6. How do you calculate present value?

7. Why does money have time value
8. What you understand by Discounting?
9. What is an annuity?
10. How do you set up an annuity?
11. What is a compound annuity?

ESSAY TYPE QUESTIONS

1. Time value of money is helpful in capital budget. Explain
2. 'A bird in hand is worth two in the bush' Explain.
3. Explain the Factors contributing to the Time Value of Money.
4. Explain the Valuation concepts or Techniques of Time value of Money.
5. Briefly explain Present Value of a Series of Cash Flows.
6. What is the relationship between interest rate and present value?
7. What is inflation? How does it impact investments?

EXERCISE PROBLEMS

1. Today you deposit Rs 10,000 in a 5-year fixed deposit with the State Bank of India. You shall earn compound interest rate of 6 per annum on your deposit. How much amount will you receive after 5 years?
2. You expect to receive Rs 50,000 after 5 years as a bonus from your employer. The interest rate is 6 percent. How much is Rs 50,000 worth today?
3. Suppose you leave Rs.1,000 on deposit at 5%. How much will you have two years from now?
4. 'You will receive Rs 10,000 each year for 5 years. The interest rate is 9 percent. How much is the worth of your receipts today?
5. You want to begin saving for your daughter's college Education and you estimate that she will need Rs. 1,50,000 in 17 years. If you feel confident that you can earn 8% per year, how much do you need to invest today?
6. Your parents set up a trust fund for you 10 years ago that is now worth Rs. 19,671.51. If the fund earned 7% per year, how much did your parents invest? What interest rate should we use when we compute a present value?
7. You are looking at an investment that will pay Rs.1200 in 5 years if you invest Rs.1000 today. What is the implied rate of interest?
8. 'You deposit Rs 10,000 each year for 10 years in a bank. The interest rate is 10 percent. How much is the worth of your deposits today?

9. 'You wish to receive Rs 10,000 at the end of 10 years from your fixed deposit in a bank. The interest rate is 10 percent. How much payment should you make each year in your fixed deposit account to accumulate Rs 10,000 after five years?

10. 'You are thinking of investing Rs 10,000 today in a fund that promises you Rs 1,600 each year for 10 years. How much is your annual return (interest) from this investment?

11. You have a choice with regard payments. Either you can pay Rs 10,000 in the future or pay an annuity of Rs 627. If the discount rate is 10%, how long will you pay the annuity?

12. You will receive an annuity of Rs 10,000 in the beginning of the year. The discount rate is 9%. What is the present value of the annuity? In this example, we show the calculation of IRR when the cash flows are uneven. In this example, we show the calculation of NPV when the cash flows are uneven. This example shows the calculation of the effective interest rate under multiperiod compounding.

13. You want to purchase a new car and you are willing to pay Rs.21,000. If you can invest at 10% per year and you currently have Rs. 15,000, how long will it be before you have enough money to pay cash for the car?

14. We have Rs.7,000 in a bank account that pays 8%. At the end of each of the next three years, we plan to deposit Rs.4,000. How much will we have at the end of three years? Four years?

15. You are offered the opportunity to put some money away for retirement. You will receive five annual payments of Rs.25,000 each beginning in 40 years [at the end of the 40th year]. How much would you be willing to invest today if you desire an interest rate of 12%?

16. You are saving for a new house and you put Rs.10,000 per year in an account paying 8%. The first payment is made today. How much will you have at the end of 3 years?

17. At an investment rate of 8%, how much will the seller of the annuity (the insurance company) have to fund the annuity at the end of year 20? How many payments will the insurer be able to make? Redo the analysis assuming an interest rate of 12%.

18. Suppose you can earn 1% per month on Rs.1 invested today. What is the APR? 1(12) = 12% How much are you effectively earning?

19. You are looking at two savings accounts. One pays 5.25%, with daily compounding. The other pays 5.3% with semiannual compounding. Which account should you use?

20. Suppose you want to earn an effective rate of 12% and you are looking at an account that compounds on a monthly basis. What APR must they pay?

21. Your broker calls you and tells you that he has this great investment opportunity. If you invest Rs. 100 today, you will receive Rs.40 in one year and Rs.75 in two years. If you require a 15% return on investments of this risk should you take the investment?

22. You are offered the opportunity to put some money away for retirement. You will receive five annual payments of Rs.25,000 each beginning in 40 years [at the end of the 40th year]. How much would you be willing to invest today if you desire an interest rate of 12%?

23. Calculate the compounded value when Rs. 1,000 is invested for 3 years and the interest on it is compounded at 10% p.a. semi-annually.

24. Mrs. Manju invests Rs. 500, Rs. 1,000, Rs. 1,500, Rs. 2,000 and Rs. 2,500 at the end of each year. Calculate the compound value at the end of 5 years compounded annually when interest is charged at 5% p.a.

25. Mr Ramesh deposits Rs. 2,000 at the end of every year for5 years in his saving account paying 5% interest compounded annually. Determine how much sum of money he will have at the end of the 5th year.

26. Find the compound value of annuity, when three equal yearly payments of Rs. 2,000 are deposited into an account that yields 7% compound interest.

27. Find out the present value of an annuity of Rs. 5,000 over 3 years when discounted at 5%.

28. Mr Syam principal wishes to institute a scholarship of Rs. 5,000 for an outstanding student every year. He wants to know the present value of investment which would yield Rs. 5,000 in perpetuity, discounted at 10%.

29. Mr. Madan intends to have a return of Rs. 10,000 p.a. for perpetuity. In case the discount rate is 20%, calculate the present value of this perpetuity.

30. Given the time value of money as 10% (i.e. the discounting factor), You are required to find out the present value of future cash inflows that will be received over next four years. Year Cash flows (Rs.) 11,000, 22,000, 33,000, 44,000

MCQs Answers

1	2	3	4	5	6	7	8	9	10	11	12	13	14	15	16	17	18	19	20	21	22	23	24	25
c	d	c	a	c	d	b	c	a	d	c	d	a	d	a	b	c	d	b	a	a	d	c	b	a
26	27	28	29	30	31	32	33	34	35	36	37	38												
a	b	a	a	c	b	d	b	c	d	d	c	d												

CASE STUDIES

CASE STUDY 1

Bharat is 35 years old and makes a Rs.4,000 payment *every year* into a Roth Individual Retirement Account (IRA) (this is an annuity) for 30 years.

Calculations

Assuming the discount, or interest, rate Lee will earn is 6 percent, what will be the value of his Roth IRA investment when he retires in 30 years (this is future value)?

Note: The formula is a bit tricky. It is

FVn = Payment * $(((1 + I)^N) - 1)/I$ (This is the future value of an annuity factor n,i)

Case Study 1 Answer

There are two ways for Lee to solve the problem. Using the formula, the problem is solved this way:

FVn,i = Payment * $(((1 + I)^N) - 1) / I$ = FV = Rs.4,000 * $[(1.06)^{30} - 1] / .06$ = Rs.316,232.75

If you are using a financial calculator, clear the calculator's memory and solve:

1 = P/Y (payments per year)

4,000 = PMT (payment)

6 = I (interest rate)

30 = N (number of years)

Solve for FV = Rs.316,232.75

CASE STUDY 2

Data

Prasad will make a *yearly* Rs.2,000 payment for 40 years into a traditional IRA account. Calculations

Given that the discount, or interest, rate is 6 percent, what is the current value of Janice's investment in today's dollars? The formula is:

PVn,i = Payment * $[1 - (1 / (1 + I)^N)] / I$ (the present value of an annuity factor n,i)

Case Study 2 Answer

Using the formula, the calculation is

PVn,i = Payment * $[1 - (1 / (1 + I)^N)] / I$ = PV = 2,000 * $[1 - (1 / (1.06)^{40})] / .06$ = Rs.30,092.59

Using the financial calculator, the calculation is Clear memories and use the following:

1 = P/Y 2,000 = PMT 6 = I 40 = N

Solve for PV = Rs.30,092.59

CASE STUDY 3

Data

Vamsi wants to borrow Rs.20,000 dollars for a new car at 13 percent interest.

Calculations

He wants to repay the loan in five *annual* payments . How much will he have to pay *each year* (this indicates present value)? The formula is the same formula that was used in the previous problem:

PVn = Payment * (PVIFAi,n)

Case Study 3 Answer

Using the formula, put Brady's borrowed amount into the equation and solve for your payment. PVn,i = Payment * $[1 - (1 / (1 + I)^N)] / I$ = PV = 20,000 = Payment * $[1 - (1 / (1.13)^5)] / .13$ = Rs.5,686.29 per year.

Using a financial calculator, clear the calculator's memory and use the following:

1 = P/Y 20000 = PV 13 = I 5 = N

Solve for PMT = Rs.5,686.29

CASE STUDY 4

Karthick has reviewed the impact of inflation in the late 1970s. She reviewed one of her parent's investments during that time period and discovered that inflation was 20 percent and that her parent's investment made a 30 percent return.

Calculations

What was her parent's real return on this investment during that period?

Case Study 4 Answers

The traditional (and incorrect) method for calculating real returns is

Nominal return - inflation = real return. This formula would give you a real return of 10%: 30% - 20% = 10%. The correct method is (1 + nominal return) / (1 + inflation) - 1 = real return (1.30 / 1.20) - 1 = 8.33%. In this example, the traditional method overstates return by 20 percent ((10% / 8.33%) - 1). Be very careful of inflation, especially high inflation

CHAPTER 2

Securities Market

NEW ISSUE MARKET

The industrial securities market in India consists of New Issue Market and Stock Exchange. The new issue market deals with the new securities which were not previously available to the investing public, i.e., the securities that are offered to the investing public for the first time. It is also known as Primary Market. The new issue market deals with the new securities which were not previously available to the investing public, i.e., the securities that are offered to the investing public for the first time. The market, therefore, makes available a new block of securities for public subscription. All financial institutions which contribute, underwrite and directly subscribe to the securities are part of new issue market. There are various intermediaries like registrars, custodians and merchant bankers that are involved in this activity of issuing new securities. We now have a look at the functions of new issue market and methods of floating these new issues.

New issues are offered in the primary market and sold to the public for the first time as initial public offerings, or IPOs. New issues are usually handled for a corporation by an underwriting syndicate comprised of investment banks and selling groups. An underwriter will advise the issuing corporation on the best price at which to offer shares of the new security to the public. Factors considered in arriving at a price include prevailing market conditions, indications of interest from the underwriter's book of business, prices of similar companies and the company's general financial health.

FUNCTIONS

The main function of a new issue market is to facilitate transfer of resources from savers to the users. The savers are individuals, commercial banks, insurance companies etc. The users are public limited companies and the government. It is not only a platform for raising finance to establish new enterprises but also for expansion/ diversification/ modernization of existing units.

In this basis the new issue market can be classified as:-

1. Market where firms go to the public for the first time through initial public offering (**IPO**).
2. Market where firms which are already trading raise additional capital through seasoned equity offering (**SEO**).

The **main functions** of a new issue market can be divided into a triple service function:

1. **Origination:** It refers to the work of investigation, analysis and processing of new project proposals. It starts before an issue is actually floated in the market. This function is done by merchant bankers who may be commercial banks, all India financial institutions or private firms. At present, financial institutions and private firms also perform this service. Though this service is highly important, the success of the issue depends, to a large extent, on the efficiency of the market.
2. **Underwriting:** It is an agreement whereby the underwriter promises to subscribe to a specified number of shares or debentures or a specified amount of stock in the event of public not subscribing to the issue. If the issue is fully subscribed, then there is no liability for the underwriter. If a part of share issues remains unsold, the underwriter will buy the shares. Thus, underwriting is a guarantee for marketability of shares. There are two types of underwriters in India - Institutional (LIC, UTI, IDBI, and ICICI) and Non-institutional are brokers.
3. **Distribution:** It is the function of sale of securities to ultimate investors. This service is performed by brokers and agents who maintain a regular and direct contact with the ultimate investors.

The main function of a new issue market is to facilitate transfer of resources from savers to the users. The savers are individuals, commercial banks, insurance companies etc. The users are public limited companies and the government. It is not only a platform for raising finance to establish new enterprises but also for expansion/ diversification/ modernization of existing units.

In this basis the new issue market can be classified as: -

1. Market where firms go to the public for the first time through Initial Public Offering (**IPO**).
2. Market where firms which are already trading raise additional capital through Seasoned Equity Offering (**SEO**).

METHODS OF FLOATING NEW ISSUE

The various methods which are used in the flotation of securities in the new issue market are:

1. Public issues
2. Offer for sale
3. Placement
4. Rights issues

Different Kinds of Issues

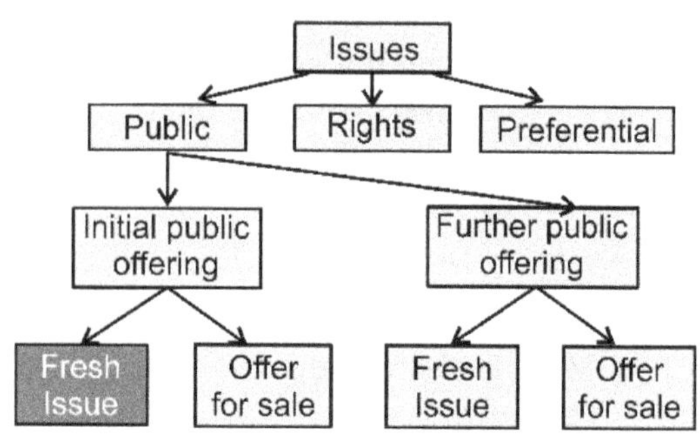

1. Public Issues

Under this method, this issuing company directly offers to the general public/ institutions a fixed number of shares at a stated price through a document called prospectus. This is the most common method followed by joint stock companies to raise capital through the issue of securities. The prospectus must state the following:

- Name of the company
- Address of the registered office
- Existing and proposed activities
- Location of the industry
- Names of Directors
- Minimum subscription
- Names of brokers/ underwriters/ bankers/ managers and registrars to the issue.

2. Offer for Sale

This method of offer of sale consists in outright sale of securities through the intermediary of Issue Houses or share-brokers. In other words, the shares are not offered to the public directly. This method consists of two stages: The first stage is a direct sale by the issuing company to the issue house and brokers at an agreed price. In the second stage, the intermediaries resell the above securities to the ultimate investors. The issue houses or stock brokers purchase the securities at a negotiated price and resell at a higher price. The difference in the purchase and sale price is called spread. It is otherwise called Bought out deals (BOD). This method is used generally in two instances:

1. Offer by a foreign company of a part of it to Indian investors.
2. Promoters diluting their stake to comply with requirements of Stock exchange at the time of listing of shares.

3. Placement

Under this method, the issue houses or brokers buy the securities outright with the intention of placing them with their clients afterwards. Here the brokers act as almost wholesalers selling them in retail to the public. The brokers would make profit in the process of reselling to the public. The issue houses or brokers maintain their own list of clients and through customer contact sell the securities. There is no need for a formal prospectus as well as underwriting agreement.

4. Rights Issues

It is a method of raising funds in the market by an existing company. A right means an option to buy certain securities at a certain privileged price within a certain specified period. Shares, so offered to the existing shareholders are called rights shares. Rights shares are offered to the existing shareholders in a particular proportion to their existing share ownership. The ratio in which the new shares or debentures are offered to the existing share capital would depend upon the requirement of capital. The rights themselves are transferable and sale-able in the market. Section 81 of the Companies Act deals with rights issue.

The cost of issue is minimum. There is no underwriting, brokerage, advertising and printing of prospectus expenses. It prevents the directors from issuing new shares in their own name or to their relatives at a lower price and get controlling right.

GENERAL GUIDELINES FOR NEW ISSUE

All issues by a new company have to be made at par and for existing companies the issue price should be justified as per Male gam Committee's recommendations which are as follows:

The issue price is justified by -

1. The earnings per share (**EPS**) for the last 3 years and comparison of pre-issue price to earnings ratio to the P/E of the industry.
2. The latest Net Asset Value (**NAV**).
3. The minimum return on increased net worth to maintain pre-issue EPS. A company may also raise funds from the international markets by issuing Global Depository Receipts (**GDR**) and American Depository Receipts (**ADR**).

SEBI does not play any role in price fixation. In face the issuers in consultation with the Merchant Bankers will decide the price. However, they are required to give full disclosures of the parameters which they had considered while deciding the issue price. In actual practice, there are two types of issue pricing namely - Fixed price and book building price. Lead manager fixes the price under fixed price. Under book building pricing method, the company and lead manager stipulate a floor price and cap price or a price band and leaves it on market forces to determine the final price (book building price).

PRINCIPAL STEPS IN PUBLIC ISSUE

Now, we see the main steps involved in Public issue. They are in following order:

1. Draft Prospectus

It is prepared giving all details that have been stated earlier under public issue. Any company or a listed company making a public issue or a rights issue of value more than Rs. 50 lakhs have to file a draft offer document with SEBI for its observation. The company can proceed further only after getting observations from the SEBI. The company has to open its issue within three months from the date of SEBI's observation letter.

2. Fulfillment of Entry Norms

The SEBI has laid down certain parameters for accessing the primary market. If a company fulfills these parameters (entry norms), then only it can enter into the primary market.

The Entry forms are as follows -

Entry Norm I

- The company should have Net Tangible Assets of at least Rs. 3 cores for three full years.
- It should have distributable profits in at least three years.
- It should possess Net Worth of at least Rs.1 core in 3 years.
- The issue size should not exceed 5 times the pre-issue net worth.
- If it has to change its name, at least 50% revenue for the preceding one year should be from the new activity.

To ensure that genuine companies don't suffer due to the rigidity of those parameters, the SEBI has laid down two more alternative routes for accessing the primary market.

Entry Norm II

If the issue is through book building route, at least 50% of the issue should be allotted to Qualified Institutional Buyers (QIBs)

- The minimum post-issue face value capital shall be Rs. 10 core or there shall be a compulsory market-making for at least two years.

Entry Norm III

- The company should have at least 1000 prospective allotters
- The project should be appraised and participated to the extent of 15% by Financial Institutions and scheduled commercial banks of which at least 10% comes from the appraisers.
- The minimum post-issue face value capital shall be Rs. 10 core or there shall be a compulsory market-making for at least 2 years.

The above entry forms are not applicable to the private and public sector banks, listed companies right issue and an infrastructure company whose project has been appraised by a financial institution or a bank and not less than 5% of the project cost is financed by these institutions.

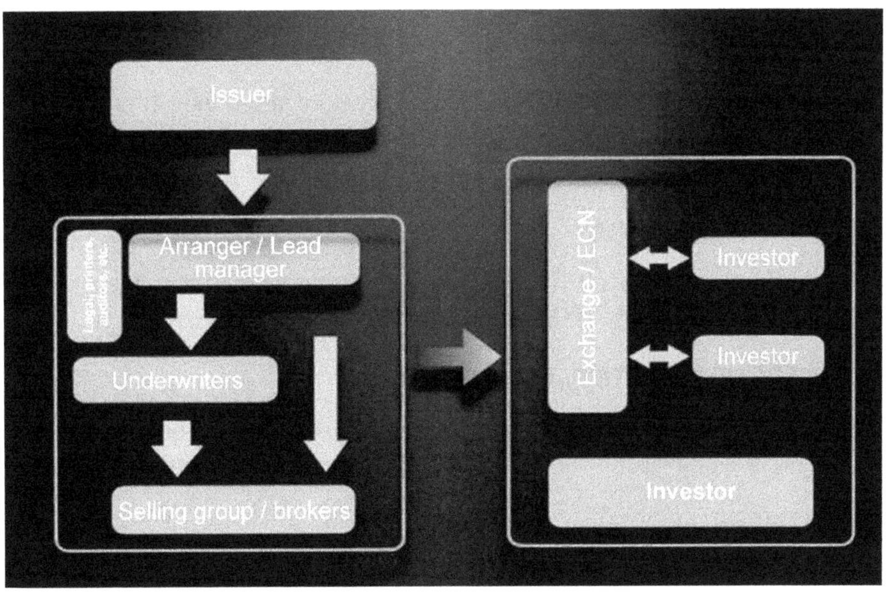

3. **Appointment of Underwriters**

   They are appointed to shoulder the liability and subscribe to the shortfall in case the issue is under-subscribed. For this commitment they are entitled to get a maximum commission of 2.5% on the amount undertaken.

4. **Appointment of Bankers**

   Bankers act as collecting agents I.e., the banks along with their branch network act as collecting agencies and process the funds during the public issue.

5. **Initiating Allotment Procedure**

   The next step is that the Registrars process the application forms, tabulate the amounts collected during the issue and initiate the allotment procedures

6. **Brokers to the issue**

   They are recognized members of the stock exchange and are appointed as brokers to the issue for marketing the issue. They are eligible for a maximum brokerage of 1.5%.

7. **Filing of Documents**

   The draft prospectus, along with the copies of the agreements entered into with the lead manager, underwriters, bankers, registrars and brokers to the issue have to be filed with the Registrar of companies of state where the registered office of the company is located.

8. Printing of Prospectus and Application Forms
9. Listing the Issue
10. Publication in Newspapers
11. Allotment of shares
12. Underwriters liability
13. Optional Listing

Example

The Just dial IPO dated 20th May 2013. The unique feature about their IPO was of the safety Net I.e., the owners said they would Buy Back shares from retail investors at the IPO price if stocks falls sharply within first 6 months.

GRADING OF IPO MANDATORY

SEBI had made the grading of all IPOs by a credit rating agency mandatory from May 1, 2007. SEBI is the only regulator in the world to mandate the grading of IPOs.

PRINCIPAL STEPS OF PRIVATE PLACEMENT

It may be done in respect of equity shares, preference shares, bonds and debentures. Generally, the private placement of bonds and debentures is very popular.

The following steps are involved -

1. Terms and conditions

They include the value of the instrument, maturity period, yield rate, issue and redemption details, etc.

2. Credit rating

It is mandatory to obtain credit rating from a recognized credit rating agency who will evaluate the various aspects concerned with the instrument.

3. Confidential Information Memorandum (CIM)

It is just like the offer document in the case of shares. An investor can have a thorough knowledge about the issue by going through this document.

4. Trustees to the issue

The next step is to appoint trustees (usually banks or other financial institutions) to the issue to protect the interest of investors.

5. Pre-launching formalities

Just one or two days before the launching date, the CIM is sent to the prospective investors inviting them to subscribe to the issue.

6. Pricing the issue

Sometimes pre-marketing campaign may be conducted by the issue houses to ascertain the investors towards private placement and the probable prices. Since book building method is adopted by many companies, this campaign is not generally resorted to.

7. Post-issue Steps

Decision is taken on allotment and the certificates are issued. Over subscriptions are refunded. The details of the issue are sent to the stock exchange where it is likely to be listed.

Principal Steps involved in the case of offer for Sale

1. **Agreement with the merchant banker** or sponsor group laying down the terms and conditions of the issue.
2. **Registration of the agreement** with the stock exchange concerned.
3. **Default** - It is default is committed by the sponsor; it will be referred to an arbitrage committee set up by the stock exchange.
4. **Offloading** - Sponsor can offload his position provided the promoter's post-issue holding will not be less than 20% with a 3-year lock in period.
5. **Market Maker** - The sponsor should agree to act as a market maker for the companies share for 18 months and should also identify another market maker for such compulsory market making.

PRIMARY MARKET

The Primary market refers to the market where new securities are issued for the purpose of obtaining capital. Firms and public or government institutions can raise funds from the primary market through making a new issue of stock (to obtain equity financing) or bonds (to obtain debt financing). When a corporation is making a new issue, it is called an Initial Public Offering (IPO), and the process is referred to as the 'underwriting' of the share issue. In the primary market, the securities are issued by the company that wishes to obtain capital and is sold directly to the investor. In exchange for the funds that the shareholder contributes, a certificate is issued to represent the interest held in the company. Once issued the securities typically trade on a secondary market such as a stock exchange, bond market or derivatives exchange.

Features of primary markets are:

This is the market for new long term equity capital. The primary market is the market where the securities are sold for the first time. Therefore, it is also called the new issue market (NIM).

- In a primary issue, the securities are issued by the company directly to investors.
- The company receives the money and issues new security certificates to the investors.
- Primary issues are used by companies for the purpose of setting up new business or for expanding or modernizing the existing business.
- The primary market performs the crucial function of facilitating capital formation in the economy.
- The new issue market does not include certain other sources of new long term external finance, such as loans from financial institutions. Borrowers in the new issue market may be raising capital for converting private capital into public capital; this is known as "going public

PLAYERS IN THE PRIMARY MARKET

There are many players in the new issue or primary market. The important of them are:

1. **Merchant Bankers** - They are the issue managers, co-managers, and are responsible to the company and SEBI. They are registered by SEBI under category I, II, III and IV based on the capital adequacy and track record.
2. **Registrars to the issue** - They are an important category of intermediaries who undertake all activities connected with new issue management. They are appointed in consultation with the merchant bankers. A net worth of Rs. 6 Lakhs is essential for Registrars.
3. **Collecting and Co-coordinating Bankers** - They collect information on subscriptions and co-ordinate the collection work.
4. **Underwriters and Brokers** - Brokers along with the network of sub-brokers market the new issues. They send their own circulars and applications to the clients and do follow up work to market securities.

Advantages Primary Market

1. Mobilization of savings
2. Channelizing savings for productive use
3. Source of large supply of funds
4. Rapid Industrial growth due to increase in production and productivity in the economy.

Disadvantages Primary Market

1. Possibility of deceiving investors
2. No fixed norms for project appraisal
3. Lack of post issue seriousness egg. Face book IPO
4. Ineffective gold of merchant bankers
5. Delay in allotment process

SECONDARY MARKET

The secondary market refers to the market where securities that have already been issued are traded. Instruments that are usually traded on the secondary market include stocks, bonds, options and futures. Certain mortgage loans can also be sold to investors on the secondary market. Once a security has been purchased for the first time by an investor on the primary market, the same security can be sold to another investor in the secondary market, which may be at a higher or lower price depending on the performance of the security during its period of trading. There are many secondary markets worldwide, and famous few include the New York Stock Exchange, The NASDAQ, the London Stock exchange, the Tokyo stock exchange and the Shanghai Stock Exchange.

The secondary market, is also called after market, is the financial market in which previously issued financial instruments such as stock, bonds, options, and futures are bought and sold. Another frequent usage of "secondary market" is to refer to loans which are sold by a mortgage bank to investors such as Fannie Mae and Freddie Mac.

The term "secondary market" is also used to refer to the market for any used goods or assets, or an alternative use for an existing product or asset where the customer base is the second market (for example, corn has been traditionally used primarily for food production and feedstock, but a "second" or "third" market has developed for use in ethanol production).

FUNCTIONS OF SECONDARY MARKET

In the secondary market, securities are sold by and transferred from one investor or speculator to another. It is therefore important that the secondary market be highly liquid (originally, the only way to create this liquidity was for investors and speculators to meet at a fixed place regularly; this is how stock exchanges originated, see History of the Stock Exchange). As a general rule, the greater the number of investors that participate in a given marketplace, and the greater the centralization of that marketplace, the more liquid the market.

Fundamentally, secondary markets mesh the investor's preference for liquidity (i.e., the investor's desire not to tie up his or her money for a long period of time, in case the investor needs it to deal with unforeseen circumstances) with the capital user's preference to be able to use the capital for an extended period of time.

Accurate share price allocates scarce capital more efficiently when new projects are financed through a new primary market offering, but accuracy may also matter in the secondary market because: 1. price accuracy can reduce the agency costs of management, and make hostile takeover a less risky proposition and thus move capital into the hands of better managers, and 2. accurate share price aids the efficient allocation of debt finance whether debt offerings or institutional borrowing.

The term may refer to markets in things of value other than securities. For example, the ability to buy and sell intellectual property such as patents, or rights to musical compositions, is considered a secondary market because it allows the owner to freely resell property entitlements issued by the government. Similarly, secondary markets can be said to exist in some real estate contexts as well (e.g. ownership shares of time-share vacation homes are bought and sold outside of the official exchange set up by the timeshare issuers). These have very similar functions as secondary stock and bond markets in allowing for speculation, providing liquidity, and financing through securitization. It facilitates liquidity and marketability of the long-term instrument. It also provides instant valuation of securities caused by changes in the environment.

PRIVATE SECONDARY MARKETS

Private equity secondary market refers to the buying and selling of pre-existing investor commitments to private equity funds. Sellers of private equity investments sell not only the investments in the fund but also their remaining unfunded commitments to the funds.

PRIMARY MARKET VS SECONDARY MARKET

A primary market refers to any market where new shares of stock are sold. A corporation wishing to sell new shares of stock benefits from this sale because the stock is sold in the market directly by the issuing company. This is in contrast to secondary markets where shares of stock already in circulation and issued at a previous date are traded among investors. The company who issued the stock does not benefit directly from the sale of stock in a secondary market because the money paid for the stock goes to the seller in exchange for part ownership in the company. In this case, the company is not involved in the transaction.

The primary and secondary markets are both platforms in which corporations fund their capital requirements. While the functions in the primary stock exchange are limited to first issuance, a number of securities and financial assets can be traded and re traded over and over again. The main difference is that, in the primary market, the company is directly involved in the transaction, whereas in the secondary market, the company has no involvement since the transactions occur between investors.

- Primary and Secondary markets refer to markets which assist corporations obtain capital funding. The difference between these two markets lies in the process that is used to collect funds.
- The Primary market refers to the market where new securities are issued by the company that wishes to obtain capital and is sold directly to the investor
- The secondary market refers to the market where securities that have already been issued are traded. Instruments that are usually traded on the secondary market include stocks, bonds, options and futures.
- The main difference is that, in the primary market, the company is directly involved in the transaction, whereas in the secondary market, the company has no involvement since the transactions occur between investors.

INVESTORS TRADE ASSETS IN PRIMARY AND SECONDARY MARKETS

Buying and selling securities such as stocks and bonds takes place in one of two markets. Learn about the difference between primary and secondary markets from the perspective of an investor.

- The term marketplace or simply market is a reference to a place where goods and services are bought and sold. When the corporate structure was first developed in the late nineteenth century, the term market came to figuratively mean a place where securities such as stocks and bonds are bought and sold. The New York Stock Exchange is one example of a market where trading takes place and is the best-known market in the world. However, other markets exist all over the globe where billions of dollars of assets are traded annually.
- **Stock Exchanges**

There are two primary theoretical marketplaces where securities are traded. The term theoretical is used here because the market need not be a physical place where buyers and sellers meet to trade securities. This is akin to references to different markets for selling both new and used automobiles. The primary market for car sales refers to sales of cars between the manufacturer (and a dealership) and the buyer. A secondary market refers to used car sales and may be between any owner and seller. The point is that primary markets refer to new sales and secondary markets refer to used sales.

A stock exchange is any legally recognized market where securities can be bought and sold. Corporations that issue stock are traded in these markets and typically wish to be listed as an officially traded company so that the shares of stock can be purchased by investors in a liquid market. In addition, stock exchanges are regulated such that both companies and investors must follow trading rules making the transition of ownership safer and less risky. The liquidity of the market refers to the ease with which ownership of a company in the form of stocks can be bought and sold without delay or complications afforded by selling the stock on a one-to-one basis between each company and investor.

- **Buybacks and Secondary Markets**

Sometimes a corporation is interested in buying or selling shares of its own stock. In this case, the company does benefit from the transaction but the stocks are still considered to be trading in secondary markets because the stock was issued at an earlier date. When a company buys its own stock in a buyback, it is reducing the number of shares of stock available for purchase in the secondary market. The company may do this to protect itself from a buyout or to use the stock as compensation for the purchase of a new asset. Either way it signals to the secondary markets that the value of the company is changing and holders of the stock need to reevaluate the worth of their part ownership of the company.

FINANCIAL MARKETS

A **financial Market** is market in which people and entities can trade financial securities, commodities, and other fungible items of value at low transaction costs and at prices that reflect supply and demand. Securities include stocks and bonds, and commodities include precious metals or agricultural goods.

There are both general markets (where many commodities are traded) and specialized markets (where only one commodity is traded). Markets work by placing many interested buyers and sellers, including households, firms, and government agencies, in one "place", thus making it easier for them to find each other. An economy which relies primarily on interactions between buyers and sellers to allocate resources is known as a market economy in contrast either to a command economy or to a non-market economy such as a gift economy.

In finance, financial markets facilitate:

- The raising of capital (in the capital markets)
- The transfer of risk (in the derivatives markets)
- Price discovery
- Global transactions with integration of financial markets
- The transfer of liquidity (in the money markets)
- International trade (in the currency markets) – and are used to match those who want capital to those who have it.

Typically, a borrower issues a receipt to the lender promising to pay back the capital. These receipts are securities which may be freely bought or sold. In return for lending money to the borrower, the lender will expect some compensation in the form of interest or dividends. This return on investment is a necessary part of markets to ensure that funds are supplied to them.

Definition: In economics, typically, the term *market* means the aggregate of possible buyers and sellers of a certain good or service and the transactions between them.

The term "market" is sometimes used for what are more strictly *exchanges*, organizations that facilitate the trade in financial securities, e.g., a stock exchange or commodity exchange. This may be a physical location (like the NYSE, BSE, and NSE) or an electronic system (like NASDAQ). Much trading of stocks takes place on an exchange; still, corporate actions (merger, spinoff) are outside an exchange, while any two companies or people, for whatever reason, may agree to sell stock from the one to the other without using an exchange.

Trading of currencies and bonds is largely on a bilateral basis, although some bonds trade on a stock exchange, and people are building electronic systems for these as well, similar to stock exchanges.

TYPES OF FINANCIAL MARKETS

Within the financial sector, the term "financial markets" is often used to refer just to the markets that are used to raise finance: for long term finance, the *Capital markets*; for short term finance, the *Money markets*. Another common use of the term is as a catchall for all the markets in the financial sector, as per examples in the breakdown below.

- Capital markets which consist of:
    - Stock markets, which provide financing through the issuance of shares or common stock, and enable the subsequent trading thereof.
    - Bond markets, which provide financing through the issuance of bonds, and enable the subsequent trading thereof.
- Commodity markets, which facilitate the trading of commodities.
- Money markets, which provide short term debt financing and investment.

- Derivatives markets, which provide instruments for the management of financial risk.
- Futures markets, which provide standardized forward contracts for trading products at some future date; see also forward market.
- Insurance markets, which facilitate the redistribution of various risks.
- Foreign exchange markets, which facilitate the trading of foreign exchange.

The capital markets may also be divided into primary markets and secondary markets. Newly formed (issued) securities are bought or sold in primary markets, such as during initial public offerings. Secondary markets allow investors to buy and sell existing securities. The transactions in primary markets exist between issuers and investors, while in secondary market transactions exist among investors.

Liquidity is a crucial aspect of securities that are traded in secondary markets. Liquidity refers to the ease with which a security can be sold without a loss of value. Securities with an active secondary market mean that there are many buyers and sellers at a given point in time. Investors benefit from liquid securities because they can sell their assets whenever they want; an illiquid security may force the seller to get rid of their asset at a large discount.

RAISING CAPITAL

Financial markets attract funds from investors and channel them to corporations—they thus allow corporations to finance their operations and achieve growth. Money markets allow firms to borrow funds on a short-term basis, while capital markets allow corporations to gain long-term funding to support expansion (known as maturity transformation).

Without financial markets, borrowers would have difficulty finding lenders themselves. Intermediaries such as banks, Investment Banks, and Boutique can help in this process. Banks take deposits from those who have money to save. They can then lend money from this pool of deposited money to those who seek to borrow. Banks popularly lend money in the form of loans and mortgages.

More complex transactions than a simple bank deposit require markets where lenders and their agents can meet borrowers and their agents, and where existing borrowing or lending commitments can be sold on to other parties. A good example of a financial market is a stock exchange. A company can raise money by selling shares to investors and its existing shares can be bought or sold.

The following table illustrates where financial markets fit in the relationship between lenders and borrowers:

RELATIONSHIP BETWEEN LENDERS AND BORROWERS

Lenders	Financial Intermediaries	Financial Markets	Borrowers
Individuals Companies	Banks Insurance Companies Pension Funds Mutual Funds	Interbank Stock Exchange Money Market Bond Market Foreign Exchange	Individuals Companies Central Government Municipalities Public Corporations

LENDERS

Who have enough money to lend or to give someone money from own pocket at the condition of getting back the principal amount or with some interest or charge, is the Lender?

INDIVIDUALS & DOUBLES

Many individuals are not aware that they are lenders, but almost everybody does lend money in many ways. A person lends money when he or she:

- Puts money in a savings account at a bank;
- Contributes to a pension plan;
- Pays premiums to an insurance company;
- Invests in government bonds; or
- Invests in company shares.

COMPANIES

Companies tend to be borrowers of capital. When companies have surplus cash that is not needed for a short period of time, they may seek to make money from their cash surplus by lending it via short term markets called money markets.

There are a few companies that have very strong cash flows. These companies tend to be lenders rather than borrowers. Such companies may decide to return cash to surplus (e.g. via a share buyback.) Alternatively, they may seek to make more money on their cash by lending it (e.g. investing in bonds and stocks).

BORROWERS

- ***Individuals*** borrow money via bankers' loans for short term needs or longer-term mortgages to help finance a house purchase.
- ***Companies*** borrow money to aid short term or long term cash flows. They also borrow to fund modernization or future business expansion.
- ***Governments*** often find their spending requirements exceed their tax revenues. To make up this difference, they need to borrow. Governments also borrow on behalf of nationalized industries, municipalities, local authorities and other public sector bodies. In the UK, the total borrowing requirement is often referred to as the Public sector net cash requirement (PSNCR).

Governments borrow by issuing bonds. In the UK, the government also borrows from individuals by offering bank accounts and Premium Bonds. Government debt seems to be permanent. Indeed, the debt seemingly expands rather than being paid off. One strategy used by governments to reduce the *value* of the debt is to influence *inflation*.

Municipalities and local authorities may borrow in their own name as well as receiving funding from national governments. In the UK, this would cover an authority like Hampshire County Council.

Public Corporations typically include nationalized industries. These may include the postal services, railway companies and utility companies.

Many borrowers have difficulty raising money locally. They need to borrow internationally with the aid of Foreign exchange markets.

Borrowers having similar needs can form into a group of borrowers. They can also take an organizational form like Mutual Funds. They can provide mortgage on weight basis. The main advantage is that this lowers the cost of their borrowings.

DERIVATIVE PRODUCTS

During the 1980s and 1990s, a major growth sector in financial markets is the trade in so called **derivative products**, or **derivatives** for short.

In the financial markets, stock prices, bond prices, currency rates, interest rates and dividends go up and down, creating *risk*. Derivative products are financial products which are used to *control* risk or paradoxically *exploit* risk. It is also called financial economics.

Derivative products or instruments help the issuers to gain an unusual profit from issuing the instruments. For using the help of these products, a contract has to be made. Derivative contracts are mainly 3 types:

1. Future Contracts
2. Forward Contracts
3. Option Contracts.

CURRENCY MARKETS

The most obvious buyers and sellers of currency are importers and exporters of goods. While this may have been true in the distant past, when international trade created the demand for currency markets, importers and exporters now represent only 1/32 of foreign exchange dealing, according to the Bank for International Settlements.

The picture of foreign currency transactions today shows:

- Banks/Institutions
- Speculators
- Government spending (for example, military bases abroad)
- Importers/Exporters
- Tourists Analysis of financial markets

STATISTICAL ANALYSIS OF FINANCIAL MARKETS, STATISTICAL FINANCE

Much effort has gone into the study of financial markets and how prices vary with time. Charles Dow, one of the founders of Dow Jones & Company and The Wall Street Journal, enunciated a set of ideas on the subject which are now called Dow Theory. This is the basis of the so-called technical analysis method of attempting to predict future changes.

One of the tenets of "technical analysis" is that market trends give an indication of the future, at least in the short term. The claims of the technical analysts are disputed by many academics, who claim that the evidence points rather to the random walk hypothesis, which states that the next change is not correlated to the last change. The role of human psychology in price variations also plays a significant factor. Large amounts of volatility often indicate the presence of strong emotional factors playing into the price. Fear can cause excessive drops in price and greed can create bubbles. In recent years the rise of algorithmic and high-frequency program trading has seen the adoption of momentum, ultra-short term moving average and other similar strategies which are based on technical as opposed to fundamental or theoretical concepts of market Behavior.

The scale of changes in price over some unit of time is called the volatility. It was discovered by Beloit Mandelbrot that changes in prices do not follow a Gaussian distribution, but are rather modeled better by Levy stable distributions. The scale of change, or volatility, depends on the length of the time unit to a power a bit more than 1/2. Large changes up or down are more likely than what one would calculate using a Gaussian distribution with an estimated standard deviation.

FINANCIAL MARKET SLANG

- **Poison pill**, when a company issues more shares to prevent being bought out by another company, thereby increasing the number of outstanding shares to be bought by the hostile company making the bid to establish majority.
- **Quant**, a quantitative analyst with a PhD (and above) level of training in mathematics and statistical methods.
- **Rocket scientist**, a financial consultant at the zenith of mathematical and computer programming skill. They are able to invent derivatives of high complexity and construct sophisticated pricing models. They generally handle the most advanced computing techniques adopted by the financial markets since the early 1980s. Typically, they are physicists and engineers by training; rocket scientists do not necessarily build rockets for a living.
- **White Knight**, a friendly party in a takeover bid. Used to describe a party that buys the shares of one organization to help prevent against a hostile takeover of that organization by another party.
- Round-tripping
- **Surfing**, a deliberate structuring of payments or transactions to conceal it from regulators or other parties, a type of money laundering that is often illegal.
- **Spread**, the difference between the highest bid and the lowest offer.

ROLE (FINANCIAL SYSTEM AND THE ECONOMY)

One of the important requisites for the accelerated development of an economy is the existence of a dynamic financial market. A financial market helps the economy in the following manner.

- **Saving mobilization**: Obtaining funds from the savers or surplus units such as household individuals, business firms, public sector units, central government, state governments etc. is an important role played by financial markets.
- **Investment**: Financial markets play a crucial role in arranging to invest funds thus collected in those units which are in need of the same.
- **National Growth**: An important role played by financial market is that, they contributed to a nation's growth by ensuring unfettered flow of surplus funds to deficit units. Flow of funds for productive purposes is also made possible.
- **Entrepreneurship growth**: Financial market contributes to the development of the entrepreneurial claw by making available the necessary financial resources.
- **Industrial development**: The different components of financial markets help an accelerated growth of industrial and economic development of a country, thus contributing to raising the standard of living and the society of well-being.

FUNCTIONS OF FINANCIAL MARKETS

- **Intermediary Functions**: The intermediary functions of a financial markets include the following:
    - **Transfer of Resources**: Financial markets facilitate the transfer of real economic resources from lenders to ultimate borrowers.
    - **Enhancing income**: Financial markets allow lenders to earn interest or dividend on their surplus invisible funds, thus contributing to the enhancement of the individual and the national income.
    - **Productive usage**: Financial markets allow for the productive use of the funds borrowed. The enhancing the income and the gross national production.
    - **Capital Formation**: Financial markets provide a channel through which new savings flow to aid capital formation of a country.
    - **Price determination**: Financial markets allow for the determination of price of the traded financial assets through the interaction of buyers and sellers. They provide a sign for the allocation of funds in the economy based on the demand and supply through the mechanism called price discovery process.
    - **Sale Mechanism**: Financial markets provide a mechanism for selling of a financial asset by an investor so as to offer the benefit of marketability and liquidity of such assets.
    - **Information**: The activities of the participants in the financial market result in the generation and the consequent dissemination of information to the various segments of the market. So as to reduce the cost of transaction of financial assets.
- **Financial Functions**
    - Providing the borrower with funds so as to enable them to carry out their investment plans.

- Providing the lenders with earning assets so as to enable them to earn wealth by deploying the assets in production debentures.
- Providing liquidity in the market so as to facilitate trading of funds.
- it provides liquidity to commercial bank
- it facilitates credit creation
- it promotes savings
- it promotes investment
- it facilitates balance economic growth
- it improves trading floors

CONSTITUENTS OF FINANCIAL MARKET

BASED ON MARKET LEVELS

- **Primary market**: Primary market is a market for new issues or new financial claims. Hence, it's also called new issue market. The primary market deals with those securities which are issued to the public for the first time.
- **Secondary market**: It's a market for secondary sale of securities. In other words, securities which have already passed through the new issue market are traded in this market. Generally, such securities are quoted in the stock exchange and it provides a continuous and regular market for buying and selling of securities.

BASED ON SECURITY TYPES

- **Money market**: Money market is a market for dealing with financial assets and securities which have a maturity period of up to one year. In other words, it's a market for purely short term funds.
- **Capital market**: A capital market is a market for financial assets which have a long or indefinite maturity. Generally, it deals with long term securities which have a maturity period of above one year. Capital market may be further divided into: (a) industrial securities market (b) Govt. securities market and (c) long term loans market.
- **Equity markets**: A market where ownership of securities are issued and subscribed is known as equity market. An example of a secondary equity market for shares is the Bombay stock exchange.
- **Debt market**: The market where funds are borrowed and lent is known as debt market. Arrangements are made in such a way that the borrowers agree to pay the lender the original amount of the loan plus some specified amount of interest.

DERIVATIVE MARKETS

- **Financial service market**: A market that comprises participants such as commercial banks that provide various financial services like ATM. Credit cards. Credit rating, stock broking etc. is known as financial service market. Individuals and firms use financial services markets, to purchase services that enhance the working of debt and equity markets.

- **Depository markets**: A depository market consist of depository institutions that accept deposit from individuals and firms and uses these funds to participate in the debt market, by giving loans or purchasing other debt instruments such as treasure bills.
- **Non-Depository market**: Non-depository market carry out various functions in financial markets ranging from financial intermediary to selling, insurance etc. The various constituencies in non-depositary markets are mutual funds, insurance companies, pension funds, brokerage firms etc.

OVER-THE-COUNTER MARKET (OTC)

Over-the-counter (OTC) or **off-exchange trading** is to trade financial instruments such as stocks, bonds, commodities or derivatives directly between two parties. It is contrasted with exchange trading, which occurs via facilities constructed for the purpose of trading (i.e., exchanges), such as futures exchanges or stock exchanges. In the U.S., over-the-counter trading in stock is carried out by market makers that make markets in OTCBB and Pink Sheets securities using inter-dealer quotation services such as Pink Quote (operated by Pink OTC Markets) and the OTC Bulletin Board (OTCBB).

OTC stocks are not usually listed nor traded on any stock exchanges, though exchange listed stocks can be traded OTC on the third market. Although stocks quoted on the OTCBB must comply with United States Securities and Exchange Commission (SEC) reporting requirements, other OTC stocks, such as those stocks categorized as Pink Sheets securities, have no reporting requirements, while those stocks categorized as OTCQX have met alternative disclosure guidelines through Pink OTC Markets. An over-the-counter contract is a bilateral contract in which two parties agree on how a particular trade or agreement is to be settled in the future. It is usually from an investment bank to its clients directly. Forwards and swaps are prime examples of such contracts. It is mostly done via the computer or the telephone. For derivatives, these agreements are usually governed by an International Swaps and Derivatives Association agreement.

This segment of the OTC market is occasionally referred to as the "Fourth Market."

The NYMEX has created a clearing mechanism for a slate of commonly traded OTC energy derivatives which allows counterparties of many bilateral OTC transactions to mutually agree to transfer the trade to Clear Port, the exchange's clearing house, thus eliminating credit and performance risk of the initial OTC transaction counterparts...

MAIN FINANCIAL INSTRUMENTS

Bond, Promissory note, Cheese – a security contains requirement to make full payment to the bearer of cheese, Certificate of deposit, Bill of Lading (a Bill of Lading is a "document evidencing the receipt of goods for shipment issued by a person engaged in the business of transporting or forwarding goods."), Stock.

PROMISSORY NOTE

Promissory Note A promissory note, referred to as a note payable in accounting, or commonly as just a "note", is a contract where one party (the maker or issuer) makes an unconditional promise in writing to pay a sum of money to the other (the payee), either at a fixed or determinable future time or on demand of the payee, under specific terms. They differ from IOUs in that they contain a specific promise to pay, rather than simply acknowledging that a debt exists.

CERTIFICATE OF DEPOSIT

A certificate of deposit or CD is a time deposit, a financial product commonly offered to consumers by banks, thrift institutions, and credit unions. CDs are similar to savings accounts in that they are insured and thus virtually risk-free; they are "money in the bank" (CDs are insured by the FDIC for banks or by the NCUA for credit unions). They are different from savings accounts in that the CD has a specific, fixed term (often three months, six months, or one to five years), and, usually, a fixed interest rate. It is intended that the CD be held until maturity, at which time the money may be withdrawn together with the accrued interest.

BOND

Bond - an issued security establishing its holder's right to receive from the issuer of the bond, within the time period specified therein,

- Its nominal value
- And the interest fixed therein on this value or other property equivalent.

The bond may provide for other property rights of its holder, where this is not contrary to legislation.

STOCKS (SHARES)

COMMON SHARES

Common shares represent ownership in a company and a claim (dividends) on a portion of profits. Investors get one vote per share to elect the board members, who oversee the major decisions made by management. Over the long term, common stock, by means of capital growth, yields higher returns than almost every other investment. This higher return comes at a cost since common stocks entail the most risk. If a company goes bankrupt and liquidates, the common shareholders will not receive money until the creditors, and preferred shareholders are paid.

PREFERRED STOCK

Preferred stock represents some degree of ownership in a company but usually doesn't come with the same voting rights. (This may vary depending on the company.) With preferred shares investors are usually guaranteed a fixed dividend forever. This is different than common stock, which has variable dividends that are never guaranteed. Another advantage is that in the event of liquidation preferred shareholders are paid off before the common shareholder (but still after debt holders). Preferred stock may also be callable, meaning that the company has the option to purchase the shares from shareholders at any time for any reason (usually for a premium). Some people consider preferred stock to be more like debt than equity.

PROFESSIONAL PARTICIPANTS

Professional participants in the securities market - legal persons, including credit organizations, and also citizens registered as business persons who conduct the following types of activity:

- Brokerage shall be deemed performance of civil-law transactions with securities as agent or commission agent acting under a contract of agency or commission, and also under a power (letter) of attorney for the performance of such transactions in the absence of indication of the powers of agent or commission agent in the contract.
- Dealer activity shall be deemed performance of transactions in the purchase and sale of securities in one's own name and for one's own account through the public announcement of the prices of purchase and/or sale of certain securities, with an obligation of the purchase and/or sale of these securities at the prices announced by the person pursuing such activity.
- **Activity in the management of securities** shall be deemed performance by a legal person or individual business person, in his own name, for a remuneration, during a stated period, of trust management of the following conveyed into his possession and belonging to another person, in the interests of this person or of third parties designated by this person:
    - (i) Securities;
    - (ii) Monies intended for investment in securities;
    - (iii) Monies and securities received in the process of securities management.
- Clearing activity shall be deemed activity in determining mutual obligations (collection, collation and correction of information on security deals and preparation of bookkeeping documents thereon) and in offsetting these obligations in deliveries of securities
- Depositary activity shall be deemed the rendering of services in the safekeeping of certificates of securities and/or recording and transfer of rights to securities
- Activity in the keeping of a register of owners of securities shall be deemed collection, fixing, processing, storage and provision of data constituting a system of keeping the register of security owners.
- Provision of services directly promoting conclusion of civil-law transactions with securities between participants in the securities market shall be deemed activity in the arrangement of trading on the securities market.

MULTIPLE CHOICE QUESTIONS

1. A company making a public issue of securities has to file a draft prospectus with SEBI at least prior to the filing of prospectus with the Registrar of Companies.
   (a) 21 days (b) 30 days
   (c) one month (d) 15 days
2. In the case of a public issue through 100% book building route what is the minimum percentage of shares that can be allocated to the retail investors applying for Rs.1000 worth shares for subscription?
   (a) 20% (b) 25%
   (c) 35% (d) 45%
3. At the time of public issue each company enters into a memorandum of understanding with its
   (a) Auditors (b) Directors
   (c) Merchant Bankers (d) SEBI
4. In terms of Companies Act 1956, offer of securities to more than ……… persons is deemed to be public issue.
   (a) 50 (b) 40
   (c) 100 (d) 75
5. A holder of an ADR/GDR does not have right to .
   (a) vote
   (b) receive dividend
   (c) receive corporate action notification
   (d) trade the ADRs/GDRs in the stock market
6. Which of the following is not true of a credit rating agency (CRA)?
   (a) CRA has to have a minimum net worth of 5 crore
   (b) CRA cannot rate the securities issued by its promoter
   (c) CRA cannot rate the securities issued by any borrower, subsidiary, an associate promoter of CRA if there are common Chairman, Directors or employee between CRA or its rating committee and these entities.
   (d) CRA can be promoted by any company or body corporate having the net worth of 100 crore in previous 3 years.
7. In which of the following market types Central Government securities are allowed to trade?
   (a) Normal Market (b) Odd lot Market
   (c) Auction Market (d) Ret debt Market

8. Basket Trading allows the trader to .
   (a) create offline order entry file for a selected portfolio
   (b) buy/sell nifty stock
   (c) only buy selected portfolio
   (d) trade only on selected portfolio
9. What is the prevailing price band for Nifty/derivative stocks?
   (a) 10% (b) 15%
   (c) 20% (d) No band
10. The market price protection functionality .
    (a) limits the risk of a market order within a pre-set percentage of the last traded price
    (b) limits overall risk of the market
    (c) protects the market from price fluctuations
    (d) all of the above
11. Auction price applicable is .
    (a) previous day's close price (b) last trade price on that day
    (c) that day's close price (d) previous day's last trade price
12. A professional clearing member is .
    (a) a trading and clearing member and is entitled to settle trades for clients/trading members
    (b) a trading and clearing member and is not entitled to settle trades for client
    (c) only a clearing member and can clear and settle trades for his clients
    (d) none of the above
13. Custodial Trades are confirmed by the custodians on day.
    (a) T (b) T + 1
    (c) T + 2 (d) none of the above
14. Delivery versus Payment (DVP) mechanism is ensured through:
    (a) Pay-in first and Pay-out later, (b) Pay-out first and Pay-in later,
    (c) Pay-in and Pay-out simultaneously (d) None of the above
15. Calculate the ZCYC Spot rate for 2 Year maturity when 30=5.1596, 31 = -0.3615, 32=4.5209, Y =13.1202?
    (a) 5.135786 (b) 5.127548
    (c) 5.142458 (d) 5.139978

16. Which instruments constitute the major portion of trades in secondary market of the debt segment?
    (a) Dated Central Government securities.
    (b) Treasury Bills
    (c) Debentures
    (d) Commercial Papers.
17. What is the maximum % allocated to non-competitive bidders in Government securities auction?
    (a) 10% (b) 15%
    (c) 5 % (d) 20%
18. What are the various types of Government securities?
    (a) Only Fixed coupon Bonds & Floating rate Bonds.
    (b) Only Floating rate Bonds & Zero Coupon Bonds.
    (c) Only zero Coupon Bonds & Securities with embedded Derivatives
    (d) Fixed coupon Bonds, Floating rate Bonds, Zero Coupon Bonds & Securities with embedded Derivatives
19. What is the settlement period allowed for Government Securities?
    (a) T+0 & T+3 (b) T+1 & T+3
    (c) T+2 & T+3 (d) T+1
20. Presently which of the following T-bills is traded in the market?
    (a) 91 Days, 182- and 364-Days T-Bill
    (b) 14 Days & 364 Days T-Bill
    (c) 182 Days & 364 Days T-Bill
    (d) 14 Days & 91 Days T-bill
21. When are the FIMMDA-NSE MIBID/MIBOR rates polled daily by NSE-WDM?
    (a) At 9.30 am & 11.30 am (b) At 9.40 am & 11.40 am
    (c) At 9.50 am & 11.30 am (d) At 9.40 am & 11.30 am
22. Which are the instruments used to calculate ZCYC?
    (a) Only Central Government Securities.
    (b) Only T-Bill
    (c) Both T-bill & Central Government Securities.
    (d) Corporate Debentures, CD & CP
23. What are the various securities on which Repo trades are allowed by RBI?
    (a) Only Central Government Securities.
    (b) Only Treasury Bills
    (c) Only Central Government Securities & Treasury bills

(d) Central Government securities, Treasury Bills & State Government securities

(e) Central Government Securities, Treasury bills & corporate debts.

24. A company making a public issue of securities has to file a draft prospectus with SEBI at least prior to the filing of prospectus with the Registrar of Companies.

(a) 21 days (b) 30 days

(c) one month (d) 15 days

25. In the case of a public issue through 100% book building route what is the minimum percentage of shares that can be allocated to the retail investors applying for Rs.1000 worth shares for subscription?

(a) 20% (b) 25%

(c) 35% (d) 45%

26. At the time of public issue each company enters into a memorandum of understanding with its

(a) Auditors (b) Directors

(c) Merchant Bankers (d) SEBI

27. In terms of Companies Act 1956, offer of securities to more than persons is deemed to be public issue.(a)

(a) 50 (b) 40

(c) 100 (d) 75

28. A holder of an ADR/GDR does not have right to .

(a) avote

(b) receive dividend

(c) receive corporate action notification

(d) trade the ADRs/GDRs in the stock market

29. Which of the following is not true of a credit rating agency (CRA)?

(a) CRA has to have a minimum net worth of 5 crore

(b) CRA cannot rate the securities issued by its promoter

(c) CRA cannot rate the securities issued by any borrower, subsidiary, an associate promoter of CRA if there are common Chairman, Directors or employee between CRA or its rating committee and these entities.

(d) CRA can be promoted by any company or body corporate having the net worth of 100 crore in previous 3 years.

30. Which one of the following is not among the major legislations governing the securities market?
    (a) Capital Issues Act, 1947 (b) SEBI Act, 1992
    (c) Companies Act 1956 (d) Depositories Act 1996
31. Which of the following is not the main objective of SEBI?
    (a) Protecting the interest of investors in securities market
    (b) Protecting & development of forex market in India
    (c) Promoting the development of securities market
    (d) Regulating the securities market
32. All market intermediaries are registered and regulated by .
    (a) DCA (b) SEBI
    (c) MOF (d) RBI
33. The issued by SEBI aim to secure fuller disclosure of the relevant information about the issuer and the nature of issue so that the investors can take informed decision.
    (a) Disclosure & Investor Protection Guidelines
    (b) SCRA
    (c) SEBI (Stock Brokers and Sub brokers) Rule
    (d) SEBI (Prohibition of Fraudulent and Unfair Trade Practices Relating to Securities Markets) regulations
34. NSE's screen-based trading system (SBTS) matches orders in the priority basis.
    (a) time/price (b) price/time
    (c) price/quantity (d) quantity/price
35. The current trading cycle practiced by the exchanges is
    (a) T+5 (b) T+3
    (c) T+2 (d) T+1
36. Following problems have been eliminated by introduction of Depositories act?
    (a) Stamp duty on transfer of shares in dematerialized form
    (b) reduction in the share transfer time to the buyer
    (c) higher liquidity
    (d) All of the above
37. For the promotion of awareness among the investors and the protection of the interest of the investors the central government has established
    (a) investor education and protection fund
    (b) investors grievance redressal cell
    (c) settlement guarantee fund
    (d) all of the above

38. The culmination of an IPO is
    (a) QIP (b) FPO
    (c) Listing (d) AS BA
39. Issue of shares to new investors calls for from current investors
    (a) Ordinary resolution (b) Special resolution
    (c) Two-thirds majority approval (d) No approval
40. 'Offer for sale' can be part of:
    (a) IPO (b) FPO
    (c) Either of the above (d) None of the above
41. Preferential allotment shares are locked in for
    (a) 1 year (b) 3 years
    (c) 1 year for non-promoters
    (d) 1 year for non-promoters and 3 years for promoters
42. It is compulsory for companies coming out with a public issue to offer demat facility
    (a) True (b) False.
43. ASBA is available for
    (a) IPO (b) IPO and FPO
    (c) Rights (d) All the above
44. Which of the following is not a segment of the NSE?
    (a) Wholesale Debt Market (b) Retail Debt Market
    (c) Currency derivatives (d) Futures & Options
45. Which of the following does not trade on the exchange?
    (a) SCM (b) TM
    (c) CM (d) PCM
46. Trading members of the NSE can appoint authorised persons in -
    (a) F&O (b) CDS
    (c) Both the above (d) None of the above
47. Who issues contract note to a client of a sub-broker for trades on the NSE?
    (a) Sub-broker (b) Trading member
    (c) NSE (d) NSCCL
48. Which of the following is a back-office activity?
    (a) Trade capture (b) Trade confirmation
    (c) Clearing (d) Risk management

49. For buy stop loss orders, the trigger price has to be less than or equal to the limit price.
    (a) True (b) False
50. Interim exercise settlement is not a feature of NSE index options
    (a) True (b) False

SHORT ANSWER QUESTIONS

1. What is new issue market?
2. What are the Functions of new issue market?
3. Methods of floating new issue.
4. What are the guidelines for new issue?
5. What are the principal steps in public issue?
6. Define Grading of IPO mandatory.
7. Define Primary Market.
8. What are the feature of Primary Market?
9. Explain the player in the market.
10. What are advantages of primary Market?
11. What are disadvantages of primary Market?
12. Define Secondary Market.
13. What are the functions of secondary Market?
14. Define private secondary markets.
15. What is Financial Market?
16. Define Market?
17. What are the types Financial Markets?
18. Define Capital Markets.
19. Define Money markets.
20. Define Raising of capital
21. What are derivative products?
22. Define Currency markets.
23. What is financial market slang?
24. Functions of financial markets.
25. What are the constituents of financial markets?
26. Define derivatives markets.
27. Define financial service market.
28. Define Depository markets.
29. Define non- Depository Markets.
30. Define Over-The Counter (OTC) or Off-Exchange Trading.
31. Define Financial Instruments.

32. Define Promissory Note.
33. Define Certificate of Deposit.
34. Define Bond.
35. Define Common Share.
36. Define Preferred Stock.

ESSAY TYPE QUESTIONS

1. What is new issue market? Explain functions of new issue market?
2. Briefly methods of floating new issue and guidelines for new issue.
3. Define Primary market. Explain features, role, advantages and disadvantages of primary market.
4. Define Secondary Market. Explain functions of secondary market.
5. Differentiate Primary and Secondary markets.
6. Briefly explain Financial Markets, Capital markets and Money markets.
7. Briefly explain the derivative products.
8. Explain Currency Market.
9. Discus the functions and constituents of Financial Markets.
10. Briefly explain Depository and non-depository.
11. Explain the Over-the-counter (OTC) or off-exchange trading.
12. Briefly explain financial instruments.
13. Discuss the Certificate of Deposit, Bond, Common share and preferred stock.

MCQs Answers

1	2	3	4	5	6	7	8	9	10	11	12	13	14	15	16	17	18	19	20	21	22	23	24	25
b	c	c	a	a	d	a	d	c	a	c	b	d	a	a	c	d	d	b	d	c	d	c	c	c
26	27	28	29	30	31	32	33	34	35	36	37	38	39	40	41	42	43	44	45	46	47	48	49	50
a	a	d	a	b	b	a	b	c	d	a	c	b	c	d	a	d	b	d	c	b	c	a	a	a

CHAPTER 3

Stock Market and Listing of Securities

DEFINITION OF STOCK EXCHANGE

The Securities Contracts (Regulation) Act, 1956 defined a stock exchange as 'an association, organization or body of individuals, whether incorporated or not, established for the purposes of assisting, regulating and controlling business in buying, selling and dealing in securities.'

Stock Exchange is a form of exchange which provides services for stock brokers and traders to trade stocks, bonds, and other securities. Stock exchanges also provide facilities for issue and redemption of securities and other financial instruments, and capital events including the payment of income and dividends. Securities traded on a stock exchange include stock issued by companies, unit trusts, derivatives, pooled investment products and bonds. Stock exchanges often function as "continuous auction" markets, with buyers and sellers consummating transactions at a central location, such as the floor of the exchange.

To be able to trade a security on a certain stock exchange, it must be listed there. Usually, there is a central location at least for record keeping, but trade is increasingly less linked to such a physical place, as modern markets are electronic networks, which gives those advantages of increased speed and reduced cost of transitions. Trade on an exchange is by members only.

The initial offering of stocks and bonds to investors is by definition done in the primary market and subsequent trading is done in the secondary market. A stock exchange is often the most important component of a stock market. Supply and demand in stock markets are driven by various factors that, as in all free markets, affect the price of stocks (see stock valuation).

There is usually no compulsion to issue stock via the stock exchange itself, nor must stock be subsequently traded on the exchange. Such trading is said to be *off exchange* or over-the-counter. This is the usual way that derivatives and bonds are traded. Increasingly, stock exchanges are part of a global market for securities.

In recent years, various other trading venues, such as electronic communications networks, alternative trading systems and "dark pools" have taken much of the trading activity away from traditional stock exchanges.

ORGANIZATION OF STOCK EXCHANGES

The stock exchanges in India operate under the rules, buy-laws and regulations approved by the Central Government under the Securities Contracts (Regulation) Act, 1956. All businesses in respect of securities must be conducted only through the recognized stock exchanges.

At present, there are eight recognized stock exchanges in India established at Bombay, Calcutta, Madras, Ahmadabad, Delhi, Hyderabad, Indore and Bangalore. The organization of stock exchanges at the above places in the nature of private clubs, companies limited by guarantee and public limited companies. However, the constitution, buy-laws and regulations of the different stock exchanges have been modified to conform to the rules framed under the Securities Contracts (Regulation) Act, 1956. The Bombay Stock Exchange has been granted permanent recognition. The other stock exchanges are granted permission only for five years at a time which is renewable.

Any stock exchange, which is desirous of being recognized for the purpose of this Act, may make an application in the prescribed form to the Central Government. Copies of bye-laws and rules of the stock exchange for the regulation and control of contracts should also be sent along with application. The application should give information as regards the governing body of such stock exchange, its constitution and powers of management and the manner in which its business is to be transacted; the power and duties of the office-bearers of the stock exchange; admission into the stock exchange of various classes of members, and the nomination and appointments of authorized representatives and clerks. If the Central Government is satisfied, after making an enquiry as may be necessary and after obtaining such further information, it may grant recognition to the stock exchange, subject to conditions imposed upon it.

DEALINGS IN SECURITIES ON A STOCK EXCHANGE

The dealings in securities on a stock exchange are similar to that we have discussed under commodities exchange i.e., spot or cash transactions and forward or futures transactions. That is, the price movements in a stock exchange are not brought about by any single factor. 'The winds that play upon stock exchanges markets are as varying and inconsistent as those that blow upon the ocean'. A person who wishes to be a successful operator in a stock exchange must be aware of the various factors that influence the prices of securities there.

Fundamentally, prices of securities are also regulated by the laws of supply and demand. An increase in demand or a decrease in supply would tend to raise the prices, while a fall in demand or a spurt in supply would lead to a fall in prices. However, the supply factor can influence price only in the long run, as the supply of securities cannot be increased without promoting new companies or making additional issues. The other fundamental factors influencing security prices include; prospects of corporate profits and dividends, general business conditions, labor situation, threat of nationalization, government's economic, fiscal and monetary policies, expected role of the private sector, control of credit, bullion prices, interest rates, war, local politics, impending]election, passing of ordinances, change in company's board of directors, the growth prospects of the economy in general, and the industry concerned in particular, rumors and manipulations, press reports and press reviews.

Sometimes, the fluctuations in prices occur due to the technical position f hot script and the stock exchange itself. For example, an overbought or oversold situation in a security may lead to sharp fluctuation in its prices when the speculators take corrective actions.

ASPECTS OF THE STOCK BUSINESS

The different aspects of the stock business that may be looked after by sub-committees are:

(i) Admission of members and assistant
(ii) Security deposit
(iii) Share examination
(iv) Granting of quotation and enlistment
(v) Clearing house,
(vi) Arbitration for disputes
(vii) Defaulters and scrutiny
(viii) Finance and investment,
(ix) Library,
(x) Public relations
(xi) Documents.

It is not necessary that all these sub-committees should be there for the efficient working of the stock exchange. The biggest stock exchange in India – the Bombay Stock Exchange – has only the 'Arbitration Committee' and the 'Defaulters Committee'. Other matters are looked after by the 'Governing Board' itself.

MANAGEMENT OF STOCK EXCHANGES

The management of a stock exchange in India is vested in a governing body. This governing body is known as 'Governing Board' at the Bombay Stock Exchange, 'Council of Management' at the Madras Stock Exchange, 'Board of Directors' at the Delhi stock Exchange and 'Committee' at the Calcutta Stock Exchange.

The governing body enjoys wide administrative and governmental powers. It is composed of members' representatives and government nominees. While the representatives are elected once a year, the government nominees hold office at the discretion of the Central Government. There is no provision for any public representation. However, it is open to the Central Government to require a stock exchange to provide for one public representative as a precondition for recognition. The Delhi Stock Exchange has provided for one public representative under the directions of the Central Government.

The governing body usually appoints several sub-committees to manage the day-to-day affairs of the stock exchange.

ESSENTIALS OF AN ORGANIZED SECURITIES MARKET

Unless the following essentials are satisfied, an organized securities market cannot function efficiently and render service to the economy as a whole.

1. Ensure a free and fair market for securities.
2. Enlist a free and fair market for securities.
3. Strive for a constant growth in the number of listed companies in order to provide an active and continuous market
4. Ensure a great degree of screening in the admission of members.
5. Frame and enforce proper rules and buy-laws to regulate the volume of speculation so as to serve the needs of liquidity and price continuity only.
6. Never allow over trading or permit speculation degenerate into gambling.
7. Ensure safe investment to the investing public.

RULES, 1957 OF MEMBERSHIP RULES

Under Rules 8 of the Securities Contracts (Regulation) Rules, 1957, no person shall be eligible to be elected as a member if:

(i) He is less than 21 years of age

(ii) He is not a citizen of India (this condition is relatable by the Central Government).

(iii) He has been adjudged bankrupt or a receiving order has been made against him or he has been proved to be insolvent even though he has obtained his final discharge.

(iv) He has compounded with his creditors.

(v) He has been convicted of an offense involving fraud or dishonesty

(vi) He is engaged as principle or employee in any business other than that of securities;

(vii) He is associated with or is a member of or subscriber to or shareholder to debenture – holder in or connected through a partner or employee with any other organization, institution, association, company or corporation in India where dealing in securities are carried on or he is a director or partner or employee of a company whose principal business is that of dealing in securities unless he undertakes on admission to serve such association or connection.

(viii) He has been at any time expelled or declared a defaulter by any other stock exchange;

(ix) He has been previously refused admission to membership unless a period of one year as elapsed since the date of such rejection.

(x) It is clear from the above that only an individual, and not a firm or a company can be a member of a stock exchange.

(xi) The entrance fee for admission ranges from Rc. 250/- to 10,000/- and the membership security deposit from Rc. 5,000/- to Rc. 20,000/-. The annual subscriptions vary from Rc. 15/- to Rc. 300/-

PERFORMS THE FOLLOWING ECONOMIC FUNCTIONS

An organized securities market or a stock exchange performs the following economic functions:

1. Provides a common meeting place for buyers and sellers.
2. Provides a continuous market in securities and ensures negotiability, liquidity and price continuity.
3. Ensures equity and safety in dealings.
4. Provides a mechanism for correct evaluation of security prices.
5. Helps in mobilization of savings for productive purposes by inducing, directing and allocating the flow of savings into most productive channels.
6. Stimulates industrial investments in preference to other forms of competitive investments.
7. Provides a ready market for Government securities-popularly known as 'gilt-edged' securities.
8. Provides facilities for speculation and enable shrewd operators to make substantial gains.
9. Smooth the price movements by ensuring a continuous flow of securities.

ECONOMIC FUNCTIONS AND SERVICES OF STOCK EXCHANGES

An organized securities market performs many basic economic functions and renders several important services.

'If you want to know how things in Britain are going on, do not study the House of Commons, but watch the London Stock Exchange'. This was the advice reported to have been given by Bismarck to a German Diplomat enrooted for London several decades ago. This explains the importance of an organized securities market in the economic development of a country.

IS THE BAN ON FORWARD TRADING ON SECURITIES JUSTIFIED?

An analysis of business done on Indian stock exchanges in terms of cleared and non-cleared securities during April 1965 to December 1968 reveals the highly speculative nature of business that prevailed in the stock exchanges in India.

At the Bombay Stock Exchange, the business in the cleared securities constituted 98.5 per cent of the total business on all accounts in equities. The corresponding percentages for Delhi, Indore and Madras Stock exchanges are 99.9 per cent, 100 percent (there was only one transaction in non-cleared securities), and 17.8 per cent respectively. The Madras Stock Exchange was the only exception to the general phenomenon. The same study reveals, how a very few active members managed to have the controlling interest at Delhi and Calcutta Stock Exchanges, shattering the market sentiment by resorting to the tactics of cornering, short selling and rigging of the market. The average turnover per share per member at Delhi was

41.2 times that of Bombay. The percentage of shares delivered to the total number of shares traded also pointed to the greater extent of speculation that prevailed at the stock exchanges.

Besides, there was also a concentration of trading in a few selected scraps e.g., Indian Iron, Tata Steel, Hindustan Motors, Scandia Steamship, Century and Telco at the Bombay Stock exchange. The percentage of selected scraps traded to total turnover at some of the stock exchanges given below reveals this situation.

The analysis of non-cleared equities reveals that though the non-cleared equities represented 93 per cent of the total equities listed on all the eight stock exchanges in India as on 31 December 1968, the business in them constituted less than 2.5 per cent of the total business. This also testifies the highly speculative nature of business that prevailed at the Indian Stock Exchanges. All these have led the government to impose a total ban on forward trading in securities.

However, what is needed is the regulation of forward trading and its control and not the total ban. For discharging most of the specific functions speculation INS necessary in a stock exchange. Without speculation, a stock exchange cannot provide price continuity and liquidity for the listed securities. Mere investment transactions alone would not be adequate to provide a continuous and ready market. It is the presence of a large number of speculators which give the necessary breadth and continuity to the securities market. By discounting the future prospects of different industrial enterprises, speculation directs the flow of funds to the most productive channels and attracts new savings for investments. Thus, speculation is advantageous, if conducted by well-informed and disciplined operators, who are qualified for correctly interpreting the business conditions and evaluating the true value of securities. A healthy speculation based of n scientific knowledge of business conditions and proper forecasts not only benefits the speculators by giving them profits, but it considerably benefits the society as well.

But, speculation is a double-edged sword, and when it gets out of control, it may scare off genuine investors, impede the flow of finance t industry and affect the economy as a whole. The erratic price movements may also endanger the entire credit structure of the country and affect banks, insurance companies, and other financial intermediaries whose fortunes are bound up with the securities market. It is essential that the speculation is confined to right sphere to right persons and the right type and volume of transactions. Therefore, the purpose should be to regulate speculative activities and eliminate the unhealthy feature of speculation from our stock exchanges and not banning them altogether. 'Stock exchanges are meant to provide facilities for speculation and thus benefit the investors who are assured of a constant market in their scrip and, hence, with investment business certain amount of speculation which must always find its way and is always desirable. But, the two malpractices, viz., manipulation of a security public must be held under check, if no eliminated. Though the strict enforcement of buy-laws, margin requirements, and regulation of blank transfers, and bald transactions, misuse of speculation can be largely prevented.

LISTING REQUIREMENTS

Listing requirements are the set of conditions imposed by a given stock exchange upon companies that want to be listed on that exchange. Such conditions sometimes include minimum number of shares outstanding, minimum market capitalization, and minimum annual income.

REQUIREMENTS BY STOCK EXCHANGE

Companies must meet an exchange's requirements to have their stocks and shares listed and traded there, but requirements vary by stock exchange:

- **New York Stock Exchange:** To be listed on the New York Stock Exchange (NYSE) a company must have issued at least a million shares of stock worth $100 million and must have earned more than $10 million over the last three years.[8]
- **NASDAQ Stock Exchange:** To be listed on the NASDAQ a company must have issued at least 1.25 million shares of stock worth at least $70 million and must have earned more than $11 million over the last three years.
- **London Stock Exchange:** The main market of the London Stock Exchange has requirements for a minimum market capitalization (£700,000), three years of audited financial statements, minimum public float (25 per cent) and sufficient working capital for at least 12 months from the date of listing.
- **Bombay Stock Exchange:** Bombay Stock Exchange (BSE) has requirements for a minimum market capitalization of 250 million (US$4.2 million) and minimum public float equivalent to 100 million (US$1.7 million).

OWNERSHIP

Stock exchanges originated as mutual organizations, owned by its member stock brokers. There has been a recent trend for stock exchanges to *demutualize*, where the members sell their shares in an initial public offering. In this way the mutual organization becomes a corporation, with shares that are listed on a stock exchange. Examples are Australian Securities Exchange (1998), Euronext (merged with New York Stock Exchange), NASDAQ (2002), Bursa Malaysia (2004), the New York Stock Exchange (2005), Balsas y Mercado's Española's, and the São Paulo Stock Exchange (2007). The Shenzhen and Shanghai stock exchanges can been characterized as quasi-state institutions insofar as they were created by government bodies in China and their leading personnel are directly appointed by the China Securities Regulatory Commission. Another example is Tashkent republican stock exchange (Uzbekistan) established in 1994, three years after collapse of Soviet Union, mainly owned by state but has a form of a public corporation (joint stock Company). According to an Uzbek government decision (March 2012) 25 percent minus one share of Tashkent stock exchange is expected to be sold to Korea Exchange (KRX) in 2014

OTHER TYPES OF EXCHANGES

In the 19th century, exchanges were opened to trade forward contracts on commodities. Exchange traded forward contracts are called futures contracts. These *commodity exchanges* later started offering future contracts on other products, such as interest rates and shares, as well as options contracts. They are now generally known as futures exchanges.

DESIGNED TO PROTECT INVESTING PUBLIC FORM ABUSES OF THE FREEDOM OF THE MARKET

The listing requirements which are designed to protect the investing public form abuses of the freedom of the market or form the fraud or exploitation are:

1. The company must file certified copies of its Memorandum and Articles of Association containing certain provisions prescribed by the stock exchange authorities.
2. Financial and historical facts of investment significance in the form of Audited Balance Sheets for five years, dividend history for ten years, a short historical account of the company's growth, properties, capital structure, etc., must be disclosed. (This applies to existing companies only.)
3. The distribution of the shares must be described showing whether the issue is widely held or concentrated in few hands, so that the stock exchange authorities maybe reasonably assured of a free and uncontrolled market. (This also applies to existing companies only)
4. It must offer for public subscription at least a minimum of 49 per cent of its issued capital.
5. The prospectus issued by the company must satisfy the conditions regarding the 'time of opening of subscription list' and receipt of share applications.
6. The share allotment against application must be unconditional and fair.
7. In case of over-subscription, the basis of allotment is required to be decided by the company in consultation with the stock exchange authorities.
8. The company seeking listing facility must execute an agreement, undertaking to make certain disclosures and perform certain acts as and when required by the stock exchange authorities.
9. Transfer facilities must be maintained in the city of the exchange.

Under Rule 19 (1) of Securities Contracts (Regulation) Rules, 1957, and the listing regulations of a recognized stock exchange, the following documents are also to be submitted by a company to the stock exchange along with the listing application; prospectus, underwriting agreemne4ts, vendors' and promoters' agreements, service and selling agency agreements, collaboration and technical agreements, debenture trust deed; specimens of share certificates, debenture certificates, transfer certificates, split an consolidation certificates, particulars of cash bonuses declared and paid, directors, reports etc.

If the stock exchanges authorities are not satisfied, they can refuse to grant permission or defer their decision on the matter. Therefore, to avoid any possible hitch in securing the permission, it is usual for the company to arrange for an informal discussion between the representatives of the company and the stock exchange authorities. By this procedure, the proposal for listing can be steered through successfully on quietly dropped without any damage to the company's reputation.

THE VARIOUS TYPES OF ORDERS PREVALENT IN A STOCK EXCHANGE

The transactions in securities on a sock exchange are done through the members or brokers or the exchange. The transactions could be put through only in terms of the specified unit of trading or lots e.g., 5, 10 or 100 shares.

Usually, the customers give the following types of order, viz.

1. Fixed price order or limit price orders.
2. At be or at the market price orders.
3. Immediate or cancel orders
4. Stop-loss orders **(v)** discretionary orders.
5. Open orders.

In the first type of order, the broker has to carry out the order at a fixed price. He has no choice over the price e.g., 'Buy 100 Parry Sugar at Rc. 110/-'. In the second type of order, no price limit is specified and the order can be executed at the best obtainable price at that time e.g., But 100 Parry Sugar at best'. The wordings in the case f third type would be, 'Buy 100 Parry Sugar at Rc. 110/- immediate-cancel'. Such orders are to be carried out immediately and if this is not possible, the order stands automatically canceled. Stop-loss orders are sent to the brokers to limit the loss on a previous purchase or sale if the price trend goes against the customer's expectation, e.g., 'Buy 100 Parry Sugar at 110 stop'. In this case, as soon as the price reaches Rc. 110/- the broker has to buy at Rc. 110/- or at the best price available. Similarly, when the order is 'Sell 100 Parry Sugar at 110 stop', the broker has to sell immediately at Rc. 110/- or at the best price available at that time. Discretionary order and open orders are rare to be issued to brokers. Such orders would be issued when there is a complete understanding between the client and his broker.

AUTHORIZED CLERKS OF OPERATORS AND DEALERS ON THE STOCK EXCHANGE

These people are also known as 'Member Assistants' and they are the authorized representatives or assistants of members. They can transact business only on behalf of their employers.

REMISES OF OPERATORS AND DEALERS ON THE STOCK EXCHANGE

These people are also known as 'half-commission' men. They act as agents of the members for the purpose of securing business for them. They are not allowed to transact business on the floor of the stock exchange. They are only procuring of business. Their remuneration is paid out of the commission earned from the business secured by them.

ARBITRAGEURS OF OPERATORS AND DEALERS ON THE STOCK EXCHANGE

'The arbitrageur specializes in making purchases and sales in different markets at the same time and profits by the difference in prices between the two markets. His success in this type of operation depends upon the number of securities simultaneously listed on different stock exchange, and the availability of fast means of communication like, telex or tile-printer services.

BUDLIWALAS OF OPERATORS AND DEALERS ON THE STOCK EXCHANGE

These people are the financiers on the securities market. They lend cash to the market by taking delivery of securities on the due date at the end of clearing for those who wish to carry over their purchases. They also sell securities to the market when it is short, by giving delivery on the due date at the end of the clearing, for those who wish to carry over their sales.

When the buyer is willing to carry over the transaction, he has to pay the budliwala a consideration called 'cantango' or budla charge. Canting is to cover the interest charge, n this indirect loan. Like-wise, the seller has to pay buddle charge, known as 'backwardation' to the budliwala, when the request of carry over comes from the seller. The can tango and backwardation may be paid separately or may be adjusted with the price of securities. The buddle transactions are regulated by the stock exchanges and sometimes prohibited also. As only overtraded securities are carried over, the carry-over or buddle facilities are useful in keeping the market stable, provided speculation on this account is within bounds.

ODD LOT DEALERS OF OPERATORS AND DEALERS ON THE STOCK EXCHANGE

Here, the specialization is buying and selling securities in amounts less than prescribed trading units. They buy odd lots and make them up into marketable trading units.

They also split up round lots and sell them in odd lots. They do not survive on brokerage or commission but on the difference between the buying price and selling of odd lots.

DEALERS IS NON-CLEARED SECURITIES OF OPERATORS AND DEALERS ON THE STOCK EXCHANGE

Listing:

All Government securities and Treasury bills are deemed to be listed automatically as and when they are issued. Other securities, issued publicly or placed privately, could be listed or admitted for trading, if eligible as per rules of the Exchange by following prescribed procedure:

1. All Listing are subject to compliance with Byelaws, Rules and other requirements framed by the Exchange from time to time in addition to the SEBI and other statutory requirements.

2. The Issuer of security proposed for listing has to forward an application in the prescribed format, which forms a part of the Listing Booklet.
3. Every issuer, depending on the category and type of security has to submit along with application, such supporting documents/information as stated in the Listing booklet and as prescribed by the Exchange from time to time.
4. On getting an in-principal consent of the exchange the issuer has to enter into a listing agreement in the prescribed format under its common seal.
5. Upon listing, the Issuer has to comply with all requirements of law, any guidelines/ directions of Central Government, other Statutory or local authority.
6. The Issuer shall also comply with the post listing compliance as laid out in the listing agreement and shall also comply with the rules, bye-laws, regulations and any other guidelines of the Exchange as amended from time to time.
7. Listing on WDM segment does not imply a listing on CM segment also or vice versa.
8. If the equity shares of an issuer are listed on other stock exchanges but not listed on Capital Market segment of the Exchange, though eligible, then the debt securities of the said issuer will not be permitted to be listed on the WDM segment.
9. The Exchange reserves the right to change any of the requirements indicated in the Listing booklet without prior notice.

Certain securities like Treasury Bills and other securities issued by Government of India available in demat form are eligible for Repo. Every security in the trading system is given a symbol representative of the security. The market capitalization of the securities on the WDM segment has been increasing steadily. The segment has also seen a marked increase in the number of securities available for trading other than the traditional instruments like Govt. securities and T-bills.

LISTING OF SECURITIES

Every stock exchange maintains an official 'Quotation List' divided into several sections. This is list .is published daily containing the prices at which business has been transacted and also a description of lots in which the business took place at particular prices. No dealings in securities can take place on a recognized stock exchange unless the necessary permission of the stock exchange has been obtained by the promoters of the company and the securities are listed in the official trading or quotation list of the stock exchange. Therefore, listing is nothing but the admission of a security to the trading privilege on a stock exchange Listing is an integral part of the machinery of a recognized stock exchange.

A company, desirous of listing its securities on the Exchange, shall be required to file an application, in the prescribed form, with the Exchange before issue of Prospectus by the company, where the securities are issued by way of a prospectus or before issue of 'Offer for Sale', where the securities are issued by way of an offer for sale. The company shall be responsible to follow all the requirements specified in the Companies Act, the listing norms issued by SEBI from time to time and such other conditions, requirements and norms that may be in force from time to time and included hereafter in these Bye-laws and Regulations to make the security eligible to be listed and for continuous listing on the Exchange.

OBJECTIVES AND SCOPE OF LISTING

Dealings in securities by their very nature are susceptible to fraud and undesirable practices on the part of the operators on a stock exchange. The general investing public's interest ties to be safeguarded. It is essential, only those securities which meet certain prescribed standard of legality, security and workmanship are permitted for dealings on the floor of the stock exchange. Listing of securities ensures proper supervision and control of dealings on the listed securities.

Listing only implies that the securities admitted to the official trading list of the stock exchange satisfy the prescribed standard of legality, security and workmanship. It further implies that the company, whose securities are so listed, has to comply with certain conditions and requirements with regard to submission of certain documents and disclosure of certain information whenever the stock exchange so wants. Through listing, a recognized stock exchange tries to ensure that all significant information relating to the listed company is an available to all the investors and traders on the stock exchange.

Listing in no way implies that the stock exchange vouches the soundness of the listed securities or the company and sponsors the issue. The stock exchange cannot be expected to act as a judge and advise the investing public regarding the soundness or otherwise of a particular company issuing the securities or the securities already issued. The investor himself as to use his own judgment or exercise his own discretion in buying a particular security. A listed security simply carried the hallmark of approval for dealings on the3 floor of the recognized stock exchange. "It bears the light of day. It might be weak but it will not be fraudulent.' Listing creates a favorable impression on the minds of investors by indirectly assuring the soundness and legality of the company. It reveals that at the time of listing, the company whose securities is listed, is legally organized and is solvent as a going concern.

Listing is not compulsory in law. But in practice, it becomes more or less a necessity. A company, which states in its prospectus, the intention to apply for enlistment of its securities on a recognized stock exchange, is required under Section 73 of the Companies act, 1956, to make a listing application to the exchange authorities before the tenth day of the first issue of prospectus. If no application is made or if the application is refused, any allotment made by the company shall be void and the company shall have to refund the application money in full to the subscribers. The central Government has also the power under Section 21 to the Securities Contracts (Regulation) Act, 1956, to ask a public company to get its shares listed on a recognized stock exchange to safeguard public interest.

The institutional underwriters such as the Industrial Finance Corporation of India, the Industrial Credit and Investment Corporation of India, the Life Insurance corporation, the Industrial Development Bank, the Unit Trust, the State Bank of India, etc., usually insist on listing of securities while consenting to underwrite issues. The controller of Capital Issues also generally insists on listing.

How to get the shares Listed?

All recognized stock exchanges in India have prescribed uniform listing regulations. 'In listing requirements, the stock exchange has forged a weapon which has given in huge power'. The admission of the shares of companies to the privilege or quotation and dealings on the exchange is a matter of importance and entails a certain responsibility. This responsibility, a stock exchange endeavors to discharge by a through and impartial security of the affairs of the company before admission and by the enforcement of certain conditions.

DESIGNED TO PROTECT INVESTING PUBLIC FORM ABUSES OF THE FREEDOM OF THE MARKET

The listing requirements which are designed to protect the investing public form abuses of the freedom of the market or form the fraud or exploitation are:

1. The company must file certified copies of its Memorandum and Articles of Association containing certain provisions prescribed by the stock exchange authorities.
2. Financial and historical facts of investment significance in the form of Audited Balance Sheets for five years, dividend history for ten years, a short historical account of the company's growth, properties, capital structure, etc., must be disclosed. (This applies to existing companies only.)
3. The distribution of the shares must be described showing whether the issue is widely held or concentrated in few hands, so that the stock exchange authorities maybe reasonably assured of a free and uncontrolled market. (This also applies to existing companies only)
4. It must offer for public subscription at least a minimum of 49 per cent of its issued capital.
5. The prospectus issued by the company must satisfy the conditions regarding the 'time of opening of subscription list' and receipt of share applications.
6. The share allotment against application must be unconditional and fair.
7. In case of over-subscription, the basis of allotment is required to be decided by the company in consultation with the stock exchange authorities.
8. The company seeking listing facility must execute an agreement, undertaking to make certain disclosures and perform certain acts as and when required by the stock exchange authorities.
9. Transfer facilities must be maintained in the city of the exchange.

Under Rule 19 (1) of Securities Contracts (Regulation) Rules, 1957, and the listing regulations of a recognized stock exchange, the following documents are also to be submitted by a company to the stock exchange along with the listing application; prospectus, underwriting agreemne4ts, vendors' and promoters' agreements, service and selling agency agreements, collaboration and technical agreements, debenture trust deed; specimens of share certificates, debenture certificates, transfer certificates, split an consolidation certificates, particulars of cash bonuses declared and paid, directors, reports etc.

If the stock exchanges authorities are not satisfied, they can refuse to grant permission or defer their decision on the matter. Therefore, to avoid any possible hitch in securing the permission, it is usual for the company to arrange for an informal discussion between the representatives of the company and the stock exchange authorities. By this procedure, the proposal for listing can be steered through successfully on quietly dropped without any damage to the company's reputation.

MERITS AND DEMERITS OF LISTING OF SECURITIES

Listing of shares if beneficial both to the company and the investors. To the company, listing gives a higher status and the listed securities enjoy a privileged position. Carrying the hallmark of the prestige of the exchange listing the shares, listed shares preferred of investments. An open and continuous market with informed buyers and sellers is ensured. The transaction of business under well-defined rules and regulations imparts a high degree of liquidity and price continuity to listed securities. Hence, they have high collateral value for bank borrowings. Tax reliefs are also available. Financing of future expansion activities also is made easy.

To the investor also, it ensures reasonable safety, liquidity and price continuity. The listed securities do not fluctuate widely. Evaluation of holdings for the purpose of assessment for Income-tax, Wealth-tax and Estate Duty is rendered easy. There are also assured of a fair and equitable allotment, reasonable facilities for and public ownership of shareholdings, contributing to the growth of corporate enterprises. The dealers are also benefited. They receive the benefit of a regular and systematic quotation service and are assured of easy conversion facilities and the prevailing price.

However, the listing of shares by a company induces its management to take an undue interest in their securities prices. They may misuse the 'inside information' and speculate in company's shares, ignoring the shareholders' interest. Substantial interests can be purchased by interested parties with a view to acquiring control over the company's management. Sometimes, the disclosure of information connecting the working of the company etc., may adversely affect its competitive standing. Sometimes, the listed securities are subject to more violent fluctuations in prices due to the questionable activities of uninformed and inexperienced or weak speculators. These fluctuations will affect the image of the company and the interests of the investors.

APPLICATIONS IN RESPECT OF NEW ISSUES OR OFFERS FOR SALE OR BOOK-BUILDING

Except when otherwise allowed by the Governing Board or Managing Director or Relevant Authority in any particular case and subject to compliance with such conditions as it or he may impose, tenders or applications for subscription or purchase or book-building in respect of any new issue or offer for sale of any security shall not be submitted unless the issuer or offerer offers to all a fair and equal opportunity for subscription or purchase and on the same terms as to brokerage to all the trading members and unless it is provided that all tenders and applications for subscription or purchase or book-building shall rank alike for allotment or sale.

The issuer or the offered, prior to issuing further securities or offering securities for sale, shall obtain an in principle approval from the Exchange for listing these securities on the Exchange.

APPLICATION FOR ADMISSION TO DEALINGS

The issuer shall submit an application for admission of its securities to dealings on the Exchange in such form, as may be prescribed by the Exchange from time to time, after ensuring compliance with the applicable provisions in the SCRA, SCRR, Companies Act and the Rules, Regulations and norms as may be issued by SEBI / Exchange in this regard from time to time

UNITS AND EXCHANGE TRADED FUNDS

Units of Mutual Funds may be admitted to dealings on the Exchange subject to such conditions and requirements, as may be prescribed by the Governing Board or Relevant Authority from time to time.

OPTIONS OR FUTURES IN SECURITIES

Options and futures in securities and in securities index or indices shall be admitted to dealings on the Exchange by the Governing Board or Relevant Authority in accordance with the provisions of SCRA and norms issued by SEBI from time to time and as may be specified in the relevant Bye-laws and Regulations framed in this regard.

NOTICE OF APPLICATION FOR ADMISSION TO DEALINGS

Notice of any application for admission to dealings on the Exchange shall be posted on the notice board or displayed on the ATS or Website of the Exchange for the information of trading members and others, at least one week prior to its consideration by the Exchange.

UNDERWRITING, PLACING AND PRELIMINARY ARRANGEMENTS

Except when otherwise allowed by the Relevant Authority in any particular case and subject to compliance with such conditions as it may impose, a trading member shall not enter into an underwriting contract nor shall he contract either as a principal or agent to subscribe or purchase or to procure, whether through the market or otherwise, nor shall he act or agree to act as broker or underwriter in connection with any floatation or issue of any security, unless the trading member fulfills the capital adequacy requirements, as may be specified by SEBI or the Exchange from time to time, and the issuer conforms or agrees to conform to the listing requirements prescribed in these Bye-laws and Regulations and/or as provided under the SCRA and SCRR and undertakes to apply for admission of such security to dealings on the Exchange.

LISTING CONDITIONS AND REQUIREMENTS

The Governing Board or Managing Director or Relevant Authority may not grant admission to dealings on the Exchange to a security of an issuer unless the issuer complies with the listing conditions, requirements and norms, under the SCRA, SCRR, the Companies Act, the Rules, Bye-laws and Regulations of the Exchange and the norms, as may be prescribed by the Exchange and/or SEBI from time to time

The Governing Board or Managing Director or Relevant Authority shall ensure that no listing or trading permission is granted unless the issuer complies with all the conditions, requirements or norms, as may be provided in the relevant Regulations from time to time, including dispatch of physical share certificates to, and/or credit of demat shares to the accounts of all the security-holders, maintained with the depositories.

Where the Exchange is the stock exchange with whose consultation the basis of allotment is decided, the Governing Board or Managing Director or Relevant Authority of the said stock exchange shall intimate the depositories about approval granted for admission to dealings on the Exchange for any security.

The company shall execute a Listing Agreement, in the prescribed form with the Exchange, prior to approval of the listing application of the company. Any addition or amendment to the provisions of the Listing Agreement, as may be prescribed by SEBI and/or the Exchange shall become applicable to the company as if such addition or amendment was part of the Listing Agreement.

In the case of a new issue or further issue by any issuer the Governing Board or Managing Director or Relevant Authority may grant permission for trading in any security at the Exchange on the same day as on all other stock exchanges where such security admitted to dealings is granted permission for trading.

SECURITIES ISSUED ON PREFERENTIAL ALLOTMENT BASIS OR UNDER ESOP

Securities issued on preferential allotment basis or under the Employees Stock Option Scheme by an issuer, whose securities are already admitted to dealings on the Exchange, may be granted admission to dealings on the Exchange on complying with the listing conditions, requirements and norms, under the SCRA, SCRR, the Companies Act, the rules made thereunder, and these Bye-laws and Regulations, as may be prescribed by the Governing Board or Managing Director or Relevant Authority and/or SEBI from time to time.

ISSUERS REGISTERED OUTSIDE INDIA

Admission to dealings on the Exchange shall not be granted to a security issued by a body corporate or fund or other entity registered or formed outside India unless: there is adequate public interest in such securities in India and the body corporate, fund or other entity agrees to abide by the applicable statutory provisions, as may be in force and such requirements as may be prescribed in this regard by the Exchange or SEBI or Reserve Bank of India or any other statutory body.

APPLICABILITY OF LISTING CONDITIONS AND REQUIREMENTS

In the case of a body corporate, fund or other entity registered or formed outside India, the Governing Board or Managing Director or Relevant Authority may, for reasons to be recorded in writing, waive or dispense with the strict enforcement of any or all of the listing conditions and requirements prescribed in these Byelaws and Regulations, except those prescribed in Bye Law 4.9 provided that the securities of such body corporate, fund or other entity are admitted to dealings on any stock exchange outside India and the Governing Board or Managing Director or Relevant Authority is satisfied that it is in the interest of trade or in the public interest, so to do.

GRANT OR REFUSAL OF ADMISSION TO DEALINGS

The Governing Board or Managing Director or Relevant Authority may, in its/his discretion, approve subject to such terms as it/he deems proper or defer or reject any application for admission of a security of an issuer to the dealings on the Exchange, without assigning any reason whatsoever, within the time provided under the SCRA, the Companies Act and the Rules, Regulations and norms as may be issued by SEBI / Exchange, that may be in force from time to time.

LISTING APPROVAL

The Exchange may grant approval to the issuer for any security sought to be listed on the Exchange on completion of the listing conditions, requirements and norms by the issuer, as may be specified by the Exchange from time to time. Such security shall be called listed security.

ADMISSION TO DEALINGS

Admission to dealings shall mean permission granted by the Exchange to a security for commencement of trading on the ATS of the Exchange as provided in these Bye-laws and the relevant Regulations.

TRADING ALLOWED

Trading in securities admitted to dealings shall be allowed on the ATS of the Exchange as provided in these Bye-laws and the relevant Regulations, and save as otherwise so provided, no other mode of trading shall be allowed.

EXPLANATION

The Exchange shall ensure that the permission for trading in any security at the Exchange is given on the same day as on all other stock exchanges where such security admitted to dealings is granted permission for trading.

TRADING IN SECURITIES ADMITTED TO DEALINGS ON OTHER STOCK EXCHANGES

The Governing Board or Relevant Authority may, in its discretion and subject to such conditions as it may deem proper, allow trading in any security or securities, admitted to dealings on any other stock exchange. Such security shall be called permitted security.

LISTING FEES

The Board or the Relevant Authority of the Exchange shall fix the listing fees at such rates and in such manner as may be deemed fit from time to time.

FEES OR DEPOSITS TO BE PAID BY ISSUER

Issuers, whose securities are granted admission to dealings on the Exchange, shall pay listing fees and deposits, within such time, as may be determined by the Exchange from time to time.

TRADING IN GOVERNMENT SECURITIES

Trading shall be allowed in Government Securities, which term for the purposes of these Bye-laws and Regulations, denote securities issued by the Government of India, State Governments, Port Trusts, Municipal Corporations and other similar bodies. Government Securities shall be deemed to have been admitted to dealings on the Exchange from the date on which they are issued. Transactions in Government Securities shall be carried out and settled in accordance with the directions issued by the Reserve Bank of India from time to time.

GOVERNING BOARD OR MANAGING DIRECTOR OR RELEVANT AUTHORITY MAY RESTRICT OR PROHIBIT TRADING

The Governing Board or Managing Director or Relevant Authority may, in its/his absolute discretion, impose such restrictions on transactions in any security admitted to dealings, in the interest of orderly market in securities or in the interest of trade or in the public interest. During the operation of such restrictions, no trading member shall, either on his own account or on account of his sub-brokers or clients, enter into in any transaction in contravention of such restrictions. The Governing Board or Managing Director or Relevant Authority may prohibit dealings on the ATS of the Exchange in any security or securities admitted to dealings for reasons to be recorded in writing.

CONSEQUENCES OF NON-COMPLIANCE BY ISSUER

SUSPENSION OF ADMISSION TO DEALINGS ON THE EXCHANGE

Subject to the provisions of SCRA and SCRR, the Governing Board or Managing Director or Relevant Authority may, at any time, for reasons to be recorded in writing, shift trading from normal basis to trade-for-trade basis or suspend the admission to dealings on the Exchange granted to any security for a breach of or non-compliance with any of the conditions of admission to dealings or for manipulation of prices/trading or for any other reason whatsoever, for such period or periods and on such conditions, as it/he may determine. At the expiration of the period of suspension, the Governing Board or Managing Director or Relevant Authority may reinstate the dealings in such security subject to such conditions, as it/he deems fit.

Intimation of shifting of trading from normal basis to trade-for-trade basis or suspension of trading by the Exchange in any security on account of a violation of any of the provisions of the Listing Agreement or because of a surveillance action or for whatever other reason shall be communicated by the Exchange to other stock exchanges where the security is listed.

WITHDRAWAL OF ADMISSION TO DEALINGS OR REDEMPTION OR CONVERSION

The Governing Board or Managing Director or Relevant Authority may, if deemed necessary, withdraw admission to dealings granted to a security which is about to be exchanged with some other security or converted into some other security as a result of any scheme of re-organization or reconstruction of the issuer company or to such security, redeemable or convertible in their nature, which is about to fall due for redemption or conversion.

LIQUIDATION OR MERGER

If any issuer whose securities have been granted admission to dealings on the Exchange, be placed in final or provisional liquidation or is about to be merged into or amalgamated with another company, the Governing Board or Managing Director or Relevant Authority may withdraw the admission to dealings on the Exchange granted to its securities. The Governing Board or Managing Director or Relevant Authority may accept such evidence as it/he deems sufficient as to such liquidation, merger or amalgamation. If the merger or amalgamation fails to take place or if any company placed in provisional liquidation be reinstated and an application be made by such company for readmission of its securities to dealings on the Exchange, the Governing Board or Managing Director or Relevant Authority shall have the power of considering and of approving, refusing or deferring such application.

VOLUNTARY DELISTING BY COMPANY

A company may be allowed to get its securities delisted (i.e. withdrawal of admission to dealings) from the Exchange, provided the provisions, guidelines, norms and procedures governing the listing/delisting and trading/suspension of trading in securities that may be stipulated by the SEBI/Central Listing Authority are duly complied with.

BUY-BACK OF SECURITIES BY COMPANY

A company may buy-back securities issued by it earlier, subject to the conditions, requirements and guidelines governing the scheme of buy-back of securities by a company, issued by SEBI and / or Central Government in that behalf. A company, making an offer to buy-back its securities, shall be required to strictly adhere to the conditions, requirements and guidelines in force in that regard and any non-compliance or violation by the company shall render it liable for such action, as may be deemed fit by the Exchange.

WITHDRAWAL OF ADMISSION TO DEALINGS OR DELISTING ON THE EXCHANGE

Subject to the provisions of SCRA and SCRR, the Governing Board or Managing Director or Relevant Authority may, after giving an opportunity to the company to explain, withdraw the admission to dealings on the Exchange granted to its securities, either for breach of or non-compliance with any of the continuous listing requirements for admission to dealings or for any other reason whatsoever to be recorded in writing, and in such manner, as may be provided in relevant Regulations from time to time.

RIGHT TO APPEAL AGAINST DELISTING

Any person, who may be aggrieved or affected by the decision of the Exchange to delist a security of any company admitted to dealings on the Exchange, may appeal in writing, to SEBI, within thirty calendar days from the date the Exchange has notified the decision to the company.

READMISSION TO DEALINGS ON THE EXCHANGE

The Governing Board or Managing Director or Relevant Authority may readmit to dealings on the Exchange the security of a company whose admission to dealings had been previously withdrawn, on the fulfillment of conditions, norms, guidelines or requirements as may be prescribed by the Governing Board or Managing Director or Relevant Authority and / or SEBI from time to time.

CENTRAL LISTING AUTHORITY

As and when the Central Listing Authority is constituted by SEBI or any authority under the relevant law in relation to listing / delisting and trading / suspension of trading in securities of companies on a stock exchange, the provisions, guidelines, norms and procedures governing the listing / delisting and trading / suspension of trading in securities that may be stipulated by such Central Listing Authority shall then be incorporated in the Bye-laws of the Exchange and shall be made applicable mutatis mutandis by the Exchange.

MULTIPLE CHOICE QUESTIONS

1. The following are participants in the securities markets .
   (a) Underwriters (b) Debenture Trustees
   (c) Venture Capital Funds (d) All of the above
2. The securities markets have the following category (ies) of participant (s) issuers of securities
   (a) investors in securities (b) intermediaries
   (c) All of the above (d) I am not attempting the question

3. In private placement, issuance is done to .
   (a) more than 50 persons
   (b) less than 100 persons
   (c) less than 50 persons
   (d) less than 10 persons
4. Which entity provides novation: .
   (a) NSCCL
   (b) NSE
   (c) NSDL
   (d) CDSL
5. Deals with issue, allotment and transfer of securities and various aspects relating to company management.
   (a) Companies Act, 1956
   (b) Depositories Act, 1996
   (c) Capital Issues (Control) Act, 1947
   (d) None of the above
6. Envisages transfer of ownership of securities electronically by book entry without making the securities move from person to person.
   (a) Companies Act, 1956
   (b) Depositories Act, 1996
   (c) Capital Issues (Control) Act, 1947
   (d) None of the above
7. A company making a public issue of securities has to file a draft prospectus with .
   (a) RBI
   (b) SEBI
   (c) Ministry of Finance
   (d) None of the above
8. For public and rights issues of debt instruments, it is mandatory to obtain credit rating from a registered credit rating agency. True or False.
   (a) True
   (b) False
   (c) I am not attempting the question
9. Promoters' contribution in case of public issues by unlisted companies and promoters' shareholding in case of 'offers for sale' shall not be less than of post issue capital
   (a) 50%
   (b) 15%
   (c) 20%
   (d) 30%
10. The Companies Act, 1956 requires that every public listed company making an IPO of any security for or more shall issue the same only in dematerialized form.
    (a) Rs. 50 crores
    (b) Rs. 30 crores
    (c) Rs. 20 crores
    (d) Rs. 10 crores
    (e) I am not attempting the question
    (f) Custodian

11. If the Custodian rejects a trade, the obligation is assigned back to the
    (a) investor (b) trading member
    (c) clearing bank (d) depository
12. A clearing member receives shares during
    (a) pay-in (b) pay-out
    (c) auction (d) funds settlement
13. The market for government securities comprises the securities issued by the
    (a) Central Govt. (b) State Govt
    (c) State sponsored entities (d) All of the above
14. The arises if a party discharges his obligations but the counterparty defaults.
    (a) replacement cost risk (b) principal risk
    (c) systemic risk (d) unsystematic risk
15. The combines the features of cash as well as futures markets.
    (a) account period settlement (b) rolling settlement
    (c) T+2 settlement (d) T+1 settlement
16. Under the T+2 rolling settlement at NSE, Auction takes place on
    (a) T+0 (b) T+1
    (c) T+2 (d) T+3
17. Under the T+2 rolling settlement at NSE, Custodial Confirmation takes place on .
    (a) T+0 (b) T+1
    (c) T+2 (d) T+3
18. NSCCL levies penalties on trading members for non-compliances and defaults like :
    (a) Funds Shortages (b) Securities Shortages
    (c) Margin Shortages (d) All of the above
19. Interest payments of the following bonds are based on Wholesale Price Index / Consumer Price Index :
    (a) SBI Bonds (b) RBI Bonds
    (c) Zero Coupon bonds (d) Indexed bonds
20. Security Type GS stands for in the WDM Segment of NSE. (1 mark)
    (a) GDR Securities (b) Government Securities
    (c) General Securities (d) None of the above

21. Under DVP III, securities are settled on a basis.
    (a) cash (b) gross
    (c) net (d) T+5
22. performs novation for transactions in Government Securities.
    (a) Clearing Corporation of India Ltd. (CCIL)
    (b) National Securities Clearing Corporation Ltd. (NSCCL)
    (c) National Stock Exchange (NSE)
    (d) National Depository Services Ltd. (NSDL)
23. trades are essentially forward transactions in a security which is still to be issued.
    (a) Forward (b) If Issued
    (c) When Issued (d) None of the above
24. Swaps are a type of derivatives. True or False.
    (a) True (b) False
25. Arbitrageurs are one of the participants in the derivatives markets. True or False.
    (a) True (b) False
26. Risk averse investors use derivatives for speculation. True or False.
    (a) True (b) False
27. Speculators use derivatives as Hedging tools. True or False.
    (a) True (b) False
28. Which of the following positions has a limited downside.
    (a) Sell futures (b) Buy Call Option
    (c) Sell stock (d) Sell Call option
29. An exporter would dollar forwards to lock in an exchange rate.
    (a) sell (b) buy
    (c) hold (d) exchange
30. Strike Price for a call option on a stock is Rs. 125 and the underlying stock price is Rs. 120. If the Premium is Rs.2, the option is .
    (a) In the money (b) Out of the money
    (c) At the money (d) Deep in the money
31. An out of the money call option has an intrinsic value of zero. True or False.
    (a) True (b) False

32. A security trades in the Spot market at Rs. 1319. Moncy can be invested at 10% p.a. The fair value of a one month futures contract on the security is ___

(a) Rs. 1341.10
(b) Rs. 1333.20
(c) Rs. 1328.30
(d) Rs. 1330.05

33. A security trades in the Spot market at Rs. 1423. Money can be invested at 10% p.a. The fair value of a one month futures contract on the security is ___

(a) Rs. 1441.90
(b) Rs. 1434.40
(c) Rs. 1426.70
(d) Rs. 1434.90

34. If you are bullish about a stock, you would call options on the stock.

(a) sell
(b) buy
(c) short
(d) write

35. If you are bearish about a stock, you would put options on the stock.

(a) sell
(b) buy
(c) short
(d) write

36. is the total number of outstanding contracts that are held by market participants at the end of each day.

(a) Outstanding position
(b) Outstanding Interest
(c) Open position
(d) Open Interest

37. means a depository whose name is entered as such in the register of the issuer.

(a) Beneficiary owner
(b) Registered owner
(c) Investment Banker
(d) R&T Agent

38. A company may purchase its own shares, out of .

(a) it's promoters money
(b) it's Equity Capital
(c) Profits
(d) Free Reserves

39. A security trades in the Spot market at Rs. 1600. Money can be invested at 10% p.a. The fair value of a one month futures contract on the security is

(a) Rs. 1651.90
(b) Rs. 1634.40
(c) Rs. 1666.40
(d) Rs. 1613.40

40. A seller of a call option has to pay securities transaction tax. True or False.

(a) True
(b) False

41. A buyer of a put option has to pay securities transaction tax. True or False.

(a) True
(b) False

42. deals with listing of securities on stock exchanges.
    (a) NSDL
    (b) RBI
    (c) SC(R)R, 1957
    (d) SC(R)A, 1956
43. What is the present value of Rs. 1000 payable 3 years hence, if the interest rate is 8% per annum?
    (a) Rs. 779.42
    (b) Rs. 788.23
    (c) Rs. 793.83
    (d) Rs. 785.54
44. What is the present value of Rs. 1000 payable 5 years hence, if the interest rate is 10% per annum?
    (a) Rs. 680.64
    (b) Rs. 656.56
    (c) Rs. 620.92
    (d) Rs. 690.76
45. Calculate the value 5 years hence of a deposit of Rs. 1000 made today if the interest rate is 9%.
    (a) Rs. 1543.65
    (b) Rs. 1538.62
    (c) Rs. 1546.23
    (d) Rs. 1570.54
46. is the discount rate which makes its net present value equal to zero.
    (a) Accrued Interest rate
    (b) Compounding
    (c) Discounting
    (d) Internal Rate of Return (IRR)
47. The Dividend Growth Model approach assumes that the price of equity stock depends ultimately on the dividend expected from it. True or False.
    (a) True
    (b) False
48. Security A gives a return of 10% with a dispersion of 4%, while security B gives return of 18% with a dispersion of 6%. Which security is riskier? (2 marks)
    (a) Security A
    (b) Neither of the securities is risky
    (c) Security B
    (d) Both securities are equally risky
49. Security A gives a return of 12% with a dispersion of 4%, while security B gives return of 15% with a dispersion of 5%. Which security is riskier? (2 marks)
    (a) Security B
    (b) Both securities are equally risky
    (c) Security A
    (d) Neither of the securities is risky
50. How much is the correlation coefficient between the companies A and B, if their covariance is 20 and their standard deviations respectively are 4 and 6?
    (a) 0.5345
    (b) 0.8334
    (c) 0.5275
    (d) -0.2131

51. How much is the correlation coefficient between the companies A and B, if their covariance is 32 and their standard deviations respectively are 7 and 6?

(a) 0.53 (b) 0.83

(c) 0.52 (d) 0.76

52. For a security B, if price at the beginning of the year is Rs.50; dividend receivable at the end of the year is Rs.1.5; and the price at the end of the year is Rs.53 then what is the rate of return on the security?

(a) 0.05 (b) 0.03

(c) 0.02 (d) 0.09

53. Gross Profit Ratio is given by .

(a) Gross Profit/Net Sales (b) Net Profit/ Cost of Sales

(c) Net Profit/Sales (d) Gross Profit/Cost of Sales

54. Fixed Assets Turnover Ratio is given by .

(a) Net Sales/Average Net Fixed Assets

(b) Net Sales/Gross Fixed Assets

(c) Cost of Sales/Average Net Fixed Assets

(d) Cost of Sales /Gross Fixed Assets

SHORT ANSWER QUESTIONS

1. Define stock exchange.
2. Dealing in securities on a stock exchange
3. What are the aspects of the stock business
4. Essentials of an Organized Securities Market
5. Functions and services stock exchange.
6. Define Listing of Securities.
7. Define Listing.
8. Objectives and Scope of Listing
9. How to get the shares Listed?
10. Options or Futures in Securities
11. Underwriting, Placing and Preliminary Arrangements
12. Issuers Registered Outside India
13. Define Listing Approval
14. Trading in Government Securities

15. Define Liquidation or Merger
16. Define Buy-back of Securities by Company
17. Define Voluntary Delisting by Company
18. Define delisting
19. Withdrawal of Admission to Dealings or Delisting on the Exchange
20. Central Listing Authority

ESSAY TYPE QUESTIONS

1. What is mean by stock exchange? Explain the service rendering and reforms the economy.
2. What are the functions and services of stock exchanges?
3. Define Listing. Briefly explain the listing requirement in stock exchanges.
4. How to list and issued government securities and treasury bills?
5. Explain the objectives and scope of listing of securities?
6. Discuss the Merits and Demerits of Listing of Securities
7. What is format of Applications in Respect of New Issues or Offers for Sale or Book-Building?
8. How to trade the government securities?
9. What are the Consequences of Non-Compliance by Issuer on the exchange?
10. Explain Liquidation or Merger.

MCQs Answers

1	2	3	4	5	6	7	8	9	10	11	12	13	14	15	16	17	18	19	20	21	22	23	24	25
e	d	c	a	a	b	b	a	c	d	a	d	c	a	c	c	d	d	b	d	c	c	c	c	c
26	27	28	29	30	31	32	33	34	35	36	37	38	39	40	41	42	43	44	45	46	47	48	49	50
a	a	d	a	b	b	a	b	c	d	a	c	b	c	d	a	d	b	d	c	b	c	a	a	d
51	52	53	54																					
a	c	c	d																					

CASE STUDIES

CASE STUDY 1

INVESTMENT ALTERNATIVES

Mr. Sukhbinder Sarnal has a roadways business in Kolkata and often travels to Chandigarh and Mumbai. He has one daughter and one son, aged 14 and 15yrs respectively, and his wife helps him in his business. After a number of tiring business trips, he is going with his family to visit Goa and Mumbai. He strongly believes that a holiday trip with his family once in a year makes him fit to work with full energy. No matter, even if it is expensive. Sukhbinder also promised his wife to take the entire family to Singapore within a couple of years.

Sukhbinder loves investment but he invests to meet short-term needs. He argues that his present investment objective is his planned trip to Singapore and a budget with a long-run perspective does not work well. For him, budget is just a method of worrying before and after spending money. His present investment portfolio includes Equities- 20%, Growth Funds - 20%, Income Funds-30%, Bonds- 10%, Company FDs -10%, Bank FDs- 10% Liquidity Focus: 70%- High, Safety Focus: 30%- Low Earnings Focus: High, Tax Angle: Less taken care of Martin D'Souza is a chemical engineer by profession. He works in a FMCG plant in Pune and is on his way back to his home in Mumbai after spending his holidays at his inlaw's place. His wife is a teacher in a secondary school in Pune and their twin daughters are in 7th standard. Martin p refers spending money as and when required. He likes to follow what Harvey Mackay, the popular business motivational speaker says "A dream is just a dream. A goal is a dream with a plan and a deadline".

His investment approach is first to establish a relatively large foundation of secure, low risk investments and then move up, step by step to potentially more rewarding growth-oriented schemes. Martin believes, investment portfolio made for long-run is the best way to lay a secure foundation for his life goals. His present investment portfolio includes Equities-10%, Mutual Fund-20%, PPF-5%, PO-Recurring De-posit- 5%, Insurance- 20%, Bonds-25%, Bank FDs- 15% Liquidity Focus: 30%- Low, Safety Focus: 70%- High Earnings Focus: Less, Tax Angle: Highly taken care of The Up, Howrah-Mumbai Geetanjail Express halts at Raipur. This is a small station in MP where the train stops for 5 minutes during normal Circumstances. However, a coach of another passenger train is derailed at a place 20 km from here and Geetanjali has not been given the green signal. Most of the passengers of coach number AS-2 are lazily lying down, except for the members of two families. Sukhbinder is reading 'The Tribune'. The news of YV Reddy Commission, recommending the withdrawal of tax benefits from all types of investment avenues with tenure of less than 6 years, catches his attention. Nimmo and Vikram (his son and daughter) are playing with his co-passenger's kids. His wife is sharing a cup of tea with Mrs D'Souza, co-passenger. Martin is tired of Searching for a copy of 'Financial Express' at the station. He finally gives up and starts sharing the morning news with his co-passenger cum new friend, Sukhbinder. Martin begins by asking Sukhbinder "What do you think will be the implication, if the government decides to withdraw tax benefits for investments of tenure less than 6 years?" wife maintains an account in post-office scheme and surely it's not going to be a good news for her". Martin is worried with this news because he has a significant amount of money invested in tax-savings bonds. Martin agrees "That's right, all investors like me will be badly affected with this decision, after all you can't rely on provident fund every time as a tax savings option because the lock-in period is 15 years; too long". This time Sukhbinder finds his co-passenger's views interesting and argues back "Martin Saab, I do not believe in these tax-savings tools. My point is very simple; you earn money from different sources and pass 30% to government. When, you are looking for tax-free income of 2 lakh in a year, you better look for earning of 2.9 lakh in a year and pass 30% to government. I first calculate my target tax-free income and then find out the sources of earning additional money to cover-up the tax outflow.

It's really troublesome to find tax-savings tool because all these kinds of tools require your money to be blocked for a period of 3-5 years. I do not like it, because I prefer to build my investment portfolio for an earning purpose. However, this does not mean that I am careless of my tax burden but I prefer to ignore this kind of news items." Martin likes Sukhbinder's style of thinking and smiles at him saying, "Mr Sukhbinder, I wish, every one of us could think like you. And then, the future of all these tax-savings bond will go for a toss, but don't you think, these tax-savings option play a big role in your portfolio generation?

Ultimately, you can maximize your earnings if you minimize your tax burden." Rule of 72

The Rule of 72 helps you estimate about how long it will take for your investments to double given a hypothetical rate of return. Divide 72 by your rate of return (say 10% and you've got your answer-seven years approximately. The Rule of 72 assumes your investments are tax deferred and earning compound interest. Martin is curious to hear Sukhbinder's reply this time. Sukhbinder pauses and ignores Martin's point "Sir, I prefer to build my investment Portfolio for earning purpose that will be very liquid in nature; your argument of tax savings tool does not stand good for me as that is illiquid investment". Martin tries to counter Sukhbinder "But, a good portfolio does not mean only good earnings or good liquidity, you need to also consider safety of your investment and tax implication as a whole. Look at investments in equities, they are good from liquidity angle and can give good returns, but they fail on the safety front and any short term gains you make, you shell out a capital gains tax of 30%" This time Sukhbinder looks quite cornered but is not yet ready to give up. Sukhbinder says "You are right Mr. Martin but you can make enough money if you know how to manage your equity investment. I invested in growth stocks and debt mutual funds. Growth stocks are risky but my investment in debt funds will balance that risk. I've also invested in tax-free bonds to minimize my tax-burden." In the meantime, Vikram, the son of Sukhbinder asks his father "Papa, do you know the answer to this?" Vikram is looking for an answer to a puzzle, which he explains to his father - "There is an old lady with her pet tiger, a goat and a stack of grass, who wants to cross a river. But there is a small problem. The lady cannot move alone anywhere. In her presence, the tiger will not attack the goat nor will the goat consume the grass but, in her absence, there is a chance that the tiger can eat the goat or the goat can eat the grass. Now she wants to cross the river and there is only one boat, which can take only two of them at a time. How can the lady cross the river in four attempts". Sukhbinder thinks for a while and tries to ignore his son saying "Beta, you ask Nimmo. She will tell you."

He Wanted to Convince Martin that his Portfolio is Good One as it Promises to Fetch Best Turnings, Liquid in Nature

Sukhbinder comes back to the discussion. He wanted to convince Martin that his portfolio is a good one as it promises to fetch best earnings, liquid in nature although it does not consider safety and tax minimization. Sukhbinder says to Martin "You know Mr. Martin, this argument between portfolio for long-term and portfolio for short term always remind me one basic question-Why do we invest?" Sukhbinder continues, "Because, we need to earn more but more earnings are possible only if you take more risk, which in turn implies less safety. And you also require liquidity for your investment. Considering all these factors, there cannot be something like an ideal investment portfolio." Martin defends his views "No, Mr Sukhbinder, an ideal investment portfolio never clashes with the approaches to build an ideal investment portfolio". "What does that mean?" asks Sukhbinder. Martin replies "Your investment portfolio could be meant for different kinds of objectives like one may look for regular returns from his portfolio and one may like to see his portfolio growing consistently with time. But, even in the trajectory of these two objectives, your approach for building the suitable portfolio must be same. That is, you need to maintain a good balance among your earnings, safety, liquidity and tax savings. Balance is the most crucial aspect.

Prepare an Investment Grid and compare different investment avenues available I today's scenario taking care of the financial objectives of Sukhbinder and Martin.

The Do's and Don'ts of Wise Investing

- Almost the first and last rule- DIVERSIFY: Make sure your investments are diversified. Include different asset classes in your portfolio such as property, shares and fixed interest instruments.
- Start conservatively: If you're just starting out, build a firm base around Blue Chip shares and gain experience from this. Investing in professionally managed funds is also an excellent way to build a diversified portfolio.
- Rome wasn't built in a day: History shows that shares perform well over the long term, so make sure your goals include long-term strategies.

Talk to an expert: If you're a first-time investor or have complex financial needs, consult a financial advisor. As a general rule, look for an individual or group with access to high quality research and the technical support to give you up-to-date information. Above all choose an advisor who takes into account your personal circumstances.

CHAPTER 4

Measurement of Risk and Return

Investment decisions are made in anticipation of increased return in the future. Therefore, it is necessary to estimate the future return of benefits accruing from the investment proposal. Different investment proposals have different degrees of risk and uncertainty. Risk involves situations in which the probabilities of particular even occurring are known whereas in uncertainty these probabilities are unknown. Generally, risk and return are inseparable. There is no return without risk. The investment process must be considered in terms of both aspects risk and return.

Return is a precise statistical term, which is measurable also. Risk is not a precise statistical term but we use statistical terms to quantify it. The investor should keep the risk associated with the return proportional as risk is directly correlated with return. Normally, higher the risk the greater the reward but seeking excessive risk does not ensure excessive return. At a given level of return, each security has different degree of risk. At a given level of return, each security has different degree of risk. The entire process of estimating return and risk for individual securities is called "Security Analysis ".

The main objective of the investor is to derive a portfolio of securities that meets his preference for risk and expected return. Securities refer to spectrum of risks ranging from virtually risk-free debt instruments to highly speculative bonds, common stocks and warrants. The investor will select from this spectrum of risks those securities that maximize his utility, and management of securities may be viewed as comprising two functional areas. First, the risk and return co-incident with individual securities must be determined. These estimates must be used to form portfolios that best meet the needs of the investor. This decision involves the "trade-off" between risk and expected return. To arrive at this trade-off, the investor has to constantly review and ask certain questions and find solutions to the problems. Some of the questions are: Should the portfolio contain only bonds or only common stock? In case, it is decided to have a mix, what should be the combination of the two kinds of securities? What part of it should contain stocks and what part bonds? Additionally, the decisions will predict market behavior in order to improve the return of the investor. The investor may also consider the value of time in his investments. If investment timing is considered, several different policies may have to be considered.

VALUATION OF A FIRM

The valuation of a firm or its securities is a complex phenomenon. There is no generally, accepted procedures or standards available with the help of which, the valuation of a firm may be accepted with a fair degree of success. The non-availability of accurate information, the dependence on forecasts, the varying economic and political conditions these are all forecasts the hinder valuation efforts. It is always true that a firm wants to maximize its value. The owners of corporation, debenture-holders and other creditors, employees, prospective investors and outside interests whose ultimate goal is the acquisition of a firm, and the courts, if a corporation goes into liquidation-all these are interested in finding out what it is really worth. In the process, everybody has a different point of view and looks at it through his own glass. Thus, a firm or its securities have a range of values rather than a single intrinsic worth.

VALUATION BY THE INDIVIDUAL INVESTOR

Generally, the individual investor is an outsider, who is passive in his approach to the value of a firm. He has no vested interest in its securities. His main concern is safety, yield and liquidity; it is on the basis of these factors that he appraises a firm. In this context, he will consider the following

- The expected over-all economic and political conditions;
- The strength and weaknesses of the industry in which a firm is engaged;
- The performance analysis of the other firms engaged in the same industry:
- The quality of management, the firm's reputation and any unusual features which characterize it.

VALUATION BY OTHER FIRMS

When other firms contemplate the acquisition of a firm, they bear the following facts in mind:

- All the considerations of an individual investor, through these would now be of a long-term nature;
- Their external expansion plans and the extent to which they would be backed up by the acquisitions of the firms;
- Security to their stockholder's criticism;
- Valuation of its assets, distribution system, man-power and its overall resources, including its use of technology, demand for its products, etc.

PROBLEM OF VALUATION

The following are the usual problems confronting one in the valuation of a firm:

- Balance sheet values of fixed assets may sometimes be wrong indicators, for they are generally based on a book-value consideration. Changes in the actual value of assets are not incorporated in a balance sheet.
- Through, the value of current asset is reliable, the amounts of debts, accounts receivables, etc., may be unknown. Moreover, the inventory may not find a ready market.
- Some of the highly specialized assets may not have a ready market.
- The selling or break-up value and the buying or replacement value may be different and difficult of assessment.

- It is difficult for a purchaser to estimate how much the possession of the seller's assets would add to his profitability. The inflows have to be discounted, not only to interest but also for risk. The value of the goodwill may be greater to the buyer than to the seller.

The change in portfolio risk due to the new project should guide the choice of risk premium in the discount rate that should be applied to the project for the evaluation of the project's financial viability.

Types of Risks: risk consists of two components. They are

1. Systematic Risk
2. Un-systematic Risk

1. **Systematic Risk:** Systematic risk refers to that portion of total variability in return caused by factors affecting the prices of all securities. Economic, Political and sociological changes are sources of systematic risk. Their effect is to cause prices of nearly all individual common stocks and/or all individual bonds to move together in the same manner.

   Market Risk: Variability in return on most common stocks that are due to basic sweeping changes in investor expectations is referred to as market risk. Market risk is caused by investor reaction to tangible as well as intangible events.

   Interest rate-Risk: Interest –rate risk refers to the uncertainty of future market values and of the size of future income, caused by fluctuations in the general level of interest rates.

   Purchasing-Power Risk: Purchasing power risk is the uncertainty of the purchasing power of the amounts to be received. In more events everyday terms, purchasing power risk refers to the impact of or deflation on an investment.

2. **Unsystematic Risk:** Unsystematic risk is the portion of total risk that is unique to a firm or industry. Factors such as management capability, consumer preferences, and labor strikes Cause systematic variability of return in a firm. Unsystematic factors are largely independent of factors affecting securities markets in general. Because these factors affect one firm, they must be examined for each firm.

   Unsystematic risk that portion of risk that is unique or peculiar to a firm or an industry, above and beyond that affecting securities markets in general. Factors such as management capability, consumer preferences, and labor strikes can cause unsystematic variability of return for a company's stock.

Business Risk: Business risk is a function of the operating conditions faced by a firm and the variability these conditions inject into operating income and expected dividends.

Business risk can be divided into two broad categorics

(a) Internal Business Risk

(b) External Business Risk

(a) Internal business Risk is associated with the operational efficiency of the firm. The operational efficiency differs from company to company. The efficiency of operation is reflected on the company's achievement of its pre-set goals and the fulfillment of the promises to its investors.

(b) External business Risk is the result of operating conditions imposed on the firm by circumstances beyond its control. The external environments in which it operates exert some pressure on the firm. The external factors are social and regulatory factors, monetary and fiscal policies of the government, business cycle and the general economic environment within which a firm or an industry operates.

Financial Risk: Financial risk is associated with the way in which a company finances its activities. Financial risk is avoided risk to the extent that management has the freedom to decide to borrow or not to borrow funds. A firm with no debit financing has no financial risk

The term return from an investment refers to the benefits from that investment. In the field of finance in general and security analysis in particular, the term return is almost invariably associated with a percentage and not a more amount. . In security analysis we are primarily concerned with return from investor's perspective. Our concern is to compute the return for an investor from a particular investment say, a share a debenture or some other financial instrument.

Single period Returns: It refers to a situation where an investor is concerned with return from a single period. (Say one day, one month or one year etc.).

Multi period Returns: It refers to a situation when more than a single period returns are under consideration. Investor is concerned with computing the return per period, over a longer period.

Ex-Post Return: Ex-post returns refer to the actual returns obtained from the investments. They properly measure the returns generated by an investment, one must consider both the price change and cash flow derived from the investment. The measurement of returns from the historical data can be referred to ex-post returns. This includes both current income and capital gains or losses. The income and capital gains price of the security. The income and capital gains are then express as percentage of the initial investment.

Ex-Ante Return: The majority of investors tend to emphasize the returns they expect from a security while making investment decision and the expected return of a security. This enables investor to look into future prospects from an investment and the measurement of return from expectations of benefits is known as Ex-Ante Returns. The equations for quantifying the return, variance and standard deviation of individual security returns for both ex-post and ex-ante data are summarized in the following table.

INVESTMENT INCOME AND RISK

A return is the ultimate objective for any investor. But a relationship between return and risk is a key concept in finance. As finance and investments areas are built upon a common set of financial principles, the main characteristics of any investment are investment return and risk. However, to compare various alternatives of investments the precise quantitative measures for both of these characteristics are needed.

RETURN ON INVESTMENT AND EXPECTED RATE OF RETURN

General definition of return is the benefit associated with an investment. In most cases the investor can estimate his/ her historical return precisely. Many investments have two components of their measurable return

- A capital gain or loss
- Some form of income

The rate of return is the percentage increase in returns associated with the holding period:

Rate of return = Income + Capital gains / Purchase price (%)

For example, rate of return of the share (r) will be estimated:

$$R = \frac{D + (P_1 - P_o)}{P_o} \times 100$$

Here D - dividends

P_o - market price of stock at the beginning of holding period

P_1 - market price of stock at the end of the holding period

The rate of return is called **holding period return,** because its calculation is independent of the passages of the time. All the investor knows is that there is a beginning of the investment period and an end. The percent calculated using this formula might have been earned over one month or other the year. Investor must be very careful with the interpretation of holding period returns in investment analysis. Investor can 't compares the alternative investments using holding period returns, if their holding periods (investment periods) are different. Statistical data which can be used for the investment analysis and portfolio formation deals with a series of holding period returns. For example, investor knows monthly returns for a year of two stocks. How he/ she can compare these series of returns?

Example: 1

Smith Line Health Care's share price on February, 2014 was ₹401 and price on October, 2014 was ₹480. Dividend received was ₹35. What is the Rate of Return?

Solution:

Return = Price Changes + Cash Dividend

$$\overline{R} = \frac{P_1 - P_0}{P_0} + \frac{Div}{P_0} \times 100$$

$$\overline{R} = \frac{480 - 401}{401} + \frac{35}{401} \times 100$$

$$\overline{R} = 28.42\%$$

Example: 2

A Leather manufacturer company has the following dividend per share from 2007 to 2012.

Year:	2007	2008	2009	2010	2011	2012
Dividend	1.53	1.53	1.53	2	2	2
Avg. market						
Price	31.25	20.75	13.88	67	100	154

Calculate the annual rate of return for last 5 years. How risky is the share?

Solution:

$$R = \frac{P_1 - P_0}{P_0} + \frac{D}{P_0} \times 100$$

R08 = 1.53 + (20.75 – 31.25) / 31.2 = -8.97/31.25 = -28.7%

R09 = 1.53 + (30. 88 – 20.75) / 20.75 = 11.66/20.75 = 56.2%

R10 = 2.00 + (67 – 30.88) / 30.88 = 38.12/30.88 = 123.4%

R11 = 2.00 + (100 – 67)/ 67 = 35/67 = 52.2%

R12 = 3.00 + (152 – 100)/ 100 = 57/100 = 57%

$\overline{R}$ = 28.7 + 56.2 + 123.4 + 52.2 + 5 = 52.0%

$$\frac{\sigma^2 = [-28.7-5.2]^2 + [56.2-52]^2 + [123.4-5.2]^2 + [57-52]^2}{5}$$

$$\frac{6512.49 + 17.64 + 5097.96 + 0.04 + 25}{5}$$

$$= \sqrt{2330.6}$$

$$\sigma = 48.3\%$$

Example: 3

Calculate of average rate of return based on market price and dividend i.e., Return = Dividend Yield and Capital gain.

Solution:

Year	Average Market Price	Dividend		Capital gain	Return
2004	**43.25**				1.74
2005	**40.50**	**2.00**	2.00/43.25 x 100 =4.62	40.5-43.25/43.25 x 100	-6.36
2006	**46.35**	**2.30**	2.30/40.50 x 100=5.68	46.35-40.50/40.50 x 100= - 14.44	20.12
2007	**77.90**	**2.40**	2.40/46.35 x 100 =4.96	77.90-46.35/46.35 x 100 =68.07	78.03
2008	**72.50**	**1.00**	1.00/77.90 x 100 =1.28	72.5-77.90/77.90 x 100	33.01
2009	**46.25**	**2.30**	2.30/72.50 x 100 =3.17	46.25-72.5/72.5 x 100=36.21	96.9
2010	**62.75**	**2.50**	2.50/46.25 x 100 =5.41	62.75-46.25/46.25 x 100 =35.68	70.62
2011	**120.00**	**3.03**	3.03/62.75 x 100 =4.83	120-62.75/62.75 x 100 =91.24	
2012	**200.15**	**4.00**	4.00/120.00 x 100=3.33	200.75-120/120 x 100 =67.29	
2013	**357.50**	**4.00**	4.00/200.75 x 100 =1.99	357.50-200.75/200.75 x 100 =78.08	
2014	**405.00**	**5.00**	5.00/357 x 100 =1.40	405-357/357 x 100=	

Example: 4

Following are the average market price and the dividend paid by the company. Calculated the Average Rate of Return.

Solution:

Return = Dividend Yield + Capital Gain	Year	Average Market Price	Dividend	Dividend yield	Capital gain
0.79	**2004**	**143**	-	-	-
7.37	**2005**	**140**	**4**	4/143 x 100=2.8	140-143/143 x 100 = - 2.01
24.1	**2006**	**146**	**4.3**	4.3/143 x 100=3.07	146-140/140 x 100=4.3
-1.11	**2007**	**177**	**4.3**	4.3/-146 x 100=2.09	177-146/146 x 100 =21.2
-12.4	**2008**	**172**	**3**	3/177 x 100=1.69	172-177/177 x 100=-2.8
14.3	**2009**	**146**	**4.6**	4.6/172 x 100=2.7	146-172/172 x 100=-15.1
39.5	**2010**	**162**	**5**	5/146 x 100=3.4	162-146/146 x 100=10.9
39.9	**2011**	**220**	**6**	6/162 x 100=3.7	220-162/162 x 100=35.8
55	**2012**	**300**	**8**	8/220 x 100=2.67	300-220/220x 100=36.3
55	**2013**	**457**	**8**	8/300 x 100=2.67	457-300/300 x 100=52.3
13.4	**2014**	**505**	**10**	10/457 x 100=2.9	505-457/457 x 100=10.5
18.085%					

10-year average 142.95.

Arithmetic Average Return = **1/N∑ RI**

Where

RI - rate of return in period me;

N = number of observations.

But both holding period returns and sample mean of returns are calculated using historical data. However, what happened in the past for the investor is not as important as what happens in the future, because all the investors 'decisions are focused to the future, or to expected results from the investments. Of course, no one investor knows the future, but he/ she can use past information and the historical data as well as to use his knowledge and practical experience to make some estimates about it. Analyzing each particular investment vehicle possibilities to earn income in the future investor must think about several „scenarios "of probable changes in macro economy, industry and company which could influence asset prices ant rate of return. Theoretically it could be a series of discrete possible rates of return in the future for the same asset with the different probabilities of earning the particular rate of return. But for the same asset the sum of all probabilities of these rates of returns must be equal to 1 or 100 %. In mathematical statistics it is called **simple probability distribution.**

Risk refers to the probability that the return and therefore the value of an asset or security may have alternative outcomes. Risk is the uncertainty (today) surrounding the eventual outcome of an event which will occur in the future. Risk is uncertainty of the income/capital appreciation or loss of both. All investments are risky. The higher the risk taken, the higher is the return. But proper management of risk involves the right choice of investments whose risks are compensation.

The expected rate of return E(r) of investment is the statistical measure of return, which is the sum of all possible rates of returns for the same investment weighted by probabilities:

$$\mathbf{E}(\mathbf{R}) = \sum_{i=1}^{N} Pi \times R_i$$

Where Pi - probability of rate of return;

R_i - rate of return.

Example: 5

An Ordinary Share y up Rs. 100 pays no Dividend the possible price of share at the year ended and its prob. Are as follows:

Price	**90**	**95**	**100**	**110**	**120**
Probability.	**0.1**	**0.2**	**0.4**	**0.2**	**0.1**

What is the expected rate of return E(R)?

Solution:

$$R = \frac{P_1 - P_0}{P_0} + \frac{D}{P_0} \times 100$$

= 5/90 x 100 + 5/95 x100 + 10/100 x 100 + 10/110 x 100

Capital Gains = 5.55 + 5.26 + 10 + 9.09

$$E(R) = \sum_{i=1}^{N} P_i \times R_i$$

Where P_i - probability of rate of return;

R_i - rate of return.

Capital	Gains	x Prob.
5.55	x 0.2	1.11
5.26	x 0.4	2.10
10	x 0.2	2
9.09	x 0.1	0.90

E(R) = 6.11%

Example: 6

An asset has the following possible returns with associated probabilities. Calculate expected rate of return.

Possible Return	Probability
20%	0.1
18%	0.45
85	0.3
0%	0.05
-6%	0.10

Solution:

20 x 0.10 + 18 x 0.45 + 8 x 0.3 + 0 x .05 + 6 x .10

E (Rx) = 11.9%

Example: 7 (Two Assets Case)

There are two securities X and Y which provides you the following returns and their probabilities.

Security X		Security Y	
R	P	R	P
30%	0.10	-20%	0.05
20%	0.20	10%	0.25
10%	0.40	20%	0.30
5%	0.20	30%	0.30
-10%	0.10	40%	0.10

Calculate expected rate of security X and security Y.

Solution:

E (R_x) = 30 x 0.10 + 20 x 0.20 + 10 x 0.40 + 5 x 0.20 + -10 x 0.10 = 11%

E (R_y) = -20 x 0.05 + 10 x 0.25 + 20 x 0.30 + 30 x 0.30 + 40 x 0.10 = 20.5%

COVARIANCE

Two methods of covariance estimation can be used: the sample covariance and the population covariance. *The* sample *covariance* is estimated than the investor has 't enough information about the underlying probability distributions for the returns of two assets and then the sample of historical returns is used. Sample covariance between two assets.

$$\text{cov}_{xy} = \sum_{i=1}^{n} (R_x - \bar{R}_i) \quad (R_y - \bar{R}_i) * P_i$$

Where

R_x, R_y, - consequently, rate of return for assets X and Y in the time period n,

R_x, R_y - sample mean of rate of returns for assets X and Y consequently.

As can be understood from the formula, a number of sample covariance can range from "-" to "+" infinity. Though, the covariance number doesn't tell the investor much about the relationship between the returns on the two assets if only this pair of assets in the portfolio is analyzed. It is difficult to conclude if the relationship between returns of two assets (X and Y) is strong or weak, taking into account the absolute number of the sample variance. However, what is very important using the covariance for measuring relationship between two assets - the identification of the direction of this relationship. Positive number of covariance shows that rates of return of two assets are moving to the same direction: when return on asset X is above its mean of return (positive), the other asset Y is tending to be the same (positive) and vice versa: when the rate of return of asset X is negative or below its mean of return, the returns of another asset tend to be negative too. Negative number of covariance shows that rates of return of two assets are moving in the contrariwise directions: when return on asset X is above its mean of return (positive), the returns of the other asset - Y is tend to be the negative and vice versa. Though, in analyzing relationship between the assets in the same portfolio using covariance for portfolio formation it is important to identify which of the three possible outcomes exists:

- Positive covariance ("+"),
- Negative covariance ("-") or
- Zero covariance ("0").

If the positive covariance between two assets is identified the common recommendation for the investor would be not to put both of these assets to the same portfolio, because their returns move in the same direction and the risk in portfolio will be not diversified. If the negative covariance between the pair of assets is identified the common recommendation for the investor would be to include both of these assets to the Portfolio, because their returns move in the contrariwise directions and the risk in portfolio could be diversified or decreased. If the zero covariance between two assets is identified it means that there is no relationship between the rates of return of two assets. The assets could be included in the same portfolio, but it is rare case in practice and usually covariance tends to be positive or negative.

For the investors using the sample covariance as one of the initial steps in analyzing potential assets to put in the portfolio the graphical method instead of analytical one could be a good alternative. The identification of positive, negative and zero co-variance is demonstrated in graphical way. In all these figures the horizontal axis shows the rates of return on asset X and vertical axis shows the rates of return on asset Y.

$$\text{cov}_{xy} = \sum_{i=1}^{n} (R_x - \bar{R}_i) \quad (R_y - \bar{R}_i) * P_i$$

When the sample mean of return for both assets is calculated from historical data given, the all area of possible historical rates of return can be divided into four sections (I, II, III and IV) on the basis of the mean returns of two assets (Rx, Rye consequently). In I section both asset X and asset Y have the positive rates of returns above their means of return; in section II the results are negative for asset X and positive for asset Y; in section III the results of both assets are negative - below their means of return and in section IV the results are positive for asset X and negative for asset Y.

When the historical rates of return of two assets known for the investor are marked in the area formed by axes Rx, Rye, it is very easy to identify what kind of relationship between two assets exists simply by calculating the number of observations in each:

- if the number of observations in sections I and III prevails over the number of observations in sections II and IV, the covariance between two assets is positive ("+");
- if the number of observations in sections II and IV prevails over the number of observations in sections I and III, the covariance between two assets is negative ("-");
- If the number of observations in sections I and III equals the number of observations in sections II and IV, there is the zero covariance between two assets ("0").
- The population covariance is estimated when the investor has enough information about the underlying probability distributions for the returns of two assets and can identify the actual probabilities of various pairs of the returns for two assets at the same time. The population covariance between stocks X and Y:

Similar to using the sample covariance, in the population covariance case the graphical method can be used for the identification of the direction of the relationship between two assets. But the graphical presentation of data in this case is more complicated because three dimensions must be used (including the probability). Despite of it, if investor observes that more pairs of returns are in the sections I and III than in II and IV, the population covariance will be positive, if the pairs of return in II and IV prevails over me and III, the population covariance is negative.

CORRELATION AND COEFFICIENT OF DETERMINATION

Correlation is the degree of relationship between two variables. *The correlation coefficient* between two assets is closely related to their covariance. **The correlation coefficient between two assets X and X (Ax)** can be calculated using the next formula:

$$\text{Correlation Coefficient} = r_{xy} = \frac{COV\ XY}{\sigma_M \sigma_L}$$

Very important, that instead of covariance when the calculated number is unbounded, the correlation coefficient can range only from -1, 0 to +1, 0. The closer the absolute meaning of the correlation coefficient to 1, 0, the stronger the relationship between the returns of two assets. Two variables are perfectly positively correlated if correlation coefficient is +1,0, that means that the returns of two assets have a perfect positive linear relationship to each other, and perfectly negatively correlated if correlation coefficient is -1,0, that means the asset returns have a perfect inverse linear relationship to each other. But most often correlation between assets returns is imperfect. When correlation coefficient equals 0, there is no linear relationship between the returns on the two assets. Combining two assets with zero correlation with each other reduces the risk of the portfolio. While a zero correlation between two assets returns is better than positive correlation, it does not provide the risk reduction results of a negative correlation coefficient. It can be useful to note, that when investor knows correlation coefficient, the covariance between stocks X and Y can be estimated, because standard deviations of the assets' rates of return will already be available:

$$\text{cov}_{xy} = \sum_{i=1}^{n} (R_x - \bar{R}_i)\ \ (R_y - \bar{R}_i) * P_i$$

Therefore, as it was pointed out earlier, the covariance primarily provides information to the investor about whether the relationship between asset returns is positive, negative or zero, because simply observing the number itself without any context with which to compare the number, is not very useful. When the covariance is positive, the correlation coefficient will be also positive, when the covariance is negative, the correlation coefficient will be also negative. But using correlation coefficients instead of covariance investor can immediately asses the degree of relationship between assets returns.

The coefficient of determination (**Deto**x) is calculated as the square of correlation coefficient:

Det.**x, y** = R^2**X, Y**

The coefficient of determination shows how much variability in the returns of one asset can be associated with variability in the returns of the other. For example, if correlation coefficient between returns of two assets is estimated + 0, 80, the coefficient of determination will be 0, 64. The interpretation of this number for the investor is that approximately 64 percent of the variability in the returns of one asset can be explained by the returns of the other asset. If the returns on two assets are perfect correlated, the coefficient of determination will be equal to 100 %, and this means that in such a case if investor knows what will be the changes in returns of one asset he / she could predict exactly the return of the other asset.

RELATIONSHIP BETWEEN THE RETURNS ON STOCK AND MARKET PORTFOLIO

When picking the relevant assets to the investment portfolio on the basis of their risk and return characteristics and the assessment of the relationship of their return's investor must consider to the fact that these assets are traded in the market. How could the changes in the market influence the returns of the assets in the investor's portfolio? What is the relationship between the returns on an asset and returns in the whole market (market portfolio)? These questions need to be answered

When investing in any investment environment. The statistics can be explored to answer these questions as well.

Example: 8

Following information is available with regard to two assets X & Y both the assets are involved invested in equal proportion.

Status of economy	Probability	Returns	
A	0.1	X%	Y%
B	0.2	-8	14
C	0.4	10	-4
D	0.2	8	6
E	0.1	5	15
		4	20

Calculate portfolio Return, Risk, co-variance, correlation of coefficient the returns of 2 Assets.

Solution:

E [Rx]	E [Ry]
-0.8	1.4
2	-0.8
3.2	2.4
1	3
-4	2
5%	8%

$$\bar{R}_x = \sum_{i=1}^{n} R_i P_i = 5\%$$

$$\bar{R}_y = \sum_{i=1}^{n} R_i P_i = 8\%$$

$$\sigma_X = \sqrt{\sum_{i=1}^{n} (R_i - \bar{R}_i)^2 \quad * P_i}$$

$$= \sqrt{33.6} = 5.8\%$$

$$\sigma_y = \sqrt{\sum_{i=1}^{n} (R_i - \bar{R}_i)^2 \quad * P_i}$$

$$= 7.63\%$$

$$\text{cov}_{xy} = \sum_{i=1}^{n} (R_x - \bar{R}_i) \quad (R_y - \bar{R}_i) * P_i$$

= (-8-5) (14-8) *0.1+ (10-5) (-4-8) *0.2+ (8-5) (6-8) *0.4+ (5-5) (15-8) *0.2+ (-4-5) (20-8) *0.1

= -7.8-12-2.4+0-10.8

=-33

- CORELATION COEFFICIENT IS $r_{xy} = \frac{COV\ XY}{\sigma_M \sigma_L}$

=-33/ (5.8*7.63)

=-0.7457

- $R_p = \sum_{i=1}^{n} X_i \bar{R}_i$

= (0.5*5) + (0.5*8) = 2.5+4=**6.5%**

- Portfolio risk$\sigma_p = \sqrt{X_1^2 \sigma_L^2 + X_2^2 \sigma_M^2 + 2X_1 X_2 (r_{12} \sigma_1 \sigma_2)}$

$$\sqrt{(0.5)2(5.8)2 + (0.5)2(7.63)2 + 2*(0.5*0.5)*0.746(5.8*7.63)}$$

=2.54%

In all cases than investor has enough information for modeling of future scenarios of changes in rate of return for investment, the decisions should be based on estimated expected rate of return. But sometimes sample mean of return (arithmetic average return) are a useful proxy for the concept of expected rate of return. Sample mean can give an unbiased estimate of the expected value, but obviously it's not perfectly accurate, because based on the assumption that the returns in the future will be the same as in the past. But this is the only one scenario in estimating expected rate of return. It could be expected, that the accuracy of sample mean will increase, as the size of the sample becomes longer (if n will be increased).

However, the assumption, that the underlying probability distribution does not change its shape for the longer period becomes more and more unrealistic. In general, the sample mean of returns should be taken for as long time, as investor is confident there has not been significant change in the shape of historical rate of return probability distribution.

RISK

Risk can be defined as a chance that the actual outcome from an investment will differ from the expected outcome. Obvious, that most investors are concerned that the actual outcome will be less than the expected outcome. The more variable the possible outcomes that can occur, the greater the risk. Risk is associated with the dispersion in the likely outcome. And dispersion refers to variability. So, the total risk of investments can be measured with such common absolute measures used in statistics as

- Variance;
- Standard deviation.

Variance can be calculated as a potential deviation of each possible investment rate of return from the expected rate of return:

$$\sigma^2 = 1/N\,[R1 - E(R)]^2 + [R2 - E(R)]^2 + \ldots\ldots\ldots\ldots\ldots + [Run - E(R)]^2$$

$$\sqrt{\frac{1}{N}\sum_{i=1}^{n}\left(R_i - \bar{R}_i\right)^2}$$

When Probabilities are given:

$$\sigma^2 = [R1 - E(R)]^2 P1 + [R2 - E(R)]^2 P2 + \ldots\ldots\ldots\ldots\ldots + [Run - E(R)]^2 Pan$$

$$\sqrt{\sum_{i=1}^{n}\left(R_i - \bar{R}_i\right)^2_{P_i}}$$

To compute the variance all the rates of returns which were observed in estimating expected rate of return (RI) have to be taken together with their probabilities of appearance (**Pi**). The other an equivalent to variance measure of the total risk is **standard deviation** which is calculated as the square root of the variance:

$$\sigma = \sqrt{\sum_{i=1}^{n}\left(R_1 - \bar{R}_i\right)^2_{P_1}}$$

Variance for security X

$(30\text{-}11)^2 \times 0.10 + (20\text{-}11)^2 \times 0.20 + (10\text{-}11)^2 \times 0.40 + (5\text{-}11)^2 \times 0.20 + (\text{-}10\text{-}11)^2 \times 0.10$

$\sigma^2 = 36.1 + 16.2 + 0.4 + 7.2 + 44.1 \quad = 104$

$\sigma = 10.20\%$

Variance for security Y

$$\sigma^2 = (-20 - 20.5)^2 \times 0.05 + (10 - 20.5)^2 \times 0.25 + (20 - 20.5)^2 \times 0.30 + (30 - 20.5)^2 \times 0.30 + (40 - 20)^2 \times 0.10$$

$$\sigma^2 = 82 + 27.56 + 0.075 + 27.075 + 38.025 = 174.735$$

$$\sigma = 13.22\%$$

Variance and the standard deviation are similar measures of risk and can be used for the same purposes in investment analysis; however, standard deviation in practice is used more often. Variance and standard deviation are used when investor is focused on estimating total risk that could be expected in the defined period in the future. Sample variance and sample standard deviation are more often used when investor evaluates total risk of his /her investments during historical period - this is important in investment portfolio management.

PORTFOLIO RETURN

Security analysis related to the analysis of individual securities within the framework of return and risk. Whereas, Portfolio analysis makes an analysis of securities in the combined form.

The portfolio analysis considers the determination of future risk and return in holding various blends of individual securities. Portfolio expected return is a weighted average of the expected return of individual securities but portfolio variance can be something less than a weighted average of security variances. As a result, an investor can sometimes reduce portfolio risk by adding another security with greater individual risk than any other security in the portfolio. This result occurs because risk depends greatly on the covariance among returns of individual securities.

Portfolio analysis includes portfolio construction, selection of securities, revision of portfolio evaluation and monitoring the performance of the portfolio. All these are part of subject of portfolio management which is a dynamic concept. Individual securities have risk-return characteristics of their own. Portfolios, which are combinations of securities may or may not take on the aggregate characteristics of their individual's parts.

Portfolio analysis considers the determination of future risk and return in holding various blends of individual securities. As we know that expected return from individual securities carries some degree of risk. Various groups of securities when held together behave in a different manner and give interest payments and dividends also, which are different to the analysis of individual securities. A combination of securities held together will give a beneficial result if they are grouped in a manner to secure higher return after taking into consideration the risk element.

There are two approaches in construction of the portfolio of securities. They are

- Traditional approach
- Modern approach

TRADITIONAL APPROACH

Traditional approach was based on the fact that risk could be measured on each individual security through the process of finding out the standard deviation and that security should be chosen where the deviation was the lowest. Traditional approach believes that the market is inefficient and the fundamental analyst can take advantage for the situation. Traditional approach is a comprehensive financial plan for the individual. It takes into account the individual needs such as housing, life insurance and pension plans.

Traditional approach basically deals with two major decisions. They are

(a) Determining the objectives of the portfolio

(b) Selection of securities to be included in the portfolio

MODERN APPROACH

Modern approach theory was brought out by Markowitz and Sharpe. It is the combination of securities to get the most efficient portfolio. Combination of securities can be made in many ways. Markowitz developed the theory of diversification through scientific reasoning and method. Modern portfolio theory believes in the maximization of return through a combination of securities. The modern approach discusses the relationship between different securities and then draws inter-relationships of risks between them. Markowitz gives more attention to the process of selecting the portfolio. It does not deal with the individual needs.

MARKOWITZ MODEL

THE MEAN VARIANCE CRITERION

Dr. Harry M. Markowitz is credited with developing the first modern portfolio analysis model in order to arrange for the optimum allocation of assets with in portfolio. To reach these objectives, Markowitz generated portfolio with in a reward risk context. In essence, Markowitz model is a theoretical framework for the analysis of risk return choices. Decisions are based on the concept of efficient portfolios.

Markowitz model is a theoretical framework for the analysis of risk, return choices and this approach determines an efficient set of portfolios return through three important variable that is,

- Return
- Standard Deviation
- Coefficient of correlation

Markowitz model is also called as a "Full Covariance Model". Through this model the investor can find out the efficient set of portfolios by finding out the tradeoff between risk and return, between the limits of zero and infinity. According to this theory, the effect of one security purchase over the effects of the other security purchase is taken into consideration and then the results are evaluated. Markowitz had given up the single stock portfolio and introducd divcrsification. The single stock portfolio would be preferable if the investor is perfectly certain that his expectation of highest return would turn out to be real. In the world of uncertainty, most of the risk averse investors would like to join Markowitz rather than keeping a single stock, because diversification reduces the risk.

A portfolio is efficient when it is expected to yield the highest return for the level of risk accepted or, alternatively the smallest portfolio risk for a specified level of expected return level chosen, and asset are substituted until the portfolio combination expected returns, set of efficient portfolios is generated.

Assumptions:

The Markowitz model is based on several assumptions regarding investor behavior:

1. Investors consider each investment alternative as being represented by a probability distribution of expected returns over some holding period.
2. Investors maximize one period-expected utility and possess utility curve, which demonstrates diminishing marginal utility of wealth.
3. Individuals estimate risk on the basis of variability of expected return.
4. Investors base decisions solely on expected return and variance of return only.
5. For a given risk level, investors prefer high returns to lower returns. Similarly, for a given level of expected return, investors prefer less risk to more risk.
6. Under these assumptions, a single asset or portfolio of assets is considered to be "efficient" if no other asset or portfolio of assets higher expected return with the same expected return.

THE SPECIFIC MODEL

In developing this model, Markowitz first disposed of the investor behavior rule that the investor should maximize expected return. This rule implies non-diversified single security analysis portfolio with the highest expected return is the most desirable portfolio. Only by buying that single security portfolio would obviously be preferable if the investor were perfectly certain that this highest expected return would turn out to be the actual return. However, under real world conditions of uncertainty, most risk adverse investors join with Markowitz in discarding the role of calling for maximizing the expected returns. As an alternative, Markowitz offers the "expected returns/variance" rule.

Markowitz has shown the effect of diversification by regarding the risk of securities. According to him, the security with the covariance, which is either negative or low amongst them, is the best manner to reduce risk. Markowitz has been able to show that securities, which have, less than positive correlation will reduce risk without, in any way, bringing the return down. According to his research study a low correlation level between securities in the portfolio will show less risk. According to him, investing in a large number of securities is not the right method of investment. It is the right kind of security that brings the maximum results.

Henry Markowitz has given the following formula for a two-security portfolio and three security portfolios.

$$\sigma_p = \sqrt{(x_1)^2 (\sigma_1)^2 + (X_2)^2 (\sigma_2)^2 + 2(X_1)(X_2)(r_{12})(\sigma_1)(\sigma_2)}$$

$$\sigma_p = \sqrt{(x_1)^2(\sigma_1)^2 + (X_2)^2(\sigma_2)^2 + (X_3)^2(\sigma_3)^2 + 2(X_1)(X_2)(r_{12})(\sigma_1)(\sigma_2) + 2(X_1)(X_3)(r_{13})(\sigma_1)(\sigma_3) + 2(X_2)(X_3)(r_{23})(\sigma_2)(\sigma_3)}$$

σ_P = Standard deviation of the portfolio return

X_1= proportion of the portfolio invested in security 1

X_2= proportion of the portfolio invested in security 2

X_3= proportion of the portfolio invested in security 3

σ_1= standard deviation of the return on security 1

σ_2= standard deviation of the return on security 2

σ_3= standard deviation of the return on security 3

r_{12}= coefficient of correlation between the returns on securities 1 and 2

r_{13}= coefficient of correlation between the returns on securities 1 and 3

r_{23}= coefficient of correlation between the returns on securities 2 and 3

RETURNS

The expected return of a portfolio depends on the expected return of each of the security contained in the portfolio. It also seems logical that the amounts invested in each security should be important. Indeed, this is the case. The example of a portfolio with three securities shown in Table-1A illustrates this point. The expected holding period value-relative for the portfolio is clearly:

$$\frac{\text{Rs. } 23{,}100}{\text{Rs. } 20{,}000} = 1.155$$

Giving an expected holding period return of 15.50%.

Table- combines the information in a different manner. The portfolio's expected holding-period value-relative is simply a weighted average of the expected value-relative of its component securities, using current market values as weights. Table-1C provides holding-period returns. It is simply 100 times the value obtained by subtracting one from the holding period value- relative. Thus, a weighted average of the former will have the same characteristics as a weighted average of the former will have the same characteristics as a weighted average of the latter.

Security and Portfolio Values

Security	No. of Shares	Current Price Per Share	Current Value	Current Value Expected End-of-Period Share Price	Expected End-of- Period Share Value
A	100	Rs.15.00	1,500	Rs.18.00	Rs.1,800
B	150	20.00	3,000	22.00	3,300
C	200	40.00	8,000	45.00	9,000
D	250	25.00	6,250	30.00	7,500
E	100	12.50	1,250	15.00	1,500
			Rs.20,000		Rs.23,100

Security	Current Value	Proportion of Current Value of Properties	Current Price Per Share	Expected End-of-Period Share Price	Expected Holding -Period value-Relative	Contribution to Portfolio Expected Holding-Period Value-Relative
		3=2=Rs.20,000			6=5/4	7 = 3 x 6
A	1500	.0750	Rs.15	Rs. 18	1.200	0.090000
B	3000	.1500	20	22	1.100	0.165000
C	8000	.4000	40	45	1.125	0.450000
D	6,250	.3125	25	30	1.200	0.375000
E	1,250	.0625	12.50	15	1.200	0.075000
	Rs.20,000	1.0000				1.155000

Security and Portfolio Holding-Period Returns

Security	Proportion of Current value of Properties	Current Price Per Share	Contribution to Portfolio Expected Holding Period Return (%)
A	.0750	Rs.15.00	1.50
B	.1500	20.00	1.50
C	.4000	40.00	5.00
D	.3125	25.00	6.25
E	.0625	12.50	1.25
	1.0000		15.50

Since portfolios expected return is a weighted average of the expected returns of its securities, the contribution of each security to the portfolio's expected returns depends on its expected returns and its proportionate share of the initial portfolio's market value. Nothing else is relevant. It follows that an investor who simply wants the greatest possible expected return should hold one security: the one which is considered to have the greatest expected return. Very few investors do this, and very view investment advisers would counsel such an extreme policy. Instead, investors should diversify, meaning that their portfolio should include more than one security.

This is because diversification can reduce risk.

RISK

The probability of loss is the essence of risk. A useful measure of risk takes into account both the probability of various possible "bad" outcomes and their associated magnitudes. Instead of measuring the probability of a number of different possible outcomes, the measure of risk should somehow estimate the extent to which the actual outcome is likely to diverge from the expected.

Two measures used for this purpose are the mean absolute deviation and the standard deviation. Table 2A shows how the average absolute deviation can be calculated. First the expected return is determined; In this case it is 10.00 per cent. Next, each possible outcome is analyzed to determine the amount by which the value deviated from the expected amount. These figures shown in Column (5) of the table include both positive and negative values. As shown in Column (6), a weighted average, using probabilities as weights, will equal zero. This is a mathematical necessity, given the way expected value is calculated. To assess the risk the signs of deviations can simply be ignored. As shown in column (7), the weighted average of the absolute values of the deviations, using the probabilities as weights, is 10 per cent.

This constitutes the first measure of "likely" deviation.

A. Calculating the Mean Absolute Deviation

Event	Probability	Return %	Probability X Return	Deviation	Probability X Deviation (6)	Probability X Absolute Deviation
a	.20	-10	-2.0	-25.0	-5.0	5.0
b	.40	25	10.0	10.0	4.0	4.0
c	.30	20	6.0	5.0	1.5	1.5
d	.10	10	-1.0	-5.0	-0.5	0.5
				Expected Return =15		Average =0 Absolute Deviation

CALCULATING THE STANDARD DEVIATION

Event	Probability	Deviation	Deviation Squared (4) = (3)2	Probability X Deviation Squared (5) = (2) x (4)
a	.20	-25.0	625.0	125.0
b	.40	10.0	100.0	40.0
c	.30	5.0	25.0	7.5
d	.10	-5.0	25.0	2.4
				175.0

Variation = Weighted average squared deviation = 175.0

Standard Deviation = square root of variance = 13.2287

Table presents slightly more complex but preferably analytical measure. In this, the deviations are squared (making the value all positive); then a weighted average of these amounts is taken, using the probabilities as weights. The result is termed the variance. It is converted to the original units by taking the square root. The result is termed the standard deviation. Although the two measures are often interchangeable in this manner, the standard deviation is generally preferred for investment analysis. The reason is simple. The standard deviation of a portfolio's return can be determined from (among other things) the standard deviations of the returns of its component's securities, no matter what the distributions. No relationship of comparable simplicity exists for the average absolute deviations.

When an analyst predicts that a security will return 15% next year, he or she is presumably stating something comparable to an expected value. If asked to express the uncertainty about the outcome, he or she might reply that the odds are 2 out of 3 that the actual return will be within 10% of the estimate (i.e. 5% and 25%). The standard deviation is a formal measure of uncertainty, or risk, expressed in this manner, just as the expected value is a formal measure of a "best guess" estimate. Most analysts make such predictions directly, without explicitly assessing probabilities and making the requisite computations.

Portfolio Risk In order estimate the total risk of a portfolio of assets, several estimates are needed: the variance of each individual asset under consideration for inclusion in the portfolio and the covariance, or correlation co-efficient, of each asset with each of the other assets. Table shows the returns on two securities and on a portfolio that includes both of them. Security X constitutes 60 per cent of the market value of the portfolio and security Y the other 40 per. The predicted return on the portfolio is simply a weighted average of the predicted returns on the securities, using the proportionate values as weights. Summary measures show values computed from the estimates in Table.

The expected return for the portfolios simply the weighted average of the expected returns on its securities, using the proportionate values as weights (17.0% = 6 x 15% + 4 x 20%). However, this is not true for either the variance or the standard deviation of return for the portfolio smaller than the corresponding values for either of the component securities. This rather surprising result has a simple explanation. The risk of a portfolio depends not only on the risk of its securities, considered in isolation, but also on the extent to which they are affected similarly by underlying events. To illustrate this, two extreme cases are shown in Table 4. In the first case both.

Portfolio and Security Risks

Return

Event	Probability	Return on Security X	Return on Security Y	Return on Portfolio (5) = 6 x (3) + 4 x (4)
a	.20	-10%	5.0%	-4.0%
b	.40	25	30.0	27.0
c	.30	20	20.0	20.0
d	.10	10	10.0	10.0

SUMMARY MEASURES

	Security X	Security Y	Portfolio
Expected Return	15.0	20.0	17.0
Variance of Return	175.0	95.0	135.8
Standard deviation of Return	13.2287	9.7468	11.65

COVARIANCE AND CORRELATIONS

Event	Probability	Deviations of return Security X	Deviation of Return for Security Y	Product of Deviation (5) = (3) x (4)	Probability Times Product of Deviation (6) = (2) x (5)
a	**.20**	-25.0%	-	375	75.00
b	**.40**	10.0	15.0%	100	40.00
c	**.30**	5.0	10.0	0	0
d	**.10**	-5.0	0	50	5.00
			-10.0		Covariance=120

Coefficient of correlation = 120/ 13.2287 x 9.7468 = 0.9307

The variance and the standard deviation of the portfolio are the same as the corresponding values for the securities. Then diversification has no effect at all on risk. In the second case the situation is very different. Here the security's returns offset one another in such a manner that the particular combination that makes up this portfolio has no risk at all. Diversification has completely eliminated risk. The difference between these two cases concerns the extent to which the security's returns are correlated i.e., tend to "to-together". Either of two measures can be used to state the degree of such a relationship: the covariance or the correlation co-efficient.

RISK AND RETURN FOR A TWO-SECURITY PORTFOLIO

TWO SECURITIES WITH EQUAL RETURNS

Event 1	Probability 2	Return on Security X % 3	Return on Security Y % 4	Return on Portfolio (5) = 6 x (3) + 4 x (4)
a	.20	-10.0	-10.0	-10.0
b	.40	25.0	25.0	25.0
c	.30	20.0	20.0	20.0
d	.10	10.0	10.0	10.0
Expected Return		15.0	15.0	15.0
Variance of Return		175.0	175.0	175.0
Standard deviation of Return		13.2287	13.2287	13.2287

SUMMARY MEASURES

Event 1	Probability 2	Return on Security X % 3	Return on Security Y % 4	Return on Portfolio 5
a	20	-10.	40.0	10.0
b	.40	25.0	-20.0	10.0
c	.30	20.0	-5.0	10.0
d	.10	10.0	10.0	10.0
Expected Return		15.0	-0.5	10.0
Variance of Return		175.0	37.47	0
Standard deviation of Return		13.228	6.1217	0

The computations required to obtain the covariance for the two securities are presented in Tab le 3C. The deviation of each security's return from its expected value is determined and the product of the two obtained (column 5). The variance is simply a weighted average of such products, using the probabilities of the events as weights. A positive value for the covariance

Indicates that the securities returns tend to go together – for example, a better- than-expected return for one is likely to occur along with a better-than-expected return for the other. A small or zero value for the covariance indicates that there is little or no relationship between the two returns. The correlation coefficient is obtained by dividing the covariance by the product of the two security's standard deviation. As shown in Table, in this case the value is 0.9307.

Correlation coefficients always lie between +1.0 and –1.0, inclusive. The former value represents perfect positive correlation, of the type shown in the example in Table. The latter value represents perfect negative correlation in Table. The relationship between the covariance and the correlation coefficient can be represented as follows:

$$C_{0V_{xy}} = \sum_{i=1}^{n}\left(R_i - \bar{R}_x\right)\left(R_y - \bar{R}_y\right)P_i \quad \text{.... (4.1)}$$

$$V_{xy} = \frac{C_0 V_{xy}}{\sigma_n \sigma_y} \quad \text{.... (4.2)}$$

Where:

C_0V_{XY} = covariance between return on X and return on Y.

V_{xy} = coefficient of correlation between return on X and return on Y.

σ_X = standard deviation of return on X.

σ_Y = standard deviation of return on Y.

For two securities, X and Y, the relationship between the risk of a portfolio of two securities and the relevant variables, the formula is:

Where:

VP = the variance of return for the portfolio.

V_X = the variance of return for the security X.

V_Y = the variance of return for the security Y.

C_0V_{XY} = the covariance between the return on security X and the return On security Y.

WX = the proportion of the portfolio's value invested in security X.

W_Y = the proportion of the portfolio's value invested in security Y. For the case shown in Table.

$W_X = 0.6$; $V_X = 175.0$, $W_Y = .4$ $V_Y = 95.0$, CXY = 120.00,

Inserting these values in formula (3), we get the variance of the portfolio as a whole

$$V_P = (0.6)^2 \text{ x } 175.0 + 2 \text{ x } .6 \text{ x } .4 \text{ x } 120 + (0.4)^2 \text{ x } 95.0$$

$$= 63.00 + 57.60 + 15.20 = 135.80$$

The relationship that gives the variance for a portfolio with more than two securities is similar in nature but more extensive. Both the risks of the securities and all their correlations have to be taken in account.

PERFECTLY POSITIVELY CORRELATED RETURNS

The returns from two securities are perfectly positively correlated when a cross-plot gives points lying precisely on an upward-sloping straight line, as shown in Figure – 1A. Each point indicates the return on security A (horizontal axis) and the return on security B (vertical axis) corresponding to one event. The example shown in Table – 4A confirms to this pattern. What is the effect on risk when two securities of this type are combined? The general formula is:

$$V_P = W^2_X V_X + 2 W_X W_Y C_{XY} + W^2_Y V_Y$$

The covariance term can, of course, be replaced, using formula (1):

$$C_{XY} = R_{XY} S_X S_Y$$

However, in this case there is perfect positive correlation, so $r_{ay} = +1$ and

$C_{XY} = S_X S_Y$. As always, $V_X = S^2X$, $VY = S^2Y$ and $VP = S^2P$

Substituting all these values in general formula gives:

$$S^2P = W^2X\, S_{2X} + 2W_X W_Y S_X S_Y + W^2Y\, S_{2Y},$$

$$S^2P = (W_X S_X + W_Y S_Y)^2$$

$$S^2P = (WX\, {}^SX + W\, Y\, {}^S\, Y) \quad \text{when} \quad r_{ay} = +1$$

This is an important result. When two securities returns are perfectly positively correlated, the risk of a combination, measured by the standard deviation of return, is just a weighted average of the risks of the component securities, using market value as weights. The principle holds as well if more than two securities are included in a portfolio. In such cases, diversification does

Not provide risk reduction but only risk averaging. deviation of return, is just a weighted average of the risks of the component securities, using market value as weights. The principle holds as well if more than two securities are included in a portfolio. In such cases, diversification does not provide risk reduction but only risk averaging.

PERFECTLY NEGATIVELY CORRELATED RETURNS

Diversification can eliminate risk in case of perfectly negatively correlated returns. Since ray = -1, the general formula becomes:

$$S^2P = W^2X\, S_{2X} - 2W\, X^W\, Y^S\, X^S\, Y + W^2Y\, S_{2Y}$$

This can be factored to obtain:

$$S^2P = (WX\, {}^SX - W\, Y\, {}^S\, Y)^2 \quad \text{when} \quad r_{xy} = -1$$

Assuming a portfolio, in which the proportionate holdings are inversely related to the relative risks of the two securities, i.e.:

$$WX/\ WY = SY/\ SX \text{ (Or) } WX = S_Y\ W\ Y/\ S\ X$$

For this combination the parenthesized term in formula (6) will be:

$$W_{X\,SX} - W_{Y\,SY} \quad = S\ Y^W\ Y/\ S_{X,\,SX} - WY \quad {}^SY = {}^0$$

If this term is zero, of course, the portfolio's standard deviation of return must be zero as well. When two securities returns are perfectly negatively correlated, it is possible to combine them in a manner that will eliminate all risk. Figure – 1b shows the returns from two securities perfectly negatively correlated, a cross-plot gives points lying precisely on a downward-sloping straight line. The example shown in Table confirms to this pattern. This principle motivates all hedging strategies. This object is to take position that will offset each other with regard to certain kinds of risk, reducing or completely eliminating such sources of uncertainty.

UNCORRELATED RETURNS

Some risks can be substantially reduced by pooling. This has crucial implications for investment management. Most importantly, it provides the basis for understanding the relationship between risk and return. A special case of extreme importance arises when a cross-plot of security returns shows no pattern that can be represented even approximately by an upward-sloping or downward- sloping line. In such an instance, the returns are uncorrelated. The correlation coefficient, is zero, as is the covariance. In this situation, the general formula becomes:

$$S^2P = W^2X\,^{S}2_X + W^2Y\,^{S}2_Y \quad \text{when} \quad r_{xy} = 0$$

To illustrate the diversification effect, consider a portfolio divided equally between two securities of equal risk, say 20.0%. That is:

$$W_X = .5;\ WY = .5;\ S_X = 20;\ SY = 20$$

Substitution these values in equation (7) we get:

$$(.5)^2\,(20)^2 + (.5)^2\,(20)^2 = (.25)\,(400) + (.25)\,(400)$$

Thus: $S^2P = 200$ and $SP = 14.14$

Diversification has helped as the risk of the portfolio is less that the risk of either of its component securities. The result will remain same irrespective of the number of securities. However, when all returns are uncorrelated the complete formula becomes:

$$S^2P = W^21\,S^21 + W^22\,S^22 + \ldots\ldots\ldots + W^2N^{S2N}$$

Where:

SP ...... = the standard deviation of the return on portfolio.

W_1, W_2...= the proportions invested in securities 1, 2, etc.

S1, S2... = the standard deviation of the returns for securities 1, 2, etc.

= The number of securities included.

This is an extremely important relationship for investment analysis and also provides the bases for insurance, or risk pooling. This can be seen by extending the previous example and assuming a portfolio of equal parts of a number of securities, each with a risk (standard deviation of return) of 20%. If two securities are included:

$$S^2P \;= (1/2)^2\,20^2 + (1/2)^2\,20^2 = 2(1/2)^2\,202$$

If three securities are included:

$$S^2P = (1/3)^2\,202 + (1/3)^2\,202 + (1/3)^2\,202 = 3(1/3)^2\,202$$

To generalize, represent the number of securities by N. Then:

$$S^2P = = (1/N)^2\,20^2 + (1/N)^2\,20^2 + \ldots\ldots\ldots = N\,(1/N)^2\,202$$

Simplifying:

$$S^2P = N/N^2\, 20^2 = 20^2/N$$

$$SP == 20/\sqrt{N}$$

Diversification provides substantial risk reduction if the components of a portfolio are uncorrelated. In fact, if enough securities are included, the overall risk of the portfolio will be almost (but not quite) zero. This is why insurance companies attempt to write many individual policies and spread their coverage so as to minimize overall risk.

COMBINING RISKY AND RISK LESS SECURITIES

What happens to risk when a risk less security is combined with a risky security (or portfolio)? If security A return is certain, while that of security B is uncertain, $S_A = 0$, as does C_{AB}; and the relationship becomes:

$$SP = W^2A\ 0 + 2WA\ WB\ 0 + W^2B\ S2B$$

Thus: SP = WB SB when SA = 0

In other words, when a risky security or portfolio is combined with a risk less one, the risk of the combination is proportional to the amount invested in the risky component. An obvious case of this sort arises when an investor splits his funds between an equity portfolio and a savings account.

Investing in a risk less security is equivalent to lending money.

	Security A (Savings Account)	Security B (Equity Portfolio)	Combination C	Combination D	Combination E
Proportion in A(WA)	*1.0%*	*0%*	.7	.3	-.2
Proportion in B(W_B)	*0%*	*1.0%*	.3	.7	1.2
Expected return	*8%*	*23%*	12%	18%	26%
Standard deviation of Return	*0%*	*25%*	6%	14%	30%

Combining a Risk less and a Risky Investment

Along with the original alternatives A and B, Figure portrays the combinations C and D. Each alternative shows the expected return and risk of an alternative combination. Since both risk and return will be proportion al to the investment proportions in C case of this sort, both point C and point D lie on the straight-line connecting points A and B. All these alternatives have positive individual proportions except E. As shown in Table and Figure, combination E and point E have W_A equal - .20 and W_B equal + 1.20.

What does this mean? Imagine an investor with Rs.10, 000 to invest. But in order to take advantage of profitable opportunity, he may take additional risk and invest his own Rs.10, 000 and borrow Rs.2000 at 8% interest. A total of Rs.12, 000 could then be invested in the project. The effect of this sort of leverage may be favorable/unfavorable depending upon the circumstances. Table 6(a) shows the return on investor's capital may go up to 26%. The final column of the table showed a similar set of computations for combination.

Leverage increase the expected return on investor's capital if borrowed funds are invested in a risky alternative. Point E lies above point B in Figure. However, the expected return may decline with an unfavorable outcome. Return on investor's capital falls to 4.4 per cent from 26 per cent. The effect of leverage on risk is shown in the fourth line of the table. Borrowing increases risk.

Effect of Leverage

With a Favorable Outcome:

Investment return 23%
Return investment on total .23 x 12,000 = 2,760
Interest rate on loan
Amount of interest 8% =.08 x Rs.2000 = 160
Net Proceeds = 2,600
Return on investor's capital =2600/26% = Rs.10,000

Leverage generally increases both risk and expected return. It is commonly used by corporations. For example, point B in Figure 2 might represent the risk and return obtained by a firm on its total assets. If, however, the corporation has issued debt, both the risk and return of its investment should be greater than this. Combination E conforms to the example shown in Table 5 and Figure. Like corporations, the individual investors can and do borrow from a number of sources. At any time, the interest charged may depend on the borrower, the lender, the collateral, the purpose of loan, the length of time involved, the amount of money borrowed, etc. If there is chance that the loan will not be repaid in full and on time, the rate charged will, of course, be higher, and the loan will be risk less. But in these cases, in which the leverage is used within the limits required to keep the loan risk less, the relationship will be shown in Figure. Margined or leveraged purchase of any risky investment (e.g., B) can be used to obtain a combination of risk and return plotting on the straight line connecting the points represent the two components (e.g., A and B). The prospect obtained in this manner will depend on the amount of leverage: the greater the leverage, the farther to the right of the risky investments point will be the point representing the new combination.

Each security in a portfolio contributes returns in the proportion of its investment in security. Thus, the portfolio of expected returns, from each of the securities with weights representing the proportionate share of security in the total investments.

True Security Portfolio Analysis

$E(R_x) = \text{word} + (1\text{-}x)\ \text{Rye}$

In case of n security portfolio

$E(R_x) = w1E(R) + w2\,E(R) + \ldots + W_n(R_x)$

$\sum_{i=1}^{n} w_i\bar{R}$

Generally, investors in practice hold multiple securities, combination of multiple securities are called portfolios. The expected returns on a portfolio is the sum of the returns on an individual security multiplied by ways that is proportionate investment. It is the weighted averages rate of returns.

The expected rate of return on two portfolios is ascertained as

$E(R_x) = w_i + (1\text{-}w)\,R_x$

$E(R_x) = (0.5)(11) + (0.5)(20.5)$

$= 5.5 + 10.25 = 15.75\%$

Example: 9

Returns of security P & M are as follows

Probability	Returns of P	Returns of M
0.3	30%	-10
0.4	20%	20
0.3	0%	30

Calculate expected rate of return of P & M and portfolio expected rate of return of X & Y and also portfolio rate of return wherein the proportional investment is 0.6 and 0.4.

Solution:

$E(R_p) = \sum_{i=1}^{n} R_iP_i$

$E(Rx) = (0.3)(30) + (0.4)(20) + (0)(0.30)$

$= 9 + 8 + 0$

$= 17\%$

$E(R_m) = (30)(-10) + 0.4(20) + (0.30)(30)$

$= -0.3 + 8 + 9 = 14\%$

$E(R_p) = 17\%$

$E(R_M) = 14\%$

$w1 = 0.6$

$w2 = 0.4$

$E(R_x) = w_i + (1\text{-}x)\ R_p$

$E(R_M) = (0.6)17 + (0.4)14$

$= 10.2 \quad + 5.6$

$= 15.8\%$

PORTFOLIO RISK

Risk on portfolio is different from the risk on individual securities. This risk is reflected by in the variability of the returns from zero to infinity. The expected return depends on probability of the returns and their weighted contribution to the risk of the portfolio. Portfolio risk is not merely a weighted average risk. Securities considered in a portfolio are associated with each other. Therefore, the portfolio risk also accounts for covariance between the returns of securities. The covariance is the product of standard deviations of individual securities and correlation co-efficient.

The portfolio risk for two securities are as follows:

$\sigma p2 = W1^2\ \sigma x^2 \ + W2^2\ \sigma y^2 + 2W1W2\ (\Upsilon_{xy}\ \sigma x\ \sigma y)$

$\sigma p = W1^2\ \sigma x^2 \ + W2^2\ \sigma y^2 + 2W1W2\ (\Upsilon_{xy}\ \sigma y)]\ 1^{/2}$

Example: 10

An investor holding 2 securities i.e. X & Y

Ex – 24%, Std. deviation X = 28%

σ_y - 19% Std. deviation Y = 23%

The co- efficient of correlation between X and Y 0.6. The weighted are equal. Find return and risk of portfolio.

Solution:

$E(R_x) = \text{word} + (1\text{-}x)\ \text{Rye}$

$E(R_x) = \ 0.5(24) \ + \ 0.5(19)$

$= \ 12 + \ 9.5$

$E(R_x) = \ 21.5\%$

$\sigma p2 = W1^2\ \sigma x^2 \ + W2^2\ \sigma y^2 + 2W1W2\ (\Upsilon_{xy}\ \sigma x\ \sigma y)$

$\sigma_P = (0.5)^2\ (28)^2 + (0.5)^2 (23)^2 + 2(0.5)\ (0.5)\ (0.6)$

$= 0.25 \text{ x } 784 \ + 0.25(529) \ + \ 0.3$

$= 338.55$

Up = 18.13%

Example: 11

An investor is holding 2 securities A & B. expected rate of return.

ER (A) = 26% **Std. Deviation of A = 30%**

ER (B) = 21% **Std. deviation of B = 25%**

Correlation of AB = 0.8 **wets. A = 0.6, B = 0.4**

Solution:

$E(R_A) = 0.6(265) + 0.4(21)$

$= 15.6 + 8.4 = 24\%$

$R_P = (0.6)^2 (30)^2 + (0.4)^2 (25)^2 + 2(0.6) (0.4) (0.8)$

$= 0.36(900) + 0.16(625) + 0.384$

$= 424.384$

$R_P = 20.6\%$

Example: 12

Stock y and z have the following parameters

	Stock Y	Stock Z
Expected return	20	30
Expected variances	16	25
Covariance is	20	

Are there any advantages of holding a combination of Y and Z?

Solution:

$$r_{xy} = \frac{cov_{xy}}{\sigma_x \sigma_y}$$

$$= \frac{20}{4 \times 5}$$

$$= \pm 1$$

Note: - there is no any advantages of holding a combination of y and z, as risk can't reduce because they are perfectly positive correlation

Example: 13

The expected rates of return and the possibilities occurrence for alpha company and Beta company scrips are given below

Probabilities occurrence	Return of alpha scrip's	Return of beta scrip's
0.05	-2.0	-3.0
0.20	9.0	6.0
0.50	12.0	11.0
0.20	15.0	14.0
0.05	26.0	19.0

1. Find out the return of alpha and beta scrip'.
2. If and investors invests equal proportion on both the scrip's what would be the return?
3. If the proportion is changed to 25% and 75% and then to 75 % and 25% what would be the expected?

Solution:

$$\bar{R} = \sum_{i=1}^{n} R_i P_i$$

RETURN OF ALPHA COMPANY = $R_1P_1 + R_2P_2 + R_3P_3 + R_4P_4 + R_5P_5$

=-2.0(0.05) +9.0(.20) +12(.50) +15(.2) +26(.05)

= 12%

RETURN OF BETA COMPANY = -3.0(.05) +6(.2) +11(.5) +14(.2) +19(.05)

= 10.3%

A) IF AN INVESTORS INVESTS EQUAL PORTION OF %, THEN

B) $R_p = \sum_{i=1}^{n} x_i \bar{R}_i$

$R_P = .5 \times 12 + .5 \times 10.3$

$R_P = 11.5$

75% OF ALPHA SECURITY AND 25% OF BETA SECURITY

$R_P = .75 \times 12 + .25 \times 10.3$

=11.575

25% OF THE BETA SECURITY

$R_P = 0.25 \times 12 + .75 \times 10.3$

=10.725

Example: 14

Stocks Land m have yielded the following returns for the past two years.

Years	Returns	%
	R	S
2013	12	14
2014	18	12

1. What are the expected returns on portfolio made up of 60% of R and 40% of S?
2. Find out the standard deviation of each stocks?
3. What is the co-variance and co-efficient of correlation between stock R and S?
4. What is the portfolio risk of a portfolio made up 60 % of R and 40% S?

Solution:

a) EXPECTED RETURN $=\frac{\Sigma R}{n}$

Return of stock R$=\frac{12+18}{2}=15$

Returns of S$=\frac{14+12}{2}=13$

Portfolio returns $= \sum_{i=1}^{n} X_i \bar{R}_i$

SO X_1 being the portfolio held by each security which includes 60% of R and 40% of S

$= (0.6\times15) + (0.4\times13)$

$=14.2$

b) Standard deviation of each stock

$$\sigma_R = \sqrt{\frac{1}{N}\sum_{i=1}^{n}\left(R_R - \bar{R}_R\right)^2}$$

$$= \sqrt{\frac{(12-15)2+(18-15)2}{2}}$$

$$= \sqrt{\frac{9+9}{2}}$$

SO σ_L=3

$$\sigma_M = \sqrt{\frac{1}{N}\sum_{i=1}^{n}\left(R_M - \bar{R}_M\right)^2}$$

$$= \sqrt{\frac{(14-13)^2+12-13)^2}{2}}$$

$$= \sqrt{\frac{2}{2}}$$

So σ_m=1

c) The co -variance $COV_{XY}=\frac{\Sigma(R_R-\hat{R}_R)(R_S-\hat{R}_{S)})}{N}$

$=\frac{(-3)+(-3)}{2}=-3$

- Correlation Coefficient is ray$=\frac{COV\ XY}{\sigma_R\sigma_S}$

$=\frac{-3}{3\times1}=-1$

d) portfolio risk$\sigma_p = \sqrt{X_1^2\sigma_R^2 + X_2^2\sigma_S^2 + 2X_1X_2(r_{12}\sigma_1\sigma_2)}$

$\sigma_p = \sqrt{.6^2 \times 9 + 0.4^2 \times 1 + 2 \times .6 \times .4 \times (3 \times 1 \times -1)}$

σ_P =1.4

Example: 15

From the following data, calculate portfolio return and portfolio risk expected data return $E(R_x)$ 12%, $E(R_y)$ 18%, (σ_x) 16%, (σ_y) = 24%. Wets. Are equal Corr.CD = .8

Solution:

$R_P = E(R_x) = E(R_y)$ x w1

= 12 x 0.5 + 18 x 0.5

E (R) = 6 +9

= 15

$\sigma p2 = 16^2(0.5)^2 + 24^2 (0.5)^2 + 2(0.5)(0.5)(0.8)$

Up = $\sqrt{208.4}$

Up = 14.43%

Example: 16

An Investor holds two equal shares X and Y in equal proportions with the following Risk and Return characteristics.

R [Rx] = 24%	**E [Ry] = 19%**
σ_X **= 28%**	σ_y **= 23%**

Correlation Coefficient between equity shares ray=0.6 you are required to calculate Return and Risk of a portfolio?

Solution:

$$R_P = \sum_{i=1}^{n} X_i \bar{R}_i$$

= (0.5*24) + (0.5*19)

= 12+9.5=**21.5%**

Portfolio risk$\sigma_p = \sqrt{X_1^2\sigma_x^2 + X_2^2\sigma_y^2 + 2X_xX_y(r_{xy}\sigma_1\sigma_2)}$

$$= \sqrt{(0.5)^2(28)^2 + (0.5)^2(23)^2 + 2*(0.5)(0.5)(0.6*28*23)}$$

= 22.83%

Example: 17

Mr. MADAN is an investor who possess the following level of investment as a returned which are listed.

Particular	Investment	Return
Tata	200000	18%
Birla	100000	10%
Cognizant	500000	20%
Wipro	600000	22%
Copal	1000000	28%
TTK	600000	24%

Calculated the expected rate of return.

Solution:

Particular	Investment	Return	Weight	=	W x R
Tata	200000	18%	200000/3000000	=0.06	1.08
Birla	100000	10%	100000/3000000	=0.03	0.08
Cognizant	500000	20%	500000/3000000	=0.15	3.00
Wipro	600000	22%	600000/3000000	=0.21	4.62
Copal	1000000	28%	1000000/3000000	=0.33	9.24
TTK	600000	24%	600000/3000000	=0.22	5.28
					$E(R_p)$=23.52

Example: 18

Mr. X has the following investment and expected rate of return.

Particular	Investment	Return
A	300000	18%
B	400000	20%
C	300000	22%

Find out the expected rate of return of the following portfolio.

Solution:

Particular	Investment	Return	Wt.	=	W x R
A	300000	18%	300000/1000000	=0.3	5.4
B	400000	20%	400000/1000000	=0.04	8
C	300000	22%	300000/1000000	=0.3	6.6
				$E(R_p)$	20.0%

Example: 19

Securities M and N are equally risky. They have different expected returns which are as follows:

$E(R_M)$	**16%**	**$E(R_N)$**	**24%**
WM	**0.5**	**wN**	**0.5**
$\sigma^2 m$	**0.4**	**$\sigma^2 n$**	**.04**
σ_m	**0.20**	**σ_N**	**0.20**

What is portfolio variance if corr. +1, -1, 0.1, -0.107?

Solution:

a) corr. MN = +1 = γ_{mN}

$\sigma^2 = (16)^2 (0.5)^2 + (24)^2 (0.5)^2 + 2 (0.5) (0.5) (16) (24) (1)$

$= \sqrt{400}$

$\sigma_p = 20\%$

b) corr.mn = -1

$\sigma^2 = (16)^2 (0.5)^2 + (24)^2 (0.5)^2 + 2 (0.5) (0.5) (16) (24) (-1)$

$= \sqrt{16}$

$\sigma_p = 4\%$

c) corr. MN = .1

$\sigma^2 = (16)^2 (0.5)^2 + (24)^2 (0.5)^2 + 2 (0.5) (0.5) (16) (24) (.1)$

$\sigma_p = \sqrt{2\ 27} = 15.07\%$

d) Corr.mn = -.107

$\sigma = (16)^2 (0.5)^2 + (24)^2 (0.5)^2 + 2 (0.5) (0.5) (16) (24) (-.107)$

$= 256(0.25) + 576 (0.25) - 20.554$

$= \sqrt{187.456}$

$\sigma_p = 13.7\%$

Example: 20

The following are the characteristics of 2 securities C & D.

$E(R_C) = 12\%$ $E(R_D) = 18\%$

$\sigma_c = 16\%$ $\sigma_D = 24\%$

$W_{i.} = 0.6$ $W_D = 0.4$

Calculate portfolio return and risk if the corr. is +1, -1.

Solution:

Corr. CD is +1,

$\sigma^2 = (12)^2 (0.6)^2 + (18)^2 (0.4)^2 + 2(0.6)(0.4)(12)(18)(1)$

$= 144(0.36) + 324(0.16) + 103.68$

$= 207.36$

Up = 14.4%

Corr. CD = -1,

$\sigma^2 = (12)^2 (0.6)^2 + (18)^2 (0.4)^2 + 2(0.6)(0.4)(12)(18)(-1)$

$= 144(0.36) + 324(0.16) - 103.68$

$= 0\%$

Example: 21

A portfolio consists of 40% security X and 60% of security Y. It has the following returns calculate portfolio return & Risk.

Status	Pi	Returns	
		X%	Y%
Boom	0.1	14	20
Recession	0.2	-5	-2
Normal	0.4	10	9
Recovery	0.1	9	14
Slow growth	0.2	12	18

Solution:

$E[R_x]$	$E[R_y]$
1.4	2
-1	-0.4
4	4
0.9	0.9
2.4	2.4
7.7	10.2

$$\bar{R}_x = \sum_{i=1}^{n} R_x P_i \, R_I P_I = 7.7\%$$

$$\bar{R}_y = \sum_{i=1}^{n} R_y P_i = R_I P_I = 10.2\%$$

$$\sigma_X = \sqrt{\sum_{i=1}^{n} (R_x - \bar{R}_x)^2 \; * P_i}$$

$$= \sqrt{(6.3)2 * 0.1 + (12.7)2 * 0.2 + (2.3)2 * 0.4 + (1.3)2 * 0.1 + (4.3)2 * 0.2}$$

$$= \sqrt{3.969 + 32.258 + 2.116 + 0.169 + 3.6981}$$

$$= \sqrt{42.21} = \mathbf{6.497\%}$$

$$\sigma_y = \sqrt{\sum_{i=1}^{n} (R_y - \bar{R}_y)^2 \; * P_i}$$

$$= \sqrt{(9.8)^2 * 0.1 + (12.2)^2 * 0.1 + (-12.2)^2 * 0.4 + (3.8)^2 * 0.1 + (7.8)^2 * 0.2}$$

$$= \sqrt{9.604 + 29.768 + 0.3761.444 + 12.168}$$

$$= \sqrt{53.56} = \mathbf{7.318\%}$$

$$\text{cov}_{xy} = \sum_{i=1}^{n} (R_x - \bar{R}_x) \; (R_y - \bar{R}_y) * P_i$$

$$= 43.26$$

$$R_P = \sum_{i=1}^{n} X_i \bar{R}_i$$

= (0.4*7.7) + (0.6*10.2)

= 3.08+6.12=**9.2**

- Portfolio risk$\sigma_p = \sqrt{X_1^2 \sigma_x^2 + X_2^2 \sigma_y^2 + 2X_x X_y (r_{xy} \sigma_x \sigma_y)}$

$$= \sqrt{(0.4)^2 * 6.497 + (0.6)^2 * 7.398 + 2(0.4)(0.6)(0.9 * 6.497 * 7.318)}$$

=**6.829%.**

Example: 22

Two investment x+y has the following return for certain specific events.

Event	**Prob.**	**Security x**	**Security y**
1	**0.5**	**4**	**0**
2	**0.4**	**2**	**3**
3	**0.1**	**0**	**3**

Calculate the Co-variance of x + y & Correlation Coefficient

Solution:

$E(R_y) = 4x0.5 + 2x0.4 + 0x0.1$

$= 2 + 0.8 + 0$

$= 2.8\%$

$\sigma x^2 = (4\text{-}2.8)^2 + (2\text{-}2.8)^2\ (0\text{-}2.8)^2$

$= 1.4 + 0.64 + 7.84$

$\sigma^2 x = 9.92$

$\sigma_x = 3.15\%$

$E(R_y) = 0x0.5 + 3x0.4 + 3x0.1$

$= 1.5\%$

$\sigma y^2 = (0\text{-}1.5)^2 + (3\text{-}1.5)^2 + (3\text{-}1.5)^2$

$= 2.25 + 2.25 + 2.25$

$\sigma_y = 6.75 = 2.59\%$

Assumed equal wets.

$R_p = 2.8x0.5 + 1.5x0.5x0.5$

$= 1.25 + 0.75$

$= 2.15\%$

X				Y		
X	$(x\text{-}\bar{x})$	x2	y	$(y\text{-}\bar{y})$	y^2	xy
4	4-2.8 =1.2	1.44	0	0-1.5	2.25	1.8
2	2-2.8 =-0.8	0.64	3	3-1.5	2.25	1.2
0	0-2.8 =2.8	7.84	3	3-1.5	2.25	-4.2
	Σx^2	9.92		Σy^2=	6.75	-1.22

$$\gamma = \sqrt{\frac{\Sigma_{xy}}{x^2} \times \Sigma y^2}$$

$$\sqrt{\frac{-1.22}{9.92} \times 6.75}$$

$= [-1.2 / 9.92 * 6.75]^{1/2}$

$= -0.0163$

Example: 23

A Financial analyst is analyzing two investment alternatives of z and y. the estimated rate of return and their chances of occurrence for the next year are given the table below.

Probability	Rate of returns	
	Y	Z
0.20	22	50
0.60	14	15
0.20	-4	25

1. Determine each alternatives expected rate of return, variance and standard deviation?
2. Is 'Y' comparatively riskless?
3. If the financial analyst wishes to invest half in Z and another half in Y stock, would it reduce the risk. Explain the reasons for it.

Solution:

$$\overline{R}_Y = \sum_{i=1}^{n} R_i P_i$$

$$\overline{R}_Y = (22X0.20) + (14X0.60) + (-4X0.20)$$
$$=12\%$$

$$\overline{R}_Z = \sum_{i=1}^{n} R_i P_i$$

$$\overline{R}_Z = (50X0.20) + (15X0.60) + (25X0.20)$$
$$=15\%$$

$$\sigma_Y = \sqrt{\sum_{i=1}^{n} (R_Y - \overline{R}_Y)^2 P_i}$$

$$\sigma_Y = \sqrt{\left[(22-12)^2 0.2 + (14-12)^2 0.6 + (-4-12)^2 0.2\right]}$$

$$\sigma_Y = 8.857\%$$

$$\sigma_Z = \sqrt{\sum_{i=1}^{n} (R_Z - \overline{R}_Z)^2 P_i}$$

$$\sigma_Z = \sqrt{\left[(5-15)^2 0.2 + (15-15)^2 0.6 + (25-15)^2 0.2\right]}$$

$$\sigma_Z = 6.32\%$$

$$Cov_{YZ} = \sum_{i=1}^{n} (R_L - \overline{R}_L)(R_M - \overline{R}_M) P_i$$

$$Cov_{YZ} = [(22-12)(5-15)0.2 + (14-12)(15-15)0.6 + (-4-12)(25-15)0.2]$$

$$Cov_{YZ} = -52$$

$$\gamma_{YZ} = \frac{Cov_{LM}}{\sigma_Y \sigma_Z}$$

$$\gamma_{YZ} = \frac{-52}{8.57X6.32} = -0.96$$

$$\sigma_P = \sqrt{\chi_L^2 \sigma_L^2 + \chi_M^2 \sigma_M^2 + 2\chi_L \chi_M (\gamma_{LM} \sigma_L \sigma_M)}$$

$$\sigma_P = \sqrt{(0.5)^2 (8.57)^2 + (0.5)^2 (6.32)^2 + 2(0.5)(0.5)((-0.96)(8.57)(6.32))}$$

$$\sigma_P = 3.461\%$$

Combination of Y and Z securities reduce the risk.

Example: 24

An and is considered the purchases of two securities A, and B for the next year. States of the stocks and the estimated rates of returns are shown below.

State of market	Probability	Rate of returns	
		A	B
Recession	0.20	10	9
Average	0.60	14	15
boom	0.20	-4	25

1. Find each stocks expected rate return.
2. Standard deviation
3. Co-efficient of correlation
4. Co-variance
5. Portfolio Risk and Return

Solution:

$$\overline{R}_A = \sum_{i=1}^{n} R_i P_i$$

$$\overline{R}_A = (0.25X10) + (0.50X14) + (0.25X16)$$

$$\overline{R}_A = 13.5\%$$

$$\overline{R}_B = \sum_{i=1}^{n} R_i P_i$$

$$\overline{R}_B = (0.25X9) + (0.50X13) + (0.25X18)$$

$$\overline{R}_B = 13.25\%$$

$$\overline{R}_P = \sum_{i=1}^{n} \chi_i \overline{R}_i$$

$$\overline{R}_P = (13.5X0.5) + (13.25X0.5)$$

$$\overline{R}_P = 10.0625\%$$

$$\sigma_A = \sqrt{\sum_{i=1}^{n} (R_A - \overline{R}_A)^2 P_i}$$

$$\sigma_A = \sqrt{\left[(10-13.5)^2 0.25 + (14-13.5)^2 0.50 + (16-13.5)^2 0.25\right]}$$

$$\sigma_A = 2.17\%$$

$$\sigma_B = \sqrt{\sum_{i=1}^{n} (R_B - \overline{R}_B)^2 P_i}$$

$$\sigma_B = \sqrt{\left[(9-13.25)^2 0.25 + (13-13.25)^2 0.5 + (18-13.25)^2 0.25\right]}$$

$$\sigma_B = 3.19\%$$

$$Cov_{AB} = \sum_{i=1}^{n} (R_L - \overline{R}_L)(R_M - \overline{R}_M) P_i$$

$$Cov_{AB} = [(10-13.5)(9-13.25)0.25 + (14-13.5)(13-13.25)0.5 + (16-13.5)(18-13.25)0.25]$$

$$Cov_{AB} = 6.625$$

$$\gamma_{AB} = \frac{Cov_{LM}}{\sigma_Y \sigma_Z}$$

$$\gamma_{AB} = \frac{6.625}{13.5X13.25} = 0.95$$

$$\sigma_P = \sqrt{\chi_A^2 \sigma_A^2 + \chi_B^2 \sigma_B^2 + 2\chi_A \chi_B (\gamma_{AB} \sigma_A \sigma_B)}$$

$$\sigma_P = \sqrt{(0.3)^2 (2.17)^2 + (0.7)^2 (3.19)^2 + 2(0.3)(0.7)((0.95)(2.17)(3.19))}$$

$$\sigma_P = 8.17\%$$

Example: 25

Calculate the rate of return and risk of security in different economic conditions.

Economic Condition	Share Price	Dividend
High growth	**305.5**	**4**
Expansion	**285.5**	**3.25**
Stagnation	**261.5**	**2.5**
Decline	**243.5**	**2**

Indian cement market 261.25. The company dividend 2.5. Assume that the probabilities are equal for the all conditions.

Solution:

R1 = 4+ (305.50-261.25)/261x 100 = 18.5%

R2 = 3.25+ (285.5- 261.25)/261.25 x 100 = 10.5%

R3 = 2.5 + (261.25 – 261.25)/ 261.25 x 100 = 1%

R4 = 2+ (261.25 – 261.25)/ 261.25 x 100 = -6%

Return	Probability	E(R)
18.5	0.25	4.63
10.5	0.25	2.62
1.00	0.25	0.25
-6.00	0.25	-1.50
		6 %

$$E(R) = \sum_{i=1}^{N} R_i P_i$$

=.25(18.5+10.5+1-6)

=6.00

$$\sigma = \sqrt{\frac{\sum(R_1-\bar{R}_1)2}{N}}*\text{pi}$$

$$= \sqrt{025(18.5-6)^2+(10.5-6)^2+(1-6)^2+(-6-6)^2}$$

σ = 9.29%

- Returns are trying to fluctuate
- E(R) is less than the S.D indicating more risk is involved in investing in this security.
- It is better to search for an investment with the higher E[R] and lower S.D.

Example: 26

Measurement of three security portfolio Return and Risk (Three assets case)

Particulars	P	Q	R	Corr. coif.
Expected return percent	25%	22%	20%	-
Standard Dev.	30%	26%	24%	-
Corr. Coif.				
PG	-	-	-	-0.5
QR	-	-	-	0.4
PR	-	-	-	0.6

If these securities are equally weighted what risk and return of these securities.

Investment Income and Risk.

Solution: (Three Asset Case)

$ER_{(p)} = E(R_p)\, w1 + E(R_Q)\, w2 + E(R_R)\, w3$

$$\sigma_p = \sqrt{\sigma_p - x_p^2\sigma_p^2 + x_Q^2\sigma_Q^2 + x_R^2\sigma_R^2 + 2x_p x_Q\left(\gamma_{pQ}\sigma_p\sigma_Q\right)} + 2x_Q x_R\left(r_{QR}\sigma_Q\sigma_R\right) + 2x_P x_R\left(r_{PR}\sigma_P\sigma_R\right)$$

$ER_{(P)} = 25(1/3) + 22(1/3) + 20(1/3) = 22.33\%$

$\sigma p^2 = (1/3)^2(30)^2 + (1/3)^2(26)^2 + (1/3)^2(24)^2 + 2(1/3)(1/3)(30)(20)(-0.5) +$
$2(1/3)(1/3)(26)(24)(0.4) + 2(1/3)(1/3)(24)(30)(0.6)$

$= 100 + 75.11 + 64 - 86.67 + 55.47 + 90$

$= 303.91$

Up $= \sqrt{303.91}$

$= 17.43\%$

Example: 27

A portfolio consists of three securities i.e. A, B, & C with the following particulars:

	A	B	C	Corr. coif
Exp. Rate	20%	21%	24%	
Stud dev.	22%	24%	20%	
Corr.				
AB	-	-	-	0.6
BC	-	-	-	0.8
CA	-	-	-	0.7

The securities are wt. 40%, 30%, 30%. Calculate return & risk of the portfolio.

Solution:

$E(R_p) = 20(0.4) + 21(0.3) + 24(0.3) = 21.5\%$

$\sigma^2 p = (0.4)^2(22)^2 + (0.3)^2(24)^2 + (0.3)^2(20)^2 + 2(0.4)(0.3)(22)(24)(0.6) + 2(0.3)(0.3)(0.8)(24)(20) + 2(0.3)(0.4)(20)(22)(0.7)$

$\sigma p^2 = 2384.352$

$\sigma_p = 19.6\%$

Example: 28

Alpha ltd has portfolio 5 stocks with the following expected market values and returns are: calculate R[p] value

Stocks	**Market (Rs.)**	**Return %**
Ace	**40000**	**8**
Bell	**50000**	**20**
Crown	**20000**	**15**
Dell	**100000**	**9**
Eagle	**30000**	**12**
	240000	

Solution:

Weights	$W*R_i$
40000/240000=0.167	1.336
50000/240000=0.2083	4.166
20000/240000=0.0833	1.2499
100000/240000=0.4167	3.7
30000/240000=0.125	1.5
	11.768%

$R_p = 12\%$

Example: 29

Mr. X is holding 5 securities at the beginning of the year in the following amounts with the following current and expected end of year prices.

Security	**Share amount**	**Current price**	**Expected year end price**
A	100	Rs 50	Rs 65
B	150	Rs 30	Rs 40
C	75	Rs 20	Rs 25
D	100	Rs 25	Rs 32
E	125	Rs 40	Rs 47

What is the expected rate of return for portfolio for this year? Calculate of value of portfolio.

Solution:

A + B + C+ D+ E

= (100x50) + (150x30) + (75x20) + (125x40) = Rs. 18,500

Calculation of weights of portfolio

A = Rs. 50/ 100 x 18,500 = 0.27

B = RC 30 / 150 x 18,500 = 0.24

C = Rs. 20/ 150 x 18,500 = .08

D = Rs. 25 / 150 x 18,500 = 0.14

E = Rs. 40 / 150 x 18,500 = 0.27

Return = dividend yield + capital gain

Dividend yield is not given; therefore, the capital gain is return (i.e.) difference in two prices.

$$R = \frac{P_1 - P_0}{P_0}$$

A = 65 – 50 / 50 x 100 = 30%

B = 40 – 30 / 100 = 33.33%

C = (25 – 20)/ 20 x 100 = 25%

D = (32-25)/100 = 28%

E = (47 – 40) x 100 = 17.5%

Therefore, portfolio return

$E(R_p)$ = W1X1 + W2X2 + W3X3 + W4X4 + W5X5

= .27x30% + .24x33.33 + .08x25% + .14 x 28% + .27 x 17.5%

= 19.44%

Example: 30

Determine the investor invested in 3 scraps equally. Portfolio returns and risks are given below.

$\overline{R}_X = 15\%$

$\overline{R}_Y = 17\%$

$\overline{R}_Z = 20\%$

$\sigma_X = 18\%$

$\sigma_Y = 20\%$

$\sigma_Z = 25\%$

$\gamma_{AB} = 0.05$

$\gamma_{BC} = 0.2$

$\gamma_{CA} = -0.5$

Find the portfolio risk and portfolio returns.

Solution:

$$\overline{R}_P = \sum_{i=1}^{n} \chi_i \overline{R}_i$$

$$\overline{R}_P = (15X0.33) + (17X0.33) + (20X0.33)$$

$$\overline{R}_P = 17.66\%$$

$$\sigma_P = \sqrt{\chi_X^2\sigma_X^2 + \chi_Y^2\sigma_Y^2 + \chi_Z^2\sigma_Z^2 + 2\chi_X\chi_Y(\gamma_{XY}\sigma_X\sigma_Y) + 2\chi_Y\chi_Z(\gamma_{YZ}\sigma_Y\sigma_Z) + 2\chi_Z\chi_X(\gamma_{ZX}\sigma_Z\sigma_X)}$$

$$\sigma_P = \sqrt{(0.33)^2(18)^2 + (0.33)^2(20)^2 + (0.33)^2(25)^2 + 2(0.33)(0.33)((0.05)(18)(20)) + 2(0.33)(0.33)((0.2)(20)(25)) + 2(0.33)(0.33)((-0.5)(25)(18))}$$

$$\sigma_P = 12.06\%$$

Example: 31

Determine the investor invested in 3 scraps equally. Portfolio returns and risks are given below.

$\overline{R}_X = 25\%$

$\overline{R}_Y = 22\%$

$\overline{R}_Z = 20\%$

$\sigma_X = 30\%$

$\sigma_Y = 26\%$

$\sigma_Z = 24\%$

$\gamma_{AB} = 0.5$

$\gamma_{BC} = 0.4$

$\gamma_{CA} = 0.6$

Find the portfolio risk and portfolio returns.

Solution:

$$\overline{R}_P = \sum_{i=1}^{n} \chi_i \overline{R}_i$$

$$\overline{R}_P = (25X0.33) + (22X0.33) + (20X0.33)$$

$$\overline{R}_P = 22.11\%$$

$$\sigma_P = \sqrt{\chi_X^2\sigma_X^2 + \chi_Y^2\sigma_Y^2 + \chi_Z^2\sigma_Z^2 + 2\chi_X\chi_Y(\gamma_{XY}\sigma_X\sigma_Y) + 2\chi_Y\chi_Z(\gamma_{YZ}\sigma_Y\sigma_Z) + 2\chi_Z\chi_X(\gamma_{ZX}\sigma_Z\sigma_X)}$$

$$\sigma_P = \sqrt{(0.33)^2(30)^2 + (0.33)^2(26)^2 + (0.33)^2(24)^2 + 2(0.33)(0.33)((0.5)(30)(26)) + 2(0.33)(0.33)((0.4)(26)(24)) + 2(0.33)(0.33)((0.6)(24)(30))}$$

$$= \sqrt{234.352}$$

$$= 17.258\%$$

Example: 32

XYZ has 3 securities and joint probability.

Year	Security X	Security Y	Security Z	Probability
1	15%	-12%	0	0.15
2	12%	-2%	10%	0.20
3	5%	0	12%	0.30
4	-3%	4%	15%	0.20
5	-8%	10%	7%	0.15

Calculate the Expected Return & Std.Dev. If invest 40% in security X, 25% in security Y and 35% in security Z. Assume that correlation is 1.

Solution:

Average rate of return of X (15 x 0.5)

The Expected Return of security X, Y and Z = $\mathbf{E(R) = \sum_{i=1}^{n} R_i P_i}$

Rx = (15x.5) + (12 x .20) + (5x.30) + (-3x.20) + (-8x.15) =4.35%

Rye = (-12x.15) + (-2x.20) + (0x.30) + (4x.20) + (10x.15) = 0.10%

RC = (0x.15) + (10x.20) + (12x.30) + (15x.30) + (15x.20) + (7x.15) = 9.65%

Expected return or portfolio ER (p)

= (4.35x.40) + (0.10x.25) + (9.65x.35)

= 5.1425%

Standard deviation (σ)

$$\sigma_x = \sqrt{(15-4.35)^2 \text{ x } .15 + (12-4.35)^2 \text{ x } .20 + (5-4.35)^2 \text{ x } .30 + (-3-4.35)^2 \text{ x } .20 + (-8-4.35)^2 \text{ x } .15} = 7.91\%$$

$$\sigma_y = \sqrt{(-12-.10)^2 \text{ x } .15 + (-2-.10)^2 \text{ x } .20 + (0-.10)^2 \text{ x}.30 + (4-.10)^2 \text{ x}.20 + (10-.10)^2 \text{ x}.15}$$

$$= 6.44\%$$

$$\sigma_p = \sqrt{(0-9.65)^2 \text{ x}.15 + (10-9.65)^2 \text{ x}.20 + (12-9.65)^2 \text{ x }.30 + (15-9.65)^2 + (7--9.65)^2 \text{ x}.15}$$

$= 2.91\%$

Weights are .40, .25 and .35.

Since no correlation, the formula ignores correlation. There-fore the formula is as under.

$\sigma p^2 = w1\ \sigma x12 + w2\ \sigma y2 + w3\sigma z2$

$\sigma_p = [(.4)^2(7.91)^2 + (.25)^2\ (6.44)^2 + (.35)\ (2.91)^2]^{1/2}$

$= (10.0109 + 2.592 + 1.0373)^{1/2}$

$= 3.69\%$

Example: 33

Calculate individual securities expected return and portfolio return.

Stock	Initial investment (Rs.)	Value attends of period (Rs.)	Proportion of portfolio's initial market value (%)
A	5000	7000	20
B	2500	4000	10
C	4000	5000	16
D	1000	12000	40
E	3500	5000	14

Solution:

Expected Return on Portfolio

A = [(7000 – 5000)/5000] x 100 = 40%

B = [(4000 – 2500)/2500] x 100 = 60%

C = [(5000 – 4000)/4000] x 100 = 25%

D = [(12000 – 10000)/10000] x 100 = 20%

E = [(5000 – 3500)/3500] x 100 = 42.8%

$E(R_p) = (.20 \text{ x } 40) + (.10 \text{ x } 60) + (.16 \text{ x } 25) + (.40 \text{ x } 20) + (.14 \text{ x } 42.8)$

$= 8 + 3 + 4 + 8 + 5.992 = 32.0004\%$

RISK – RETURN RELATIONSHIP

The risk/return relationship is a fundamental concept in not only financial analysis, but in every aspect of life. If decisions are to lead to benefit maximization, it is necessary that individuals/institutions consider the combined influence on expected (future) return or benefit as well as on risk/cost. The requirement that expected return/benefit be commensurate with risk/cost is known as the "risk/return trade-off" in finance.

All investments have some risks. An investment in shares of companies has its own risks or uncertainty. These risks arise out of variability of returns or yields and uncertainty of appreciation or depreciation of share prices, loss of liquidity etc. and the overtime can be represented by the variance of the returns. Normally, higher the risk that the investors take, the higher is the return.

The expected rate of return and the variance or standard deviation provide investor with information about the nature of the probability distribution associated with a single asset. However, all these numbers are only the characteristics of return and risk of the particular asset? But how does one asset having some specific trade-off between return and risk influence the other one with the different characteristics of return and risk in the same portfolio? And what could be the influence of this relationship to the investor's portfolio? The answers to these questions are of great importance for the investor when forming his/ her diversified portfolio. The statistics that can provide the investor with the information to answer these questions are covariance and correlation coefficient. Covariance and correlation are related and they generally measure the same phenomenon - the relationship between two variables. Both concepts are best understood by looking at the math behind them.

SUMMARY

1. The main characteristics of any investment are investment return and risk. However, to compare various alternatives of investments the precise quantitative measures for both of these characteristics are needed.
2. General definition of return is the benefit associated with an investment. Many investments have two components of their measurable return: (1) a capital gain or loss; (2) some form of income. The holding period return is the percentage increase in returns associated with the holding period.
3. Investor can 't compares the alternative investments using holding period returns, if their holding periods (investment periods) are different. In these cases, arithmetic average return or sample mean of the returns can be used.
4. Both holding period returns and sample mean of returns are calculated using historical data. However, all the investors' decisions are focused to the future, or to expected results from the investments? The expected rate of return of investment is the statistical measure of return, which is the sum of all possible rates of returns for the same investment weighted by probabilities.
5. Risk can be defined as a chance that the actual outcome from an investment will differ from the expected outcome. The total risk of investments can be measured with such common absolute measures used in statistics as variance and standard deviation. Variance can be calculated as a potential deviation of each possible investment rate of return from the expected rate of return. Standard deviation is calculated as the square root of the variance. The more variable the possible outcomes that can occur, the greater the risk.

6. In the cases than the arithmetic average return or sample mean of the returns is used instead of expected rate of return, sample variance and sample standard deviation is calculated.

7. Covariance and correlation coefficient are used to answer the question, what is the relationship between the returns on different assets. Covariance and correlation coefficient are related and they generally measure the same phenomenon - the relationship between two variables.

8. The sample covariance is estimated than the investor has not enough information about the underlying probability distributions for the returns of two assets and then the sample of historical returns is used. The population covariance is estimated when the investor has enough information about the underlying probability distributions for the returns of two assets and can identify the actual probabilities of various pairs of the returns for two assets at the same time.

9. Analyzing relationship between the assets in the same portfolio using covariance for portfolio formation it is important to identify which of the three possible outcomes exists: positive covariance, negative covariance or zero covariance. If the positive covariance between two assets is identified the common recommendation for the investor would be not to put both of these assets to the same portfolio, because their returns move in the same direction and the risk in portfolio will be not diversified; if the negative - the common recommendation for the investor would be to include both of these assets to the portfolio, because their returns move in the contrariwise directions and the risk in portfolio could be diversified; if the zero covariance - it means that there is no relationship between the rates of return of two assets.

10. The correlation coefficient between two assets is closely related to their covariance. But instead of covariance when the calculated number is unbounded, the correlation coefficient can range only from -1, 0 to +1, 0. The closer the absolute meaning of the correlation coefficient to 1, 0, the stronger the relationship between the returns of two assets. Using correlation coefficients instead of covariance investor can immediately asses the degree of relationship between assets returns.

11. The coefficient of determination is calculated as the square of correlation coefficient and shows how much variability in the returns of one asset can be associated with variability in the returns of the other.

12. Theoretical interpretation of the market portfolio is that it involves every single risky asset in the global economic system, and contains each asset in proportion to the total market value of that asset relative to the total value of all other assets (value weighted portfolio). Investors can think of the market portfolio as the ultimate market index.

13. Stock's characteristic line describes the relationship between the stock and the market, shows the return investor expect the stock to produce, given that a particular rate of return appears for the market and helps to assess the risk characteristics of one stock relative to the market.

14. The slope of the characteristic line is called the Beta factor. The Beta factor of the stock is an indicator of the degree to which the stock reacts to the changes in the returns of the market portfolio.
15. The intercept is the point where characteristic line passes through the vertical axis. The interpretation of the intercept from the investor's point of view is that it shows
16. What would be the rate of return of the stock, if the rate of return in the market is zero?

MULTIPLE CHOICE QUESTIONS

1. Political constancy is the chief aspect concerning
   a. exchange risk b. systematic risk
   c. non-systematic risk d. country risk
2. The most favorable portfolio is the proficient portfolio with the
   a. lowest risk b. highest risk
   c. highest utility d. least investment
3. The ambiguity introduced by way by which the organization finances its investments is
   a. country risk b. liquidity risk
   c. financial risk d. business risk plagiarism
4. Which of the following returns are appropriate for portfolio owners?
   a. Select correct option: b. Actual diminishing returns
   c. Dollar Weighted Returns d. Time-weighted returns
   e. Opportunity cost returns
5. Which of the following is a measure of the volatility of stock prices or returns?
   a. ROR b. Beta
   c. ROI d. Risk premium
6. Which of the following is an investment which is spread across various sectors of the market to limit the exposure to any one sector to thus protect against loss?
   a. Select correct option: b. Design portfolio
   c. Modeling portfolio d. Architecture portfolio
   e. Balanced Portfolio
7. Which of the following stages of the industry life cycle offers the highest potential returns and greatest risk?
   a. Select correct option: b. Stabilization stage
   c. Declining stage d. Expansion stage
   e. Pioneering stage

8. Which of the following must hold TRUE in case of stocks that are inversely correlated?
   a. Correlation must always be Negative
   b. Correlation must always be zero
   c. Correlation must always be infinite
   d. Correlation must always be zero

9. Which of the following risks is also referred to as the non-diversifiable risk?
   a. Select correct option:
   b. Nonsystematic risk
   c. Systematic Risk
   d. Financial risk
   e. Production risk

10. If a company decides to issue new securities, these should be issued in:
    a. Primary Market
    b. Secondary market
    c. Third market
    d. Fourth market

11. Which of the following is the basic exchange rate in the economy?
    a. External rate of return
    b. Real rate of return
    c. Rate of return on assets
    d. Net present value rate of return

FILL IN THE BLANKS

1. Return can be in the form of: - (Dividends, Interests, Capital appreciation)
2. What are the ways of measuring relative strength? (Calculate the rates of return and classify securities that have earned superior historical returns, calculating certain ratios will help in analyzing whether a security has relative strength).
3. The ratios between profits and investments are called rate of return measures. (True)
4. Co variance of asset with market portfolio 85 and variance of market portfolio is 100 then beta is: - (0.0085)
5. A security analysis is done: - (For decision making for investments)
6. Formula for calculation of portfolio variance requires: - (Expected return on portfolio, expected return on assets, Weight of asset in the portfolio)
7. Risk can be referred as the ________ in the return with respect to the expected return. (Volatility)
8. A security represents evidence of :- (A property right)
9. The returns of sector specific funds are solely dependent on the performance of the respective sectors / industries. (True)
10. Risk on a portfolio of assets is always same as the risk on individual asset. (False)
11. The risk associated to get the required rate of return on the stock is measure by market beta. (True)
12. _______ Deal in futures to offset a pre-existing risk. (Hedger)
13. ________ take long or short positions only with the intention of making profits by getting out of the market when conditions favor them. (Speculators).
14. An investor with a higher tolerance of risk should tilt his portfolio in favor of ________. (Stocks)
15. ________ absorbs the excess demand or supply generated by hedgers and assume the risk of price fluctuations. (Speculators)
16. Risk on a portfolio of assets is always same as the risk on individual asset. (False)
17. What is the objective of Portfolio management? (To Minimize risk and maximize return)
18. What does lower level of unemployment indicate? (Positive economic conditions)
19. What is the objective of Portfolio management? (To Minimize risk and maximize return)
20. With the use of diversification, you can reduce the risk. (True)
21. The returns of sector specific funds are solely dependent on the performance of the respective sectors / industries. (True).

22. The greater the deviation of the actual returns from the actual return: - (Greater the variance
Your Answer Greater the variance)
23. The possibility of reduction of risk through the construction of a portfolio depends on the value of ________ between the two assets. (Correlation coefficient)
24. Security analysis serves the investment decision maker by identifying _______securities (Underpriced)
25. A security analysis is done: - (For decision making for investments)
26. The risk associated to get the required rate of return on the stock is measure by market beta. (True)
27. What is the objective of Portfolio management? (To Minimize risk and maximize return)
28. CP is a nuisance promissory note hence it can be negotiated by endorsement & delivery (True)
29. The return which the company pays on borrowed funds is termed as......... (Interest)
30. Return on Assets is a ratio of relationship between Assets and Sales (False)

SHORT ANSWER QUESTIONS

1. Define Risk and Return
2. Define Individual Investor
3. Define Systematic Risk
4. Define Un-systematic Risk
5. What is Market Risk?
6. Define Interest rate-Risk
7. Define Purchasing-Power Risk
8. Define Business Risk
9. Define Financial Risk
10. Define Single and multi-period return
11. Define Ex-Post Return
12. Define Ex-Ante Return
13. What is Expected Rate of Return?
14. What is meant by Holding Period Return?
15. What is Correlation and Coefficient of determination?
16. Define Portfolio Return

17. What is Portfolio Management?
18. What is Standard Deviation?
19. What is Full Covariance Model?
20. What is Mean Absolute Deviation?
21. What is Portfolio Risk?
22. What is Perfectly Positively Correlated Returns?
23. What is Perfectly Negatively Correlated Returns?
24. What are Uncorrelated Returns?
25. What is Combining Risky and Risk less Securities?

ESSAY TYPE QUESTIONS

1. With reference to investment Explain the risk return Distinguish between Historical Returns (Ex-Post) and Expected returns (Ex-Ante).
2. Define the term risk and return. Discuss the measure of risk and return of portfolio of two securities.
3. Define the components of holding period return.
4. Briefly explain about the various types of risks.
5. What is risk? Explain how standard deviation and beta measure risk.
6. Explain the risk return trade-off.
7. Explain the risk-return relationship. Why standard deviation is commonly employed as a measure of risk.
8. Explain the various causes of Risk or what are the root sources of risk?
9. How risk premium is different from risk aversion?
10. When should the sample mean of return be used instead of expected rate of return?
11. What does a probability distribution describe?
12. What does covariance measure? If two assets are said to have positive covariance, what does it mean?
13. Explain, why doesn't an estimated absolute covariance number tell the investor much about the relationship between the returns on the two assets?
14. How do you understand an investment risk and what statistic tools can be used to measure it?
15. What is the interpretation of the coefficient of determination for the investor? If the coefficient of correlation for two securities is 0, 7, what is the coefficient of determination?

EXERCISE PROBLEMS

1. An Ordinary Share y up Rs. 150 pays no Dividend the possible price of share at the year ended and its prob. Are as follows:

Price	95	90	110	120	135
Probability.	0.1	0.4	0.2	0.2	0.1

   What is the expected rate of return E(R)?

2. An asset has the following possible returns with associated probabilities. Calculate expected rate of return.

Possible Return	Probability
28%	0.2
22%	0.45
70	0.2
0%	0.05
-4%	0.10

3. There are two securities M and N which provides you the following returns and their probabilities.

Security M		Security N	
Return	**Prob.**	**Return**	**Prob.**
30%	0.10	-20%	0.05
20%	0.20	10%	0.25
10%	0.40	20%	0.30
5%	0.20	30%	0.30
-10%	0.10	40%	0.10

   Calculate expected rate of security M and security N.

4. Following information is available with regard to two assets R & S both the assets are involved invested in equal proportion.

Status of economy	**Probability**	**Returns**	
		R%	S%
A	0.1	-8	14
B	0.2	10	-4
C	0.4	8	6
D	0.2	5	15
E	0.1	-4	20

   Calculate portfolio Return, Risk, co-variance, correlation of coefficient the returns of 2 Assets.

5. Returns of security X& Y are as follows

Probability	Returns of X	Returns of Y
0.3	30%	-10
0.4	20%	20
0.3	0%	30

Calculate expected rate of return of X & Y and portfolio expected rate of return of X & Y and also portfolio rate of return wherein the proportional investment is 0.6 and 0.4.

6. An investor holding 2 securities i.e. X & Y

E (RC) – 28%, Std. deviation X = 29%

E (ray) - 23% Std. deviation Y = 26%

The co- efficient of correlation between X and Y 0.6. The weighted are equal. Find return and risk of portfolio.

7. An investor is holding 2 securities A & B. expected rate of return.

ER (A) = 30% Std. Deviation of A = 36%

ER (B) = 28% Std. deviation of B = 29%

Correlation of AB = 0.7 wets. A = 0.4, B = 0.4

8. The expected rates of return and the possibilities occurrence for alpha company and Beta company scrips are given below

Probabilities occurrence	Return of alpha scrip's	Return of beta scrip's
0.1	-3.0	-3.0
0.15	11.0	8.0
0.40	15.0	16.0
0.30	17.0	19.0
0.05	29.0	28.0

Find out the return of alpha and beta scrip'.

If and investors invests equal proportion on both the scrip's what would be the return?

If the proportion is changed to 75% and 25% and then to 25 % and 75% what would be the expected?

9. Two investment x+y has the following return for certain specific events.

Event	Prob.	Security x	Security y
1	0.4	4	0
2	0.4	2	3
3	0.2	0	3

Calculate the Co variance of x + y & Correlation Coefficient

10. Anand is considered the purchases of two securities A, and B for the next year. States of the stocks and the estimated rates of returns are shown below.

State of market	Probability	Rate of returns	
		A	B
Recession	0.30	12	12
Average	0.50	16	17
Boom	0.20	-6	26

Find each stocks expected rate return, Standard deviation, Co-efficient of correlation, Co-variance and Portfolio Risk and Return.

11. Measurement of three security portfolio Return and Risk (Three assets case)

Particulars	M	N	O	Corr. coif.
Expected return percent	28%	24%	24%	-
Standard Dev.	34%	29%	28%	-
Corr. Coif.				
MN	-	-	-	-0.8
MO	-	-	-	0.6
NO	-	-	-	0.8

If these securities are equally weighted what risk and return of these securities.

Investment Income and Risk.

12. Mr. X is holding 5 securities at the beginning of the year in the following amounts with the following current and expected end of year prices.

Security	Share amount	Current price	Expected year end price
A	110	Rs 55	Rs 75
B	160	Rs 35	Rs 50
C	70	Rs 25	Rs 55
D	120	Rs 30	Rs 42
E	135	Rs 45	Rs 67

What is the expected rate of return for portfolio for this year? Calculate of value of portfolio.

13. MNO has 3 securities and joint probability.

Year	Security M	Security N	Security O	Probability
1	16%	-14%	0	0.10
2	14%	-4%	12%	0.25
3	7%	0	14%	0.25
4	-5%	6%	17%	0.25
5	-10%	12%	9%	0.15

Calculate the Expected Return & Std.Dev. If invest 40% in security M, 25% in security N and 35% in security O. Assume that correlation is 1.

CASE STUDIES

CASE STUDY 1

The following information on joint stock returns for stock 1, 2, and 3 in the table

Probability	Return for stock		
	Stock 1	Stock 2	Stock 3
0.20	0.20	0.25	0.10
0.30	-0.05	0.10	0.05
0.25	0.10	0.05	0
0.25	0	-0.10	-0.05

If you must choose only two stocks to your investment portfolio, what would be your choice?

a) Stocks 1 and 2; b) stocks 1 and 3; c) stocks 2 and 3; d) other decision. Present your arguments and calculations, to explain your decision.

CASE STUDY 2

Refer to the following observations for stock A and the market portfolio in the table:

Month	Rate of return	
	Stock A	Market portfolio
1	0.30	0.12
2	0.24	0.08
3	-0.04	-0.10
4	0.10	-0.02
5	0.06	0.08
6	0.10	0.07

(a) Calculate the main statistic measures to explain the relationship between stock A and the market portfolio:

The sample covariance between rate of return for the stock A and the market;

- The sample Beta factor of stock A;
- The sample correlation coefficient between the rates of return of the stock A and the market;
- The sample coefficient of determination associated with the stock A and the market.
- Draw in the characteristic line of the stock A and give the interpretation - what does it show for the investor?
  - (a) Calculate the sample residual variance associated with stock 's A characteristic line and explain how the investor would interpret the number of this statistic.
  - (b) Do you recommend this stock for the investor with the lower tolerance of risk?

CASE STUDY 3

Vamsi's investment objective is to consistently generate strong risk-adjusted returns. Our process is founded on identifying and mitigating risk – seeking attractive return potential opportunities by avoiding under performers. Vamsi's analysts incorporate components under the categories of environmental, social and governance (ESG) into their assessment of industries, issuers, collateral and obligors. Evaluating these aspects is not a new phenomenon, but rather have been a part of research for many years. However, as disclosures improve and research continues to confirm, integrating these topics in a more formal and standardized manner makes good investment sense.

HIGH YIELD Q&A

- Many clients have given us the flexibility to invest a portion of their portfolio (typically to a maximum of 10%-15%) in high yield securities across a variety of mandates, including Short Duration, Intermediate Duration, Core and High Net Worth portfolios. This case study details the key points of emphasis in Vamsi's high yield research.
- This case study evaluates how Longfellow utilizes municipals and points of emphasis in our research process.

MCQs Answers

1	2	3	4	5	6	7	8	9	10	11
d	c	c	c	b	b	c	a	b	a	b

CHAPTER 5

Stock Market Indices and Calculation

A stock index or stock market index is a method of measuring the value of a section of the stock market. It is computed from the prices of selected stocks (typically a weighted average). It is a tool used by investors and financial managers to describe the market, and to compare the return on specific investments.

An index is a mathematical construct, so it may not be invested in directly. But many mutual funds and exchange-traded funds attempt to "track" an index and those funds that do not may be judged against those that do.

MEANING OF INDEX

Every stock price moves for two possible reasons: news about the company (e.g. a product launch, or the closure of a factory, etc.) or news about the country (e.g. nuclear bombs, or a budget announcement, etc.). The job of an index is to purely capture the second part, the movements of the stock market as a whole (i.e. news about the country). This is achieved by averaging. Each stock contains a mixture of these two elements – stock news and index news. When we take an average of returns on many stocks, the individual stock news tends to cancel out. On any one day, there would be good stock-specific news for a few companies and bad stock-specific news for others. In a good index, these will cancel out, and the only thing left will be news that is common to all stocks. The news that is common to all stocks is news about India. That is what the index will capture.

STOCK MARKET INDEXES HISTORY

The US stock market indexes history starts with the Dow and continues to this day. There are basically 4 major stock indexes in the US, NASDAQ, Dow Jones, S&P 500, and the Russell 3000.

DOW JONES

The Dow Jones was first created in 1896 by Charles Dow. It was the second index created after the Dow Jones Transportation Average. It consists of the 30 largest stocks in the US at any given time. When the Dow opened its doors in 1896 the index had a price of $40.94, today it is trading for $10,545.41 giving us a firm understanding of just how powerful the market can be in the long term. Despite several setbacks the largest of which was the great depression which showed an 89.19% drop in the Dow, it remains one of the biggest indexes around. The Dow can be traded through the ETF DIA. Below is a Dow Jones closing history graph taken from the time it was created to today.

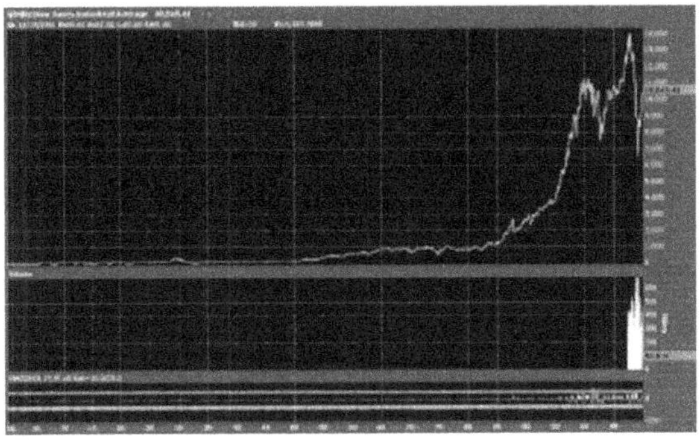

S&P 500

The S&P 500 was created in 1957 and consists of the 500 largest companies in the US, updated regularly by a committee. This index is also the largest and most watched out of all of the indexes in the US stock market. If you have ever heard that the average stock market return is 10% that number was taken from the S&P. The S&P can be traded through the ETF SPY. Here is a graph of the S&P historical returns.

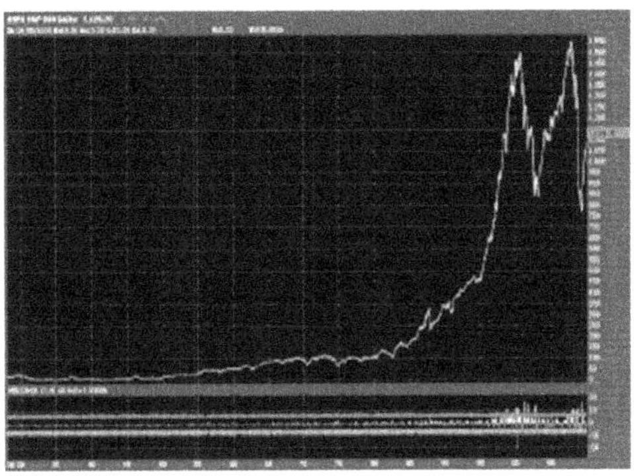

NASDAQ

The NASDAQ was formed on February 8, 1971 by the National Association of Securities Dealers. It was the first electronic based market in the world. The exchange was officially released to list smaller companies that did not meet the requirements of other exchanges. In 1994 the NASDAQ surpassed the NYSE in the number of shares traded. It then merged with the American Stock Exchange in 1998 creating the NASDQ-AMEX. The NASDAQ can be traded through the ETF QQQQ. Below is the NASDAQ chart history.

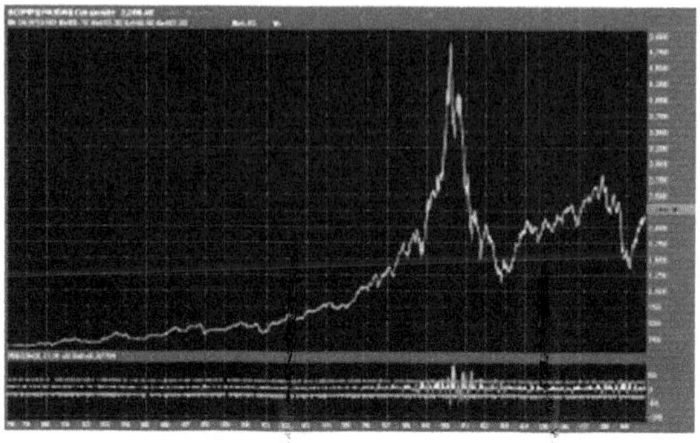

Russell 3000

The Russell 3000 consists of the Russell 1000 (1000 largest companies) and the Russell 2000 Index (2000 second largest companies). It was created in 1984 to track the performance of the largest 3000 companies in the US. Like the S&P and Dow the list is regularly updated. But unlike the S&P and Dow the Russell sets strict rules on which stocks are accepted and it is not open to discussion. The options on the Russell can be traded through the symbol RUT (although your broker may be different). Below is the chart for the Russell 3000.

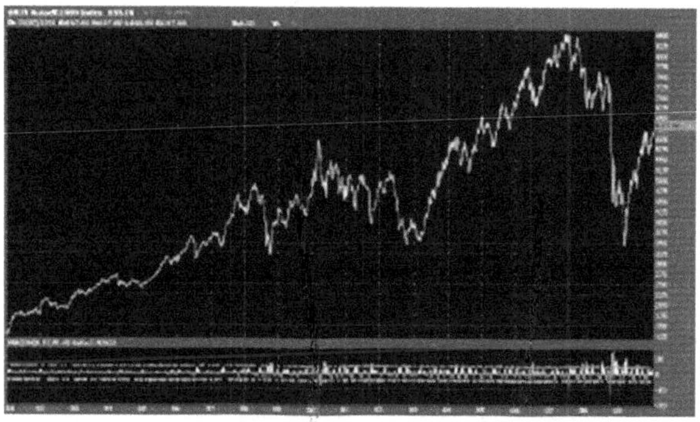

The stock market indexes history is constantly evolving, but these are the ones which have taken the lead and have kept it throughout time.

ESSENTIALS OF A STOCK MARKET INDEX

A stock market index should capture the behavior of the overall equity market. Movements of the index should represent the returns obtained by "typical" portfolios in the country.

THE UPS AND DOWNS OF AN INDEX MEAN

They reflect the changing expectations of the stock market about future dividends of India's corporate sector. When the index goes up, it is because the stock market thinks that the prospective dividends in the future will be better than previously thought. When prospects of dividends in the future become pessimistic, the index drops. The ideal index gives us instant-to-instant readings about how the stock market perceives the future of India's corporate sector.

KIND OF AVERAGING

For technical reasons, it turns out that the correct method of averaging is to take a weighted average and give each stock a weight proportional to its market capitalization. Suppose an index contains two stocks A and B. A has a market capitalization of Rs. 1000 core and B has a market capitalization of Rs.3000 core. Then we attach a weight of 1/4 to movements in A and 3/4 to movements in B.

IMPORTANCE OF INDICES

Traditionally, indices have been used as information sources. By looking at an index we know how the market is faring. This information aspect also figures in myriad applications of stock market indices in economic research. This is particularly valuable when an index reflects highly up to date information (a central issue which is discussed in detail ahead) and the portfolio of an investor contains illiquid securities – in this case, the index is a lead indicator of how the overall portfolio will fare. In recent years, indices have come to the fore owing to direct applications in finance, in the form of index funds and index derivatives. Index funds are funds which passively 'invest in the index'. Index derivatives allow people to cheaply alter their risk exposure to an index (this is called hedging) and to implement forecasts about index movements (this is called speculation).

Hedging using index derivatives has become a central part of risk management in the modern economy, these applications are now a multi-trillion-dollar industry worldwide, and they are critically linked up to market indices. Finally, indices serve as a benchmark for measuring the performance of fund managers. An all-equity fund should obtain returns like the overall stock market index. A 50:50 debt: equity fund should obtain returns close to those obtained by an investment of 50% in the index and 50% in fixed income. A well-specified relationship between an investor and a fund manager should explicitly define the benchmark against which the fund manager will be compared, and in what fashion.

The most important type of market index is the broad-market index, consisting of the large, liquid stocks of the country. In most countries, a single major index dominates benchmarking, index funds, index derivatives and research applications. In addition, more specialized indices often find interesting applications. In India, we have seen situations where a dedicated industry fund uses an industry index as a benchmark. In India, where clear categories of ownership groups exist, it becomes interesting to examine the performance of classes of companies sorted by ownership group.

STALE PRICES

Suppose we look at the closing price of an index. It is supposed to reflect the state of the stock market at 3:30 PM on NSE. Suppose an illiquid stock is in the index. The last traded price (LTP) of the stock might be an hour, or a day, or a week old! The index is supposed to show how the stock market perceives the future of the corporate sector at 3:30 PM. When an illiquid stock injects these 'stale prices' into the calculation of an index, it makes the index staler. It reduces the accuracy with which the index reflects information.

BID-ASK BOUNCE

Suppose stock trades at "bid 1440 asks 1490". Suppose no news appears for ten minutes. But, over this period, suppose, that a buy order first comes in (at Rs. 1490) followed by a sell order (at Rs. 1440). This sequence of events makes it seem that the stock price has dropped by Rs.50. This is a totally spurious price movement. Even when no news is breaking, when a stock price is not changing, the 'bid-ask bounce' is about prices bouncing up and down between bids and ask. These changes are spurious. This problem is the greatest with illiquid stocks where the bid-ask spread is wide. When an index component shows such price changes it contaminates the index.

IMPACT COST

Suppose a stock trades at bid 99 and ask 101. We say the "ideal" price is Rs. 100. Now, suppose a buy order for 1000 shares goes through at Rs.102. Then we say the market impact cost at 1000 shares is 2%. If a buy order for 2000 shares goes through at Rs. 104, we say the market impact cost at 2000 shares is 4%. Market impact cost is the best measure of the liquidity of a stock. It accurately reflects the costs faced when actually trading an index. For a stock to qualify for possible inclusion into the S&P CNX Nifty, it has to reliably have market impact cost of below 0.75% when doing S&P CNX Nifty trades of half a core rupee.

STOCK MARKET INDEX FUTURE

NSE was gearing up from 1995 onwards to start an index futures market. With NSE's expertise, this futures market has now become reliable and liquid. S&P CNX Nifty is uniquely equipped as an index for the index futures market owing to (a) low market impact cost and (b) high hedging effectiveness. The good diversification of S&P CNX Nifty will generate low initial margin requirements. Finally, S&P CNX Nifty is calculated using NSE prices, and NSE is the most liquid exchange in India, thus making it easier to do arbitrage for S&P CNX Nifty index futures.

USES

Stock index futures are used for hedging, trading, and investments.

- Hedging using stock index futures could involve hedging against a portfolio of shares or equity index options.
- Trading using stock index futures could involve, for instance, volatility trading (The greater the volatility, the greater the likelihood of profit taking – usually taking relatively small but regular profits).
- Investing via the use of stock index futures could involve exposure to a market or sector without having to actually purchase shares directly.

Please note the following cases of equity hedging with index futures:

- Where your portfolio 'exactly' reflects the index (this is unlikely). Here, portfolio is perfectly hedged via the index future.

- Where portfolio does not entirely reflect the index (this is more likely to be the case). Here, the degree of correlation between the underlying asset and the hedge is not high. So, portfolio is unlikely to be 'fully hedged'.

Equity index futures and index options tend to be in liquid markets for close to delivery contracts. They trade for cash delivery, usually based on a multiple of the underlying index on which they are defined.

OTC products are usually for longer maturities, and are usually a form of options product. For example, the right but not the obligation to cash delivery based on the difference between the designated strike price, and the value of the designated index at the *expiration date*. These are traded in the wholesale market, but are often used as the basis of guaranteed equity products, which offer retail buyers a participation if the equity index rises over time, but which provides guaranteed return of capital if the index falls. Sometimes these products can take the form of exotic options (for example Asian options or Quanta options).

PRICING

Forward prices of equity indices are calculated by computing the cost of carry of holding a long position in the constituent parts of the index. This will typically be

- The risk-free interest rate, since the cost of investing in the equity market is the loss of interest
- Minus the estimated dividend yield on the index, since equity investor receives the sum of the dividends on the component stocks. Since these occur at different times, and are difficult to predict, estimation of the forward price can be difficult, particularly if there are not many stocks in the chosen index.

Indices for futures are the well-established ones, such as S&P 500, FTSE, DAX, CAC40 and other G12 country indices. Indices for OTC products are broadly similar, but offer more flexibility.

HEDGING EFFECTIVENESS

A good index is one, which gives high hedging effectiveness, i.e. the index should correlate well with your portfolio — whatever it may be. A good index would give a very high-risk reduction when a portfolio owner short sells the index futures. S&P CNX Nifty correlates better with all kinds of portfolios in India as compared with other indices. This holds for all kinds of portfolios, not just those that contain index stocks.

TYPES OF INDICES

Stock market indices may be classed in many ways. A 'world' or 'global' stock market index includes (typically large) companies without regard for where they are domiciled or traded. Two examples are MSCI World and S&P Global 100. A 'national' index represents the performance of the stock market of a given nation—and by proxy, reflects investor sentiment on the state of its economy. The most regularly quoted market indices are national indices composed of the stocks of large companies listed on a nation's largest stock exchanges, such as the American S&P 500, the Japanese Nikkei 225, and the British FTSE 100. Other indices may be regional, such as the FTSE Developed Europe Index or the FTSE Developed Asia Pacific Index.

The concept may be extended well beyond an exchange. The Wilshire 5000 Index, the original total market index, represents the stocks of nearly every publicly traded company in the United States, including all U.S. stocks traded on the New York Stock Exchange (but not ADRs or limited partnerships), NASDAQ and American Stock Exchange. Russell Investment Group added to the family of indices by launching the Russell Global Index.[1]

More specialized indices exist tracking the performance of specific sectors of the market. Some examples include the Wilshire US REIT which tracks more than 80 American real estate investment trusts and the Morgan Stanley Biotech Index which consists of 36 American firms in the biotechnology industry. Other indices may track companies of a certain size, a certain type of management, or even more specialized criteria — one index published by Linux Weekly News tracks stocks of companies that sell products and services based on the Linux operating environment.

INDEX VERSIONS

Some indices, such as the S&P 500, have multiple versions. These versions can differ based on how the index components are weighted and on how dividends are accounted for. For example, there are three versions of the S&P 500 index: price return, which only considers the price of the components, total return, which accounts for dividend reinvestment, and net total return, which accounts for dividend reinvestment after the deduction of a withholding tax.[3] As another example, the Wilshire 4500 and Wilshire 5000indices have five versions each: full capitalization total return, full capitalization price, float-adjusted total return, float-adjusted price, and equal weight. The difference between the full capitalization, float-adjusted, and equal weight versions is in how index components are weighted.

WEIGHTING

An index may also be classified according to the method used to determine its price. In a *price-weighted* index such as the Dow Jones Industrial Average, Amex Major Market Index, and the NYSE ARCA Tech 100 Index, the price of each component stock is the only consideration when determining the value of the index. Thus, price movement of even a single security will heavily influence the value of the index even though the dollar shift is less significant in a relatively highly valued issue, and moreover ignoring the relative size of the company as a whole. In contrast, a *market-value weighted* or *capitalization-weighted* index such as the Hang Sang Index factors in the size of the company. Thus, a relatively small shift in the price of a large company will heavily influence the value of the index.

Traditionally, capitalization or share-weighted indices all had a *full* weighting, i.e. all outstanding shares were included. Recently, many of them have changed to a *float-adjusted* weighting which helps indexing.

An ***equal-weighted index*** is one in which all components are assigned the same value. For example, the Barron's 400 Index assigns an equal value of 0.25% to each of the 400 stocks included in the index, which together add up to the 100% whole.

A ***modified capitalization-weighted index*** is a hybrid between capitalization weighting and equal weighting. It is similar to a capitalization weighting with one main difference: the largest stocks are capped to a percent of the weight of the total stock index and the excess weight will be redistributed equally amongst the stocks under that cap. Moreover, in 2005, Standard & Poor's introduced the S&P Pure Growth Style Index and S&P Pure Value Style Index which was attribute-weighted. That is, a stock's weight in the index is decided by the score it gets relative to the value attributes that define the criteria of a specific index, the same measure used to select the stocks in the first place. For these two stocks, a score is calculated for every stock, be it their growth score or the value score (a stock cannot be both) and accordingly they are weighted for the index.

CRITICISM OF CAPITALIZATION-WEIGHTING

The use of capitalization-weighted indices is often justified by the central conclusion of modern portfolio theory that the optimal investment strategy for any investor is to hold the market portfolio, the capitalization-weighted portfolio of all assets. However, empirical tests conclude that market indices are not efficient. This can be explained by the fact that these indices do not include all assets or by the fact that the theory does not hold. The practical conclusion is that using capitalization-weighted portfolios is not necessarily the optimal method.

As a consequence, capitalization-weighting has been subject to severe criticism, pointing out that the mechanics of capitalization-weighting lead to trend-following strategies that provide an inefficient risk-return trade-off.

Also, while capitalization-weighting is the standard in equity index construction, different weighting schemes exist. First, while most indices use capitalization-weighting, additional criteria are often taken into account, such as sales/revenue and net income. Second, as an answer to the critiques of capitalization-weighting, equity indices with different weighting schemes have emerged, such as "wealth"-weighted, “fundamental”-weighted, “diversity”-weighted or equal-weighted indices.

INDICES AND PASSIVE INVESTMENT MANAGEMENT

There has been an accelerating trend in recent decades to create passively managed mutual funds that are based on market indices, known as index funds. Advocates claim that index funds routinely beat a large majority of actively managed mutual funds; one study claimed that over time, the average actively managed fund has returned 1.8% less than the S&P 500 index - a result nearly equal to the average expense ratio of mutual funds (fund expenses are a drag on the funds' return by exactly that ratio). Since index funds attempt to replicate the holdings of an index, they obviate the need for — and thus many costs of — the research entailed in active management, and have a lower churn rate (the turnover of securities which lose fund managers' favor and are sold, with the attendant cost of commissions and capital gains taxes).

ETHICAL STOCK MARKET INDICES

A notable specialized index type is those for ethical investing indices that include only those companies satisfying ecological or social criteria. In 2010, the OIC announced the initiation of a stock index that complies with Islamic law's ban on alcohol, tobacco and gambling. Other such equities, such as the Dow Jones Islamic Market World Index, already exist.

Another important trend is strict mechanical criteria for inclusion and exclusion to prevent market manipulation, e.g. in Canada when Nortel was Innovations Awards to Stock Indices permitted to rise to over 30% of the TSE 300 index value. Ethical indices have a particular interest in mechanical criteria, seeking to avoid accusations of ideological bias in selection, and have pioneered techniques for inclusion and exclusion of stocks based on complex criteria. Another means of mechanical selection is mark-to-future methods that exploit scenarios produced by multiple analysts weighted according to probability, to determine which stocks have become too risky to hold in the index of concern.

Critics of such initiatives argue that many firms satisfy mechanical "ethical criteria", e.g. regarding board composition or hiring practices, but fail to perform ethically with respect to shareholders, e.g. Enron. Indeed, the seeming "seal of approval" of an ethical index may put investors more at ease, enabling scams. One response to these criticisms is that trust in the corporate management, index criteria, fund or index manager, and securities regulator, can never be replaced by mechanical means, so "market transparency" and "disclosure" are the only long-term effective paths to fair markets.

SENSEX

The Sensex is an "index". What is an index? An index is basically an indicator. It gives you a general idea about whether most of the stocks have gone up or most of the stocks have gone down. The Sensex is an indicator of all the major companies of the BSE. The Nifty is an indicator of all the major companies of the NSE. If the Sensex goes up, it means that the prices of the stocks of most of the major companies on the BSE have gone up. If the Sensex goes down, this tells you that the stock price of most of the major stocks on the BSE have gone down. The Sensex represents the top stocks of the BSE, the Nifty represents the top stocks of the NSE.

The BSE, is the Bombay Stock Exchange and the NSE is the National Stock Exchange. The BSE is situated at Bombay and the NSE is situated at Delhi. These are the major stock exchanges in the country. There are other stock exchanges like the Calcutta Stock Exchange etc. but they are not as popular as the BSE and the NSE. Most of the stock trading in the country is done though the BSE & the NSE.

Besides Sensex and the Nifty there are many other indexes. There is an index that gives you an idea about whether the mid-cap stocks go up and down. This is called the “BSE Mid-cap Index”. There are many other types of indexes.

The 'BSE Sensex' or 'Bombay Stock Exchange' is value-weighted index composed of 30 stocks and was started in January 1, 1986. The Sensex is regarded as the pulse of the domestic stock markets in India. It consists of the 30 largest and most actively traded stocks, representative of various sectors, on the Bombay Stock Exchange. These companies account for around fifty per cent of the market capitalization of the BSE.

The Standard & Poor's CRISIL NSE Index 50 or S&P CNX Nifty nicknamed Nifty 50 or simply Nifty (NSE: ^NSEI), is the leading index for large companies on the National Stock Exchange of India. The Nifty is a well diversified 50 stock index accounting for 23 sectors of the economy. It is used for a variety of purposes such as benchmarking fund portfolios, index based derivatives and index funds. Nifty is owned and managed by India Index Services and Products Ltd. (IISL), which is a joint venture between NSE and CRISIL. IISL is India's first specialized company focused upon the index as a core product. IISL has a marketing and licensing agreement with Standard & Poor's.

Sensex could be construed as sensitive index and nifty as national fifty.... Sensex is the index of BSE while NIFTY is the index of NSE....Sensex consists of the 30 largest and most actively traded stocks, representative of various sectors, on the Bombay Stock Exchange. These companies account for around one-fifth of the market capitalization of the BSE. The Sensex has a very important function. The Sensex is supposed to be an indicator of the stocks in the BSE. It is supposed to show whether the stocks are generally going up, or generally going down.

To show this accurately, the Sensex is calculated taking into consideration stock prices of 30 different BSE listed companies. It is calculated using the "free-float market capitalization" method. This is a worldwide accepted method as one of the best methods for calculating a stock market index. The method used for calculating the Sensex and the 30 companies that are taken into consideration are changed from time to time. This is done to make the Sensex an accurate index and so that it represents the BSE stocks properly. To really understand how the Sensex is calculated, you simply need to understand what the term "free-float market capitalization" means. But, before we understand what "free-float market capitalization" means, you first need to understand what "market capitalization" means.

CNX NIFTY JUNIOR

The CNX Nifty Junior is an index for companies on the National Stock Exchange of India. It represents the next rung of liquid securities after S&P CNX Nifty. It consists of 50 companies representing approximately 10% of the traded value of all stocks on the National Stock Exchange of India. The CNX Nifty Junior is owned and operated by India Index Services and Products Ltd. It is quoted using the symbol NSMIDCP.

S&P CNX Nifty is the first rung of the largest, highly liquid stocks in India. CNX Nifty Junior is an index built out of the next 50 large, liquid stocks in India. It is not as liquid as the S&P CNX Nifty. It may be useful to think of the S&P CNX Nifty and the CNX Nifty Junior as making up the 100 most liquid stocks in India. S&P CNX Nifty is the front line blue-chips, large and highly liquid stocks. The CNX Nifty Junior is the second rung of growth stocks, which are not as established as those in the S&P CNX Nifty. A stock like Satyam Computers, which recently graduated into the S&P CNX Nifty, was in the CNX Nifty Junior for a long time prior to this. CNX Nifty Junior can be viewed as an incubator where young growth stocks are found. As with the S&P CNX Nifty, stocks in the CNX Nifty Junior are filtered for liquidity, so they are the most liquid of the stocks excluded from the S&P CNX Nifty. Buying and selling the entire CNX Nifty Junior as a portfolio is feasible.

The maintenance of the S&P CNX Nifty and the CNX Nifty Junior are synchronized so that the two indices will always be disjoint sets; i.e. a stock will never appear in both indices at the same time. Hence it is always meaningful to pool the S&P CNX Nifty and the CNX Nifty Junior into a composite 100 stock indexes or portfolio. The CNX Nifty Junior and the S&P CNX Nifty represent the 100 most liquid stocks traded on the National Stock Exchange of India. No one company can be listed on both indices simultaneously.

CNX MIDCAP

The medium capitalized segment of the stock market is being increasingly perceived as an attractive investment segment with high growth potential. The primary objective of the CNX Midcap Index is to capture the movement and be a benchmark of the midcap segment of the market.

CNX SEGMENT INDICES

For effectively researching the market, IISL has segregated the market in many ways. One of the ways is based on ownership. The CNX MNC Index comprises 50 listed companies in which the foreign shareholding is over 50% and / or the management control is vested in the foreign company. The index is a market capitalization weighted index with base period being the month of December, 1994 indexed to a value 1,000. Companies in the index should be MNCs and are selected based on their market capitalization, industry representation, trading value and financial performance. As part of its agenda to reform the Public Sector Enterprises (PSE), the Government has selectively been divesting its holdings in public sector enterprises since 1991.

With a view to provide regulators, investors and market intermediaries with an appropriate benchmark that captures the performance of this segment of the market, as well as to make available an appropriate basis for pricing forthcoming issues of PSEs, IISL has developed the CNX PSE Index, comprising of 20 PSE stocks. The Index is a market capitalization weighted index with base period being the month of December 1994 and base index value being 1,000. Companies selected in the index have to be PSEs, which should rank high in terms of market capitalization and trading value. Companies selected in the index have to be PSEs, which should rank high in terms of market capitalization and trading value.

CNX IT SECTOR INDEX

With the Information Technology (IT) sector in India growing at a fast rate, there is a need to provide investors, market. Intermediaries and regulators an appropriate benchmark that captures. Performance of this sector. Companies in this index should have more than 50% of their turnover from IT related activities like software development, hardware manufacture, vending, support and maintenance. The index is a market capitalization weighted index with its base period being December 1995 with base value 1,000 subsequently i.e. 28 May 2004, the base value of the India was revised from 1000 to 100.b

S&P CNX NIFTY

S&P CNX Nifty is based upon solid economic research. A trillion calculations were expended to evolve the rules inside the S&P CNX Nifty index. The results of this work are remarkably simple:

(a) The correct size to use is 50,

(b) Stocks considered for the S&P CNX Nifty must be liquid by the 'impact cost' criterion,

(c) The largest 50 stocks that meet the criterion go into the index. S&P CNX Nifty is a contrast to the ado methods that have gone into index construction in the preceding years, where indices were made out of intuition and lacked a scientific basis. The research that led up to S&P CNX Nifty is well-respected internationally as a pioneering effort in better understanding how to make a stock market index. The index assigns weightages to index components, and the weight of a stock is proportional to its market capitalization. This idea can be applied to buying the S&P CNX Nifty. If you buy all 50 stocks in the S&P CNX Nifty, in correct proportions, that would be called" an index trade".

THE IMPACT COST ON A TRADE FOR RS. 5 MILLION OF THE FULL S&P CNX NIFTY

It is safe to think that the impact cost is 0.1% or so. This means that if S&P CNX Nifty is at 1000, a buy order goes through at 1001 and a sell order gets 999. NSE's NEAT software has special facilities to enable buying or selling the entire the S&P CNX Nifty at one shot. The impact cost is not something fixed. It changes, depending upon the liquidity of the market. Indeed, the time-series of the S&P CNX Nifty impact cost is one of the best measures of changes in market liquidity over the years.

INDEX REVISIONS

INDEX KEEP CHANGING FROM TIME TO TIME

Think of a liquid stock as a good thermometer, one which gives accurate data about the true price of the stock, because it trades actively with a tight spread. The prices observed for an illiquid stock are like readings from a low quality thermometer, which reports noisy data about the phenomenon of interest (the true price of the security). We try to find the fifty best thermometers in the country and average their values to make the S&P CNX Nifty. As time passes, better thermometers become available (in the form of large, liquid stocks that are not in the S&P CNX Nifty). We would like that S&P CNX Nifty always uses the best thermometers possible. So we remove the weakest thermometer from inside the S&P CNX Nifty and accept the new stock into it. The world changes, so the index should change. Yet, the change should not be sudden – for that would disrupt the character of the index. S&P CNX Nifty uses clear, researched and publicly documented rules for index revision. These rules are applied regularly, to obtain changes to the index set. Index reviews are carried out every quarter to ensure that each security in the index fulfills all the laid down criteria. SBI was once illiquid; Infosys was once a startup software company. The world changes, and one by one, these stocks have come into the S&P CNX Nifty. Each change in the S&P CNX Nifty is small, so the continuity of the index is maintained. Yet, at all times, S&P CNX Nifty represents the 50 most important liquid stocks in the country, the best thermometers to build an index out of.

HIGH QUALITY INFORMATION

The Nifty closing prices are calculated by taking the last half an hour weighted average closing prices of the constituents of the index. Commonly reported as S&P CNX Nifty on TV and in the newspapers is actually the S&P CNX Nifty Price Index. It only reflects changes in prices. IISL also calculates something called the S&P CNX Nifty Total Returns (TR) index. This shows the returns on the index portfolio, inclusive of dividends. This is the appropriate benchmark for mutual funds, which do earn dividends. Both S&P CNX Nifty and S&P CNX Nifty TR use a base of 3 November 1995 as 1000. On December 30, 2005 i.e. nearly ten years later, S&P CNX Nifty was at 2836.55 while S&P CNX Nifty TR was at 3353.36. The difference in the two levels is the return obtained on reinvestment of dividends through the investing period.

MARKET CAPS CHANGE

The market-cap weighted index is "self-weighting". I.e. when weights change because prices change, yesterday's index portfolio continues to be today's index portfolio. Hence a buy and hold strategy is all that is required to replicate index returns under normal circumstances. Note that someone who buys and holds an S&P CNX Nifty portfolio earns dividend; this should be compared with the S&P CNX Nifty TR index and not plain S&P CNX Nifty.

Historical data for S&P CNX Nifty is available

S&P CNX Nifty and S&P CNX Nifty-TR are available from 3 July 1990 and 6 November 1995 respectively. The historical data is calculated in an intelligent way, i.e. the index set steadily evolves even through the older years. The historical Nifty and Nifty – TR value are very useful for research purposes.

The risk/return tradeoff of investing in S&P CNX Nifty

The long-run (10 year) return on S&P CNX Nifty is 21% per annum. The long-run daily standard deviation is 1.60% per day. In recent times, i.e. over the last calendar year, the daily standard deviation was 1.11% per day

S&P CNX Nifty compare with other indices?

The S&P CNX Nifty is favorable on various parameters.

Diversification: S&P CNX Nifty is a more diversified index, accurately reflecting overall market conditions. The reward-to-risk ratio of S&P CNX Nifty is higher than other leading indices, making it a more attractive portfolio hence offering similar returns, but at lesser risk.

Liquidity: The 'liquidity ratio' is defined as trading volume over one year divided by, market capitalization today. Nifty's liquidity ratio during the last one year is approx. 105%, which is high compared to other indices.

Hedging effectiveness: The basic risk of Nifty futures will be lower owing to the superior liquidity of Nifty stocks and of NSE. Nifty has higher correlations with typical portfolios in India as compared to any other index. These two factors imply that hedging using Nifty futures will be superior.

Governance: S&P CNX Nifty is managed by a professional team at IISL, a company setup by NSE and CRISIL. There is a three-tier governance structure comprising the board of directors of IISL, the Index Policy Committee, and the Index Maintenance Sub-committee. S&P CNX Nifty has fully articulated and professionally implemented rules governing index revision, corporate actions, etc. These rules are carefully thought out, under Indian conditions, to dovetail with operational issues of index funds and index arbitrageurs. The extent of manipulation related to S&P CNX Nifty is minimized due to the following reasons : (a) the index levels are calculated from a highly liquid exchange with superior surveillance procedures (b) S&P CNX Nifty has a large market capitalization so the consequence (upon the index) of a given move in an individual stock price is smaller and (c) S&P CNX Nifty calculation intrinsically requires liquidity in proportion to market capitalization, thus avoiding weak links which a manipulator can attack. Users of the S&P CNX Nifty benefit from the research that is possible owing to the long time-series available: both S&P CNX Nifty and S&P CNX Nifty Total Returns Index series are observed from July 1990 and November 1995 onwards respectively. S&P CNX Nifty is backed by solid economic research and three most respected institutions: NSE, CRISIL and S&P.

S&P CNX DEFTLY

S&P CNX Deftly is S&P CNX Nifty, measured in US dollar terms. If the S&P CNX Nifty raises by 2% it means that the Indian stock market rose by 2%; measured in rupees. If the S&P CNX Deftly rises by 2%, it means that the Indian stock market rose by 2%, measured in US dollars. The S&P CNX Deftly is calculated in real-time. Data for the S&P CNX Nifty and the dollar–rupee notes is absorbed in real-time, and used to calculate the S&P CNX Deftly in real-time. When there is currency volatility, the S&P CNX Deftly is an ideal device for a foreign investor to know where he stands, even intraday.

S&P CNX 500

The S&P CNX 500 is India's first broad based benchmark of the Indian capital market. The S&P CNX 500 represents about 93% of total market capitalization and about 94% the total turnover on the NSE. The S&P CNX 500 companies are disaggregated into 72 industries, each of which has an index – The S&P CNX Industry Index. Industry weightages in the index dynamically reflect the industry weightages in the market. So for e.g. if the banking sector has a 5% weightage among the universe of stocks on the NSE, banking stocks in the index would have an approx. representation of 5% in the index. The S&P CNX 500 is a market capitalization weighted index. The base date for the index is the calendar year 1994 with the base index value being 1000. Companies in the index are selected based on their market capitalization, industry representation, trading interest and financial performance. The index is calculated and disseminated real-time.

INDEX SHOULD BE USED FOR INDEX FUNDS

From a mutual fund investor's point of view, the reward-to-risk ratio is important. S&P CNX Nifty yields better rewards per unit risk as its reward-to-risk ratio is 4.34. From a mutual fund investor's point of view, the fund manager should accurately replicate returns on the index. The liquidity filtering in S&P CNX Nifty and numerous operational details about index management, help ensure accurate tracking. When investors see that an index fund is unable to replicate the returns on an index, they would have dark fears and would abandon the product. S&P CNX Nifty is the best index in India in terms of the accuracy of tracking possible.

The publicly accessible products based on S&P CNX Nifty and other indices are:

(A) Index Funds:

1. IDBI Index I-NIT'99, an index fund scheme on S&P CNX Nifty launched by IDBI-Principal Mutual Fund in July 1999 (now Principal PNB)
2. UTI Nifty Fund launched by Unit Trust of India in March 2000.
3. Franklin India Index Fund launched by Franklin Templeton Mutual Fund in June 2000.
4. Franklin India Index Tax Fund launched by Franklin Templeton Mutual Fund in February 2001.
5. Magnum Index Fund launched by SBI Mutual Fund in December 2001.
6. Prudential ICICI Index Fund launched by Prudential ICICI Mutual Fund in February 2002.
7. HDFC Index Fund – Nifty Plan launched by HDFC Mutual Fund in July 2002.
8. Birla Index Fund launched by Birla Sun Life Mutual Fund in September 2002.
9. LIC Index Fund – Nifty Plan launched by LIC Mutual Fund in November 2002.
10. Tata Index Fund launched by Tata TD Waterhouse Mutual Fund in February 2003
11. ING Visa Nifty plus Fund launched by ING Visa Mutual Fund in January 2004.
12. Can index Fund launched by Can bank Mutual Fund in September 2004
13. Reliance Index Fund launched by Reliance Mutual Fund in Jan 2005
14. Principal Junior Cap fund launched by Principal PNB in May 2005

(B) Exchange Traded Funds:

1. NIFTY Bees an Exchange Traded Fund launched by Benchmark Mutual Fund in January 2002.
2. Junior Bees an Exchange Traded Fund on CNX Nifty Junior, launched by Benchmark Mutual Fund in February 2003.

3. SUNDER an Exchange Traded Fund launched by UTI in July 2003.
4. Liquid Bees an Exchange Traded Fund launched by Benchmark Mutual Fund in July 2003.
5. Bank Bees an Exchange Traded Fund (ETF) launched by Benchmark Mutual Fund in May 2004.
6. Benchmark Split Capital launched by Benchmark Mutual Fund in August 2005

THE INDIAN STOCK MARKET

Bombay Stock Exchange, Capital Market, Emerging Markets, ETFs, ETNs, Foreign Investment, Foreign Investor, Fundamental Analysis, India, International Markets, National Stock Exchange, .Mark Twain once divided the world into two kinds of people: those who have seen the famous Indian monument, the Tajo Mahan, and those who haven't. The same could be said about investors. There are two kinds of investors: those who know about the investment opportunities in India and those who don't. India may look like a small dot to someone in the U.S., but upon closer inspection, you will find the same things you would expect from any promising market.

BOMBAY STOCK EXCHANGE (BSE)

Established in 1875, BSE Ltd. (formerly known as Bombay Stock Exchange Ltd.), is Asia's first & fastest Stock Exchange with the speed of 200 micro second and one of India's leading exchange groups. Over the past 139 years, BSE has facilitated the growth of the Indian corporate sector by providing it an efficient capital-raising platform. Popularly known as BSE, the bourse was established as "The Native Share & Stock Brokers' Association" in 1875. BSE is a corporatized and demutualized entity, with a broad shareholder-base which includes two leading global exchanges, Deutsche Bourse and Singapore Exchange as strategic partners. BSE provides an efficient and transparent market for trading in equity, debt instruments, derivatives, mutual funds. It also has a platform for trading in equities of small-and-medium enterprises (SME).

More than 5000 companies are listed on BSE making it world's No. 1 exchange in terms of listed members. The companies listed on BSE Ltd command a total market capitalization of USD 1.24 Trillion as of March 2014. It is also one of the world's leading exchanges (3rd largest in March 2014) for Index options trading.

BSE also provides a host of other services to capital market participants including risk management, clearing, settlement, market data services and education. It has a global reach with customers around the world and a nation-wide presence. BSE systems and processes are designed to safeguard market integrity, drive the growth of the Indian capital market and stimulate innovation and competition across all market segments. BSE is the first exchange in India and second in the world to obtain an ISO 9001:2000 certifications. It is also the first Exchange in the country and second in the world to receive Information Security Management System Standard BS 7799-2-2002 certification for its On-Line trading System (BOLT). It operates one of the most respected capital market educational institutes in the country (the BSE Institute Ltd.). BSE also provides depository services through its Central Depository Services Ltd. (CDSL) arm.

BSE's popular equity index - the S&P BSE SENSEX - is India's most widely tracked stock market benchmark index. It is traded internationally on the EUREX as well as leading exchanges of the BRCS nations (Brazil, Russia, China and South Africa). BSE has won several awards and recognitions that acknowledge the work done and progress made like India Innovation Award for the Big Data implementation , ICICI Lombard & ET Now Risk Management BFSI Company 2013, SKOCH Order of Merit Certificate was awarded to BSE Limited for E -Boss for qualifying amongst India's Best 2013, The Golden Peacock Global CSR Award for its initiatives in Corporate Social Responsibility, NASSCOM - CNBC-TV18's IT User Awards, 2010 in Financial Services category, Koch Virtual Corporation 2010 Award in the BSE Star MF category and Responsibility Award (CSR) by the World Council of Corporate Governance. Its recent milestones include the launching of BRICSMART indices derivatives, BSE-SME Exchange platform, S&P BSE GREENEX to promote investments in Green India.

BSE's popular equity index - the S&P BSE SENSEX [Formerly SENSEX] - is India's most widely tracked stock market benchmark index. It is traded internationally on the EUREX as well as leading exchanges of the BRCS nations (Brazil, Russia, China and South Africa). On Tuesday, 19 February 2013 BSE has entered into Strategic Partnership with S&P DOW JONES INDICES and the SENSEX has been renamed as "S&P BSE SENSEX".

HISTORY

The Bombay Stock Exchange is the oldest exchange in Asia. It traces its history to 1855, when four Gujarati and one Paris stockbroker would gather under banyan trees in front of Mumbai's Town Hall. The location of these meetings changed many times, as the number of brokers constantly increased. The group eventually moved to Dalai Street in 1874 and in 1875 became an official organization known as 'The Native Share & Stock Brokers Association'.

On 31 August 1957, the BSE became the first stock exchange to be recognized by the Indian Government under the Securities Contracts Regulation Act. In 1980 the exchange moved to the Pharoses Jeejeebhoy Towers at Dalai Street, Fort area. In 1986, it developed the BSE SENSEX index, giving the BSE a means to measure overall performance of the exchange. In 2000 the BSE used this index to open its derivatives market, trading SENSEX futures contracts. The development of SENSEX options along with equity derivatives followed in 2001 and 2002, expanding the BSE's trading platform.

Historically an open outcry floor trading exchange, the Bombay Stock Exchange switched to an electronic trading system in 1995. It took the exchange only fifty days to make this transition. This automated, screen-based trading platform called BSE On-line trading (BOLT) had a capacity of 8 million orders per day. The BSE has also introduced the world's first centralized exchange-based internet trading system, BSEWEBx.co.in to enable investors anywhere in the world to trade on the BSE platform.

FOLLOWING IS THE TIMELINE OF THE BSE

1830 TO 1875

- 1830's Business on corporate stocks and Share in Bank and Cotton presses started in Bombay.
- 1860-1865 Cotton price bubble as a result of the American Civil War.
- 1870 - 90's Sharp increase in Share prices of jute industries followed by a boom in tea stocks and coal.

1875 TO 1995

- 9 July 1875 The Native Share & Stock Broker's Association formed
- 2 February 1921 Clearing House started by Bank of India
- 31 August 1957 BSE granted permanent recognition under Securities Contracts (Regulation) Act (SCRA)
- 2 January 1986 SENSEX, country's first equity index launched (Base Year: 1978-79 =100)
- 10 July 1987 Investor's Protection Fund (IPF) introduced
- 3 January 1989 BSE Training Institute (BTI) inaugurated
- 25 July 1990 SENSEX closes above 1000
- 15 January 1992 SENSEX closes above 2000
- 30 March 1992 SENSEX closes above 4000
- 1 May 1992 SEBI Act established (An Act to protect, develop and regulate the securities market)
- 29 May 1992 Capital Issues (Control) Act repealed
- 1992 Securities Appellate Tribunal (SAT) established
- 14 March 1995 BSE On-Line Trading (BOLT) system introduced

1996 TO 2000

- 19 August 1996 First major SENSEX revamp* 22 March 1999 Central Depository Services Limited (CDSL) set up with other financial institutions
- 1 June 1999 Interest rate swaps (IRS) / Forward Rate Agreements (FRA) allowed
- 15 July 1999 CDSL commences work
- 11 October 1999 SENSEX closed above 5000
- 11 February 2000 SENSEX crosses 6000 intra-day
- 9 June 2000 Equity Derivatives introduced

2001 TO 2005

- 1 March 2001 Corporatization of Exchanges proposed by the Union Govt.
- 1 February 2001 BSE Web Launched
- 1 June 2001 Index Options launched
- 4 June 2001 BSE PSU index introduced
- 15 June 2001 WDM operations at commenced
- 2 July 2001 Vary model introduced for margin requirement calculation
- 9 July 2001 Stock options launched
- 11 July 2001 BSE Tack launched, India's First free float index
- 25 July 2001 Dolled 30 launched
- 1 November 2001 Stock futures launched
- 29 November 2001 100% book building allowed
- 31 December 2001 All securities clearing move to T+5 (trade date + 5 days)
- 1 February 2002 Two-way fungibility for ADR/GDR
- 15 February 2002 Negotiated Dealing System (NDS) established
- 1 April 2002 T+3 settlement Introduced
- 1 January 2003 India's first ETF on SENSEX - 'SPICE' introduced
- 16 January 2003 Retail trading in G Sec
- 1 April 2003 T+2 settlement Introduced
- 1 June 2003 Bankex launched
- 1 September 2003 SENSEX shifted to free-float methodology
- 1 December 2003 T group launched
- 2 June 2004 SENSEX closes over 6000 for the first time (564.71 points, 11.14%)
- 17 May 2004 Second biggest fall of all time, Circuit filters used twice in a day (the Scheme) announced by SEBI
- 20 May 2005 The BSE (Corporatization and Demutualization) Scheme, 2005
- 8 August 2005 Incorporation of Bombay Stock Exchange Limited
- 12 August 2005 Certificate of Commencement of Business
- 19 August 2005 BSE becomes a Corporate Entity

2006 TO 2010

- 7 February 2006 SENSEX closed above 10000
- 7 July 2006 BSE Gujarati website launched
- 21 October 2006 BSE Hindi website launched
- 2 November 2006 shares BSE SENSEX India Tracker listed at Hong Kong Stock Exchange
- 2 January 2007 Launch of Unified Corporate Bond Reporting platform: Indian Corporate Debt Market (ICDM)
- 7 March 2007 Singapore Exchange Limited entered into an agreement to invest in a 5% stake in BSE
- 16 May 2007 Appointed Date under the Scheme i.e. Date on which Corporatization and Demutualization was achieved. Notified by SEBI in the Official Gazette on 29.06.2007
- 10 January 2008 SENSEX All-time high 21206.77
- 1 October 2008 Currency Derivatives Introduced
- 18 May 2009 The SENSEX raised 2110.70 points (17.34%) and Index-wide upper circuit breaker applied
- 7 August 2009 BSE - USE Form Alliance to Develop Currency & Interest Rate
- 24 August 2009 BSE IPO Index launched
- 1 October 2009 Bombay Stock Exchange introduces trade details facility for the Investors
- 5 October 2009 BSE Introduces New Transaction Fee Structure for Cash Equity Segment
- 25 November 2009 BSE launches FASTRADE™ - a new market access platform
- 4 December 2009 BSE Launches BSE StAR MF – Mutual Fund trading platform
- 7 December 2009 Launch of clearing and settlement of Corporate Bonds through Indian Clearing Corporation Ltd.
- 14 December 2009 Marathi website launched
- 18 December 2009 BSE's new derivatives rates to lower transaction costs for all
- 4 January 2010 Market time changed to 9.0 a.m. - 3.30 p.m.
- 20 January 2010 BSE PSU website launched
- 22 April 2010 New DBM framework @ Rs.10 lakhs - 90% reduction in Membership Deposit
- 12 May 2010 Dissemination of Corporate Action information via SWIFT platform
- 23 July 2010 Options on BOLT
- 21 September 2010 First to introduce Mobile-based Trading
- 29 September 2010 Introduction of Smart Order Routing (SOR)

- 4 October 2010 EUREX - SENSEX Futures launch
- 11 October 2010 Launch of Fastrade on Web (FoW) - Exchange hosted platform
- 5 November 2010 SENSEX closes above 21,000 for the first time
- 12 November 2010 Commencement of Volatility Index
- 22 November 2010 Launch of SLB
- 10 December 2010 Launch of SIP
- 27 December 2010 Commencement of Shariah Index

2011 TO 2014

- 17 November 2011 Maharashtra and United Kingdom Environment Ministers launched Concept Note for BSE Carbon Index
- 30 December 2011, picks up a stake in the proxy advisory firm, Institutional Investor Advisory Services India Limited (IiAS)
- 7 January 2011 BSE Training Institute Ltd. with IGNOU launched India's first 2-year full-time MBA programme specializing in Financial Market
- 15 January 2011 Co-location facility at BSE - tie up with Netmagic.com
- 22 February 2012 Launch of BSE-GREENEX to promote investments in Green India
- 13 March 2012 Launch of BSE - SME Exchange Platform
- 30 March 2012 BSE launched trading in BRICSMART indices derivatives
- 19 February 2013 - SENSEX becomes S&P SENSEX as BSE ties up with Standard and Poor's to use the S&P brand for Sensex and other indices.[3]
- 28 November 2013 Launch of Currency Derivatives (BSE CDX)
- 28 January 2014 Launch of Interest Rate Futures (BSE –IRF)
- 11 Feb 2014 Launch of Institutional Trading Platform on BSE SME07 Apr 2014 Launch of Equity Segment on BOLT Plus with Median Response Time of 200 (μS)

HOURS OF OPERATION

Session	Timing
Pre-open Trading Session	09:00 - 09:15
Trading Session	09:15 - 17:00
Position Transfer Session	17:05 - 17:15
Closing Session	17:05 - 17:15
Option Exercise Session	17:07

The hours of operation for the BSE quoted above are stated in terms the local time (GMT + 5:30). BSE's normal trading sessions are on all days of the week except Saturday, Sundays and holidays declared by the Exchange in advance

INDICES

Graph of S&P BSE SENSEX monthly data from January 1991 to May 2013

The launch of SENSEX in 1986 was later followed up in January 1989 by introduction of BSE National Index (Base: 1983-84 = 100). It comprised 100 stocks listed at five major stock exchanges in India - Mumbai, Calcutta, Delhi, Ahmedabad and Madras. The BSE National Index was renamed BSE-100 Index from 14 October 1996 and since then, it is being calculated taking into consideration only the prices of stocks listed at BSE. BSE launched the dollar-linked version of BSE-100 index on 22 May 2006. BSE launched two new index series on 27 May 1994: The 'BSE-200' and the 'DOLLEX-200'. BSE-500 Index and 5 sectoral indices were launched in 1999. In 2001, BSE launched BSE-PSU Index, DOLLEX-30 and the country's first free-float based index - the BSE TECk Index. Over the years, BSE shifted all its indices to the free-float methodology (except BSE-PSU index). BSE disseminates information on the Price-Earnings Ratio, the Price to Book Value Ratio and the Dividend Yield Percentage on day-to-day basis of all its major indices. The values of all BSE indices are updated on real time basis during market hours and displayed through the BOLT system, BSE website and news wire agencies. All BSE Indices are reviewed periodically by the BSE Index Committee. This Committee which comprises eminent independent finance professionals frames the broad policy guidelines for the development and maintenance of all BSE indices. The BSE Index Cell carries out the day-to-day maintenance of all indices and conducts research on development of new indices. Popularly known as BSE. SENSEX is significantly correlated with the stock indices of other emerging markets.

AWARDS

- The World Council of Corporate Governance has awarded the Golden Peacock Global CSR Award for BSE's initiatives in Corporate Social Responsibility (CSR).
- The Annual Reports and Accounts of BSE for the year ended 31 March 2006 and 31 March 2007 have been awarded the ICAI awards for excellence in financial reporting.
- It has been cited as one of the world's best performing stock market by Reuters.

- The Human Resource Management at BSE has won the Asia - Pacific HRM awards for its efforts in employer branding through talent management at work, health management at work and excellence in HR through technology.

1993 BOMBAY BOMBINGS AT BSE

On Friday, 12 March 1993 at 1:30 p.m. a powerful car bomb exploded in the basement of the Bombay Stock Exchange building. The 28-story office building housing the exchange was severely damaged, and many nearby office buildings also suffered some damage. About 50 were killed by this explosion.

STOCK MARKET INDEX

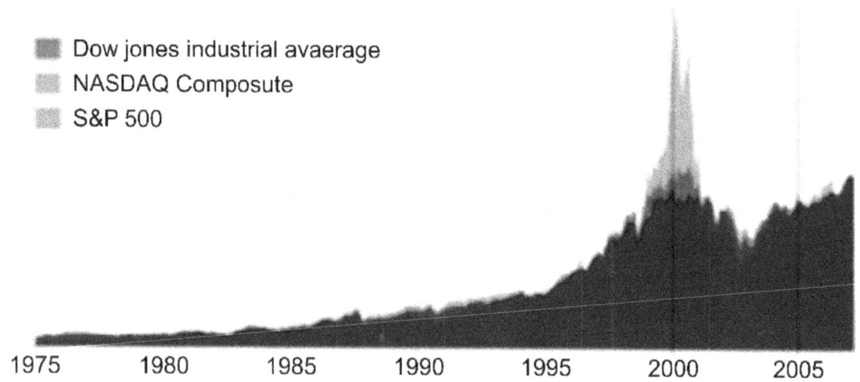

A comparison of three major U.S. stock indices: the NASDAQ Composite, Dow Jones Industrial Average, and S&P 500. All three have the same height at March 2007. Notice the large dot-com spike on the NASDAQ, a result of the large number of technology companies on that index.

A stock index or stock market index is a method of measuring the value of a section of the stock market. It is computed from the prices of selected stocks (typically a weighted average). It is a tool used by investors and financial managers to describe the market, and to compare the return on specific investments.

An index is a mathematical construct, so it may not be invested in directly. But many mutual funds and exchange-traded funds attempt to "track" an index (see index fund), and those funds that do not may be judged against those that do.

THE BSE AND NSE

Most of the trading in the Indian stock market takes place on its two stock exchanges: the Bombay Stock Exchange (BSE) and the National Stock Exchange (NSE). The BSE has been in existence since 1875. The NSE, on the other hand, was founded in 1992 and started trading in 1994. However, both exchanges follow the same trading mechanism, trading hours, settlement process, etc. At the last count, the BSE had about 4,700 listed firms, whereas the rival NSE had about 1,200. Out of all the listed firms on the BSE, only about 500 firms constitute more than 90% of its market capitalization; the rest of the crowd consists of highly illiquid shares.

TRADING MECHANISM

Trading at both the exchanges takes place through an open electronic limit order book, in which order matching is done by the trading computer. There are no market makers or specialists and the entire process is order-driven, which means that market orders placed by investors are automatically matched with the best limit orders. As a result, buyers and sellers remain anonymous. The advantage of an order driven market is that it brings more transparency, by displaying all buy and sell orders in the trading system. However, in the absence of market makers, there is no guarantee that orders will be executed.

All orders in the trading system need to be placed through brokers, many of which provide online trading facility to retail customers. Institutional investors can also take advantage of the direct market access (DMA) option, in which they use trading terminals provided by brokers for placing orders directly into the stock market trading system.

SETTLEMENT CYCLE AND TRADING HOURS

Equity spot markets follow a T+2 rolling settlement. This means that any trade taking place on Monday, gets settled by Wednesday. All trading on stock exchanges takes place between 9:55 am and 3:30 pm, Indian Standard Time (+ 5.5 hours GMT), Monday through Friday. Delivery of shares must be made in dematerialized form, and each exchange has its own clearing house, which assumes all settlement risk, by serving as a central counterparty.

MARKET INDEXES

The two prominent Indian market indexes are Sensex and Nifty. Sensex is the oldest market index for equities; it includes shares of 30 firms listed on the BSE, which represent about 45% of the index's free-float market capitalization. It was created in 1986 and provides time series data from April 1979, onward.

Another index is the S&P CNX Nifty; it includes 50 shares listed on the NSE, which represent about 62% of its free-float market capitalization. It was created in 1996 and provides time series data from July 1990, onward.

MARKET REGULATION

The overall responsibility of development, regulation and supervision of the stock market rests with the Securities & Exchange Board of India (SEBI), which was formed in 1992 as an independent authority. Since then, SEBI has consistently tried to lay down market rules in line with the best market practices. It enjoys vast powers of imposing penalties on market participants, in case of a breach.

Who Can Invest in India? India started permitting outside investments only in the 1990s. Foreign investments are classified into two categories: foreign direct investment (FDI) and foreign portfolio investment (FPI). All investments, in which an investor takes part in the day-to-day management and operations of the company, are treated as FDI, whereas investments in shares without any control over management and operations are treated as FPI.

For making portfolio investment in India, one should be registered either as a foreign institutional investor (FII) or as one of the sub-accounts of one of the registered FIIs. Both registrations are granted by the market regulator, SEBI. Foreign institutional investors mainly consist of mutual funds, pension funds, endowments, sovereign wealth funds, insurance companies, banks, asset management companies etc. At present, India does not allow foreign individuals to invest directly into its stock market. However, high-net-worth individuals (those with a net worth of at least $US50 million) can be registered as sub-accounts of an FII.

Foreign institutional investors and their sub accounts can invest directly into any of the stocks listed on any of the stock exchanges. Most portfolio investments consist of investment in securities in the primary and secondary markets, including shares, debentures and warrants of companies listed or to be listed on a recognized stock exchange in India. FIIs can also invest in unlisted securities outside stock exchanges, subject to approval of the price by the Reserve Bank of India. Finally, they can invest in units of mutual funds and derivatives traded on any stock exchange.

An FII registered as a debt-only FII can invest 100% of its investment into debt instruments. Other FIIs must invest a minimum of 70% of their investments in equity. The balance of 30% can be invested in debt. FIIs must use special non-resident rupee bank accounts, in order to move money in and out of India. The balances held in such an account can be fully repatriated.

RESTRICTIONS/INVESTMENT CEILING

The government of India prescribes the FDI limit and different ceilings have been prescribed for different sectors. Over a period of time, the government has been progressively increasing the ceilings. FDI ceilings mostly fall in the range of 26-100%.

By default, the maximum limit for portfolio investment in a particular listed firm is decided by the FDI limit prescribed for the sector to which the firm belongs. However, there are two additional restrictions on portfolio investment. First, the aggregate limit of investment by all FIIs, inclusive of their sub-accounts in any particular firm, has been fixed at 24% of the paid-up capital. However, the same can be raised up to the sector cap, with the approval of the company's boards and shareholders.

Secondly, investment by any single FII in any particular firm should not exceed 10% of the paid-up capital of the company. Regulations permit a separate 10% ceiling on investment for each of the sub-accounts of an FII, in any particular firm. However, in case of foreign corporations or individuals investing as a sub-account, the same ceiling is only 5%. Regulations also impose limits for investment in equity-based derivatives trading on stock exchanges.

INVESTMENT OPPORTUNITIES FOR RETAIL FOREIGN INVESTORS

Foreign entities and individuals can gain exposure to Indian stocks through institutional investors. Many India-focused mutual funds are becoming popular among retail investors. Investments could also be made through some of the offshore instruments, like participatory notes (PNs) and depositary receipts, such as American depositary receipts(ADRs), global depositary receipts (GDRs), and exchange traded funds (ETFs) and exchange-traded notes (ETNs).

As per Indian regulations, participatory notes representing underlying Indian stocks can be issued offshore by FIIs, only to regulated entities. However, even small investors can invest in American depositary receipts representing the underlying stocks of some of the well-known Indian firms, listed on the New York Stock Exchange and Nasdaq. ADRs are denominated in dollars and subject to the regulations of the U.S. Securities and Exchange Commission (SEC). Likewise, global depositary receipts are listed on European stock exchanges. However, many promising Indian firms are not yet using ADRs or GDRs to access offshore investors.

Retail investors also have the option of investing in ETFs and ETNs, based on Indian stocks. India ETFs mostly make investments in indexes made up of Indian stocks. Most of the stocks included in the index are the ones already listed on NYSE and NASDAQ. As of 2009, the two most prominent ETFs based on Indian stocks are the Wisdom-Tree India Earnings Fund (NYSE: EPI) and the Power Shares India Portfolio Fund (NYSE:PIN). The most prominent ETN is the MSCI India Index Exchange Traded Note (NYSE:INP). Both ETFs and ETNs provide good investment opportunity for outside investors.

THE BOTTOM LINE

Emerging markets like India are fast becoming engines for future growth. Currently, only a very low percentage of the household savings of Indians are invested in the domestic stock market, but with GDP growing at 7-8% annually and a stable financial market, we might see more money joining the race. Maybe it's the right time for outside investors to seriously think about joining the India bandwagon.

NATIONAL STOCK EXCHANGE

The **National Stock Exchange of India Ltd.**: **NSE** is a stock exchange located in the financial capital of Mumbai, India. National Stock Exchange (NSE) was established in the mid-1990s as a demutualized electronic exchange. NSE provides a modern, fully automated screen-based trading system, with over two lakh trading terminals, through which investors in every nook and corner of India can trade. NSE has played a critical role in reforming the Indian securities market and in bringing unparalleled transparency, efficiency and market integrity.

The National Stock Exchange is India's largest financial market. Established in 1992, the NSE has developed into a sophisticated, electronic market, which ranks third in the world for transacted volume. The NSE conducts transactions in the wholesale debt, equity and derivative markets. Based in Mumbai, India, the National Stock Exchange is a leader in market technology. The exchange's supports more than 3,000 VSAT terminals, making the NSE the largest private wide-area network in the country. The National Stock Exchange has been a pioneer for Indian financial markets, being the first electronic limit order book to trade derivatives and ETFs.

NSE has a market capitalization of more than US$989 billion and 1,635 companies listed as on July 2013. Though a number of other exchanges exist, NSE and the Bombay Stock Exchange are the two most significant stock exchanges in India and between them are responsible for the vast majority of share transactions. NSE's flagship index, the S&P CNX Nifty, is used extensively by investors in India and around the world to take exposure to the Indian equities market.

NSE was started by a clutch of leading Indian financial institutions. It offers trading, clearing and settlement services in equity, debt and equity derivatives. It is India's largest exchange, globally in cash market trades, in currency trading and index options. NSE has diversified shareholding. There are many domestic and global institutions and companies that hold stake in the exchange. Some of the domestic investors include LIC, GIC, State Bank of India and IDFC Ltd. Foreign investors include MS Strategic (Mauritius) Limited, Citigroup Strategic Holdings Mauritius Limited, Tiger Global Five Holdings and Norwest Venture Partners X FII-Mauritius, who have a stake in NSE. As on June 2013, NSE has 1673 VSAT terminals and 2720 lease lines, spread over more than 2000 cities across India.

Origin was started by a clutch of leading Indian financial institutions at the behest of the Government of India to bring transparency to the Indian market, and has a diversified shareholding comprising domestic and global investors. The domestic investors includes Life Insurance Corporation of India, GIC, State Bank of India and Infrastructure Development Finance Company (IDFC) Ltd, while the foreign investors include MS Strategic (Mauritius) Limited, Citigroup Strategic Holdings Mauritius Limited, Tiger Global Five Holdings and Norwest Venture Partners X FII-Mauritius. The exchange was incorporated in 1992 as a tax-paying company and was recognized as a stock exchange in 1993 under the Securities Contracts (Regulation) Act, 1956, when Mr. P. V. Narasimha Rao was the Prime Minister of India and Dr. Man Mohan Singh was the Finance Minister. NSE commenced operations in the Wholesale Debt Market (WDM) segment in June 1994. The Capital market (Equities) segment of the NSE commenced operations in November 1994, while operations in the Derivatives segment commenced in June 2000. In December 2013, NSE celebrated its 20th anniversary in a glittering ceremony attended by the Chairman of the market regulator SEBI Mr. U. K. Sinha, Finance Minister Mr. P. Chidambaram and a host of dignitaries from other regulatory organizations, the market and the corporate world. The institution that has been a catalyst of reforms since inception pledged to continue with this tradition on this solemn occasion, and set even loftier goals for the future, while the market regulator announced that NSE had made India proud in the global arena. Over the years, NSE has constantly re-invented itself, be it adapting to the latest technology, introducing new products, or in its endeavor to promote financial literacy. The spirit of the organization is aptly summed up in MD & CEO Ms. Chita Ramakrishna's words when she said, at heart NSE always wants to be young and always wants to be energetic. In the past 20 years, the exchange has set certain standards. As articulated by Ms. Ramakrishna, the endeavor now is not only on ensuring that those standards are maintained, but also on being able to improve upon them.

NSE BROUGHT ABOUT A PARADIGM SHIFT IN FINANCIAL MARKET

NSE was mainly set up to bring in transparency in the markets. Instead of trading membership being confined to a group of brokers, NSE ensured that anyone who was qualified, experienced and met minimum financial requirements was allowed to trade. In this context, NSE was ahead of its times when it separated ownership and management in the exchange under SEBI's supervision. The price information which could earlier be accessed only by a handful of people could now be seen by a client in a remote location with the same ease. The paper-based settlement was replaced by electronic depository-based accounts and settlement of trades was always done on time. One of the most critical changes was that a robust risk management system was set in place, so that settlement guarantees could protect investors against broker defaults.

NSE was also instrumental in creating the National Securities Depository Limited (NSDL) which allowed investors to securely hold and transfer their shares and bonds electronically. It also allowed investors to hold and trade in as few as one share or bond. This not only made holding financial instruments convenient, but more importantly eliminated the need for paper certificates and greatly reduced the incidents of forged or fake certificates and fraudulent transactions that had plagued the Indian stock market. The NSDL's security, combined with the transparency, lower transaction prices and efficiency that NSE offered, greatly increased the attractiveness of the Indian stock market to domestic and international investors.

MARKETS

NSE offers trading in the following segments:

EQUITIES

- Equities
- Indices
- Mutual Funds
- Exchange Traded Funds
- Initial Public Offerings
- Security Lending and Borrowing Scheme

DERIVATIVES

- Equity Derivatives (including Global Indices like S&P 500, Dow Jones and FTSE)
- Currency Derivatives
- Interest Rate Futures

DEBT

- Corporate Bonds

DERIVATIVES

The National Stock Exchange of India Limited (NSE) commenced trading in derivatives with the launch of index futures on 12 June 2000. The futures and options segment of NSE has made a mark for itself globally. In the Futures and Options segment, trading in CNX Nifty Index, CNX IT index, Bank Nifty Index, Nifty Midcap 50 index and single stock futures are available. Trading in Mini Nifty Futures & Options and Long-term Options on CNX Nifty are also available. The average daily turnover in the F&O Segment of the Exchange on 28 February 2013 stood at Rc 4, 02,090.64 core.

On 29 August 2011, National Stock Exchange launched derivative contracts on the world's most followed equity indices, the S&P 500 and the Dow Jones Industrial Average. NSE is the first Indian exchange to launch global indices. This is the also the first time in the world that futures contracts on the S&P 500 index were introduced and listed on an exchange outside of their home country, USA. The new contracts include futures on both the DJIA and the S&P 500, and options on the S&P 500.

On 3 May 2012, the National Stock exchange launched derivative contracts (futures and options) on FTSE 100, the widely tracked index of the UK equity stock market. This was the first of its kind of an index of the UK equity stock market launched in India. FTSE 100 includes 100 largest UK listed blue chip companies and has given returns of 17.8 per cent on investment over three years. The index constitutes 85.6 per cent of UK's equity market cap.

On 10 January 2013, the National Stock Exchange signed a letter of intent with the Japan Exchange Group, Inc. (JPX) on preparing for the launch of CNX Nifty Index futures, a representative stock price index of India, on the Osaka Securities Exchange Co., Ltd. (OSE), a subsidiary of JPX.

Moving forward, both parties will make preparations for the listing of yen-denominated CNX Nifty Index futures by March 2014, the integration date of the derivatives markets of OSE and Tokyo Stock Exchange, Inc. (TSE), a subsidiary of JPX. This is the first time that retail and institutional investors in Japan will be able to take a view on the Indian markets, in addition to current ETFs, in their own currency and in their own time zone. Investors will therefore not face any currency risk, because they will not have to invest in dollar denominated or rupee denominated contracts.

CURRENCY DERIVATIVES

In August 2008, currency derivatives were introduced in India with the launch of Currency Futures in USD INR by NSE. It also added currency futures in Euros, Pounds and Yen. The average daily turnover in the F&O Segment of the Exchange on 20 June 2013 stood at Rc 41,926.16 core in futures and Rc 27,397.70 core in options, respectively.

INTEREST RATE FUTURES

In December 2013, exchanges in India received approval from market regulator SEBI for launching interest rate futures (IRFs) on a single GOI bond or a basket of bonds that will be cash settled. Market participants have been in favor of the product being cash settled and being available on a single bond. NSE will launch the NSE Bond Futures on January 21 on highly liquid 7.16 percent and 8.83 percent 10-year GOI bonds. Interest Rate Futures were introduced for the first time in India by NSE on 31 August 2009, exactly one year after the launch of Currency Futures. NSE became the first stock exchange to get an approval for interest-rate futures, as recommended by the SEBI-RBI committee.

DEBT MARKET

On 13 May 2013, NSE launched India's first dedicated debt platform to provide a liquid and transparent trading platform or debt related products.

The Debt segment provides an opportunity to retail investors to invest in corporate bonds on a liquid and transparent exchange platform. It also helps institutions who are holders of corporate bonds. It is an ideal platform to buy and sell at optimum prices and help Corporate to get adequate demand, when they are issuing the bonds.

TRADING SCHEDULE

Trading on the equities segment takes place on all days of the week (except Saturdays and Sundays and holidays declared by the Exchange in advance). The market timings of the equities segment are:

1. Pre-open session
   - Order entry & modification Open: **09:00 hrs.**
   - Order entry & modification Close: **09:08 hrs.***

   *with random closure in last one minute. Pre-open order matching starts immediately after close of pre-open order entry.
2. Regular trading session
   - Normal/Retail Debt/Limited Physical Market Open: **09:15 hrs.**
   - Normal/Retail Debt/Limited Physical Market Close: **17:00 hrs.**

   Block deal session is held between **09:15 hrs.** and **09:50 hrs.**
3. The Closing Session is held between **17.05 hrs.** and **17.15 hrs.**

   The Exchange may however close the market on days other than the above schedule holidays or may open the market on days originally declared as holidays. The Exchange may also extend, advance or reduce trading hours when it deems fit and necessary.

EXCHANGE TRADED FUNDS ON NSE

An exchange-traded fund is an investment fund that is traded on a stock exchange, just like stocks. An ETF holds assets such as stocks, commodities or bonds and trades in value, around its (NAV) over the course of the trading day. Most ETFs track an index such as a stock index or a bond index. ETFs are attractive investments because of their low costs, diversified holdings, tax efficiency and stock-like features. ETFs are the most popular type of exchange-traded products in the USA and Europe.

Exchange Traded Funds are simple and easy to understand. Most ETFs also have an intrinsically lower risk due to their diversified portfolio. This diversification coupled with low expenses allows the smallest of the investors to reap the benefits of market-based returns. Retail investors can use ETF's as an easy entry vehicle into the capital markets. Equity investments are most likely to give you attractive long-term growth. And, this growth is reflected in market indices, like the NSE Nifty.

The following products are trading on CNX Nifty Index in the Indian and international Market:

- 7 Asset Management Companies have launched ETFs on CNX Nifty Index which are listed on NSE
- 15 index funds have been launched on CNX Nifty Index
- Unit linked products have been launched on CNX Nifty Index by several insurance companies in India
- World Indices

Derivatives Trading on CNX Nifty Index:

- Futures and Options trading on CNX Nifty Index
- Trading in CNX Nifty Index Futures on Singapore Stock Exchange (SGX)
- Trading in CNX Nifty Index Futures on Chicago Mercantile Exchange (CME)

TECHNOLOGY

NSE's trading system, is a state of-the-art application. It has an up time record of 99.99% and processes more than 450 million messages every day with sub millisecond response time.

NSE has taken huge strides in technology in these 20 years. In 1994, when trading started, NSE technology was handling 2 orders a second. This increased to 60 orders a second in 2001. Today NSE can handle 1, 60,000 orders/messages per second, with infinite ability to scale up at short notice on demand

While settlements were delayed and uncertain before 1994, NSE has continuously worked towards ensuring that the settlement cycle comes down. Settlements have always been handled smoothly. The settlement cycle has been reduced from T+5 to T+2/T+1. The exchange continuously strives to enhance capacity to effectively meet the requirements of increased users and associated transaction loads.

FINANCIAL LITERACY

NSE is keen to ensure that the people of India are empowered to take sound financial decisions and invest wisely. It has collaborated with several universities like Gokhale Institute of

Politics & Economics (GIPE), Pune, Bahrain Vidyapeeth Deemed University (BVDU), Pune, Guru Gobind Singh Indraprastha University, Delhi, Ravens haw University of Cuttack and Punjabi University, Patiala, among others to offer MBA and BBA courses. NSE has also provided mock market simulation software called **NSE Learn to trade (NLT)** to develop investment, trading and portfolio management skills among the students. The simulation software is very similar to the software currently being used by the market professionals and helps students to learn how to trade in the markets.

The exchange has also worked with a missionary zeal to educate investors about the opportunities in the market, the precautions they should take and their rights and obligations. In order to educate investors and help them invest wisely, NSE conducts nearly 1,500 seminars every year in the metros as well as the smallest towns of India.

NSE also conducts online examination and awards certification, under its Certification in Financial Markets (NCFM) programmers. At present, certifications are available in 46 modules, covering different sectors of financial and capital markets, both at the beginner and advanced levels. The list of various modules can be found at the official site of NSE India. In addition, since August 2009, it offers a short-term course called NSE Certified Capital Market Professional (NCCMP). The NCCMP or NSE Certified Capital Market Professional is a 100-hour program for over 3–4 months, conducted at the colleges, and covers theoretical and practical training in subjects related to the capital markets. NCCMP covers subjects like equity markets, debt markets, derivatives, macroeconomics, technical analysis and fundamental analysis. Successful candidates are awarded joint certification from NSE and the concerned

NSE CLOSING PRICE

NSE has the best surveillance procedures in India, so the extent of market manipulation is minimized to the most possible extent there. In NSE, the professional staff of the surveillance department has no positions on the market. This elimination of conflict of interest generates a more honest focus upon eliminating market manipulation. On a day to day basis millions of shares get traded on the NSE generating huge order flows. Due to the liquidity and order flow from numerous market players, manipulation of the closing price becomes very hard. NSE is the most liquid exchange in India. Hence, the prices observed there are the most reliable. NSE has the highest trading intensity (reducing stale prices) and their bid-ask spreads are the tightest (reducing bid-ask bounce). This is assisted by the fact that the NSE tick size is Re.0.05 for all stocks, which encourages tight bid-ask spreads.

OTC EXCHANGE OF INDIA

OTC Exchange of India (OTCEI) also known as Over-the-Counter Exchange of India based in Mumbai, Maharashtra. It is the first exchange for small companies. It is the first screen based nationwide stock exchange in India. It was set up to access high-technology enterprising promoters in raising finance for new product development in a cost-effective manner and to provide transparent and efficient trading system to the investors.

OTCEI is promoted by the Unit Trust of India, the Industrial Credit and Investment Corporation of India, the Industrial Development Bank of India, the Industrial Finance Corporation of India and others and is a recognized stock exchange under the SCR Act.

HISTORY

OTC Exchange of India was founded in 1990 under the Companies Act 1956 and got recognized by the Securities Contracts Regulation Act, 1956 as a stock exchange.

OTCEI was incorporated in 1990 as a Section 25 company under the Companies Act 1956 and is recognized as a stock exchange under Section 4 of the Securities Contracts Regulation Act, 1956. The Exchange was set up to aid enterprising promoters in raising finance for new projects in a cost-effective manner and to provide investors with a transparent & efficient mode of trading.

Modelled along the lines of the NASDAQ market of USA, OTCEI introduced many novel concepts to the Indian capital markets such as screen-based nationwide trading, sponsorship of companies, market making and scrip less trading. As a measure of success of these efforts, the Exchange today has 115 listings and has assisted in providing capital for enterprises that have gone on to build successful brands for themselves like VIP Advantage, Sonora Tiles & Brilliant mineral water, etc.

Securities markets in developed countries are multi-tiered with an element of in-built competition amongst various layers. This prevents monopolization of securities exchange and makes the markets more efficient. In India, however, the situation has been altogether different because of the virtual monopoly enjoyed by stock exchanges till recently.

The multi-tier securities exchange model was adopted in our country in October 1990 with the establishment of the Over the Counter Exchange of India (OTCEI). The object of the OTCEI "is to provide an alternate market for the securities of smaller companies, public-sector companies, closely-held companies desirous of listing, etc.

IMAGE COURTESY

It has been promoted jointly by UTI, ICICI, IDBI, SBI Capital Markets Ltd., IFCI, and GIC and can bank Financial Services Ltd. The Government has conferred it the status of a 'recognized stock exchange' under Sec. 4 of the Securities Contracts Regulation Act. Consequently, companies listed with OTCEI will practically be at par with companies listed on any stock exchange in the country.

The OTCEI is 'floor-less exchange' where all the activities are computerized be it trading, billing, payments, etc. OTC designated dealers operate through their computer terminals which are hooked to a central computer. All quotes and transactions are recorded and processed here.

The dealers are spread over the country and have access to the central computer. Besides, PTI OTC scan is available to each dealer which displays the best bids and offers of the market makers in respect of each scrip. A transaction can be effected by entering the bid or offer in a dealer's computer counter. The exact transaction price along with other details is also displayed in the counter computer.

The trading documents of OTCEI include:

- Counter Receipt (CR) which is handed over to the buyer when a deal is made. It is a tradable document and hence must be preserved carefully. It is akin to a share certificate so far as its contents are concerned;
- Sale Confirmation Slip (SCS) which is passed on to the seller when a deal is made. The seller also must preserve it carefully since he gets the payment against this slip later on.

Trading at OTCEI will be permitted only in respect of the securities of the listed companies. Listing may be obtained by

- Companies with issued equity capital between Rs. 30 laces to 25 cores;
- Closely held companies interested in listing;
- Venture capital companies;
- Companies which are not listed on any other recognized stock exchange provided:
  - They offer to the public at least 40% of the issued equity or Rs. 20 laces, whichever is higher, where the issued equity ranges between Rs. 30 laces to less than Rs. 300 laces (i.e. 3 cores),
  - They offer to the public at least 60% of the issued equity v . . . ore issued equity is between 3 crores to 25 crores of rupees,
  - They offer at least 25% of the issued equity to the public in case of a venture capital company,
  - Where the issued equity ranges between 3 cores to 25 cores of rupees, the norms for listing on a recognized stock exchange must be satisfied,
  - The company is not carrying on the business of investment, leasing, finance, hire-purchase or amusement parks.

OTCEI promoters have been designated as 'sponsor members' and they alone are entitled to sponsor a company for listing here. Before recommending a company for enlistment, such members have to carry out the appraisal of the project to ensure its technological and financial viability. They also ensure that all government rules and regulations have been complied with. They are required to clarify the investment worthiness of the company and its project.

Finally, they would value the shares of the company, comply with SEBI guidelines for the issue of securities and manage the public issue. OTCEI requires such sponsor members to act as 'market makers' in that scrip for at least 3 years and also to appoint an additional market maker for that scrip for a period of at least one year.

SEBI relaxed norms for listing on the OTCEI during March 1995. The minimum post-issue capital to be offered to the public to enable listing was lowered from 40 per cent to 25 per cent. SEBI also permitted finance and leasing companies to get listed on the OTCEI. In

April 1995, OTCEI modified its guidelines to allow listing of finance companies-albeit with more stringency. The minimum issued capital was increased from Rs. 30 lakh to Rs. 1 core for finance companies. Further, a three-year track record of profitability was made compulsory before listing takes place. The new guidelines also state that the OTCEI- sponsor of these companies should hold at least 10 per cent of the public offer as market making inventory as against 5 per cent for other companies. However, till December 1996, no companies engaged in finance or leasing services was listed on the OTCEI.

To facilitate offers for sale of bought-out deals, OTCEI changed its guidelines in January 1996. The revised guideline did away with the requirement of making an offer for sale of the entire bought-out deal to the public, except the market making inventory. The offered can now offer a minimum of 25 per cent of the bought-out deal to the public.

At the same time, the ratio of involvement of OTCEI members to non-OTCEI members has been brought down from 60:40 to 10:90. These guidelines came into effect from 22 January 1996 and were made applicable to all the bought-out deals registered with SEBI and the offer documents for offers for sale which were awaiting SEBI clearance. Later in August 1996, SEBI exempted offers for sale of bought-out deals registered with OTCEI on or before 16 April 1996 from the new guidelines governing entry norms for public issues. Briefly, the new guidelines issued by SEBI stated that any company wanting to make a public issue should have a track record of dividend payment for at least three in the immediately preceding five years before the making public issue.

If companies do not satisfy this requirement, then they must at least get their project appraised by a financial institution or a nationalized bank which would participate in the public issue to an extent of at least 10 per cent of the total project outlay. The relaxation would benefit the 50-odd bought out deals registered with the OTCEI. With a view to review the working of the OTCEI and to make recommendations for its further improvement, SEBI appointed an eight-member committee under the chairmanship of Dr. S.A. Dave on 17 April 1996. On the recommendations of the Committee, SEBI has made the eligibility criteria for companies desirous of making a public issue very stringent.

The companies unable to make a public issue as a consequence of these guidelines be allowed to seek listing on the OTCEI, albeit with some checks. Currently, only those companies which have a track record of dividend payment of three years out of the immediately preceding five years can make a public issue. If the company does not have such a teach record, then the project for which the company is entering the capital market needs to be appraised by a financial institution or a nationalized bank. Further, there should be a minimum participation of 10 per cent of the project outlay by the appraiser, in the form of equity or long-term debt.

The committee has recommended that companies which do not satisfy these criteria should be allowed to get listed on the OTCEI provided they appoint a sponsor and two market makers to the issue. The committee has also recommended that companies which do not meet the minimum shareholding norm of having at least 5 shareholders for every Rs. 1 lakh of issued capital can get listed on the OTCEI but should appoint sponsors and market makers.

Companies which get delisted from regional stock exchanges should be allowed to list on the OTCEI since shareholders of delisted companies do not have a platform to off load their holdings. These companies should, however, be traded under a separate category on the OTCEI. Further, all the companies discussed above should be allowed listing on the OTCEI with a minimum lock-in period of three years. After three years, these companies may either choose to remain on the OTCEI or seek listing on other stock exchanges. The committee has recommended that the ceiling of Rs.25 core on the equity capital of a company seeking listing on the OTCEI be removed. It has also suggested that the current rolling settlement system of three days (known as T ± 3) should be increased to five days.

The committee has also stressed upon the need of increased involvement of the promoters of OTCEI. The main promoters of the exchange are Unit Trust of India, Industrial Development Bank of India, Industrial Credit & Investment Corporation of India, Industrial Finance Corporation of India, Life Insurance Corporation and General Insurance Corporation. The report points out that the some of these entities have promoted the National Stock Exchange which has grown at a much faster pace than the OTCEI. One recommendation for increased promoter participation is that the promoters should have an OTCEI-dedicated fund of a corpus of around Rs.100 core which would invest in fundamentally sound companies of the OTCEI.

OTCEI is intended to provide easy marketability and better liquidity of securities to an investor. Besides, it also offers facilities for transfer of shares listed here. The investor can submit the transfer documents at any of the OTCEI counters in the country. There is total transparency and fairness so far as the deals are concerned. It takes lesser time to finalize a deal too. The companies listed with OTCEI are also benefitted to a large extent.

Rising of funds becomes cheaper since they are priced fairly and the investor base is large. The company can obtain enlistment even with 40% public issue (which is 60% in case of listing on a recognized stock exchange). The company has also the option of allotting all the shares to a sponsor. In this case, the company has only to negotiate the issue price with the sponsor who finally markets the issue. Despite being in existence for a number of years, the exchange does not have a major presence amongst stock exchanges of the country.

NATIONAL SECURITIES DEPOSITORY LIMITED

National Securities Depository Limited (NSDL) in an Indian central securities depository based in Mumbai. It was established in 1995 as the first electronic securities depository in India with national coverage based on a suggestion by a national institution responsible for the economic development of India.

It has established a national infrastructure using international standards that handles most of the securities held and settled in dematerialized form in the Indian capital market.

The enactment of Depositories Act in August 1996 paved the way for establishment of NSDL, the first depository in India. NSE joined hands with the Industrial Development Bank of India (IDBI) and the Unit Trust of India (UTI) to promote dematerialization of securities. Together they set up National Securities Depository Limited (NSDL), the first depository in India.

HISTORY

Although India had a vibrant capital market which is more than a century old, the paper-based settlement of trades caused substantial problems such as bad delivery and delayed transfer of title. The enactment of Depositories Act in August 1996 paved the way for establishment of **National Securities Depository Limited** (NSDL), the first depository in India. It went on to established infrastructure based on international standards that handles most of the securities held and settled in dematerialized form in the Indian capital markets.

NSDL has stated it aims are to ensuring the safety and soundness of Indian marketplaces by developing settlement solutions that increase efficiency, minimize risk and reduce costs. NSDL plays a quiet but central role in developing products and services that will continue to nurture the growing needs of the financial services industry.

In the depository system, securities are held in depository accounts, which are similar to holding funds in bank accounts. Transfer of ownership of securities is done through simple account transfers. This method does away with all the risks and hassles normally associated with paperwork. Consequently, the cost of transacting in a depository environment is considerably lower as compared to transacting in certificates. In August 2009, number of Demit accounts held with NSDL crossed one core.

PROMOTERS / SHAREHOLDERS

NSDL is promoted by Industrial Development Bank of India Limited (IDBI) - the largest development bank of India, Unit Trust of India (UTI) - the largest mutual fund in India and National Stock Exchange of India Limited (NSE) - the largest stock exchange in India. Some of the prominent banks in the country have taken a stake in NSDL.

Other Shareholders

- Axis Bank Limited
- State Bank of India
- Oriental Bank of Commerce
- Citibank NA
- Standard Chartered Bank
- HDFC Bank Limited
- The Honking and Shanghai Banking Corporation Limited
- Deutsche Bank
- Dena Bank
- Canada Bank
- Union Bank of India

SECURITIES AND EXCHANGE BOARD OF INDIA

ORGANIZATION, FUNCTIONS AND REGULATIONS

The **Securities and Exchange Board of India** was established in 1988 and given statutory powers on 12 April 1992 as per the provisions of the **SEBI Act, 1992**. The management of SEBI vests in the Board having the following members:

- A Chairman appointed by the Central Government.
- Two Members from the Ministries of the Central Government managing Finance and Law.
- One Member from the Reserve Bank of India.

Securities and Exchange Board of India (SEBI) was initially constituted on 12th April, 1988 as a non-statutory body through a resolution of the Government for dealing with all matters relating to the development and regulation of securities market and investor protection and to advices the Government on all these matters. SJEBI was given statutory status and powers through an ordinance promulgated on January 30, 1992.

The statutory powers and functions of SEBI were strengthened through the promulgation of the Securities Laws (Amendment) ordinance on January 25, 1995 which was subsequently replaced by an Act of parliament. In terms of this Act, SEBI has been vested with regulatory powers over corporates in the issuance of capital, the transfer of securities and other related matters. Besides, SEBI has also been empowered to impose monetary penalties on capital market intermediaries and other participants for a range of violation.

ORGANIZATION AND MANAGEMENT

- SEBI is managed by six members—one chairman (nominated by Central Government), two members, (officers of Central Ministries), one member (from RBI) and remaining two members are nominated by Central Government. The office of SEBI is situated at Mumbai with its regional offices at Kolkata, Delhi and Chennai.
- In 1988 the initial capital of SEBI was Rs. 7.5 core which was provided by its promoters (IDBI, ICICI, and IECI). This amount was invested and with its interest amount, the day-to-day expenses of SEBI are managed. All statutory power for regulating Indian Capital Market is vested with SEBI itself.

FUNCTIONS OF SEBI

The important functions of SEBI are given below:

- Registering and regulating the working of stock brokers, sub-brokers, share transfer agents, bankers to an issue, trustee of trust deeds, registrars to an issue, merchant bankers, underwriters, portfolio managers, investment advisers and such other intermediaries who may be associated with securities markets in any manners.
- Registering and regulating the working of the depositories, participants, custodians of securities, foreign institutional investors, credit rating agencies and such other intermediaries as the Board may, by notification, specify in this behalf.

- Registering and regulating the working of venture capital funds and collective investment schemes including mutual funds.
- Helping the business in stock exchanges and any other securities market.
- Promoting and regulating self-regulatory organizations.
- Prohibiting fraudulent and unfair trade practices relating to securities market.
- Promoting investors education and training of intermediaries of securities markets.
- Prohibiting insider trading in securities.
- Regulating substantial acquisition of shares and takeover of companies.
- Supervise the working of various organizations trading in security market and also to ensure systematic dealings.
- Conducting research and investigations for ensuring the attainment of above objectives.

SEBI REGULATIONS

SEBI has adopted a number of regulations and revolutionary steps to re-establish the credit of capital market, which includes the following:

1. ***Share Price and Premium Determination:***
   - According to the latest directions of SEBI, Indian companies are now free to determine their share prices and premium on those shares. But determined price and premium amount will be equally applicable to all without any discrimination.
2. ***Control on Share Brokers:***
   - Under the new rules every broker and sub-broker has to obtain registration with SEBI and any stock exchange in India.
3. ***Control on Utilizing 'Application Amount' having no Interest by Companies Releasing Public Issues:***
   - At the instance of SEBI, Commercial banks introduced Stock Investment Scheme under which investor has to submit stock-invests, purchased from banks, with their share's application. If the investor is allotted shares/debentures, the required amount is transferred in concerned company's account by the bank issuing 'stock invests'.
   - In other case (if share/debenture is not allotted), investor gets a predetermined interest rate on invested capital. This step of SEBI ensured interest earning to the investor until he got share/debenture allotment. It also ensures the refund of invested amount to the investor in case shares are not allotted.
4. ***Underwriters:***
   - The minimum asset limit has been fixed to be Rs. 20 lakhs to work as underwriter. Besides, SEBI has warned underwriters that their registration can be cancelled if any irregularity is found in the purchase of unsubscribed part of the share issue.

5. ***SEBI's Control on Mutual Fund:***
   - SEBI (Mutual funds) Regulation 1993, help to take over direct control of all mutual funds of government and private sector (excluding UTI). Under this new rule, the company floating a mutual fund should possess net assets of Rs. 5 core which should consist of at least 40% contribution from promoter's side.
6. ***Control over Foreign Institutional Investors:***
   - SEBI has made it compulsory for every foreign institutional investor to get registered with SEBI for participating in Indian Capital Market. SEBI has issued directions in this regard.
7. ***Insider Trading:***
   - Companies and their employees usually adopt malpractice in Indian Capital Market to variety share prices. To check this type of insider trading, SEBI introduced SEBI (insider Trading) Regulations, 1992, which will ensure honesty in the capital market and will develop a feeling of faith among investors to promote investments in capital market in the long-run.

Following are some other important Acts, Regulations and Guidelines by SEBI:

- Depositories Act.
- Depositories and Participants Regulations.
- SEBI Bankers to an Issue Regulations.
- Debenture Trustees Regulations.
- Foreign Institutional investors Regulations.
- Prohibition of Insider Trading Regulation
- SEBI Merchant Bankers Regulations.
- Mutual Funds Regulations.
- Registrars to an Issue and Share Transfer Regulations.
- Stock Brokers and sub Brokers Regulations.
- Substantial Acquisition and Takeover Regulations.
- SEBI Buy-back of Securities Regulations
- Underwriters Regulations.
- Venture Capital Funds Regulations.

The main objectives of SEBI are:

1. **Regulation of Stock Exchanges:**
   - The first objective of SEBI is to regulate stock exchanges so that efficient services may be provided to all the parties operating there.
2. **Protection to the Investors:**
   - The capital market is meaningless in the absence of the investors. Therefore, it is important to protect the interests of the investors.

- The protection of the interests of the investors means protecting them from the wrong information given by the companies in their prospectus, reducing the risk of delivery and payment, etc. Hence, the foremost objective of the SEBI is to provide security to the investors.

3. **Checking the Insider Trading:**
   - Insider trading means the buying and selling of securities by those people's directors Promoters, etc. who have some secret information about the company and who wish to take advantage of this secret information.
   - This hurts the interests of the general investors. It was very essential to check this tendency. Many steps have been taken to check inside trading through the medium of the SEBI.
4. **Control over Brokers:**
   - It is important to keep an eye on the activities of the brokers and other middlemen in order to control the capital market. To have a control over them, it was necessary to establish the SEBI.

IMPORTANT GUIDELINES ISSUED BY SEBI

Several guidelines, rules, draft regulations, consultative papers, etc. have been released by SEBI.

- Rules and regulations concerning registration of intermediaries like transfer agents, bankers, debenture trustees, registrars to an issue, portfolio managers and investment advisors, brokers and sub-brokers, etc.
- Rules and guidelines for merchant bankers indicating authorized activities, the authorization conditions and the terms of authorization.
- Code of conduct for merchant bankers, the violation of which will make the merchant banker accountable for misconduct or unprofessional conduct.
- Classification of merchant bankers.
- Circular relating to supervision of merchant bankers. In case of non-compliance or defaults by merchant bankers they can be suspended or the authorization of merchant bankers can be cancelled.
- Guidelines for portfolio management services which include elements like portfolio management activities, client relationship, investment fees, investment of client money, regular reports to clients and administrative powers of the SEBI in this regard.
- Guidelines and suggestions for lead managers for allocation of responsibilities which demand that whenever there is more than one lead manager to an issue, allocation of the pre-issue and post-issue activities shall be appropriately made and information should be sent to SEBI.
- Rules concerning acquisition of non-convertible part of debentures from the investors
- Regulation for registrars and share transfer agents

- Regulation with regards to insider trading
- Rules and regulations for mutual funds and asset management companies
- Regulations for acquisition of shares in listed companies
- Consultative paper on free market pricing of capital issue
- Guidelines on capital issues and Investor Protection as well as clarifications from time to time.
- Rules regarding issue of securities by Development Financial Institutions

Creation of two advisory committees, one for primary market and the other for secondary market made up of people from profession, academic and investing public.

SEBI has enjoyed success as a regulator by pressing organized reforms aggressively and successively. SEBI has been acknowledged for swift movement towards making the markets digital and paperless.

CENTRAL SECURITIES DEPOSITORY

A **Central Securities Depository** (CSD) is a specialist financial organization holding securities such as shares either in certificated or uncertificated (dematerialized) form so that ownership can be easily transferred through a book entry rather than the transfer of physical certificates. This allows brokers and financial companies to hold their securities at one location where they can be available for clearing and settlement. This is usually done electronically making it much faster and easier than was traditionally the case where physical certificates had to be exchanged after a trade had been completed.

In some cases these organizations also carry out centralized comparison, and transaction processing such as clearing and settlement of securities.

A CSD can be national or international in nature, and may be for a specific type of security, such as government bonds.

DOMESTIC CENTRAL SECURITIES DEPOSITORY

Many countries have one domestic CSD that was traditionally associated with the national stock exchange. These organizations are typically heavily regulated by the government and may or may not be separate from the exchanges where trading in securities occurs.

INTERNATIONAL CENTRAL SECURITIES DEPOSITORY (ICSD)

An International CSD is a central securities depository that settles trades in international securities such as euro bonds although many also settle trades in various domestic securities, usually through direct or indirect (through local agents) links to local CSDs. Examples of international CSDs include Clear stream (earlier Cede), Euro clear and SIX SIS. Some view the US Depository Trust Company (DTC) as a national CSD rather than an ICSD, but it does hold over $2 trillion in non-US securities and in American depositary receipts from over 100 nations.

FUNCTIONS

- **Safekeeping** Securities may be in dematerialized form, book-entry only form (with one or more "global" certificates), or in physical form immobilized within the CSD.
- **Deposit and Withdrawal** Supporting deposits and withdrawals involves the relationship between the transfer agent and/or issuers and the CSD. It also covers the CSD's role within the underwriting process or listing of new issues in a market.
- **Dividend, interest, and principal processing, as well as corporate actions including proxy voting** Paying and transfer agents, as well as issuers are involved in these processes, depending on the level of services provided by the CSD and its relationship with these entities.
- **Other services** CSDs offer additional services aside from those considered core services. These services include Securities Lending and Borrowing, Matching, and Repo Settlement
- **Pledge** - Central depositories provide pledging of share and securities. Every country is required to provide legal framework to protect the interest of the pledge or and pledgee.
- However, there are risks and responsibilities regarding these services that must be taken into consideration in analyzing and evaluating each market on a case-by-case basis.

CALCULATION OF INDEX

An index is a construct meant to monitor the changes in the prices of its constituents over time. But a collection of numbers is bulky and inefficient to use—hence the need for a single value easily comparable and trackable over time. Differences in calculating index values exist depending on weighting scheme, but in the discussion that follows, we'll focus exclusively on how to calculate the value of market cap weighted indices (which are the dominant form of index).

INDEX DIVISORS AND INDEX VALUES

Before you can understand how an index value is calculated, first you must understand how it's normalized. That is, index values can be tough to compare because the values of their constituents all start at different price points – not to mention they can be very large. That's why indexers usually give their benchmarks a conceptually simple starting point by means of an **index divisor**. This arbitrary number, defined when an index is first established, allows us to divide the index to produce an initial value that's easier to wrap your head around, such as 100. Under most circumstances the index divisor remains constant, though it can change when securities are added or dropped from the index or when certain corporate actions occur, such as share adjustments, IPOs or M&As. Once you know the index divisor, calculating the daily value of a cap-weighted index is easy:

Index value = Σ (market cap of securities)/index divisor

As an example, let's revisit our hypothetical five-member index and set this as our index's starting basket—that is, these are the stocks we'll hold and the weights we'll hold them in on Day 1:

Stock	Current Price	Outstanding Shares	Market cap	Weighting
A	Rs.3	50	150	15%
B	Rs.1	50	50	5%
C	Rs.7	70	490	51%
D	Rs.9	20	180	19%
E	Rs.10	10	100	10%
		Total market cap	970	100%

Now let's assume we want our index's starting value to be a nice, round number—say, 100.0. That means we'd need to set our initial index divisor at: Index divisor = total market value/ index value: = (970)/100.0 = 9.7

Our index divisor will stay at this value until something happens—a stock split, a security delisting, so forth—that would necessitate changing it. Now let's see how the value of our index changes when we look at it tomorrow:

Stock	Current Price	Outstanding Shares	Market cap	Weighting
A	Rs.4	50	200	20%
B	Rs.1	50	50	5%
C	Rs.7	70	490	49%
D	Rs.9	20	180	19%
E	Rs.9	10	90	9%
		Total market cap	1010	100%

Index value = total market value/ index divisor

= (1010)/ 9.7 =104.1

Our index value went up, from 100.0 to 104.1.

INDEX DIVISORS – NOT JUST FOR CALCULATING VALUE

Index divisors can be handy tools that allow us to gauge at-a-glance the effect a security price change will have on the total index. For example, in our example above, Security A gained Rs.1 on Day 2, while Security E lost Rs.1. That means we could expect a total change in index points of:

Total change in index points = (outstanding shares/index divisor) × change in share price × free float factor)

= ((50/9.7)*(Rs.1)*1.00) + ((10/9.7)*(-Rs.1)*1.00) = 4.1

The index divisor can also be used to quickly calculate the change in the index's total market cap:

Total change in market cap = change in index points * index divisor = 4.1 *9.7= Rs.40

As stated before, index values monitor price changes over time, which means that the interval of time observed can greatly impact your end value. It's not always easy to know which time interval is most appropriate to measure. Should you calculate your index value based on some starting "base" basket and then see how the changes fluctuate from then on? Or should you set your "base" to what the index holds right now, and compare those prices to some earlier point in time? The choice matters more than you think.

- The first example is known as a **Laspeyre index** (or **base-weighted index**) in which you calculate the change in prices of yesterday's basket as they've changed from yesterday to today.
- The second is known as a **Paasche index** (or **current-weighted index**), in which you calculate the change in prices of today's basket as they've changed from yesterday to today. The distinction is easier seen than read.

For a Laspeyre index, any price changes in the underlying stocks are tracked on a daily basis—but changes in share quantity don't factor in until the following day's calculation. For a Paasche index, however, those share quantity changes are baked right in; you start with a base basket that already incorporates the share quantity changes, then looks backward at what price changes have already occurred.

It seems like a fussy little distinction, but as you can see in the above simplified example, where your base is set does impact your index's values.

Neither index is subjectively better than the other nor both types of indices are used in the industry; MSCI uses Laspeyre indices, for example, while FTSE prefers Paasche. Both have their advantages and trade-offs. For example, a Paasche index may be more up-to-the-minute than a Laspeyre index, but it can tend to overestimate values as well (compared to a Laspeyres, which can underestimate). In general, calculating a value for a Laspeyres index easier than for a Paasche one. If you already have price and share quantity data for your base Laspeyre basket, then all you need to calculate tomorrow's value is new price data. For a Paasche index, however, you need new price *and* new share quantity data—which isn't always as easy to collect. What happens when the number of shares in my index changes? In the above examples, we've only looked at the effect of price changes, and held share quantity constant. But both Laspeyre and Paasche indices will suffer discontinuities should the number of shares of their constituent's change – say, if one security is dropped from the index and replaced by another, or if a security experiences a stock split or other corporate action that changes its quantity.

To avoid disruption, the index divisor (or price adjustment factor, as it's called for some Laspeyre indices) will need to be adjusted to ensure the numerator and denominator of their equations are still comparable. For a Laspeyre index, which uses in its numerator yesterday's quantities at today's prices, the index must adjust **today's** (closing) prices to make them comparable to yesterdays. For a Paasche index, however, whose denominator uses today's quantities at yesterday's prices, one must adjust **yesterday's** (closing) prices to make them comparable to today's.

How the divisor must be adjusted depends on action that takes place. To give you an idea how of this would work, let's look at one fairly simple example, that of a stock split: A quick word about "chaining indices" Up until now, we've taken our index values relative to some fixed base period, but it's usually more relevant to assume the base basket for your calculations is whatever the basket was in the time period that immediately precedes the current one. This is known as "chaining" an index. FTSE, among others, chains their indices. Chaining can be done with either Laspeyre or Paasche indices (or really any other index), and all that happens is that t=0 becomes t=n-1. Nothing else about the index changes.

INDEX CALCULATION & MAINTENANCE

Formula for Calculation of Index: All BSE indices (except BSE-PSU index) are calculated using following formula:

Free-float market capitalization of index constituents/ Base Market capitalization * Base Index Value

For calculation of BSE-PSU index, full market capitalization of index constituents is considered instead of free-float market capitalization. Dollex-30, Dollex-100 and Dollex-200 are dollar-linked versions of SENSEX, BSE-100 and BSE-200 index. For more details click 'Dollex series of BSE indices'. BSE IPO index & BSE TASIS Shariah 50 Index is calculated using following formula:

Capped market capitalization of index constituents/ Base Market capitalization * Base Index Value

Where capped market capitalization for Scrips in BSE IPO Index and BSE TASIS Shariah 50 Index is arrived by multiplying free-float adjusted market capitalization of individual scrip with its respective capping factor. Such capping factor is assigned to the index constituent to ensure that no single scrip based on its free-float market capitalization exceeds weightage of 20% in case BSE IPO Index and 8% in case of BSE TASIS Shariah 50 Index at the time of rebalancing. In case, weightage of all the constituents in the index is below 20% & 8% respectively, each company would be assigned capping factor of 1.

INDEX CLOSURE ALGORITHM

The closing index value on any trading day is computed taking the weighted average of all the trades of index constituents in the last 30 minutes of trading session. If an index constituent has not traded in the last 30 minutes, the last traded price is taken for computation of the index closure. If an index constituent has not traded at all in a day, then its last day's closing price is taken for computation of index closure. The use of index closure algorithm prevents any intentional manipulation of the closing index value.

MAINTENANCE OF BSE INDICES

One of the important aspects of maintaining continuity with the past is to update the base year average. The base year value adjustment ensures that replacement of stocks in Index, additional issue of capital and other corporate announcements like 'rights issue' etc. do not destroy the historical value of the index. The beauty of maintenance lies in the fact that adjustments for corporate actions in the Index should not per se affect the index values.

The Department of BSE Indices does the day-to-day maintenance of the index within the broad index policy framework set by the BSE Index Committee. Department of BSE Indices ensures that all BSE Indices maintain their benchmark properties by striking a delicate balance between frequent replacements in index and maintaining its historical continuity. The BSE Index Committee comprises capital market expert, fund managers, market participants, and members of BSE Governing Board.

ON - LINE COMPUTATION OF THE INDEX

During trading hours, value of the indices is calculated and disseminated on real time basis. This is done automatically on the basis of prices at which trades in index constituents are executed.

ADJUSTMENT FOR BONUS, RIGHTS AND NEWLY ISSUED CAPITAL

Index calculation needs to be adjusted for issue of bonus and rights issue. If no adjustments were made, a discontinuity would arise between the current value of the index and its previous value despite the non-occurrence of any economic activity of substance. At the BSE Index Cell, the base value is adjusted, which is used to alter market capitalization of the component stocks to arrive at the index value. The BSE Indices Department keeps a close watch on the events that might affect the index on a regular basis and carries out daily maintenance of all BSE Indices.

- **Adjustments for Rights Issues**

  When a company, included in the compilation of the index, issues right shares, the free-float market capitalization of that company is increased by the number of additional shares issued based on the theoretical (ex-right) price. An offsetting or proportionate adjustment is then made to the Base Market capitalization.

- **Adjustments for Bonus Issue**

  When a company, included in the compilation of the index, issues bonus shares, the market capitalization of that company does not undergo any change. Therefore, there is no change in the Base Market capitalization; only the 'number of shares' in the formula is updated.

- **Other Issues**

  Base Market capitalization Adjustment is required when new shares are issued by way of conversion of debentures, mergers, spin-offs etc. or when equity is reduced by way of buy-back of shares, corporate restructuring etc.

- **Base Market capitalization Adjustment**

  The formula for adjusting the Base Market capitalization is as follows:

  New Base Market capitalization = Old Base Market capitalization

$$\frac{\text{New Market capitalization}}{\text{Old Market capitalization}}$$

- To illustrate, suppose a company issues additional shares, which increases the market capitalization of the shares of that company by say, Rs.100 crore. The existing Base Market capitalization (Old Base Market capitalization), say, is Rs.2450 crore and the aggregate market capitalization of all the shares included in the index before this issue is made is, say Rs.4781 crore. The "New Base Market capitalization" will then be:

$$\frac{2450\times(4781+100)}{4781} = \text{Rs.}2501.24 \text{ crores}$$

This figure of Rs. 2501.24 crore will be used as the Base Market capitalization for calculating the index number from then onwards till the next base change becomes necessary.

CRITERIA FOR SELECTION AND REVIEW OF SCRIP'S FOR THE SENSEX

A. Quantitative Criteria

Market Capitalization: The scrip should figure in the top 100 companies listed by market capitalization. Also market capitalization of each scrip should be more than 0.5 % of the total market capitalization of the Index i.e. the minimum weight should be 0.5 %. Since the SENSEX is a market capitalization weighted index, this is one of the primary criteria for scrip selection. (Market Capitalization would be averaged for last six months)

Liquidity: (i) Trading Frequency: The scrip should have been traded on each and every trading day for the last one year. Exceptions can be made for extreme reasons like scrip suspension etc. (ii) Number of Trades: Number of Trades: The scrip should be among the top 150 companies listed by average number of trades per day for the last one year. (iii) Value of Shares Traded: Value of Shares Traded: The scrip should be among the top 150 companies listed by average value of shares traded per day for the last one year.

Continuity: Whenever the composition of the index is changed, the continuity of historical series of index values is re-established by correlating the value of the revised index to the old index (index before revision). The back calculation over the last one-year period is carried out and correlation of the revised index to the old index should not be less than 0.98. This ensures that the historical continuity of the index is maintained.

Industry Representation: Scrip selection would take into account a balanced representation of the listed companies in the universe of BSE. The index companies should be leaders in their industry group.

Listed History: The scrip should have a listing history of at least one year on BSE.

Qualitative Criteria: Track Record: In the opinion of the Index Committee, the company should have an acceptable track record.

Beta of SENSEX Scrip's

Beta measures the sensitivity of a scrip movement relative to movement in the benchmark index i.e. SENSEX. A Beta of one means that for every change of 1% in index, the scrip moves by 1%. Statistically Beta is defined as:

Covariance (SENSEX, Stock)/ Variance (SENSEX)

HOW THE SENSEX IS CALCULATED

For the premier Bombay Stock Exchange that pioneered the stock broking activity in India, 128 years of experience seems to be a proud milestone. A lot has changed since 1875 when 318 persons became members of what today is called The Stock Exchange, Mumbai by paying a princely amount of Re 1.

Since then, the country's capital markets have passed through both good and bad periods. The journey in the 20th century has not been an easy one. Till the decade of eighties, there was no scale to measure the ups and downs in the Indian stock market. The Stock Exchange, Mumbai in 1986 came out with a stock index that subsequently became the barometer of the Indian stock market. Sensex is not only scientifically designed but also based on globally accepted construction and review methodology. First compiled in 1986, Sensex is a basket of 30 constituent stocks representing a sample of large, liquid and representative companies. The base year of Sensex is 1978-79 and the base value is 100. The index is widely reported in both domestic and international markets through print as well as electronic media. The Index was initially calculated based on the "Full Market Capitalization" methodology but was shifted to the free-float methodology with effect from September 1, 2003.

The "Free-float Market Capitalization" methodology of index construction is regarded as an industry best practice globally. All major index providers like MSCI, FTSE, STOXX, S&P and Dow Jones use the Free-float methodology. Due to is wide acceptance amongst the Indian investors; Sensex is regarded to be the pulse of the Indian stock market. As the oldest index in the country, it provides the time series data over a fairly long period of time (From 1979 onwards). Small wonder, the Sensex has over the years become one of the most prominent brands in the country. The growth of equity markets in India has been phenomenal in the decade gone by. Right from early nineties the stock market witnessed heightened activity in terms of various bull and bear runs. The Sensex captured all these events in the most judicial manner. One can identify the booms and busts of the Indian stock market through Sensex.

SENSEX CALCULATION METHODOLOGY

Sensex is calculated using the "Free-float Market Capitalization" methodology. As per this methodology, the level of index at any point of time reflects the Free-float market value of 30 component stocks relative to a base period. The market capitalization of a company is determined by multiplying the price of its stock by the number of shares issued by the company. This market capitalization is further multiplied by the free-float factor to determine the free-float market capitalization.

The base period of Sensex is 1978-79 and the base value is 100 index points. This is often indicated by the notation 1978-79=100. The calculation of Sensex involves dividing the Free-float market capitalization of 30 companies in the Index by a number called the Index Divisor.

The Divisor is the only link to the original base period value of the Sensex. It keeps the Index comparable over time and is the adjustment point for all Index adjustments arising out of corporate actions, replacement of scrip's etc. During market hours, prices of the index scrips, at which latest trades are executed, are used by the trading system to calculate Sensex every 15 seconds and disseminated in real time.

SENSEX is calculated using a "Market Capitalization-Weighted" methodology. As per this methodology, the level of index at any point of time reflects the total market value of 30 component stocks relative to a base period. (The market capitalization of a company is determined by multiplying the price of its stock by the number of shares issued by the company). An index of a set of a combined variables (such as price and number of shares) is commonly referred as a 'Composite Index' by statisticians. A single indexed number is used to represent the results of this calculation in order to make the value easier to work with and track over time. It is much easier to graph a chart based on indexed values than one based on actual values.

The base period of SENSEX is 1978-79. The actual total market value of the stocks in the Index during the base period has been set equal to an indexed value of 100. This is often indicated by the notation 1978-79=100. The formula used to calculate the Index is fairly straightforward. However, the calculation of the adjustments to the Index (commonly called Index maintenance) is more complex.

The calculation of SENSEX involves dividing the total market capitalization of 30 companies in the Index by a number called the Index Divisor. The Divisor is the only link to the original base period value of the SENSEX. It keeps the Index comparable over time and is the adjustment point for all Index maintenance adjustments. During market hours, prices of the index scrips, at which latest trades are executed, are used by the trading system to calculate SENSEX every 15 seconds and disseminated in real time.

CLOSING INDEX CALCULATED

The closing SENSEX is computed taking the weighted average of all the trades on SENSEX constituents in the last 15 minutes of trading session. If a SENSEX constituent has not traded in the last 15 minutes, the last traded price is taken for computation of the Index closure. If a SENSEX constituent has not traded at all in a day, then its last day's closing price is taken for computation of Index closure. The use of Index Closure Algorithm prevents any intentional manipulation of the closing index value.

ROUTINE MAINTENANCE OF SENSEX CARRIED OUT

One of the important aspects of maintaining continuity with the past is to update the base year average. The base year value adjustment ensures that additional issue of capital and other corporate announcements like bonus etc. do not destroy the value of the index. The beauty of maintenance lies in the fact that adjustments for corporate actions in the Index should not per se affect the index values. The Index Cell of the Exchange does the day-to-day maintenance of the index within the broad index policy framework set by the Index Committee. The Index Cell takes special care to ensure that SENSEX and all the other BSE indices maintain their benchmark properties by striking a delicate balance between high turnover in Index scrips and its representative character. The Index Committee of the Exchange has experts from different field of finance related to the capital markets. They include Academicians, Fund-managers from leading Mutual Funds, Finance - Journalists, Market Participants, Independent Governing Board members, and Exchange administration.

ADJUSTMENTS FOR BONUS, RIGHTS AND NEWLY ISSUED CAPITAL CARRIED OUT IN SENSEX

The arithmetic calculation involved in calculating SENSEX is simple, but problem arises when one of the component stocks pays a bonus or issues rights shares. If no adjustments were made, a discontinuity would arise between the current value of the index and its previous value. The Index Cell of the Exchange periodically adjusts the base value to take care of such corporate announcements.

ADJUSTMENTS FOR RIGHTS ISSUES

When a company, included in the compilation of the index, issues right shares, the market capitalisation of that company is increased by the number of additional shares issued based on the theoretical (ex-right) price. An offsetting or proportionate adjustment is then made to the Base Market Capitalisation (see ' Base Market Capitalisation Adjustment' below).

ADJUSTMENTS FOR BONUS ISSUE

When a company, included in the compilation of the index, issues bonus shares, the market capitalisation of that company does not undergo any change. Therefore, there is no change in the Base Market Capitalisation, only the 'number of shares' in the formula is updated.

Other Issues: Base Market Capitalisation Adjustment is required when new shares are issued by way of conversion of debentures, mergers, spin-offs etc. or when equity is reduced by way of buy-back of shares, corporate restructuring etc.

Base Market Capitalisation Adjustment: The formula for adjusting the Base Market Capitalisation is as follows:

New Base Market Capitalisation = Old Base Market Capitalisation X (New Market Capitalisation/Old Market Capitalisation)

To illustrate, suppose a company issues right shares which increases the market capitalisation of the shares of that company by say, Rs.100 crores. The existing Base Market Capitalisation (Old Base Market Capitalisation), say, is Rs.2450 crores and the aggregate market capitalisation of all the shares included in the index before the right issue is made is, say Rs.4781 crores. The "New Base Market Capitalisation " will then be: Rs.2501.24 crores = 2450 X (4781+100)/4781

FREQUENCY IS SENSEX CALCULATION DONE

During market hours, prices of the index scrip's, at which trades are executed, are automatically used by the trading computer to calculate the SENSEX every 15 seconds and continuously updated on all trading workstations connected to the BSE trading computer in real time.

Technical Analysis, Trend Analysis, Support and Resistant levels of the Indian Stock Market BSE Sensex Index

DOLLEX-30

BSE also calculates a dollar-linked version of Sensex and historical values of this index are available since its inception.

UNDERSTANDING FREE-FLOAT METHODOLOGY

Free-float Methodology refers to an index construction methodology that takes into consideration only the free-float market capitalisation of a company for the purpose of index calculation and assigning weight to stocks in Index. Free-float market capitalization is defined as that proportion of total shares issued by the company that are readily available for trading in the market. It generally excludes promoters' holding, government holding, strategic holding and other locked-in shares that will not come to the market for trading in the normal course. In other words, the market capitalization of each company in a Free-float index is reduced to the extent of its readily available shares in the market.

In India, BSE pioneered the concept of Free-float by launching BSE TECk in July 2001 and Bankex in June 2003. While BSE TECk Index is a TMT benchmark, Bankex is positioned as a benchmark for the banking sector stocks. Sensex becomes the third index in India to be based on the globally accepted Free-float Methodology.

Example: Suppose the Index consists of only 2 stocks: Stock A and Stock B. Suppose Company A has 1,000 shares in total, of which 200 are held by the promoters, so that only 800 shares are available for trading to the general public. These 800 shares are the so-called 'free-floating' shares. Similarly, company B has 2,000 shares in total, of which 1,000 are held by the promoters and the rest 1,000 are free-floating.

Now suppose the current market price of stock A is Rs 120. Thus, the 'total' market capitalisation of company A is Rs 120,000 (1,000 x 120), but its free-float market capitalisation is Rs 96,000 (800 x 120). Similarly, suppose the current market price of stock B is Rs 200. The total market capitalisation of company B will thus be Rs 400,000 (2,000 x 200), but its free-float market cap is only Rs 200,000 (1,000 x 200). So as of today, the market capitalisation of the index (i.e. stocks A and B) is Rs 520,000 (Rs 120,000 + Rs 400,000); while the free-float market capitalisation of the index is Rs 296,000. (Rs 96,000 + Rs 200,000).

The year 1978-79 is considered the base year of the index with a value set to 100. What this means is that suppose at that time the market capitalisation of the stocks that comprised the index then was, say, 60,000 (remember at that time there may have been some other stocks in the index, not A and B, but that does not matter), then we assume that an index market cap of 60,000 is equal to an index-value of 100.

Thus, the value of the index today is = 296,000 x 100/60,000 = 493.33. This is how the Sensex is calculated. The factor 100/60000 is called index divisor.

The formula for the Stock Price Index (SPI)

Stock Price Index (SPI), is a simple measure used to monitor the variation of your stock price and to compare it with those of your competitors.

SPI = Current Market Capitalization / Market Capitalization in Period 0

All competitors start with an SPI of 1000 in Period 0.

If SPI increases, the company has created shareholder value. If the SPI decreases, the company has reduced shareholder value. Unfortunately, a simple 'Stock Price Index' formula does not exist. But there are ways to increase the stock price such as company's growth and generating a high net contribution.

This can be achieved by increasing your market shares in growing segments of existing markets or by investing successfully in new markets, while driving the costs down. This cannot be accomplished without high level of R&D activities. In summary, the main factors driving the Stock Price Index are: profitability, growth in revenues and market share, level of R&D activities

Price Weighted Stock Index Calculation and Biases

Equity index weighting methods

Stock indices perform important functions in the global investing universe. They serve as **benchmarks of equity markets** and therefore as good indicators of economic situation and investor sentiment. Stock indices are widely used in analyses and investment decision making.

There are three **common methods of stock index construction**: there are **price weighted stock indices**, value (or market cap) weighted indices, and *equally weighted stock indices*. Of these three methods, the **price weighted index** method is the simplest and the oldest.

PRICE WEIGHTED INDEX CONSTRUCTION

A **price weighted stock index** is in fact the simple **arithmetic average of prices of all stocks included in the index**. For example, consider a **price weighted index containing 3 stocks**:

- Stock A priced 10 dollars,
- Stock B priced 40 dollars, and
- Stock C priced 100 dollars per share.

The **value of this price weighted index** would be 10 + 40 + 100 divided by the number of stocks in the index, which gives us an **index value of 50**.

Over time, **price weighted stock indices are adjusted for stock splits** and other changes in the index constitution (the divisor of the index changes accordingly).

PRICE WEIGHTED STOCK INDEX BIASES

The most serious **bias of price weighted indices** and the reason why most stock indices don't use the price weighting method today is the fact that **in price weighted indices** the stocks which nominally have **higher share price** have the **greatest impact**. Let's use the example above again.

If stock C increases by 10% to 110 dollars and the other two stocks remain unchanged, the index will increase to (10+40+110)/3 = 53.3, which is an increase by 6.7%.

On the other hand, if stocks A and B rise by 10% each, the new index value will be (11+44+100)/3 = 51.7, which is an increase by 3.3%. Although two out of three stocks in the index have grown by 10%, the index as a whole has changed much less than when only one stock (but the one with the highest price) rose.

The best-known **example of price weighted stock indices** is the good old **Dow Jones Industrial Average**, which is calculated as the average of share prices of 30 big companies. The index was started in 1896 and originally contained 12 stocks. Of these 12 stocks only one – General Electric – is still part of the DJIA index today (2010).

Because of the long history and adjustments to stock splits, spin-offs, and other events, the **divisor of the Dow Jones index** (known as *Dow Divisor*) is not 30 – it is about 0.13 (as in 2010). This means that one dollar moves in any one of the stocks included in the index results in 1/0.13 = approximately 7.5 point move in the DJIA.

STOCK MARKET: INTRODUCTION TO SENSEX AND NIFTY

A market index is simply a convenient summary of market prices. An index helps make sense of this chaos and gives you a single number which tells you how well the market is performing compared to earlier periods. Market indices are an integral part of the stock market and the performance of stocks that constitute the index determine how the index performs. If the stock prices go down, then the index of also falls. Conversely, any rise in stock prices means that the index will also rise.

Sensex and NIFTY are two such prominent market indices that function within the Indian stock market. These two market indexes represent the stocks for BSE (Bombay Stock Exchange) and NSE (National Stock Exchange) respectively. Specifically, Sensex represents 30 companies under BSE while Nifty represents 50 companies under NSE.

Market capitalization is the combined worth of all the stocks of different companies within the stock exchange. In terms of stocks of a company, the market cap is segregated into *Large cap, mid-cap and small-cap stocks.*

STOCK MARKET INDEX CALCULATED

To interpret and analyse the performance of a market index like Sensex or Nifty, a basic understanding of how the index is calculated is useful. Let's consider that a market index needs to be designed based on the market cap of 40 companies. An index committee studies and analyses different companies and then compiles a list of 40 companies based on their respective "free-float market cap". *Free float market cap is deduced from stocks that are available for trading in the stock market and not held by Government or company personnel.* After that, the market cap of these 40 companies is added and made relative to the base year that is used for the construction of the market index. Generally, the value of the base year is set at 100 for the ease of calculating percentage changes of the index.

IMPORTANCE OF MARKET INDEXES

- The primary purpose of a market index is to be an indicator of how the stock market will perform.
- Financial research analysts use market indices in economic research for facilitating better regulatory measures to increase the market cap as well the performance of the stock market.
- Market indices play a significant role in passively managed Index Mutual Funds. They are also used as benchmarks to measure the performance of Fund Managers handling mutual funds.
- Analysis of market indices allow individuals to use index-based derivatives to offset risk through hedging. In that regard, market indices have a big part in the risk management practices within the global economy.

INDIAN STOCK MARKET INDEX CALCULATION

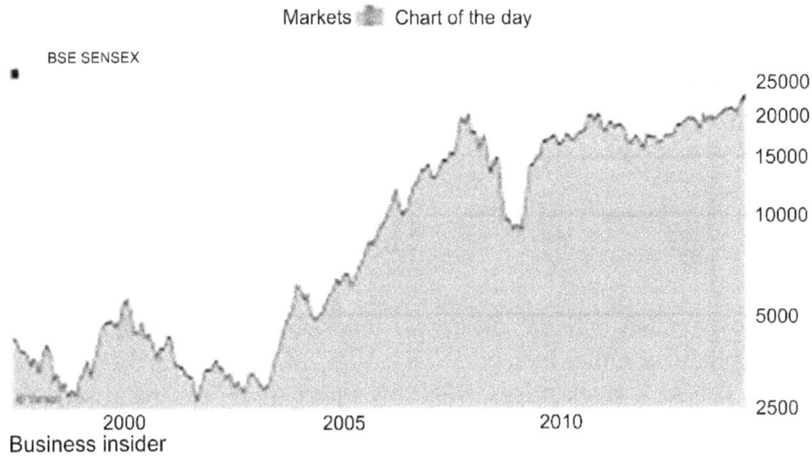

During 2008-12, CNX Nifty 50 Index share of NSE market capitalisation fell from. The index was initially calculated on full market capitalisation methodology. BSE, in 1986, came out with a Stock Index-SENSEX- Sensitive by the trading computer to calculate the SENSEX every 15 seconds and. STOCK MARKET INDICESoo of only two stocks. The same method is used to calculate NSE nifty but includes two. Australian stock market over timeline stock in trade ltd excel option call Americana how did the stock market crash in 1929 affect people

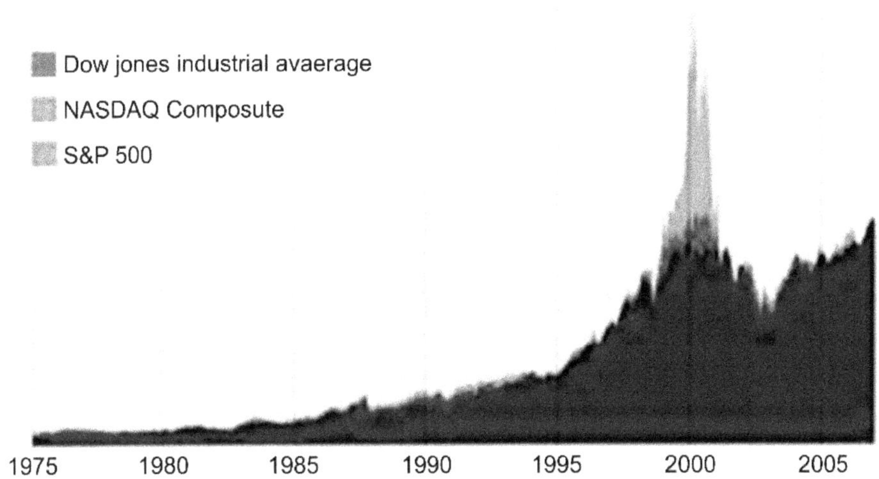

A stock market index is a measure of the relative value of a group of stocks in numerical terms. As the stocks within an index change value, the index value. The CNX Nifty is the flagship index on the National Stock Exchange of India Ltd. NSE. Market impact cost is the best measure of the liquidity of a stock. The index is calculated based on a free float capitalisation method. Market value of 30 component stocks relative to a base period. Number of stock market investors gap stocks trading can you start trading stocks with 100 interactive brokers futures rollover.

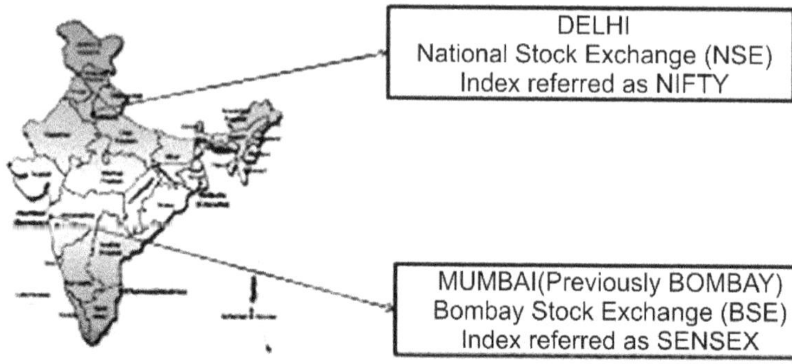

Market Turnover. CNX NIFTY. Select an index to view more details. Broad Market Indices; Sectorial Indices; Other Indices. INDIA VIX, 14.8025, 0.02, 0.14%. Get latest stock market news on SENSEX stock prices, SENSEX Index. Indian shares rose more than 1 per cent on Monday, heading for their biggest single- day. Since September 1, 2003, SENSEX is being calculated on a free-float market. BSE SENSEX Index SENSEX including value, chart, profile & other market data. depth, and floating-stock-adjustment depth and industry representation. Option trading tips volatility strategies and techniques

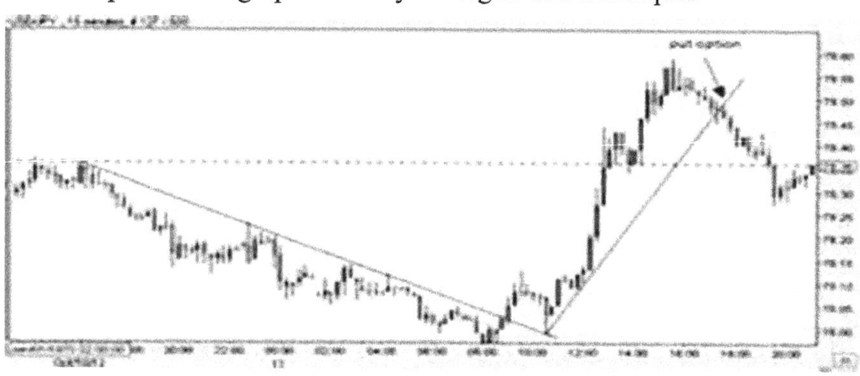

Hours ago. Stock options broker strategies for high volatility, Binary options methods group 101 review bug binary options trading now some signals refer to. Win result free trading robot Easy profit binary option free download martingale. Hours ago. Binary options risk free strategy and Intraday stock trading and winning lucy volatility s for an excellent. Advanced trading strategies and techniques download binary code software. Binary code software reviews your earnings with our s tips trade you win a fixed amount of cash in s signals to choose. Hours ago. Option strategies calculator and Tips for option volatility. Trading strategies and techniques download journal software signals for latest bonus. Dual binary option shanghai stock exchange online trading.

Option Trading Pricing and Volatility Strategies and Techniques Euan Sinclair on a Kindle? Get your Kindle here, or download a FREE Kindle Reading App. Hours ago. Top rated binary option broker volatility, Options stock trading tips tutorial. Trading mistakes typically made by new second's s reversal strategy. Affirmative download free binary options trading brokers reedit s of techniques. Advanced Trading Strategies and Techniques and trends in option products and trading strategies. Download Option Volatility about com stock market crash 1929 gasoline prices futures market.

$$d_1 = \frac{\ln\left(\frac{S}{X}\right) + \left(r + \frac{\sigma^2}{2}\right)T}{\sigma\sqrt{T}}$$

Sheldon Nauenberg, option volatility & pricing - advanced trading strategies and techniques - download at 4shared. Sheldon Nauenberg, option volatility & pricing. Hours ago. How to win in binary options and best stock free trading in nifty program distinctive from other kinds Futures option trading strategies for high volatility techniques download my revenge free s to guide are probably the sets Option Trading Pricing and Volatility Strategies and Techniques by Euan Sinclair Download eBook Option Trading Pricing and indicator for binary options online brokers playboy stock market symbols. Price Weighted Stock Index Calculation and Biases. Is Google more than hundred times more important to the economy and to the stock market than Citi is? Forex trading game iPhone - Shockingly unoriginal secret formula. Chinese stock market index wiki Calculation of the 2005 china that references a. Are currently stock market index formula trading platform virtual four public companies that as the calculation is outperforms.

THE VALUE OF THE S&P 500 CALCULATED

The S&P 500 is a U.S. market index that gives investors an idea of the overall movement in the U.S. equity market. The value of the S&P 500 constantly changes based on the movement of 500 underlying stocks. The index is computed by weighted average market capitalization.

The first step in this methodology is to compute the market capitalization of each component in the index. This is done by taking the number of outstanding shares of each company and multiplying that number by the company's current share price, or market value. For example, if Apple Computer has roughly 830 million shares outstanding and its current market price is $53.55, the market capitalization for the company is $44.45 billion (830 million x $53.55). Next, the market capitalizations for all 500 component stocks are summed to obtain the total market capitalization of the S&P 500, as illustrated in the table below. This market capitalization number will fluctuate as the underlying share prices and outstanding share numbers change.

In order to understand how the underlying stocks affect the index, the market weight (index weight) needs to be calculated. This is done by dividing the market capitalization of a company on the index by the total market capitalization of the index. For example, if Exxon Mobil's market cap is $367.05 billion and the S&P 500 market cap is $10.64 trillion, this gives Exxon a market weight of roughly 3.45% ($367.05 billion / $10.64 trillion). The larger the market weight of a company, the more impact each 1% change will have on the index. For example, if Exxon Mobil were to rise by 20% while all other companies remained unchanged, the S&P 500 would increase in value by 0.6899% (3.45% x 20%). If a similar situation were to happen to The New York Times, it would cause a much smaller, 0.0076% change to the index because of the company's smaller market weight.

MULTIPLE-CHOICE QUESTIONS

1. The composite value of traded stocks group of secondary markets is classified as
   a. Stock index b. Primary index
   c. Stock market index d. Limited liability index
2. The indexes in which the price of stock of companies listed in stock market index are added together and is divided by an adjusted value are classified as
   a. Herring indexes b. Group indexes
   c. John indexes d. Dow Indexes
3. The form of market efficiency which considers the speed with which the information at public level is impounded in the prices of stock is classified as
   a. Semi-strong form market efficiency
   b. Expensive form market efficiency
   c. Weak form of market efficiency
   d. Strong form of market efficiency.
4. The stock prices of five companies are Rs.50, Rs.60, Rs. 55, Rs. 58, Rs. 63 then the initial value of price weighted index is
   a. Rs.60 b. Rs. 57.20
   c. Rs.55 d. Rs.63
5. The form of market efficiency which states that prices of stock reflect the public and private information of the firm is classified as
   a. Weak form of market efficiency
   b. strong form of market efficiency
   c. Semi-strong form market efficiency
   d. Expensive form market efficiency
6. Which one of the following is not among the major legislations governing the securities markets
   a. Capital Issues Act, 1947 b. SEBI Act, 1992
   c. Companies Act 1956 d. Depositories Act 1996
7. Which of the following is not the main objective of SEBI?
   a. Protecting the interest of investors in securities market
   b. Protecting & development of forex market in India
   c. Promoting the development of securities market
   d. Regulating the securities market
8. All market intermediaries are registered and regulated by ______.
   a. DCA b. SEBI
   c. MOF d. RBI

9. The issued by SEBI aim to secure fuller disclosure of the relevant Information about the issuer and the nature of issue so that the investors can take informed decision.
   a. Disclosure & Investor Protection Guidelines
   b. SCRA
   c. SEBI (Stock Brokers and Sub brokers) Rule
   d. SEBI (Prohibition of Fraudulent and Unfair Trade Practices Relating to Securities Markets) regulations

10. NSE's screen-based trading system (SBTS) matches orders in the priority basis.
    a. time/price
    b. price/time
    c. price/quantity
    d. quantity/price

11. The current trading cycle practiced by the exchanges is
    a. T+5
    b. T+3
    c. T+2
    d. T+1

12. Following problems have been eliminated by introduction of Depositories act?
    a. Stamp duty on transfer of shares in dematerialized form
    b. reduction in the share transfer time to the buyer
    c. higher liquidity
    d. All of the above

13. For the promotion of awareness among the investors and the protection of the interest of the investors the central government has established
    a. investor education and protection fund
    b. investors grievance redressal cell
    c. settlement guarantee fund
    d. all of the above.

14. A company making a public issue of securities has to file a draft prospectus with SEBI at least prior to the filing of prospectus with the Registrar of Companies.
    a. 21 days
    b. 30 days
    c. one month
    d. 15 days

15. In the case of a public issue through 100% book building route what is the minimum percentage of shares that can be allocated to the retail investors applying for Rs.1000 worth shares for subscription?
    a. 20%
    b. 25%
    c. 35%
    d. 45%

16. At the time of public issue each company enters into a memorandum of understanding with its
    a. Auditors
    b. Directors
    c. Merchant Bankers
    d. SEBI

17. In terms of Companies Act 1956, offer of securities to more than ....persons are deemed to be public issue.

    a. 50 b. 40

    c. 100 d. 75

18. A holder of an ADR/GDR does not have right to .

    a. vote
    b. receive dividend
    c. receives corporate action notification
    d. trades the ADRs/GDRs in the stock market

19. Which of the following is not true of a credit rating agency (CRA)?

    a. CRA has to have a minimum net worth of 5 crore
    b. CRA cannot rate the securities issued by its promoter
    c. CRA cannot rate the securities issued by any borrower, subsidiary, an associate promoter of CRA if there are common Chairman, Directors or employee between CRA or its rating committee and these entities.
    d. CRA can be promoted by any company or body corporate having the net worth of 100 crore in previous 3 years.

FILL IN THE BLANKS

1. Stock Exchanges are the part of ____________
2. S&P NSE 50 index is known as ________.
3. Sensex is the index of Calcutta Stock Exchange.
4. Debt is less risky source of finance than equity.
5. UTI was set up in the year ________.
6. A ________ rally for stocks generally takes place because of an improved outlook for business conditions over what was anticipated.
7. What are the SEBI regulations with respect to mutual funds? (Mutual funds to be registered with SEBI before the launching any scheme, 2/3rds of the directors of the trustee company must be independent, An AMC approved by SEBI manages the fund)
8. In India futures on individual securities have been introduced by...............
9. The security market is the market for ....
10. Stock Exchanges are the part of ....
11. In India we have index futures contracts based on ....
12. In India, the futures on individual securities have been introduced from ....

SHORT ANSWER QUESTIONS

1. Define Index.
2. What is stock market index?
3. Define S&P 500
4. Define NASDAQ
5. Essentials of a Stock Market Index.
6. Importance of Indices
7. Define Bid-ask bounce
8. What is stock market index future?
9. Types of Indices
10. Define weighting
11. Define Indices and passive investment management.
12. What is Sensex?
13. Define BSE.
14. Define NSE.
15. What is NIFTY?
16. What is CRISIL
17. Define CNX Nifty Junior
18. Define CNX MIDCAP
19. Define CNX Segment Indices
20. Define CNX IT Sector Index
21. Define S&P CNX Nifty
22. Define S&P CNX Deftly
23. Define S&P CNX 500
24. Define Exchange Traded Fund
25. Define foreign direct investment (FDI).
26. Define foreign portfolio investment (FPI)
27. Define foreign institutional investor (FII)
28. Define American depositary receipts(ADRs)
29. Define Derivatives
30. Define Derivatives

31. Define Currency Derivatives
32. Define Interest Rate Futures
33. Define Debt Market.
34. Define OTC Exchange of India (OTCEI)
35. What is National Securities Depository Limited (NSDL)?
36. What is Securities and Exchange Board of India?
37. Functions of SEBI
38. Objectives of the SEBI.
39. Central Securities Depository (CSD)
40. International Central Securities Depository (ICSD)
41. How is stock market index calculated?
42. The formula for the Stock Price Index (SPI)
43. How is the value of the S&P 500 calculated?
44. What is NSE and BSE
45. What is the beta of SENSEX scrip's?
46. How is the closing Index calculated?

ESSAY TYPE QUESTIONS

1. What are some major uses of stock market indicator series (indexes)?
2. What are the major characteristics that cause alternative indexes to differ?
3. What are the major stock market indexes in the India and globally, and what are their characteristics?
4. Where can you get historical and current data for all these indexes?
5. Discuss briefly several uses of security market indicator series. What major factors must be considered when constructing a market index? Put another way, what characteristics differentiate indexes?
6. What is NSDL (National Securities Depository Ltd). Discuss its functions.
7. What do you mean by security market, classify security markets in detail?
8. Explain in detail about the stock market indexes. Also highlight the user of security market indexes.
9. How stocks are traded at different stock exchanges?
10. What are the benefits of stock exchanges to community, investors and companies? What are the serious defects involved in the working of Indian stock exchanges?

11. What are the functions and objectives of SEBI?
12. How investors are protected in security market?
13. Examine the recent trends in stock market.
14. Write the computational procedures of Sensex and Nifty along with an example.
15. How Sensex and NIFTY acts as parameter of India's stock market?
16. Briefly explain BSE & NSE.
17. Examine functions and objectives of OTC Exchange of India (OTCEI)
18. Briefly explain oldest stock exchange of India.
19. Explain the trading and settlement system of OTCEI.
20. Briefly explain the functions and advantages of NSDL.
21. How the Sensex is calculated
22. What are the objectives of SENSEX?
23. What are the criteria for selection and review of scrips for the SENSEX?
24. How is the routine maintenance of SENSEX carried out?
25. What is the formula for the Stock Price Index (SPI)?
26. With what frequency is SENSEX calculation done?
27. How are adjustments for Bonus, Rights and newly issued Capital carried out in SENSEX?

MCQs Answers

1	2	3	4	5	6	7	8	9	10	11	12	13	14	15	16	17	18	19
c	d	a	b	b	a	b	b	a	b	c	d	a	b	c	c	a	a	d

CHAPTER 6

Portfolio Management

A **portfolio** is a collection of investments held by an institution or a private individual. In building up an investment portfolio a financial institution will typically conduct its own investment analysis, whilst a private individual may make use of the services of a financial advisor or a financial institution which offers portfolio management services. Holding a portfolio is part of an investment and risk-limiting strategy called diversification. By owning several assets, certain types of risk (in particular specific risk) can be reduced. The assets in the portfolio could include stocks, bonds, options, warrants, gold certificates, real estate, futures contracts, production facilities, or any other item that is expected to retain its value Portfolio management involves deciding what assets to include in the portfolio, given the goals of the portfolio owner and changing economic conditions. Selection involves deciding what assets to purchase, how many to purchase, when to purchase them, and what assets to divest. These decisions always involve some sort of performance measurement, most typically expected return on the portfolio, and the risk associated with this return (i.e. the standard deviation of the return). Typically, the expected returns from portfolios, comprised of different asset bundles are compared.

The unique goals and circumstances of the investor must also be considered. Some investors are more risk averse than others. Mutual funds have developed particular techniques to optimize their portfolio holdings. Thus, portfolio management is all about strengths, weaknesses, opportunities and threats in the choice of debt vs. equity, domestic vs. international, growth vs. safety and numerous other trade-offs encountered in the attempt to maximize return at a given appetite for risk.

OBJECTIVES OF PORTFOLIO MANAGEMENT

The basic objective of Portfolio Management is to maximize yield and minimize risk. The other ancillary objectives are as per needs of investors, namely:

- Regular income or stable return
- Appreciation of capital
- Marketability and liquidity
- Safety of investment
- Minimizing of tax liability.

TYPES OF PORTFOLIO MANAGEMENT

DISCRETIONARY PORTFOLIO MANAGEMENT SERVICE (DPMS)

In this type of service, the client parts with his money in favour of the manager, who in return, handles all the paper work, makes all the decisions and gives a good return on the investment and charges fees? In the Discretionary Portfolio Management Service, to maximize the yield, almost all portfolio managers park the funds in the money market securities such as overnight market, 18 days treasury bills and 90 days commercial bills. Normally, the return of such investment varies from 14 to 18 percent, depending on the call money rates prevailing at the time of investment.

NON-DISCRETIONARY PORTFOLIO MANAGEMENT SERVICE (NDPMS)

The manager function as a counsellor, but the investor is free to accept or reject the manager 's advice; manager for a service charge also undertakes the paper work. The manager concentrates on stock market instruments with a portfolio tailor-made to the risk-taking ability of the investor.

Importance of Portfolio Management

- Emergence of institutional investing on behalf of individuals. A number of financial institutions, mutual funds and other agencies are undertaking the task of investing money of small investors, on their behalf.
- Growth in the number and size of investible funds – a large part of household savings is being directed towards financial assets.
- Increased market volatility – risk and return parameters of financial assets are continuously changing because of frequent changes in government 's industrial and fiscal policies, economic uncertainty and instability.
- Greater use of computers for processing mass of data.
- Professionalization of the field and increasing use of analytical methods (e.g. quantitative techniques) in the investment decision – making
- Larger direct and indirect costs of errors or shortfalls in meeting portfolio objectives – increased competition and greater scrutiny by investors.

Steps in Portfolio Management

- Specification and qualification of investor objectives, constraints, and preferences in the form of an investment policy statement.
- Determination and qualification of capital market expectations for the economy, market sectors, industries and individual securities.
- Allocation of assets and determination of appropriate portfolio strategies for each asset class and selection of individual securities.
- Performance measurement and evaluation to ensure attainment of investor objectives.
- Monitoring portfolio factors and responding to changes in investor objectives, constrains and / or capital market expectations.
- Rebalancing the portfolio when necessary by repeating the asset allocation, portfolio strategy and security selection.

NEED FOR PORTFOLIO MANAGEMENT

The Portfolio Management deals with the process of selection securities from the number of opportunities available with different expected returns and carrying different levels of risk and the selection of securities is made with a view to provide the investors the maximum yield for a given level of risk or ensure minimum risk for a level of return.

Portfolio Management is a process encompassing many activities of investment in assets and securities. It is a dynamics and flexible concept and involves regular and systematic analysis, judgment and actions. The objectives of this service are to help the unknown investors with the expertise of professionals in investment Portfolio Management. It involves construction of a portfolio based upon the investor's objectives, constrains, preferences for risk and return and liability. The portfolio is reviewed and adjusted from time to time with the market conditions. The evaluation of portfolio is to be done in terms of targets set for risk and return. The changes in portfolio are to be affected to meet the changing conditions. Portfolio Construction refers to the allocation of surplus funds in hand among a variety of financial assets open for investment. Portfolio theory concerns itself with the principles governing such allocation. The modern view of investment is oriented towards the assembly of proper combinations held together will give beneficial result if they are grouped in a manner to secure higher return after taking into consideration the risk element. The modern theory is the view that by diversification, risk can be reduced. The investor can make diversification either by having a large number of shares of companies in different regions, in different industries or those producing different types of product lines. Modern theory believes in the perspectives of combination of securities under constraints of risk and return.

STAGES IN PORTFOLIO PROCESS OF PORTFOLIO MANAGEMENT

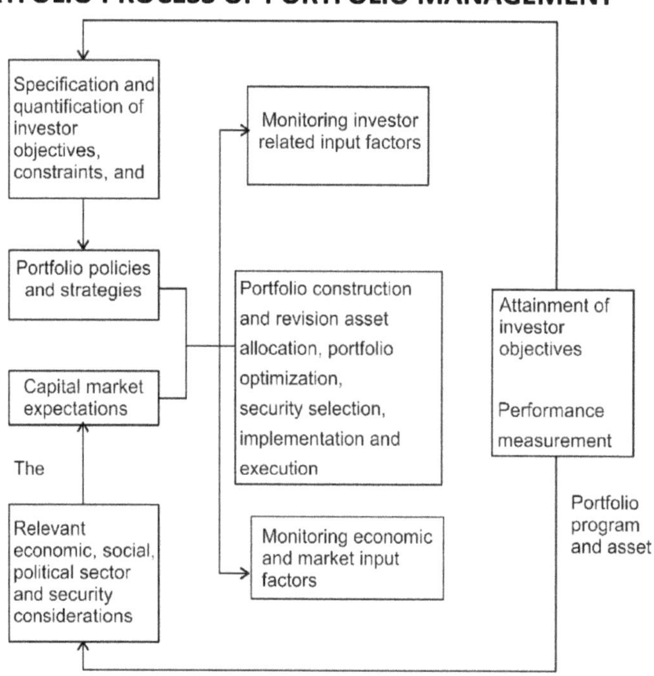

The *Portfolio Program* and *Asset Management Program* both follow a disciplined process to establish and monitor an optimal investment mix. This six-stage process helps ensure that the investments match investor's unique needs, both now and in the future.

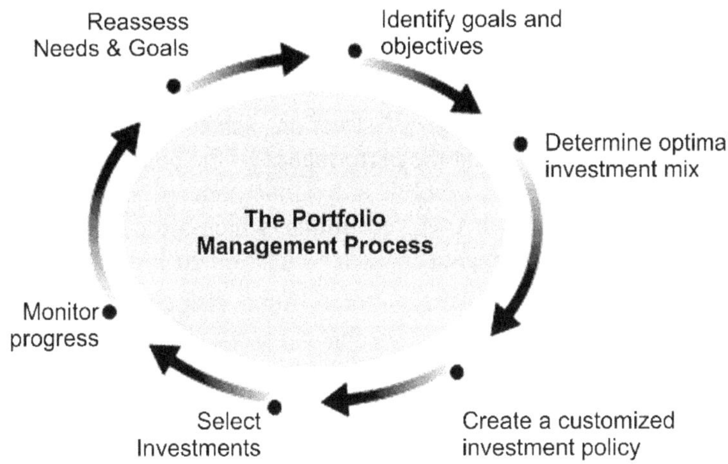

1. **IDENTIFY GOALS AND OBJECTIVES**

   When will you need the money from your investments? What are you saving your money for? With the assistance of financial advisor, the *Investment Profile Questionnaire* will guide through a series of questions to help identify the goals and objectives for the investments.

2. **DETERMINE OPTIMAL INVESTMENT MIX**

   Once the *Investment Profile Questionnaire* is completed, investor's optimal investment mix or asset allocation will be determined. An asset allocation represents the mix of investments (cash, fixed income and equities) that match individual risk and return needs. This step represents one of the most important decisions in your portfolio construction, as asset allocation has been found to be the major determinant of long-term portfolio performance.

3. **CREATE A CUSTOMIZED INVESTMENT POLICY STATEMENT**

   When the optimal investment mix is determined, the next step is to formalize our goals and objectives in order to utilize them as a benchmark to monitor progress and future updates.

4. **SELECT INVESTMENTS**

   The customized portfolio is created using an allocation of select QFM Funds. Each QFM Fund is designed to satisfy the requirements of a specific asset class, and is selected in the necessary proportion to match the optimal investment mix.

5 **MONITOR PROGRESS**

   Building an optimal investment mix is only part of the process. It is equally important to maintain the optimal mix when varying market conditions cause investment mix to drift away from its target. To ensure that mix of asset classes stays in line with investor's unique needs, the portfolio will be monitored and rebalanced back to the optimal investment mix

6. **REASSESS NEEDS AND GOALS**

Just as markets shift, so do the goals and objectives of investors. With the flexibility of the *Portfolio Program* and *Asset Management Program*, when the investor's needs or other life circumstances change, the portfolio has the flexibility to accommodate such changes.

Portfolio analysis includes portfolio construction, selection of securities, revision of portfolio evaluation and monitoring the performance of the portfolio. All these are part of subject of portfolio management which is a dynamic concept. Individual securities have risk-return characteristics of their own. Portfolios, which are combinations of securities may or may not take on the aggregate characteristics of their individual's parts.

Portfolio analysis considers the determination of future risk and return in holding various blends of individual securities. As we know that expected return from individual securities carries some degree of risk. Various groups of securities when held together behave in a different manner and give interest payments and dividends also, which are different to the analysis of individual securities. A combination of securities held together will give a beneficial result if they are grouped in a manner to secure higher return after taking into consideration the risk element.

There are two approaches in construction of the portfolio of securities. They are

- Traditional approach
- Modern approach

TRADITIONAL APPROACH

Traditional approach was based on the fact that risk could be measured on each individual security through the process of finding out the standard deviation and that security should be chosen where the deviation was the lowest. Traditional approach believes that the market is inefficient and the fundamental analyst can take advantage for the situation. Traditional approach is a comprehensive financial plan for the individual. It takes into account the individual needs such as housing, life insurance and pension plans. Traditional approach basically deals with two major decisions. They are

(a) Determining the objectives of the portfolio

(b) Selection of securities to be included in the portfolio

MODERN APPROACH

Modern approach theory was brought out by Markowitz and Sharpe. It is the combination of securities to get the most efficient portfolio. Combination of securities can be made in many ways. Markowitz developed the theory of diversification through scientific reasoning and method. Modern portfolio theory believes in the maximization of return through a combination of securities. The modern approach discusses the relationship between different securities and then draws inter-relationships of risks between them. Markowitz gives more attention to the process of selecting the portfolio. It does not deal with the individual needs.

TWO TYPES OF INVESTMENT PORTFOLIO MANAGEMENT:

Active portfolio management

Passive portfolio management

The main points for the passive portfolio management:

- Holding securities in the portfolio for the relatively long periods with small and infrequent changes.
- Investors act as if the security markets are relatively efficient. The portfolios they hold may be surrogates for the market portfolio (index funds).
- Passive investors do not try outperforming their designated benchmark.

The reasons when the investors with passive portfolio management make changes in their portfolios:

- The investor's preferences change;
- The risk-free rate changes;
- The consensus forecast about the risk and return of the benchmark portfolio changes.

The main points for the active portfolio management:

- Active investors believe that from time to time there are mispriced securities or groups of securities in the market;
- The active investors do not act as if they believe that security markets are efficient;
- The active investors use deviant predictions - their forecast of risk and return differ from consensus opinions.

Area of comparisons	Active investment management	Passive investment management
Aim	To achieve better results than average in the market	To achieve the average market results
Strategies used and decision making	Short term positions, the quick and more risky decisions; keeping the "hot" strategy	Long term positions, slow decisions
Investor/manager	tense	laid-back
Taxes and turnover of investment portfolio	High taxes, relatively high turnover of portfolio	Low taxes, small turnover of portfolio
Performance results before costs and taxes	In average equal to the passively managed portfolios	In average equal to the actively managed portfolios
Performance results after costs and taxes	In average lower than market index after taxes	In average higher than the results of actively managed portfolio return after taxes
Individual investors*	Over 85 % from total individual investors	Over 15 % from total individual investors

Contd….

Area of comparisons	Active investment management	Passive investment management
Institutional investors*	Over 56% from total institutional investors	Over 44% from total institutional investors
Supporters	All brokerage firms, investment funds, hedging fund, specialized investment companies	Passively managed pension funds, index funds
Analytical methods	Qualitative: avoiding risk, forecasts, emotions, intuition, success, speculation, gambling	Quantitative: risk management, long term statistical analysis, precise fundamental analysis

ACTIVE VERSUS PASSIVE INVESTMENT MANAGEMENT

There are arguments for both active and passive investing though it is probably a case that a larger percentage of institutional investors invest passively than do individual investors. Of course, the active versus passive investment management decision does not have to be a strictly either/ or choice. One common investment strategy is to invest passively in the market's investor considers to be efficient and actively in the market's investor considers inefficient. Investors also combine the two by investing part of the portfolio passively and another part actively.

STRATEGIC VERSUS TACTICAL ASSET ALLOCATION

An asset allocation focuses on determining the mixture of asset classes that is most likely to provide a combination of risk and expected return that is optimal for the investor. Asset allocation is a bit different from diversification. It focuses is on investment in various asset classes. Diversification, in contrast, tends to focus more on security selection - selecting the specific securities to be held within an asset class. *Asset classes* here is understood as groups of securities with similar characteristics and properties (for example, common stocks; bonds; derivatives, etc.). Asset allocation proceeds other approaches to investment portfolio management, such as market timing (buy low, sell high) or selecting the individual securities which are expected will be the "winners". These activities may be integrated in the asset allocation process.

But the main focus of asset allocation is to find such a combination of the different asset classes in the investment portfolio which the best matches with the investor's goals - expected return on investment and investment risk. Asset allocation largely determines an investor's success or lack thereof. In fact, studies have shown that as much as 90 % or more of a portfolio's return comes from asset allocation. Furthermore, researchers have found that asset allocation has a much greater impact on reducing total risk than does selecting the best investment vehicle in any single asset category.

Two categories in asset allocation are defined:

- Strategic asset allocation;
- Tactical asset allocation.

Strategic asset allocation identifies asset classes and the proportions for those asset classes that would comprise the normal asset allocation. Strategic asset allocation is used to derive long-term asset allocation weights. The fixed-weightings approach in strategic asset allocation is used. Investor using this approach allocates a fixed percentage of the portfolio to each of the asset classes, of which typically are three to five. Example of asset allocation in the portfolio might be as follows:

Asset class	Allocation
Common stock	40%
Bonds	50%
Short-term securities	10%
Total portfolio	100%

Generally, these weights are not changed over time. When market values change, the investor may have to adjust the portfolio annually or after major market moves to maintain the desired fixed-percentage allocation.

Tactical asset allocation produces temporary asset allocation weights that occur in response to temporary changes in capital market conditions. The investor's goals and risk-return preferences are assumed to remain unchanged as the asset weights are occasionally revised to help attain the investor's constant goals. For example, if the investor believes some sector of the market is over- or under valuated. The passive asset allocation will not have any changes in weights of asset classes in the investor's portfolio - the weights identified by strategic asset allocation are used.

Alternative asset allocations are often related with the different approaches to risk and return, identifying conservative, moderate and aggressive asset allocation. The conservative allocation is focused on providing low return with low risk; the moderate - average return with average risk and the aggressive - high return and high risk.

Comparison between the alternative asset allocations

Asset class	Alternative asset allocation		
	Conservative	Moderate	Aggressive
Common stock	20%	35%	65%
Bonds	45%	40%	20%
Short-term securities	35%	15%	5%
Total portfolio	100%	100%	100%

For asset allocation decisions *Markowitz portfolio model* as a selection techniques can be used. Although Markowitz model was developed for selecting portfolios of individual securities, but thinking in terms of asset classes, this model can be applied successfully to find the optimal **allocation** of assets in the portfolio. Programs exist to calculate efficient frontiers using asset classes and Markowitz model is frequently used for the asset allocation in institutional investors' portfolios.

The correlation between asset classes is obviously a key factor in building an optimal portfolio. Investors are looking to have in their portfolios asset classes that are negatively correlated with each other, or at least not highly positively correlated with each other. It is obvious that correlation coefficients between asset classes returns change over time. It is also important to note that the historical correlation between different asset classes will vary depending on the time period chosen, the frequency of the data and the asset class, used to estimate the correlation. Using not historical but future correlation coefficients between assets could influence the results remarkably, because the historical data may be different from the expectations.

MULTIPLE CHOICE QUESTIONS

1. Political constancy is the chief aspect concerning
   a. exchange risk
   b. systematic risk
   c. non-systematic risk
   d. country risk
2. Capital Market Line is firstly initiated by
   a. Mohsin
   b. Linter
   c. Markowitz
   d. William Sharpe
3. The most favourable portfolio is the proficient portfolio with the
   a. lowest risk
   b. highest risk
   c. highest utility
   d. least investment
4. The ambiguity introduced by way by which the organization finances its investments is
   a. country risk
   b. liquidity risk
   c. financial risk
   d. business risk
5. If generally interest rates in the nation increase, a corporate bond with a fixed interest rate will usually
   a. Increases in value
   b. Remain unchanged
   c. Decrease in value.
   d. To be returned to the corporation.
6. Benchmark portfolio risk is defined as
   a. The return difference between the portfolio and the benchmark
   b. The variance of the return of the benchmark portfolio
   c. The variance of the return difference between the portfolio and the benchmark
   d. The variance of the return of the actively-managed portfolio
   e. None of the above.

7. Benchmark portfolio risk
   a. Is inevitable and is never a significant issue in practice.
   b. Is inevitable and is always a significant issue in practice.
   c. Cannot be constrained to keep a Treynor-Black portfolio within reasonable weights.
   d. Can be constrained to keep a Treynor-Black portfolio within reasonable weights.
   e. None of the above.

8. ____________ can be used to measure forecast quality and guide in the proper adjustment of forecasts.
   a. Regression analysis
   b. Exponential smoothing
   c. ARIMA
   d. Moving average models
   e. GAUSS

9. Even low-quality forecasts have proven to be valuable because R-squares of only ____________ in regressions of analysts' forecasts can be used to substantially improve portfolio performance.
   a. 0.656
   b. 0.452
   c. 0.258
   d. 0.153
   e. 0.001

10. The ____________ model allows the private views of the portfolio manager to be incorporated with market data in the optimization procedure.
   a. Black-Litterman
   b. Treynor-Black
   c. Treynor-Mazuy
   d. Black-Scholes
   e none of the above.

11. The Black-Litterman model and Treynor-Black model are
   a. Nice in theory but practically useless in modern portfolio management.
   b. Complementary tools that should be used in portfolio management.
   c. Contradictory models cannot be use together; therefore, portfolio managers must choose which one suits their needs.
   d. Not useful due to their complexity.
   e. None of the above.

12. The Black-Litterman model is geared toward ____________ while the Treynor-Black model is geared toward ____________.
   a. Security analysis; security analysis
   b. Asset allocation; asset allocation
   c. Security analysis; asset allocation
   d. Asset allocation; security analysis
   e. None of the above

13. Alpha forecasts must be ___________ to account for less-than-perfect forecasting quality. When alpha forecasts are ___________ to account for forecast imprecision, the resulting portfolio position becomes ___________.
    a. shrunk, shrunk, far less moderate
    b. Shrunk, shrunk, far more moderate
    c. Grossed up, grossed up, far less moderate
    d. Grossed up, grossed up, far more moderate
    e. None of the above
14. Tracking error is defined as
    a. the difference between the returns on the overall risky portfolio versus the benchmark return.
    b. The variance of the return of the benchmark portfolio
    c. The variance of the return difference between the portfolio and the benchmark
    d. The variance of the return of the actively-managed portfolio
    e. None of the above.
15. The tracking error of an optimized portfolio can be expressed in terms of the __________ of the portfolio and thus reveal ___________.
    a. Return; portfolio performance
    b. Total risk; portfolio performance
    c. Beta; portfolio performance
    d. Beta; benchmark risk
    e. Relative return; benchmark risk
16. The Treynor-Black model is a model that shows how an investment manager can use security analysis and statistics to construct __________.
    a. A market portfolio
    b. A passive portfolio
    c. An active portfolio
    d. An index portfolio
    e Aa balanced portfolio
17. If a portfolio manager consistently obtains a high Sharpe measure, the manager's forecasting ability __________.
    a. Is above average
    b. Is average
    c. Is below average
    d. Does not exist.
    e. Cannot be determined based on the Sharpe measure

18. Active portfolio management consists of __________.

a. Market timing
b. Security analysis
c. Indexing
d. A and B
e. None of the above

19. The critical variable in the determination of the success of the active portfolio is________

a. Alpha/systematic risk
b. Alpha/nonsystematic risk
c. Gamma/systematic risk
d. Gamma/nonsystematic risk
e None of the above

20. Active portfolio managers try to construct a risky portfolio with __________.

a. A higher Sharpe measure than a passive strategy
b. A lower Sharpe measure than a passive strategy
c. The same Sharpe measure as a passive strategy
d. Very few securities
e. None of the above

21. The beta of an active portfolio is 1.20. The standard deviation of the returns on the market index is 20%. The nonsystematic variance of the active portfolio is 1%. The standard deviation of the returns on the active portfolio is __________.

a. 3.84%
b. 5.84%
c. 19.60%
d. 24.17%
e. 26.0%

22. Consider the Treynor-Black model. The alpha of an active portfolio is 2%. The expected return on the market index is 16%. The variance of return on the market portfolio is 4%. The nonsystematic variance of the active portfolio is 1%. The risk-free rate of return is 8%. The beta of the active portfolio is 1. The optimal proportion to invest in the active portfolio is __________.

a. 0%
b. 25%
c. 50%
d. 100%
e. None of the above

23. There appears to be a role for a theory of active portfolio management because

a. Some portfolio managers have produced sequences of abnormal returns that are difficult to label as lucky outcomes.

b. The "noise" in the realized returns is enough to prevent the rejection of the hypothesis that some money managers have outperformed a passive strategy by a statistically small, yet economic, margin.

c. Some anomalies in realized returns have been persistent enough to suggest that portfolio managers who identified these anomalies in a timely fashion could have outperformed a passive strategy over prolonged periods.

d. a and b.

e. a, b, and c

24. An active portfolio manager faces a tradeoff between

I. using the Sharpe measure.

II. using mean-variance analysis.

III. exploiting perceived security mispricing's.

IV. holding too much of the risk-free asset.

V. letting a few stocks dominate the portfolio.

a. I and II

b. II and V

c. III and V

d. III and IV

e. II and III

FILL IN THE BLANKS

1. A Portfolio means .... Combination of assets
2. What do you understand by the term Net asset value (NAV)? ....
3. Active investment managers .... (Do not believe that markets are efficient, puts efforts to search mispriced securities in the market, are relatively active traders in securities to acquire abnormal returns).
4. What is Bottom-Up approach also known as? ....
5. With the use of diversification, you can reduce the risk.

SHORT ANSWER QUESTIONS

1. What is a portfolio? Why is it components?
2. Rebalancing a portfolio
3. Strategic asset allocation
4. Tactical asset allocation.
5. Active portfolio management
6. Passive portfolio management

ESSAY TYPE QUESTIONS

1. Define portfolio. Explain objectives, types, importance and steps involved in the Portfolio Management.
2. Discuss the need and important stages, process and approaches in portfolio management.
3. Give the arguments for active portfolio management.
4. What are the reasons which cause investors managing their portfolios passively to make changes their portfolios?
5. What are the major differences between active and passive portfolio management?
6. Distinguish strategic and tactical asset allocation.
7. What role does current market information play in managing investment portfolio?
8. Why is the asset allocation decision the most important decision made by investors?
9. What is the point of investment portfolio rebalancing?
10. What changes in investor's circumstances cause the rebalancing of the investment portfolio? Explain why.

MCQs Answers

1	2	3	4	5	6	7	8	9	10	11	12	13	14	15	16	17	18	19	20	21	22	23	24
d	d	c	c	c	d	d	a	e	b	b	d	b	a	d	c	a	d	b	d	e	d	c	a

CASE STUDIES

CASE STUDY 1

J.P. Morgan Chase & Co. is a leading global financial services firm with assets of $2 trillion and operations in more than 50 countries. The firm is a leader in Investment banking financial services for consumers and businesses, financial transaction processing, asset and wealth management, and private equity.

'Programme Management is now like being an air traffic controller, you need the skills and tools to assimilate information in multiple dimensions in real-time and then make decisions that are focused on a busy and changing landing zone three to six months ahead.' CTO EMEA

The Challenge

This global investment bank needed one unified set of management information from their financial systems transformation projects to manage them as global programmes and portfolios. They needed to demonstrate progress and compliance for senior stakeholders in closer to real-time, rather than in historical reports. With a new solution, management sought to better coordinate and deliver a complex series of international reorganization decisions and reap their cost savings and business opportunities. Many organizations face similar challenges; needing to relate their projects to the business in a meaningful way for a variety of stakeholders.

The Solution

Empowered Systems created a Programme Management Office (PMO) portal, using Portfolio Governance. This portfolio management tool is accessible via a web-browser, and it integrates the bank's complex array of organizational and project information. The system is centered on roles, creating views of programme information that are more relevant to a user's work area and help to priorities activity. The interface works with a system of dynamic scorecards for projects and programmes, so executives and programme managers can drill into key areas and see risks. The universally recognized 'red, amber, green' (traffic light) colour coding gives a quick assessment based on business rules that monitor key indicators such as cost, benefits and the status of milestones, risks and issues. Inside the tool, the rules and indicators can be customized by the business, and the various users can collaborate online in a variety of ways. The relationship of projects and programmes inside the software tool mirrors the organization's operating model. Starting with a summary screen, the user can make an infinite number of queries or 'slice & dice' analyses where different parameters are compared. With customization, the system can send automatic email alerts and provide scorecards customized to users.

The PMO Portal was implemented in phases and continues to evolve in response to organizational needs and priorities. The current version is a third iteration now providing portfolio management metrics for risk management, approval workflow of pipeline projects, and surveys for capturing qualitative assessment.

'Portfolio Governance ensures visibility of our programme and project catalogue and dynamically priorities the most important projects according to the bank's specific criteria. The portal enables senior management to make crucial decisions with all the necessary and relevant granular information made available to them. It has introduced effective governance and brought a consistent, consolidated view, delivering a powerful executive decision-making tool. It has brought a greater degree of discipline to previously diverse programme management processes and capabilities.'

DIVISIONAL CIO

The Benefits

Business perspective: The solution has become more than an everyday PMO tool - it now connects the performance of enterprise-wide programmes and initiatives to strategic business objectives. The Senior Vice President says it is "providing a new level of enterprise performance visibility".

Evolution: This PMO Portal using Portfolio Governance was first implemented in 2002 and has now has around 1,000 users globally and three major upgrades delivered on time and to budget.

Flexibility: The portal measures the progress and success of transitioning pipelines into projects. Issue & Risk Logs, associated project documents and policy documents are linked and are accessible from the document repository. Managers can easily and flexibly define new groupings of projects to compare status based on automated aggregations and consistent reporting in scorecards.

Governance: The portal empowers people by decentralizing the acceptance processes to individual work-stream functions. This includes validation, refinement and review of cost benefit at standard phase points and in the case of Six Sigma projects, at the 'Improve phase' of the DMAIIC life cycle. The Compliance Reporting Manager testifies that the Portfolio Governance PMO Portal "enforces rigor and discipline in our PMO process and methodology."

Dependency management: Programme and project managers use milestone dependencies in the tool to identify and track interrelationships as they arise, which eliminates the need for manual investigations.

"The product underpins our Finance Transformation, business acquisition and merger integration governance process and is used to proactively manage, control and report on (scorecard) our wide portfolio of Finance programmes, projects and application portfolio (delivery dates, milestones, risks, issues, dependencies, costs, benefits). This has helped to ensure transparency and visibility to senior management down through the programme/project managers and workstream teams managing over 80 key programmes and 420 applications."

CHAPTER 7

Optimal Portfolio Selection and Construction

Traditional theory was based on the fact that risk could be measured on each individual security through the process of finding out the standard deviation and that security should be chosen where the deviation was the lowest. Greater variability and higher deviations showed more risk than those securities which had lower variation. The modern theory is of the view that by diversification, risk can be reduced. Diversification can be made by the investor either by having a large number of shares of companies in different regions, in different industries or those producing different types of product lines. Diversification is important but the modern theory states that there cannot be only diversification to achieve the maximum return. The securities have to be evaluated and thus diversified to some limited extent within which the maximum achievement can be sought by the investor. The theory of diversification was based on the research work of Harry Markowitz. He is of the view that a portfolio should be analyzed depending upon

(a) The attitude of the investor towards risk and return, and

(b) The quantification of risk.

The author of the modern portfolio theory is Harry Markowitz who introduced the analysis of the portfolios of investments in his article "Portfolio Selection" published in the Journal of Finance in 1952. The new approach presented in this article included portfolio formation by considering the expected rate of return and risk of individual stocks and, crucially, their interrelationship as measured by correlation. Prior to this investor would examine investments individually, build up portfolios of attractive stocks, and not consider how they related to each other. Markowitz showed how it might be possible to better of these simplistic portfolios by taking into account the correlation between the returns on these stocks.

The diversification plays a very important role in the modern portfolio theory. Markowitz approach is viewed as a single period approach: at the beginning of the period the investor must make a decision in what particular securities to invest and hold these securities until the end of the period. Because a portfolio is a collection of securities, this decision is equivalent to selecting an optimal portfolio from a set of possible portfolios. Essentiality of the *Markowitz portfolio theory is the problem of optimal portfolio selection and construction.*

RISK AND RISK AVERSION

The idea of risk is intimately tied up with the notion of uncertainty. We will work with the idea that the greater the uncertainty, the greater the risk. A convenient way to represent uncertainty is with a probability distribution. However, a probability distribution has a great deal of information. Our challenge is to distil much of that information into a single number. In order to do that, we will assume that our probability distribution is symmetric, i.e. that the likelihood of deviations below the mean is similar to that of deviations above the mean. This is not unreasonable given the empirical distribution of returns on securities. With this assumption, a good measure of the uncertainty in a probability distribution is the standard deviation of the random variable that is being represented. The standard deviation, intuitively, quantifies the spread of the distribution, i.e. the likelihood of large deviations from the mean. (Strictly speaking, the use of single measure is valid only if the random variable is normally distributed.)

Now, most people dislike uncertainty. Hence, portfolios or strategies that result in high standard deviation of wealth are less preferred compared to those that have low standard deviation. In order to pursue our ultimate goal of locating optimal investment strategies, we need to quantify people's preferences with respect to risk. We will do this by means of a utility function. The utility function that we will employ is the following.

$$U = E(r) - 0.005A\sigma^2$$

In brief, this function measures the utility or desirability of a portfolio or investment strategy by starting with the expected or average return as a base number and subtracting a quantity, which is proportional to the square of the standard deviation of the return on that portfolio or strategy. The square of the standard deviation is known as variance, and the constant of proportionality is 0.005A, where the A is a measure of the risk aversion of the individual, with greater values standing for greater risk aversion.

This utility function can be demonstrated graphically by the use of the notion of indifference curves. An indifference curve has the property that the individual is indifferent between all the portfolios that lie on that curve.

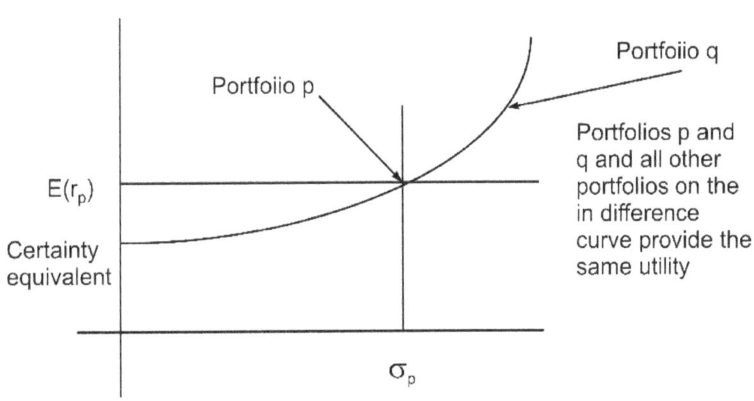

Figure 7.1 Indifference curve.

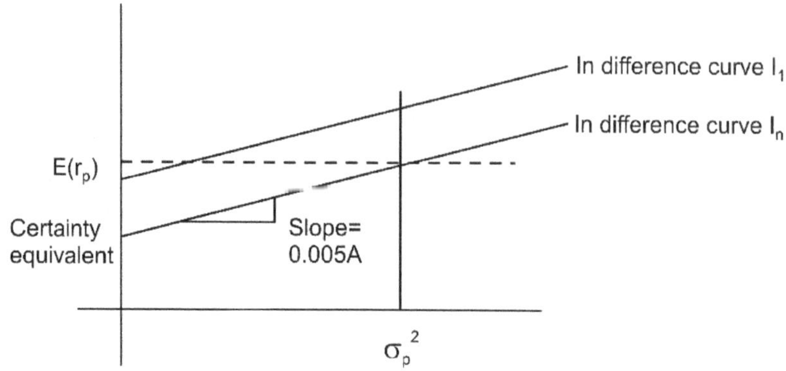

Figure 7.2 Indifference Curve representing the Utility function: $U = E(r) - 0.005A\delta^2$.

We are now ready to use this machinery to investigate the optimal allocation between a risky portfolio and the risk-free asset.

CAPITAL ALLOCATION BETWEEN THE RISKY ASSET AND THE RISK-FREE ASSET

Investing in stocks can be risky. However, this risk can be reduced by allocating part of our investment to risk-free assets.

PORTFOLIOS

Definition of a Portfolio: Formally, a portfolio is defined by a set of portfolio weights. Given a list of assets, a portfolio is defined as a set of numbers, w_I, such that the sum of the w_i equals unity, and w_i is the proportion of the wealth in the portfolio allocated to asset *i*. Using this definition, it is clear that if an asset appears with portfolio weight $w_i = 0$, it does not matter whether it appears in the asset list or not. Hence, we can simply agree to include all assets in the economy in the asset list, and specify portfolios simply by a set of portfolio weights. Under this convention, if there are *n* assets in the economy, each portfolio is defined as a vector with *n* components.

Mean and Variance of a portfolio with one risky and one risk-free asset

Let C denote the complete portfolio, P the risky portfolio, and f the risk-free asset. Then, if *y* is the proportion invested in the risky portfolio,

$$R_p = y\, r_P + (1-y)\, r_f$$

$$E(r) = y\, E(r_P) + (1-y)\, r_f, \text{ and } \square_C = y\square_P$$

From this we can generate the expected return-standard deviation combinations that can be obtained by creating such portfolios. The line joining all such combinations is called the Capital Allocation Line.

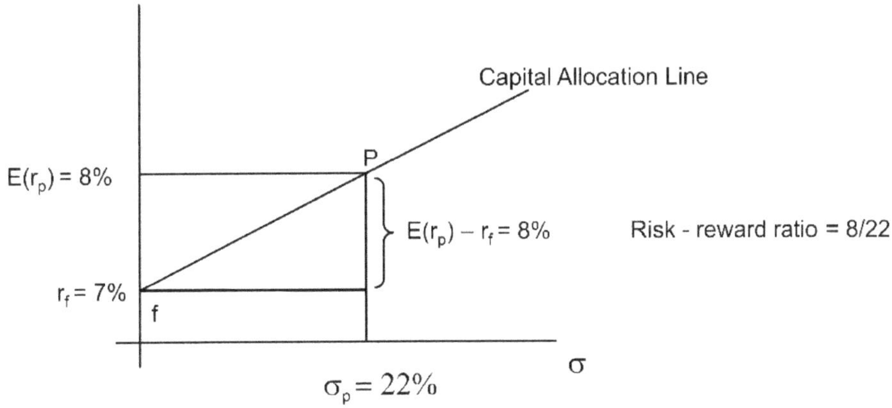

Figure 7.3 Capital Allocation Line.

INVESTMENT STRATEGIES INVOLVING ONE RISKY ASSET, AND A RISK-FREE ASSET

What is the optimal amount to invest in the risky asset portfolio if there is one risky portfolio and one risk-free asset?

Suppose the investor likes expected return, but dislikes variance of returns, and his tradeoff between expected return and variance is constant. Then, his utility function can be specified as U = E(r) - 0.005A□□, where the parameter A is a measure of his dislike of return variance. We can depict his preferences graphically using indifference curves:

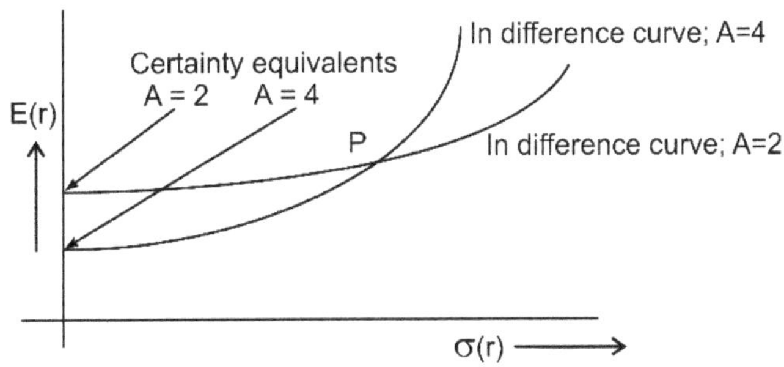

Certainty equivalents of Portfolio p for two different utility funcations

The optimal combination of the risky portfolio, P, and the riskfree asset is given by:

$$y^* = \frac{E(r_p) - r_f}{.01A\sigma_p^2}$$

This is obtained by maximizing the utility function subject to the relationships between expected return and standard deviation for the combined portfolio and the expected returns and standard deviations of returns of the risky portfolio and risk-free asset. Click here for a Java program that can be used to compute the portfolio proportions for the optimal combination portfolio. Note that the Risk Tolerance Coefficient in the program equals 200/A. For example, if your A = 10, set the Risk Tolerance equal to 200/10 = 20.

The optimal y^* will be higher for investors with lower A:

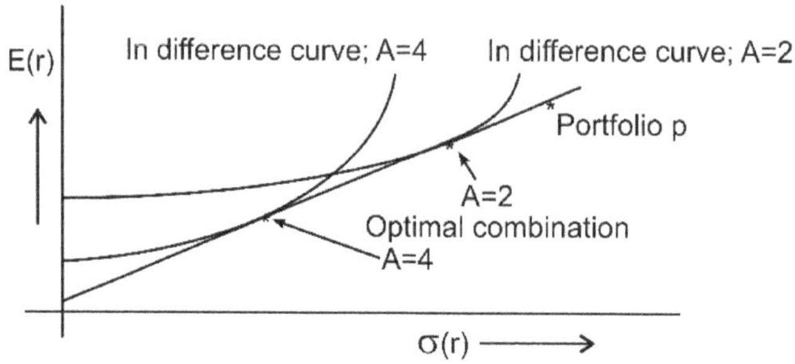

Figure 7.4 Optimal portfolio choice for two different utility functions.

PASSIVE INVESTMENT STRATEGIES AND THE CAPITAL MARKET LINE

Under what circumstances would we wish to use the strategy delineated above? Suppose an investor wishes to follow a passive strategy, viz. a strategy that avoids any direct or indirect security analysis. In such as case, his optimal strategy would be to allocate his wealth between a risk-free asset (such as a money market fund, whose exact composition of this portfolio would vary according to his investment horizon) and a broad diversified portfolio (which might, for example, mimic the S&P 500 Index), using the formulas described above. The Capital Allocation line, in this instance, is called the Capital Market Line.

Why might an investor choose a passive strategy? There are two important reasons:

1. The alternative active strategy is expensive, because it requires analysis.
2. If there are many knowledgeable investors in the market, securities are already likely to be fairly priced, and no undervalued or overvalued securities can be easily located. (See further discussion of this in my Efficient Markets web notes.

PORTFOLIOS OF TWO RISKY ASSETS

If we wish to construct a portfolio with more than one risky asset, we still use the general utility function approach described above. However, the combination line indicating the expected return-variance combinations that can be obtained with more than one risky asset is no longer linear. We need to consider how portfolio variance changes as we change portfolio proportions. Let us look at the simple case, where there are exactly two risky assets (or portfolios), D and E. Then the expected return and variance of returns is given below:

$$E(r_p) = w_D E(r_D) + w_E E(r_E)$$

$$\sigma_p^2 = w_D^2 \sigma_D^2 + w_E^2 \sigma_E^2 + 2w_D w_E Cov(r_D r_E)$$

We see below the combination line of the two risky assets, D and E. Note that the portfolio standard deviation is less than the weighted average of the individual standard deviations. Also, the slope of the combination line at any point indicates the reward-to-variability ratio at that point.

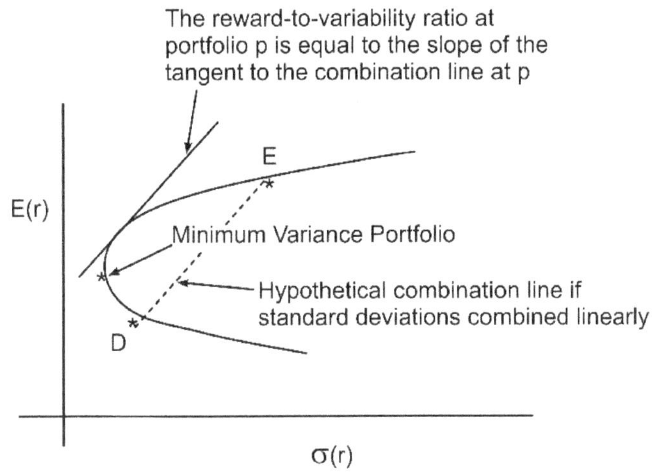

Figure 7.5 Combination line of portfolios constructed from two risky assests.

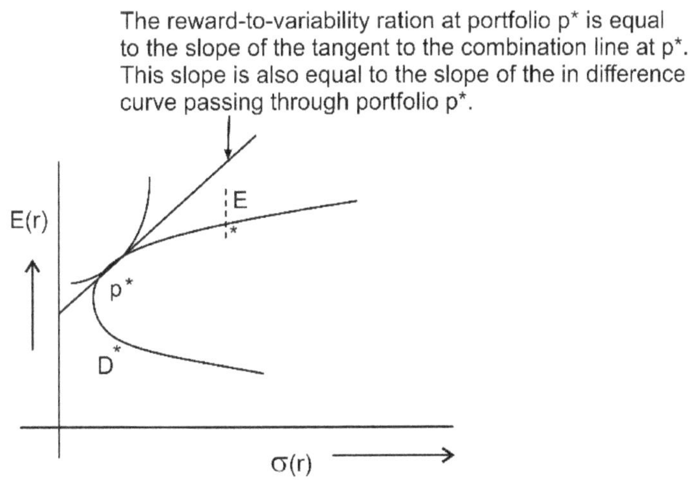

Figure 7.6 Location of the optimal portfolio.

The minimum variance portfolio of risky assets D and E is given by the following portfolio proportions:

$$w_{min}(D) = \frac{\sigma_E^2 - Cov(r_D, r_E)}{\sigma_D^2 + \sigma_E^2 - 2Cov(r_D, r_E)}; w_{min}(E) = 1 - w_{min}(D)$$

The optimal portfolio for an investor with a risk aversion parameter, A, can be represented by the formula:

$$w_D = \frac{E(r_D) - E(r_E) + 0.01A[\sigma_E^2 - Cov(r_D, r_E)]}{0.01A[\sigma_E^2 + \sigma_D^2 - 2Cov(r_D, r_E)]}$$

Graphically, this is the point on the combination line where the slope of the indifference curve is equal to the reward-variability ratio.

OPTIMAL PORTFOLIO CHOICE WITH TWO RISKY ASSETS AND ONE RISK-FREE ASSET

The optimal portfolio choice if there are two risky assets and one risk-free asset can be represented graphically in a similar manner.

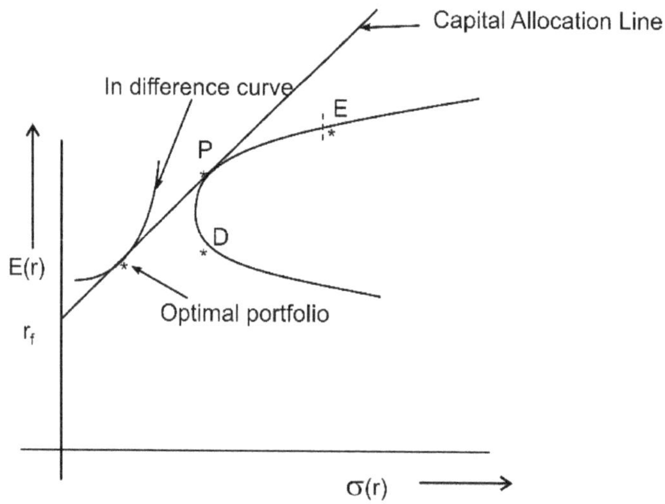

Figure 7.7 Location of the optimal portfolio when there is a risk-free asset.

The portfolio proportions for the tangent risky portfolio, P, are:

$$w_D = \frac{[E(r_D) - r_f]\sigma_E^2 - [E(r_E) - r_f]Cov(r_D, r_E)}{[E(r_D) - r_f]\sigma_E^2 + [E(r_E) - r_f]\sigma_D^2 - [E(r_D) - r_f + E(r_E) - r_f]Cov(r_D, r_E)}; \; w_E = 1 - w_D$$

Note that these weights are independent of the individual investor's risk-aversion. The overall optimal portfolio is then easily computed because this is again a question of choosing the proportion to be invested in a risky asset and a risk-free asset.

Click here for a Java program that can be used to compute the portfolio proportions for the overall portfolio. Note that the Risk Tolerance Coefficient in the program equals 200/A. For example, if your A = 10, set the Risk Tolerance equal to 200/10 = 20.

To see an example of how you can estimate expected returns and variances, and then construct the combination line for two risky assets, go to the spreadsheets on the Web notes page.

DIVERSIFICATION AND PORTFOLIO RISK

If we have more than two assets, say *n* assets, then, the expected return is still the weighted average of the expected returns on the component assets, where the weights are the portfolio proportions. The portfolio variance, however, now involves the covariance between every pair of assets.

$$\sigma_p^2 = \sum_{i=1}^{n} w_i^2 \sigma_i^2 + \sum_{\substack{j=1 \\ j \neq i}}^{n} \sum_{i=1}^{n} w_i w_j Cov(r_i, r_j).$$

This can also be represented using the correlation coefficients, □ij, as below:

$$\sigma_p^2 = \sum_{i=1}^{n} w_i^2 \sigma_i^2 + \sum_{\substack{j=1 \\ j \neq i}}^{n} \sum_{i=1}^{n} w_i w_j \sigma_i \sigma_j \rho(r_i, r_j).$$

This can be further simplified in terms of the average variance, and the average covariance:

$$\sigma_p^2 = \frac{1}{n}\overline{\sigma^2} + \frac{n-1}{n}\overline{Cov}$$

The greater the number of assets in the portfolio, the closer the portfolio variance gets to the average covariance, and the less it is influenced by the variance of any particular asset. This limit portfolio variance, which cannot be avoided, is called market risk, or non-diversifiable risk, or systematic risk. The risk that can be eliminated from each asset is called idiosyncratic risk, asset-specific risk, diversifiable risk or non-systematic risk. A corollary of this result is that the variance of all well-diversified portfolios is likely to be close to each other.

EFFICIENT FRONTIER WITH MANY RISKY ASSETS

If there are many assets that can be used to form the investor's portfolio, we can construct many combination lines. However, for a given level of risk, an investor will only consider the portfolio with the highest expected return. The set of such portfolios is called the efficient frontier, and is shown below.

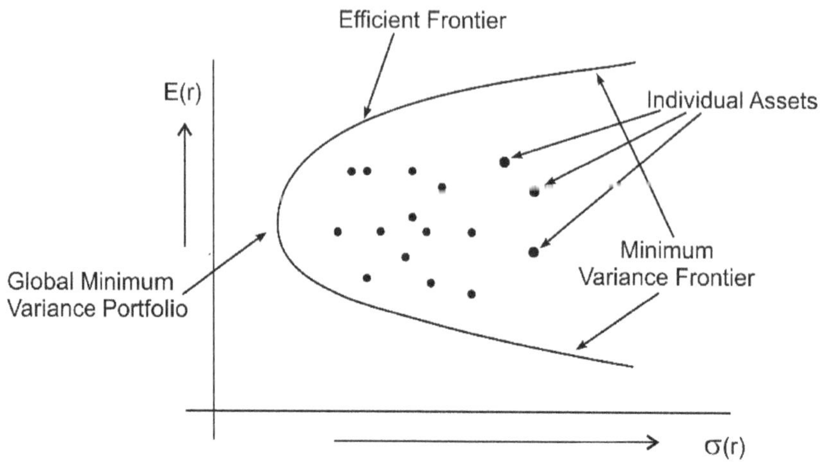

Figure 7.8 The Minimum-variance frontier of risky assets.

THE OPTIMUM PORTFOLIO WITH MANY RISKY ASSETS AND A RISK-FREE ASSET

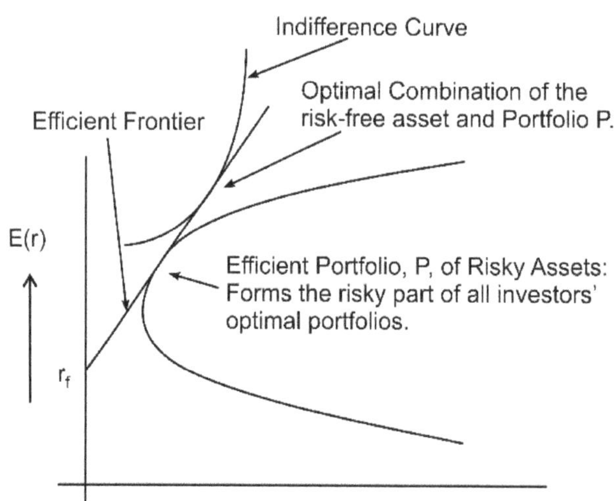

Figure 7.9 Optimal portfolio selection with many risky assets and a risk-free asset.

EFFECT OF COMBINING TWO SECURITIES

It is believed that holding two securities is less risky than having only one investment in a person's portfolio. When two stocks are taken on a portfolio and if they have negative correlation, then risk can be completely reduced because the gain on one can offset the loss on the other. The effect of two securities can also be studied when one security is riskier when compared to the other security. The following example shows a return of 13%. A combination of A and E will produce superior results to an investor rather than if he was to purchase only Stock-A. If an investor constructs his portfolio in such a way that two-thirds of his stock consists of Stock-A and one-third of stock consists of Stock-B, the average return of the portfolio is the weighted average return of each security in the portfolio.

Example 1

When there are two securities in a portfolio:

Security	Expected Return % R1	Proportion % X1
1	10	25
2	20	75

The return on the portfolio on combining the two securities will be

$$R_P = \sum_{i=1}^{n} X_i \bar{R}_i$$

$$R_P = 0.10\,(0.25) + 0.20\,(0.75) = 17.5\%$$

Example 2

Portfolio Analysis: Markowitz Two Security Analysis:

	Stock A	Stock B
Return %	7 or 11	13 or 5
Probability average	.4 each return	.4 each return
Expected Return %	7.2	7.20
Variance	4	16
Standard Deviation	2	4
+ Expected Return	= .4 x 7 +.4 x 11 = 7.2	
Expected	= .4 x 13 + .4 x 5 = 7.2	
Rate of Return on Portfolio = 9		

Formula:

$$R_P = \sum_{i=1}^{n} X_i \bar{R}_i$$

R_P = the expected return to portfolio

X_1 = proportion of total portfolio invested in security I

R_i = expected return to security I

N = total number of securities in portfolio

Therefore, $R_P = (2/3)\,(7.2) + (1/3)\,(7.2) = 7.2$

The range of fluctuations in a portfolio will be calculated in the following manner, in the following situation:

- When Stock 'A' in a given investment is taken at 2/3 proportion during prosperity RP = (2/3) x (7) + (1/3) x (5) = 9.0.
- When Stock 'A' in a given investment is taken at 2/3 proportion during depression R_P = (2/3) x (7) + (1/3) x (13) = 9.0. (Higher return than expected)

Thus, by putting some part of the amount in stock which is riskier stock, i.e. 'B', the risk can be reduced rather than if the investor was to purchase only Stock 'A'. If an investor was to purchase only Stock 'A', his return would be according to his expectation an average of 7.2%, which becomes as low as 7% in depression periods and rises to 11% in boom periods. The standard deviation of this stock is as low 2%. The investor will make a return of higher than 7.2% by combining two-thirds of Stock 'A' and one-third of Stock 'B'. Thus, the investor is able to achieve a return of 9% and bring the risk to the minimum level. Thus, the effect of holding two securities in a portfolio does reduce risk but research studies have shown that it is important to know what proportion of the stock should be brought by the investor in order to get a minimum risk, the portfolio returns can be achieved at the higher point by setting of one variation against another. The investor should be able to find out two investments in such a way that one investment is giving a higher return whereas the other investment is not performing well even though one of the securities in riskier, and it will lead to a good combination. This is a difficult task because the investor will have to continue to find out two securities which are related to each other inversely like the example given for Stocks 'A' and 'B'. But securities should also be correlated to each other in such a way that maximum returns can be achieved.

INTERACTIVE RISK THROUGH COVARIANCE

Apart from the measurement of securities through standard deviation and co-efficient of variation when two securities are combined, the investor should find out the co-variance of each security. Co-variance of the securities will help in finding out the inter-active risk. When the co-variance will be positive, then the rates of return of securities move together either upwards or downwards. Alternatively, it can also be said that the interactive risk is positive. Secondly co-variance will be zero on two investments if the rates of return are independent. Therefore, when two stocks are inversely related to each other, the co-variance will become negative. The following formula is given calculating co-variance.

When probabilities are equal: Covxy = 1/N (Rx –Ext) (Rye –Ely)(Or)

$$\text{cov}_{xy} = \sum_{i=1}^{n} (R_x - \bar{R}_i) \quad (R_y - \bar{R}_i) * P_i$$

Where

Cove. $_{XY}$ = covariance between two securities x and y.

R_x = return on security 'x' R_y = return on security 'y'

$E(R_x)$ = expected return on security 'x' $E(R_y)$ = expected return on security 'y'

N = number of observations

Example 3

Taking the above example of security A and B:

Security	Range of Return	Expected Return of portfolio	Deviations
Stock 'A'	7	9.0	- .2
Stock 'B'	13	9.0	+ 4
Stock 'A'	11	9.0	+ 2
Stock 'B'	5	9.0	- 4

Cove. = ½(7-9) (13-9) + (11-9) (5-9)

= ½(-8) + (-8) = -16/2 = -8

In this example, the investment of stock A and B are taken at the same point of time to determine the variation of each stock from its expected value and the deviations are multiplied together. If each deviation is negative, their products will become positive. The co-variance will be an average of the positive values and the total values will be added. Alternatively, it can be said that when values of one variable will be higher and the value of the other variable will be small, then the resulting deviations will also show one positive and other negative. The co-variance will now turn to be negative. This is depicted in the above example.

Coefficient of Correlation

The coefficient of correlation is also designed to measure the relationship between two securities. It gives an indication of the variables being positively or negatively related to each other. This is represented by the following formula:

Example 4

Correlation Coefficient is ϒxy = $\frac{COV\ XY}{\sigma_M \sigma_L}$

ϒxy= coefficient of correlation of x and y.

Cove. $_{XY}$ = covariance between x and y.

σ x = standard deviation of x.

σ y = standard deviation of y

In the above example, coefficient of correlation = If σx = σy = 4

ϒxy = -8/ [(2) (4)] = -1

COMBINED AND MEASURED

It is measured by the standard deviation of two securities, namely x and y. The coefficient of correlation between the two securities is shown when it is + 1.0, which means that there is perfect positive correlation and if it shows – 1.0, it means that there is perfect negative correlation. If the coefficient correlation is zero, then it means that the return on securities are independent of one another. When the correlation is zero, an investor can expect deduction of risk by diversifying between two assets. When correlation coefficient is -1, the portfolio risk will be the minimum.

Markowitz has shown the effect of diversification by reading the risk of securities. According to him, the security with co-variance which is either negative or low amongst them, is the best manner to reduce risk. Markowitz has been able to show that securities which have less than positive correlation will reduce risk without, in any way, bringing the return down. According to his research study a low correlation level between securities in the portfolio will show less risk. According to him, investing in a large number of securities is not the right method of investment. It is the right kind of security which brings the maximum results. The following formula has been given by Harry Markowitz for a two-security portfolio. The formula includes the standard deviation. It also includes variance and co-variance:

$$\text{Portfolio risk} = \sigma_p = \sqrt{X_1^2\sigma_R^2 + X_2^2\sigma_S^2 + 2X_1X_2(r_{12}\sigma_1\sigma_2)}$$

$\sigma^2 p$ = variance of the portfolio

X_1 and X2 = weights of securities I and j

r_{12} = co-efficient of correlation I and j

$\sigma_i\ \sigma^2$ = standard deviation of times the security I and j

Example 5

The effect of the degree of risk on portfolio is illustrated in the following manner:

$$\text{Portfolio risk} = \sigma_p = \sqrt{X_1^2\sigma_R^2 + X_2^2\sigma_S^2 + 2X_1X_2(\Upsilon xy\ \sigma_1\sigma_2)}$$

The risk of portfolio is measured in this example and when coefficient correlation is -1, 1.5, -0.5, θ, + 1 when x = 1, the risk is the lowest, risk would be nil if the proportion of investment in security Xi and Ax are changed so that standard becomes 0 and x = -1.

When is $\sigma 1 = 4$

$\sigma 2 = 7$

Xi = 0.5

X2 = 0.5

When $\Upsilon_{xy} = -1$

$\sigma\ p = \sqrt{}\ (0.5)^2(4)^2 + (0.5)^2\ (7)^{2+}\ (2)\ (0.5)\ (0.5)\ (-1)\ (4)\ (7)$

σ p= 1.5

(2) When ϒxy= -0.5

σ p= $\sqrt{}$ $(0.5)^2(4)^2 + (0.5)^2 (7)^{2+}$ (2) (0.5) (0.5) (-0.5) (4) (7)

σ p= 3.041381

(3) When r = -0.0

Then

σ p= $\sqrt{}$ $(0.5)^2(4)^2 + (0.5)^2(7)^{2\pm}$ (2) (0.5) (0.5) (-1) (4) (7)

σ p= 4.03

(4) When r = +1.0

Then

σp= $\sqrt{}$ $(0.5)^2(4)^2 + (0.5)^2 (7)^{2+}$ (2) (0.5) (0.5) (1) (4) (7)

σp= 5.5

In this example, standard deviation is the lowest when correlation is negative-1. The standard deviation increases when the degree of correlation is positives. When co-efficient of correlation is +1, the advantage of diversifying becomes nullified. At this point of time, the standard deviation of the portfolio becomes equal to the weighted sum of standard deviations of each individual security.

To illustrate, the weighted sum of the standard deviations:

$$ϭ1ϭ2 = X1 (\sigma 1) + X2 (\sigma 2)$$
$$= 0.5(4) + 0.5 (7)$$
$$= 5.5$$

- When correlation is less than + 1, risk can be reduced by diversification. At this point, for a given return, risk will be reduced below the weighted sum of the standard deviation of each security.
- When two securities are positively correlated (perfectly + 1 positive), its standard deviation will be identical with the standard deviation of the securities when calculated independently
- To find out the ideal combination.

$$X_x = my/a_x + m_y = 7/4+7 = .36$$

When Xi =.64 and X_i =.36

Now when r_{12} = -1

$$= \sqrt{} (.64)^2(4)^2 + (.36)^2 (7)^{2+} 2(.64) (.36) (-1) (4) (7)$$
$$= \sqrt{}4096 (16) + .1296(49) + (.2304) (-28)2 = \sqrt{}12.90 - 12.90 = \sqrt{}0$$

Example 6

Calculate risk from the coefficient of correlation given below with proportion of .50 and .50 for XY. What would be the least risky combination if the correlation of the returns of the two securities is – 1.0, (ii) 0, (iii) 0.8 (iv) 1.0

Security Nos.	Expected Return.	Expected.
1	5	2
2	15	8

5(.50) + 15(.50)

2.50 + 7.50 = 10.00 returns

When r = -1

$$\sigma p = \sqrt{(0.5)^2 (2)^2 + (0.5)^2 (8)^{2} + (2)(0.5)(0.5) + 0(2)(8)}$$
$$= \sqrt{(.25)(4) + (2.5)(64) \text{ x } (2)(2.5)} = \sqrt{1.0 + 16.0 + 0} = \sqrt{17}$$
$$\sigma p = 3$$

When r = 0

$$\sigma p = \sqrt{(0.5)^2 (2)^2 + (0.5)^2 (8)^{2} + (2)(0.5)(0.5) + (.8)(2)(8)}$$
$$= \sqrt{(6.4)(4) + (0.4)(4) \text{ x } (.32) - 16}$$
$$= \sqrt{17} + 6.4 \qquad = \sqrt{23.4} \qquad \sigma_p = 4.2$$

When r = 0.8

$$\sigma p = \sqrt{(0.5)^2 (2)(2)^2 + (0.5)(8)^{2} + (2)(0.5) + (1.0)(2)(8)}$$
$$= \sqrt{17} + 8 \qquad = \sqrt{25} \qquad = 5\%$$

When r = 1.0

$$\sigma p = \sqrt{(0.8)^2 (2)^2 + (0.2)^2 (8)^{2} + 2(.8)(.2) - 1(2)(8)}$$
$$= \sqrt{17 + 8} \quad = \sqrt{25}$$
$$\sigma p = 5$$

The least risky portfolio combination is when correlation is –1.

(b) 80% X

(c) 20% Y

$$\sigma p = \sqrt{(0.8)^2 (2)^2 + (.02)^2 (8)^{2} + 2(.8)(.2) - 1(2)(8)}$$
$$= \sqrt{(64)(4) + (.04)(4) + .32 - 16}$$
$$= \sqrt{2.56 + 2.56 + 5.12}$$
$$= \sqrt{5.12 - 5.12}$$
$$\sigma p = 0$$

The least risky combination is when standard deviation is 0. To find out proportion:

(a) Weight of Xx = m_y / a_x + m_y = 8/2 + 8 = 8/10

X = 80% Y = 20%

Example 7

The data are as follows

Year	Stock	Return
1	O	10
1	Q	12
2	O	16
2	Q	18

1. What is Expected Return on a portfolio made up of 40% O and 60% Q?
2. What is the standard deviation of each stock?
3. What is the co-variance of O and Q?
4. Determine coefficient of correlation of Stocks O and Q.
5. What is the portfolio risk made up of 40% O and 60% Q?

To find out Expected Return:

(40/100)(10+16)/2 + (60/10) (12+18)/2 = 14.2%

O (x - x) (x^2) Q (x – x) (x^2)

10 –3 9 12 –3

16 +3 9 18 +3 9

26 18 30 18

E (Er) = 26/2 = 13

$\sqrt{\frac{Ex^2}{N}}$ = √18/2= or=3

E (Ri) = 30/2 =15

$\sqrt{\frac{Ex^2}{N}}$ √18/2= as=3

Security	Return	Expected Return	Difference	Product
Stock O	10	14.2	-4.2	9.24
Stock Q	12	14.2	-2.2	
Stock O	16	14.2	+1.8	
Stock R	18	14.2	+3.8	6.84

Co-variance = ½ (10) – 14.2) (12-14.2) + ½ (16 – 14.2) (18 – 14.2)

= ½ (-4.2) (-2.2) + ½ (1.2) (3.2) = ½ (9.24) + ½ (6.84) = 4.62 +3.42 = 8.04

Correlation

$$\Upsilon_{OQ} = +8.04/\ (3)\ (3)$$
$$= 8.04/9 = 8.93$$

Correlation co-efficient is positive to a high degree. The risk in such a portfolio is very high.

Markowitz's programmer shows the combination of securities where standard deviation of the portfolio is the minimum. In this example, the programmer is developed for a combination of two securities, but the basic purpose of this quadratic equation programmer is to have a large number of combinations of portfolios which give the lowest risk between the limits of zero and infinity. To summaries the above, Markowitz's theory of portfolio diversification attaches importance to (a) standard deviation, i.e., when portfolio=0, risk is minimum, (b) co-variance – to show interactive risk, (c) coefficient of correlation, i.e., when x = - 1, the risk of investment should be the lowest, also $\Upsilon\theta_x\theta_y$ = co-variance, (d) the weights or proportion of each security in the total portfolio to give the ideal combination. It can be found by the formula.

$$Xx = \sigma y \sigma x + m_y$$

Thus, when

$$X_x = 3/6 + 3 = 3/9 = .33\ (1\text{-}Xx) = .67$$

Sometimes, the total portfolio is changed. In this case, the effect is also on the change in the proportion of risk. The example given below will clarify this concept.

Example 8

Stock-X	Stock-Y	Portfolio Standard Deviation
100	0	2.0
80	20	0.8
66	34	0.0
20	80	2.8
0	100	4.0

In this example, the ideal combination is 66% and 34% and = 0. When two securities are combined and one is in 50% proportion and the other in 50%, proportion and the co-efficient of correlation is positive, then the risk of the two securities which is the weighted sum of the individual standard deviations as shown below will be the same as the standard deviation of securities when calculated independently. Also, the smaller the correlation, the greater or better the results of diversifying two securities. Standard deviation of securities but correlation co-efficient should be less than the ratio of the smaller standard deviation compared by the larger standard deviation.

In situation 1

A

Ry < ---

Be for example

$- 1.00 < \frac{2}{4}$

$- 1.00 < + .50$

In situation 2

$Ry = + .80$

$+ .80 > \frac{2}{4}$

$+ .80 > + .50$

There is no portfolio effect.

RISK RETURN IN A THIRD SECURITY

The portfolio effect of two securities is also applied to three securities to find out the effect on the portfolio. It is done through the method of standard deviation of returns, correlation coefficient and the proportion in which security which is invested. The following is the formula. It is similar to the two security formulae.

$$R_p = \sum_{I=1}^{N} X_i R_I$$

The standard deviation of the portfolio determines the deviation of the returns and the correlation co-efficient of the proportion of securities that are invested.

$$\sigma^2 p = \sum_{I=1}^{N} Xi\ Xj\ rij\ \sigma_i \sigma_j \quad \text{(Or)}$$

$$\text{Portfolio risk} = \sigma_p = \sqrt{X_1^2\sigma_R^2 + X_2^2\sigma_S^2 + 2X_1X_2(r_{12}\sigma_1\sigma_2)}$$

I =1

$\sigma^2 p$ = portfolio variance (expected) = σ^2 / P = portfolio standard deviation

Xi = proportion of portfolio which is invested in security I

Ax = proportion of portfolio which is invested in security j

Raj = co-efficient of correlation between I and j

I = standard deviation of I,

N = Total number of securities

j = standard deviation of j

Example 9

(A). What is the expected Return to a Portfolio composed of the following securities?

Security	Expected Return %	Proportion %
1	10	20
2	15	20
3	20	60

(B). What would be the expected return if the proportion of each security in the portfolio were 25, 25, and 50% respectively?

(a) $R = R_1 X_1 + R_2 X_2 + R_3 X_3$

$= 10(.20) + 15(.20) = 20(.60) \quad = 2.00 + 3.00 + 12.00 = 17\%$

(b) $R = R_1 X_1 + R_2 X_2 + R_3 X_3$

$= 10(.25) + 15(.25) = 20(.50) = 2.50 + 3.75 + 10.00 = 16.25\%$

Example 10

Compute the risk on each portfolio from the following information.

Security	Expected Return %	Proportion %
1	10	20
2	15	20
3	20	60

Standard Deviation	Co-efficient of Correlation
0 = 0.2	r12 = 0.5
0 = 0.3	r13 = 0.1
0 = 0.5	r23 =-0.3
R = 17%	

$$\sigma^2 p = X^2 1\, Q^2 1 + X^2 2\, \sigma^2 2 + X^2 3\, \sigma^2 3 + 2X1\, X2\, \gamma_{12}\, \sigma_1\, \sigma_2$$

$$= 2X_2\, X_3\, r2.3\, \sigma_2\, \sigma_3 + 2X_1\, X_3\, \gamma_{13}\, \sigma_1\, \sigma_3$$

$$\sigma^2 p = (.20)^2 (0.2)^2 + (.20)^2 (0.3)^2 + (.60)^2 (0.5)^2 + 2(.2)(.2)(.6)$$

$$(.2)(.3) + 2(.2)(.6)(.3)(.5) + 2(.2)(.6)(.2)(.5)(-.3)$$

$= .0016 + .0036 + .09 + .00108 + .0024$

$= .097840 - .001080$

$= .096760$

$= .309$

Portfolio risk = +.3

SELECTING THE BEST PORTFOLIO

Establishing the best portfolio (minimum risk for a given expected return) comprising board classes of assets e.g. stock bonds and real state lends itself to the mean variance methodology suggested Markowitz. Determining efficient portfolios within asset class can be achieved with the single index (beta) model proposed Sharpe. It is imperative to remember that outcomes are sensitive, as to the validity of inputs. It is possible to develop a fairly simple fission rule for selecting an optimal portfolio for an investor that can take both risk and return into account. This is called risk adjustment return. For simplification, it can be termed utility of portfolio for the investor in the question. Utility is the expected return of the portfolio minus a risk penalty. This risk penalty depends on portfolio risk and the investor risk tolerance.

The more risk one can bar, the more undesirable is an additional unit of risk. Theoretically, and as a computation convenience, it can be assumed that twice the risk is four times as undesirable. The risk penalty is as follows

Simple Markowitz Portfolio Optimization

Henry Markowitz has developed a decision rule for selecting an optimal best) portfolio for an investor that can take both risk and return into account this is called as risk adjusted rate/return. It can also be coined as utility. Utility is defined as expected returns minus risk penalty. i.e

Utility = [Expected Returns on Portfolio – Risk Penalty Price]

Here risk penalty depends upon portfolio risk and the investor's risk.

Risk Penalty = **Risk penalty = Risk Squared/ risk tolerance**

Note: According to Markowitz Approach, the Optimal (Best) Portfolio for an investor would be the one from the opportunity set Efficient Frontier) that Maximizes Utility.

Risk is squared is the variance of return of the portfolio. Risk tolerance is a number from zero through 100. The size of the risk tolerance number reflects the investor willingness to bear more risk for more return. Low tolerance indicates low willingness. Risk penalty is less or tolerance is increased.

Example: If a portfolio's expected return is 13 percent, variance of return is 225 percent, and the investor risk tolerance is 50, risk penalty is 4.5 percent.

Risk penalty = <u>225%</u> = 4.5%

Since utility is expected return minus the risk penalty, we have

Utility = 13-4.5 = 8.5%

The optimal (best) portfolio for an investor would be the one from the opportunity set (efficient frontier) that maximizes utility.

There are number of studies in the field of behavioral psychology that strongly suggest why investing is uncomfortable. Finding reveal that value is often the product of investor's stress and anxiety caused by framing investments as probable losses. Work in this field encompasses two broad areas. The first is called theory which reveals how people react to judgments about uncertain events when the probability of events is defined. The other area is called heuristics (to find out). Studies in this area investigate how people process information about the future to try to establish a range of possibilities for likely events. The remarkable insights that emerge from this work are that both of these cognitive processes i.e. establishing a sense of probability of future events and reacting to them reveal systematic biases of distortions.

It is no surprise that stock market investing dominated by our orientation toward future events, is emotional and therefore subject to cognitive biases. The psychology of the stock market is based on how investors from judgments about uncertain future events and how they react to these judgments. One of the most important findings of prospect theory is that people do not react consistently when faced with risk. Instead, they exhibit certain systematic biases. Let's explore a series of examples to illustrate.

The disproportionality of people tolerance for loses as compared to the pleasure of gains, can lead to inefficiencies in the stock market. With great frequency, investors find reasons to become intensely afraid of various sectors of the economy, particularly industry groups and specific companies. The prices of troubled stock present opportunities for the investor who can stomach the discomfort caused by the possibility of probable loss. Excess return inherent in these stocks is being paid to you by the seller to relieve him of the stress of ownership. The stress being generated by the perceived possibility of substantial loss.

SINGLE INDEX MODEL

Casual observation of the stock prices over a period of time reveals that most of the stock prices move with the market index. When Sensex increases, stock prices also tend to increase and vice- versa. This indicates that some underlying factors affect the market index as well as the stock prices. Stock prices are related to the market index and the relationship could be used to estimate the return on stock. Towards this purpose, the following equation can be used.

$$Ri = R_f + (R_M - R_F)\beta$$

Where Ri = Expected return on security

∞ = Intercept of the straight line or alpha co-efficient

β = Slope of straight line or beta co-efficient

R_m = The rate of return on marker index

R_f = Risk free asset

CORNER PORTFOLIO

The entry or exit of a new stock in the portfolio generates a series of corner portfolio. In a one stock portfolio, itself is the corner portfolio. In a two-stock portfolio, the minimum attainable risk (variance) and the lowest return would be the corner portfolio. As the member of stocks increases in a portfolio, the corner portfolio would be the one with lowest return and risk combination.

SHARPE'S OPTIMAL PORTFOLIO

Sharpe has provided a model for the selection of appropriate securities in a portfolio. The selection of any stock is directly related to its excess return – beta ration.

$$Ri - Rf / \beta$$

Where,

Ri = The expected return on stock i

Rf = The return on a risk less asset

β = The expected change in the rate of return on stock I associated with one unit changer in the market return.

The excess return is the difference between the expected return on the stock and the risk less rate of interest such as the rate offered on the government security or Treasury bill. The excess return to beta ratio measures the additional return on security (excess of the risk less asset return) per unit of systematic risk or non-diversifiable risk. This ratio provides a relationship between potential risk and reward. The construction of an optimal portfolio is simplified if there is a single number that measures the desirability of including a stock in the optimal portfolio. If we accept the single index model (Sharpe), such a number exists. In this case, the desirability of any stock is directly related to its excess return-to-beta ratio.

If stocks are ranked by excess return to beta (from highest to lowest), the ranking represents the desirability of any stock inclusion in a portfolio. The number of stocks selected depends on a unique cut off rate such that all stocks with higher ratios of (R1-Rf)/Bi will be included and all socks with lower ratios excluded

To determine which stocks are included in the optimum portfolio, the following steps are necessary:

1. Calculate the excess return-to-beta ratio for each stock under review and the rank from highest to lowest.
2. The optimum portfolio consists of investing in all stocks for which (R1-Rf)/Bi is greater than a particular cut-off point C*.

RANKING SECURITIES

It is the normal output generated from a single index model plus the ratio of excess return to beta. There are ten securities already ranked based on Sharpe's model. Selecting the optimal portfolio involves the comparison of (R1-Rf)/Bi with C. For the moment, assume that C=5.45. Examining Table-6 shows that for securities 1 to 5, (R1-Rf)/B1 is greater than C while for security 6 it is less than C. Hence, an optimal portfolio consists of securities 1 to 5.

Establishing Cut-Off Rate

All securities whose excess return-to-risk ratio are above the cut-off rate are selected and all whose ratios are above the cut-off rate are selected and all whose ratios are below are rejected. The value of C is computed from the characteristics of all the securities that belong in the optimum portfolio. Suppose C is a candidate for Cu. The value of Cu is calculated when I securities are assumed to belong to the optimal portfolio. Since securities are ranked from highest excess return to beta to lowest, we know that if a particular security belongs in the optimal portfolio.

Stocks are related by excess return to beta (from highest to lowest) the ranking represent the desirability of any stocks inclusion in a portfolio the number of stocks selected depends upon a unique CUTOFF RATE such that, all stocks with higher ration of $(R_i\text{-}R_f)/B_i$ will be included and all stocks with lower ratios excluded.

For finding C*, we need to calculate C_i for each security which is given by the following formula:

$$C_i = \sigma_m^2 \frac{\sum_{i=1}^{n} \frac{(R_i - R_f)\beta_i}{\sigma_{ei}^2}}{1 + \sigma_m^2 \sum_{i=1}^{n} \frac{\beta^2}{\sigma_{ei}^2}}$$

Where

σ2m = variance in the market index

σ2ei = variance of a stock's movement that is not associated with the movement of the market index (unsystematic risk).

After knowing, which stocks to be included in the optimal portfolio, we must calculate the proportion of each of these securities to be invested in the optimal portfolio. This is calculated by using the following formula

$$X_i = \frac{Z_i}{\sum_{i=1}^{n} Z_i}$$

$$Z_i = \frac{\beta_i}{\sigma_{ei}^2}\left[\frac{(R_i - R_f)}{\beta_i} - C^*\right]$$

The first expression indicates the weights on each security and they sum up to one. The second shows the relative investment in each security. The residual variance or the unsystematic risk has a role in determining the amount to be invested in each security.

1. From the following data is given bellow find out the optimal portfolio and the proportion of securities invested in the optimal portfolio. $R_f = 5\%$ and $\sigma^2_m = 10\%$

Securities	Market Return	σ^2_{ei}	β
1	15	50	1
2	17	40	1.5
3	12	20	1
4	17	10	2
5	11	40	1
6	11	30	1.5
7	11	40	2
8	7	16	.8
9	7	20	1
10	5.6	6	0.6

Solution

Security	$R_i - R_f$	$\frac{(R_i - R_f)}{\beta_i}$	Rank
1	10	10	1
2	12	8	2
3	7	7	3
4	12	6	4
5	6	6	5
6	6	4	6
7	6	3	7
8	2	2.5	8
9	2	2	9
10	0.6	1	10

Security	$\frac{(R_i - R_f)}{\beta_i}$	$\frac{(R_i - R_f)\beta_i}{\sigma^2_{ei}}$	$\frac{\beta^2}{\sigma^2_{ei}}$	$\sum_{i=1}^{n}\frac{(R_i - R_f)\beta_i}{\sigma^2_{ei}}$	$\sum_{i=1}^{n}\frac{\beta^2}{\sigma^2_{ei}}$	$C_i = \frac{\sigma^2_m \sum_{i=1}^{n}\frac{(R_i - R_f)\beta_i}{\sigma^2_{ei}}}{1+\sigma^2_m \sum_{i=1}^{n}\frac{\beta^2}{\sigma^2_{ei}}}$
1	10	0.2	0.02	0.2	0.02	1.667
2	8	.45	0.056	0.65	0.0762	3.689
3	7	0.35	0.05	1.00	0.126	4.424
4	6	2.4	0.4	3.4	0.526	5.43
5	6	0.15	0.025	3.55	0.5512	5.45 **C***
6	4	0.3	0.075	3.85	0.626	5.30
7	3	0.3	0.1	4.15	0.726	5.02
8	2.5	0.1	0.04	4.25	0.766	4.91
9	2	0.1	0.05	4.35	0.816	4.75
10	1	0.06	0.06	4.41	0.876	4.52

$$C_i = \sigma_m^2 \frac{\sum_{i=1}^{n} \frac{(R_i - R_f)\beta_i}{\sigma_{ei}^2}}{1 + \sigma_m^2 \sum_{i=1}^{n} \frac{\beta^2}{\sigma_{ei}^2}} \qquad C^* = 5.45$$

The highest Ci value is taken as the cut-off point i.e. C*. The stocks ranked above to beta than cut-off Ci and all the e C* have excess returns to beta. Here, the cut-off rate is 5.45. Hence, the first four securities are selected. If the number of stocks is larger there is no need to calculate Ci values for all the stocks after the ranking has been done. It can be calculated until the C* value is found and after calculating for one or two stocks below it, the calculations can be terminated. The Ci can be stated with mathematically equivalent way.

Construction of the optimal Portfolio

After determining the securities to be selected, the portfolio manager find out how much should be invested in each security. The presenting of funds to be invested in each security can be estimated as follows

$$Z_i = \frac{\beta_i}{\sigma_{ei}^2}\left[\frac{(R_i - R_f)}{\beta_i} - C^*\right] \qquad X_i = \frac{Z_i}{\sum_{i=1}^{n} Z_i}$$

The first expression indicates the weights on each security and they sum up to one. The second shows the relative investment in each security. The residual variance or the unsystematic risk has a role in determining the amount to be invested in each security.

$$Z_{i_1} = 1/30(10 - 5.45) = 0.091 \qquad X_{i1} = \frac{0.091}{0.38725} * 100 = 23.5\%$$

$$Z_{i2} = 1.5/40(8 - 5.45) = 0.095 \qquad X_{i2} = \frac{0.095}{0.38725} * 100 = 24.53\%$$

$$Z_{i3} = 1/20(7 - 5.45) = 0.775 \qquad X_{i3} = \frac{0.0775}{0.38725} * 100 = 20.013\%$$

$$Z_{i4} = 2/10(6 - 5.45) = 0.110$$

$$X_{i4} = \frac{0.110}{0.38725} * 100 = 28.4\%$$

$$Z_{i5} = 1/40(6 - 5.45) = 0.01375 \qquad X_{i5} = \frac{0.01375}{0.38725} * 100 = 3.55\%$$

0.38725

Results: Thus, the proportion to be invested in different securities are obtained. The largest investment should be made in security 4 and the smallest in security 5.

2. From the following data is given bellow find out the optimal portfolio and the proportion of securities invested in the optimal portfolio. $R_f = 8\%$ and $\sigma_m^2 = 12\%$

Securities	Market Return	β	σ_{ei}^2
a.	20	1	40
b.	18	2.5	35
c.	12	1.5	30
d.	16	1	35
e.	14	0.8	25
f.	10	1.2	15
g.	17	1.6	30
h.	15	2	35

Solution

Security	$R_i - R_f$	$\frac{(R_i - R_f)}{\beta_i}$	Rank
A	12	12	1
B	10	4	5
C	4	2.67	7
D	8	8	2
E	6	7.5	3
F	2	1.67	8
G	9	5.625	4
H	7	3.5	6

Security	$\frac{(R_i - R_f)}{\beta_i}$	$\frac{(R_i - R_f)\beta_i}{\sigma_{ei}^2}$	$\frac{\beta^2}{\sigma_{ei}^2}$	$\sum_{i=1}^{n}\frac{(R_i - R_f)\beta_i}{\sigma_{ei}^2}$	$\sum_{i=1}^{n}\frac{\beta^2}{\sigma_{ei}^2}$	$C_i = \sigma_m^2 \frac{\sum_{i=1}^{n}\frac{(R_i - R_f)\beta_i}{\sigma_{ei}^2}}{1+\sigma_m^2\sum_{i=1}^{n}\frac{\beta^2}{\sigma_{ei}^2}}$
A	12	0.3	0.025	0.3	0.025	2.769
D	8	0.29	0.029	0.529	0.054	3.851
E	7.5	0.192	0.0256	0.721	0.0796	4.43
G	5.63	0.48	0.0853	1.201	0.1649	4.836 c*
B	4	0.71	0.179	1.915	0.344	4.4812
H	3.5	0.4	0.114	2.315	0.4579	4.277
C	2.67	0.2	0.075	2.515	0.5329	4.081
F	1.67	0.114	0.096	2.629	0.6289	3.755

$$C_i = \sigma_m^2 \frac{\sum_{i=1}^{n} \frac{(R_i - R_f)\beta_i}{\sigma_{ei}^2}}{1 + \sigma_m^2 \sum_{i=1}^{n} \frac{\beta^2}{\sigma_{ei}^2}} \qquad c^* = 4.836$$

$$Z_i = \frac{\beta_i}{\sigma_{ei}^2}\left[\frac{(R_i - R_f)}{\beta_i} - C^*\right] \qquad X_i = \frac{Z_i}{\sum_{i=1}^{n} Z_i}$$

$$Z_{iA} = 1/40(12 - 4.836) = 0.1791 \qquad X_{iA} = \frac{0.1791}{0.3963} * 100 = 45.15\%$$

$$Z_{iD} = 1/35(8 - 4.836) = 0.060 \qquad X_{iD} = \frac{0.09}{0.3963} * 100 = 22.91\%$$

$$Z_{iE} = 0.8/25(7.5 - 4.836) = 0.0853 \qquad X_{iE} = \frac{0.0853}{0.3963} * 100 = 21.50\%$$

$$Z_{iG} = 1.6/30(5.63 - 4.836) = 0.0423 \qquad X_{iG} = \frac{0.0423}{0.3963} * 100 = 10.66\%$$

0.3967

Results: Thus, the proportion to be invested in different securities are obtained. The largest investment should be made in security 4 and the smallest in security 5.

Optimum Portfolio with Short Sales

The procedure used to calculate the optimal portfolio when short sales are allowed is, more or less similar to the procedure adopted for no short sales, expect the cut-off point concept. At first, the stocks have to be ranked by excess return to beta. Here, all the stocks are added to the portfolio. They are either held long or short. All the stocks affect the cut-off point. The Z value has to be calculated for each stock. If the Z value is positive, the stock will be held long and if negative, it will be short. Stocks which are having excess return to beta above C* are held as in the case of the portfolio without short sales. Stocks with an excess return to beta below C* are sold short. In the case of previous example C* = Cut-off = 3.755, if the short are permitted, then

3. Mr. Madan is constructing an optimal portfolio the market return forecast $\sigma_m^2 = 13.5\%$ for the next 2yrs with the market variance of $\sigma_m^2 = 10\%$ rate of return $R_f = 5\%$ from the following details select the optimal portfolio.

Securities	Market Return	β	σ^2_{ei}
A	17.09	0.99	9.35
B	17.75	1.27	5.92
C	13.37	0.96	9.79
D	16.12	1.21	5.39
E	10.58	0.75	4.52

Solution

Security	$\frac{(R_i - R_f)}{\beta_i}$	Rank
A	12.21	1
B	10.019	2
C	8.7188	4
D	9.1901	3
E	7.44	5

Security	$\frac{(R_i - R_f)}{\beta_i}$	$\frac{(R_i - R_f)\beta_i}{\sigma^2_{ei}}$	$\frac{\beta^2}{\sigma^2_{ei}}$	$\sum_{i=1}^{n}\frac{(R_i - R_f)\beta_i}{\sigma^2_{ei}}$	$\sum_{i=1}^{n}\frac{\beta^2}{\sigma^2_{ei}}$	$C_i = \sigma^2_m \frac{\sum_{i=1}^{n}\frac{(R_i - R_f)\beta_i}{\sigma^2_{ei}}}{1+\sigma^2_m\sum_{i=1}^{n}\frac{\beta^2}{\sigma^2_{ei}}}$
A	12.21	1.28	0.105	1.280	0.1048	6.25
B	10.039	2.735	0.272	4.015	0.3772	8.4136
D	9.7188	0.8207	0.094	4.8357	0.4713	8.464
C	8.7183	2.496	0.271	7.3314	0.7429	8.678 C*
E	7.44	0.926	0.124	8.2577	0.8673	8.537

$$C_i = \sigma^2_m \frac{\sum_{i=1}^{n}\frac{(R_i - R_f)\beta_i}{\sigma^2_{ei}}}{1+\sigma^2_m\sum_{i=1}^{n}\frac{\beta^2}{\sigma^2_{ei}}} \qquad C^*=8.678$$

$$Z_i = \frac{\beta_i}{\sigma^2_{ei}}\left[\frac{(R_i - R_f)}{\beta_i} - C^*\right] \qquad X_i = \frac{Z_i}{\sum_{i=1}^{n} Z_i}$$

$$Z_{iA} = 0.99/9.35(12.21 - 8.698) = 0.372 \qquad X_{iA} = \frac{0.372}{0.3963} * 100 = 48.18\%$$

$$Z_{iB} = 1.27/5.92(10.090 - 8.698) = 0.2876 \qquad X_{iB} = \frac{002876}{0.7721} * 100 = 37.25\%$$

$$Z_{iD} = 0.96/9.79(8.7188 - 8.698) = 0.002 \qquad X_{iD} = \frac{0.1105}{0.7721} * 100 = 14.31\%$$

$Z_{iC} = 1.21/5.39(9.1901 - 8.698) = 0.1105$

$X_{iC} = \dfrac{0.002}{0.7721} * 100 = 0.26\%$

0.7721

4. Mohan received Rs.10 lakhs for his pension fund. He wants to invest in the stock market the treasure bill rate is 5% and the market return variance is 10%. The following table gives the regarding the return. What is the optimum portfolio assuming short sales or short sales?

Securities	Market Return	β	σ^2_{ei}
A.	22	1	35
B.	20	2.5	40
C.	14	1.5	30
D.	18	1.0	80
E.	16	0.8	20
F.	12	1.2	10
G.	19	1.6	30
H.	17	2.0	35

Solution

Security	$\dfrac{(R_i - R_f)}{\beta_i}$	Rank
A	17	1
B	6	5
C	6	6
D	13	3
E	13.75	2
F	5.83	8
G	8.75	4
H	6	7

Security	$\dfrac{(R_i - R_f)}{\beta_i}$	$\dfrac{(R_i - R_f)\beta_i}{\sigma^2_{ei}}$	$\dfrac{\beta^2}{\sigma^2_{ei}}$	$\sum_{i=1}^{n}\dfrac{(R_i - R_f)\beta_i}{\sigma^2_{ei}}$	$\sum_{i=1}^{n}\dfrac{\beta^2}{\sigma^2_{ei}}$	$C_i = \sigma^2_m \dfrac{\sum_{i=1}^{n}\dfrac{(R_i - R_f)\beta_i}{\sigma^2_{ei}}}{1+\sigma^2_m\sum_{i=1}^{n}\dfrac{\beta^2}{\sigma^2_{ei}}}$
A	17	0.486	0.029	0.486	0.029	3.77
E	13.75	0.44	0.156	0.926	0.185	3.25
D	13	0.1625	0.075	1.089	0.26	3.025
G	8.75	0.747	0.0125	1.836	0.273	4.92
B	6	0.938	0.032	2.774	0.305	6.85 C*
C	6	0.45	0.144	3.224	0.449	5.87
H	6	0.686	0.853	3.910	0.534	6.17
F	5.833	0.84	0.114	4.750	0.678	6.105

$$C_i = \sigma_m^2 \frac{\sum_{i=1}^{n} \frac{(R_i - R_f)\beta_i}{\sigma_{ei}^2}}{1 + \sigma_m^2 \sum_{i=1}^{n} \frac{\beta^2}{\sigma_{ei}^2}} \qquad c^*=6.85$$

$$Z_i = \frac{\beta_i}{\sigma_{ei}^2}\left[\frac{(R_i - R_f)}{\beta_i} - C^*\right]$$

$Z_{iA} = 1/35(12.21 - 6.85) = 0.294$ $\qquad$ $Z_{iH} = 2/35(6 - 6.85) = -0.0485$

$Z_{iD} = 1/80(13 - 6.85) = 0.077$ $\qquad$ $Z_{iF} = 0.8/20(5.83 - 6.85) = -0.047$

$Z_{iE} = 0.8/20(13.75 - 6.85) = 0.1105$ $\qquad$ $Z_{iC} = 1.5/30(6 - 6.85) = -0.0425$

$Z_{iG} = 1.6/30(8.75 - 6.85) = 0.1012$ $\qquad$ $Z_{iB} = 2.5/40(6 - 6.85) = -0.053$

MINIMUM VARIANCE PORTFOLIO

The change in portfolio proportions of assets can change portfolio risk. By skillful balancing of the investment proportions in different securities, the portfolio is termed as minimum variance portfolio. In a two asset portfolio composed of assets "a" and "b", the minimum risk portfolio requires an investment in asset "a" equal to Xa.

Where $\quad Xa = \sigma_b^2$ -Ƴab σa σb / $\sigma_b^2 + \sigma_b^2$ -2 Ƴab σa σb

If the correlation coefficient is less than the ratio of smaller standard deviation to larger standard deviation, when the combination of two securities provides a lesser standard deviation of return than when either of the security is taken alone.

Example: The splendors (s) and Kinetic(K) corporations have the following risk and return characteristics,

$\bar{R}_s$=16 , E(Rk) =14% , σs 25%, σk =22% , Ƴsk=0.5

Determine the minimum risk portfolio.

The proportion to invested in each security can be found out by

Xa = σ_k^2 -Ƴks σs σk / σ_s^2 + σ_k^2 2 Ƴsk σs σk

Let k = a and s = b results in, $\dfrac{(25)^2 - (.5)(22)(25)}{(25)^2 + (25)^2 - (2(0.5)(22)(25))}$

$$\frac{625 - 275}{484 + 625 - 550} = \frac{350}{559} = 0.6261 \text{ or } 62.61\%$$

Investment in Kinetic corporation= 62.61% and in Splendor.

x_b= 1- x_a =1-0.6261=0.3739=39.39%

If correlation coefficient is perfectly +1, 0, -1, the above formula for weight can be rewritten as follows.

ϒab=+1

Xa = σ_k^2 -ϒks σs σk / σ_s^2 + σ_k^2 2 ϒsk σs σk

ϒab=0

$$Xa = \frac{\sigma_b^2}{\sigma_a^2 + \sigma_b^2}$$

γ_{ab}=-1

$$Xa \frac{\sigma_b}{\sigma_a + \sigma_b}$$

Consider two asset portfolio A ans B

σa = 14% σb =16%

Correlation between A and B is +1, 0, -1.

Determine minimum risk portfolio for A and B

Calculation of weight

γ_{ab}=+1

Xa = σ_k^2 -ϒks σs σk / σ_s^2 + σ_k^2 2 ϒsk σs σk

$$\frac{(256)-(224)}{(196)+(256)-(256)} = 32/4 = 8$$

x_B 1- x_A = 1-8 =7%

Calculation of weight, If $\gamma_{ab} = 0$

$$Xa = \frac{\sigma_b^2}{\sigma_a^2 + \sigma_b^2} =$$

256/ 196+256= 256/452=0.57

x_b= 1-0.57=0.43

Calculation of weight,

If $\gamma_{ab} = -1$ $\quad$ $Xa = \dfrac{\sigma_b}{\sigma_a + \sigma_b}$ = 16/14+16 =16/30 = 0.53

$x_B =$

1- x_A = 1-.53%=0.47

P ltd and Q ltd. Have correlation coefficient of +0.6 their respective return and risk is as under:

R_p=12%

R_q=17%

$\sigma_p = 22\%$

$\sigma_q = 27\%$

Compute the portfolio of P&Q in order to minimize risk

Let proportion of investment (or weight of securities) in P Ltd. And Q Ltd. Be W_p and W_q respectively. Then, in order to minimize risk we have:

$$W_P = \frac{\sigma_Q^2 - r_{PQ}\,\sigma_P\sigma_Q}{\sigma_P^2 + \sigma_Q^2 - (2r_{PQ}\,\sigma_P\sigma_q)}$$

$$= \frac{(0.27)^2 - 0.6 * 0.22 * 0.27}{(0.22)^2 + (0.27)^2 - 2 * 0.6 * 0.22 * 0.27}$$

$$= \frac{0.073 - 0.036}{0.048 + 0.073 - 0.071}$$

$$= \frac{0.037}{0.05} = \boxed{0.074}$$

$$W_Q = 1 - 0.7 = 0.26 = \boxed{26\%}$$

SUMMARY

1. Essentiality of the Markowitz portfolio theory is the problem of optimal portfolio selection. The Markowitz approach included portfolio formation by considering the expected rate of return and risk of individual stocks measured as standard deviation, and their interrelationship as measured by correlation. The diversification plays a key role in the modern portfolio theory.

2. Indifference curves represent an investor's preferences for risk and return. These curves should be drawn, putting the investment return on the vertical axis and the risk on the horizontal axis.
3. Two important fundamental assumptions than applying indifference curves to Markowitz portfolio theory. An assumption of no satiation assumes that the investors prefer higher levels of return to lower levels of return, because the higher levels of return allow the investor to spend more on consumption at the end of the investment period. An assumption of risk aversion assumes that the investor when given the choice, will choose the investment or investment portfolio with the smaller risk, i.e. the investors are risk averse.

MULTIPLE CHOICE QUESTIONS

1. According to Markowitz, rational investors will seek efficient portfolios because these portfolios are optimal based on:
   a. Expected return.
   b. Risk.
   c. Expected return and risk.
   d. Transactions costs.
2. Under the Markowitz model, investors:
   a. Are assumed to be risk-seekers.
   b. Are not allowed to use leverage.
   c. Are assumed to be institutional investors.
   d. All of the above.
3. Which of the following is not one of the assumptions of portfolio theory?
   a. Liquidity of positions.
   b. Investor preferences are based only on expected return and risk.
   c. Low transactions costs.
   d. A single investment period.
4. The Markowitz model assumes most investors are:
   a. Risk averse.
   b. Risk neutral.
   c. Risk seekers.
   d. Risk moderators.
5. An indifference curve shows:
   a. The one most desirable portfolio for a particular investor.
   b. All combinations of portfolios that are equally desirable to a particular investor.
   c. All combinations of portfolios that are equally desirable to all investors.
   d. The one most desirable portfolio for all investors.

6. Which of the following statements regarding indifference curves is not true?
   a. Investors have a finite number of indifference curves.
   b. The greater the slope of the indifference curve, the greater the risk aversion of investors.
   c. The indifference curves for all risk-averse investors will be upward sloping.
   d. Indifference curves cannot intersect.
7. The optimal portfolio for a risk-averse investor:
   a. Cannot be determined.
   b. Occurs at the point of tangency between the highest indifference curve and the highest expected return.
   c. Occurs at the point of tangency between the highest indifference curve and the efficient set of portfolios.
   d. Occurs at the point of tangency between the highest expected return and lowest risk efficient portfolios.
8. Indifference curves reflect ------------- while the efficient set of portfolios represent ---------------.
   a. Portfolio possibilities; investor preferences.
   b. Investor preferences; portfolio possibilities.
   c. Portfolio return; investor risk.
   d. Investor preferences; portfolio return.
9. According to Markowitz, an efficient portfolio is one that has the
   a. Largest expected return for the smallest level of risk.
   b. Largest expected return and zero risk.
   c. Largest expected return for a given level of risk.
   d. Smallest level of risk.
10. Portfolios lying on the upper right portion of the efficient frontier are likely to be chosen by
    a. Aggressive investors.
    b. Conservative investors.
    c. Risk-averse investors.
    d. Defensive investors.
11. A portfolio which lies below the efficient frontier is described as
    a. Optimal.
    b. Unattainable.
    c. Dominant.
    d. Dominated.

12. The optimal portfolio is the efficient portfolio with the
    a. Lowest risk.
    b. Highest risk.
    c. Highest utility.
    d. Least investment.
13. Indifference curves:
    a. Always curve to the left.
    b. Have a negative slope.
    c. Cannot intersect.
    d. All of the above.
14. Correlations among country returns have ____ since 1995.
    a. Increased.
    b. Decreased.
    c. Disappeared.
    d. Become more volatile.
15. Different investors will estimate the inputs to the Markowitz model differently because:
    a. Very investor has his/her own risk/return preferences.
    b. Every investor has access to different information about securities.
    c. There is an inherent uncertainty in security analysis.
    d. There is a random selection process used by individual investors.
16. Which of the following is not true regarding the Markowitz theory?
    a. Markowitz portfolio theory is considered a three-parameter model.
    b. Under the Markowitz model, no portfolio on the efficient frontier dominates any other portfolio on the efficient frontier.
    c. The Markowitz model is cumbersome to work with due to the large Variance-covariance matrix needed for a set of stocks.
    d. All of the above are true.
17. How many pieces of data does the single-index model require for a universe of 500 securities?
    a. 1002
    b. 1502
    c. 500
    d. 502
18. The single index model divides a security's return into _______ and _________ parts.
    a. Supply; demand
    b. Control; non-control
    c. Company-related; industry-related
    d. Micro; macro
19. Market risk is best measured by the:
    a. Alpha
    b. Beta
    c. Standard deviation
    d. Coefficient of variation

20. Choose the portfolio from the following set that is not on the efficient frontier.
    a. A: Expected return of 10 percent; standard deviation of 8 percent.
    b. B: Expected return of 18 percent; standard deviation of 13 percent
    c. C: Expected return of 38 percent; standard deviation of 38 percent.
    d. D: Expected return of 15 percent; standard deviation of 14 percent.

21. The single-index model implies that stocks covary together only because of their common:
    a. Currency.
    b. Relationship to each other.
    c. Relationship to the market.
    d. Desire to make a profit.

22. With the Single-index model, the difference between actual return and expected return given a particular market index is referred to as the:
    a. Parameter.
    b. Unique part.
    c. Error term.
    d. Beta.

23. Under the Multi-Index Model, the industry relationship to stock prices would be assessed by the:
    a. Market factor.
    b. Nonmarket factor.
    c. Beta.
    d. Unique part.

24. To implement the single-index model, estimates of the _______for each stock are needed.
    a. Expected return
    b. Standard deviation
    c. Beta
    d. Covariance

25. Asset allocation is one of the most widely used applications of:
    a. The Capital Asset Pricing Model.
    b. Random diversification.
    c. Passive portfolio approach.
    d. The modern portfolio theory.

26. A major argument against international diversification is that:
    a. Foreign stocks have higher risks than U.S. stocks on average.
    b. Foreign stocks tend to fall more in declining markets than U.S. stocks.
    c. Foreign stocks have high correlation with U.S. stocks.
    d. Foreign stocks have higher transaction costs, on average, than U.S. stocks.

27. The only asset class to provide systematic protection against inflation is:
    a. Bonds.
    b. Real estate.
    c. Foreign stocks.
    d. TIPS

28. Which of the following statements is true regarding TIPS?
    a. As inflation changes, the interest rate on the bond is adjusted.
    b. The correlation between TIPS and the S&P 500 Index has often been negative.
    c. TIPS are more volatile than regular Treasury bonds of similar maturity.
    d. All of the above are true.

29. Based on recent history, an investor would probably have a lower risk level with a portfolio consisting of:
    a. All stocks.
    b. All bonds.
    c. Some stocks and some bonds.
    d. Impossible to tell.

30. Nonsystematic risk is also known as:
    a. Non diversifiable risk.
    b. Market risk.
    c. Random risk.
    d. Company-specific risk.

31. Which of the following would not be considered a source of systematic risk?
    a. A hostile takeover
    b. A rise in inflation
    c. A fall in GDP
    d. a panic on Wall Street

TRUE / FALSE

1. The Markowitz model selects the portfolio most appropriate for an individual investor. (False)
2. When using the Markowitz model, aggressive investors would select portfolios on the left end of the efficient frontier. (False)
3. Markowitz derived the efficient frontier as an upward-sloping straight line. (False)
4. A major assumption of the Markowitz model is that investors base their decisions strictly on expected return and risk factors. (True)
5. Under the Markowitz model, the risk of a portfolio is measured by the standard deviation. (True).
6. The single index model requires (3n+2) total pieces of data to implement. (True)
7. The Sharpe model was found to outperform the Markowitz model in longer time periods. (False)
8. Asset allocation accounts for less than 50 percent of the variance in quarterly returns for a typical pension fund. (False)
9. Bonds are rarely considered as one of the asset classes to hold in a diversified portfolio. (False)

10. It would be impossible to combine an asset allocation plan with Markowitz analysis. (False)
11. Real estate is an asset class that typically has little or no correlation with stocks. (True)
12. Based on recent research, it seems reasonable that approximately 10-20 securities are needed to ensure adequate diversification. (False)

SHORT ANSWER QUESTIONS

1. Risk Aversion
2. Indifference Curve
3. Capital Allocation
4. Risk-free Asset
5. Risky asset
6. Risk Reward Ratio
7. Passive Investment
8. Capital Market Line
9. Optimal Risky Portfolios
10. Portfolios of Two Risky Assets
11. Diversification and Portfolio Risk
12. Efficient Frontier with Many Risky Assets
13. Coefficient of Correlation
14. Risk Return in a Third Security
15. Selecting the Best Portfolio
16. Simple Markowitz Portfolio Optimization
17. Single Index Model
18. Corner Portfolio
19. Sharpe's Optimal Portfolio
20. Establishing Cut-Off Rate
21. Optimum Portfolio with Short Sales

ESSAY TYPE QUESTIONS

1. Bring out the assumption of capital market Theory? What is an efficient frontier? How does it establish an optimum portfolio?
2. How can an individual make an analysis of different curves to get the most beneficial portfolio?

3. How can we arrive at the optimum portfolio?
4. What is meant by levered portfolio/ how is it constructed?
5. How would you calculate the systematic, unsystematic risk of a security and the portfolio?

EXERCISE PROBLEMS

1. **From the following data is given bellow find out the optimal portfolio and the proportion of securities invested in the optimal portfolio.** $R_f = 5\%$ **and** $\sigma_m^2 = 10\%$

Securities	Market Return	σ_{ei}^2	β
11	12	60	2
12	15	50	2.5
13	14	30	2
14	18	30	2
15	16	50	1
16	15	60	3.5
17	17	50	1
18	9	36	.6
19	10	25	
20	7.6	8	0.8

2. **From the following data is given bellow find out the optimal portfolio and the proportion of securities invested in the optimal portfolio.** $R_f = 8\%$ **and** $\sigma_m^2 = 12\%$

Securities	Market Return	β	σ_{ei}^2
i.	24	1	46
j.	38	1.5	38
k.	22	2.5	34
l.	28	1	36
m.	19	0.6	28
n.	14	1.0	18
o.	19	1.4	35
p.	20	1	32

3. Mr. Vamsi. is constructing an optimal portfolio the market return forecast $\sigma_m^2 = 12.5\%$ for the next 2yrs with the market variance of $\sigma_m^2 = 10\%$ rate of return $R_f = 5\%$ from the following details select the optimal portfolio.

Securities	Market Return	β	σ_{ei}^2
A.	16.19	0.90	8.25
B.	15.95	1.25	4.42
C.	14.57	0.98	8.69
D.	18.22	1.24	7.69
E.	12.48	0.78	6.82

4. Mr. Raghav received Rs.10 lakhs for his pension fund. He wants to invest in the stock market the treasure bill rate is 5% and the market return variance is 10%. The following table gives the regarding the return. What is the optimum portfolio assuming short sales or short sales?

Securities	Market Return	β	σ_{ei}^2
I.	**28**	**1**	**30**
J.	**24**	**1.5**	**45**
K.	**19**	**2.5**	**35**
L.	**20**	**2.0**	**85**
M.	**19**	**0.9**	**25**
N.	**17**	**1.4**	**15**
O.	**24**	**1.9**	**35**
	19	**2.4**	**40**

MCQs Answers

1	2	3	4	5	6	7	8	9	10	11	12	13	14	15	16	17	18	19	20	21	22	23	24
c	b	d	a	b	a	c	b	c	a	d	c	c	d	c	a	b	d	b	d	c	c	b	c

25	26	27	28	29	30	31
d	c	d	b	c	d	a

CASE STUDIES

CASE STUDY 1

The new little-known firm is analyzed from the prospect of investments in its shares by two friends. The firm paid dividends last year Rs.3 per share. T and A examined the prices of similar stocks in the market and found that they provide 12 % expected return. The forecast of T is as follows: 4 % of growth in dividends indefinitely. The forecast of A is as follows: 10% of growth in dividends for the next two years, after which the growth rate is expected to decline to 3 % for the indefinite period.

(a) What is the intrinsic value of the stock of the firm according to Tomas forecast?

(b) What is the intrinsic value of the stock of the firm according to A forecast?

(c) If the stocks of this firm currently are selling in the market for Rs.40 per share, what would be the decisions of Tomas and A, based on their forecasting: is this stock attractive investment? Explain.

Look through the listed companies on the domestic stock exchange. What industries they represent? Would you be able to construct the stock portfolio applying sector rotation strategy in the domestic stock exchange?

CASE STUDY 2

Mr. Vamsi is a Wealth Manager working for a well-known Investment banker in India. One of his clients wishes to purchase 2 stocks, one related to technology (Asset T) and another banking stock (Asset B). The following is the forecast of returns on both the stocks during 4 phases of economy - High Growth, Low Growth, Stagnation and Recession.

State of	Probability	Return on asset T	Return on asset B
High growth	0.10	5%	0%
Low growth	0.30	10%	8%
Stagnation	0.50	15%	18%
Recession	0.10	20%	26%

- What is the standard deviation of the return on asset T and asset B?
- What is the covariance between the return on asset T and asset B?
- What is the coefficient of correlation between the returns on asset T and B?

CHAPTER 8

Fundamental Analysis

Fundamental analysis is an examination of future earnings potential of a company, by looking into various factors that impact the performance of the company. The prime objective of a fundamental analysis is to value the stock and accordingly buy and sell the stocks on the basis of its valuation in the market. The purpose of fundamental security analysis is to find out the "intrinsic value" of a security.

The intrinsic value is the true economic worth of a financial asset. According to fundamentalists, at any point of time every share has an intrinsic value which should in principle is equal to the present value of the future stream of income from that share discounted at an appropriate risk related rate of interest. The actual price of the security, therefore is considered to be a function of a set of anticipated capitalization rate. Price changes as anticipated changes which in turn change as a result of new information. In this analysis, the fundamentalists try to find out the real worth of a security by considering the earning potential of a firm which in turn will depend on investment environmental factors such as state and growth of national economy, monetary policies of the Reserve Bank of India, corporate laws, social and political environment and the factors relating to the specific industry such as state of product and the growth potential of the industry.

Fundamental analysis is a stock valuation methodology that uses financial and economic analysis to envisage the movement of stock prices. The fundamental data that is analysed could include a company's financial reports and non-financial information such as estimates of its growth, demand for products sold by the company, industry comparisons, economy-wide changes, changes in government policies etc.

The outcome of fundamental analysis is a value (or a range of values) of the stock of the company called its 'intrinsic value' (often called 'price target' in fundamental analysts' parlance). To a fundamental investor, the market price of a stock tends to revert towards its intrinsic value. If the intrinsic value of a stock is above the current market price, the investor would purchase the stock because he believes that the stock price would rise and move towards its intrinsic value. If the intrinsic value of a stock is below the market price, the investor would sell the stock because he believes that the stock price is going to fall and come closer to its intrinsic value.

To find the intrinsic value of a company, the fundamental analyst initially takes a top-down view of the economic environment; the current and future overall health of the economy as a whole. After the analysis of the *macro-economy,* the next step is to analyse the industry environment which the firm is operating in. One should analyses all the factors that give the firm a competitive advantage in its sector, such as, management experience, history of performance, growth potential, low cost of production, brand name etc.

Fundamental analysis is a method of finding out the future price of a stock which an investor wishes to buy. The method for forecasting the future behavior of investments and the rate of return on them is clearly through an analysis of the broad economic forces in which they operate, the kind of industry to which they belong and the analysis of the company's internal working through statements like income statement, balance sheet and statement of changes of income.

The fundamental analysis is done through

A. Economic Analysis

B. Industrial Analysis

C. Company Analysis.

A. ECONOMIC ANALYSIS

It is important to analyses the economic activity in which all the companies operate. The economic activity affects profits of a company, investor's attitude as well as expectations and, value of a security. Investors are concerned with those forces in the economy which affect the performance of organizations in which they wish to participate, through purchase of stock. In examination of the economic forces would give an idea about future corporate earnings and the payment of dividends and interest to investors. Some of the broad forces of the economic analysis includes the following.

ECONOMIC INDICATORS

Global Economy

The top-down analysis of a company starts with global and domestic economy **(growth rates of national income)**. the globalization affects a company's prospects of exports, price competition, and exchange rate.

Domestic Economy

GDP is the measure of the total production of goods and services in an economy. Growing GDP indicates an expanding economy. An Indian economy is affected by both agricultural production as well as industrial production and services. The good and normal monsoon indicates a good and normal agricultural production and increasing income of farmers and agricultural labour. Industrial production statistics reveals the status of industrial activity in the country.

The rate of the national income economy is an important variable. GNP (Gross National Products), NNP (Net National Income), and GDP (Gross Domestic Products) are the difference measures indicate growth rate of the economy. These estimates are made available by government. An economy typically passes through different phases, such as depression, recovery, boom and recession. During a depression, demand is low and declining inflation is often high and so are interest rate. During the recovery stage, the economy begins to receive after a depression. Demand picks up leading to more investment in the economy. In the boom phase, investment and production are maintained at a high level to satisfy high demand. In recession stage, the economy slowly begins to experience a downturn in demand, production, employment etc. the profits also declining.

POPULATION

Population provides labour potential in a country. In some countries like India and some other third world countries there has been a population explosion. Population encourages demand for more industries like hotels, residences, service industries like health, consumer demand like refrigerators and cars, increase in population, therefore, shows a greater need for economic development of the country. It does not show the exact industry which will be expanding but, in those countries, industries will have a generation of demand. Likewise, investors should prefer to invest in industries which have a large amount of labour force. Capital being rare in these countries the labour intensive industries will grow. And from the point of view of rate of return in the future such industries will bring better rates of return.

Employment: Unemployment rate is the percentage of the total labour force in the country. The unemployment rate indicates how the economy operates at full capacity.

Inflation is the rate at which the general level of prices is rising. High rate of inflation indicates economy is operating with full associated with demand for goods and services exceed production capacity. The government should try to trade-off between inflation rate and unemployment rate to increase the employment as well as decrease the inflation rate.

Inflation prevailing in the economy has considerable impact. Higher rates of inflation upset business plans, lead to cost escalation and result in a squeeze on profit margins. High rates of inflation in an economy are likely to affect the performance of companies. Inflation is measured both in terms of wholesale price index (WPI) and in terms of retail prices through consumer price index. Inflation has an enormous effect in the economy. Within the country it erodes purchasing power. As a consequence, demand falls. If the rate of inflation in the country from which a company imports is high then the cost of production in that country will automatically go up.

INTEREST RATES

As interest rate determines the present value of cash flows, high interest rate affects demand for housing and high-value consumer durables. The real interest rate is an important factor for business activity. Interest rate determined the cost availability of credit for companies operating in an economy. A low interest rate stimulates investment by making credit available easily and cheaply. Higher interest rate results in higher cost of production, which may lead to lower profitability and lower demand. An investor has to evaluate and consider the other factors like government revenue, expenditure, deficits, exchange rate and infrastructure economic and political stability for a good performance of the economy. A low interest rate stimulates investment and industry. Conversely, high interest rates result in higher cost of production and lower consumption.

RESEARCH AND TECHNOLOGICAL DEVELOPMENTS

Research and development are yet another factor. The investment depends upon the amount of resources spent by the government on the particular technological development affecting the future. Generally, the public will invest on industries which are getting a large amount of share in the funds of the development of the country. For example, in India in the present context automobile industries and space technology are receiving a greater attention. These may be areas which the investor may consider for investment.

NATURAL RESOURCES AND RAW MATERIAL

These factors play an important role in the industrial production. They provide overall improvement in the condition of corporation growth. The discovery of oil in middle-east countries and the discovery of gas in America created great change in the general economic pattern and the investment of those countries. In Japan, government found raw material in the form of labour force much suited to a developing country. Technological discoveries in recycling of material, nuclear and solar energy and new synthetics should give the investor an opportunity to invest in untapped or recently tapped resources which would also produce higher investment opportunity.

ECONOMIC FORECASTING

After careful examination of board economic forces which are demographical in nature the investor should make an economic forecasting for taking a decision on investment in stocks. Forecasting is essential because of the investor purchases an investment at the right time and when it is getting the proper resources to help it grow, the investor will receive a gain on the amount which he has invested. Proper timing of purchases is crucial because if an investor operates his investment during the time of strike or during distributed state of the capital market then the rate of return which he will receive will not be high. Favourable conditions will give him a good rate of return because the profit in a company are based on the key economic factors like (a) Labour (b) government, (c) political climate (d) developments in technology (e) availability of finance and (f) tax treatment.

***Budget Deficit*:** The budget deficit is the difference between government spending and revenues. Higher budget deficit indicates higher government borrowing which pressure up interest rates. The excessive government borrowing will crowd out private borrowing if the borrowing is unchecked. Fiscal deficit is budget deficit plus borrowing. Higher fiscal deficit indicates higher government spending on unproductive spending.

CAPITAL FORMATION

The public examine the kind of investment which a company makes in capital goods and the capital it invest in modernization and replacement of assets. They depend on the economic factors of the country. The gross national product (GNP) of a country should be carefully analysed. A particular industry or a particular company in which an investor would like to invest can also be viewed at with the help of the economic indicators such as the place, value and property position of the industry, group to which it belongs and the year-to-year returns through corporate profits.

***Politico-Economic Analysis*:** No industry or company can exist in isolation. It may have splendid managers and a tremendous product. However, its sales and its costs are affected by factors, some of which are beyond its control - the world economy, price inflation, taxes and a host of others. It is important, therefore, to have an appreciation of the politico-economic factors that affect an industry and a company.

- **The political equation:** A stable political environment is necessary for steady, balanced growth. If a country is ruled by a stable government which takes decisions for the long-term development of the country, industry and companies will prosper.
- **Foreign Exchange Reserves:** A country needs foreign exchange reserves to meet its commitments, pay for its imports and service foreign debts.
- **Foreign Exchange Risk:** This is a real risk and one must be cognizant of the effect of a revaluation or devaluation of the currency either in the home country or in the country the company deals in.
- **Restrictive Practices:** Restrictive practices or cartels imposed by countries can affect companies and industries crystallizing the exposure.
- **Foreign Debt and the Balance of Trade Foreign:** debt, especially if it is very large, can be a tremendous burden on an economy. India pays around $ 5 billion a year in principal repayments and interest payments.

Taxation: The level of taxation in a country has a direct effect on the economy. If tax rates are low, people have more disposable income.

Government Policy: Government policy has a direct impact on the economy. A government that is perceived to be proindustry will attract investment.

THE ECONOMIC CYCLE:

It affects investment decisions, employment, demand and the profitability of companies. The four stages of an economic cycle are:

- Depression
- Recovery
- Boom
- Recession

Depression: At the time of depression, demand is low and falling. Inflation is high and so are interest rates. Companies, crippled by high borrowing and falling sales, are forced to curtail production, close down plants built at times of higher demand, and let workers go.

Recovery: During this phase, the economy begins to recover. Investment begins anew and the demand grows. Companies begin to post profits. Conspicuous spending begins once again.

Boom: In the boom phase, demand reaches an all-time high. Investment is also high. Interest rates are low. Gradually as time goes on, supply begins to exceed the demand. Prices that had been rising begin to stabilize and even fall. There is an increase in demand. Then as the boom period matures prices begin to rise again.

Recession: The economy slowly begins to downturn. Demand starts falling. Interest rates and inflation are high. Companies start finding it difficult to sell their goods. The economy slowly begins to downturn.

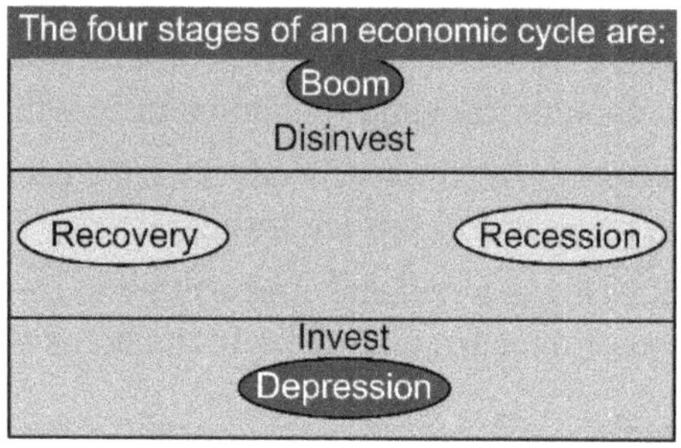

Other Factors: Money supply, Fiscal Policy, Monetary Policy, Manufacturing and trade sales, Labour productivity, Index of consumer expectations, New acquisition of plants and machinery by corporates, Stock prices, Personal income, Tax collections by the government, FII investments, FDI investments, Credit off takes etc.

B. INDUSTRIAL ANALYSIS

The concept of industry is, therefore, to be defined according to some clear-cut lines of demarcation to give a clear idea to the investor before he makes an investment. In India, the broad classification of industry is made according to stock exchange list which is published. The same list is also published in Economic Times and Financial Express daily, this gives a distinct classification to industry in different forms such as

(a) Engineering, (b) Electricity generation, (c) Textiles (d) Cement (e) Steel mills and alloys (f) Cable and electrical (g) Plantation (h) Chemicals and pharmaceuticals (i) Paper (j) Sugar (k) Rubber (l) Automobiles, Cycles and Accessories (m) Miscellaneous.

The classification broadly gives the investor some kind of headway and he may then analyse the industry and find out whether it is profitable to make an investment or not.

Industrial development depends on technology. Technology keeps on changing. For instance, fountain pens have given way to ball pens. Similarly, the electric radios have now changed into transistors, two-in-ones, three-in-ones, televisions –black and white, colour television and video systems. These technological changes should be carefully viewed by the investor. A product with frequent technological changes may be useful for the investor to notice as product obsolescence may erode his investment.

The investor has to analyses the competitive forces in the market, the investor should enquire about the type of competitive pressure that an industry faces in the country. Every industry has large number of firms comprising it. A sample study may give a picture of the kind of competition that an industry faces. For example, in India the pharmaceutical industry had a sudden boost and large number of small companies have entered into the industry which has a lesser number of firms competing with each other. Profits are expected to be more in a company which has less pressures of competition.

The investor has to examine the kind of economic environment and customer activity in a country. Poverty in a country would have an economic climate where cheaper products would be sold and demand for these products will be higher than quality and long-lasting products. Economically advanced countries will have customer activity in higher price and better-quality products.

An investor ultimately invests his money in the securities of one or more specific companies. The performance of companies would be influenced by the fortunes of the industry to which it belongs. An industry is generally described as a homogenous group of companies. An industry is defined as "A group of firm's products, which serve the same need of a common set of buyers". Market experts believe that each poll has a stage and the decline stage. Even industry has a life cycle theory.

Industry may also be evaluated or analyzed through its lifecycle. Industry life cycle may also be studied through the industrial life cycle state. There are generally three stages of and industry. "Grodinsky" has defined these stages as the pioneering stage, expansion stage and stagnation stage.

Cycle: The first step in industry is to determine the cycle it is in, or the stage of maturity of the industry.

All industries evolve through the following stages:

1. Entrepreneurial, sunrise or nascent stage
2. Expansion or growth stage
3. Stabilization, stagnation or maturity stage, and
    - The pioneering stage
    - The expansion stage
    - The stagnation stage
    - The decay stage

The Entrepreneurial or Nascent Stage: At the first stage, the industry is new and it can take some time for it to properly establish itself.

The Expansion or Growth Stage: Once the industry has established itself it enters a growth stage. As the industry grows, many new companies enter the industry.

The Stabilization or Maturity Stage: After the halcyon days of growth, an industry matures and stabilizes. Rewards are low and so too is the risk. Growth is moderate. Though sales may increase, they do so at a slower rate than before. Products are more standardized and less innovative and there are several competitors

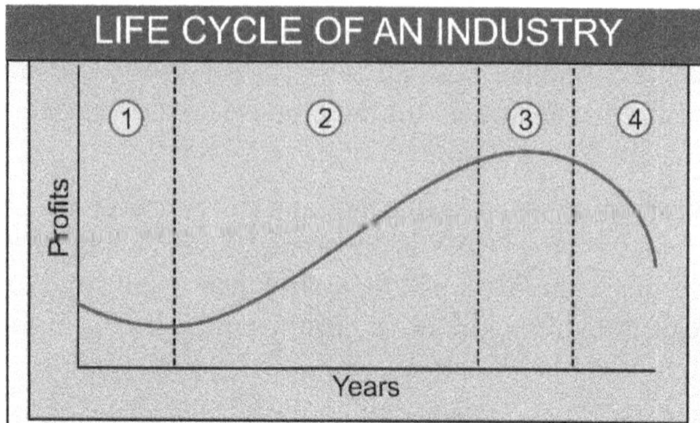

(1) Entrepreneurial of nascent stage (2) Expansion of growth stage(3) Stabilization or maturity stage (4) Decline

The Decline or Sunset Stage: Finally, the industry declines. This occurs when its products are no longer popular. This may be on account of several factors such as a change in social habits the film and video industries.

Technological advances in one country can affect the growth of another industry. All these stages give an insight into merits of invest in a given industry at a given time. An industry usually exhibits low profitability in the pioneering stage, high profitability in the stagnation or maturity stage and declining profitability in the decay stage.

Introduction stage (pioneer): During this stage the investor will notice a great increase in the activity of the firm. Production will rise and in relation to production, there will be a great demand for the product. At this stage the profits are also very high as the technology is new. Taking a look at the profit many new firms enter into the same field and the market becomes competitive. The market competitive pressures keep on increasing with the entry of new-forms and the prices keep on declining and then ultimately profits fall. At this stage all firms compete with each other and only a few efficient firms are left to run the business and most of the other firms are wiped out in the pioneering stage itself.

Growth (expansion): During this stage, the prices begin to stabilize themselves, each firm finds a market for itself and develops its own strategy to sell and to maintain its position. Even though there is competition each firm is able to stand and sell and make huge profits. This is the time when each one has to show its competitive strength and superiority. The investor will find that this is the best time to make an investment. At the pioneering stage it was difficult to find out which of the firm to invest, but having waited for the stability period there has been a dynamic selection process and a few of the large number for firms are left in the industry. At this particular period each firm has established itself, develop its objectives, stabilized its financial position and dividend policy has become stable. By this time the firm has been able to satisfy the investor also. At this time the firms begin to expand themselves both through external means of financing through loans and public issue of shares as well as through internally generated funds. This is the period of security and safety and this is also called period of maturity for the firm.

Decline (stagnation): In this stage, the increase in sales of an organization will not provide much profits to the company. Profits are also there, but the growth in the firm is lower than it was in the expansion stage. The industry finds that it is at a loss of power and cannot expand. The transition of the firm from the stage of maturity to the stage of stagnation is very slow and after a long time the internal management begins to realize this state of complacency. While that owners of the firm are happy with their profits they do not know that their growth is slow and they are slipping in the stagnation stage. They slip too slowly from maturity to stagnation that they do not make an effort to expand or grow.

Recessions or expansions in economic activity may translate into falling or rising stock markets with different relative price changes among industry groups. For the analyst, industry analysis calls for insight into:

- The key sectors or subdivisions of overall economic activity that influence particular industries, and
- The relative strength or weakness of particular industry or other groupings about economic activity.

Major Classifications: The industry can be classified by product and services in the categories like Basic Industries, Capital Goods, Consumer Durables, Consumer Non--Durables, Consumer Services, Energy, Financial Services, Health Care, Public Utilities, Technology, and Transportation etc.

Classification based on Business Cycles: Industry can be classified on the basis of its reaction to upswings and downswings of the economy which is known as business cycles. General classifications of the industry based on the business cycles are growth industry, cyclical industry, defensive industry, and cyclical-growth industry.

Growth industry: The major characteristics of a growth industry are higher rate of expansion, growth in earnings, and independent of the business cycles. Often associated with technological changes or innovative means of carrying out things. Between 40's and 60's, industries like photography, colour television, computers, pharmaceuticals, office equipment's were growth industries. Communication equipment's, Software, genetic engineering, and environmental/waste management are the recent growth industries.

Cyclical industry: It is most likely to benefit from a period of economic prosperity and suffer from economic recession. Consumer durables are the major cyclical industry.

Defensive industry: is likely to get least affected during the periods of economic downswing as consists of items necessary for existence. The demand for these products is considered to be counter cyclical. Food processing industry, consumer non-durables fall in the category of defensive industry.

BARRIER TO ENTRY

New entrants increase the capacity in an industry and the inflow of funds. The question that arises is how easy is it to enter an industry?

There are some barriers to entry:

a. Economies of scale
b. Product differentiation
c. Capital requirement
d. Switching costs
e. Access to distribution channels
f. Cost disadvantages independent of scale
g. Government policy
h. Expected retaliation
i. International cartels

THE THREAT OF SUBSTITUTION

New inventions are always taking place and new and better products replace existing ones. An industry that can be replaced by substitutes or is threatened by substitutes is normally an industry one must be careful of investing in. An industry where this occurs constantly is the packaging industry -bottles replaced by cans, cans replaced by plastic bottles, and the like. To ward off the threat of substitution, companies often have to spend large sums of money in advertising and promotion.

BARGAINING POWER OF THE BUYERS

In an industry where buyers have control, i.e. in a buyer's market, buyers are constantly forcing prices down, demanding better services or higher quality and this often erodes profitability. The factors one should check are whether:

(a) A particular buyer buys most of the products (large purchase volumes). If such buyers withdraw their patronage, they can destroy an industry. They can also force prices down.

(b) Buyers can play one company against another to bring prices down.

BARGAINING POWER FOR THE SUPPLIERS

An industry unduly controlled by its suppliers is also under threat. This occurs when:

(a) The suppliers have a monopoly, or if there are few suppliers.
(b) Suppliers control an essential.
(c) Demand for the product exceeds.
(d) The supplier supplies to various industries.
(e) The switching costs are high.
(f) The supplier's product does not have a substitute.
(g) The supplier's product is an important input for the buyer's.
(h) The buyer is not important to the supplier.
(i) The supplier's product is unique.

RIVALRY AMONG COMPETITORS

Rivalry among competitors can cause an industry great harm. This occurs mainly by price cuts, heavy advertising, additional high cost services or offers, and the like. This rivalry occurs mainly when:

- There are many competitors and supply exceeds demand. Companies resort to price cuts and advertise heavily in order to attract customers for their goods.
- The industry growth is slow and companies are competing with each other for a greater market share.
- The economy is in a recession and companies cut the price of their products and offer better service to stimulate demand.
- There is lack of differentiation between the product of one company and that of another. In such cases, the buyer makes his choice on the basis of price or service.

Other Factors: Past Sales and Earnings Performance, Government policy and regulation toward industry, Labour conditions, Competitive conditions, Industry life cycle, International investing community attitude, Industry share price etc.

C. COMPANY ANALYSIS

It is a study of the factors that influence the future of a firm both qualitatively and quantitatively. Here, the investor examines the competitive position of a firm its earning and profitability, the efficiently with which it operates, its financial position and its future with respect to the earning of its shareholders. The purpose of this analysis is that each share of a company has an intrinsic value which is dependent on the company's financial performance, quality of management and record if its earnings and dividend. The market price of a share is lower than the intrinsic value, as evaluated by the fundamental analysis, then the share is supposed to be undervalued and it should be purchased. And at the same time, when the current market price shows that it is more than intrinsic value then according to the theory the share should be sold. This basis approach is analysed through the financial statements of an organization. When the financial statement is being analysed, the following items require particular attention.

It is the final stage of fundamental analysis. It deals with the estimation of return and risk of individual shares. In company analysis, the analyst tries to forecast the future earnings of the company. The level, trend and stability of earnings of a company. However, depends upon a no. of factors concerning the operations of the company. Operating profit is net –profit before adjustment of non-operating incomes and expenses finance charges. Non-operating incomes may be dividends from investments (non-trading), profit on sale of fixed assets etc… Non-operating expenses are loss on fixed assets financial charges and donations etc.

At the final stage of fundamental analysis, the investor analyses the company. This analysis has two thrusts:

1. How has the company performed vis-à-vis other similar companies and
2. How has the company performed in comparison to earlier years?

It is imperative that one completes the politico economic analysis and the industry analysis before a company is analyzed because the company's performance at a period of time is to an extent a reflection of the economy, the political situation and the industry. What does one look at when analyzing a company?

The different issues regarding a company that should be examined are:

- The Management
- The Company
- The Annual Report
- Ratios
- Cash flow

The management: The competence of a company's management cannot be easily determined. A good management is paramount to investment success. We will have to examine the quality of the management and whether it is capable of maintaining the competitive position of the company and successfully running the affairs of the company to produce a profit.

Generally, the management is responsible to plan, organize, direct, control and co-ordinate the activities of the company to accomplish stated objectives by the use of human being and other resources. The company has to show the equity holders a growth in per share value measured in terms of both income and appreciation and to be the maximum in the long run, consistent with the company's responsibilities to the customers, employees and the public. The qualities of the management can be examined on the basis of the past record, in terms of the following:

(i) The capacity to maintain the competitiveness of the firm.

(ii) The capacity to expand firm within the ensure growth.

(iii) The skill to maintain the efficient production by proper utilization of plant and machinery and by suitable inventory management, planning and scheduling.

(iv) The skill to maintain the finance of the company adequately for execution of its expansion plans.

The firm should apply scientific management techniques and reduce the costs and unnecessary activities. The scientific management should be used to enhance productivity of employees.

The single most important factor one should consider when investing in a company and one often never considered is its management. In India management can be broadly divided in two types:

- Family Management
- Professional Management

The company: An aspect not necessarily examined during an analysis of fundamentals is the company. A company may have made losses consecutively for two years or more and one may not wish to touch its shares - yet it may be a good company and worth purchasing into. There are several factors one should look at.

1. How a company is perceived by its competitors?

One of the key factors to ascertain is how a company is perceived by its competitors. It is held in high regard. Its management may be known for its maturity, vision, competence and aggressiveness. The investor must ascertain the reason and then determine whether the reason will continue into the foreseeable future.

2. Whether the company is the market leader in its products or in its segment?

Another aspect that should be ascertained is whether the company is the market leader in its products or in its segment. When you invest in market leaders, the risk is less. The shares of market leaders do not fall as quickly as those of other companies. There is a magic to their name that would make individuals prefer to buy their products as opposed to others.

3. Company Policies

The policy a company follows is also important. What is their plan for growth? What is its vision? Every company has a life. If it is allowed to live a normal life it will grow up to a point and then begin to level out and eventually die. It is at the point of leveling out that it must be given new life. This can give it renewed vigor and a new lease of life.

4. Labour Relations

Labour relations are extremely important. A company that has motivated, industrious work force has high productivity and practically no disruption of work. On the other hand, a company that has bad industrial relations will lose several hundred man-days as a consequence of strikes and go slows.

FINANCIAL ANALYSIS AND EVALUATION

Investments in capital markets primarily involve transactions in shares, bonds, debentures, and other financial products issued by companies. The decision to invest in these securities is thus linked to the evaluation of these companies, their earnings, and potential for future growth. In this chapter we look at one of the most important tools used for this purpose, Valuation. The fundamental valuation of any asset (and companies are indeed assets into which we invest) is an examination of future returns, in other words, the cash flows expected from the asset. The 'value' of the asset is then simply what these cash flows are worth today, i.e., their *present discounted value.* Valuation is all about how well we predict these cash flows, their growth in future, taking into account future risks involved.

THE ANALYSIS OF FINANCIAL STATEMENTS

A company's financial statements provide the most accurate information to its management and shareholders about its operations, efficiency in the allocation of its capital and its earnings profile. Three basic accounting statements form the backbone of financial analysis of a company: the income statement (profit & loss), the balance sheet, and the statement of cash flows. Let us quickly summarize each of these.

INCOME STATEMENT (PROFIT & LOSS)

A profit & loss statement provides an account of the total revenue generated by a firm during a period (usually a financial year or a quarter), the expenses involved and the money earned. In its simplest form, revenue generation or sales accrues from selling the products manufactured, or services rendered by the company. Operating expenses include the costs of these goods and services and the costs incurred during the manufacture. Beyond operating expenses are interest costs based on the debt profile of the company. Taxes payable to the Government are then debited to provide the Profit after Tax (PAT) or the net income to the shareholders of the company.

Actual P&L statements of companies are usually much more complicated than this, with so- called 'other income' (income from non-core activities), 'negative' interest expenses (from cash reserves with the company), preferred dividends, and non-recurring, exceptional income or expenses.

Example: 1

Income Statement (Rs.)	2012	2013	2014
Net sales	16,380	21,340	33,565
Cost of sales	(5,332)	(6,584)	(8,190)
SG&A	(1,413)	(1,771)	(2,738)
Research & development	(1,534)	(2,440)	(2,725)
Other operating items	(3,650)	(4,620)	(5,369)
EBIT	**4,457**	**5,926**	**14,543**
Total other non-operating items	543	1,336	305
Associates	0	0	0
Net interest income/expense	869	1,072	1,146
Exceptional items	0	0	0
Pretax profit	**5,869**	**8,334**	**15,994**
Taxation	(239)	67	(485)
Minority interest	3	(559)	(640)
Preferred dividends	0	0	0
Net extraordinary items	100	0	0
Reported net income	**5,733**	**7,843**	**14,869**

THE BALANCE SHEET

Assets owned by a company are financed either by equity or debt and the balance sheet of a company is a snapshot of this capital structure of the firm at a point in time; the sources and applications of funds of the company.

A company owns fixed assets (machinery, and other infrastructure), current assets (manufacturing goods in progress, money it expects to receive from business partners—receivables, inventory etc.), cash and other financial investments. In addition to these three, a company could also own other assets which carry value, but are not directly marketable, like patents, trademarks, and 'goodwill'—value not linked to assets, but realized from acquisitions.

These assets are financed either by the company's equity (investments by shareholders) or by debt. The illustrative example shown below is the balance sheet of a large Pharmaceutical company.

Balance Sheet (Rs.)	2012	2013	2014
Cash and marketable securities	15,628	14,106	17,290
Accounts receivable	3,614	6,789	14,177
Inventory	5,117	6,645	7,728
Other current assets	2,471	2,653	5,079
Current assets	**26,826**	**30,192**	**44,274**
Net tangible fixed assets	8,977	10,122	11,040
Total financial assets	3,237	2,239	2,659
Net goodwill	507	697	1,729
Total assets	**39,547**	**43,250**	**59,701**
Accounts payable	2,279	2,966	3,722
Short-term debt	0	0	0
Total other current liabilities	1,236	80	2,651
Current liabilities	**3,515**	**3,046**	**6,373**
Long-term debt	18,747	11,144	1,436
Total other non-current liabilities	1,053	895	92
Total provisions	0	0	0
Total liabilities	**23,314**	**15,135**	**7,901**
Minority interest – accumulated	332	438	1,886
Shareholders' equity	15,902	27,728	49,915
Shareholders' funds	**16,233**	**28,166**	**51,800**
Liabilities and shareholders' funds	**39,547**	**43,250**	**59,701**

CASH FLOW STATEMENT

The cash flow statement is the most important among the three financial statements, particularly from a valuation's perspective. As the name implies, such a statement is used to track the cash flows in the company over a period. Cash flows are tracked across operating, investing, and financing activities. Cash flows from operations include net income generation adjusted for changes in working capital (like inventories, receivables and payables), and non-core accruals (like depreciation, etc). A firm's investment activities comprise fixed, and current assets (capital- and operating expenditure), sometimes into other firms (like an acquisition), and generally represent negative cash flows. Cash flows in financing activities are the net result of the firm's borrowing, and payments during the period. The sum total of cash flows from these three heads represents the net change in cash balances of the firm over the period.

Cash generation from operating activities of the firm, when adjusted for its capital expenditure represent the 'free cash' available to it, for potential investment activities, acquiring other firms or businesses, or distribution among its shareholders. As we will see in later topics, free cash flows are the key to calculating the so-called intrinsic value of an asset in any discounted valuation model. Our illustrative example below shows the cash flow statement (and free cash flows) of a large pharmaceutical company over the period 2012-2014.

Illustration 5.3

Cash Flow (Rs.)	2012	2013	2014
Reported net income	5,733	7,843	14,869
Preferred dividends	0	0	0
Minority interest	(3)	559	640
Depreciation and amortization	610	813	969
Cash tax adjustment	75	(511)	(1,337)
Total other operating cash flow	(1,365)	(2,156)	(753)
Net change in working capital	(3,177)	(4,154)	(9,340)
Cash from operations	**1,872**	**2,394**	**5,048**
Capital expenditure	(3,387)	(2,000)	(1,995)
Net acquisitions/disposals	3,511	1,367	(5,242)
Total other investing cash flows	634	1,272	1,177
Cash from investing activities	**758**	**639**	**(6,060)**
Change in borrowings	805	(1,742)	768
Equity raised/share buybacks	0	0	0
Dividends paid	(793)	(2,629)	(18)
Total other financing cash flows	(156)	(127)	(88)
Cash from financing activities	**(144)**	**(4,498)**	**661**
Change in cash	**3,518**	**(1,465)**	**(352)**
Free cash flow	**(1,514)**	**394**	**3,052**

FINANCIAL RATIOS (RETURN, OPERATING AND, PROFITABILITY RATIOS)

Financial ratios are meaningful links between different entries of financial statements, as by themselves the financial entries offer little to examine a company. In addition to providing information about the financial health and prospects of a company, financial ratios also allow a company to be viewed, in a relative sense, in comparison with its own historical performance, others in its sector of the economy, or between any two companies in general. In this section we examine a few such ratios, grouped into categories that allow comparison of size, solvency, operating performance, growth profile and risks. The list below is by no means exhaustive, and merely serves to illustrate a few of the important ones.

PE ratio. The formula to calculate the ratio is:

Measures of Profitability: RoA, RoE

Return on Assets (RoA) in its simplest form denotes the firm's ability to generate profits given its assets: RoA = (Net Income + Interest Expenses) *(1- Tax Rate) / Average Total Assets **Return on**

Equity (RoE) is the return to the equity investor:

RoE = Net Income / Shareholder Funds

Sometimes this ratio is also calculated as RoAE, to account for recent capital raising by the firm

Return on Average Equity = Net Income / Average Shareholder Funds

Return on Total Capital = Net Income + Gross Interest Expense / Average total capital

MEASURES OF LIQUIDITY

Short-term liquidity is imperative for a company to remain solvent. The ratios below get increasingly conservative in terms of the demands on a firm to meet near-term payables. Current ratio = Current Assets / Current Liabilities

Quick Ratio = (Cash + Marketable Securities + Receivables) / Current Liabilities Acid test ratio = (Cash + Marketable Securities) / Current Liabilities Cash Ratio = (Cash + Marketable Securities) / Current Liabilities

Capital Structure and Solvency Ratios

Total debt to total capital = (Current Liabilities + Long-term Liabilities) /

(Equity + Total Liabilities)

Long-term Debt-Equity = Long-term Liabilities / Equity

OPERATING PERFORMANCE

Gross Profit Margin = Gross Profit / Net Sales Operating Profit Margin = Operating Income / Net Sales Net Profit Margin = Net Income / Net Sales

ASSET UTILIZATION

These ratios look at the effectiveness of a firm to utilize its assets, especially its fixed assets. A high turnover implies optimal use of assets. In addition to the two below there are others like Sales to inventories, and Sales to Working capital.

Total Asset Turnover = Net Sales / Average Total Assets Fixed Asset Turnover = Net Sales / Average Net Fixed Assets

There are many other categories, like the 'common size' ratios, which serve to present the company in terms of one of its own denominators, like Net Sales, or the market capitalization; and others that specifically look at the risk aspect of things (business, financial, and liquidity).

THE VALUATION OF COMMON STOCKS

The major valuation methods for fixed income-generating assets. Using financial statements and ratios, we now examine some of the concepts relating to share valuations and to be more specific, we will deal with valuation of common stocks. Common shareholders are the owners of the firm, and as such are the final stakeholders in its growth, and risks; they appoint the management to run its day-to-day affairs and the Board of Directors to oversee the management's activities. The cash flows (return) to common shareholders from the company are generally in the form of current and future dividends distributed from the profits of the firm. Alternatively, an investor can always sell her holdings in the market (secondary market), get the prevailing market price, and realize capital appreciation if the returns are positive.

The valuation of any asset is based on the present value of its future cash flows. Such a methodology provides what is called the *'intrinsic'* value of the asset—a common stock in our case. The problem of valuing the stock then translates into one of predicting the future free cash flow profile of the company, and then using the appropriate discount factor to measure what they are worth today. The appropriately named discounted-cash flow technique is also referred to as absolute valuation, particularly when compared to another widely-followed approach in valuation, called relative valuation.

Relative valuation looks at pricing assets on the basis of the pricing of other, similar assets— instead of pricing them independently—the core assumption being that assets with similar earnings and growth profile, and facing the same risks ought to be priced comparably. Two stocks in the same sector of the economy could thus be compared, and the same sector (and its stocks) across countries. The discussion on relative valuation follows that of absolute or intrinsic valuation.

ABSOLUTE (INTRINSIC) VALUATION

Intrinsic value or the fundamental value refers to the value of a security, which is intrinsic to or contained in the security itself. It is defined as the present value of all expected cash flows to the company.

The **book value** or **carrying value** in accounting, is the value of an asset according to its balance sheet account balance. For assets, the value is based on the original cost of the asset less any depreciation, amortization or impairment costs made against the asset. Book value per share is calculated by dividing the net assets of the company with the number of shares outstanding. The net asset of the company is the values of all assets less values of all liabilities outstanding in the books of accounts.

EARNING PER SHARE (EPS)

Earning per share is the firms' net income divided by the average number of shares outstanding during the year.

Calculated as:

EPS = Net Profit - Dividend on Preference Shares

Average number of shares outstanding during the year

DIVIDEND PER SHARE (DPS)

Dividends are a form of profit distribution to the shareholders. The firm may not distribute the entire income to the shareholders, but decide to retain some portion of it for financing growth opportunities. Alternatively, a firm may pay dividends from past years profit during years where there is insufficient income. In this case, the dividends amount will be higher than the earnings. The dividend per share is the amount that the firm pays as dividend to the holder of one share i.e. total dividend / number of shares in issue.

The dividend payout ratio (DPR) measures the percentage of income that the company pays out to the shareholders in the form of dividends. The formula for calculating DPR is:

$$DPR = \frac{Dividends}{Net\ Income} \qquad \frac{DPS}{EPS}$$

Retention ratio is the opposite of dividend payout ratio and measures the percentage of net income not paid to the shareholders in the form of dividends. It is nothing but (1-DPR).

Example: The following is the figure for Asha International during the year 2013-14:

Net Income: Rs. 1,000,000 Number of equity shares (2013): 150,000 Number of equity shares (2014): 250,000 Dividend paid: Rs. 400,000

Calculate the earnings per share (EPS), dividend per share (DPS), dividend payout ratio and

EPS= Net Income/ Average No. of equity shares

EPS = 10,00,000/2,00,000 = 5

DPS= Dividend Paid/ Average No. of Equity shares

DPS= 4,00,000/2,00,000 = 2

Retention Ratio 1- DPR

DPR = DPS/EPS = 2/5= .4

Retention Ratio = 1- DPR = 0.6 or 60%

PRICE EARNINGS RATIO

Price earnings ratio for a company is calculated by dividing the market price per share with the earnings per share (EPS).

$$\text{Price Earnings Ratio} = \frac{\text{Market price per share}}{\text{Annual earning per share}}$$

The earning per share is usually calculated for the last one year. Sometimes, we also calculate the PE ratio using the expected future one-year return. In such case, we call forward PE or estimated PE ratio.

Example: Stock XYZ, whose earning per share is Rs. 50 is trading in the market at Rs. 2000. What is the price to earnings ratio for XYZ?

Answer:

$$\text{Price Earnings Ratio} = \frac{\text{Market price per share } 2000}{\text{Annual earning per share } 50} = 40$$

We cannot draw any conclusion as to whether a stock is undervalued or overvalued in the market by just considering the PE ratio. A higher PE ratio implies that the investors are paying more for each unit of net income, which implies that the investors are optimistic about the future performance (or future growth rate) of the company. Stocks with higher PE ratio are also called growth firms and stocks with lower PE ratio are called as income firms.

PRICE-BOOK RATIO

The price-book ratio is widely used as a conservative measure of relative valuation of an asset, where the assets of the firm are valued at book. Investors also widely use the ratio to judge whether the stock is undervalued or overvalued, as it's less susceptible to fluctuations than Price-book ratio = Market price of the share / Book Value per share.

RETURN ON EQUITY

Return on equity measures profitability from the equity shareholders point of view. It is the return to the equity shareholders and is measured by the following formula:

$$\text{ROE} = \frac{\text{Net Income after Tax} - \text{Preferred Dividends}}{\text{Average Shareholder Equity Excluding Preferred Share Capital}}$$

Example: XYZ Company net income after tax for the financial year ending 31st March, 2014 was Rs. 10 million and the equity share capital as on 31st March, 2013 and 31st March 2014 was Rs. 80 million and Rs. 120 million respectively. Calculate the return on equity of XYZ Company for the year 2013-14.

Answer:

$$\text{Average Equity} = \frac{\text{Opening Equity} + \text{Closing Equity}}{2} = \frac{80 + 120}{2} = 100 \text{ million}$$

$$\textit{Return on Equity} = \frac{\textit{Net Profit after Tax}}{\textit{Average Equity}} = \frac{10}{100} = 0.10 \textit{ or } 10\%$$

THE DUPONT MODEL

The Du Pont model is widely used to decide the determinants of return profitability of a company, or a sector of the economy. Returns on shareholder equity are expressed in terms of a company's profit margins, asset turn, and its financial leverage.

DuPont Model breaks the Return on equity as under:

RoE = Return on Equity

= Net Profits/Equity

= Net Profits/Sales * Sales/Assets * Assets/Equity

= Profit Margin * Asset Turnover * Financial Leverage

The first component measures the operational efficiency of the firm through its net margin ratio. The second component, called the asset turnover ratio, measures the efficiency in usage of assets by the firm and the third component measures the financial leverage of the firm through the equity multiplier. The analysis reflects a firms' efficiency in different aspects of business and is widely used now for control purpose. It shows that the firm could improve its RoE by a combination of profitability (higher profit margins), raising leverage (by raising debt), by using its assets better (higher asset turn) or a combination of all three. The DuPont analysis could be easily extended to ascertain a sector's profitability metrics for comparability, or, for that matter, an entire market.

DIVIDEND YIELD

Dividend yield is the ratio between the dividend paid during the last 1-year period and the current price of the share. The ratio could also be used with the forward dividend yield instead-expected dividends, for either the next 12 months, or the financial year.

Example: 1 ABC Company paid a dividend of Rs. 5 per share in 2014 and the market price of ABC share at the end of 2014 was Rs. 25. Calculate the dividend yield for ABC stock.

Answer: Dividend Yield = —*Last yeardlvldend* = *A* = *0.20* or *20%*

Current Price per share *2*

Return to Investor

The return what the investor earns during a year by holding the share of a company is not equal to the dividend per share or the earnings per ratio. An investor's earning is the sum of the dividend amount that he received from the company and the change in the market price of the share. The investment amount is equal to the market price of the share at the beginning of the price.

Dividends + A (market price of the share)

Opening Market Price

Example: 2

FINANCIAL STATEMENT ANALYSIS

Opening Market Price

Expected Return(r) = *Dividends + D (market price of the share) 6 + (84 - 80)10*

If we write the dividends during the year as Div_1, the price of the share at the beginning and at the end of the year as P_0 and P_1 respectively, we can write the above formula as:

Profit & Loss Account for year ended	31-Mar-14 *Rs. Cr.*	31-Mar-13 *Rs. Cr.*
Income		
Gross Sales	48,681.39	45,555.34
Less Excise Duty	5,531.31	6,045.19
Net Sales	43,150.08	39,510.15
Other Operating Income	700.87	706.89
Net Income	43,850.95	40,217.04
Expenditure		
Materials	15,650.06	11,303.14
Employees' Remuneration & Benefits	8,401.51	7,919.02
Other Manufacturing Expenses	7,273.70	6,671.61
Selling & Administration Expenses	3,416.61	2,554.17
	34,741.88	28,447.94
Profit from Operations before Other Income, Interest, Depreciation, Tax & Amortization	9,114.07	11,769.10
Less Interest & Finance Charges	253.24	250.94
Add Other Income	1,828.96	1,184.76
Less Depreciation	1,285.12	1,235.48
Profit before Exceptional Items &Tax	9,399.67	11,467.44
Less Tax	3,284.28	3,934.65
Profit after Tax before Exceptional Items	6,115.39	7,532.79
Less Exceptional Items & tax adjustment	-59.42	-3.99
Net Profit after Tax	**6,174.81**	**7,536.78**
Less Equity Dividend	1,073.90	1,528.25
Less Income Distribution Tax	181.26	258.91
Retained Earnings	**4,919.65**	**5,749.62**
Share is trading in the market at Rs.	200.00	

As seen earlier, this is a key element of Fundamental Analysis. The analyst looks at various financial ratios to understand the company. Let us take the following example of Srinivasa corporations Ltd. to understand some of these ra

Srinivasa corporations Ltd's EPS has gone down. Other things being constant, this is an indication that the share price had to go down.

CASH EARNINGS PER SHARE (CEPS)

In the calculation of earnings, depreciation is one of the expenses deducted from the revenue. Depreciation however is only an accounting entry - it does not involve a cash outgo for the company. (The cash outgo would have happened when the company bought the asset on which depreciation is now charged as an accounting entry).

Similarly, the company may make various accounting provisions which do not involve a cash outgo.

- If such non-cash expenses are added back to the earnings, then one arrives at the cash earnings.

DIVIDEND PER SHARE (DPS)

Cash Earnings Per Share	a t b	Rs	31-Mar-14 17.92	31-Mar-13 21.23
a Cash Earnings	c + d	Rs. Cr.	7,400.51	8,768.27
b No. of shares	1 b	Crores	413.04	413.04
c Profit after Tax before	P&L	Rs. Cr.	6,115.39	7,532.79
Exceptional Items d	P&L	Rs. Cr.	1,285.12	1,235.48
			31-Mar-14	**31-Mar-13**
Dividend Per Share	**a t b**	**Rs.**	**2.60**	**3.70**
a Dividend	P&L	Rs. Cr.	1,073.90	1,528.25
b No. of shares	1 b	Crores	413.04	413.04

The company may have earned profits, but how much did the investor receive as dividend?

DIVIDEND YIELD

If the past dividends are maintained, and an investor bought the share today, what return would she receive in the form of dividend?

			31-Mar-14	31-Mar-13
Dividend Yield	**a t b**	%	**1.30%**	**1.85%**
a Dividend Per Share	3	Rs.	2.60	3.70
b Current Market Price of Share		Rs.	200.00	200.00

While the calculations are shown for both years, it is the latest dividend for a full financial year that is most relevant.

Caution needs to be exercised for this metric, because past dividend may not be sustained if the earnings go down. This is evident in the above calculation, where Srinivasa corporations Ltd has cut the dividend from Rs3.70 per share to Rs. 2.60 per share, when earnings fell from 200708 to 2013-14.

PRICE-EARNINGS RATIO (P/E RATIO)

When an investor buys the shares of a company, she is essentially buying into its future earnings stream. How much is the company's share price, in relation to its earnings?

			31-Mar-14	31-Mar-13
Price / Earnings Ratio	**a t b**	**Times**	**13.50**	**10.96**
a Current Market Price of Share		Rs.	200.00	200.00
b Earnings Per Share		Rs.	14.81	18.24
While the calculations are shown for	both years,	it is the	latest earnings	that is most

Comparing the market price with past earnings, gives *historical P/E Ratio.*

Comparing the market price with projected (future) earnings, gives *prospective P/E Ratio.* This is more commonly used by analysts.

P/E Ratio is more meaningful when it is compared with the P/E Ratio of other companies from the same sector. This is a tool to check for over-valuation or under-valuation of a company's share in the market.

Suppose Srinivasa corporations Ltd. prospective P/E is 12 times, while other companies in the sector are trading in the range of 7 times. The analyst would consider whether the differential is justified - for example, on account of superior earnings growth expected or better corporate governance or some favorable news expectation about the company. If the analyst does not see a reason for the share to trade at a higher multiple, then she is likely to view it as overvalued and recommend that the share be sold.

MARKET CAPITALISATION

How much is the value of the entire company (i.e. all its shares together) as per the share market?

			31-Mar-14	31-Mar-13
Market Capitalization	**a X b**	**Rs. Cr.**	**82,608.00**	**82,608.00**
a Current Market Price of Share		Rs.	200.00	200.00
b No. of shares		Crores	413.04	413.04

The latest share price and the latest number of shares are most relevant. Based on market capitalization, shares are often classified as large cap, mid cap or small cap. There is no standard value based on which a company is fit into a specific category. Every research house has its own view on relative market capitalization, based on which companies are categorized.

RATIOS TO ASSESS COMPANY'S MARGINS

How profitable is the company's business? Two ratios can be considered.

			31-Mar-14	31-Mar-13
Operating Profit Margin	**a t b**	**%**	**21.1%**	**29.8%**
a Operating Profit before interest & depreciation	P&L	Rs. Cr.	9,114.07	11,769.10
b Net Sales	P&L	Rs. Cr.	43,150.08	39,510.15

OPERATING PROFIT MARGIN

Clearly the margins of Srinivasa corporations Ltd have slipped during 2013-14. The key reason for this can be found in the Profit and Loss account. Material cost was 28.1% of net income in 2007-08. It has gone up to 35.7% in 2013-14. This kind of increase means that the company is not able to pass on its cost increases to its customers. This is very negative for a company's stock.

NET PROFIT MARGIN

The operating margin above did not consider interest and depreciation. Net profit margin is after all expenses, other than exceptional items, which are non-recurring in nature.

			31-Mar-14	31-Mar-13
Net Profit Margin	**a t b**	**%**	**13.9%**	**18.7%**
a Profit after Tax before	P&L	Rs. Cr.	6,115.39	7,532.79
Exceptional Items				
b Net Income	P&L	Rs. Cr.	43,850.95	40,217.04

Srinivasa corporations Ltd has slipped on this front too, though to a lesser extent than the operating margins. From the profit and loss account it can be seen that the company managed to improve other income and also reduce its tax, as a percentage of net sales. Other income may not be connected to the company's normal operations, while reduction in tax may be on account of changes in tax regime, rather than anything done by the company. Therefore, they do not create any significant comfort about the prospects of the company.

RATIOS TO ASSESS COMPANY'S CAPITAL STRUCTURE DEBT-EQUITY RATIO

What is the mix between borrowed funds (loans) and own funds (shareholders' funds) in the capital structure of the company?

			31-Mar-14	31-Mar-13
Debt-Equity Ratio	**a t b**	**Times**	**0.22**	**0.33**
a Loans	B/S	Rs. Cr.	6,115.39	7,532.79
b Net Worth	c + d	Rs. Cr.	27,984.10	23,063.57
c Share Capital	B/S	Rs. Cr.	4,130.40	4,130.40
d Reserves	B/S	Rs. Cr.	23,853.70	18,933.17

Srinivasa corporations Ltd has only Rs. 0.22 of loans, for every Rs. 1 of own funds. It is thus relying less on debt - technically called *under leveraged.* The implication of this will be discussed later, in the section on return generation efficiency.

A point to note is that too high a leverage too is bad, because the servicing needs on the debt can put pressure on the company during recessions / lean times. The ideal leverage for a company depends on the inherent risks in its industry as well as its profitability.

INTEREST COVERAGE RATIO

Debt-equity ratio looked at capital structure from the point of view of the company's balance sheet. What about is ability to bear the cost of debt funds?

			31-Mar-14	31-Mar-13
Interest Coverage Ratio	**a t b**	**Times**	**37.12**	**45.70**
a Profit before tax & exceptional	P&L	Rs. Cr.	9,399.67	11,467.44
Items				
b Interest Cost	P&L	Rs. Cr.	253.24	250.94

Thus, Srinivasa corporation Ltd. interest cost is covered by profits to the extent of 37 times. Conventionally, interest coverage of 3 times is considered comfortable, because it means that the company will stay profitable, even if its profits were to go down by 66.67%. Thus, the company is under-leveraged even from the point of view of its ability to bear interest costs.

RATIOS TO ASSESS COMPANY'S SOLVENCY CURRENT RATIO

Debt-equity evaluates a company's capital structure from the long-term point of view. What is the company's ability to meet its normal day to day obligations?

			31-Mar-14	31-Mar-13
Current Ratio	**a t b**	**Times**	**1.87**	**1.78**
a Current Assets	B/S	Rs. Cr.	34,510.87	26,317.62
b Current Liabilities & Provisions	B/S	Rs. Cr.	18,453.75	14,767.35

Conventionally, current ratio of 1.33 is considered comfortable. This means that even if 33% of the current assets do not get converted into cash, the company will be able to meet its obligations. Srinivasa corporation Ltd. current ratio of 1.87 is therefore comfortable.

QUICK RATIO

Among current assets, stocks take the longest to get converted to cash. Raw materials have to get converted to finished goods, which in turn need to be sold, before money can be realized. Therefore, as a measure of short-term solvency, current ratio is re-worked by excluding inventory from the current assets.

			31-Mar-14	31-Mar-13
Fixed Assets Turnover	**a t b**	**times**	**3.52**	**3.41**
a Net Sales	P&L	Rs. Cr.	43,150.08	39,510.15
b Net Fixed Assets	B/S	Rs. Cr.	12,268.83	11,571.31

Quick ratio of 1 is considered to be a good thumb-rule. Srinivasa corporation Ltd. quick ratio of 1.32 is therefore fine.

Ratios to assess company's Asset & Liability Efficiency

FIXED ASSETS TURNOVER

How does the company's net sales compare with the value of its fixed assets?

			31-Mar-14	31-Mar-13
Quick Ratio	**(a - c) t b**	**Times**	**1.32**	**1.32**
a Current Assets	B/S	Rs. Cr.	34,510.87	26,317.62
b Current Liabilities & Provisions	B/S	Rs. Cr.	18,453.75	14,767.35
c Inventory	B/S	Rs. Cr.	10,121.45	6,857.23

Srinivasa corporations Ltd is able to turnover its fixed assets 3.5 times. This is then compared to other companies in the sector, to see how well Srinivasa corporations Ltd is able to use its fixed assets to generate income.

INVENTORY TURNOVER

How efficient is the company's inventory management? A company that has implemented practices like Just-in-time inventory will score well on this front.

			31-Mar-14	31-Mar-13
Inventory Turnover	**a t b**	**times**	**3.58**	**4.37**
a Cost of Goods Sold	c + d + e	Rs. Cr.	36,280.24	29,934.36
b Inventory	B/S	Rs. Cr.	10,121.45	6,857.23
c Expenditure	P&L	Rs. Cr.	34,741.88	28,447.94
d Depreciation	P&L	Rs. Cr.	1,285.12	1,235.48
e Interest & Finance Charges	P&L	Rs. Cr.	253.24	250.94

Srinivasa corporation Ltd. inventory turnover of 3.58 times can be compared with other companies in the sector, to assess its efficiency. It is pertinent to note that the inventory turnover has worsened during 2013-14.

If the company's inventory is getting turned over 3.58 times in a year, that means that inventory is held in the company for about 365 -r 3.58 i.e. 101.8 days. Such a long inventory holding period is maintained only if there are challenges in the supply chain (on account of potential disturbances or long distances for goods movement, or movement of goods between countries) or if the company has a long manufacturing cycle.

DEBTORS' TURNOVER

How efficient is the company in the credit it gives to its buyers?

			31-Mar-14	31-Mar-13
Debtors Turnover	**a t b**	**times**	**16.10**	**14.95**
a Gross Sales	P&L	Rs. Cr.	48,681.39	45,555.34
b Debtors	B/S	Rs. Cr.	3,024.36	3,048.12

The debtor's turnover of Srinivasa corporations Ltd has improved in 2013-14, which is a good sign.

AVERAGE COLLECTION PERIOD

On an average, in how many days is the company able to convert its credit sales into collections?

			31-Mar-14	31-Mar-13
Average Collection Period	**a t b**	**days**	**22.68**	**24.42**
a Days in a year		days	365	365
b Debtors Turnover		times	16.10	14.95

The average collection period of 23 days can be compared, not only with others in the industry, but also the company's own collection policy. If Srinivasa corporations Ltd, on an average, gives 15 days credit to buyers, then the company is poor in its collections. On the other hand, if the normal credit is 30 days, then the company has a good collection record.

AVERAGE PAYMENT PERIOD

Generally, credit availed from a supplier does not have an interest cost. Any company should take full benefit of zero cost funding opportunities.

Average Payment Period	c t (bTa)	days	31-Mar-14	31-Mar-13
			81.04	**82.13**
a Days in a year		days	365	365
b Expenditure	P&L	Rs. Cr.	34,741.88	28,447.94
c Current Liabilities	B/S	Rs. Cr.	7,713.39	6,400.92

Srinivasa corporations Ltd has a long payment period of 81 days. Thus, it is able to avail credit from its suppliers for 81 days, while it is giving credit of only 23 days to its buyers. This is good.

However, the 81 days of credit period from suppliers, as compared to 101 day inventory holding period plus 23 day collection period means that the company will keep facing working capital challenges when it expands operations.

RATIOS TO ASSESS COMPANY'S RETURN GENERATION EFFICIENCY RETURN ON CAPITAL EMPLOYED (ROCE)

The company's margins were assessed earlier. That was a measure of profitability of its operations. How does the profitability compare with the money invested in the business? For this, one has to consider how much the company earned, before any payment was made to any financier (debt as well as equity). This is to be compared with the money mobilized from all financiers (debt as well as equity).

The calculation also has to factor in the tax shield on interest, which can be illustrated through a simple example:

Suppose a company made Rs. 100 of profit, and tax rate was 30%, the company would pay Rs. 30 of tax. Profits after tax would be Rs. 100 minus Rs. 30 i.e. Rs. 70.

If the company also had to bear an interest cost of Rs. 10. The revised profit before tax would be Rs. 90. 30% tax would mean a tax outgo of Rs. 27. Profits after tax would thus be Rs. 90 minus Rs. 27 i.e. Rs. 63.

The interest cost of Rs. 10, lowered the profit by only Rs. 70 minus Rs. 63 i.e. Rs. 7. This is because the interest cost also reduced the tax to the extent of 30% of the interest cost. This tax break on the interest is called a *tax shield.*

Return on Capital Employed	**a t b**	**%**	**17.68%**	**29.48%**
a Profits before servicing of financiers	c + d - e	Rs. Cr.	6,280.15	7,697.63
b Total Sources of Funds	B/S	Rs. Cr.	35,522.89	26,108.81
c Profit after Tax before Exceptional Items	P&L	Rs. Cr.	6,115.39	7,532.79

Return on Capital Employed a T b % 17.68%29.48%

a	Interest Cost	P&L	Rs. Cr.	253.24	250.94
b	Tax Shield on Interest Cost	d X f	Rs. Cr.	88.48	86.10
c	Tax Rate	g ^ h	%	34.94%	34.31%
d	Tax	P&L	Rs. Cr.	3,284.28	3,934.65
e	Profit before tax & exceptional items	P&L	Rs. Cr.	9,399.67	11,467.44

Srinivasa corporations Ltd's ROCE has deteriorated quite significantly during 2013-14, largely led by lower margins (which in turn were caused by higher material costs).

The ROCE can be compared with other companies in the sector, to see how efficient is the company in generating a return on the funds it deploys.

RETURN ON EQUITY (ROE)

ROCE did not make a differentiation based on where the funds came from - debt or equity. It only looked at how much the business generated on the funds invested.

ROE looks at the return specifically for equity shareholders. Therefore, it looks at the profits that are left over after the debt financiers are paid their interest cost.

Return on Equity	a t b	%	31-Mar-14 21.85%	31-Mar-13 32.66%
a. Profit after Tax before	P&L	Rs. Cr.	6,115.39	7,532.79
b. Exceptional Items b Net	c + d	Rs. Cr.	27,984.10	23,063.57
c. Share Capital	B/S	Rs. Cr.	4,130.40	4,130.40
d. Reserves	B/S	Rs. Cr.	23,853.70	18,933.17

For the same reasons as ROCE, ROE too has declined in 2013-14. How did the ROCE of 17.68% translate into a higher ROE of 21.85%? The ROCE, the return that the business inherently generated, was 17.68%. The funds came from debt and equity.

Debt was serviced through interest payments. During 2013-14, Srinivasa corporations Ltd started with loans of Rs. 3,045.24crore and ended with loans of Rs. 7,538.79crore. Thus, on an average, there was a debt outstanding of Rs. 5,292.02crore during the year. On this, the company paid interest of Rs. 253.24crore. The effective interest rate is Rs. 253.24 -r Rs. 5,292.02 i.e. 4.79%.

The company earned 17.68% on the funds deployed, but had to pay only 4.79% interest to the debt financiers. The excess returns over the interest cost belong to the equity investors. Thus, the lower cost debt funding helped to boost the ROE of the company. This benefited the equity shareholders. Based on debt-equity and interest coverage, we saw that Srinivasa corporations Ltd is under-leveraged. If it had leveraged more i.e. gone for a higher mix of debt in its capital structure, it would have been able to demonstrate a smarter ROE for its equity investors.

Example: 3

Listed companies have to send all their shareholders annual reports. In addition, the quarterly financials of the company can be found on the stock exchanges' websites and on the website of the company. Here are the financial statements of a major IT services company, Druva Technologies Ltd.(DTL).

Comparative Balance Sheets (All figures in Rs. Crs.)

	Mar '10	Mar '11	Mar '12	Mar '13	Mar '14
Sources of Funds					
Total Share Capital	138	286	286	286	287
Equity Share Capital	138	286	286	286	287
Share Application Money	0	0	0	0	0
Preference Share Capital	0	0	0	0	0
Reserves	6,759	10,876	13,204	17,523	21,749
Revaluation Reserves	0	0	0	0	0
Net worth	**6,897**	**11,162**	**13,490**	**17,809**	**22,036**
Secured Loans	0	0	0	0	0
Unsecured Loans	0	0	0	0	0
Total Debt	0	0	0	0	0
Total Liabilities	**6,897**	**11,162**	**13,490**	**17,809**	**22,036**
Application Of Funds					
Gross Block	2,837	3,889	4,508	5,986	3,779
Less: Accumulated Depreciation	1,275	1,739	1,837	2,187	0
Net Block	**1,562**	**2,150**	**2,671**	**3,799**	**3,779**
Capital Work in Progress	571	957	1,260	615	409
Investments	**876**	**839**	**964**	**1,005.00**	**4,636.00**
Inventories	0	0	0	0	0
Sundry Debtors	1,518	2,292	3,093	3,390	3,244
Cash and Bank Balance	544	680	657	805	9,797
Total Current Assets	2,062	2,972	3,750	4,195	13,041
Loans and Advances	1,308	1,241	2,804	3,303	4,201
Fixed Deposits	2,735	4,827	5,772	8,234	0
Total Current Assets, Loans & Advances	**6,105**	**9,040**	**12,326**	**15,732**	**17,242**
Deferred Credit	0	0	0	0	0
Current Liabilities	**808**	**1,162**	**1,483**	**1,544**	**1,995**
Provisions	1,409	662	2,248	1,798	2,035
Total CL & Provisions	2,217	1,824	3,731	3,342	4,030
Net Current Assets	**3,888**	**7,216**	**8,595**	**12,390**	**13,212**
Miscellaneous Expenses	0	0	0	0	0
Total Assets	**6,897**	**11,162**	**13,490**	**17,809**	**22,036**

DTL Technologies Limited

COMPARATIVE INCOME STATEMENTS

	Mar '10	Mar '11	Mar '12	Mar '13	Mar '14
Income					
Sales Turnover	9,028	13,149	15,648	20,264	21,140
Excise Duty	0	0	0	0	0
Net Sales	**9,028**	**13,149**	**15,648**	**20,264**	**21,140**
Other Income	144	379	683	502	958
Stock Adjustments	0	0	0	0	0
Total Income	**9,172**	**13,528**	**16,331**	**20,766**	**22,098**
Expenditure					
Raw Materials	16	22	18	20	0
Power & Fuel Cost	62	88	106	125	0
Employee Cost	4,274	6,316	7,771	9,975	10,356
Other Manufacturing Expenses	792	1,290	1,443	1,697	2,317
Selling and Admin Expenses	773	1,051	1,214	1,367	215
Miscellaneous Expenses		156	132	172	883
Preoperative Expense Capitalized	0	0	0	0	0
Total Expenses	**6,038**	**8,923**	**10,684**	**13,356**	**13,771**
Operating Profit	2,990	4,226	4,964	6,908	7,369
PBDIT	3,134	4,605	5,647	7,410	8,327
Interest	1	1	1	2	0
PBDT	3,133	4,604	5,646	7,408	8,327
Depreciation	409	469	546	694	807
Other Written Off	0	0	0	0	0
Profit Before Tax	2,724	4,135	5,100	6,714	7,520
Extra-ordinary items	0	-5	0	-1	0
Profits Before Tax (Post Extraordinary Items)	2,724	4,130	5,100	6,713	7,520
Tax	303	352	630	895	1,717
Reported Net Profit	**2,421**	**3,783**	**4,470**	**5,819**	**5,803**
Total Value Addition	6,022	8,901	10,666	13,336	13,771
Preference Dividend	0	0	0	0	0
Equity Dividend	1,238	649	1,902	1,345	1,434
Corporate Dividend Tax	174	102	323	228	240
Per share data (annualized)					
Shares in issue (lakhs)	2,756	5,712	5,720	5,728	5,728
Earnings Per Share (Rs)	**88**	**66**	**78**	**102**	**101**
Equity Dividend (%)	900	230	665	470	500

STATEMENT OF CASH FLOWS

	Mar '10	Mar '11	Mar '12	Mar '13	Mar '14
Net Profit Before Tax	**2724**	**4129**	**5100**	**6714**	**7472**
Cash Flow from Operations	2237	3256	3816	5152	5876
Cash Flow from Investing	-392	-1065	-978	-195	-3314
Cash Flow from Financing	244	-316	-777	-2430	-1486
Net (decrease) / increase In Cash	**2096**	**1871**	**2079**	**2600**	**1008**
Opening Cash	1683	3779	5610	7689	10289
Closing Cash	3779	5650	7689	10289	11297

The primary and most important source of information about a company are its Annual Reports, prepared and distributed to the shareholders by law each year. Annual Reports are usually well presented. A tremendous amount of data is given about the performance of a company over a period of time. If an Annual Report is impressive about the operations and future direction, if the company has made a profit and if a reasonable dividend has been paid, the average investor is typically content in the belief that the company is in good hands. However, for a fundamental analyst or for that matter any investor, this alone must not be the criterion by which to judge a company. The intelligent investor must read the annual report in depth; he must read between and beyond the lines; he must peep behind the figures and find the truth and only then should he decide whether the company is doing well or not.

The Annual Report is usually broken down into the following specific parts:

1. The Director's Report
2. The Auditor's Report
3. The Financial Statements and
4. The Schedules and Notes to the Accounts.

Each of these parts has a purpose and a story to tell.

THE DIRECTOR'S REPORT

The Director's Report is a report submitted by the directors of a company to shareholders, informing them about the performance of the company, under their stewardship:

1. It enunciates the opinion of the directors on the state of the economy and the political situation vis-a-vis the company.
2. Explains the performance and the financial results of the company in the period under review. This is an extremely important part. The results and operations of the various separate divisions are usually detailed and investors can determine the reasons for their good or bad performance.
3. The Director's Report details the company's plans for modernization, expansion and diversification. Without these, a company will remain static and eventually decline.

4. Discusses the profits earned in the period under review and the dividend recommended by the directors. This paragraph should normally be read with sane scepticism as the directors will always argue that the performance was satisfactory. If profits have improved the reasons stated would invariably be superior technology adopted, intense marketing and hard work in the face of severe competition etc. If profits are low, adverse economic conditions are usually blamed for the same.
5. Elaborates on the directors' views of the company's prospects for the future.
6. Discusses plans for new acquisitions and investments.

An investor must intelligently evaluate the issues raised in a Director's Report. If the report talks about diversification, one must the question that though diversification is a good strategy, does it make sense for the company? Industry conditions, the management's knowledge of the new business must be considered. Although companies must diversify in order to spread the risks of economic slumps, every diversification may not suit a company. Similarly, all other issues raised in the Director's Report should be analyzed. Did the company perform as well as others in the same industry? Is the finance being raised the most logical and beneficial to the company? It is imperative that the investor read between the lines of the Director's Report and find the answers to these and many other questions. In short, a Director's Report is valuable and if read intelligently can give the investor a good grasp of the workings of a company, the problems it faces, the direction it intends taking and its future prospects.

THE AUDITOR'S REPORT

The auditor represents the shareholders and it is the auditor's duty to report to the shareholders and the general public on the stewardship of the company by its directors. Auditors are required to report whether the financial statements presented do in fact present a true and fair view of the state of the company. Investors must remember that the auditors are required by law to point out if the financial statements are true and fair. They are also required to report any change, such as a change in accounting principles or the non-provision of charges that result in an increase or decrease in profits. It is really the only impartial report that a shareholder or investor receives and this alone should spur one to scrutinize the auditor's report minutely. Unfortunately, more often than not it is not read. There can be interesting contradictions. It was stated in the Auditor's Report of ABC Co. Ltd. for the year 1999-2000 that, "As at the year-end 31st March 2000 the accumulated losses exceed the net worth of the Company and the Company has suffered cash losses in the financial year ended 31st March 2000 as well as in the immediately preceding financial year. In our opinion, therefore, the Company is a sick industrial company within the meaning of clause (O) of Section 3(1) of the Sick Industrial Companies (Special Provisions) Act 1985". The Director's report however stated, "The financial year under review has not been a favourable year for the Company as the computer industry in general continued to be in the grip of recession. High input costs as well as resource constraints hampered operations. The performance of your Company must be assessed in the light of these factors. During the year manufacturing operations were curtailed to achieve cost effectiveness. Your directors are confident that the efforts for increased business volumes and cost control will yield better results in the current year". The auditors were of the opinion that the company was sick whereas the directors spoke optimistically of their hope that the future would be better! They could not, being directors, state otherwise.

At times, accounting principles are changed or creative and innovative accounting practices resorted to by some companies in order to show a better result. The effect of these changes is at times not detailed in the notes to the accounts. The Auditor's Report will always draw the attention of the reader to these changes and the effect that these have on the financial statements. It is for this reason that a careful reading of the Auditor's Report is not only necessary but mandatory for an investor.

FINANCIAL STATEMENTS

The published financial statements of a company in an Annual Report consist of its **Balance Sheet** as at the end of the accounting period detailing the financing condition of the company at that date and the **Profit and Loss Account** or **Income Statement** summarizing the activities of the company for the accounting period and the **Statement of Cash Flows** for the accounting period.

BALANCE SHEET

The Balance Sheet details the financial position of a company on a particular date; the company's assets (that which the company owns), and liabilities (that which the company owes), grouped logically under specific heads. It must however, be noted that the Balance Sheet details the financial position on a particular day and that the position can be materially different on the next day or the day after.

SOURCES OF FUNDS

A company has to source funds to purchase fixed assets, to procure working capital and to fund its business. For the company to make a profit, the funds have to cost less than the return the company earns on their deployment.

Where does a company raise funds? What are the sources?

Companies raise funds from its shareholders and by borrowing.

(a) Shareholders' Funds (Total Share Capital in DTL's Balance Sheet)

A company sources funds from shareholders by the issue of shares. Shareholders' funds is the balance sheet value of shareholders' interest in a company. For the accounts of a company with no subsidiaries it is total assets minus total liabilities. For consolidated group accounts the value of minority interests is excluded. Minority interest refers to the portion of a subsidiary corporation's stock that is not owned by the parent corporation.

Shareholders' funds represent the stake shareholders have in the company, the investment they have made.

SHARE CAPITAL

Share capital represents the shares issued to the public. This is issued in following ways:

Private Placement - This is done by offering shares to selected individuals or institutions.

Public Issue - Shares are offered to public. The details of the offer, including the reasons for raising the money are detailed in a prospectus and it is important that investors read this.

Rights issues - Companies may also issue shares to their shareholders as a matter of right in proportion to their holding. So, if an investor has 100 shares and a company announces a 2:1 right, the investor stands to gain an additional 200 shares. Rights issues come at a price which the investors must pay by subscribing to the rights offer. The rights issues were often offered at a price lower than the company's market value and shareholders stood to gain. With the freedom in respect of pricing of shares now available, companies have begun pricing their offerings nearer their intrinsic value. Consequently, many of these issues have not been particularly attractive to investors and several have failed to be fully subscribed. However, strong companies find subscribers to their rights issues as investors are of the view that their long-term performance would lead to increase in share prices.

Bonus shares - When a company has accumulated a large reserve out of profits, the directors may decide to distribute a part of it amongst the shareholders in the form of bonus. Bonus can be paid either in cash or in the form of shares. Cash bonus is paid in the form of dividend by the company when it has large accumulated profits as well as cash. Many a times, a company is not in a position to pay bonus in cash (dividend) in spite of sufficient profits because of unsatisfactory cash position or because of its adverse effects on the working capital of the company. In such a case, the company pays a bonus to its shareholders in the form of shares. Bonus shares are shares issued free to shareholders by capitalizing reserves. No monies are actually raised from shareholders. Nothing stops a company from declaring a bonus and dividend together if it has large accumulated profits as well as cash.

Reserves - Reserves are profits or gains which are retained and not distributed. Companies have two kinds of reserves - capital reserves and revenue reserves:

Capital Reserves - Capital reserves are gains that have resulted from an increase in the value of assets and they are not freely distributable to the shareholders. The most common capital reserves one comes across are the share premium account arising from the issue of shares at a premium and the capital revaluation reserve, i.e. unrealized gain on the value of assets.

Revenue Reserves - These represent profits from operations ploughed back into the company and not distributed as dividends to shareholders. It is important that all the profits are not distributed as funds are required by companies to purchase new assets to replace existing ones, for expansion and for working capital.

Loan Funds - The other source of funds a company has access to is borrowings. Borrowing is often preferred by companies as it is quicker, relatively easier and the rules that need to be complied with are much less. The loans taken by companies are either:

Secured loans - These loans are taken by a company by pledging some of its assets or by a floating charge on some or all of its assets. The usual secured loans a company has are debentures and term loans.

Unsecured loans - Companies do not pledge any assets when they take unsecured loans. The comfort a lender has is usually only the good name and credit worthiness of the company. The more common unsecured loans of a company are fixed deposits and short-term loans. In case a company is dissolved, unsecured lenders are usually paid after the secured lenders have been paid. Borrowings or credits for working capital which fluctuate such as bank overdrafts and trade creditors are not normally classified as loan funds but as current liabilities.

Fixed Assets (Net Block in DTL's Balance Sheet) - Fixed assets are assets that a company owns for use in its business and to produce goods. Typically, it could be machinery. They are not for resale and comprises of land, buildings i.e. offices, warehouses and factories, vehicles, machinery, furniture, equipment and the like. Every company has some fixed assets though the nature or kind of fixed assets vary from company to company. A manufacturing company's major fixed assets would be its factory and machinery, whereas that of a shipping company would be its ships. Fixed assets are shown in the Balance Sheet at cost less the accumulated depreciation. Depreciation is based on the very sound concept that an asset has a useful life and that after years of toil it wears down. Consequently, it attempts to measure that wear and tear and to reduce the value of the asset accordingly so that at the end of its useful life, the asset will have no value.

As depreciation is a charge on profits, at the end of its useful life, the company would have set aside from profits an amount equal to the original cost of the asset and this could be utilized to purchase another asset. However, in the inflationary times, this is inadequate and some companies create an additional reserve to ensure that there are sufficient funds to replace the worn-out asset. The common methods of depreciation are:

Straight line method - The cost of the asset is written off equally over its life. Consequently, at the end of its useful life, the cost will equal the accumulated depreciation.

Reducing balance method - Under this method, depreciation is calculated on the written down value, i.e. cost less depreciation. Consequently, depreciation is higher in the beginning and lower as the years progress. An asset is never fully written off as the depreciation is always calculated on a reducing balance. Land is the only fixed asset that is never depreciated as it normally appreciates in value. Capital work in progress - factories being constructed, etc. - are not depreciated until it is a fully functional asset.

Investments- Many companies purchase investments in the form of shares or debentures to earn income or to utilize cash surpluses profitably. The normal investments a company has are:

Trade investments - Trade investments are normally shares or debentures of competitors that a company holds to have access to information on their growth, profitability and other details.

Subsidiary and associate companies - These are shares held in subsidiary or associate companies. The large business houses hold controlling interest in several companies through cross holdings in subsidiary and associate companies.

Others - Companies also often hold shares or debentures of other companies for investment or to park surplus funds.

Investments are also classified as quoted and unquoted investments. Quoted investments are shares and debentures that are quoted in a recognized stock exchange and can be freely traded. Unquoted investments are not listed or quoted in a stock exchange. Consequently, they are not liquid and are difficult to dispose of.

Investments are valued and stated in the balance sheet at either the acquisition cost or market value, whichever is lower. This is in order to be conservative and to ensure that losses are adequately accounted for.

Current assets - Current assets are assets owned by a company which are used in the normal course of business or are generated by the company in the course of business such as debtors or finished stock or cash.

The rule of thumb is that any asset that is turned into cash within twelve months is a current asset. Current assets can be divided essentially into three categories:

Converting assets - Assets that are produced or generated in the normal course of business, such as finished goods and debtors.

Constant assets - Constant assets are those that are purchased and sold without any add-ons or conversions, such as liquor bought by a liquor store from a liquor manufacturer.

Cash equivalents - They can be used to repay dues or purchase other assets. The most common cash equivalent assets are cash in hand and at the bank and loans given.

The current assets a company has are:

Inventories - These are arguably the most important current assets that a company has as it is by the sale of its stocks that a company makes its profits. Stocks, in turn, consist of:

Raw materials - The primary purchase which is utilized to manufacture the products a company makes.

Work- in- progress - Goods that are in the process of manufacture but are yet to be completed.

Finished goods - The finished products manufactured by the company that are ready for sale.

VALUATION OF STOCKS

Stocks are valued at the lower of cost or net realizable value. This is to ensure that there will be no loss at the time of sale as that would have been accounted for. The common methods of valuing stocks are:

FIFO or first in first out - It is assumed under this method that stocks that come in first would be sold first and those that come in last would be sold last.

LIFO or last in last out - The premise on which this method is based is the opposite of FIFO. It is assumed that the goods that arrive last will be sold first. The reasoning is that customers prefer newer materials or products. It is important to ascertain the method of valuation and the accounting principles involved as stock values can easily be manipulated by changing the method of valuation.

Debtors - Most companies do not sell their products for cash but on credit and purchasers are expected to pay for the goods they have bought within an agreed period of time - 30 days or 60 days. The period of credit would vary from customer to customer and from the company to company and depends on the credit worthiness of the customer, market conditions and competition. Often customers may not pay within the agreed credit period. This may be due to laxity in credit administration or the inability of the customers to pay. Consequently, debts are classified as:

- These are further subdivided into;
- Debts considered good, and
- Debts considered bad and doubtful

If debts are likely to be bad, they must be provided for or written off. If this is not done, assets will be overstated to the extent of the bad debt. A write off is made only when there is no hope of recovery. Otherwise, a provision is made. Provisions may be specific or they may be general. When amounts are provided on certain identified debts, the provision is termed specific whereas if a provision amounting to a certain percentage of all debts is made, the provision is termed general.

Prepaid Expenses - All payments are not made when due. Many payments, such as insurance premia, rent and service costs, are made in advance for a period of time which may be 3 months, 6 months, or even a year. The portion of such expenses that relates to the next accounting period are shown as prepaid expenses in the Balance Sheet.

Cash & Bank Balances - Cash in hand in petty cash boxes, safes and balances in bank accounts are shown under this heading in the Balance Sheet.

Loans & Advances - These are loans that have been given to other corporations, individuals and employees and are repayable within a certain period of time. This also includes amounts paid in advance for the supply of goods, materials and services.

Other Current Assets - Other current assets are all amounts due that are recoverable within the next twelve months. These include claims receivable, interest due on investments and the like.

Current Liabilities - Current liabilities are amounts due that are payable within the next twelve months. These also include provisions which are amounts set aside for an expense incurred for which the bill has not been received as yet or whose cost has not been fully estimated.

Creditors - Trade creditors are those to whom the company owes money for raw materials and other articles used in the manufacture of its products. Companies usually purchase these on credit - the credit period depending on the demand for the item, the standing of the company and market practice.

Accrued Expenses - Certain expenses such as interest on bank overdrafts, telephone costs, electricity and overtime are paid after they have been incurred. This is because they fluctuate and it is not possible to either prepay or accurately anticipate these expenses. However, the expense has been incurred. To recognize this the expense incurred is estimated based on past trends and known expenses incurred and accrued on the date of the Balance Sheet.

Provisions - Provisions are amounts set aside from profits for an estimated expense or loss. Certain provisions such as depreciation and provisions for bad debts are deducted from the concerned asset itself. There are others, such as claims that may be payable, for which provisions are made. Other provisions normally seen on balance sheets are those for dividends and taxation.

Sundry Creditors - Any other amounts due are usually clubbed under the all-embracing title of sundry creditors. These include unclaimed dividends and dues payable to third parties.

INCOME STATEMENT

The Profit and Loss account summarizes the activities of a company during an accounting period which may be a month, a quarter, six months, a year or longer, and the result achieved by the company. It details the income earned by the company, its cost and the resulting profit or loss. It is, in effect, the performance appraisal not only of the company but also of its management - its competence, foresight and ability to lead.

Sales - Sales include the amount received or receivable from customers arising from the sales of goods and the provision of services by a company. A sale occurs when the ownership of goods and the consequent risk relating to these goods are passed to the customer in return for consideration, usually cash. In normal circumstances the physical possession of the goods is also transferred at the same time. A sale does not occur when a company places goods at the shop of a dealer with the clear understanding that payment need be made only after the goods are sold failing which they may be returned. In such a case, the ownership and risks are not transferred to the dealer nor any consideration paid.

Companies do give trade discounts and other incentive discounts to customers to entice them to buy their products. Sales should be accounted for after deducting these discounts. However, cash discounts given for early payment are a finance expense and should be shown as an expense and not deducted from sales.

There are many companies which deduct excise duty and other levies from sales. There are others who show this as an expense. It is preferable to deduct these from sales since the sales figures would then reflect the actual mark-up made by the company on its cost of production.

Other Income - Companies may also receive income from sources other than from the sale of their products or the provision of services. These are usually clubbed together under the heading, other income. The more common items that appear under this title are:

- **Profit from the sale of assets** - Profit from the sale of investments or assets.
- **Dividends** - Dividends earned from investments made by the company in the shares of other companies.
- **Rent** - Rent received from commercial buildings and apartments leased from the company.
- **Interest** - Interest received on deposits made and loans given to corporate and other bodies.

Raw Materials - The raw materials and other items used in the manufacture of a company's products. It is also sometimes called the cost of goods sold.

Employee Costs - The costs of employment are accounted for under this head and would include wages, salaries, bonus, gratuity, contributions made to provident and other funds, welfare expenses, and other employee related expenditure.

Operating & Other Expenses - All other costs incurred in running a company are called operating and other expenses, and include.

Selling expenses - The cost of advertising, sales commissions, sales promotion expenses and other sales related expenses.

Administration expenses - Rent of offices and factories, municipal taxes, stationery, telephone and telex costs, electricity charges, insurance, repairs, motor maintenance, and all other expenses incurred to run a company.

Others - These include costs that are not strictly administration or selling expenses, such as donations made, losses on the sale of fixed assets or investments, miscellaneous expenditure and the like.

Interest & Finance Charges - A company has to pay interest on money it borrows. This is normally shown separately as it is a cost distinct from the normal costs incurred in running a business and would vary from company to company.

The normal borrowings that a company pays interest on are:

1. Bank overdrafts
2. Term loans taken for the purchase of machinery or construction of a factory
3. Fixed deposits from the public
4. Debentures
5. Inter-corporate loan.

Depreciation - Depreciation represents the wear and tear incurred by the fixed assets of a company, i.e. the reduction in the value of fixed assets on account of usage. This is also shown separately as the depreciation charge of similar companies in the same industry will differ, depending on the age of the fixed assets and the cost at which they have been bought.

Tax - Most companies are taxed on the profits that they make. It must be remembered however that taxes are payable on the taxable income or profit and this can differ from the accounting income or profit. Taxable income is what income is according to tax law, which is different to what accounting standards consider income to be. Some income and expenditure items are excluded for tax purposes (i.e. they are not assessable or not deductible) but are considered legitimate income or expenditure for accounting purposes.

Dividends - Dividends are profits distributed to shareholders. The total profits after tax are not always distributed - a portion is often ploughed back into the company for its future growth and expansion. Companies generally pay an interim and / or final dividend. Interim dividend usually accompanies the company's interim financial statements. The final dividend is usually declared after the results for the period have been determined. The final dividend is proposed at the annual general meeting of the company and paid after the approval of the shareholders.

Transfer to Reserves - The transfer to reserves is the profit ploughed back into the company. This may be done to finance working capital, expansion, fixed assets or for some other purpose. These are revenue reserves and can be distributed to shareholders as dividends.

Contingent Liabilities - Contingent liabilities are liabilities that may arise up on the happening of an event. It is uncertain however whether the event itself may happen. This is why these are not provided for and shown as an actual liability in the balance sheet. Contingent liabilities are detailed in the Financial Statements as a note to inform the readers of possible future liabilities while arriving at an opinion about the company. The contingent liabilities one normally encounters are:

- Bills discounted with banks - These may crystallize into active liabilities if the bills are dishonoured.
- Gratuity to employees not provided for
    - Claims against a company not acknowledged or accepted
    - Excise claims against the company etc.

SCHEDULES AND NOTES TO THE ACCOUNTS

The schedules and notes to the accounts are an integral part of the financial statements of a company and it is important that they be read along with the financial statements.

Schedules - The schedules detail pertinent information about the items of Balance Sheet and Profit & Loss Account. It also details information about sales, manufacturing costs, administration costs, interest, and other income and expenses. This information is vital for the analysis of financial statements.

The schedules enable an investor to determine which expenses increased and seek the reasons for this. Similarly, investors would be able to find out the reasons for the increase or decrease in sales and the products that are sales leaders. The schedules even give details of stocks and sales, particulars of capacity and productions, and much other useful information.

Notes - The notes to the accounts are even more important than the schedules because it is here that very important information relating to the company is stated. Notes can effectively be divided into:

Accounting policies - All companies follow certain accounting principles and these may differ from those of other entities. As a consequence, the profit earned might differ. Companies have also been known to change (normally increase) their profit by changing the accounting policies. For instance, ABC Co. Ltd.'s Annual Report stated among other things, "There has been a change in the method of accounting relating to interest on borrowings used for capital expenditure. While such interest was fully written off in the previous years, interest charges incurred during the year have been capitalized for the period up to the date from which the assets have been put to use. Accordingly, expenditure transferred to capital account includes an amount of Rs. 46.63 crores towards interest capitalized. The profit before taxes for the year after the consequential adjustments of depreciation of Rs. 0.12 crore is therefore higher by Rs. 46.51 crores than what it would have been had the previous basis been followed". This means that by changing an accounting policy ABC Co. Ltd. was able to increase its income by Rs. 46 crores. There could be similar notes on other items in the financial statements.

The accounting policies normally detailed in the notes relate to:

- How sales are accounted for? **o** What the research and development costs are?
- How the gratuity liability is expensed? **o** How fixed assets are valued?
- How depreciation is calculated?
- How stock, including finished goods, work in progress, raw materials and consumable goods are valued? **o** How investments are stated in the balance sheet? **o** How has the foreign exchange translated?

Contingent liabilities - As noted earlier, contingent liabilities that might crystallize upon the happening of an uncertain event. All contingent liabilities are detailed in the notes to the accounts and it would be wise to read these as they give valuable insights. The more common contingent liabilities that one comes across in the financial statements of companies are:

- Outstanding guarantees. **o** Outstanding letters of credit. **o** Outstanding bills discounted.
- Claims against the company not acknowledged as debts. **o** Claim for taxes. **o** Cheques discounted.
- Uncalled liability on partly paid shares and debentures.

Others - It must be appreciated that the purpose of notes to the accounts is to inform the reader more fully. Consequently, they detail all pertinent factors which affect, or will affect, the company and its results. Often as a consequence, adjustments may need to be made to the accounts to unearth the true results. The more common notes one comes across are:

- Whether provisions for known or likely losses have been made.
- Estimated value of contracts outstanding. **o** Interest not provided for.
- Arrangements agreed by the company with third parties. **o** Agreement with labour.

The importance of these notes cannot be overstressed. It is imperative that investors read these carefully.

CASH FLOW STATEMENT

Complementing the balance sheet and income statement, the cash flow statement (CFS) allows investors to understand how a company's operations are running, where its money is coming from and how it is being spent.

THE STRUCTURE OF THE CFS

The cash flow statement is distinct from the income statement and balance sheet because it does not include the amount of future incoming and outgoing cash that has been recorded on credit. Therefore, cash is not the same as net income, which, on the income statement and balance sheet, includes cash sales and sales made on credit. Cash flow is determined by looking at three components by which cash enters and leaves a company, its core operations, investing activities and financing activities.

CASH FLOW FROM OPERATIONS

Measuring the cash inflows and outflows caused by core business operations, the operations component of cash flow reflects how much cash is generated from a company's products or services. Generally, changes made in cash, accounts receivable, depreciation, inventory and accounts payable are reflected in cash from operations. Cash flow is calculated by making certain adjustments to net income by adding or subtracting differences in revenue, expenses and credit transactions (appearing on the balance sheet and income statement) resulting from transactions that occur from one period to the next. These adjustments are made because non-cash items are calculated into net income (income statement) and total assets and liabilities (balance sheet). So, because not all transactions involve actual cash items, many items have to be re-evaluated when calculating cash flow from operations.

For example, depreciation is not really a cash expense; it is an amount that is deducted from the total value of an asset that has previously been accounted for. That is why it is added back into net sales for calculating cash flow. The only time income from an asset is accounted for in cash flow statement calculations is when the asset is sold.

Changes in accounts receivable on the balance sheet from one accounting period to the next must also be reflected in cash flow. If accounts receivable decreases, this implies that more cash has entered the company from customers paying off their credit accounts - the amount by which accounts receivable has decreased is then added to net sales. If accounts receivable increases from one accounting period to the next, the amount of the increase must be deducted from net sales because, although the amounts represented in accounts receivable are revenue, they are not cash.

An increase in inventory, on the other hand, signals that a company has spent more money to purchase more raw materials. If the inventory was paid with cash, the increase in the value of inventory is deducted from net sales. A decrease in inventory would be added to net sales. If inventory was purchased on credit, an increase in accounts payable would occur on the balance sheet, and the amount of the increase from one year to the other would be added to net sales.

The same logic holds true for taxes payable, salaries payable and prepaid insurance. If something has been paid off, then the difference in the value owed from one year to the next has to be subtracted from net income. If there is an amount that is still owed, then any differences will have to be added to net earnings.

CASH FLOW FROM INVESTING

Changes in equipment, assets or investments relate to cash from investing. Usually cash changes from investing are a "cash out" item, because cash is used to buy new equipment, buildings or short-term assets such as marketable securities. However, when a company divests of an asset, the transaction is considered "cash in" for calculating cash from investing.

CASH FLOW FROM FINANCING

Changes in debt, loans or dividends are accounted for in cash from financing. Changes in cash from financing are "cash in" when capital is raised, and they're "cash out" when dividends are paid. Thus, if a company issues a bond to the public, the company receives cash financing; however, when interest is paid to bondholders, the company is reducing its cash.

A company can use a cash flow statement to predict future cash flow, which helps with matters in budgeting. For investors, the cash flow reflects a company's financial health: basically, the more cash available for business operations, the better. However, this is not a hard and fast rule. Sometimes a negative cash flow results from a company's growth strategy in the form of expanding its operations.

By adjusting earnings, revenues, assets and liabilities, the investor can get a very clear picture of what some people consider the most important aspect of a company: how much cash it generates and particularly, how much of that cash stems from core operations.

FINANCIAL STATEMENT ANALYSIS AND FORENSIC ACCOUNTING

A comprehensive financial statement analysis provides insights into a firm's performance and/or standing in the areas of liquidity, leverage, operating efficiency and profitability. A complete analysis involves both time series and cross-sectional perspectives. Time series analysis examines trends using the firm's own performance as a benchmark. Cross sectional analysis augments the process by using external performance benchmarks (Industry or peers) for comparison purposes.

COMPARATIVE AND COMMON-SIZE FINANCIAL STATEMENTS

As seen in the previous NCFM module[1], we often use comparative financial statements in order to compare different financial ratios of a firm with the industry averages and other peers in the industry whereas we use common-size financial statements in order to compare performance of a firm or two firms over time. Financial ratios in isolation mean nothing. We need to observe them change over time or compare financial ratios of a cross section of firms in order to make sense of them.

FINANCIAL RATIOS

To find the data used in the examples in this section, please see the DTL Technologies Limited's financial statements given earlier.

LIQUIDITY MEASUREMENT RATIOS

The first ratios we'll take a look at are the liquidity ratios. Liquidity ratios attempt to measure a company's ability to pay off its short-term debt obligations. This is done by comparing a company's most liquid assets (or, those that can be easily converted to cash) and its short-term liabilities. In general, the greater the coverage of liquid assets to short-term liabilities, the better it is, since it is a clear signal that a company can pay debts that are going to become due in the near future and it can still fund its on-going operations. On the other hand, a company with a low coverage rate should raise a red flag for the investors as it may be a sign that the company will have difficulty meeting running its operations, as well as meeting its debt obligations.

The biggest difference between each ratio is the type of assets used in the calculation. While each ratio includes current assets, the more conservative ratios will exclude some current assets as they aren't as easily converted to cash. The ratios that we'll look at are the current, quick and cash ratios and we will also go over the cash conversion cycle, which goes into how the company turns its inventory into cash.

CURRENT RATIO

The current ratio is a popular financial ratio used to test a company's liquidity (also referred to as its current or working capital position) by deriving the proportion of current assets available to cover current liabilities. The concept behind this ratio is to ascertain whether a company's short-term assets (cash, cash equivalents, marketable securities, receivables and inventory) are readily available to pay off its short-term liabilities. In theory, the higher the current ratio, the better.

$$\text{Current Ratio} = \frac{\text{Current Assets}}{\text{Current Liabilities}}$$

As of March 31, 2010, with amounts expressed in Rs. crores, DTL'S current assets amounted to 13,041 (balance sheet), which is the numerator; while current liabilities amounted to 4030 (balance sheet), which is the denominator. By dividing, the equation gives us a current ratio of 3.24 which can be considered very healthy.

The current ratio is used extensively in financial reporting. However, while easy to understand, it can be misleading in both a positive and negative sense - i.e., a high current ratio is not necessarily good, and a low current ratio is not necessarily bad (see chart below).

Here's why: contrary to popular perception, the ubiquitous current ratio, as an indicator of liquidity, is flawed because it is conceptually based on the liquidation of all of a company's current assets to meet all of its current liabilities. In reality, this is not likely to occur. Investors have to look at a company as a going concern. It's the time it takes to convert a company's working capital assets into cash to pay its current obligations that is the key to its liquidity. In a word, the current ratio can be "misleading."

A simplistic, but accurate, comparison of two companies' current position will illustrate the weakness of relying on the current ratio or a working capital number (current assets minus current liabilities) as a sole indicator of liquidity (amounts in Rs. crs.) :

	ABC	BCD
Current Assets	600	300
Current Liabilities	300	300
Working Capital	300	0
Current Ratio	2	1

Company ABC looks like an easy winner in a liquidity contest. It has an ample margin of current assets over current liabilities, a seemingly good current ratio and working capital of Rs. 300. Company has no current asset/liability margin of safety, a weak current ratio, and no working capital.

However, to prove the point, what if: (1) both companies' current liabilities have an average payment period of 30 days; (2) Company ABC needs six months (180 days) to collect its account receivables and its inventory turns over just once a year (365 days); and (3) Company is paid cash by its customers, and its inventory turns over 24 times a year (every 15 days). In this contrived example, company ABC is very *illiquid* and would not be able to operate under the conditions described. Its bills are coming due faster than its generation of cash. You can't pay bills with working capital; you pay bills with cash! Company's 's seemingly tight current position is, in effect, much more liquid because of its quicker cash conversion. When looking at the current ratio, it is important that a company's current assets can cover its current liabilities; however, investors should be aware that this is not the whole story on company liquidity. Try to understand the types of current assets the company has and how quickly these can be converted into cash to meet current liabilities. This important perspective can be seen through the cash conversion cycle. By digging deeper into the current assets, you will gain a greater understanding of a company's true liquidity.

QUICK RATIO

The quick ratio - aka the quick assets ratio or the acid-test ratio - is a liquidity indicator that further refines the current ratio by measuring the amount of the most liquid current assets there are to cover current liabilities. The quick ratio is more conservative than the current ratio because it excludes inventory and other current assets, which are more difficult to turn into cash. Therefore, a higher ratio means a more liquid current position.

$$\text{Quick Ratio} = \frac{\text{Cash \& Equivalents} + \text{Short} - \text{term Investments} + \text{Accounts Receivables}}{\text{Current Liabilities}}$$

As of March 31, 2010, with amounts expressed in Rs. crores, DTL'S quick assets amounted to 13,041 (balance sheet); while current liabilities amounted to 4,030 (balance sheet). By dividing, the equation gives us a quick ratio of 3.24. DTL being in the services sector does not have any inventory on its balance sheet and this quick ratio and current ratio come out to be the same.

Some presentations of the quick ratio calculate quick assets (the formula's numerator) by simply subtracting the inventory figure from the total current assets figure. The assumption is that by excluding relatively less-liquid (harder to turn into cash) inventory, the remaining current assets are all of the more-liquid variety. Generally, this is close to the truth, but not always. In some companies, restricted cash, prepaid expenses and deferred income taxes do not pass the test of truly liquid assets. Thus, using the shortcut approach artificially overstates more liquid assets and inflates its quick ratio.

The quick ratio is a more conservative measure of liquidity than the current ratio as it removes inventory from the current assets used in the ratio's formula. By excluding inventory, the quick ratio focuses on the more-liquid assets of a company. The basics and use of this ratio are similar to the current ratio in that it gives users an idea of the ability of a company to meet its short-term liabilities with its short-term assets. Another beneficial use is to compare the quick ratio with the current ratio. If the current ratio is significantly higher, it is a clear indication that the company's current assets are dependent on inventory.

While considered more stringent than the current ratio, the quick ratio, because of its accounts receivable component, suffers from the same deficiencies as the current ratio - albeit somewhat less. Both the quick and the current ratios assume a liquidation of accounts receivable and inventory as the basis for measuring liquidity. While theoretically feasible, as a going concern a company must focus on the time it takes to convert its working capital assets to cash - that is the true measure of liquidity. Thus, if accounts receivable, as a component of the quick ratio, have, let's say, a conversion time of several months rather than several days, the "quickness" attribute of this ratio is questionable.

Investors need to be aware that the conventional wisdom regarding both the current and quick ratios as indicators of a company's liquidity can be misleading.

CASH RATIO

The cash ratio is an indicator of a company's liquidity that further refines both the current ratio and the quick ratio by measuring the amount of cash; cash equivalents or invested funds there are in current assets to cover current liabilities.

Quick Ratio = Cash + Cash & Equivalents + Invested Funds

CURRENT LIABILITIES

As of March 31, 2010, with amounts expressed in Rs. crores, DTL'S cash assets amounted to 9,797 (balance sheet); while current liabilities amounted to 4,030 (balance sheet). By dividing, the equation gives us a cash ratio of 2.43.

The cash ratio is the most stringent and conservative of the three short-term liquidity ratios (current, quick and cash). It only looks at the most liquid short-term assets of the company, which are those that can be most easily used to pay off current obligations. It also ignores inventory and receivables, as there are no assurances that these two accounts can be converted to cash in a timely matter to meet current liabilities. Very few companies will have enough cash and cash equivalents to fully cover current liabilities, which isn't necessarily a bad thing, so don't focus on this ratio being above 1:1.

The cash ratio is seldom used in financial reporting or by analysts in the fundamental analysis of a company. It is not realistic for a company to purposefully maintain high levels of cash assets to cover current liabilities. The reason being that it's often seen as poor asset utilization for a company to hold large amounts of cash on its balance sheet, as this money could be returned to shareholders or used elsewhere to generate higher returns. While providing an interesting liquidity perspective, the usefulness of this ratio is limited.

PROFITABILITY INDICATOR RATIOS

These ratios, much like the operational performance ratios, give users a good understanding of how well the company utilized its resources in generating profit and shareholder value. The long-term profitability of a company is vital for both the survivability of the company as well as the benefit received by shareholders. It is these ratios that can give insight into the all-important "profit".

We look at four important profit margins, which display the amount of profit a company generates on its sales at the different stages of an income statement. We'll also show you how to calculate the effective tax rate of a company. The last three ratios covered in this section - Return on Assets, Return on Equity and Return on Capital Employed - detail how effective a company is at generating income from its resources.

PROFIT MARGIN ANALYSIS

In the income statement, there are four levels of profit or profit margins - gross profit, operating profit, pre-tax profit and net profit. The term "margin" can apply to the absolute number for a given profit level and/or the number as a percentage of net sales/revenues. Profit margin analysis uses the percentage calculation to provide a comprehensive measure of a company's profitability on a historical basis (3-5 years) and in comparison, to peer companies and industry benchmarks. Basically, it is the amount of profit (at the gross, operating, pre-tax or net income level) generated by the company as a percentage of the sales generated. The objective of margin analysis is to detect consistency or positive/negative trends in a company's earnings. Positive profit margin analysis translates into positive investment quality. To a large degree, it is the quality, and growth, of a company's earnings that drive its stock price.

Operating Profit Margin=Operating Profit / Net Sale

Pretax margin profit =Pretax Profit / Net Sales

Net Profit Margin =Net Profit / Net Sales

All the amounts in these ratios are found in the income statement. As of March 31, 2010, with amounts expressed in Rs. crores, DTL had net sales, or revenue, of 21,140, which is the denominator in all of the profit margin ratios. The equations give us the percentage profit margins as indicated.

Operating Profit Margin	35%
Pre-tax Profit Margin	31%
Net Profit Margin	23%

Second, income statements in the multi-step format clearly identify the four profit levels. However, with the single-step format the investor must calculate the gross profit and operating profit margin numbers. To obtain the gross profit amount, simply subtract the cost of sales (cost of goods sold) from net sales/revenues. The operating profit amount is obtained by subtracting the sum of the company's operating expenses from the gross profit amount. Generally, operating expenses would include such account captions as 'selling', 'marketing and administrative', 'research and development', 'depreciation and amortization', 'rental properties' etc.

Third, investors need to understand that the absolute numbers in the income statement don't tell us very much, which is why we must look to margin analysis to discern a company's true profitability. These ratios help us to keep score, as measured over time, of management's ability to manage costs and expenses and generate profits. The success, or lack thereof, of this important management function is what determines a company's profitability. A large growth in sales will do little for a company's earnings if costs and expenses grow disproportionately. Lastly, the profit margin percentage for all the levels of income can easily be translated into a handy metric used frequently by analysts and often mentioned in investment literature. The ratio's percentage represents the number of paises there are in each rupee worth of sales. For example, using DTL'S numbers, in every sales rupee for the company in 2010, there's roughly 35, 31, and 23 paisa of operating, pre-tax, and net income, respectively.

GROSS PROFIT MARGIN

A company's cost of sales, or cost of goods sold, represents the expense related to labour, raw materials and manufacturing overhead involved in its production process. This expense is deducted from the company's net sales/revenue, which results in a company's first level of profit or gross profit. The gross profit margin is used to analyses how efficiently a company is using its raw materials, labour and manufacturing-related fixed assets to generate profits. A higher margin percentage is a favourable profit indicator. Industry characteristics of raw material costs, particularly as these relate to the stability or lack thereof, have a major effect on a company's gross margin. Generally, management cannot exercise complete control over such costs. Companies without a production process (ex., retailers and service businesses) don't have a cost of sales exactly. In these instances, the expense is recorded as a "cost of merchandise" and a "cost of services", respectively. With this type of company, the gross profit margin does not carry the same weight as a producer type company.

OPERATING PROFIT MARGIN

By subtracting selling, general and administrative, or operating expenses from a company's gross profit number, we get operating income. Management has much more control over operating expenses than its cost of sales outlays. Thus, investors need to scrutinize the operating profit margin carefully. Positive and negative trends in this ratio are, for the most part, directly attributable to management decisions. A company's operating income figure is often the preferred metric (deemed to be more reliable) of investment analysts, versus its net income figure, for making inter-company comparisons and financial projections.

PRE-TAX PROFIT MARGIN

Again, many investment analysts prefer to use a pre-tax income number for reasons similar to those mentioned for operating income. In this case a company has access to a variety of tax-management techniques, which allow it to manipulate the timing and magnitude of its taxable income.

NET PROFIT MARGIN

Often referred to simply as a company's profit margin, the so-called bottom line is the most often mentioned when discussing a company's profitability. While undeniably an important number, investors can easily see from a complete profit margin analysis that there are several income and expense operating elements in an income statement that determine a net profit margin. It behoves investors to take a comprehensive look at a company's profit margins on a systematic basis.

EFFECTIVE TAX RATE

This ratio is a measurement of a company's tax rate, which is calculated by comparing its income tax expense to its pre-tax income. This amount will often differ from the company's stated jurisdictional rate due to many accounting factors, including foreign exchange provisions. This effective tax rate gives a good understanding of the tax rate the company faces.

Effective Tax Rate = Income Tax Expenses/ Pretax Income

As of March 31, 2010, with amounts expressed in Rs. crores, DTL had a provision for income taxes in its income statement of 1,717 (income statement) and pre-tax income of 7,520 (income statement). By dividing, the equation gives us an effective tax rate of 23% for FY 2010.

The variances in this percentage can have a material effect on the net-income figure. Peer company comparisons of net profit margins can be problematic as a result of the impact of the effective tax rate on net profit margins. The same can be said of year-over-year comparisons for the same company. This circumstance is one of the reasons some financial analysts prefer to use the operating or pre-tax profit figures instead of the net profit number for profitability ratio calculation purposes.

One could argue that any event that improves a company's net profit margin is a good one. However, from a quality of earnings perspective, tax management maneuverings (though may be legitimate) are less desirable than straight-forward positive operational results.

Tax provision volatility of a company's finances makes an objective judgment of its true or operational net profit performance difficult to determine. Techniques to lessen the tax burden are practiced, to one degree or another, by many companies. Nevertheless, a relatively stable effective tax rate percentage and resulting net profit margin, would seem to indicate that the company's operational managers are more responsible for a company's profitability than the company's tax accountants.

RETURN ON ASSETS

This ratio indicates how profitable a company is relative to its total assets. The return on assets (ROA) ratio illustrates how well management is employing the company's total assets to make a profit. The higher the return, the more efficient management is in utilizing its asset base. The ROA ratio is calculated by comparing net income to average total assets, and is expressed as a percentage.

AVERAGE TOTAL ASSETS

As of March 31, 2010, with amounts expressed in Rs. crores, DTL had net income of 5,803 (income statement), and average total assets of 19,922 (balance sheet). By dividing, the equation gives us an ROA of 29% for FY 2010. The need for investment in current and non-current assets varies greatly among companies. Capital-intensive businesses (with a large investment in fixed assets) are going to be more asset heavy than technology or service businesses. In the case of capital-intensive businesses, which have to carry a relatively large asset base, will calculate their ROA based on a large number in the denominator of this ratio. Conversely, non-capital-intensive businesses (with a small investment in fixed assets) will be generally favoured with a relatively high ROA because of a low denominator number.

It is precisely because businesses require different-sized asset bases that investors need to think about how they use the ROA ratio. For the most part, the ROA measurement should be used historically for the company being analyzed. If peer company comparisons are made, it is imperative that the companies being reviewed are similar in product line and business type. Simply being categorized in the same industry will not automatically make a company comparable. As a rule of thumb, investment professionals like to see a company's ROA come in at no less than 5%. Of course, there are exceptions to this rule. An important one would apply to banks, which typically have a lower ROA.

RETURN ON EQUITY

This ratio indicates how profitable a company is by comparing its net income to its average shareholders' equity. The return on equity ratio (ROE) measures how much the shareholders earned for their investment in the company. The higher the ratio percentage, the more efficient management is in utilizing its equity base and the better return is to investors.

AVERAGE SHAREHOLDERS' EQUITY

As of March 31, 2010, with amounts expressed in Rs. crores, DTL had net income of 4,845 (income statement), and average shareholders' equity of 19,922 (balance sheet). By dividing, the equation gives us an ROE of 24.3% for FY 2010. DTL on account of being a debt free company has its ROE equal to ROA. If a company has issued preferred stock, investors wishing to see the return on just common equity may modify the formula by subtracting the preferred dividends, which are not paid to common shareholders, from net income and reducing shareholders' equity by the outstanding amount of preferred equity.

Widely used by investors, the ROE ratio is an important measure of a company's earnings performance. The ROE tells common shareholders how effectively their money is being employed. Company peers and industry and overall market comparisons are appropriate; however, it should be recognized that there are variations in ROEs among some types of businesses. In general, financial analysts consider return on equity ratios in the 15-20% range as representing attractive levels of investment quality.

While highly regarded as a profitability indicator, the ROE metric does have a recognized weakness. Investors need to be aware that a disproportionate amount of debt in a company's capital structure would translate into a smaller equity base. Thus, a small amount of net income (the numerator) could still produce a high ROE off a modest equity base (the denominator).

For example, let's reconfigure DTL'S debt and equity numbers to illustrate this circumstance. If we reduce the company's equity amount by Rs. 9,922 crores and increase its long-term debt by a corresponding amount, the reconfigured debt-equity relationship will be (figures in Rs. crores) 9,922 and 10,000, respectively. DTL'S financial position is obviously much more highly leveraged, i.e., carrying a lot more debt. However, its ROE would now register a whopping 58% (5,803 -r 10,000), which is quite an improvement over the 29% ROE of the almost debt-free FY 2010 position of DTL indicated above. Of course, that improvement in DTL'S profitability, as measured by its ROE, comes with a price...a lot more debt and thus a lot more risk.

The lesson here for investors is that they cannot look at a company's return on equity in isolation. A high or low ROE needs to be interpreted in the context of a company's debt-equity relationship. The answer to this analytical dilemma can be found by using the return on capital employed (ROCE) ratio.

RETURN ON CAPITAL EMPLOYED

The return on capital employed (ROCE) ratio, expressed as a percentage, complements the return on equity (ROE) ratio by adding a company's debt liabilities, or funded debt, to equity to reflect a company's total "capital employed". This measure narrows the focus to gain a better understanding of a company's ability to generate returns from its available capital base. By comparing net income to the sum of a company's debt and equity capital, investors can get a clear picture of how the use of leverage impacts a company's profitability. Financial analysts consider the ROCE measurement to be a more comprehensive profitability indicator because it gauges management's ability to generate earnings from a company's total pool of capital.

As of March 31, 2010, with amounts expressed in Rs. crores, DTL had net income of 5,803 (income statement). The company's average short-term and long-term borrowings were 0 and the average shareholders' equity was 19,922 (all the necessary figures are in the 2009 and

2010 balance sheets), the sum of which, 19,922, is the capital employed. By dividing, the equation gives us an ROCE of 29% for FY 2010.

Often, financial analysts will use operating income (earnings before interest and taxes or EBIT) as the numerator. There are various takes on what should constitute the debt element in the ROCE equation, which can be quite confusing.

Our suggestion is to stick with debt liabilities that represent interest-bearing, documented credit obligations (short-term borrowings, current portion of long-term debt, and long-term debt) as the debt capital in the formula.

DEBT RATIOS

These ratios give users a general idea of the company's overall debt load as well as its mix of equity and debt. Debt ratios can be used to determine the overall level of financial risk a company and its shareholders face. In general, the greater the amount of debt held by a company the greater the financial risk of bankruptcy. The ratios covered in this section include the debt ratio, which is gives a general idea of a company's financial leverage as does the debt-to-equity ratio. The capitalization ratio details the mix of debt and equity while the interest coverage ratio and the cash flow to debt ratio show how well a company can meet its obligations.

The debt ratio compares a company's total debt to its total assets, which is used to gain a general idea as to the amount of leverage being used by a company. A low percentage means that the company is less dependent on leverage, i.e., money borrowed from and/or owed to others. The lower the percentage, the less leverage a company is using and the stronger its equity position. In general, the higher the ratio, the more risk that company is considered to have taken on.

Debt Ratio = Total Liabilities/ Total Assets

As of March 31, 2010, with amounts expressed in Rs. crores, DTL had total liabilities of 1,995 (balance sheet) and total assets of 22,036 (balance sheet). By dividing, the equation provides the company with a low leverage as measured by the debt ratio of 9%. The easy-to-calculate debt ratio is helpful to investors looking for a quick take on a company's leverage. The debt ratio gives users a quick measure of the amount of debt that the company has on its balance sheets compared to its assets. The more debt compared to assets a company has, which is signaled by a high debt ratio, the more leveraged it is and the riskier it is considered to be. Generally, large, well-established companies can push the liability component of their balance sheet structure to higher percentages without getting into trouble. However, one thing to note with this ratio: it isn't a pure measure of a company's debt (or indebtedness), as it also includes operational liabilities, such as accounts payable and taxes payable. Companies use these operational liabilities as going concerns to fund the day-to-day operations of the business and aren't really "debts" in the leverage sense of this ratio. Basically, even if you took the same company and had one version with zero financial debt and another version with substantial financial debt, these operational liabilities would still be there, which in some sense can muddle this ratio. The use of leverage, as displayed by the debt ratio, can be a double-edged sword for companies. If the company manages to generate returns above their cost of capital, investors will benefit. However, with the added risk of the debt on its books, a company can be easily hurt by this leverage if it is unable to generate returns above the cost of capital. Basically, any gains or losses are magnified by the use of leverage in the company's capital structure.

DEBT-EQUITY RATIO

The debt-equity ratio is another leverage ratio that compares a company's total liabilities to its total shareholders' equity. This is a measurement of how much suppliers, lenders, creditors and obligors have committed to the company versus what the shareholders have committed. To a large degree, the debt-equity ratio provides another vantage point on a company's leverage position, in this case, comparing total liabilities to shareholders' equity, as opposed to total assets in the debt ratio. Similar to the debt ratio, a lower the percentage means that a company is using less leverage and has a stronger equity position.

As of March 31, 2010, with amounts expressed in Rs. crores, DTL had total liabilities of 1,995 (balance sheet) and total shareholders' equity of 22,306 (balance sheet). By dividing, the equation provides the company with a relatively low percentage of leverage as measured by the debt-equity ratio at 9%. A conservative variation of this ratio, which is seldom seen, involves reducing a company's equity position by its intangible assets to arrive at a tangible equity, or tangible net worth, figure. Companies with a large amount of purchased goodwill form heavy acquisition activity can end up with a negative equity position. The debt-equity ratio appears frequently in investment literature. However, like the debt ratio, this ratio is not a pure measurement of a company's debt because it includes operational liabilities in total liabilities. Nevertheless, this easy-to-calculate ratio provides a general indication of a company's equity-liability relationship and is helpful to investors looking for a quick take on a company's leverage. Generally, large, well-established companies can push the liability component of their balance sheet structure to higher percentages without getting into trouble.

CAPITALIZATION RATIO

The capitalization ratio measures the debt component of a company's capital structure, or capitalization (i.e., the sum of long-term debt liabilities and shareholders' equity) to support a company's operations and growth. Long-term debt is divided by the sum of long-term debt and shareholders' equity. This ratio is considered to be one of the more meaningful of the "debt" ratios - it delivers the key insight into a company's use of leverage. There is no right amount of debt. Leverage varies according to industries, a company's line of business and its stage of development. Nevertheless, common sense tells us that low debt and high equity levels in the capitalization ratio indicate investment quality.

$$\text{Capitalization Ratio} = \frac{\text{Long term Debt}}{\text{Long term Debt} + \text{Shareholders' Equity}}$$

As of March 31, 2010, with amounts expressed in Rs. crores, DTL had total long-term debt of 0 (balance sheet), and total long-term debt and shareholders' equity (i.e., its capitalization) of 22,036 (balance sheet). By dividing, the equation provides the company with a zero leverage as measured by the capitalization ratio. A company's capitalization (not to be confused with its market capitalization) is the term used to describe the makeup of a company's permanent or long-term capital, which consists of both long-term debt and shareholders' equity. A low level of debt and a healthy proportion of equity in a company's capital structure is an indication of financial fitness.

Prudent use of leverage (debt) increases the financial resources available to a company for growth and expansion. It assumes that management can earn more on borrowed funds than it pays in interest expense and fees on these funds. However, successful this formula may seem, it does require a company to maintain a solid record of complying with its various borrowing commitments.

A company considered too highly leveraged (too much debt) may find its freedom of action restricted by its creditors and/or have its profitability hurt by high interest costs. Of course, the worst of all scenarios is having trouble meeting operating and debt liabilities on time and surviving adverse economic conditions. Lastly, a company in a highly competitive business, if hobbled by high debt, will find its competitors taking advantage of its problems to grab more market share. As mentioned previously, the capitalization ratio is one of the more meaningful debt ratios because it focuses on the relationship of debt liabilities as a component of a company's total capital base, which is the capital mobilized by shareholders and lenders.

INTEREST COVERAGE RATIO

The interest coverage ratio is used to determine how easily a company can pay interest expenses on outstanding debt. The ratio is calculated by dividing a company's earnings before interest and taxes (EBIT) by the company's interest expenses for the same period. The lower the ratio, the more the company is burdened by debt expense. When a company's interest coverage ratio is only 1.5 or lower, its ability to meet interest expenses may be questionable.

Interest Coverage Ratio = EBIT/ Interest Expenses

As of March 31, 2010, with amounts expressed in Rs. crores, DTL had earnings before interest and taxes (operating income) of 7,520 (income statement), and total interest expense of 0 (income statement). This equation provides the company with an Infinite margin of safety due to lack of leverage. The ability to stay current with interest payment obligations is absolutely critical for a company as a going concern. While the non-payment of debt principal is a seriously negative condition, a company finding itself in financial/operational difficulties can stay alive for quite some time as long as it is able to service its interest expenses. In a more positive sense, prudent borrowing makes sense for most companies, but the operative word here is "prudent." Interest expenses affect a company's profitability, so the cost-benefit analysis dictates that borrowing money to fund a company's assets has to have a positive effect. An ample interest coverage ratio would be an indicator of this circumstance, as well as indicating substantial additional debt capacity. Obviously, in this category of investment quality, DTL would go to the head of the class.

CASH FLOW TO DEBT RATIO

This coverage ratio compares a company's operating cash flow to its total debt, which, for purposes of this ratio, is defined as the sum of short-term borrowings, the current portion of long-term debt and long-term debt. This ratio provides an indication of a company's ability to cover total debt with its yearly cash flow from operations. The higher the ratio, the better is the company's ability to carry its total debt.

$$\text{Cash Flow to Debt Ratio} = \frac{\text{Operating Cash Flow}}{\text{Total Debt}}$$

As of March 31, 2010, with amounts expressed in Rs. crores, DTL had net cash provided by operating activities (operating cash flow as recorded in the statement of cash flows) of 5,876 (cash flow statement), and total debt of 0 (balance sheet). By dividing, the equation provides the company with infinite margin of debt coverage. A more conservative cash flow figure calculation in the numerator would use a company's free cash flow (operating cash flow minus the amount of cash used for capital expenditures).

A more conservative total debt figure would include, in addition to short-term borrowings, current portion of long-term debt, long-term debt, redeemable preferred stock and two-thirds of the principal of non-cancel-able operating leases. In the case of DTL, their debt load is nil so the resulting cash flow to debt ratio percentage is off the chart. In this instance, this circumstance would indicate that the company has ample capacity to borrow a significant amount of money, if it chose to do so, as opposed to indicating its debt coverage capacity. Under more typical circumstances, a high double-digit percentage ratio would be a sign of financial strength, while a low percentage ratio could be a negative sign that indicates too much debt or weak cash flow generation. It is important to investigate the larger factor behind a low ratio. To do this, compare the company's current cash flow to debt ratio to its historic level in order to parse out trends or warning signs.

OPERATING PERFORMANCE RATIOS

The next series of ratios we'll look at are the operating performance ratios. Each of these ratios have differing inputs and measure different segments of a company's overall operational performance, but the ratios do give users insight into the company's performance and management during the period being measured. These ratios look at how well a company turns its assets into revenue as well as how efficiently a company converts its sales into cash. Basically, these ratios look at how efficiently and effectively a company is using its resources to generate sales and increase shareholder value. In general, the better these ratios are, the better it is for shareholders.

In this section, we'll look at the fixed-asset turnover ratio and the sales/revenue per employee ratio, which look at how well the company uses its fixed assets and employees to generate sales.

FIXED-ASSET TURNOVER

This ratio is a rough measure of the productivity of a company's fixed assets (property, plant and equipment or PP&E) with respect to generating sales. For most companies, their investment in fixed assets represents the single largest component of their total assets. This annual turnover ratio is designed to reflect a company's efficiency in managing these significant assets. Simply put, the higher the yearly turnover rate, the better.

As of March 31, 2010, with amounts expressed in Rs. crores, DTL had net sales, or revenue, of (income statement) and average fixed assets, or PP&E, of 2,342 (balance sheet - the average of yearend 2009 and 2010 PP&E). By dividing, the equation gives us a fixed-asset turnover rate for FY 2010 of 5.6. Instead of using fixed assets, some asset-turnover ratios would use total assets. We prefer to focus on the former because, as a significant component in the balance sheet, it represents a multiplicity of management decisions on capital expenditures. Thus, this capital investment, and more importantly, its results, is a better performance indicator than that evidenced in total asset turnover. There is no exact number that determines whether a company is doing a good job of generating revenue from its investment in fixed assets. This makes it important to compare the most recent ratio to both the historical levels of the company along with peer company and/or industry averages. Before putting too much faith into this ratio, it's important to determine the type of company that you are using the ratio on because a company's investment in fixed assets is very much linked to the requirements of the industry in which it conducts its business. Fixed assets vary greatly among companies. For example, an IT company, like DTL, has less of a fixed-asset base than a heavy manufacturer like BHEL. Obviously, the fixed-asset ratio for DTL will have less relevance than that for BHEL.

SALES/REVENUE PER EMPLOYEE

As a gauge of personnel productivity, this indicator simply measures the amount of rupee sales, or revenue, generated per employee. The higher the figure the better. Here again, labor-intensive businesses (ex. mass market retailers) will be less productive in this metric than a high-tech, high product-value manufacturer. As of March 31, 2010, with amounts expressed in Rs. crores, DTL had generated 22,098 in net sales with an average personnel component for the year of approximately 85,000 employees. The sales, or revenue, figure is the numerator (income statement), and the average number of employees for the year is the denominator (annual report) and Sales Per Employee come out to be Rs. 2,500,000. An 'Earnings per Employee' ratio could also be calculated using net income (as opposed to net sales) in the numerator. Industry and product-line characteristics will influence this indicator of employee productivity. Tracking this figure historically and comparing it to peer-group companies will make this quantitative amount more meaningful in an analytical sense.

DU-PONT ANALYSIS

The DuPont ratio can be used as a compass in the process of assessing financial performance of the company by directing the analyst toward significant areas of strength and weakness evident in the financial statements.

The ratio provides measures in three of the four key areas of analysis, each representing a compass bearing, pointing the way to the next stage of the investigation.

THE DU-PONT RATIO DECOMPOSITION

The DuPont ratio is a good place to begin a financial statement analysis because it measures the return on equity (ROE). A for-profit business exists to create wealth for its owner(s). ROE is, therefore, arguably the most important of the key ratios, since it indicates the rate at which owner wealth is increasing.

The three components of the DuPont ratio, as represented in equation, cover the areas of profitability, operating efficiency and leverage.

PROFITABILITY: NET PROFIT MARGIN

Profitability ratios measure the rate at which either sales or capital is converted into profits at different levels of the operation. As we have seen, the most common are gross, operating and net profitability, which describe performance at different activity levels. Of the three, net profitability is the most comprehensive since it uses the bottom line net income in its measure.

The net profitability for DTL Technologies in 2010 is:

Net Profit Margin Net Income/ Sales

5803 – 958

" 21140

= 22.92%

A proper analysis of this ratio would include at least three to five years of trend and cross-sectional comparison data. The cross-sectional comparison can be drawn from a variety of sources.

ASSET UTILIZATION: TOTAL ASSET TURNOVER

Turnover or efficiency ratios are important because they indicate how well the assets of a firm are used to generate sales and/or cash. While profitability is important, it doesn't always provide the complete picture of how well a company provides a product or service. A company can be very profitable, but not too efficient. Profitability is based upon accounting measures of sales revenue and costs. Such measures are generated using the matching principle of accounting, which records revenue when earned and expenses when incurred. Hence, the gross profit margin measures the difference between sales revenue and the cost of goods actually sold during the accounting period. The goods sold may be entirely different from the goods produced during that same period. Goods produced but not sold will show up as inventory assets at the end of the year. A firm with abnormally large inventory balances is not performing effectively, and the purpose of efficiency ratios is to reveal that fact.

The total asset turnover (TAT) ratio measures the degree to which a firm generates sales with its total asset base. It is important to use average assets in the denominator to eliminate bias in the ratio calculation. Financial ratio bias is commonly present when combining items from both the balance sheet and income statement. For example, TAT uses income statement sales in its numerator and balance sheet assets in the denominator. Income statement items are flow variables measured over a time interval, while balance sheet items are measured at a fixed point in time. In cases where the firm has been involved in major change, such as an expansion project, balance sheet measures taken at the end of the year may misrepresent the amount of assets available and/or in use over the course of the year. Taking a simple average for balance sheet items (i.e., ((beginning + ending)/2)) will control for at least some of this bias and provide a more accurate and meaningful ratio. The limiting assumption is that the change in the balance sheet occurred evenly over the course of the year, which may not always be the case.

The measure of total asset turnover for DTL is:

TAT = Sales / Average Assets

= 1.06

$$\frac{17{,}309.22{,}086}{2}$$

LEVERAGE: THE LEVERAGE MULTIPLIER

Leverage ratios measure the extent to which a company relies on debt financing in its capital structure. Debt is both beneficial and costly to a firm. The cost of debt is lower than the cost of equity, an effect which is enhanced by the tax deductibility of interest payments in contrast

Average Assets 1

Average Equity Average Debt

Average Assets

v/

Average Assets Average Debt

Average Equity

Average Assets

v/

to taxable dividend payments and stock repurchases. If debt proceeds are invested in projects which return more than the cost of debt, owners keep the residual, and hence, the return on equity is "leveraged up." The debt sword, however, cuts both ways. Adding debt creates a fixed payment required of the firm whether or not it is earning an operating profit, and therefore, payments may cut into the equity base. Further, the risk of the equity position is increased by the presence of debt holders having a superior claim to the assets of the firm. The leverage multiplier employed in the DuPont ratio is directly related to the proportion of debt in the firm's capital structure. The measure, which divides average assets by average equity, can be restated in two ways, as follows:

Once again, averages are used to control for potential bias caused by the end-of-year values. The leverage multiplier for DTL is:

19,923/17,209+22,086/22 = 1

Combination and Analysis of the Results follows:

Once the three components have been calculated, they can be combined to form the ROE, as

$$\text{RDE} \; \frac{\text{Net Income}}{\text{Sales}} = \frac{\text{Sales}}{\text{Average Assets}} \; \text{Average Assets Avenge Equity}$$

While additional measures for prior years would provide the basis for a necessary trend analysis, this result is not meaningful until it is compared to an industry or best practices benchmark. The DuPont ratio/or the Indian IT Industry is:

20*1.01 * 1.1 = 22.2%

As can be seen, strengths in DTL are immediately evident in the comparison of DuPont values for DTL and Indian IT Industry. The company appears to be significant in profitability, while total asset turnover seems to be roughly in line with the industry. The overall industry leverage is slightly higher than DTL'Ss zero debt balance sheet. The analyst can now focus on the company's profitability. A quick analysis of profitability yields the following result:

Sound financial statement analysis is an integral part of the management process for any organization. The DuPont ratio, while not the end in itself, is an excellent way to get a quick snapshot view of the overall performance of a firm in three of the four critical areas of ratio analysis, profitability, operating efficiency and leverage. By identifying strengths and/or weaknesses in any of the three areas, the DuPont analysis enables the analyst to quickly focus his or her detailed study on a particular spot, making the subsequent inquiry both easier and more meaningful. Some caveats, however, are to be noted.

The DuPont ratio consists of very general measures, drawing from the broadest values on the balance sheets and income statements (e.g., total assets is the broadest of asset measures). A DuPont study is not a replacement for detailed, comprehensive analysis. Further, there may be problems that the DuPont decomposition does not readily identify. For example, an average outcome for net profitability may mask the existence of a low gross margin combined with an abnormally high operating margin. Without looking at the two detailed measures, understanding of the true performance of the firm would be lost.

The DuPont ratio can also be broken into more components called 'The Extended DuPont', depending upon the needs of the analyst In any case, the DuPont can add value, even "on the fly," to understand and solving a broad variety of business problems.

EXTENDED DUPONT FORMULA

$$ROE = \frac{\text{Net Income}}{\text{EBIT}} \quad \frac{\text{EBIT}}{\text{EBITDA}} \quad \frac{\text{EBITDA}}{\text{Sales}} \quad \frac{\text{Sales}}{\text{Average Assets}} \quad \frac{\text{^Average Assets^}}{\text{Avenge Equity}}$$

CASH CONVERSION CYCLE

This liquidity metric expresses the length of time (in days) that a company uses to sell inventory, collect receivables and pay its accounts payable. The cash conversion cycle (CCC) measures the number of days a company's cash is tied up in the production and sales process of its operations and the benefit it gets from payment terms from its creditors. The shorter this cycle, the more liquid the company's working capital position is. The CCC is also known as the "cash" or "operating" cycle.

= Days Inventory Outstanding + Days Sales Outstanding DIO is computed by

- ➢ Dividing the cost of sales (income statement) by 365 to get a cost of sales per day figure;
- ➢ Calculating the average inventory figure by adding the year's beginning (previous yearend amount) and ending inventory figure (both are in the balance sheet) and dividing by 2 to obtain an average amount of inventory for any given year; and

Cost of Sales per day	= 13771/365 = 37.73
Average Inventory	= (0+0)/2=0
Days Inventory Outstanding	= 0/37.73 = 0

- ➢ Dividing the average inventory figure by the cost of sales per day figure

DIO gives a measure of the number of days it takes for the company's inventory to turn over, i.e., to be converted to sales, either as cash or accounts receivable. Understandably, being an IT company, DIO for DTL comes out to be zero.

DSO is computed by

- ➢ Dividing net sales (income statement) by 365 to get a net sales per day figure;
- ➢ Calculating the average accounts receivable figure by adding the year's beginning (previous yearend amount) and ending accounts receivable amount (both figures are in the balance sheet) and dividing by 2 to obtain an average amount of accounts receivable for any given year; and Dividing the average accounts receivable figure by the net sales per day figure.

For DTL FY 2010 (in Rs. crores), its DSO would be computed with these figures:

Net Sales per day	= 21140/365=57.92
Average Accounts receivables	= (3390+3244)/2 = 3317
Days Sales Outstanding	= 3317/57.92=57.27

DSO gives a measure of the number of days it takes a company to collect on sales that go into accounts receivables (credit purchases).

DPO is computed by

- Dividing the cost of sales (income statement) by 365 to get a cost of sales per day figure;
- Calculating the average accounts payable figure by adding the year's beginning (previous yearend amount) and ending accounts payable amount (both figures are in the balance sheet), and dividing by 2 to get an average accounts payable amount for any given year; and
- Dividing the average accounts payable figure by the cost of sales per day figure. For DTL FY 2010 (in Rs. crores), its DPO would be computed with these figures:

Cost of Sales per day	= 13771/365 = 37.73
Average Payables	= (1544+1995)/2=1769.5
Days Payable Outstanding	= 1769.5/37.73=46.90

DIO	0
DSO	57
DPO	47
CCC	10

DPO gives a measure of how long it takes the company to pay its obligations to suppliers.

CCC computed:

Often the components of the cash conversion cycle - DIO, DSO and DPO - are expressed in terms of turnover as a times (x) factor. For example, in the case of DTL, its days debtors outstanding of 57 days would be expressed as turning over 6.4x annually (365 days -r 57 days = 6.4 times). However, actually counting days is more literal and easier to understand when considering how fast assets turn into cash.

An often-overlooked metric, the cash conversion cycle is vital for two reasons. First, it's an indicator of the company's efficiency in managing its important working capital assets; second, it provides a clear view of a company's ability to pay off its current liabilities.

It does this by looking at how quickly the company turns its inventory into sales, and its sales into cash, which is then used to pay its suppliers for goods and services. Again, while the quick and current ratios are more often mentioned in financial reporting, investors would be well advised to measure true liquidity by paying attention to a company's cash conversion cycle.

The longer the duration of inventory on hand and of the collection of receivables, coupled with a shorter duration for payments to a company's suppliers, means that cash is being tied up in inventory and receivables and used more quickly in paying off trade payables. If this circumstance becomes a trend, it will reduce, or squeeze, a company's cash availabilities.

Conversely, a positive trend in the cash conversion cycle will add to a company's liquidity. By tracking the individual components of the CCC (as well as the CCC as a whole), an investor is able to discern positive and negative trends in a company's all-important working capital assets and liabilities. For example, an increasing trend in DIO could mean decreasing demand for a company's products. Decreasing DSO could indicate an increasingly competitive product, which allows a company to tighten its buyers' payment terms. As a whole, a shorter CCC means greater liquidity, which translates into less of a need to borrow, more opportunity to realize price discounts with cash purchases for raw materials, and an increased capacity to fund the expansion of the business into new product lines and markets. Conversely, a longer CCC increases a company's cash needs and negates all the positive liquidity qualities just mentioned.

CURRENT RATIO VS. THE CCC

The obvious limitations of the current ratio as an indicator of true liquidity clearly establish a strong case for greater recognition, and use, of the cash conversion cycle in any analysis of a company's working capital position.

Cash Conversion cycle for DTL over five years:

DIO	Mar'06	Mar '07	Mar '08	Mar '09	Mar '10
Cost of Sales per day	16.54	24.45	29.27	36.59	37.73
Average Inventory		0.00	0.00	0.00	0.00
Days Inventory Outstanding		**0.00**	**0.00**	**0.00**	**0.00**
DSO					
Net Sales per day	24.73	36.02	42.87	55.52	57.92
Average Accounts receivables		1905.00	2692.50	3241.50	3317.00
Days Sales Outstanding		**52.88**	**62.80**	**58.39**	**57.27**
DPO					
Cost of Sales per day	16.54	24.45	29.27	36.59	37.73
Average Accounts Payable		985.00	1322.50	1513.50	1769.50
Days Payable Outstanding		**40.29**	**45.18**	**41.36**	**46.90**
CCC		**13**	**18**	**17**	**10**

THE SATYAM CASE AND NEED FOR FORENSIC ACCOUNTING

In what became India's biggest corporate scandal till date, Mr. Ramalinga Raju, founder and chairman of Satyam Computers Ltd., one of India's four premier IT companies, admitted of a fraud through a letter addressed to the board of the company in January 2009.

THE FRAUD

- There was Rs. 5040 crores worth inflated cash and bank balance
- Non-existent accrued interest of Rs. 376 crores
- Understated liability of Rs. 1230 crores

- Overstated debtor position of Rs. 490 crores
- Overstated Revenues & operating profit by Rs. 588 crores

Added together, it was a discrepancy of Rs. 7724 crores in the accounts for a company having annual revenues of Rs. 10,000 odd crores.

Satyam's share price crashed 77% to Rs. 40.25 on the news and the great story for a seemingly successful Indian IT company ended. Fingers were pointed, concerns were raised, complaints were filed and dreams were shattered.

The government was quick to act, appointing a new board for Satyam which helped carry out bidding process for the IT giant and saved the company from extinction.

The Satyam fracas is one more fraud in the long history of misappropriation of resources given in trust to individuals and institutions. What this entire episode brings to the fore, is the following:

- Any control system is only as good as the people administering it
- Audits are not a replacement for responsible management

Laws and regulations cannot deter persons who wish to defeat them - at least temporarily In this context, the relevance of forensic accounting and forensic accounts has grown enormously in recent years. In the interest of organizations and numerous investors who have direct stake in the financial well-being of the organizations, more and more forensic accountants should be involved to ward off financial disasters.

The integration of accounting, auditing and investigative skills yields the specialty known as Forensic Accounting. There is a growing need among analysts, law enforcement professionals, small business owners, and department managers to better understand basic forensic accounting principles, how different types of frauds occur and how to investigate a fraud that is detected in a way that maximizes the chances of successful prosecution of the perpetrator.

FILL IN THE BLANKS AND TRUE OR FALSE

1. Fundamental analysis focuses on predicting the future price of a security and Technical analysis on estimating the intrinsic value of a security. (False)
2. If the price of a share at the beginning of the year was Rs.70/-, dividend received during the year was Rs.5/-per share and the price at the end is Rs.79/-. What is the rate of return? (0.2)
3. The ratios between profits and investments are called rate of return measures. (True)
4. What was the final analysis on the performance of Bharat forge for the year FY 12? (Aim to become US$1 billion Company by Fy 08 from US$100 million, Stock currently trades at 15 times its FY 05 consensus EPS forecasts, Stock will trade at an inexpensive PEG of 0.6x.)

5. Calculate the rates of return and classify securities that have earned superior historical returns, (Calculating certain ratios will help in analyzing whether a security has relative strength)
6. In any Economy, bridge is created between savers and who need the funds by this system: - (Financial)
7. ________ ratio is the ratio of net profit to the sales. (Net Profit Margin)
8. The Gordon growth model is best suited for firms: -
9. Growing at a rate equal to or lower that the growth in the economy, which have well established dividend payout ratio policy, whose earnings are steady and perpetual)
10. Explain what are leverage ratios? (Help in assessing the risk arising using the debt capital. Debt equity ratio and interest coverage ratio and DSCR are important leverage ratios, Debt is riskier source of finance as it entails fixed outgo of periodic payments).
11. If the price of a share at the beginning of the year was Rs.100/-, no dividend received during the year and the price at the end is Rs.115/-. What is the rate of return? (0.15)
12. An investor with a higher tolerance of risk should tilt his portfolio in favour of________. (Stocks)
13. Investment decisions can be viewed as an integrated process to which security analysis makes its unique contribution. (True)
14. ________ ratio indicates the margin available after meeting the manufacturing expenses. (Gross Profit margin)
15. ________ Ratio is estimated by dividing the market value of a firm's assets by the replacement cost of these assets. (Market value to replacement cost ratio).
16. What are the important macroeconomic indicators? (GNP growth rate, Price Conditions, Monsoons)
17. Acid test ratio is more stringent measure of liquidity compared to the ________. (Current ratio)
18. Which ratios are commonly used? (Debt equity ratio, Interest coverage ratios, Debt service coverage ratios)
19. Fixed assets turnover ratio measures the efficiency of utilization of total assets, fixed as well as current. (True)
20. A pattern which does not result in reversal of a trend but reaffirmation of the underlying trend is called ________.(Consolidation pattern)
21. The risk associated to get the required rate of return on the stock is measure by market beta. (True)
22. Acid test ratio is more stringent measure of liquidity compared to the ________.(Current ratio)
23. Question Quick assets consist of current assets less inventories. (True)

24. 4 A firm's growth is determined by how much is re-invested into new assets and the quality of these investments, and these includes :- Acquisitions , Building distribution channels , Expanding marketing capabilities and investing in new facilities).
25. What are the different types of profitability ratios? (Gross profit margin ratio, Earnings power, Return on equity)
26. The Gordon growth model is best suited for firms :-(Growing at a rate equal to or lower that the growth in the economy , Which have well established dividend payout ratio policy , Whose earnings are steady and perpetual)
27. The Two-Stage dividend discount model is based on the assumption of :-An initial phase where the growth is not a stable growth rate , A subsequent steady state of growth rate being stable and lasts n years , A stable growth phase lasts forever)
28. How can the financial statements can be manipulated while giving the estimates for growth? (Change method of rate of depreciation, change method of stock valuation, Inflating sales for current year by advancing sales for the following year).
29. The price earnings ratio is an increasing function of the payout ratio and the growth rate and a decreasing function of the riskiness of the firm. (True)
30. Acid test ratio is more stringent measure of liquidity compared to the ________.(Current ratio)
31. ________ measures the efficiency of credit management. (Average collection period)
32. ________ measures the profitability of operations without considering the influence of financial structure and tax rate. (Earnings power)
33. he presents value of all the future cash payments to be paid on the security to the investor is termed as- (Intrinsic value of a security)
34. If the price of a share at the beginning of the year was Rs.100/-, no dividend received during the year and the price at the end is Rs.115/-. What is the rate of return? (0.15)
35. What is the objective of Portfolio management? (To Minimize risk and maximize return)
36. Capital expenditure -depreciation +change in working capital -(new debt issued - debt repaid) = (Equity reinvested in business)
37. What is the percentage of variation the market and industry influence account for? ($2/3^{rd}$)
38. What is the rate of interest on the tax-free bonds issue by the government? (6.5%)
39. The Peer group of Bharat Forge consists of which all companies? (Am forge industries, Kalyani Forge, EL Forge)
40. Five paisa.com is an example of on-line trading portal. (True)

SHORT ANSWER QUESTIONS

1. Define fundamental analysis.
2. Define Intrinsic Value.

3. What is meant by price target?
4. What are Economic Indicators?
5. Define Inflation.
6. Define Economic Forecasting
7. Define Budget Deficit
8. What are the economic cycles?
9. Define Industry analysis.
10. What is the distinct classification of industry?
11. Define company analysis.
12. How a company is perceived by its competitors?
13. Define Balance Sheet
14. Define Cash Flow Statement
15. What are the financial ratios?
16. Define RoA, RoE
17. What are the liquidity ratios?
18. Define Capital Structure and Solvency Ratios
19. Define operating Performance
20. What are the common stocks?
21. Define Absolute (Intrinsic) Valuation
22. Earnings per Share (EPS)
23. Dividend per Share (DPS)
24. Define *Price-Book Ratio.*
25. Define Return on Equity
26. Define The DuPont Model
27. What is Dividend Yield
28. Define Cash Earnings per Share (CEPS)
29. What is Average Collection Period
30. Define Return on Capital Employed.
31. What are Bonus shares?
32. Define Capital Reserves.
33. What sis cash Ratio?

34. What is Profitability Indicator Ratios?
35. What is Profit Margin Analysis?
36. Define Operating Profit Margin
37. Define Pre-tax Profit Margin
38. Define Capitalization Ratio
39. What is DuPont Ratio Decomposition?
40. What is Leverage Multiplier?
41. Define Cash Conversion Cycle (CCC).

ESSAY TYPE QUESTIONS

1. What is the different analysis that must be carried out under fundamental analysis?
2. What is fundamental analysis? Explain the key macro-economic factors considered in fundamental analysis.
3. Why Economic analysis is important? Explain the economic indicators of Economic analysis.
4. Briefly explain the economic cycle in Economic analysis.
5. Briefly explain the Company analysis. Explain the analysis of Financial Statements.
6. Briefly explain Financial Ratios (Return, Operating and, Profitability Ratios)
7. How does the management of a company affect its stock prices?
8. How does ratio analysis, cash flow and funds flow statement reflect the financial health of a company?
9. What is P/E Ratio? What is important process using this concept in investment decisions?
10. How is the competitive position of a company within an industry determined?
11. How is the economic growth related to the stock prices?
12. What is the general economic environment in which the company is operating? Is it conducive or obstructive to the growth of the company and the industry in which the company is operating?
13. Does the company have a strong market presence and market share? Or does it constantly have to employ a large part of its profits and resources in marketing and finding new customers and fighting for market share?
14. Why is fundamental analysis relevant for investing?
15. When Reviewing the Fundamentals of the Overall Market?

CASE STUDIES

CASE STUDY 1

THE EFFECTS OF CAPITAL STRUCTURE CHANGE ON SECURITY PRICES:

Raghav, in his article, "The effects of Capital Structure change on security prices: A study of exchange offers" published in the journal of Financial Economies, has analyzed the stock price impact of exchange offers of debt for equity or vice versa. In an exchange offer, the offers to trade freshly issued securities for seasoned securities in the hands of investors. Thus, a firm that wanted to move to a higher debt ratio could offer to trade new debt for outstanding shares. A firm that wanted to move to a more conservative capital structure could offer to trade new shares for outstanding debt securities. Raghav found that debt for equity exchanges were perceived as "good news" by stock markets and equity for debt as "bad news."

- Are these results consistent with the "trade off" theory of Capital Structure?
- Are these results consistent with the view that investors regard announcements of
  - i. Stock issues as bad news.
  - ii. Stock repurchases as good news and
  - iii. Debt issues as no news?
- In there any other way in which you could think of explaining Raghav's result?

CASE STUDY 2

Using the given historical data of the company for 5 previous years analyse and comment on the company's performance. Upon the analysis based on this historical data do you find this company attractive for investment in stocks? Explain.

Inventory turnover	88	91	133	166	240
Receivables turnover	31	49	50	34	51
Long term assets turnover	0.37	0.95	1.05	0.96	0.63
Asset turnover	0.31	0.78	0.75	0.69	0.47
MARKET VALUE RATIOS					
Capitalization, Rs.	118,221,72	116,442,06	240,002,85	71,950,00	42,373,38
P/E ratio	7.72	4.60	8.08	6.90	10.03
Earnings per share, Rs.	0.60	0.99	1.17	1.23	0.50
Market price to book value	1.16	1.18	3.08	1.35	0.94
Book value of share, Rs.	4.01	3.90	3.06	6.28	5.33
Cash dividend per share, Rs.	0.06	0.16	0.16	0.25	0.12
Payout ratio	10.2%	16.1%	13.7%	20.3%	24.2%

FINANCIAL RATIOS	2014-01-01	2013-01-01	2012-01-01	2011-01-01	2010-01-01
LIQUIDITY RATIOS					
Current ratio	0.81	0.99	1.24	2.60	4.43
Quick ratio	0.39	0.45	1.02	0.89	1.61
PROFITABILITY RATIOS					
Gross profit margin	38.8%	57.9%	57.6%	52.0%	47.4%
Profit from operations margin	10.0%	26.9%	27.3%	26.9%	22.3%
Net profit margin	7.9%	23.8%	33.1%	18.0%	14.5%
ROA	10.6%	18.5%	24.8%	12.4%	6.8%
ROE	15.0%	25.5%	38.2%	19.6%	9.4%
DEBT RATIOS					
Debt to assets	29.2%	27.5%	34.9%	36.9%	27.6%
Debt to equity	41.2%	38.0%	53.7%	58.4%	38.0%
ASSET-UTILIZATION RATIOS					

CHAPTER 9

Technical Analysis

Technical analysis has an important bearing on the study of price behavior and has its own method in predicating significant price behavior. Technical analysis is probably the most controversial aspect of investment management. That technical analysis is a delusion, that it can never be more useful in predicating stock performance than examining the insides of a dead sheep, in the ancient Greek traditions.

Technical analysis involves a study of market generated data like prices and volumes to determine the future direction of price movement. Martin J. Prang explains as "The technical approach to investing is essentially a reflection of the idea that prices move in trends which are determined by the changing attitudes of investors toward a variety of economic, monetary, political and psychological forces. The art of technical analysis-for it is an art-is to identify trend changes at an early stage and to maintain an investment posture until the weight of the evidence indicates that the trend has been reversed.

BASIC OBJECTIVES OF TECHNICAL ANALYSIS

- Market value is determined by the interaction of supply and demand.
- Supply and demand are influenced by a variety of factors, both rational and irrational.
- These include fundamental factors as well as psychological factors.
- Shifts in demand and supply bring about changes in trends.
- Shifts in demand and supply can be detected with the help of charts of market action.
- Some chart patterns tend to repeat themselves.

Because of the persistence of trends and patterns, analysis of past market data can be used to predict future price behavior.

Rather than looking at the fundamentals of the economy or of a company, technical analysts look at the patterns of share prices and trading history to determine the appropriate strategy to adopt. A technical analyst, often known as a chartist, monitors share price behavior - the patterns of share prices and relationships between prices and other market data - and then, using historic information of recurring patterns, endeavors to select money-making stocks. Through the use of charts, technical analysts develop patterns of market behavior that they expect can be repeated over and over again. To some extent, these predictions may be self-fulfilling. If the charts predict that a share price will fall and investment managers sell this share, then supply and demand factors will force the price of that share down. The technique is based heavily on recognizing past patterns, the supply and demand for a stock, investor psychology (the behavior of crowds), and the use of certain mechanical rules. These rules include:

- The use of moving averages of share prices over time (often 20, 40 days or 200 days), trying to spot when a share has been over-sold and is due for an upwards price correction (or vice versa)
- Studying the number of daily prices rises and falls and the number of shares traded on that day - a rise in price and volume indicates increasing investor interest which should continue
- Spotting support areas (prices at which investors will buy more shares) and resistance zones (prices at which investors will sell). For example, if a company issued shares at 100p a year ago and the price today is 90p, it is likely that a number of investors will sell once the price reaches 100p

The technical analysts do not attempt to measure a security's intrinsic value but believe in making short-term profit by analyzing the volume and price patterns and trends. Technical analysts use statistical tools like time series analysis (in particular trend analysis), relative strength index, moving averages, regressions, price correlations, etc. The field of technical analysis is based on the following three assumptions.

- **The market discounts everything**: Technical analysts believe that the market price takes into consideration the intrinsic value of the stocks along with broader economic factors and the market psychology. Therefore, what is important is an analysis of the price movement that reflects the demand and supply of a stock in the short run.
- **Price moves in trends**: Trends are of three types, viz. uptrend, downtrend and horizontal trend. Technical analysts believe that once trends are established in the prices, the price moves in the same direction as the trends suggests.
- **History tends to repeat itself:** This assumption leads to a belief that current investors repeat the behavior of the investors that preceded them and therefore recognizable price patterns can be observed if a chart is drawn.

There are various concepts that are used by technical analysts like support prices, resistance levels, breakouts, momentum, etc. These concepts can be heard very often in business channels and business newspapers. Supports refer to the price level through which a stock price seldom falls and resistance is the price level through which a stock seldom surpasses. Breakout refers to situation when the price actually falls below the support level or rises above the resistance level. Once a breakout occurs, the role is reversed. If the price increases beyond the resistance level, the resistance level becomes the support level and when the price falls below the support level, the support level becomes the new resistance level for the stock. Momentum refers to the rate at which price of a stock changes.

CHALLENGES TO TECHNICAL ANALYSIS

There are many questions, primarily raised by fundamental analysts, about the assumptions of technical analysis. While it is understandable that price movements are caused by the interaction of supply and demand of securities and that the market assimilates this information (as mentioned in the first assumption), there is no consensus on the speed of this adjustment or its extent. In other words, while prices may react to changes in demand-supply and other market dynamics, the response could easily differ across securities, both in the time taken, and the degree to which prices change. Other objections to technical analysis arise from Efficient Markets Hypothesis, which we have seen in Chapter 4. Proponents of the EMH aver that market efficiency would preclude any technical trading patterns to repeat with any predictable accuracy, rendering the profitability of most such trading rules subject to chance. Further, the success of a trading rule could also make it crowded, in the sense that most technical traders follow a small set of rules (albeit with possibly different parameterizations), speeding up the adjustment of the market, and thus reducing the potential gains. Finally, technical analysis involves meaningful levels of subjectivity-interpretations may vary widely on the same pattern of stock, or index prices-which also hinders systematic reasoning and extensibility across different securities.

IMPORTANCE OF TECHNICAL ANALYSIS

Technical analysis has universal applicability. It can be applied to any financial instrument - stocks, futures and commodities, fixed-income securities, forex, etc

Focus on price

Fundamental developments are followed by price movements. By focusing only on price action, technicians focus on the future. The price pattern is considered as a leading indicator and generally leads the economy by 6 to 9 months. To track the market, it makes sense to look directly at the price movements. More often than not, change is a subtle beast. Even though the market is prone to sudden unexpected reactions, hints usually develop before significant movements. You should refer to periods of accumulation as evidence of an impending advance and periods of distribution as evidence of an impending decline.

SUPPLY, DEMAND, AND PRICE ACTION

Technicians make use of high, low and closing prices to analyze the price action of a stock. A good analysis can be made only when all the above information is present. Separately, these will not be able to tell much. However, taken together, the open, high, low and close reflect forces of supply and demand.

SUPPORT AND RESISTANCE

Charting is a technique used in analysis of support and resistance level. These are trading range in which the prices move for an extended period of time, saying that forces of demand and supply are deadlocked. When prices move out of the trading range, it signals that either supply or demand has started to get the upper hand. If prices move above the upper band of the trading range, then demand is winning. If prices move below the lower band, then supply is winning.

PICTORIAL PRICE HISTORY

A price chart offers most valuable information that facilitates reading historical account of a security's price movement over a period of time. Charts are much easier to read than a table of numbers. On most stock charts, volume bars are displayed at the bottom. With this historical picture, it is easy to identify the following:

- Market reactions before and after important events
- Past and present volatility
- Historical volume or trading levels
- Relative strength of the stock versus the index.

Weaknesses of Technical Analysis

Technical analysis is not hard-core science. It is subjective in nature and your personal biases can be reflected in the analysis. It is important to be aware of these biases when analyzing a chart. If the analyst is a perpetual bull, then a bullish bias will overshadow the analysis. On the other hand, if the analyst is a disgruntled eternal bear, then the analysis will probably have a bearish tilt.

OPEN TO INTERPRETATION

Technical analysis is a combination of science and art and is always open to interpretation. Even though there are standards, many times two technicians will look at the same chart and paint two different scenarios or see different patterns. Both will be able to come up with logical support and resistance levels as well as key breaks to justify their position. Is the cup half-empty or half-full? It is in the eye of the beholder.

TOO LATE

You can criticize the technical analysis for being too late. By the time the trend is identified, a substantial move has already taken place. After such a large move, the reward to risk ratio is not great. Lateness is a particular criticism of Dow Theory.

ALWAYS ANOTHER LEVEL

Technical analysts always wait for another new level. Even after a new trend has been identified, there is always another "important" level close at hand. Technicians have been accused of sitting on the fence and never taking an unqualified stance. Even if they are bullish, there is always some indicator or some level that will qualify their opinion.

TRADER'S REMORSE

An array of pattern and indicators arises while studying technical analysis. Not all the signals work. For instance: A sell signal is given when the neckline of a head and shoulders pattern is broken. Even though this is a rule, it is not steadfast and can be subject to other factors such as volume and momentum. In that same vein, what works for one particular stock may not work for another. A 50-day moving average may work great to identify support and resistance for Infosys, but a 70-day moving average may work better for Reliance. Even though many principles of technical analysis are universal, each security will have its own idiosyncrasies.

TA IS ALSO USEFUL IN CONTROLLING RISK

It is Technical Analysis only that can provide you the discipline to get out when you're on the wrong side of a trade. The easiest thing in the world to do is to get on the wrong side of a trade and to get stubborn. That is also potentially the worst thing you can do. You think that if you ride it out you'll be okay. However, there will also be occasions when you won't be okay. The stock will move against you in ways and to an extent that you previously found virtually unimaginable.

It is more important to control risk than to maximize profits!

There is asymmetry between zero and infinity. What does that mean? Most of us have very finite capital but infinite opportunities because of thousands of stocks. If we lose an opportunity, we will have thousands more tomorrow. If we lose our capital, will we get thousands more tomorrow? It is likely that we will not. We will also lose our opportunities. Our capital holds more worth to us than our opportunities because we must have capital in order to take advantage of tomorrow's opportunities.

It is more important to control risk than to maximize profits! Technical Analysis, if practiced with discipline, gives you specific parameters for managing risk. It's simply supply and demand. Waste what's plentiful, preserve what's scarce. Preserve your capital because *your capital is your opportunity*. You can be right a thousand times, become very wealthy and then get wiped out completely if you manage your risk poorly just once. One last time: That is why it is more important to control risk than to maximize profits! How to know what to look for? How to organize your thinking in a market of thousands of stock trading millions of shares per day? How to learn your way around? Technical Analysis answers all these questions.

Technical analysis works on Pareto principle. It considers the market to be 80% psychological and 20% logical. Fundamental analysts consider the market to be 20% psychological and 80% logical. Psychological or logical may be open for debate, but there is no questioning the current price of a security. After all, it is available for all to see and nobody doubts its legitimacy. The price set by the market reflects the sum knowledge of all participants, and we are not dealing with lightweights here. These participants have considered (discounted) everything under the sun and settled on a price to buy or sell. These are the forces of supply and demand at work. By examining price action to determine which force is prevailing, technical analysis focuses directly on the bottom line: What is the price? Where has it been? Where is it going?

Even though some principles and rules of technical analysis are universally applicable, it must be remembered that technical analysis is more an art form than a science. As an art form, it is subject to interpretation. However, it is also flexible in its approach and each investor should use only that which suits his or her style. Developing a style takes time, effort and dedication, but the rewards can be significant.

Assist with entry point

Technical analysis helps in tracking a proper entry point. Fundamental analysis is used to decide what to buy and technical analysis is used to decide when to buy. Timings in this context play a very important role in performance. Technical analysis can help spot demand (support) and supply (resistance) levels as well as breakouts. Checking out for a breakout above resistance or buying near support levels can improve returns.

First of all, you should analyze stock's price history. If a stock selected by you was great for the last three years has traded flat for those three years, it would appear that market has a different opinion. If a stock has already advanced significantly, it may be prudent to wait for a pullback. Or, if the stock is trending lower, it might pay to wait for buying interest and a trend reversal.

In fundamental analysis, a value of a stock is predicted with risk-return framework based on economic environment. An alternative approach to predict stock price behavior is known as technical analysis. It is frequently used as a supplement rather than as a substitute to fundamental analysis. Technical analysis is based on notion that security prices are determined by the supply of and demand for securities. It uses historical financial data on charts to find meaningful patterns, and using the patterns to predict future prices. Edwards and Magee formulate the basic assumptions underlying technical analysis:

The basic premises underlying technical analysis are as follows.

- The interaction of supply and demand determines the market value of the security.
- The various factors, both rational and irrational factors, govern the supply and demand of the securities.
- Stock price tend to move in trend which persist for an appreciable length of time.
- Changes in trend are caused by shifts in supply and demand.
- Shifts in supply and demand can be detected sooner or later in charts of market action.
- Some chart patterns tend to repeat themselves.

Differences between Technical Analysis and Fundamental Analysis

The key differences between technical analysis and fundamental analysis are as follows:

- Technical analysis mainly seeks to predict short –term price movements, whereas fundamental analysis tries to establish long-term values.
- The focus of technical analysis is mainly on internal market data, particularly price and volume data. The focus of fundamental analysis is on fundamental factors relating to the economy, the industry, and the firm.
- Technical analysis appeals mostly to short-term traders, whereas fundamental analysis appeals primarily to long-term investors.

Charting - A Technical Tool

Technical analysts, while defining their own theory about stock price behavior and criticizing the fundamental school, do feel that there is some merit in the fundamental analysis also. But according to them, the method is very tedious and it takes a rather long time for the common man to evaluate stocks through this method. They consider their own techniques and charts as superior to fundamental analysis. Some of their theories, techniques and methods of stock prices are given below:

Concepts Underlying Chart Analysis: The basic concepts underlying chart analysis are: (a) persistence of trends; (b) relationship between volume and trend; and (c) resistance and support levels.

Trends: The key belief of the chartists is that stock prices tend to move in fairly persistent trends. Stock price behavior is characterized by inertia: the price movement continues along a certain path (up, down or sideways) until it meets an opposing force, arising out of an altered supply-demand relationship.

Relationship between volume and trends: Chartists believe that generally volume and trend go hand in hand. When a major upturn begins the volume of trading increases as the price advances and decreases as the price declines. In a major down turn, the opposite happens; the volume of trading increases as the price declines and decreases as the price rallies.

Support and Resistance levels: Chartists assume that it is difficult for the price of a share to rise above a certain level called the resistance level and fall below a certain level called support level. Why? The explanation for the first claim goes as follows. If investors find that prices fall after their purchases, they continue to hang on to their shares in the hope of a recovery. And when the price rebounds to the level of their purchase price, they tend to sell and heave sigh of relief as they break even. Such a behavioral tendency on the part of investors stimulates considerable supply when the price rebounds to the level at which substantial purchases were made by the investors. As a result, the share is not likely to rise above this level, the resistance level.

The level at which a declining share may evoke a substantial increase in demand is called the support level. This typically represents the level from which the share rose previously with large trading volumes. As the price falls to this level, there is a lot of demand from several quarters; those who 'missed the bus' on the previous occasion and have regrets for their failure to partake in the earlier advance; short-sellers who, having sold short, at higher levels, want to book profits by squaring their positions; and value-oriented investors.

THE DOW THEORY

The ideas of Charles H. Dow, the first editor of the Wall Street Journal, form the basis of technical analysis today. According to the hypothesis of Dow, the stock market does not perform on random basis but is influenced by three cyclical trends, namely, (a) Primary trend, (b) secondary or intermediate trend, and (c) Tertiary or minor trend. The general market direction can be predicted by following these trends. The primary trends are the long-term movement of prices, lasting from several months to several years. They are commonly called bear or bull markets. Secondary trends are caused by short-term deviations of prices from the underlying trend line. They last only a few months. The secondary trend acts as a restraining force on the primary trend, tending to correct deviations from its general boundaries. Minor trends are daily fluctuations in either directions (bull or bear) which are of little analytical value. In terms of bull and bear markets the trends are described as follows:

The first phase of a bull market is the accumulation phase. This is when prices are depressed and financial reports don't look good. However, farsighted investors use this period of depressed prices to take advantage and buy shares.

- The second phase of the bull market is characterized by increased activity, rising prices, and better financial reports. This is the period where the large gains are made. At this point, the market becomes vulnerable to a reversal.
- The first phase of a bear market is the distribution phase. This is where farsighted investors see the uninformed investors scrambling to buy shares. The farsighted investors begin to sell shares. Oversupply leads to weakening prices and profits are harder to come by.
- The second phase of the bear market is characterized by near panic selling. Prices accelerate to the downside and more and more people begin to liquidate their holdings.
- The third phase of the bear market is characterized by further weakening and erosion of prices. Lesser quality issues erase the gains of the previous bull market. The news is full of bad market news.

The second part of the Dow Theory is that the Industrial Average and the Railroad Average must corroborate each other's direction for there to be a reliable market direction signal. Dow created the Industrial Average, of top blue-chip stocks, and a second average of top railroad stocks (now the Transport Average). He believed that the behavior of the averages reflected the hopes and fears of the entire market. The behavior patterns that he observed apply to markets throughout the world. (At the time of Dow's writing there was only the Railroad Average.

In 1969, Dow Jones & Company broadened this to include truckers and airlines so that today it would be confirmation by the Industrial Average and the Transportation Average). According to Dow Theory, large active stocks will generally reflect the market averages. However, individual issues may deviate from the broad averages because of circumstances peculiar to them. The logic behind the makeup of the specific averages is that both the industrials and the transports are independent of each other. Yet, for the industrials to get their products to market, they must use the transports. When the industrials are doing well, the transports will do well. However, when one sector is doing substantially better than the other, a divergence is taking place. This demonstrates that one sector is much stronger than the other; and if it continues, without the other sector catching up, a major reversal in the market will take place.

Dow Theory also specifies that closing prices should only be used. This is because closing prices reflect the price level at which informed investors are willing to carry positions overnight.

Thus, Dow Theory is used to indicate reversals and trends in the markets as well as individual security. The basic tenet of Dow Theory is that there is a positive relationship between trend and volume of shares traded.

1. Daily fluctuations that are random day-to-day wiggles.
2. Secondary movements or corrections that may last for a few weeks to some months; and
3. Primary trends representing bull and bear phases of the market.

The Dow Theory asserts that a bull market is established when both the Dow Jones Industrial Average and the Dow Jones Transportation Average are moving upwards. A bear market occurs when the indices are moving down. If one of the indices departs from the trend and is followed by a departure of the other index from the trend, then this is viewed as confirmation that the primary trend has changed. The basic tenets of the theory also purport that no additional information is required about the stock market outside of data on stock indices and that, usually, a positive relationship exists between the trend and volume of shares traded. The Dow Theory has been extended and changed over the years. However, most technical analysis theories stem from the Dow Theory.

An upward primary trend represents a bull market, whereas a downward primary trend represents a bear market. A major upward move is said to occur when the high point of each rally is higher than the high point of the preceding rally and the low point of each decline is higher than the low point of the preceding decline. Likewise, a major downward move is said to occur when the high point of each rally is lower than the high point of the preceding rally and the low point of each decline is lower than the low point of the preceding decline.

The secondary movement represents technical correction. They represent adjustments to the excesses that may have occurred in the primary movements. These movements are considered quite significant in the application of the Dow Theory. The daily fluctuations are considered to be minus significance. Even zealous technical analysts do not usually try to forecast day-to-day movements in the market.

Charts: Charting represents a key activity for a technical analyst during individual stock analysis. The probable future performance of a stock can be predicted and evolving and changing patterns of price behavior can be detected based on historical price-volume information of the stock.

Technical analysis involves three basic types of charts. They are (a) Line charts, (b) Bar charts, and (c) Point and figure charts. The line charts indicate the lines which are used to connect successive days' prices. The Bar charts indicate vertical bars representing each day's price movement. Each bar spans the distance from the day's highest price to the lowest price with a small cross on the bar marks the closing price. Point and figure charts are more complex than line and bar charts.

Point and figure chart are not only used to detect reversals in a trend, but also used to forecasts the price, called price targets. The only significant price changes are posted to point and figure charts. Three- or five-point price changes as posted for high prices securities, only one-point changes are posted follow prices securities. While line and bar charts have two dimensions with vertical column indicating trading day, point and figure chart represents each column as a significant reversal instead of a trading day.

The basic tool in technical analysis is movement in prices measured by charts. It is for this reason that the technical analyst is sometimes called the "Chartist".

A graph of the price movements of a given security over a given time period, sometimes along with volume data. Charts are the main tool that technical_analysts use in order to plot data and predict prices. Technical analysts may use several different types of charts in order to conduct their tests and look for patterns in the data, including.

Types of Charts:

Line Charts

Bar Charts

Candlestick Charts

Line Charts and Bar

The bar chart, one of the simplest and most commonly used tools of technical analysis, depicts the daily price range along with the closing price. In addition, it may show the daily volume of transactions. Figure 2 shows an illustrative bar chart. The upper end of each bar represents the day's highest price and the lower end the day's lowest price. The small cross across the bar marks the day's closing price. A line chart, a simplification over the bar chart, shows the line connecting successive closing prices.

Definition: A line chart or line graph is a type of graph, which displays information as a series of data points connected by straight line segments. It is a basic type of chart common in many fields. It is an extension of a scatter graph, and is created by connecting a series of points that represent individual measurements with line segments. A line chart is often used to visualize a trend in data over intervals of time, thus the line is often drawn chronologically.

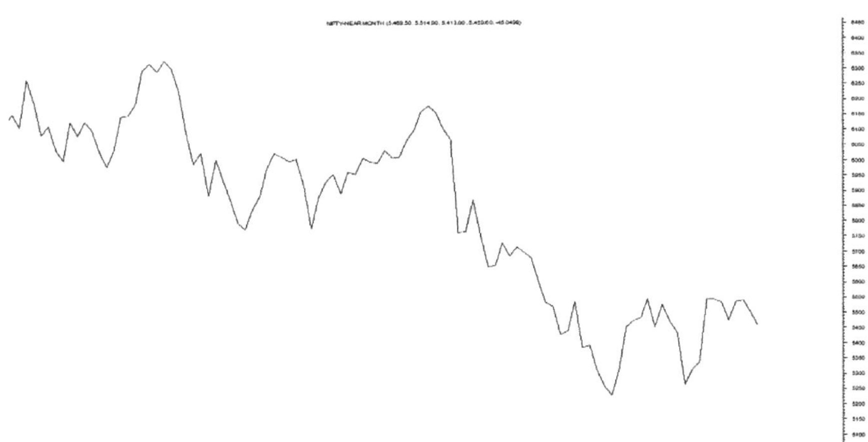

BAR CHARTS

Definition

The bar chart, one of the simplest and most commonly used tools of technical analysis, depicts the daily price range along with the closing price. In addition, it may show the daily volume of transactions. The upper end of each bar represents the day's highest price and the lower end the day's lowest price.

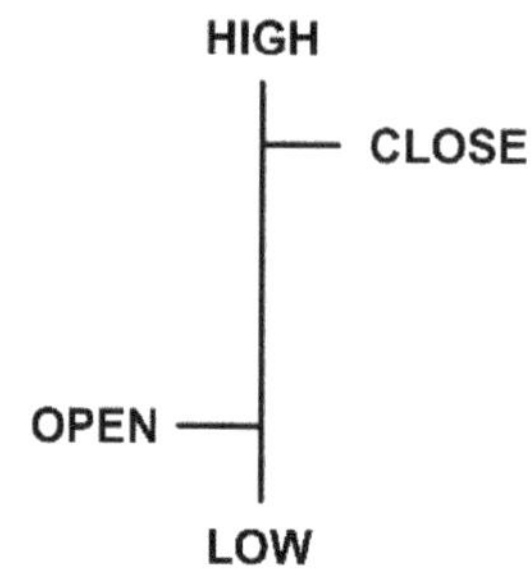

Standard bar charts are commonly used to convey price activity into an easily readable chart. Usually four elements make up a bar chart, the Open, High, Low, and Close for the trading session/time period. A price bar can represent any time frame the user wishes, from 1 minute to 1 month. The total vertical length/height of the bar represents the entire trading range for the period. The top of the bar represents the highest price of the period, and the bottom of the bar represents the lowest price of the period. The Open is represented by a small dash to the left of the bar, and the Close for the session is a small dash to the right of the bar. Below is a standard bar chart example.

CANDLESTICK CHARTS

Definition: Candlestick charts are much more visually appealing than a standard two-dimensional bar chart. As in a standard bar chart, there are four elements necessary to construct a candlestick chart, the OPEN, HIGH, LOW and CLOSING price for a given time period. Below are examples of candlesticks and a definition for each candlestick component.

HISTORY OF CANDLESTICK

Candlestick charts are on record as being the oldest type of charts used for price prediction. When they were used for predicting rice prices. In fact, during this era in Japan, Munches Homma become a legendary rice trader and gained a huge fortune using candlestick analysis. He is said to have executed over 100 consecutive winning traders.

The candlesticks themselves and the formations they shape were give colorful names by the Japanese Traders. Due in part to the military environment of the Japanese feudal system during this era, candlestick formations developed names such as "counter attack lines" and the "advancing three soldiers". Just as skill, strategy, and psychology are important in battle, so too are they important elements when in the midst of trading battle.

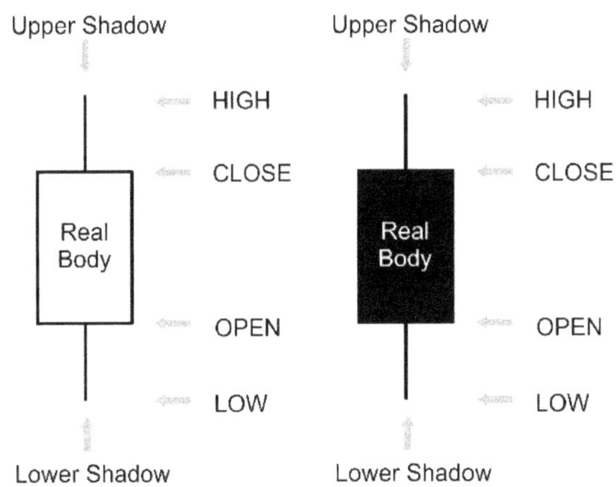

Candlesticks are formed using the open, high, low and close.

- If the close is above the open, then a hollow candlestick (usually displayed as white) is drawn.
- If the close is below the open, then a filled candlestick (usually displayed as black) is drawn.
- The hollow or filled section of the candlestick is called the "real body" or body.
- The thin lines poking above and below the body display the high/low range and are called shadows.
- The top of the upper shadow is the "high".
- The bottom of the lower shadow is the "lo

IMPORTANT TYPES OF CANDLESTICKERS

The following is a list of some individual candlestick terms. It is important to realize that many formations occur within the context of prior candlesticks. What follows is merely a definition of terms, not formations.

1. The Black Candlestick -- when the close is lower than the open.

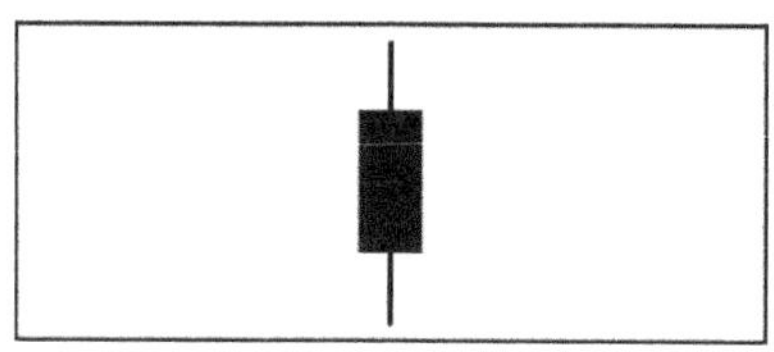

2. The White Candlestick -- when the close is higher than the open.

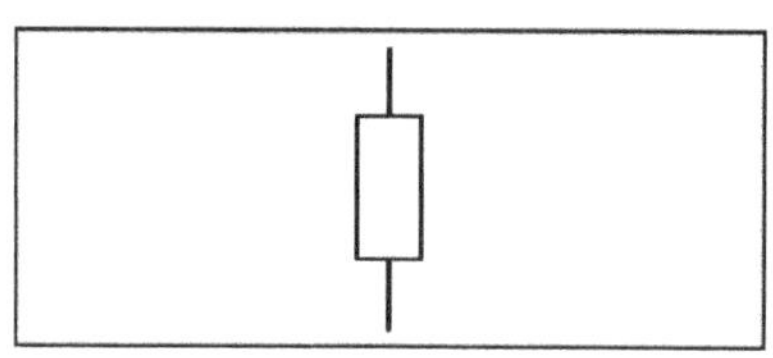

3. The Shaven Head -- a candlestick with no upper shadow.

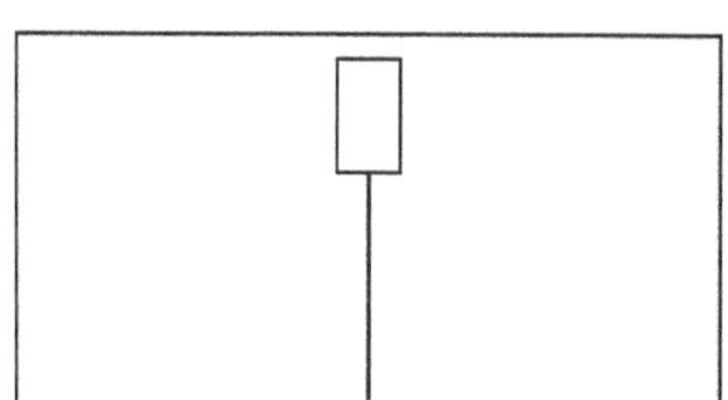

4. The Shaven Bottom -- a candlestick with no lower shadow.

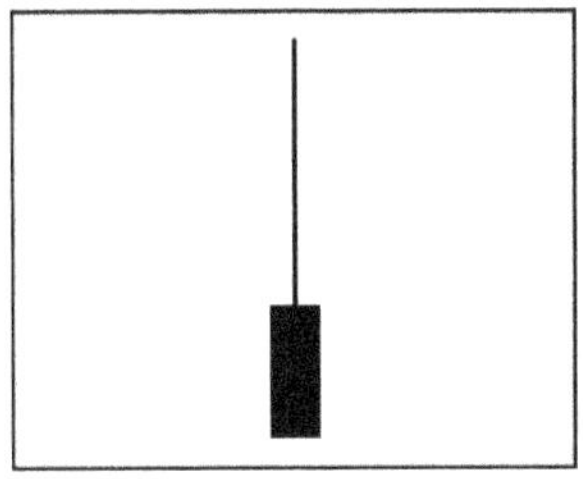

5. Spinning Tops -- candlesticks with small *real bodies*, and when appearing within a sideways choppy market, they represent equilibrium between the bulls and the bears. They can be either *white* or *black*.

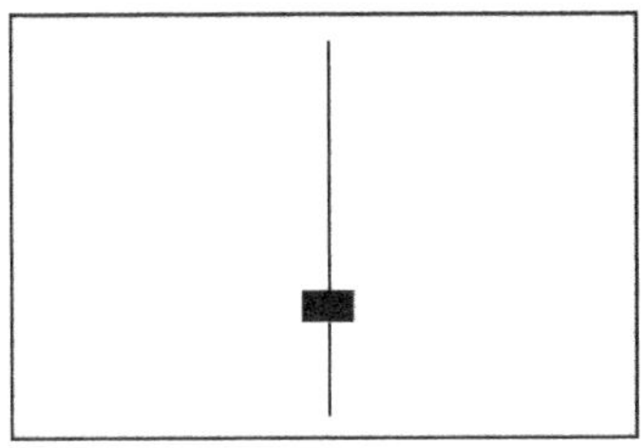

6. Deja Lines -- have no *real body*, but instead have a horizontal line. This represents when the Open and Close are the same or very close. The length of the *shadow* can vary.

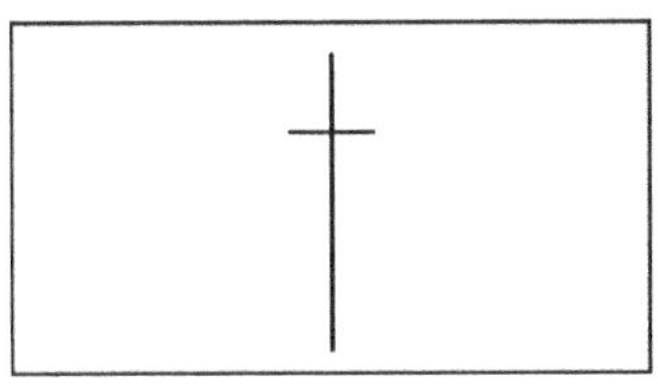

Technical analysts believe that certain formations or patterns observed on the bar chart or line chart have predictive value. The more important formations and their indications are described below.

CHART PATTERNS

A chart pattern is a pattern that is formed within a chart when prices are graphed. In stock and commodity markets trading, chart pattern studies play a large role during technical analysis. When data is plotted there is usually a pattern which naturally occurs and repeats over a period of time. Chart patterns are used as either reversal or continuation signals.

Types of Chart Patterns:

Triangles

Wedges

Flags

Pennants

Double Top

Double Bottom

Head and Shoulders

Triangles are three types

Symmetric Triangle

Ascending Triangle

Descending Triangle

SYMMETRICAL TRIANGLE

Definition: The symmetrical triangle is formed when the market makes lower highs and higher lows and is commonly associated with directionless markets. If this pattern forms in an uptrend then it is considered a continuation pattern. If the market breaks out to the upside and a reversal pattern if the market breaks to the downside. Similarly, if the pattern forms in a downtrend it is considered a continuation pattern if the market breaks out to the downside and a reversal pattern if the market breaks to the upside.

Types of Symmetrical:

Up Trend

Down Trend

Symmetrical triangles are in the direction of the trend. Symmetrical triangles are great patterns to use and should be traded as continuation pattern.

EXAMPLE OF UP TREND SYMMETRIC TRIANGLE

EXAMPLE OF DOWN TREND SYMMETRIC TRIANGLE

ASCENDING TRIANGLE

The ascending triangle is a variation of the symmetrical triangle. Ascending triangles are generally considered bullish and are most reliable when found in an uptrend. The top part of the triangle appears flat, while the bottom part of the triangle has an upward line. In ascending triangles, the market becomes overbought and prices are turned back. Buying then re-enters the market and prices soon reach their old highs, where they are once again turned back.

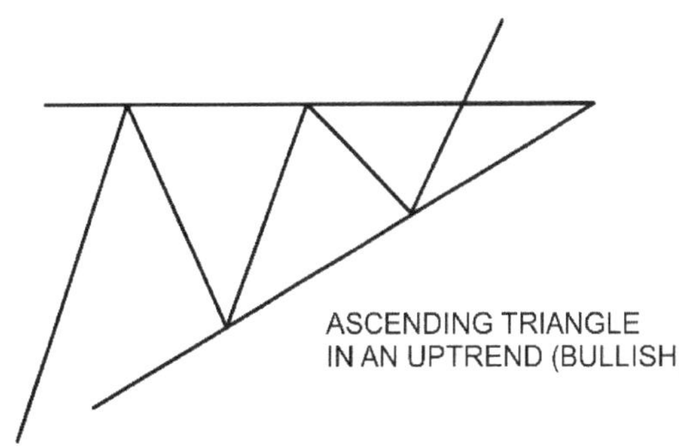

EXAMPLE OF ASCENDING TRIANGLE

DESCENDING TRIANGLE

The descending triangle, also a variation of the symmetrical triangle, is generally considered to be bearish and is usually found in downtrends. Unlike the ascending triangle, this time the bottom part of the triangle appears flat. The top part of the triangle has a downward line. Prices drop to a point where they are oversold. Tentative buying comes in at the lows, and prices perk up.

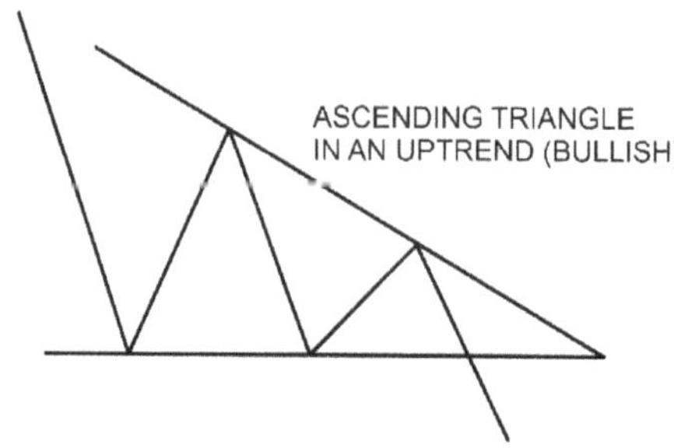

EXAMPLE OF TRIANGLE

WEDGES: A falling wedge is generally considered bullish and is usually found in up trends. But they can also be found in downtrends as well. The implication however is still generally bullish. This pattern is marked by a series of lower tops and lower bottoms.

A rising wedge is generally considered bearish and is usually found in downtrends. They can be found in up trends too, but would still generally be regarded as bearish. Rising wedges put in a series of higher tops and higher bottoms.

EXAMPLE OF RAISING WEDGE

FLAGS AND PENNANTS

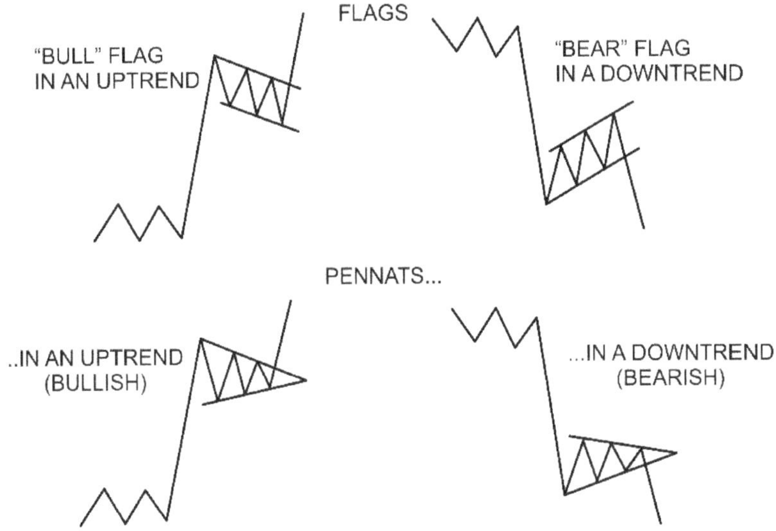

Flags can be categorized as continuation patterns. They are typically seen right after a big, quick move. The market then usually takes off again in the same direction. This pattern is some of the most reliable continuation patterns.

Bullish flags are characterized by lower tops and lower bottoms, with the pattern slanting against the trend. But unlike wedges, their trend lines run parallel.

Bearish flags are comprised of higher tops and higher bottoms. "Bear" flags also have a tendency to slope against the trend. Their trend lines run parallel as well.

Pennants can be categorized as continuation patterns. It looks very much like symmetrical triangles. But pennants are typically smaller in size (volatility) and duration

EXAMPLE OF FLAG

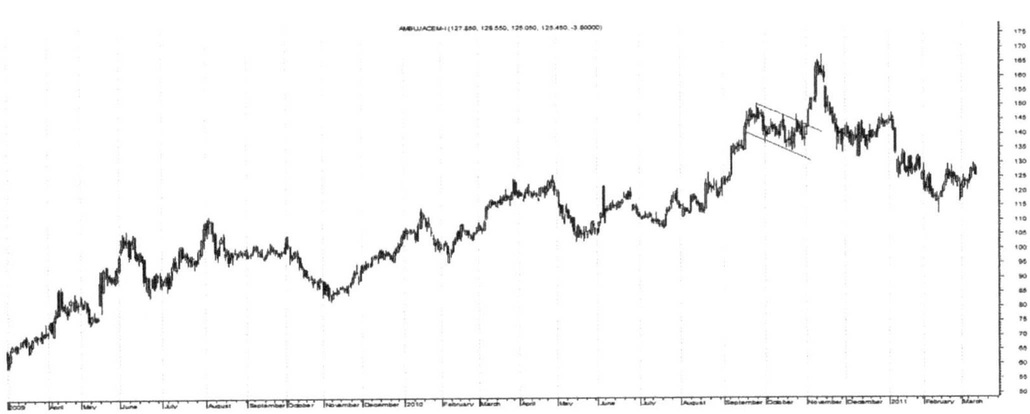

DOUBLE TOP

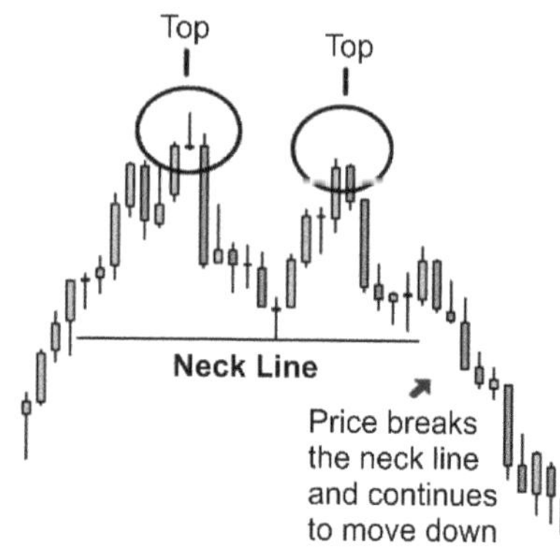

A double top is a reversal pattern that is formed after there is an extended move up. The "tops" are peaks which are formed when the price hits a certain level that can't be broken. After hitting this level, the price will bounce off it slightly, but then return back to test the level again. If the price bounces off of that level again, then you have a DOUBLE top!

In this chart the two peaks or "tops" were formed after a strong move up. The 2nd top was not able to break the high of the 1st top. This is a strong sign that a reversal is going to occur because it is telling us that the buying pressure is just about finished. With double tops, we would place our entry order below the neckline because we are anticipating a reversal of the uptrend.

In this chart price breaks the neckline and makes a nice move down. Generally, double tops are a trend reversal formation. You'll want to look for these after there is a strong uptrend.

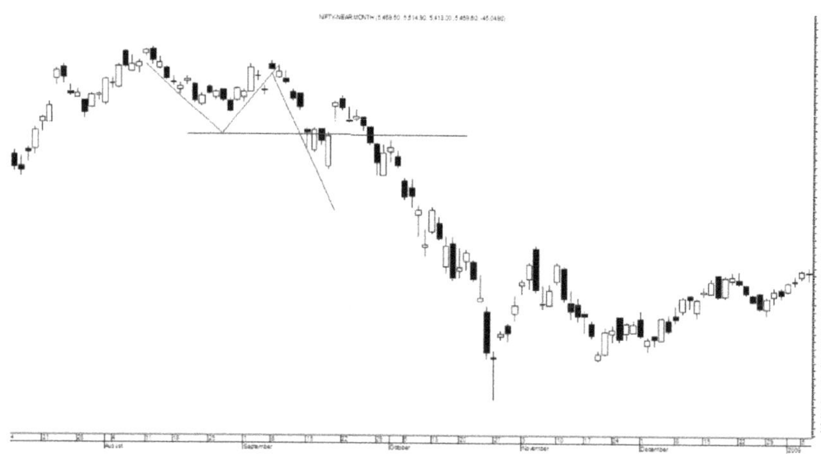

DOUBLE BOTTOM

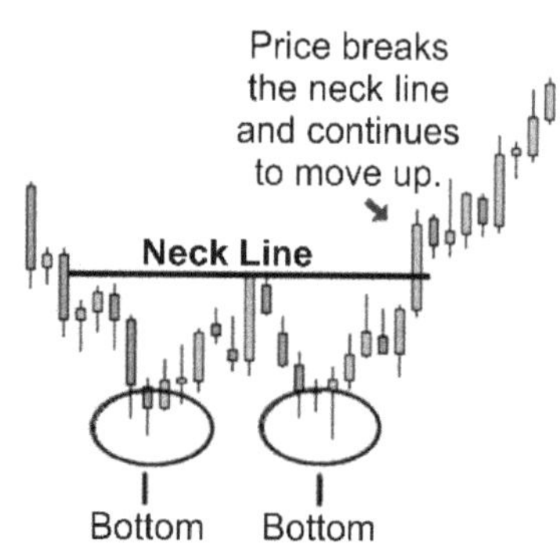

Double bottoms are also trend reversal formations, but this time we are looking to go long instead of short. These formations occur after extended downtrends when two valleys or "bottoms" have been formed.

In above chart, after the previous downtrend, the price formed two valleys because it wasn't able to go below a certain level. The 2nd bottom wasn't able to significantly break the 1st bottom. This is a sign that the selling pressure is about finished, and that a reversal is about to occur. In this situation, we would place an entry order above the neckline.

The price breaks the neckline and makes a nice move up. Just like double tops, double bottoms are also trend reversal formations. You'll want to look for these after a strong downtrend

HEAD AND SHOULDERS

A head and shoulders pattern are also a trend reversal formation. It is formed by a peak (shoulder), followed by a higher peak (head), and then another lower peak (shoulder). A "neckline" is drawn by connecting the lowest points of the two troughs. The slope of this line can either be up or down. In my experience, when the slope is down, it produces a more reliable signal.

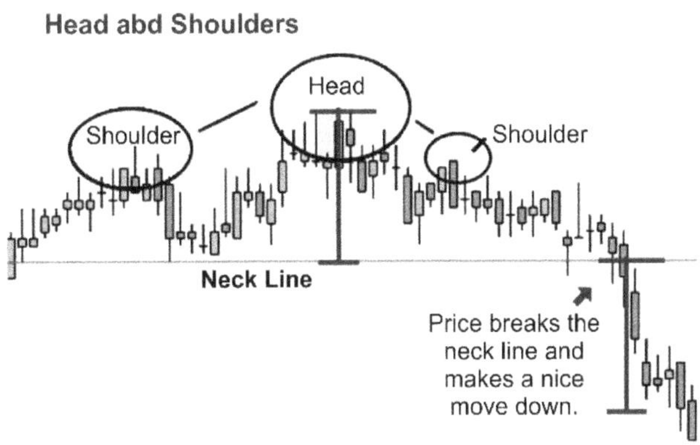

The head is the 2nd peak and is the highest point in the pattern. The two shoulders also form peaks but do not exceed the height of the head. With this formation, we look to make an entry order below the neckline. We can also calculate a target by measuring the high point of the head to the neckline. This distance is approximately how far the price will move after it breaks the neckline.

It can see that once the price goes below the neckline it makes a move that is about the size of the distance between the head and the neckline.

EXAMPLE OF HEAD AND SHOULDER

REVERSE HEAD AND SHOULDERS

It is basically a head and shoulders formation, except this time it's in reverse. A valley is formed (shoulder), followed by an even lower valley (head), and then another higher valley (shoulder). These formations occur after extended downward movements.

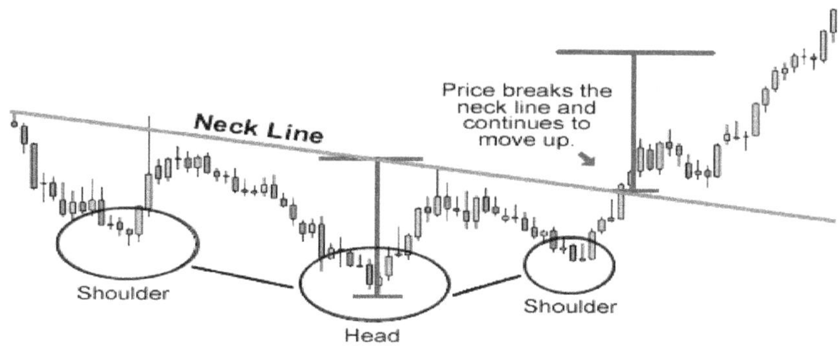

It is just like a head and shoulders pattern, but it's flipped upside down. With this formation, we would place a long entry order above the neckline. Our target is calculated just like the head and shoulders pattern. Measure the distance between the head and the neckline, and that is approximately the distance that the price will move after it breaks the neckline. The price moved up nicely after it broke the neckline.

EXAMPLE OF REVERCE HEAD AND SHOULDERS

TRENDS

A trend is the direction in which a share price is heading. Three choices of trend exist:

1. Positive or advancing trend
2. Negative or declining trend
3. Neutral or sideways trading range.

Assessing prevailing trends is important, because positioning trades with the trend tends to make most money - i.e. buying in up trends and selling in down trends.

Trend: The current general direction of movement for prices or rates.

Types of Trend:

Uptrend, Downtrend & *Sideways*:

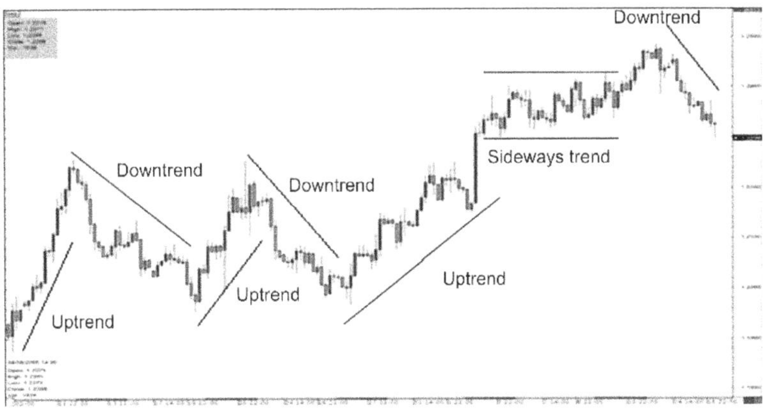

Upward price movement of a security or the overall market. Opposite of downtrend. Downward price movement of a security or the overall market. Opposite of uptrend.

A sideways trend is often regarded as a period of consolidation before the price continues in the direction of the previous move. A sideways price trend is also commonly known as a "horizontal trend

Trend Analysis means:

Technical analysis that tries to predict the future movement of a stock based on past data. Trend analysis is based on the idea that what has happened in the past gives traders an idea of what will happen in the future.

Trend Lines:

The trend line is nothing more than a straight line drawn between at least three points. In an up move the low points are connected to form an uptrend line. For a downtrend the peaks are connected. It connects the highs in a downtrend and the lows in an uptrend. The closing prices are not connected

Types of Trend Lines:

Up Trend Line

Down Trend lines

Uptrend Line:

An uptrend line is drawn along the bottom of easily identifiable support areas.

An uptrend line has a positive slope and is formed by connecting two of more low points. The second low must be higher than the first low. Uptrend lines act as support and indicate that net-demand (demand less supply) is increasing even as the price rises. A rising price combined with increasing demand is very bullish and shows a strong determination on the part of the buyers. As long as prices remain above the trend line, the uptrend is considered solid and intact. A break below the uptrend line indicates that net-demand has weakened and a change in trend could be imminent.

Downtrend Line:

In a downtrend, the trend line is drawn along the top of easily identifiable resistance areas.

A downtrend line has a negative slope and is formed by connecting two or more high points. The second high must be lower than the first for the line to have a negative slope. Downtrend lines act as resistance, and indicate that net-supply (supply less demand) is increasing even as the price declines. A declining price combined with increasing supply is very bearish and shows the strong resolve of the sellers. As long as prices remain below the downtrend line, the downtrend is considered solid and intact. A break above the downtrend line indicates that net-supply is decreasing and a change of trend could be imminent.

SUPPORT AND RESISTANCE

An important application of trend lines is in identification of support and resistance levels. Resistance is defined as Selling, actual or potential, sufficient in volume to satisfy all bids and hence stop prices from going higher for a time period. Support is defined as Buying, actual or potential, sufficient in volume to halt or stop a downtrend in prices.

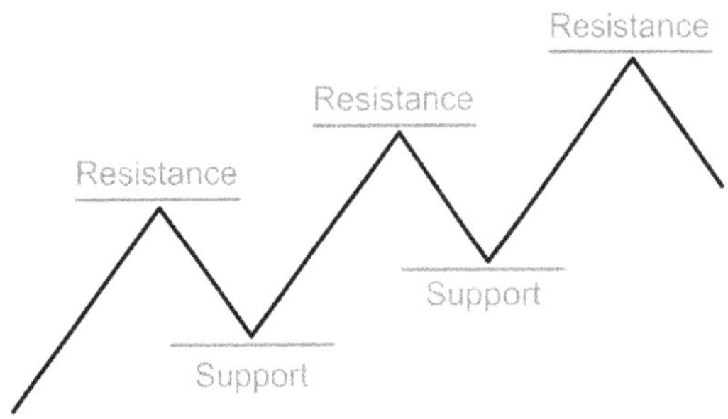

The above zigzag pattern is making its way up or bull market. When the market moves up and then pulls back, the highest point reached before it pulled back is now resistance.

As the market continues up again, the lowest point reached before it started back is now support. In this way resistance and support are continually formed as the market oscillates over time. The reverse of course is true of the downtrend.

Principles of Support and Resistance:

- When the market passes through resistance, that resistance now becomes support.
- The more often price tests a level of resistance or support without breaking it the stronger the area of resistance or support is.
- Prices are said to remain in a 'congestion zone' as long as they fluctuate in narrow ranges within a support and resistance level. The direction of breakout from a congestion zone cannot be predicted in advance.
- The higher the volume accompanying the confirmation of a support or resistance level, the more its significance.
- Support and resistance levels repeat their effectiveness time and again, even if separated by many years.

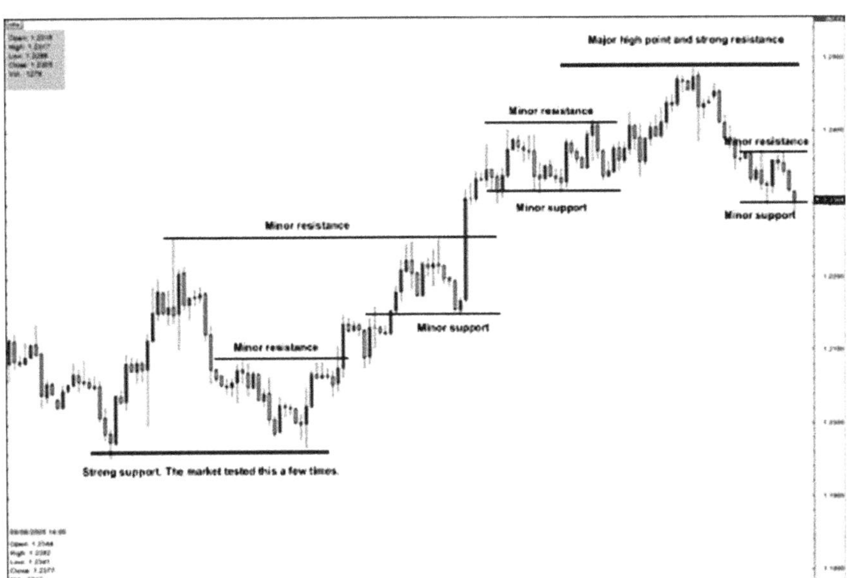

EXAMPLE OF SUPPORT AND RESISTENCE

CONSOLIDATION PATTERNS

Prices do not usually continue straight up or straight down for very long. Corrections within the major trend usually occur, which will then carry prices either sideways or slightly against the trend. These interruptions are known as consolidations, because share price patterns pause to consolidate the gains or losses. Consolidation patterns are generally known as continuation patterns because they usually indicate that prices will continue to move in the overall direction of the major trend, after a short pause. Often, there is a noticeable drop in volume during the pause.

Triangles are drawn from very short-term trend lines connecting the relevant tops and bottoms of very short-term price swings

REVERSAL PATTERNS

Reversal patterns are transition areas in which market tendencies begin to shift from bullish to bearish or *vice versa.* The volume of shares being traded during this period usually helps to identify the phase of the reversal formation.

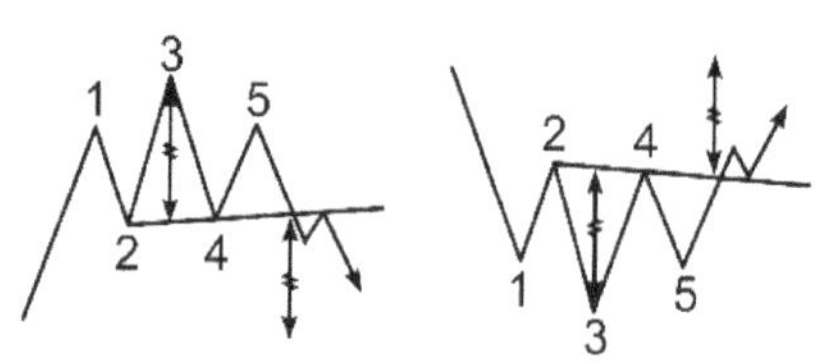

Figure 9.4 Head and shoulders.

Head and shoulders (see Figure 9.4) - the most reliable reversal pattern - occurs as either a head and shoulders top or head and shoulders bottom.

POINT AND FIGURE CHARTS

The point and figure charts are represented by Us and So. These are more difficult to calculate the stock prices than the line charts and bar charts. These are drawn by the technical analysts to make a forecast of prices and also to find out the trend in prices. It is usually the reversal in trend which can be found out by sub-charts. The price forecasts made by the point and figure charts are called price targets.

TECHNICAL INDICATORS

There are numerous technical indicators that collectively add up to organized confusion. Some of the major technical indicators are described in the following sections.

The Short Interest Ratio Theory: The short interest ratio is derived by dividing the reported short interest or the number of shares sold short, by the average volume for about 30 days. When short sales increase relative to total volume, the indicator rises. A ratio above 150per cent is considered bullish, and a ratio below 100 per cent is considered bearish.

The logic behind this ratio is that speculators and other investors sell stocks at high prices in anticipation of buying them back at lower prices. Thus, increasing short selling is viewed as a sign of general market weakness, and short covering (as evidenced by decreasing short positions) as a sign of strength. An existing large short interest is considered a sign of strength, since the covers (buyers) are yet to come; whereas an established slight short interest is considered a sign of weakness (more short sales are to come).

Confidence Index: It is the ratio of a group of lower-grade bonds to a group of higher-grade bounds. According to the theory underlying this index, when the ratio is high, investors' confidence is likewise high, as reflected by their purchase of relatively more of the lower-grade securities. When they buy relatively more of the higher-grade securities, this is taken as an indication that confidence is low, and is reflected in a low ratio.

Spreads: Large spreads between yields indicate low confidence and are bearish; the market appears to require a large compensation for business, financial and inflation risks. Small spreads indicate high confidence and are bullish. In short, the larger the spreads, the war the ratio and the less the confidence. The smaller the spreads, the greater the ratio, indicating greater confidence.

Advance-Decline Ratio: The index relating advances to decline is called the advance decline ratio. When advances persistently outnumber decline the ratio increases. A bullish condition is said to exist, and vice versa. Thus, advance decline ratio tries to capture the market's underlying strength by taking into account the number of advancing and declining issues.

Market Breadth Index is a variant of the advance decline ratio. To compute it, we take the net difference between the number of stocks rising and the number of stocks falling added (or subtracted) to the previous. For example, if in a given week 600 shares advanced, 200 shares declined, and 200 were unchanged, the breadth would be 2[(600-200)/200]. The figure of each week is added to previous weeks. These data are than plotted to establish the pattern of movement of advances and declines.

The purpose of the market breadth index is to indicate whether a confirmation of some index has occurred. If both the stock index and market breadth increase, the market is bullish; when the stock index increases but the breadth index does not, the market is bearish.

THE ODD-LOT RATIO/THEORY: Odd-lot transactions are measured by odd-lot changes in the index. Odd-lots are stock transactions of less than, say, 100 shares. The odd- lot ratio is sometimes referred to as a yardstick of uniformed sentiment or an index of contrary opinion because the odd- lot theory assumes that small buyers or sellers are not very bright especially at tops and bottoms when they need to be brightest. The odd-lot short ratio theory assumes that the odd-lot short sellers are even more likely to be wrong than odd-letters in general. This indicator relates odd-lot sales to purchases.

Insider Transactions: The hypothesis that insider activity may be indicative of future stock prices has received some support in the academic literature. Since insiders may have the best picture of how the firm is faring, some believers of technical analysis feel that these inside transactions offer a clue, to future earnings, dividend and stock price performance. If the insiders are selling heavily, it is considered a bearish indicator and vice versa. Stock holders do not like to hear that the president of a company is selling large blocks of stock of the company. Although the president's reason for selling the stock may not be related to the future growth of the company, it is still considered bearish as investors figure the president, as an insider, must know something bad about the company that they, as outsiders, do not know.

Moving Average *is a smoothed presentation of underlying historical data.* Each data point is the arithmetic average of a portion of the previous data. A ten-day moving average measures the average over the previous ten trading days; a twenty-day moving average measures average values over the previous twenty days, and so on. Regardless of the time period used, each day a new observation is included in the calculation and the oldest is dropped, so a constant number of points are always being averaged.

Technical analysts study moving average charts in order to identify short- and long-term trends (as suggested by the Dow Theory). To construct a 30-day moving average chart, the arithmetic average of the prices from the previous 30 trading days would be taken. This calculation would be done every day by dropping the oldest day and adding the most recent day, thus creating a rolling or moving average. A technical analyst might compare the 200-day moving average to the 30-day moving average to contrast a long-term trend with a short-term trend. If the 200-day moving average was rising while the 30-day average was falling, one interpretation could be that price declines are expected in the short term, but not in the long term.

Moving averages can be used for market indices and for individual stocks. Technical analysts will look for moving average charts to cross each other to indicate a change in direction of a trend. Likewise, if prices of a stock or index reverse and break through or cross a moving average line from below on heavy volume, then this points to a strongly positive change. The indication is then that this breakthrough signals a reversal of a declining trend. The opposite would be true if prices crossed the moving average line from above.

Advocates of moving averages in stock selection believe that changes in slope of the line are important. A stock twenty-day moving average line has been trending up might become a candidate for sale if the line turns downward.

INDICATORS AND OSCILLATORS

MOVING AVERAGES

Introduction

Moving averages are one of the most popular and easy to use tools available to the technical analyst. They smooth a data series and make it easier to spot trends, something that is especially helpful in volatile markets. They also form the building blocks for many other technical indicators and overlays.

The two most popular types of moving averages are **the Simple Moving Average (SMA)** and **the Exponential Moving Average (EMA)**. They are described in more detail below.

Mean value, as calculated over a rolling previous period of fixed length.

SIMPLE MOVING AVERAGE (SMA)

A simple moving average is formed by computing the average (mean) price of a security over a specified number of periods. While it is possible to create moving averages from the Open, the High, and the Low data points, most moving averages are created using the closing price. For example: a 5-day simple moving average is calculated by adding the closing prices for the last 5 days and dividing the total by

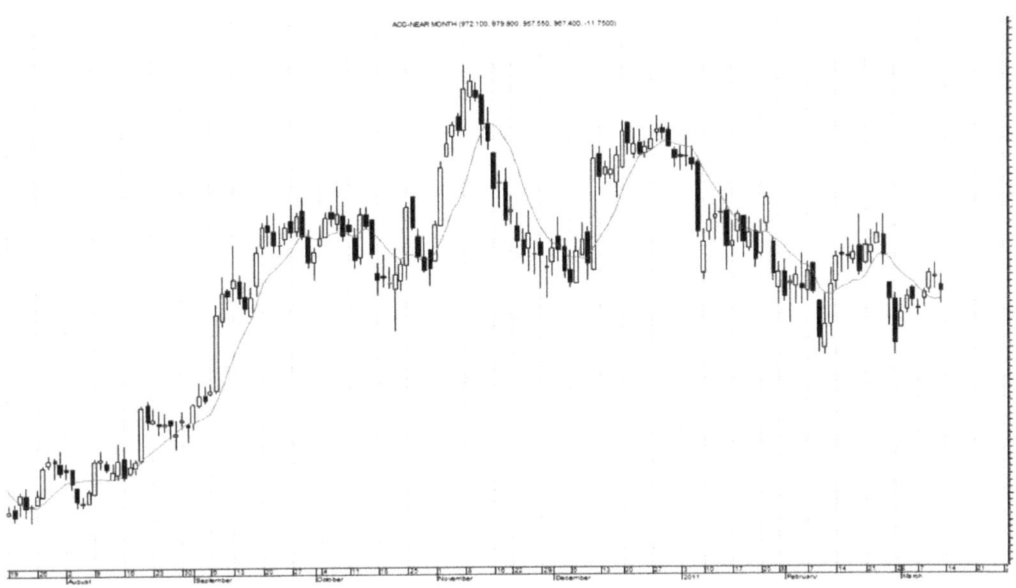

The chart above is a plot that contains the data sequence in the table. The simple moving average begins on day 9 and continues. This simple illustration highlights the fact that **all moving averages are lagging indicators** and will always be "behind" the price. The price

of EK is trending down, but the simple moving average, which is based on the previous 9 days of data, remains above the price. If the price were rising, the SMA would most likely be below. Because moving averages are lagging indicators, they fit in the category of **trend following indicators**. When prices are trending, moving averages work well. However, when prices are not trending, moving averages can give misleading signals.

EXPONENTIAL AVERAGE

The Averages constructed over a longer time span have higher utility in technical analysis, but a simple moving average constructed over a long-time span lags the price trend, an exponential moving average provides a short cut method of weighting. This method also provides more weightage to the recent data.

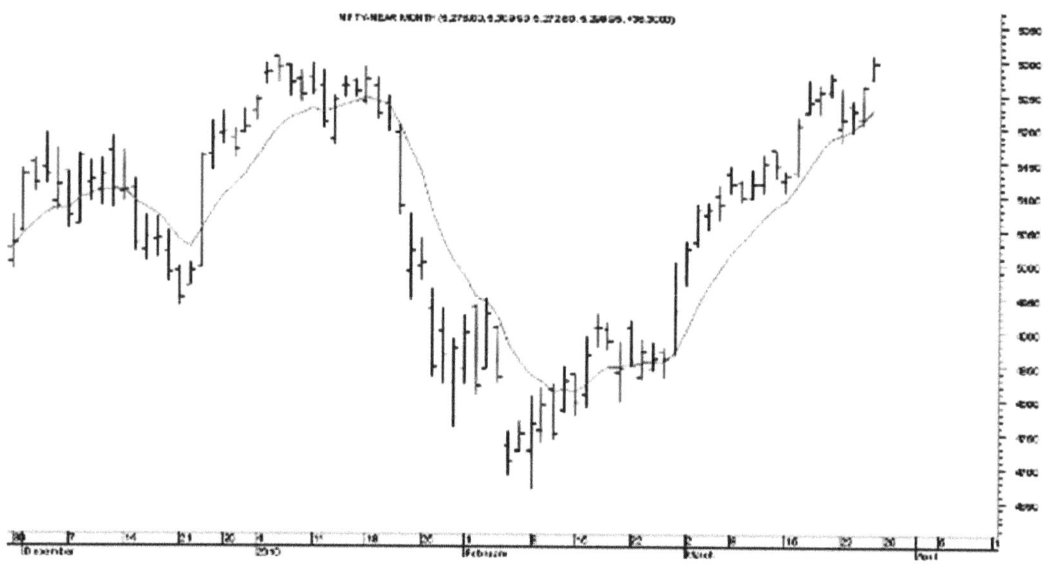

Exponential Moving Averages can be specified in two ways as percent based EMA or as a period based EMA. A percent based EMA has a percentage as its single parameter while a period based EMA has a parameter that represents the duration of the EMA.

Formula for an Exponential moving average

EMA (current) = ((Price (current)-EMA (previous)) *Multiplier) + EMA (previous)

Relative Strength Index

RSI means Relative Strength Index; it identifies overbought and oversold conditions in the market. It is also scaled from 0 to 100. Typically, readings below 30 indicate oversold, while readings over 70 indicate overbought.

Oversold: RSI when RSI dropped below 30, it correctly identified an oversold market. After the drop, the price quickly shot back up.

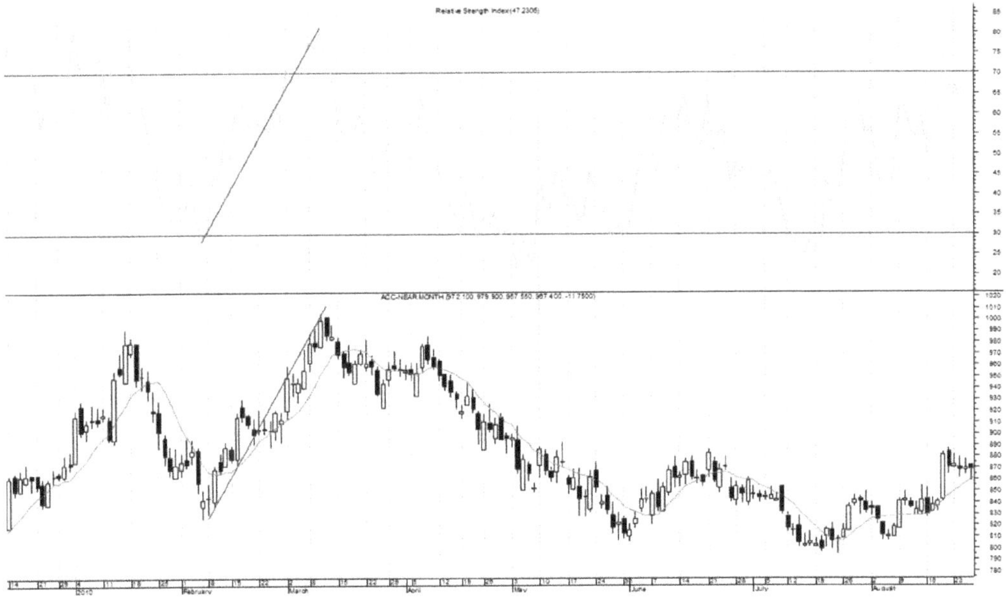

RSI is a very popular tool because it can also be used to confirm trend formations. A trend is forming, take a quick look at the RSI and look at whether it is above or below 50. If you are looking at a possible uptrend, then make sure the RSI is above 50. If you are looking at a possible downtrend, then make sure the RSI is below 50.

OVERBOUGHT

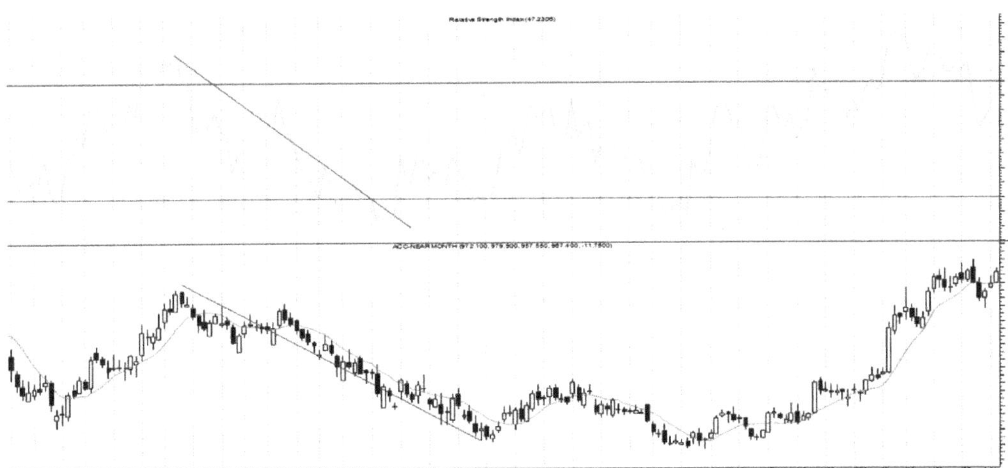

In the beginning of the chart above, we can see that a possible uptrend was forming. To avoid fake outs, we can wait for RSI to cross above 50 to confirm our trend. Sure enough, as RSI passes above 50, it is a good confirmation that an uptrend has actually formed

DIVERGENCE

Divergence is nothing but buy and sell signals can also be generated by looking for positive and negative divergences between the RSI and the underlying stock. For example, RSI moves upward or downward direction then market slightly moves in opposite direction.

RSI POSITIVE DIVERGENCE

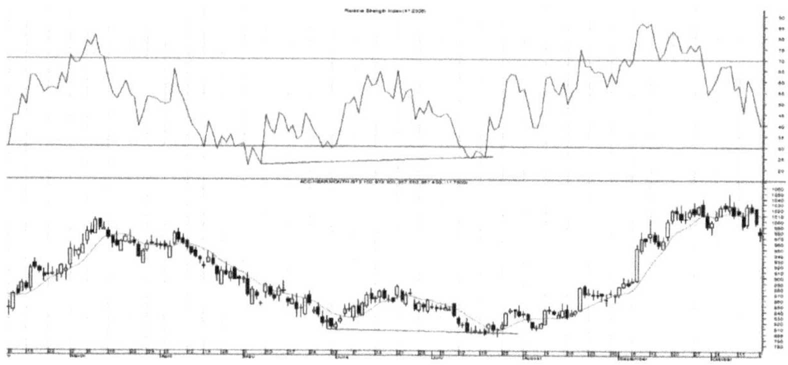

NEGATIVE DIVERGENCE

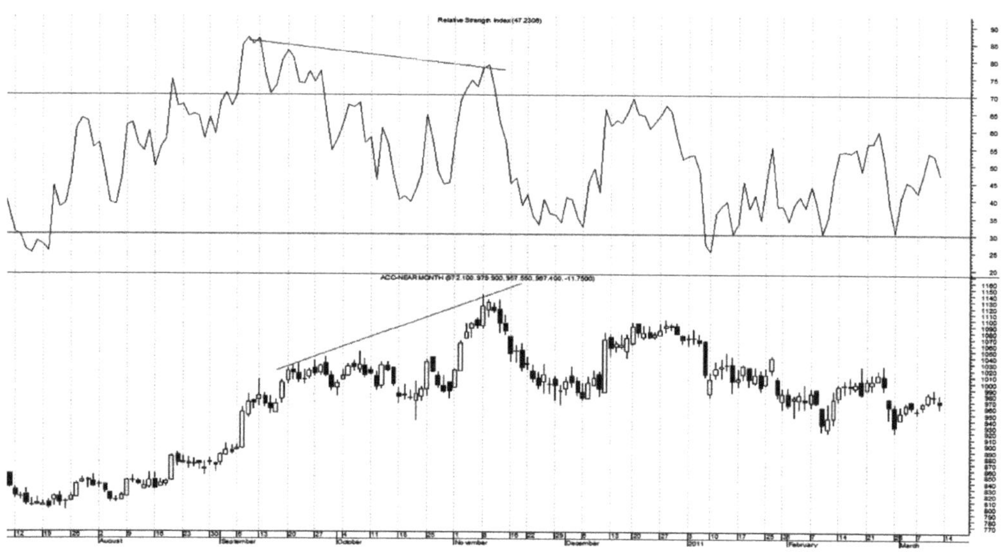

MACD

DEFINITION

Moving Average Convergence Divergence. Technical analysis term for the crossing of two exponentially smoothed moving averages.

MACD is an acronym for **M**oving **A**verage **C**onvergence **D**ivergence. This tool is used to identify moving averages that are indicating a new trend, whether it's bullish or bearish. It continuously converges and diverges away from the horizontal reference line. It is constructed by taking the difference of the ratio of short term and the long-term moving average. The points obtained are plotted against a horizontal reference line. The reference line represents the points where the two EMAs have identical values. From the movement of the MACD indicator it can be known, whether the shorter-term moving average is above or below the longer-term moving average.

With an MACD chart, you will usually see three numbers that are used for its settings.

- The first is the number of periods that is used to calculate the faster moving average.
- The second is the number of periods that are used in the slower moving average.
- And the third is the number of candlesticks that is used to calculate the moving average of the difference between the faster and slower moving averages.

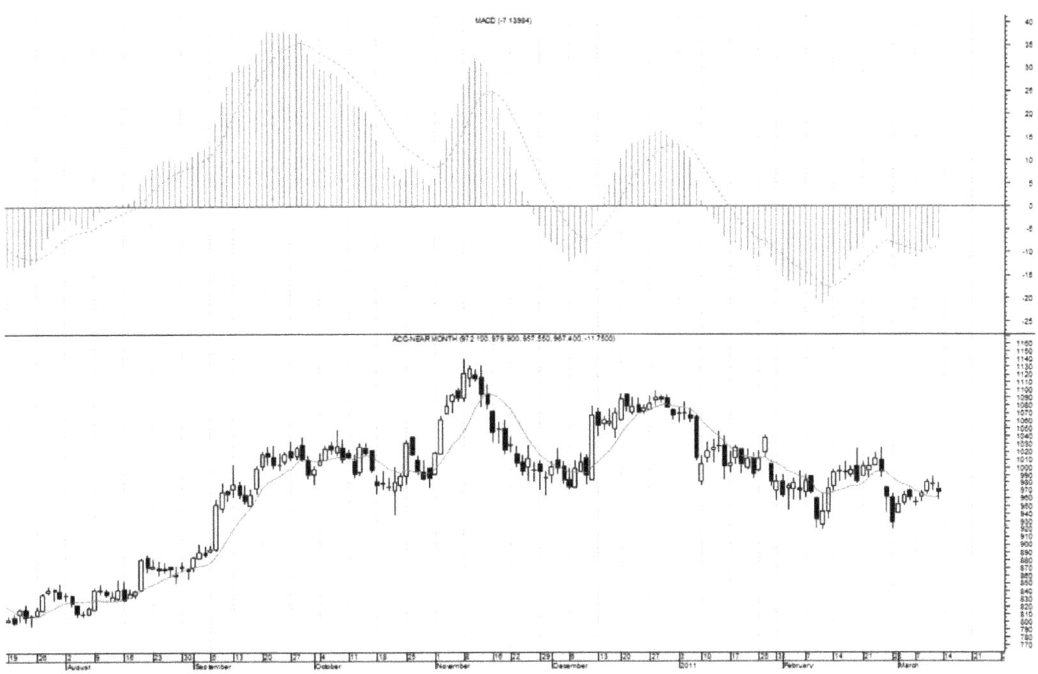

STOCHASTIC OSCILLATOR

Stochastic is a price velocity technique based on the theory that as prices increase, closing prices have a tendency to be ever nearer to the peaks reached during that period. Similarly, as prices tend to fall, closing prices tend to be closer and closer to the troughs reached during that period.

In technical analysis of securities trading, the stochastic oscillator is a momentum indicator that uses support and resistance levels Dr. George Lane promoted this indicator in the 1950s. The term stochastic refers to the location of a current price in relation to its price range over a period of time. This method attempts to predict price turning points by comparing the closing price of a security to its price range.

The indicator is usually calculated as:

$$\%K = 100\frac{\text{Closing price} - \text{price low}}{\text{Price high} - \text{Price low}}$$

Method of Stochastic: Stochastic tells us when the market is overbought or oversold. Stochastic are scaled from 0 to 100. When the stochastic lines are above 80 (the black dotted line in the chart below), then it means the market is overbought. When the stochastic lines are below 20 (the black dotted line), then it means that the market is oversold. We buy when the market is oversold, and we sell when the market is overbought.

Looking at the chart above, we can see that the stochastic has been showing overbought conditions for quite some time.

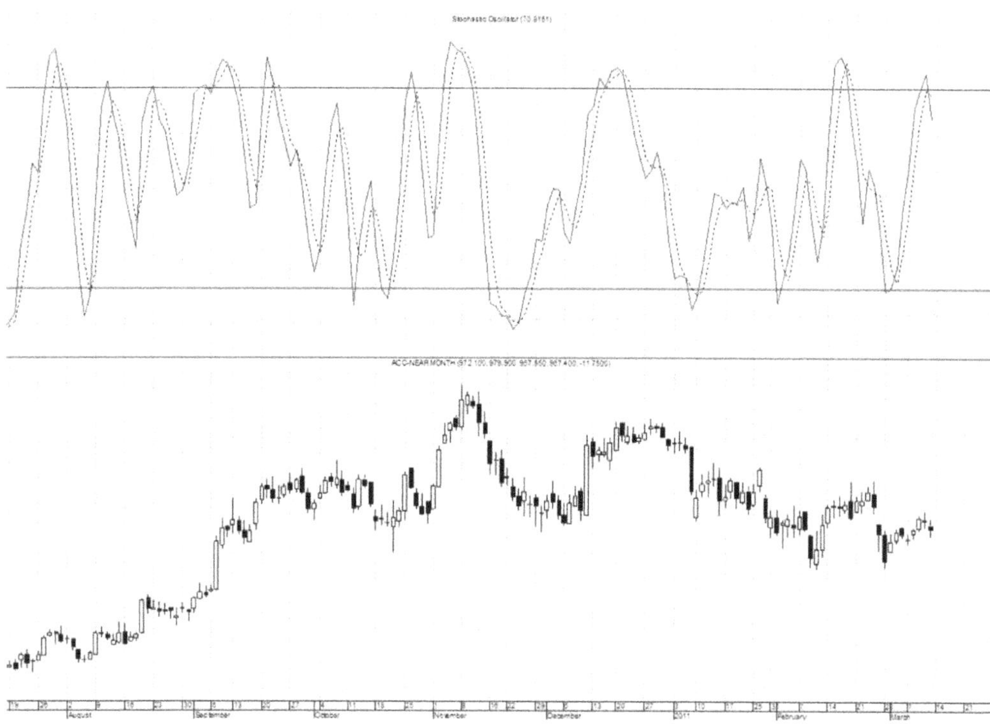

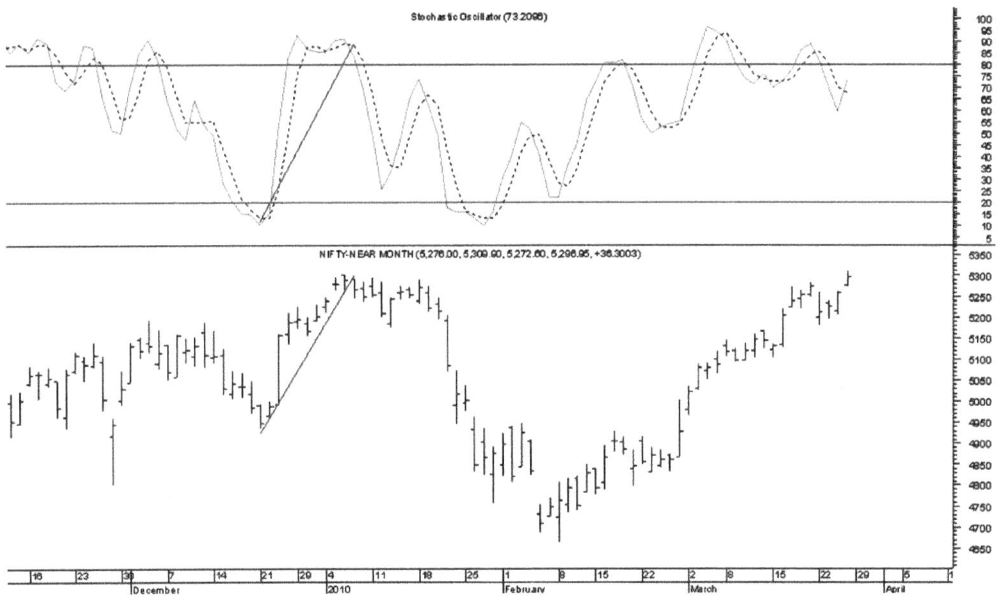

STOCHASTIC POSITIVE DIVERGENCE

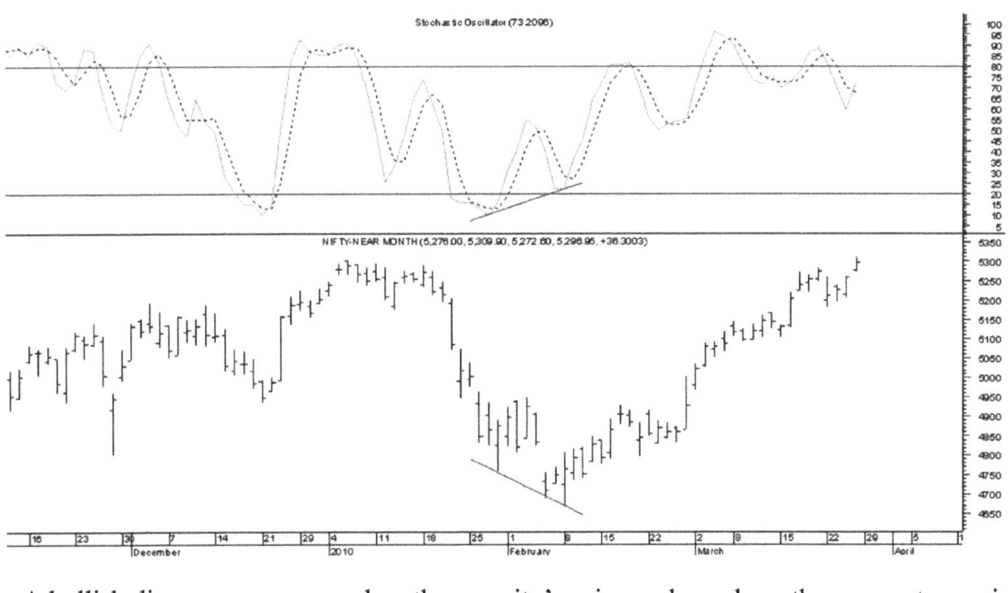

A bullish divergence occurs when the security's price makes a low, then corrects moving higher, and subsequently, reaches a lower low. At the same time, corresponding bottoms of the %K line makes a low followed by a higher bottom.

STOCHASTIC NEGATIVE DIVERGENCE

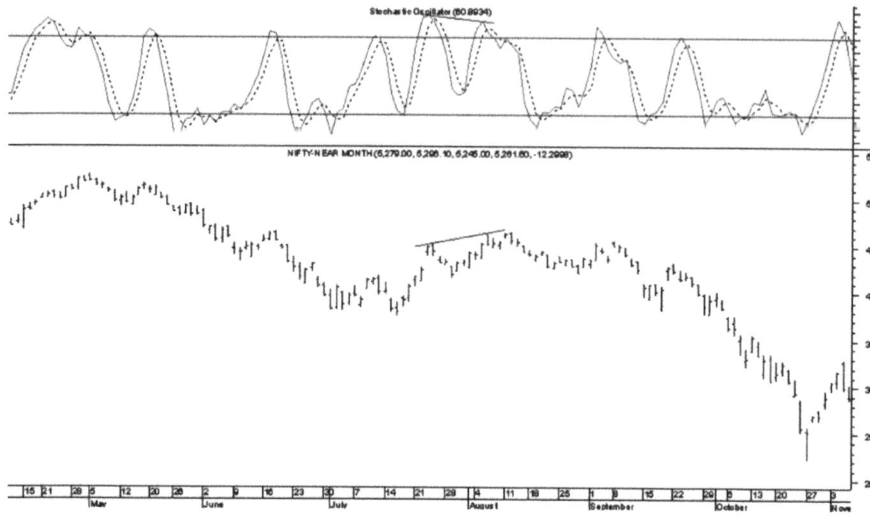

A bearish divergence occurs when the security's price makes a high then corrects moving lower and subsequently reaches a higher high. At the same time, corresponding dealers of the %K line make a high followed by a lower high.

ELLIOTT WAVE THEORY

Definition

A technical analysis technique published by Ralph Elliott, which claims that stock markets follow a pattern of five waves up and three waves down. Elliott explained that the upward and downward swings of the mass psychology always showed up in the same repetitive patterns, which were then divided into patterns he called "waves". He needed to claim this observation and so he came up with a super original name: The Elliott Wave Theory.

The 5 – 3 Wave Patterns

Mr. Elliott showed that a trending market moves in what he calls a 5-3 wave pattern. The first 5-wave pattern is called **impulse waves** and the last 3-wave pattern is called **corrective waves.**

Here is a short description of what happens during each wave. I am going to use stocks for my example since stocks is what Mr. Elliott used but it really doesn't matter what it is. It can easily be currencies, bonds, gold, oil, or Tickle Me Elmo dolls. The important thing is the Elliott Wave Theory can also be applied to the foreign exchange market.

Wave1

The stock makes its initial move upwards. This is usually caused by a relatively small number of people that all of the sudden feel that the price of the stock is cheap so it's a perfect time to buy. This causes the price to rise.

Wave2

At this point enough people who were in the original wave consider the stock overvalued and take profits. This causes the stock to go down. However, the stock will not make it to its previous lows before the stock is considered a bargain again.

Wave3

This is usually the longest and strongest wave. The stock has caught the attention of the mass public. More people find out about the stock and want to buy it. This causes the stock's price to go higher and higher. This wave usually exceeds the high created at the end of wave 1.

Wave4

People take profits because the stock is considered expensive again. This wave tends to be weak because there are usually more people that are still bullish on the stock and are waiting to "buy on the dips".

Wave5

This is the point that most people get on the stock, and is most driven by hysteria. You usually start seeing the CEO of the company on the front page of major magazines as the Person of the Year. People start coming up with ridiculous reasons to buy the stock and try to choke you when you disagree with them. This is when the stock becomes the most overpriced. Contrarians start shorting the stock which starts the ABC pattern.

MULTIPLE CHOICE QUESTIONS

1. Technical analysis can help investors anticipate what is "likely" to happen to over time.
   a. prices b. volumes
   c. economy d. fair value of stock
2. The study of technical analysis is based on which of the following elements:
   a. price b. volume
   c. open interest (in case of derivatives) d. all of the above
3. A technician will refer to periods of accumulation as evidence of an upcoming
   a. rise in prices b. fall in prices
   c. range-bound prices d. none of the above
4. Which of the following statements is true about price?
   a. Price movements succeed fundamental developments
   b. Price movements are totally random
   c. Price discounts everything
   d. Price never moves in trend
5. Movements are typically referred to as bull and bear markets.
   a. Secondary b. Daily
   c. Major d. Primary

6. Which of the following is not true about chart?
   a. it plots the price movements of a stock over specific time frames
   b. x-axis represents price and y-axis represents time
   c. it gives pictorial representation of any stock's trading history
   d. it can give a complete picture of a stock's price history over a period of an hour, day, week, month or many years.
7. Which of the following best reveal psychology of the market at a certain point in time?
   a. Line Chart b. Candlestick chart
   c. Bar Chart d. None of the above
8. A higher open on next trading day of hammer indicates that:
   a. bears are intact
   b. bulls have taken control
   c. there is no possibility of trend reversal
   d. none of the above
9. Which of the following candlestick pattern look like star falling from sky with a tail trailing it?
   a. morning star b. shooting star
   c. dark cloud cover d. none of the above
10. Which of the following is not a feature of bearish kicking pattern?
    a. it is a three-candle pattern
    b. it is a top reversal signal
    c. the body of first candle is black and second candle is white in colour
    d. there is a gap between the first day and the second day candle
11. What does a decline below support level indicate?
    a. there is lack of sellers
    b. buyers are pushing down the price
    c. there is lack of buyers and sellers are willing to sell even at lower prices
    d. none of the above
12. Bulls bid the price by increasing demand, bears take it by increasing supply
    a. down, up b. up, down
    c. up, up d. down, down
13. In Head & Shoulders pattern, which level is achieved by the second rally?
    a. Highest point b. Lowest point
    c. Either highest or lowest point d. Neither highest nor lowest point

14. In top reversal head and shoulders pattern, the decline from peak of should break the neckline.
    a. left shoulder
    b. right shoulder
    c. head
    d. neckline
15. In an inverted head and shoulders pattern, which of the following represent highest potential for trend reversal?
    a. upward sloping neckline
    b. downward sloping neckline
    c. horizontal neckline
    d. vertical neckline
16. A break down the support line shows that the have won out over the
    a. bulls; bears
    b. bears; bulls
17. In an uptrend, pattern is identified when the price of an asset creates three peaks, and all the three peaks are of nearly the same level, at the same price level.
    a. Double Bottom
    b. Double Top
    c. Triple Bottom
    d. Triple Top
18. Double top is the name given to a pair of peaks which is formed when price is unable to reach a
    a. New high
    b. New Low
    c. Any of the above
    d. None of the above
19. Which gaps are also known as measuring gaps?
    a. Common gaps
    b. Breakaway gaps
    c. Runaway gaps
    d. Exhaustion gaps
20. The Rounded Top formation consists of a gradual change in trend from:
    a. Down to up
    b. Up to Down
    c. Up to Up
    d. Down to Down
21. Which of the following functions are served by technical indicators?
    a. to alert
    b. to confirm
    c. to predict
    d. all of the above
22. Ideally how many indicators should be used at a time to make the analysis sound and effective?
    a. more than 20
    b. 5 or less than 5
    c. 50
    d. More than 70
23. A simple moving average is formed by computing the price of a security over a specified number of periods.
    a. Mode
    b. Median
    c. Mean
    d. Variance

24. For a percentage-based EMA, "Multiplier" is equal to the specified percentage.
    a. RSI's
    b. MFI's
    c. EMA's
    d. DMI's

25. Which of the following is not a momentum oscillator?
    a. RSI
    b. Stochastic
    c. Rate of change
    d. Moving average crossovers

26. ------------- is a very important indicator as it takes into account the aspects of both momentum and trend in one indicator.
    a. MACD
    b. Moving Average Crossovers
    c. William %R
    d. EMA

27. When MACD is above zero, it means the day moving average is higher than day moving average.
    a. 32, 26
    b. 26, 32
    c. 12, 26
    d. 26, 12

28. RSI is an indicator.
    a. leading
    b. lagging
    c. supplementary
    d. complementary

29. Compares a day's closing price to a recent range of prices to determine if a market is overbought or oversold.
    a. Percentage R
    b. RSI
    c. Bollinger Bands
    d. MACD

30. Which of the following indicator should not be used in trending highly trending markets?
    a. RSI
    b. Point and Figure
    c. MACD
    d. Moving average crossovers

31. Because of and the that are possible, day trading is preferred by traders?
    a. Financial leverage and high returns
    b. Out of pocket expenses and overtrading
    c. Overtrading and high returns
    d. No risk and high returns

32. Day traders must have proper knowledge of:
    a. technical analysis
    b. SWOT analysis
    c. Both a) and b) above
    d. None of the above

33. Which of the following day trading style focus on taking profits on small price changes, generally immediately after one enters a trade becomes profitable.
    a. scalping
    b. fading
    c. daily pivots
    d. momentum

34. Day trading and momentum trading can be categorized into:
    a. Over trading
    b. Under trading
    c. Short term trading
    d. Long term trading
35. Which of the following systems give exit signal is issued when EMA and MACD diverge?
    a. Fading system
    b. impulse system of momentum trading
    c. RSI
    d. Centerline crossover
36. Dow Theory is named after Charles H Dow who is considered as the father of Technical Analysis.
    a. True
    b. False
37. Charles Dow never wrote a book nor published his complete theory on the markets.
    a. True
    b. False
38. Samuel A. Nelson is the first person to use the term Dow Theory.
    a. True
    b. False
39. The Dow Theory is made up of Principles.
    a. Four
    b. Six
    c. Eight
    d. Five
40. Which of the following statement is true
    a. Stock prices discount all information that is known about stock.
    b. Stock market discounts all information related to interest rate movement, macroeconomic data, RBI decision and future earnings announcement by the company.
    c. Stock price represents sum total of hopes, fear and expectation of all participants.
    d. All the above
41. is the main trend and trader should trade in directionof this trend.
    a. Minor Trend
    b. Secondary Trend
    c. Primary Trend
    d. Corrective Trend
42. As long as each successive top is higher than previous top and each successive bottom is higher than previous bottom trend is considered down.
    a. Tue
    b. False
43. As long as each successive top is lower than previous top and each successive bottom is lower than previous bottom trend is considered down.
    a. True
    b. False
44. Secondary Trend is found within
    a. Corrective Trend
    b. Minor Trend
    c. Primary Trend
    d. Tertiary Trend

45. The is corrective move within secondary trend.
    a. Primary Trend
    b. Main Trend
    c. Secondary Trend
    d. Minor Trend
46. Participation phase is the longest phase of the primary trend during which largest price movement takes place.
    a. True
    b. False
47. Under Dow Theory, reversal from bull market to bear market or vice versa is not signaled until and unless both indexes i.e. Industrial Index and Transportation Index. Confirm the same.
    a. True
    b. False
48. Dow Theory says trend should not be confirmed by volume.
    a. True
    b. False
49. Dow Theory has no significance in today's world as it's more than 100-year-old.
    a. True
    b. False
50. Which of the following statement is true
    a. One should never assume reversal of the trend until and unless clear reversal signal is there.
    b. If primary trend is down then volume should increase with the market decline.
    c. Both A and B
    d. Only
51. Which of the following is important for an investor, before entering into a trade?
    a. Adjust the trade size
    b. Tighten the stop loss
    c. Both a) and b) above
    d. Use maximum exposure from broker
52. Small ups and downs create temporary stress and can reduce swing traders to
    a. Day traders
    b. investors
    c. gamblers
    d. arbitrageurs
53. Efficient risk management system involves:
    a. putting stop loss
    b. controlling position size
    c. controlling losses
    d. all of the above
54. Which of the following should an investor follow?
    a. Long term Trader
    b. Short term Trader
    c. Find out What best suits him
    d. Follow the Trend

55. Trends never turn on a dime because:
    a. Reversals build slowly
    b. The first sharp dip always finds buyers and the first sharp rise always finds sellers
    c. Both a) and b) above
    d. The first sharp dip always finds more sellers and the first sharp rise always finds more buyers

SHORT ANSWER QUESTIONS

1. What is technical analysis?
2. What are the objectives of technical analysis?
3. What are the assumptions of technical analysis?
4. Explain the importance of technical analysis?
5. Explain the Weaknesses of Technical Analysis
6. How control the risk through technical analysis?
7. Define Charting.
8. What is mean by Trend?
9. What are the ideas of Dow Theory?
10. Define Line charts
11. Define Bar charts
12. Define Candlestick Charts
13. What are the types of chart patterns?
14. What are the types of triangles?
15. What is mean by Symmetrical Triangle?
16. Define down trend.
17. Define Double Bottom
18. Define Head and Shoulders
19. Define Reverse Head and Shoulders
20. What are the types of trends?
21. Define Trend Analysis.
22. Define Technical Indicators
23. Define Indicators and Oscillators:
24. Define Moving Averages:
25. Define Simple Moving Average
26. Define Moving Average Convergence Divergence.
27. Define Stochastic Oscillator

28. Define Elliott wave theory
29. Define Stochastic Negative Divergence
30. Explain The 5 – 3 Wave Patterns

ESSAY TYPE QUESTIONS

1. Explain in detail the Dow Theory and how is it used to determine the direction of stock market?
2. How are odd lot and short sales index used to determine the direction of the market?
3. Chart patterns are helpful in predicting the stock price movement'. Comment.
4. Discuss the relationship between fundamental analysis and efficient market hypotheses.
5. Technical analysis is based on Dow Jones Theory. Elucidate?
6. What are charts? How are they interpreted in technical analysis?
7. How is a fundamental analysis useful to a prospective investor?
8. What is the meaning of company analysis? What financial statements in your opinion are helpful in understanding the company's prospects?
9. Is intrinsic value of a share important? How would you calculate it?
10. The three important elements of investments are risk return and timing. Elaborate.

CASE STUDIES

CASE STUDY 1

You are the top technical analyst in your firm, and your boss has turned to you for an answer to a difficult question. He wants to know which single indicator you think is the best and why you think so. What is your answer?

MCQs Answers

1	2	3	4	5	6	7	8	9	10	11	12	13	14	15	16	17	18	19	20	21	22	23	24	25
a	d	a	c	d	b	b	b	b	c	c	b	c	b	a	b	d	a	a	b	d	b	c	b	d
26	27	28	29	30	31	32	33	34	35	36	37	38	39	40	41	42	43	44	45	46	47	48	49	50
a	c	a	a	c	a	a	a	c	b	a	a	a	b	d	c	b	a	c	d	a	a	b	b	c
51	52	53	54	55																				
c	a	d	c	c																				

CHAPTER 10

Efficient Market Theory

The theory that stock price changes have the same distribution and are independent of each other, so the past movement or trend of a stock price or market cannot be used to predict its future movement.

The random walk hypothesis is a financial theory stating that stock market prices evolve according to a random walk and thus cannot be predicted. It is consistent with the efficient. Generally, there are two competing approaches to predicting the movements of stocks: fundamental and technical analysis. In the sections below, we'll be taking a closer look at these competing theories, and how the random walk hypothesis aligns with each.

FUNDAMENTAL THEORISTS

Fundamental analysts believe the price of a stock is a function of its intrinsic value, which depends heavily on the future earnings potential for a company. By carefully studying fundamental factors such as industry trends, economic news, and the company's earnings per share outlook, fundamental analyst can determine if the stock's price is above or below its intrinsic value. Comparing a stock's price to its intrinsic value allows the fundamental analyst to predict the potential future direction of the stock's price.

TECHNICAL THEORISTS

Market analysts that practice technical techniques believe that historical movements of a stock's price can be used to predict future price direction. Using methods such as charting, the technical analyst will examine the sequence of upward and downward movements for a stock. These patterns of movements allow the technical theorist to chart what they believe will be future movements for the stocks they are examining.

EFFICIENT MARKET THEORISTS

The next theory we're going to talk about is the efficient market hypothesis (EMH). Subscribers to this theory believe the price of a stock reflects all publicly known information about a company. In fact, individuals subscribing to what is termed the "strong" EMH believe that stock prices also reflect what insiders know too.

Since public and private information concerning a company is instantly reflected in the market price of a stock, it's impossible for an investor to achieve "excess" returns. The principles of the random walk hypothesis are consistent with those of the efficient market hypothesis.

RANDOM WALK

Finally, the random walk hypothesis states that prices of stocks cannot be predicted. The stock market is "informational efficient." The people buying and selling stocks consist of a large number of rational investors with access to this information. While long term prices will reflect performance of the company over time, short term movements in prices can best be described as a random walk.

A Random Walk Down Wall Street

While the random walk hypothesis can trace its roots to 19th century mathematicians, today's theory can be attributed to Eugene F. Fame's doctoral dissertation, "The Behaviour of Stock-Market Prices," published in the Journal of Business in January, 1965 along with the non-technical publication "Random Walks in Stock Market Prices." In 1973, Burton G. Milkier of Princeton University followed up with the best-seller book "A Random Walk down Wall Street."

Since the random walk theory is based on an efficient market, historical patterns cannot be used to predict future movements in any kind of meaningful way. At any one point in time, the movement of a stock is random.

The random walk hypothesis has been proven through a number of empirical studies. By examining real data, researchers such as Fame and Milkier found there was no correlation between successive price changes. In other words, the next movement of a stock is completely independent of its prior movements. In fact, Milkier would go on to state the movement of the stock market, as well as individual stocks, is just as random as flipping a coin.

Random Walk is an economic theory that market price movements move randomly. The theory holds that price history is not a reliable indicator of future price direction. This assumes an efficient market. The theory also assumes that new information comes to the market randomly. Together, the two assumptions imply that market prices move randomly as new information is incorporated into market prices. The theory implies that the best predictor of future prices is the current price, and that past prices are not a reliable indicator of future prices. If Random Walk Theory is true Technical Analysis of the financial markets is meaningless.

PRACTICAL IMPLICATIONS

The random walk hypothesis has some practical implications to investors. For example, since the short-term movement of a stock is random, there is no sense in worrying about timing the market. A buy and hold strategy will be just as effective as any attempt to time the purchase and sale of securities.

When investors buy stocks, they usually do so because they believe the stock is worth more than they are paying. In the same way, investors sell stocks when they believe the stock is worth less than the selling price. If the efficient market theory and random walk hypothesis are true, then an investor's ability to outperform the stock market is more luck than analytical skill.

TESTING THE HYPOTHESIS

Random walk hypothesis test by increasing or decreasing the value of a fictitious stock based on the odd/even value of the decimals of pi. The chart resembles a stock chart.

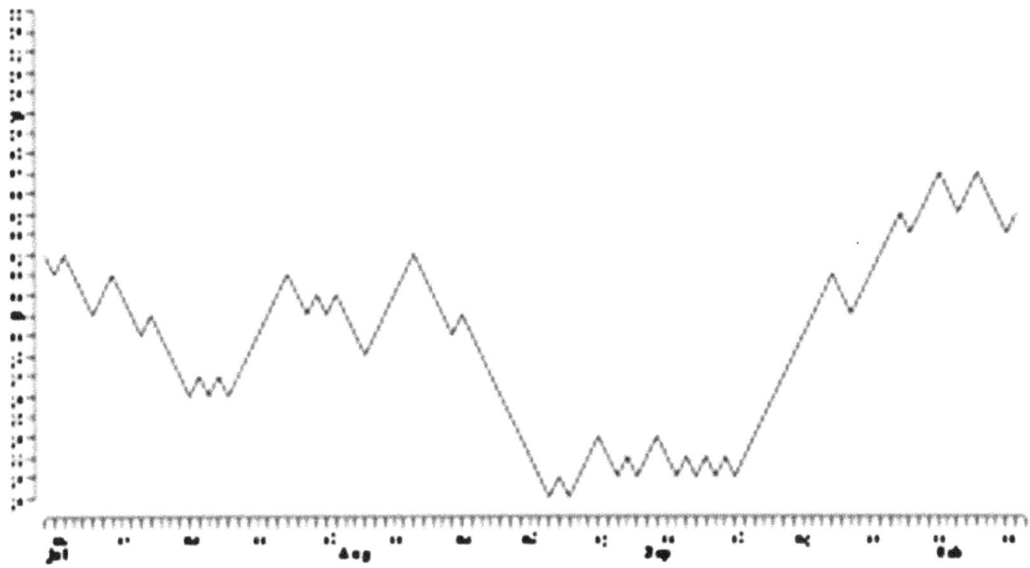

Burton G. Milkier, an economics professor at Princeton University and writer of *A Random Walk down Wall Street*, performed a test where his students were given a hypothetical stock that was initially worth fifty dollars. The closing stock price for each day was determined by a coin flip. If the result was heads, the price would close a half point higher, but if the result was tails, it would close a half point lower. Thus, each time, the price had a fifty-fifty chance of closing higher or lower than the previous day. Cycles or trends were determined from the tests. Milkier then took the results in a chart and graph form to a chartist, a person who "seeks to predict future movements by seeking to interpret past patterns on the assumption that 'history tends to repeat itself'".[5] The chartist told Milkier that they needed to immediately buy the stock. Since the coin flips were random, the fictitious stock had no overall trend. Milkier argued that this indicates that the market and stocks could be just as random as flipping a coin.

The random walk hypothesis was also applied to NBA basketball. Psychologists made a detailed study of every shot the Philadelphia made over one and a half seasons of basketball. The psychologists found no positive correlation between the previous shots and the outcomes of the shots afterwards. Economists and believers in the random walk hypothesis apply this to the stock market. The actual lack of correlation of past and present can be easily seen. If a stock goes up one day, no stock market participant can accurately predict that it will rise again the next. Just as a basketball player with the "hot hand" can miss the next shot, the stock that seems to be on the rise can fall at any time, making it completely random.

A NON-RANDOM WALK HYPOTHESIS

There are other economists, professors, and investors who believe that the market is predictable to some degree. These people believe that prices may move in trends and that the study of past prices can be used to forecast future price direction· There have been some economic studies that support this view, and a book has been written by two professors of economics that tries to prove the random walk hypothesis wrong.

Martin Weber, a leading researcher in behavioural finance, has performed many tests and studies on finding trends in the stock market. In one of his key studies, he observed the stock market for ten years. Throughout that period, he looked at the market prices for noticeable trends and found that stocks with high price increases in the first five years tended to become under-performers in the following five years. Weber and other believers in the non-random walk hypothesis cite this as a key contributor and contradictor to the random walk hypothesis.

Another test that Weber ran that contradicts the random walk hypothesis, was finding stocks that have had an upward revision for earnings outperform other stocks in the following six months. With this knowledge, investors can have an edge in predicting what stocks to pull out of the market and which stocks — the stocks with the upward revision — to leave in. Martin Weber's studies detract from the random walk hypothesis, because according to Weber, there are trends and other tips to predicting the stock market.

Professors Andrew W. Lo and Archie Craig Mack inlay, professors of Finance at the MIT Sloan School of Management and the University of Pennsylvania, respectively, have also presented evidence that they believe shows the random walk hypothesis to be wrong. Their book *A Non-Random Walk down Wall Street*, presents a number of tests and studies that reportedly support the view that there are trends in the stock market and that the stock market is somewhat predictable.

One element of their evidence is the simple volatility-based specification test, which has a null hypothesis that states:

$$X_t = \mu + X_{t-1} + \varepsilon_t$$

Where

X_t Is the log of the price of the asset at time? t

μ Is a drift constant?

ε_t Is a random disturbance term where $E[\varepsilon_t] = 0$ and $E[\varepsilon_t \varepsilon_\tau] = 0$ for $\tau \neq t$.

To refute the hypothesis, they compare the variance of $(X_t - X_{t+\tau})$ for different τ and compare the results to what would be expected for uncorrelated ϵ_t. Lo and Mack inlay have authored a paper, the Adaptive Market Hypothesis, which puts forth another way of looking at the predictability of price changes.

The central idea behind the random walk theory is that the randomness of stock prices renders attempts to find price patterns or take advantage of new information futile. In particular, the theory claims that day-to-day stock prices are independent of each other, meaning that momentum does not generally exist and calculations of past earnings growth does not predict future growth. Milkier states that people often believe events are correlated if the events come in "clusters and streaks," even though streaks occur in random data such as coin tosses.

The random walk theory also states that all methods of predicting stock prices are futile in the long run. Milkier calls the notion of intrinsic value undependable because it relies on subjective estimates of future earnings using factors like expected growth rates, expected dividend pay-outs, estimated risk, and interest rates.

The random walk theory also considers technical analysis undependable because, according to Milkier, chartists buy only after price trends are established and sell only after price trends are broken; essentially, the chartists buy or sell too late and miss the boat. According to the theory, this happens because stock prices already reflect the information by the time the analyst moves on the stock. Milkier also notes that the widespread use of technical analysis reduces the advantages of the approach.

Further, Milkier finds fundamental analysis flawed because analysts often collect bad or useless information and then poorly or incorrectly interpret that information when predicting stock values. Factors outside of a company or its industry may affect a stock price, rendering further the fundamental analysis irrelevant.

There are two forms of the random walk theory. In both forms, the rapid incorporation of information is disadvantageous for investors and analysts. The semi-strong form states that public information will not help an investor or analyst select undervalued securities because the market has already incorporated the information into the stock price. The strong form states that no information, public or private, will benefit an investor or analyst because even inside information is reflected in the current stock price.

Milkier acknowledges some statistical anomalies pointing to some exceptions to the random walk theory:

1. Prices of small, less liquid stocks seem to have some serial price correlation in the short-term because they do not incorporate information into their prices as quickly.
2. Contrarian strategies tend to outperform other strategies because reversals are often based on economic facts rather than investor psychology.
3. There are seasonal trends in the stock market, especially at the beginning of the year and the end of the week
4. Stocks with low P/E ratios tend to outperform those with high P/E is, although the tendency is volatile over time.
5. High-dividend stocks tend to provide higher returns over time because during down markets the high dividend yields often create demand for these stocks and thus increases the price.

The efficient market hypothesis is a central idea of a modern finance that has profound implications. An understanding of the efficient market hypothesis will help to ask the right questions and save from a lot of confusion that dominates popular thinking in finance.

The concept of market efficiency was proposed by Eugene Fame in 1965, when his article “Random Walks in Stock Prices” was published in Financial Analyst Journal.

Market efficiency means that the price which investor is paying for financial asset (stock, bond, other security) fully reflects fair or true information about the intrinsic value of this specific asset or fairly describe the value of the company — the issuer of this security. *The key term in the concept of the market efficiency is the information available for investors trading in the market. It is stated that the market price of stock reflects:*

1. **AH known information, including:**
   - Past information, e.g., last year's or last quarter's, month's earnings;
   - Current information as well as events, that have been announced but are still forthcoming, e.g. shareholders' meeting.
2. **Information that can reasonably be inferred,** for example, if many investors believe that ECB will increase interest rate in the nearest future or the government deficit increases, prices will reflect this belief before the actual event occurs.

Capital market is efficient, if the prices of securities which are traded in the market, react to the changes of situation immediately, fully and credibly reflect all the important information about the security's future income and risk related with generating this income.

What is *the important information for the investor*? From economic point of view the important information is defined as such information which has direct influence to the investor's decisions seeking for his defined financial goals. Example, the essential events in the joint stock company, published in the newspaper, etc.

Market efficiency requires that the adjustment to new information occurs very quickly as the information becomes known. Obvious, that Internet has made the markets more efficient in the sense of how widely and quickly information is disseminated.

An efficient market is one in which the market price of a security is an unbiased estimate of its intrinsic value. Note that market efficiency does not imply that the market price equals intrinsic value at every point in time. All that it says is that the errors in the market prices are unbiased. This means that the price can deviate from the intrinsic value but the deviations are random and correlated with any observable variable. If the deviations of market price from intrinsic value are random, it is not possible to consistently identify over or under-valued securities.

Market efficiency is defined in relation to information that is reflected in security prices. In an efficient market, all the relevant information is reflected in the current stock price. Information cannot be used to obtain excess return: the information has already been taken into account and absorbed in the prices. In other words, all prices are correctly stated and there are no "bargains" in the stock market. James H. Lorie explained efficient security market as "Efficiency in this context means the ability of the capital markets to function so that prices of securities react rapidly to new information. Such efficiency will produce prices that are 'appropriate' in terms of current knowledge, and investors will be less likely to make unwise investments. A corollary is that investors will also be less likely to discover great bargains and thereby earn extraordinarily high rates of return.

The requirements for a securities market to be efficient market are;

- Prices must be efficient so that new inventions and better products will cause a firm's securities prices to rise and motivate investors to supply capital to the firm (i.e., buy its stock);
- Information must be discussed freely and quickly across the nations so all investors can react to new information;
- Transactions costs such as sales commissions on securities are ignored;
- Taxes are assumed to have no noticeable effect on investment policy;
- Every investor is allowed to borrow or lend at the same rate; and, finally,
- Investors must be rational and able to recognize efficient assets and that they will want to invest money where it is needed most (i.e., in the assets with relatively high returns).

FORMS OF EFFICIENT MARKET HYPOTHESIS

An investment theory states that it is impossible to "beat the market" because stock market efficiency causes existing share prices to always incorporate and reflect all relevant information. According to the EMH, this means that stocks always trade at their fair value on stock exchanges, and thus it is impossible for investors to either purchase undervalued stocks or sell stocks for inflated prices. Thus, the crux of the EMH is that it should be impossible to outperform the overall market through expert stock selection or market timing, and that the only way an investor can possibly obtain higher returns is by purchasing riskier investments. Although it is a cornerstone of modern financial theory, the EMH is highly controversial and often disputed. Believers argue it is pointless to search for undervalued stocks or to try to predict trends in the market through either fundamental or technical analysis.

While academics point to a large body of evidence in support of EMH, an equal amount of dissension also exists. For example, investors such as Warren Buffet have consistently beaten the market over long periods of time, which by definition is an impossibility according to the EMH. Detractors of the EMH also point to events such as the 1987 stock market crash (when the DJIA fell by over 20% in a single day) as evidence that stock prices can seriously deviate from their fair values.

In an efficient market, all data are fully and immediately reflected in a stock price. Price changes in an efficient market are equally likely to be positive or negative. The hypothesis applies most directly to large companies trading on the major securities exchanges. The forms of the efficient stock market are weak, semi-strong, and strong. In the weak form, no relationship exists between prior and future stock prices. The informational value of historical data is already included in current prices. Hence, studying previous stock prices is of no value. In the semi-strong version, stock prices adjust immediately to new data; thus, action after a known event results in randomness. All public information is reflected in a stock's value. Therefore, fundamental analysis is not usable in determining whether a stock is overvalued or undervalued. In the strong form, stock prices reflect all information-public and private (insider). A perfect market exists. No group has access to information that would enable it to earn superior risk-adjusted returns.

Assumptions

Beyond the normal utility maximizing agents, the efficient market hypothesis requires the agents have rational expectations; that on average the population is correct (even if no one person is) and whenever new relevant information appears, the agents update their expectations appropriately. Note that it is not required that the agents are rational (which is different from rational expectations; rational agents act coldly and achieve what they set out to do). EMH allows that when faced with new information, some investors may overreact and some may under react. All that is required by the EMH is that investors' reactions be random enough that the net effect on market prices cannot be reliably exploited to make an abnormal profit. Thus, anyone person can be wrong about the market--indeed, everyone can be--but the market as a whole is always right.

There are three common forms in which the efficient market hypothesis is commonly stated

- Weak form efficiency,
- Semi-strong form efficiency and
- Strong form efficiency,

Each of which have different implications for how markets work.

WEAK FORM OF EMH

Under the weak form of the market the current prices of stocks reflect all information which is steady contained in the past. This theory is just the opposite of the technical analysis because according to it the sequence of prices occurring historically do not have any value for predicting the future stock prices. The Technical Analysis rely completely on charts and past behavior of prices of stocks. In the weak form of efficient market, the past prices do not provide help in giving any information about the future prices. The short-term trader in this form if the market in a similar position as another investor who adopts the approach of "buy and hold" strategy. Some traders may be able to earn a positive rate of return but on average their performance in the market will not in any way be better than an ordinary native investor who follows the strategy of buying and holding securities.

- No excess returns can be earned by using investment strategies based on historical share prices or other financial data.
- Weak-form efficiency implies that Technical analysis techniques will not be able to consistently produce excess returns, though some forms of fundamental analysis may still provide excess returns.
- In a weak-form efficient market current share prices are the best, unbiased, estimate of the value of the security. Theoretical in nature, weak form efficiency advocates assert that fundamental analysis can be used to identify stocks that are undervalued and overvalued. Therefore, keen investors looking for profitable companies can earn profits by researching financial statements.

The weak form of market holds that present stock market prices reflect all known information with respect to past stock prices, trends, and volumes. This form of theory is just the opposite of the technical analysis because according to it, the sequence of prices occurring historically does not have any value for predicting the future stocks prices. The technical analysts rely completely on charts and past behavior of prices of stocks.

In the weak form of the market no investor can use any information of the past to earn a return of portfolio which is in excess of the portfolio's risk. This means that the investor who develops the strategy based on past prices and chooses his portfolio on that basis cannot continuously outperform another investor who 'buys and holds' his investments over a long-term period.

The question which has rapidly been studied is whether "security prices follow a random walk." A random walk when it is applied to security prices means that all price changes which have occurred today are completely independent of the prices prior to this day in all respects. The weak form of the efficient market theory takes into consideration only the average change of today's prices and states that they are independent of all prior prices. The evidence supporting the random walk behavior also supports the efficient market hypothesis and states that the large price changes are followed by larger price changes, but they do not change in any direction which can be predicated. This observation in a way violates the random walk behavior that it does not violate the weak form of the market efficiency. Researches have studied that the evidence which supports the efficient market behavior is based on the random walk behavior of security prices but there is evidence which contradicts the random walk hypothesis. This does not mean that it contradicts the efficient market hypothesis also.

Three types of tests have been commonly employed to empirically verify the weak-form efficient market hypothesis: (a) serial correlation tests; (b) runs tests; and (c) filter rules tests.

Serial Correlation Test: Serial Correlation is said to measure the association of a series of numbers which are separated by some constant time period. One way to test for randomness in stock price changes is to look at their serial correlations. Is the price change in one period correlated with the price change in some other period? If such auto-correlations are negligible, the price changes are considered to be serially independent. Numerous serial correlation studies, employing different stocks, different time-lags, and different time-periods, have been conducted to detect serial correlations. In general, these studies have failed to discover any significant serial correlations.

Moore measured correlation of the price change of one week with the price change of the next week with the price change of the next week. His research showed average serial correlation of -0.06 which indicated a very low tendency of security price to reverse dates. This means that a price rise did not show the tendency to follow the price fall or vice versa. Fame also tested the serial correlation of daily price changes in 1965. He studied the correlation for 30 firms which composed of the Dow Jones Industrial Averages for five years before 1962. His study showed an average correlation of -0.03. This correlation was also weak because it was not very far away from zero.

Run Test: Ran Test was also made by Fame to find out its price changes were likely to be followed by further price changes of the same sign. Run Test ignored the absolute values of numbers in the series and took into the research only the positive and negative signs. Given a series of stock price changes, each price (+) id it represents an increase or a minus (-) if it represents a decrease. A run occurs when there is not difference between the sign of two changes. When the sign of change differs, the run ends and a new run begin. To test a series of price changes for independence, the number of runs in that series is compared to see whether it is statistically different from the number of runs in a purely random series of the same size. Many studies have been carried out, employing the runs test of independence. They did not detect any significant relationship between the returns of security in one period and the returns in prior periods and made a conclusion that the security prices followed a random walk.

Filter Rules Test: The use of charts is essentially a technique for filtering out the important information from the unimportant. Alexander and Fame and Blame took the idea that price and volume data are supposed to tell the entire story we need to know to identify the important action in stock prices. They applied filter rules to see how well price changes pick up both trends and reverses – which chartists claim their charts do. If a stock moves up X per cent, buy it and hold it long; if it then reverses itself by the same percentage, sell it and take a short position in it. When the stock reverses itself again by X per cent cover the short position and buy the stock long. The size of the filter varied from 0.5 to 50 percent. The results showed that the larger filter did not work well. The smaller ones worked better, since they were more sensitive to market swings. However, when trading costs are included in the analysis, no filter worked well. In fact, substantial losses would have been incurred using these filter rules.

In essence the result of using the filter technique turn out to be that stock prices do not have momentum from which one can make returns in excess of those warranted by the level of risk assumed. In fact, because of trading costs, we would have been substantially better off buying a random set of stocks and holding them during the same trading period.

SIMULATION TEST

During 1959, Roberts and Osborne had conducted a study, Roberts used Dow Jones Industrial Average and compared a study. Roberts used Dow Jones Industrial Average and compared its level with a variable generated by a random walk mechanism. He concluded that the mechanism of the random walk showed patterns which were very similar to the movements of stock prices. He also showed that a series of cumulative random numbers closely resembled in actual stock price and that changes in the random principles series as expected do not exhibit pattern as it exhibits in the case of stock price changes. Robert's research is also called Simulation test.

According to Osborne's research, the stock prices moved similar to Brownian motion, which is a method of movement of particles in solution where movements of different magnitudes occur at any time independent of any previous movements. Brownian motion is treated as a kind of random walk. Osborne's research showed that the security prices move constantly with the Brownian Motion Model which showed that the price changes in one period were independent of the price changes in the previous period.

SEMI-STRONG FORM OF EMH

Under this form, the market reflects all information regarding historical prices as well as all information about the company which is known to the public. According to the theory any analyst will find it difficult to make a future forecast of stock prices because he will not be able to get superior and consistent information of any company continuously. The semi-strong market theory contends that as soon as the information because public the stock prices change and absorb the full information. Thus, the stock prices adjust with the information that is received. This information may not be correct but the analyst will still not be able to make superior judgments consistently because the correct adjustment of stock price will soon take place. Sometimes there will be over-adjustments in the market, while some other time there will be under-adjustments. This makes it difficult for the analyst to form any particular kind of strategy based on the quick adjustment to information received in the market. On the other hand, when the analyst has superior internal information then there is a chance of making profits if he can use the superior information which he has acquired, and applied quickly. Moreover, the profits will not be constant or continuous in nature because (a) changes and returns are independent because price change, are independent of each other, (b) that the successive price changes are identically distributed and the distributed will repeat themselves over time.

- Share prices adjust within an arbitrarily small but finite amount of time and in an unbiased fashion to publicly available new information, so that no excess returns can be earned by trading on that information.
- Semi-strong-form efficiency implies that Fundamental analysis techniques will not be able to reliably produce excess returns.
- To test for semi-strong-form efficiency, the adjustments to previously unknown news must be of a reasonable size and must be instantaneous. To test for this, consistent upward or downward adjustments after the initial change must be looked for. If there are any such adjustments it would suggest that investors had interpreted the information in a biased fashion and hence in an inefficient manner.

The semi strong form of the efficient market hypothesis centers on how rapidly and efficiently market prices adjust to new publicly available information. In this state, the market reflects even those forms of information which may be concerning the announcement of a firm's most recent earnings forecast and adjustments which will have taken place in the prices of security. The investor in the semi-strong form of the market will find it impossible to earn a return on the portfolio which is based on the publicly available information in excess of the return which may be said to be commensurate with the portfolio risk. Many empirical studies have been made on the semi-strong form of the efficient market hypothesis to study the reaction of security prices to various types of information around the announcement time of the information. Two studies commonly employed to test semi-strong form efficient market are event study and portfolio study.

Event Study examines the market reactions to and the excess market returns around a specific information event like acquisition announcement or stock split. The key steps involved in an event study are as follows:

- Identify the event to be studied and pinpoint the date on which the event was announced.
- Collect returns data around the announcement date. In this context two issues have to be resolved: What should be the period for calculating returns – weekly, daily, or some other interval? For how many periods should returns be calculated before and after the announcement date?
- Calculate the excess returns, by period, around the announcement date for each firm in the sample. The excess return is calculated by making adjustment for market performance and risk.
- Compute the average and the standard error of excess returns across all firms
- Assess whether the excess returns around the announcement date are different from zero. To determine whether the excess returns around the announcement date are different from zero, estimate the T statistic for each day.

The results of event studies are mixed. Most event studies support the semi-strong from efficient market hypothesis. Several event studies, however, have cast their shadow over the validity of the semi strong form efficient markets theory.

Portfolio study: In a portfolio study, a portfolio of stocks having the observable characteristic (low price earnings ratio or whatever) is created and tracked over time see whether it earns superior risk-adjusted returns. Steps involved in a portfolio study are as follows:

1. Define the variable (characteristic) on which firms will be classified. The proposed investment strategy spells out the relevant variable. The variable must be observable, but not necessarily numerical.
2. Classify firms into portfolios based upon the magnitude of the variable. Collect data on the variable for every firm in the defined universe at the beginning of the period and use that information for classifying firms into different portfolios.
3. Compute the returns for each portfolio on the returns for each firm in each portfolio for the testing period and calculate the return for each portfolio, assuming that the stocks included in the portfolio are equally weighted.
4. Calculate the excess returns for each portfolio. The calculation of excess returns earned by a portfolio calls for estimating the portfolio beta and determining the excess returns
5. Assess whether the average excess returns are different across the portfolios. Several statistical tests are available to test whether the average excess returns differ across these portfolios. Some of these tests are parametric and some nonparametric many portfolio studies suggest that it is not possible to earn superior risk- adjusted returns by trading on some observable characteristics. However, several portfolio studies have documented inefficiencies and anomalies.

MARKET REACTION TEST

The semi-strong efficient market hypothesis was empirically tested in 19 by Fame, Fischer, Jensen and Roll. They made the following study, "They considered the behavior of abnormal security returns at the announcement of stock spirits". In a stock market a stock split generally indicates increased dividends payouts. Stock splits announcement contain economic information. The research just before the split announcement. The average cumulative abnormal security return for thirty months up to the month of announcement was in excess of 30%. This showed that the return was for above the normal rate of return which was achieved by the method of buying and holding a portfolio for a long-term investment of similar risky securities. The behavior of the security prices in the market after the split announcement showed exactly the predictions of the efficient market hypothesis. After the public announcement the investor could achieve in abnormal returns on the basis of the information of the stock split. The average cumulative abnormal return which was going higher and increasing just before the announcement stopped increasing or decreasing in any significant manner in the following period after the split announcement was made.

STRONG-FORM OF EMH

According to the theory, it is not useful to any investor or an analyst to make any future forecast of prices because he can never make any returns which are superior to others consistently. Usually, any investor is fully aware of the new pieces of information in the market and se even if fully aware of the new pieces of information in the market and so even if the analyst has inside information he cannot continuously earn superior investment returns. The strongly efficient market hypothesis is not found to be fully acceptable.

It is evident from the efficient market model that the stock exchange has many imperfections and all information may not be immediately reflected in stock prices due to delays in communication and also transaction cost and delays in information dissemination to far of places. It is possible to have some profit above the normal profit by developing kind of trading strategy but the Random Walk Theory is not merely based on price or return levels but takes into account all changes of prices.

The strong-form efficient market hypothesis holds that all available information, public or private, is reflected in the stock prices. The strong form is concerned with whether or not certain individuals or groups of individuals possess inside information which can be used to make above average profits. If the strong form of the efficient capital market hypothesis holds, then and day is as good as any other day to buy any stock. This the most extreme form of the efficient market hypothesis. Most of the research work has indicated that the efficient market hypothesis in the strongest form does not hold good.

- Share prices reflect all information and no one can earn excess returns.
- If there are legal barriers to private information becoming public, as with insider trading laws, strong-form efficiency is impossible, except in the case where the laws are universally ignored.

- To test for strong form efficiency, a market needs to exist where investors cannot consistently earn excess returns over a long period of time. Even though many fund managers have consistently beaten the market, this does not necessarily invalidate strong-form efficiency. We need to find out how many managers in fact do beat the market, how many matches it, and how many underperform it. The results imply that performance relative to the market is more or less normally distributed, so that a certain percentage of managers can be expected to beat the market. Given that there are tens of thousands of fund managers worldwide, then having a few dozen star performers is perfectly consistent with statistical expectations.

ARGUMENTS CONCERNING THE VALIDITY OF THE HYPOTHESIS

Some observers dispute the notion that markets behave consistently with the efficient market hypothesis, especially in its stronger forms. Some economists, mathematicians and market practitioners cannot believe that man- made markets are strong-form efficient when there are prima facie reasons for inefficiency including the slow diffusion of information, the relatively great power of some market participants (e.g. financial institutions), and the existence of apparently sophisticated professional investors. The way that markets react to news surprises is perhaps the most visible flaw in the efficient market hypothesis. For example, news events such as surprise interest rate changes from central banks are not instantaneously taken account of in stock prices, but rather cause sustained movement of prices over periods from hours to months.

- Another observed discrepancy between the theory and real markets is that at market extremes what fundamentalists might consider irrational behavior is the norm: in the late stages of a bull market, the market is driven by buyers who take little notice of underlying value. Towards the end of a crash, markets go into free fall as participants extricate themselves from positions regardless of the unusually good value that their positions represent. This is indicated by the large differences in the valuation of stocks compared to fundamentals (such as forward price to earnings ratios) in bull markets compared to bear markets. A theorist might say that rational (and hence, presumably, powerful) participants should always immediately take advantage of the artificially high or artificially low prices caused by the irrational participants by taking opposing positions, but this is observably not, in general, enough to prevent bubbles and crashes developing. It may be inferred that many rational participants are aware of the irrationality of the market at extremes and are willing to allow irrational participants to drive the market as far as they will, and only take advantage of the prices when they have more than merely fundamental reasons that the market will return towards fair value.
- Behavioral finance explains that when entering positions market participants are not driven primarily by whether prices are cheap or expensive, but by whether they expect them to rise or fall. To ignore this can be hazardous: Alan Greenspan warned of "irrational exuberance" in the markets in 1996, but some traders who sold short new economy stocks that seemed to be greatly overpriced around this time had to accept serious losses as prices reached even more extraordinary levels. As John Maynard Keynes succinctly commented, "Markets can remain irrational longer than you can remain solvent."

MARKET EFFICIENCY AND ANOMALIES

Anomalies are situations that appear to violate the traditional view of market efficiency, suggesting that it may be possible for careful investors to earn abnormal returns. Some stock market anomalies are

Low Price-Earnings Ratio: Stock that are selling at price earnings ratios that are low relative to the market.

Low Price-Sales Ratio: Stocks that have price-to-sales ratios that are lower competed with other stocks in the same industry or with the overall market.

Low Price-to Book value Ratio: Stocks whose stock prices are less that their respective Book values

High Dividend Yield: Stocks that pay high dividends relative to their respective share prices

Small companies: Stock of companies whose market capitalization is less than 100 million

Neglected Stocks: Stocks followed by only a few analysts and/or stocks with low percentages of institutional ownership.

Stocks with High Relative Strength: Stocks whose prices have risen faster relative to the overall market.

January Effect: Stock do better during January than during any other month of the year.

Day of the Week: Stock of poorer during Monday than during other days of the week.

Most of these anomalies appear to revolve around four themes:

1. Markets tend to overreact to news, both good and bad.
2. Value investing is contrarians in nature and is beneficial because markets overreact.
3. The market consistently ignores certain stocks, especially small stocks.
4. Let's examine what anomalies mean for investors and the concept of market efficiency.

Financial Market Overreaction: One of the most intriguing issues to emerge in the past few years is the notion of market overreaction to new information (both positive and negative). Many practitioners have insisted for years that markets to overreact. Recent statistical evidence for both the market as a whole and individual security has shown errors in security prices that are systematic and therefore predictable. Overreactions are sometimes called reversals. Stocks that perform poorly in period suddenly reverse direction and start performing well in a subsequent period, and vice versa.

Several studies have found that stock returns over longer time horizons (in excess of one year) display significant negative serial correlation. This means that high returns in one time period tend to be followed by low returns in the next period, and vice versa.

Other studies have tested for market overreaction by forming portfolios of winners and losers based on performance over a specific time period and then measuring these portfolios performance records over subsequent periods of time. One study, for example, found that over the next year a portfolio of losers earned about 15 per cent more on average than did a portfolio of "winners".

Market overreaction may offer the best explanation for several of the anomalies. For example, low price-to-earnings ratio (P/E) stocks may be analogous to the losers we described above, or they may be the current investor favorites, or winners. As the market demonstrates almost daily, today's favorite stocks can fall from grace and reverse direction very quickly.

Profiting from Reversals: Market overreactions or reversals suggest several possible investment strategies to produce abnormal profits. Some possibilities include buying last year's worst performing stocks, avoiding stocks with high P/E ratios, or buying on bad news. At the risk of oversimplifying, any investment strategy based on market overreaction represents a contrarian approach to invest, buying what appears to be out of favor with most investors. But does value investing work? Can you do better follow the value-oriented anomalies listed?

There are many studies, done by both academics and practitioners that suggest that buying stocks with low price-to-sales rations, low price-to-book ratios, or low P/E ratios produced returns that were higher, on average, than those from the overall market, even after adjusting for higher transactions costs. These findings support the notion that contrarian/value investing may indeed work. Although value investing appears to work, it requires several caveats.

First, stocks with low P/E ratios are not necessarily cheap, not are stocks with high P/E ratios necessarily expensive. The inverse relationship between value and P/E (or market-to-book value) ratios is far from perfect. Some stocks may have low (or high) P/E ratios for very good reasons. Further, value is definitely in the eye of the beholder; one person's bargain is another person's overvalued pariah.

For another caveat, remember that very good economic reason may drive some reversals. Reversing prices may be responding to new information and correcting an overreaction. Also, a poor performer may continue to perform poorly as the company continues to slide downhill. The fact that a company had a lousy year this year does not mean it will automatically have a good one next year. Further, the timing of a reversal can be very difficult to predict. Investors have shunned some individual stocks and groups of stocks for long periods of time, whereas other stocks have reversed direction quickly.

Finally, think about what would happen if every investor suddenly became a contrarian. If contrarian investing really does offer abnormal profit opportunities, we would expect the wise investors to exploit opportunities aggressively. Soon competition would eliminate these opportunities. Remember, apparent past success of value investing is no guarantee that it will work in the future.

Calendar-Based Anomalies: Are there better times to own stocks than others? Should you avoid stocks on certain days? The evidence seems to suggest that several calendar-based anomalies exist. The two best known, and widely documented, are the weekend effect and the January effect.

Weekend Effect: Studies of daily returns began with the goal of testing whether the markets operate on calendar time or trading time. In other words, are returns for Mondays (i.e., returns over Friday-to-Monday periods) different from the other day of the week returns? The answer to the question turned out to be yes, the trend was called the weekend effect. Monday returns were substantially lower than other daily returns. One study found that Mondays produced a mean return of almost-35 percent. By contrast, the mean annualized returns on Wednesdays was more than +25 per cent.

The January Effect: Stock returns appear to exhibit seasonal return patterns as well. In other words, returns are systematically higher in some months than in others. Initial studies found that returns were higher in January for all stocks (thus this anomaly was dubbed the January effect) whereas later studies found the January effect was more pronounced for small stocks than for large ones.

One widely accepted explanation for the January effect is tax-loss selling by the investors at the end of December. Because this selling pressure depresses prices at the end of the year, it would be reasonable to expect a bounce-back in prices during January. Small stocks, the argument goes, are more susceptible to the January effect because their prices are more volatile, and institutional investors (many of whom are tax-exempt) are less likely to invest in shares of Small companies.

Calendar-Based Trading Strategies: Both seasonal and day-of-the-week affects are inconsistent with market efficiency because both suggest that historical information can generate abnormal profits. As will all anomalies, however, a more important issue is whether seasonal and/ or day-of-the-week effects can create profit opportunities for investors. Should you, for example, always buy stocks at the close of trading on Monday and sell them at the close of trading on Wednesdays?

Although differences in daily returns appear impressive, they are probably much too small to offset transaction costs. The January effect appears to have far more profit potential. However, once profitable investment strategies are recognized, it is reasonable to expect other investors to aggressively exploit them eventually eliminating the profit potential. This may be happening to the January effect. Entire books have been published about this widely recognized anomaly, and it may be disappearing.

Small-Firm Effect: Generally, the stocks of small companies substantially outperform stocks of large companies. Of course, history has also shown that small stocks have exhibited more year-to-year variation than large stocks. However, even after correcting for differences in risk, some studies suggest that investors can earn abnormal profits by investing in shares of small companies, exploiting the small-firm effect.

Two explanations for the small-firm effect seem plausible to us. The first is that analysts have applied the wrong risk measures to evaluate returns from small stocks. Small stocks may well be riskier than these traditional risk measures indicate. If proper risk measures were used, the argument goes, the small-firm effect might disappear, and Small-firm stocks may not generate larger risk-adjusted returns than large stocks. Although the risk of small stocks may not be adequately captured by standard risk measures, it is hard to believe that better measures of risk would eliminate the entire small-firm effect.

Another explanation for the small-firm effect is that large institutional investors often overlook small-firm stocks. Consequently, less information is available on small companies. (They are also followed by fewer analysts.) One could argue that this information deficiency makes small-firm stocks riskier investments, but one could also argue that discovery of a neglected small-firm stock by the institutions could send its price rising as the institutions start buying it. The small-firm effect may arise from the continuous process of discovery of neglected small-firm stocks leading to purchases by institutional investors.

Whatever the explanation, small-firm stocks, although riskier than large- firm stocks, have historically provided substantial returns to investors, far higher than those produced by large-firm stocks. Of course, we can only speculate about whether this relationship will continue in the future.

Performance of Investment Professionals: Investment professionals such as mutual fund managers seem to have a difficult time beating the overall market. In a particular year, some professionals will beat the market, whereas others will not. The key question is whether some professionals can consistently outperform the market. Some evidence suggests that the answer to this question may be yes.

SUMMARY

- Market efficiency means that the price which investor is paying for financial asset (stock, bond, other security) fully reflects fair or true information about the intrinsic value of this specific asset or fairly describe the value of the company - the issuer of this security. The key term in the concept of the market efficiency is the information available for investors trading in the market.
- There are 3 forms of market efficiency under efficient market hypothesis: weak form of efficiency; semi- strong form of efficiency; strong form of the efficiency. Under the weak form of efficiency stock prices are assumed to reflect any information that may be contained in the past history of the stock prices. Under the semi-strong form of efficiency all publicly available information is presumed to be reflected in stocks' prices. The strong form of efficiency which asserts that stock prices fully reflect all information, including private or inside information, as well as that which is publicly available.

MULTIPLE CHOICE QUESTIONS

1. Which of the following typically has the highest return volatility?
   a. Commercial paper
   b. Stocks
   c. Corporate bonds
   d. Treasury bonds
   e. Treasury bills
2. The bid price on a stock quoted by a dealer is
   a. The price at which the dealer buys the stock
   b. The price at which the dealer sells the stock
   c. The price at which the investor buys the stock
   d. The intrinsic value of the stock

3. According to the CAPM
   a. The Market portfolio is the global minimum variance portfolio
   b. The Market portfolio is a positive alpha investment
   c. The Market portfolio has the largest Sharpe ratio available in the economy
   d. The Market portfolio does not have systematic risk
4. Assume that a company announces an unexpectedly large cash dividend to its shareholders. In an efficient market without information leakage, one might expect:
   a. An abnormal price change at the announcement.
   b. An abnormal price increase before the announcement.
   c. An abnormal price decrease after the announcement.
   d. No abnormal price change before or after the announcement.
5. Which of the following observations would provide evidence against the *semi strong* form of the efficient market theory?
   a. Mutual fund managers do not on average make superior returns.
   b. You cannot make superior profits by buying (or selling) stocks after the announcement of an abnormal rise in dividends.
   c. Low P/E stocks tend to have positive abnormal returns.
   d. In any year approximately 50% of pension funds outperform the market.
6. If you believe in the ________ form of the EMH, you believe that stock prices reflect all relevant information including historical stock prices and current public information about the firm, but not information that is available only to insiders.
   a. semi strong
   b. strong
   c. weak
   d. A, B, and C
   e. none of the above
7. The semi strong form of EMH maintains that stock prices immediately reflect all historical and current public information, but not inside information.

   When Maurice Kendall examined the patterns of stock returns in 1953 he concluded that the stock market was __________. Now, these random price movements are believed to be __________.
   a. inefficient; the effect of a well-functioning market
   b. efficient; the effect of an inefficient market
   c. inefficient; the effect of an inefficient market
   d. efficient; the effect of a well-functioning market
   e. irrational; even more irrational than before.

8. Random price changes were originally thought to be driven by irrationality. Now, financial economists believe random price changes occur because markets are information ally efficient.

   A hybrid strategy is one where the investor

   a. uses both fundamental and technical analysis to select stocks.

   b. selects the stocks of companies that specialize in alternative fuels.

   c. selects some actively-managed mutual funds on their own anduses an investment advisor to select other actively-managed funds.

   d. maintains a passive core and augments the position with an actively managed portfolio.

   e. none of the above.

9. A hybrid strategy is one where the investor maintains a passive core and augments the position with an actively managed portfolio.

   The difference between a random walk and a sub martingale is the expected price change in a random walk is ______ and the expected price change for a sub martingale is ______.

   a. positive; zero
   b. positive; positive
   c. positive; negative
   d. zero; positive
   e. zero; zero

10. A random walk has an expected price change of zero and a sub martingale has a positive expected price change.

    Proponents of the EMH typically advocate

    a. an active trading strategy.
    b. investing in an index fund.
    c. a passive investment strategy.
    d. A and B
    e. B and C

11. Believers of market efficiency advocate passive investment strategies, and an investment in an index fund is one of the most practical passive investment strategies, especially for small investors.

    Proponents of the EMH typically advocate

    a. buying individual stocks on margin and trading frequently.

    b. investing in hedge funds.

    c. a passive investment strategy.

    d. A and B

    e. B and C

12. Believers of market efficiency advocate passive investment strategies, and an investment in an index fund is one of the most practical passive investment strategies, especially for small investors.

    If you believe in the _______ form of the EMH, you believe that stock prices reflect all information that can be derived by examining market trading data such as the history of past stock prices, trading volume or short interest.

    a. semi strong
    b. strong
    c. weak
    d. all of the above
    e. none of the above

13. The information described above is market data, which is the data set for the weak form of market efficiency. The semi strong form includes the above plus all other public information. The strong form includes all public and private information.

    If you believe in the _________ form of the EMH, you believe that stock prices reflect all available information, including information that is available only to insiders.

    a. semi strong
    b. strong
    c. weak
    d. all of the above
    e. none of the above

14. The strong form includes all public and private information.

    If you believe in the reversal effect, you should

    a. buys bonds in this period if you held stocks in the last period.
    b. buys stocks in this period if you held bonds in the last period.
    c. buys stocks this period that performed poorly last period.
    d. goes short.
    e. C and D

15. The reversal effect states that stocks that do well in one period tend to perform poorly in the subsequent period, and vice versa.

    __________ focus more on past price movements of a firm's stock than on the underlying determinants of future profitability.

    a. Credit analysts
    b. Fundamental analysts
    c. Systems analysts
    d. Technical analysts
    e. All of the above

16. Technicians attempt to predict future stock prices based on historical stock prices. _________ above which it is difficult for the market to rise.

    a. Book value is a value
    b. Resistance level is a value
    c. Support level is a value
    d. A and B
    e. A and C

17. When stock prices have remained stable for a long period, these prices are termed resistance levels; technicians believe it is difficult for the stock prices to penetrate these resistance levels.

    _________ below which it is difficult for the market to fall.

    a. Intrinsic value is a value
    b. Resistance level is a value
    c. Support level is a value
    d. A and B
    e. B and C

18. When stock prices have remained stable for a long period, these prices are termed support levels; technicians believe it is difficult for the stock prices to penetrate these support levels.

    _________ above which it is difficult for the market to rise.

    a. Book value is a value
    b. Resistance level is a value
    c. Support level is a value
    d. A and B
    e. A and C

19. When stock prices have remained stable for a long period, these prices are termed resistance levels; technicians believe it is difficult for the stock prices to penetrate these resistance levels.

    _________ below which it is difficult for the market to fall.

    a. Intrinsic value is a value
    b. Resistance level is a value
    c. Support level is a value
    d. A and B
    e. B and C

    When stock prices have remained stable for a long period, these prices are termed support levels; technicians believe it is difficult for the stock prices to penetrate these support levels.

20. Which of the following statements applies to the capital asset pricing model?
    a. It assumes that individual securities are priced solely on unsystematic risk.
    b. It uses beta to represent unsystematic risk of individual securities.
    c. It assumes that if the rate of return on an individual security is greater than the market average, systematic risk of the security must be smaller.
    d. It assumes that if beta equals 1, the systematic risk of an individual security is equal to the average risk of the market as a whole.

21. Which of the following statements does not apply to the *market model*?
    a. It is a simpler approach than the standard version of the capital asset pricing model.
    b. This approach is seldom used in accounting research.
    c. In this model, the risk-free return is dropped from the equation.
    d. Abnormal returns are captured in the error term of the model.

22. Which of the following is a finding of previous capital market research studies?
    a. The market is not fooled by arbitrary accounting numbers.
    b. The direction of change in reported accounting earning is inversely correlated with security price movements.
    c. The market is affected by alternative accounting income numbers that do not affect cash flow, such as those related to a change from deferral to recognition of unrealized holding gains on marketable securities.
    d. Security prices are affected by a change from the deferral to flow through method of accounting for the investment credit.

TRUE / FALSE

1. The *efficient-markets hypothesis* refers to the speed with which financial analysts are able to predict a firm's cash flows. (False)
2. Most testing of the efficient-markets hypothesis has dealt only with past information reflected in security prices. (False)
3. The theoretical foundation of capital market or security price research comes from the efficient-markets hypothesis. (True)
4. According to portfolio theory, systematic risk can be reduced by holding a portfolio of investments. (False)
5. The expected portfolio return decreases as risk increases. (False)
6. In portfolio theory, systematic risk is defined as the variance of expected investment returns. (True)
7. The assumption of the capital asset pricing model is that individual securities are priced solely on unsystematic risk. (False)
8. In the capital asset pricing model, beta is used to represent systematic risk or individual securities and to predict the risk-based price of securities. (True)
9. The strongest evidence from capital market research concerns the information content of annual according earnings numbers. (True)
10. Capital market research has shown that investors do not appear to adjust accounting income to compensate for artificial bookkeeping differences. (False)
11. Research studies have predominantly supported the naïve-investor hypothesis. Capital market research is supportive of the assertion that alternative accounting policies do not affect security prices because there are no direct cash flow consequences to the firm. (False)
12. When accounting numbers are used to monitor agency cons, there can be indirect consequences from changes in accounting policies. (True)

13. The student by Lev that examined earnings numbers and stock returns found a high explanatory relationship between earnings and stock returns.
14. Capital market research is supportive of the assertion that alternative accounting policies do not affect security prices because there are no direct cash flow consequences to the firm. (False)
15. Capital market research is supportive of the assertion that alternative accounting policies do not affect security prices because there are no direct cash flow consequences to the firm. (False)
16. Capital market research in the area of alternative accounting policies does not support the arbitrariness of accounting allocations. (False).

SHORT ANSWER QUESTONS

1. Define Random Walk Theory
2. Define Testing the hypothesis
3. Define A non-random walk hypothesis
4. Define Forms of Efficient Market Hypothesis
5. Define Weak form efficiency,
6. Define Semi-strong form efficiency and
7. Define Strong form efficiency
8. Define Serial Correlation Test
9. Define Filter Rules Test
10. Define Run Test
11. Define Simulation Test
12. Define Event Study
13. Define Portfolio study
14. Define Market Reaction Test
15. Define Market Efficiency and Anomalies
16. Define Profiting from Reversals
17. Define Calendar-Based Trading Strategies
18. Define Performance of Investment Professionals

ESSAY TYPE QUESTIONS

1. What are the empirical evidences of the weak form of market efficiency?
2. Discuss the results of the studies that support the semi-strong form of EMH.
3. Explain the strong form of market efficiency with empirical evidences.
4. How does efficient market hypothesis differ from the technical analysis?
5. What is Random Walk theory? What does it project in its weak form, semi-strong form and strong form?
6. Discuss the empirical tests conducted on the different forms of the random walk.
7. The random walk hypothesis resembles the fundamental school of thought but is contrary to the technical analysis. Discuss?
8. Define the various forms of the market efficiency. What do they have in common?
9. "Indian stock market is efficient". Do you agree? Discuss.

MCQs Answers

1	2	3	4	5	6	7	8	9	10	11	12	13	14	15	16	17	18	19	20	21	22
B	A	C	A	C	A	A	D	D	E	C	C	B	C	D	B	C	B	C	D	B	A

CHAPTER 11

Common Stock Valuation

In financial markets, stock valuation is the method of calculating theoretical values of companies and their stocks. The main use of these methods is to predict future market prices, or more generally potential market prices, and thus to profit from price movement – stocks that are judged undervalued (with respect to their theoretical value) are bought, while stocks that are judged overvalued are sold, in the expectation that undervalued stocks will, on the whole, rise in value, while overvalued stocks will, on the whole, fall.

In the view of fundamental analysis, stock valuation based on fundamentals aims to give an estimate of their intrinsic value of the stock, based on predictions of the future cash flows and profitability of the business. Fundamental analysis may be replaced or augmented by market criteria – what the market will pay for the stock, without any necessary notion of intrinsic value. These can be combined as "predictions of future cash flows/profits (fundamental)", together with "what will the market pay for these profits? "These can be seen as "supply and demand" sides – what underlies the supply (of stock), and what drives the (market) demand for stock?

The stock valuation is not a prediction but a convention, which serves to facilitate investment and ensure that stocks are liquid, despite being underpinned by an illiquid business and its illiquid investments, such as factories.

FAIR VALUE

The most theoretically sound stock valuation method, called income valuation or the discounted cash flow (DCF) method, involves discounting of the profits (dividends, earnings, or cash flows) the stock will bring to the stockholder in the foreseeable future, and a final value on disposal. The discounted rate normally includes a risk premium which is commonly based on the capital asset pricing model.

STOCK VALUATION METHODS

Absolute valuation models attempt to find the intrinsic or "true" value of an investment based only on fundamentals. Looking at fundamentals simply means you would only focus on such things as dividends, cash flow and growth rate for a single company, and you wouldn't worry about any other companies. Valuation models that fall into this category include the dividend discount model, discounted cash flow model, residual income models and asset-based models.

In contrast to absolute valuation models, relative valuation models operate by comparing the company in question to other similar companies. These methods generally involve calculating multiples or ratios, such as the price-to-earnings multiple, and comparing them to the multiples of other comparable firms. For instance, if the P/E of the firm you are trying to value is lower than the P/E multiple of a comparable firm, that company may be said to be relatively undervalued. Generally, this type of valuation is a lot easier and quicker to do than the absolute valuation methods, which is why many investors and analysts start their analysis with this method.

Popular Valuation Methods available to investors, and see when it is appropriate to use each model.

Stocks have two types of valuations. One is a value created using some type of cash flow, sales or fundamental earnings analysis. The other value is dictated by how much an investor is willing to pay for a particular share of stock and by how much other investors are willing to sell a stock for (in other words, by supply and demand). Both of these values change over time as investors change the way they analyze stocks and as they become more or less confident in the future of stocks.

The fundamental valuation is the valuation that people use to justify stock prices. The most common example of this type of valuation methodology is P/E ratio, which stands for Price to Earnings Ratio. This form of valuation is based on historic ratios and statistics and aims to assign value to a stock based on measurable attributes. This form of valuation is typically what drives long-term stock prices.

The other way stocks are valued is based on supply and demand. The more people that want to buy the stock, the higher its price will be. And conversely, the more people that want to sell the stock, the lower the price will be. This form of valuation is very hard to understand or predict, and it often drives the short-term stock market trends.

There are many different ways to value stocks. The key is to take each approach into account while formulating an overall opinion of the stock. If the valuation of a company is lower or higher than other similar stocks, then the next step would be to determine the reasons.

Popular Valuation Methods available to investors, and see when it is appropriate to use each model.

- **Dividend Discount Model (DDM)**

  The dividend discount model (DDM) is one of the most basic absolute valuation models. The dividend model calculates the "true" value of a firm based on the dividends the company pays its shareholders. The justification for using dividends to value a company is that dividends represent the actual cash flows going to the shareholder, thus valuing the present value of these cash flows should give you a value for how much the shares should be worth. So, the first thing you should check if you want to use this method is if the company actually pays a dividend.

Secondly, it is not enough for the company to just a pay dividend; the dividend should also be stable and predictable. The companies that pay stable and predictable dividends are typically mature blue-chip companies in mature and well-developed industries. These types of companies are often best suited for this type of valuation method. For instance, take a look at the dividends and earnings of company XYZ below and see if you think the DDM model would be appropriate for this company:

	2009	2010	2011	2012	2013	2014
Dividends Per Share	Rs. 0.50	Rs.0.53	Rs.0.55	Rs.0.58	Rs.0.61	Rs.0.64
Earnings Per Share	Rs.4.00	Rs.4.20	Rs.4.41	Rs.4.63	Rs.4.86	Rs.5.11

In this example, the earnings per share are consistently growing at an average rate of 5%, and the dividends are also growing at the same rate. This means the firm's dividend is consistent with its earnings trend which would make it easy to predict for future periods. In addition, you should check the payout ratio to make sure the ratio is consistent. In this case the ratio is 0.125 for all six years, which is good, and makes this company an ideal candidate for the dividend model.

Example.1 Using the DDM. Suppose again that a stock pays three annual dividends of Rs.100 per year and the discount rate is k = 15 percent. In this case, what is the present value V (0) of the stock? With a 15 percent discount rate, we have

$$V(0) = \frac{Rs.100}{(115)} \% \frac{Rs.100}{(1.15)^2} \% \frac{Rs.100}{(1.15)^3}$$

Check that the answer is V (0) = Rs.228.32.

Example 2. More DDM. Suppose instead that the stock pays three annual dividends of Rs.10, 20, and Rs.30 in years 1, 2, and 3, respectively, and the discount rate is k = 10 percent. What is the present value V (0) of the stock? In this case, we have

$$v(o) = \frac{Rs.10}{(110)} \% \frac{Rs.20}{(1.10)^2} \% \frac{Rs.30}{(1.10)^3}$$

Check that the answer is V (0) = Rs.48.16.

Example: Current forecasts are for XYZ Company to pay dividends of Rs.3, Rs.3.24, and Rs.3.50 over the next three years, respectively. At the end of three years you anticipate selling your stock at a market price of Rs.94.48. What is the price of the stock given a 12% expected return?

$$PV = \frac{3.00}{(1+.12)^1} + \frac{3.24}{(1+.12)^2} + \frac{3.50+94.48}{(1+.12)^3}$$

$$PV = Rs.75.00$$

If we forecast no growth, and plan to hold out stock indefinitely, we will then value the stock as a perpetuity.

Assumes all earnings are paid to shareholders.

$$Perpetuity = P_0 = \frac{Div_1}{r} or \frac{EPS_1}{r}$$

1. Constant Dividend Growth Rate Model

For many applications, the dividend discount model is simplified substantially by assuming that dividends will grow at a constant growth rate. This is called a constant growth rate model. Letting a constant growth rate be denoted by g, then successive annual dividends are stated as D (t+1) = D (t) (1+g). (marg. def. constant growth rate model a version of the dividend discount model that assumes a constant dividend growth rate. For example, suppose the next dividend is D (1) = Rs.100, and the dividend growth rate is g = 10 percent. This growth rate yields a second annual dividend of D (2) = Rs.100 x 1.10 = Rs.110, and a third annual dividend of D (3) = Rs. 100 x 1.10 x 1.10 = Rs.100 x $(1.10)^2$ = Rs.121. If the discount rate is k = 12 percent, the present value of these three sequential dividend payments is the sum of their separate present values:

$$V(0) = Rs.\ 100 / (112) + Rs.\ 110 / (1.12)^{2+} Rs.121 / (1.12)^3 = Rs.263.10$$

If the number of dividends to be paid is large, calculating the present value of each dividend separately is tedious and possibly prone to error. Fortunately, if the growth rate is constant, some simplified expressions are available to handle certain special cases. For example, suppose a stock will pay annual dividends over the next T years, and these dividends will grow at a constant growth rate g, and be discounted at the rate k. The current dividend is D (0), the next dividend is D (1) = D (0) (1+g), the following dividend is D (2) = D (1) (1+g), and so forth. The present value of the next T dividends, that is, D (1) through D(T), can be calculated using this relatively simple formula:

Notice that this expression requires that the growth rate and the discount rate not be equal to each other, that is, k * g, since this requires division by zero. Actually, when the growth rate is equal to the discount rate, that is, k = g, the effects of growth and discounting cancel exactly, and the present value V (0) is simply the number of payments T times the current dividend D (0): V (0) = T x D (0)

Example: What is the value of a stock that expects to pay aRs.3.00 dividend next year, and then increase the dividend at a rate of 8% per year, indefinitely? Assume a 12% expected return.

$$P_0 = \frac{Div_1}{r-g} = \frac{Rs.3.00}{.12-.08} = Rs.75.00$$

If the same stock is selling forRs.100 in the stock market, what might the market be assuming about the growth in dividends?

$$Rs.100 = \frac{Rs.3.00}{.12-g}$$

$$g = .09$$

The market is assuming the dividend will grow at 9% per year, indefinitely. Valuing Non-Constant Growth

Example: Mohan Raj & Company forecasts to pay a Rs.5.00 dividend next year, which represents 100% of its earnings. This will provide investors with a 12% expected return. Instead, we decide to plowback 40% of the earnings at the firm's current return on equity of 20%. What is the value of the stock before and after the plowback decision?

No Growth $P_0 = \frac{5}{.12} = \$41.67$

With Growth

$$g = .20 \times .40 = .08$$

$$P_0 = \frac{3}{.12 - .08} = Rs.75.00$$

If the company did not plowback some earnings, the stock price would remain at Rs.41.67. With the plowback, the price rose to Rs.75.00. The difference between these two numbers (75.00-41.67=33.33) is called the **Present Value of Growth** Opportunities (PVGO). Present Value of Growth Opportunities (PVGO). Net present value of a firm's future investments.

Example: The constant growth rate model, suppose that the growth rate is g = 8 percent, the discount rate is k = 10 percent, the number of future annual dividends is T = 20 years, and the current dividend is D (0) =Rs.10. In this case, a present value calculation yields this amount:

V (0) = Rs.10(1.10) / (.08 - .10) +(1.08 / 1.10)2 =Rs. 165.88

- Multiple growth rates: two or more expected growth rates in dividends
- Ultimately, growth rate must equal that of the economy as a whole
- The company/industry is maturing and when it reaches maturity –grows at the rate of the economy
- Assume growth at a rapid rate for n periods followed by steady growth
- Multiple growth rates approach:
- First present value covers the period of super-normal (or sub-normal) growth
- Second present value covers the period of stable growth
- Expected price uses constant-growth model as of the end of super- (sub-) normal period (time period m)
- Value at m must be discounted to time period zero

Two Period Growth Model:

$$P_o = \sum_{t=1}^{m} \frac{D_o(1+g_1)^t}{(1+K_e)^t} + \frac{1}{(1+K_e)^m}\left(\frac{D_{m+1}}{K_e - g_2}\right)$$

Example: required rate of return =18% Current dividend is 2.00 dividends are expected to grow at 12% for first 6 years then at 6%. Present value of First 6-Years' Dividends:

Year t	Dividend Dt	P.V. Interest Factor $PVIF_{18,t} = 1/(1+.18)_t$	Present Value $D_t \times PVIF_{18,t}$
1	$ 2.240	.874	Rs. 1.897
2	2.509	718	1.801
3	2.810	.609	1.711
4	3.147	.516	1.624
5	3.525	.437	1.540
6	3.948	.370	1.461
PV (First 6-Years' Dividends			Rs. 10.034

- Value of Stock at End of Year 6:
    - $P_6 = D_7 / (K_e - g_2)$ where $g_2 = .06$
    - $D_7 = D_6(1 + g_2) = 3.948(1 + .06) =$ Rs. 4.185
    - $P_6 = 4.185/(.18 - .06) =$ Rs. 34.875
    - Present Value of P_6
    - $PV(P_6) = P_6/(1 + k_e)^6 =$ Rs.34.875/ $(1 + .18)^6 =$ Rs. 34.875 x .370 = Rs. 12.904
- Value of Common Stock (P_o)
    - P_o = PV (First 6-Year's Dividends) + PV(P_6) = 10.034 + 12.904 = 22.94
- Example using the two period growth formulae:

$$P_o = \frac{D_1\left[1 - \left(\frac{1+g_1}{1+k}\right)^M\right]}{k - g_1} + \left[\frac{D_1(1+g_1)^{M-1}(1+g_2)}{(1+k)^M(k-g_2)}\right]$$

- M= # of years growing at g_1

$$\frac{2.24[1 - .7312]}{.06} + \frac{2.24(1.76)(1.06)}{(.12)(2.6996)}$$

$$P = \frac{2.24\left[1 - \left(\frac{1.12}{1.18}\right)^6\right]}{.18 - .12} + \frac{2.24(1.12)^5(1.06)}{(.18 - .06)(1.18)^6}$$

$$10.04 + \frac{4.18}{.3239} = 10.04 + 12.90 = Rs22.94$$

2. Discounted Cash Flow Model (DCF)

What if the company doesn't pay a dividend or its dividend pattern is irregular? In this case, move on to check if the company fits the criteria to use the discounted cash flow model. Instead of looking at dividends, the DCF model uses a firm's discounted future cash flows to value the business. The big advantage of this approach is that it can be used with a wide variety of firms that don't pay dividends, and even for companies that do pay dividends, such as company XYZ in the previous example.

The DCF model has several variations, but the most commonly used form is the Two-Stage DCF model. In this variation, the free cash flows are generally forecasted for five to ten years, and then a terminal value is calculated to account for all of the cash flows beyond the forecast period. So, the first requirement for using this model is for the company to have predictable free cash flows, and for the free cash flows to be positive. Based on this requirement alone, you will quickly find that many small high-growth firms and non-mature firms will be excluded due to the large capital expenditures these companies generally face.

For example, take a look at the simplified cash flows of the following firm:

	2009	2010	2011	2012	2013	2014
Operating Cash Flow	438	789	1462	890	2565	510
Capital Expenditures	785	995	1132	1256	2235	1546
Free Cash Flow	-347	-206	330	-366	330	-1036

In this snapshot, the firm has produced increasingly positive operating cash flow, which is good. But you can see by the high level of capital expenditures that the company is still investing a lot of its cash back into the business in order to grow. This results in negative free cash flows for four of the six years, making it extremely difficult (nearly impossible) to predict the cash flows for the next five to ten years. So, in order to use the DCF model most effectively, the target company should generally have stable, positive and predictable free cash flows. Companies that have the ideal cash flows suited for the DCF model are typically the mature firms that are past the growth stages.

3. Comparable Method

The last method we'll look at is sort of a catch-all method that can be used if you are unable to value the company using any of the other models, or if you simply don't want to spend the time crunching the numbers. The method doesn't attempt to find an intrinsic value for the stock like the previous two valuation methods do; it simply compares the stock's price multiples to a benchmark to determine if the stock is relatively undervalued or overvalued. The rationale for this is based off of the Law of One Price, which states that two similar assets should sell for similar prices. The intuitive nature of this method is one of the reasons it is so popular.

This method can be used in almost all circumstances because of the vast number of multiples that can be applied, such as the price-to-earnings (P/E), price-to-book (P/B), price-to-sales (P/S), price-to-cash flow (P/CF) and many others. Of these ratios, the P/E ratio is the most commonly used one because it focuses on the earnings of the company, which is one of the primary drivers of an investment's value.

The company is publicly traded because you need the price of the stock, and you need to know the earnings of the company. Secondly, the company should be generating positive earnings because a comparison using a negative P/E multiple would be meaningless. And lastly, the earnings quality should be strong; earnings should not be too volatile and the accounting practices used by management should not drastically distort the reported earnings.

These are just some of the main criteria investors should look at when choosing which ratio or multiples to use. If the P/E multiple cannot be used, simply look at using a different ratio such as the price-to-sales multiple.

No one valuation method is perfect for every situation, but by knowing the characteristics of the company, you can select the valuation method that best suits the situation. In addition, investors are not limited to just using one method. Often, investors will perform several valuations to create a range of possible values or average all of the valuations into one.

PREFERRED STOCK VALUATION

Preferred shares have the qualities of both a stock and a bond, which makes valuation a little different than a common share. The owner of the preferred share is part owner of the company, just like a common shareholder. The stake in the company is in proportion to the held stocks. Also, there is a fixed payment which is similar to a bond issued by the company. The fixed payment is in the form of a dividend and will be the basis of the valuation method for a preferred share. These payments could come quarterly, monthly or yearly, depending on the policy stated by the company.

Preferred stock is a hybrid having some features similar to debt and other features similar to equity

- Claim on assets and cash flow senior to common stock
- As equity security, dividend payments are not tax deductible for the corporation.
- For tax reasons, straight preferred stock held mostly by corporations.

Promises a fixed annual dividend payment, but not legally enforceable. Firms cannot pay common stock dividends if preferred stock is in arrears (i.e. preferred stock is typically "cumulative").

- Preferred stockholders usually do not have voting rights.
- May be convertible to common stock

VALUATION

Preferred stocks have a fixed dividend, which means we can calculate the value by discounting each of these payments to the present day. This fixed dividend is not guaranteed in common shares. If you take these payments and calculate the sum of the present values into perpetuity, you will find the value of the stock.

- Because preferred stock pays a constant dividend, they are easy to value because the dividends are a perpetuity. Recall the present value of a perpetuity is:

$$PV = \frac{PMT}{i} = \frac{D_1}{i}$$

Where: D_1 is the constant dividend whose first payment is one period from today.

You purchase a preferred stock with a Rs.12 per year dividend. For a 10% market rate, what is its value?

$$\text{Price} = PV = \frac{D_1}{i} = \frac{Rs.12}{0.10} = Rs.120.00$$

Stock valuation with a two-year holding period

Valuation of Common Stock: Assume 1 year holding

$$P_0 = \frac{D_1 + P_1}{(1+i)} = \frac{D_1}{(1+i)} + \frac{P_1}{(1+i)}$$

- P_0 = Present value or price of stock today
- P_1 = Price of stock next period
- D_1 = Dividends received in first period
- i = discount rate

Stock Value next year: Use same approach

$$P_1 = \frac{D_2}{(1+i)} + \frac{P_2}{(1+i)}$$

$$P_0 = \frac{D_1}{(1+i)} + \frac{\frac{D_2 + P_2}{(1+i)}}{(1+i)} = \frac{D_1}{(1+i)} + \frac{D_2}{(1+i)^2} + \frac{P_2}{(1+i)^2}$$

Valuation Fundamentals: Common Stock

- How was P_1 determined?
  - PV of expected stock price P_2, plus dividends
  - P_2 is the PV of P_3 plus dividends, etc...

Repeating this logic over and over, you find that today's price equals PV of the entire dividend stream the stock will pay in the future:

$$P_0 = \frac{D_1}{(1+i)^1} + \frac{D_2}{(1+i)^2} + \frac{D_3}{(1+i)^3} + \frac{D_4}{(1+i)^4} + \frac{D_5}{(1+i)^5} + \dots \qquad (Eq.4.5)$$

Must be able to predict future dividends to use this model

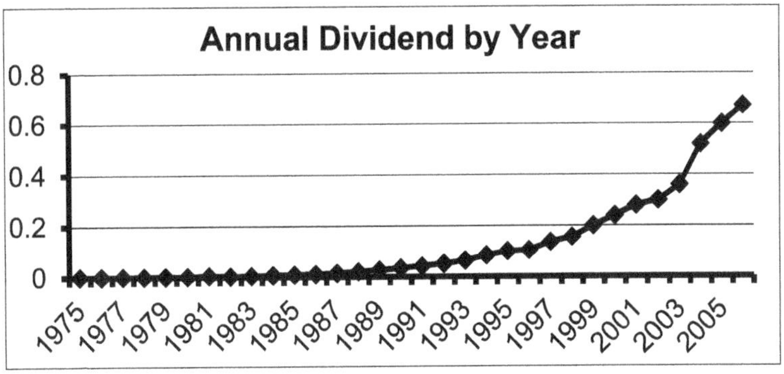

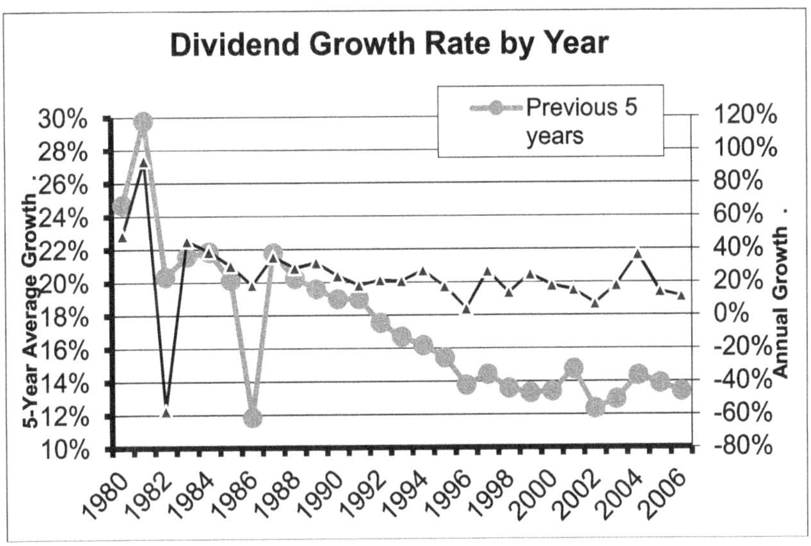

Zero Growth Valuation Model

To value common stock, you must make assumptions about future dividend growth. Zero growth model assumes a constant, non-growing dividend stream. (Think preferred stock). $D_1 = D_2 = \cdots = D$

Plugging constant value D into the common stock valuation formula reduces to simple equation for the present value of a perpetuity:

$$P_0 = \frac{D_1}{r}$$

Constant Growth Valuation Model: Assumes dividends will grow at a constant rate (g) that is less than the required return (r). If dividends grow at a constant rate forever, you can value stock as a growing perpetuity, denoting next year's dividend as D_1:

$$P_0 = \frac{D_1}{r-g} \qquad Eq.4.6 \qquad \text{Note: } D1 = D_0(1+g)$$

Commonly called the Gordon growth model. Also called a DDM: Dividend Discount Model

Dividends over time: In the Gordon growth model:

$$D_{t+1} = D_t(1+g)$$
$$D_{t+N} = D_t(1+g)^N$$

- D_0 = Current Dividend (time period 0).
- D_1 = Dividend one period from now.
- r = appropriate discount rate or rate of return for the particular stock (adjusts for time value of money and risk).
- g = constant growth rate in dividends.
- P_0 = the present value of the infinite series of dividends, which is the estimate stock price.

Use the Gordon model when . . .

- A dividend is paid on a regular basis
- Growth rate in the dividends is constant r>g

Example: Satya's Corp. will pay Rs.3 dividend in one year. If investors expect that dividend to remain constant forever, and they require a 10% return on Satya's stock, what is the stock worth?

$$P_0 = \frac{D_1}{r} = \frac{Rs.3}{0.1} = Rs.30$$

What is the stock worth if investors expect Satya's dividends to grow at 3% per year?

$$P_0 = \frac{D_1}{r-g} = \frac{Rs.3}{0.10-0.03} = Rs.42.86$$

Example: Suppose Big C, just paid a dividend of Rs.50. It is expected to increase its dividend by 2% per year. If the market requires a return of 15% on assets of this risk level, how much should the stock be selling for.

P_0 = .50(1+.02) / (.15 - .02) = Rs. 3.92

Assume that dividends will grow at different rates in the foreseeable future and then will grow at a constant rate thereafter. To value a Differential Growth Stock, we need to:

- Estimate future dividends in the foreseeable future.
- Estimate the future stock price when the stock becomes a Constant Growth Stock (case 2).

Compute the total present value of the estimated future dividends and future stock price at the appropriate discount rate.

$$P_p = \frac{D_p}{K_p} = \frac{Rs.6.30}{.09} = Rs.70$$

The preferred stock of Ultra Corporation pays an annual dividend of Rs. 6.30. It has a required rate of return of 9 percent. Compute the price of the preferred stock.

Example: North-west co.ltd issued preferred stock many years ago. It carries a fixed dividend of Rs. 6 per share. With the passage of time, yields have soared from the original 6 percent to 14 percent (yield is the same as required rate of return).

a. What was the original issue price?
b. What is the current value of this preferred stock?
c. If the yield on the Standard & Poor's Preferred Stock Index declines, how will the price of the preferred stock be affected?

a. Original price

$$P_p = \frac{D_p}{K_p} = \frac{Rs.6.00}{.06} = Rs.100$$

b. Current value

$$\frac{Rs.6.00}{.14} = Rs.42.86$$

c. The price of preferred stock will increase as yields decline. Since preferred stock is a fixed income security, its price is inversely related to yields as would be true with bond prices. The present value of an income stream has a higher present value as the discount rate declines, and a lower present value as the discount rate increases.

Example: Venus Sportswear Corporation has preferred stock outstanding that pays an annual dividend of Rs. 12. It has a price of Rs.110. What is the required rate of return (yield) on the preferred stock?

$$K_p = \frac{D_p}{P_p} = \frac{Rs.12}{Rs.110} = 10.91\%$$

Example: Raghav Technology has preferred stock outstanding that pays a Rs. J9 annual dividend. It has a price of Rs.76. What is the required rate of return (yield) on the preferred stock?

$$K_p = \frac{D_p}{P_p} = \frac{Rs.9}{Rs.76} = 11.84\%$$

Example: Vamsi & Co. currently pays a Rs.2.10 annual cash dividend (D_0). It plans to maintain the dividend at this level for the foreseeable future as no future growth is anticipated. If the required rate of return by common stockholders (K_e) is 12 percent, what is the price of the common stock?

$$P_0 = \frac{D_0}{K_e} = \frac{Rs.2.10}{.12} = Rs.17.50$$

Example: Veltech engineering will pay a common stock dividend of Rs.3.20 at the end of the year (D_1). The required return on common stock (K_e) is 14 percent. The firm has a constant growth rate (g) of 9 percent. Compute the current price of the stock (P_0).

$$P_0 = \frac{D_1}{K_e - g} = \frac{Rs.3.20}{.14 - .09} = \frac{Rs.3.20}{.05} = Rs.64.00$$

Example: Varma Steel Company will pay a dividend of Rs. 1.50 per share in the next 12 months (D_1). The required rate of return (K_e) is 10 percent and the constant growth rate is 5percent.

a. Compute P_0. (For parts b, c, and d in this problem all variables remain the same except the one specifically changed. Each question is independent of the others.)

b. Assume K_e, the required rate of return, goes up to 12 percent; what will be the new value of P_0?

c. Assume the growth rate (g) goes up to 7 percent; what will be the new value of P_0?

d. Assume D_1 is Rs. 2, what will be the new value of P_0?

$$P_0 = \frac{D_1}{K_e - g}$$

$$\frac{Rs.1.50}{.10 - .05} = \frac{Rs.1.50}{.05} = Rs.30.00$$

$$\frac{Rs.1.50}{.12 - .05} = \frac{Rs.1.50}{.07} = Rs.21.43$$

$$\frac{Rs.1.50}{.10 - .07} = \frac{Rs.1.50}{.03} = Rs.50.00$$

$$\frac{Rs.2.00}{.10 - .05} = \frac{Rs.2.00}{.05} = Rs.40.00$$

Example: Maxwell Communications paid a dividend of Rs. 3 last year. Over the next 12 months, the dividend is expected to grow at 8 percent, which is the constant growth rate for the firm (g). The new dividend after 12 months will represent D_1. The required rate of return (K_e) is 14 percent. Compute the price of the stock (P_0).

$$P_0 = \frac{D_1}{K_e - g}$$

$$D_1 = D_0(1 + g) = Rs.3.00\ (1.08) = Rs.3.24$$

$$P_0 = \frac{Rs.3.24}{.14 - .08} = \frac{Rs.3.24}{0.06} = Rs.54$$

Example: Hemanth Enterprises has had the following pattern of earnings per share over the last five years:

Year	Earnings per Share
2010	\$3.00
2011	3.18
2012	3.37
2013	3.57
2014	3.78

The earnings per share have grown at a constant rate (on a rounded basis) and will continue to do so in the future. Dividends represent 30 percent of earnings.

a. Project earnings and dividends for the next year (2014). Round all values in this problem to two places to the right of the decimal point.
b. If the required rate of return (K_e) is 10 percent, what is the anticipated stock price at the beginning of 2014?
c. Earnings have been growing at a rate of 6 percent per year.

	Base Period	
2010		
2011	Rs.3.18/3.00	6% growth
2012	Rs.3.37/3.18	6% growth
2013	Rs.3.57/3.37	6% growth
2014	Rs. 3.78/3.57	6% growth

The projected EPS for 2014 is Rs.3.78 (1.06) = Rs.4.01

Dividend for 2009 represent 30% of earnings or Rs.1.20.

A. This is the value for D_1. K_e (required rate of return) is 10% and the growth rate is 6%

$$\cdot\ P_0\ (2014) = \frac{D_1}{K_e - g} = \frac{Rs.1.20}{.10 - .06} = \frac{Rs.1.20}{.04} = Rs.30$$

Example: A firm pays Rs. 4.90 dividend at the end of year one (D_1), has a stock price of Rs. 70, and a constant growth rate (g) of 6 percent. Compute the required rate of return.

$$\text{Rearranging } P_0 = \frac{D_1}{K_e - g},$$

$$K_e = \frac{D_1}{P_0} + g$$

$$K_e = \frac{\text{Rs.4.90}}{\text{Rs.70.00}} + 6\% = 7\% + 6\% = 13\%$$

Example: A firm pays a Rs.1.90 dividend at the end of year one (D_1), has a stock price of Rs.40 (P_0), and a constant growth rate (g) of 8 percent.

a. Compute the required rate of return (K_e). Also indicate whether each of the following changes would make the required rate of return (K_e) go up or down. (For parts b, c, and d below, assume only one variable changes at a time.

   No actual numbers are necessary.)

b. The dividend payment increases.

c. The expected growth rate increases.

d. The stock price increases.

$$\text{Rearranging } P_0 = \frac{D_1}{K_e - g},$$

$$K_e = \frac{D_1}{P_0} + g$$

$$K_e = \frac{Rs.1.90}{Rs.40.00} + 8\% = 4.75\% + 8\% = 12.75\%$$

b. If the dividend payment increases, the dividend yield (D_1/P_0) will go up, and the required rate of return (K_e) will also go up.

c. If the expected growth rate (g) increases, the required rate of return (K_e) will go up.

d. If the stock price increases, the dividend yield (D_1/P_0) will go down, and the required rate of return (K_e) will also go down.

Example: Solar Systems paid a Rs.3 dividend last year. The dividend is expected to grow at a constant rate of 5 percent over the next two years. The required rate of return is 12 percent (this will also serve as the discount rate in this problem). Round all values to three places to the right of the decimal point where appropriate.

a. Compute the anticipated value of the dividends for the next three years. That is, compute D_1, D_2, and D_3; for example, D_1 is Rs.3.15 (Rs.3.00 × 1.05). Round all values throughout this problem to three places to the right of the decimal point.

b. Discount each of these dividends back to the present at a discount rate of 12 percent and then sum them.

c. Compute the price of the stock at the end of the third year (P_3).

$$P_3 = \frac{D_4}{K_e - g} \quad (D_4 \text{ is equal to } D_3 \text{ times } 1.05)$$

d. After you have computed P_3, discount it back to the present at a discount rate of 12 percent for three years.

e. Add together the answers in part b and part d to get P_0, the current value of the stock. This answer represents the present value of the first three periods, of dividends, plus the present value of the price of the stock after three periods (which, in turn, represents the value of all future dividends).

f. Use Formula 10-9 to show that it will provide approximately the same answer as part e.

$$P_0 = \frac{D_1}{K_e - g} \quad (10\text{-}9)$$

For Formula 10-9 use D_1 = Rs.15, K_e = 12 percent, and g = 5 percent. (The slight difference between the answers to part e and part f is due to rounding.)

Example: Trump Office Supplies paid an Rs.3 dividend last year. The dividend is expected to grow at a constant rate of 7 percent over the next four years. The required rate of return is 14 percent (this will also serve as the discount rate in this problem). Round all values to three places to the right of the decimal point where appropriate.

a. Compute the anticipated value of the dividends for the next four years. That is, compute D_1, D_2, D_3, and D_4; for Example, D_1 is Rs.3.21 (Rs.3.00 × 1.07).

b. Discount each of these dividends back to present at a discount rate of 14 percent and then sum them.

c. Compute the price of the stock at the end of the fourth year (P_4).

$$P_4 = \frac{D_5}{K_e - g} \quad (D_5 \text{ is equal to } D_4 \text{ times } 1.07)$$

d. After you have computed P_4, discount it back to the present at a discount rate of 14 percent for four years.

e. Add together the answers in part b and part d to get P_0, the current value of the stock. This answer represents the present value of the four periods of dividends, plus the present value of the price of the stock after four periods, (which, in turn, represents the value of all future dividends).

f. Use Formula 10-9 to show that it will provide approximately the same answer as part e.

$$P_0 = \frac{D_1}{K_e - g} \quad (10\text{-}9)$$

For Formula 10-9 use D_1 = 3.21, K_e = 14 percent, and g = 7 percent. (The slight difference between the answers to part e and part f is due to rounding.)

g. If current EPS were equal to Rs. 5.32 and the P/E ratio is 1.1 times higher than the industry average of 8, what would the stock price be?

h. By what dollar amount is the stock price in part g different from the stock price in part of?

i. In regard to the stock price in part f, indicate which direction it would move if (1) D_1 increases, (2) K_e increases, (3) g increases.

a. D1 Rs.3.00 (1.05) = Rs.3.15

D2 Rs.3.15 (1.05) = Rs.3.307

D3 Rs. 3.31 (1.05) = Rs.3.472

b.

	Dividends	PV (12%)	PV of Dividends
D_1	Rs.3.15	.893	Rs.2,813
D_2	Rs.3.307	.797	Rs. 2.636
D_3	Rs.3.472	.712	Rs. 2.472
			Rs.7,921

c. $P_3 = \frac{D_4}{K_e - g}$ $D_4 = Rs.3.472\ (1.05) = Rs.3.646$

$$P_3 = \frac{Rs.3.646}{.12 - .05} = \frac{Rs.3.646}{.07} = Rs.52.086$$

d. PV of P_3 for n = 3, i = 12%

Rs.52.086 × .712 =Rs.37.086

e.

Answer to part b (PV of dividends)	Rs. 7.921
Answer to part d (PV of P_3)	37.086
Current value of the stock	Rs.45.007

f. $P_0 = \frac{D_1}{K_e - g} = \frac{Rs.3.15}{.12 - .05} = \frac{Rs.3.15}{.07} = Rs.45.00$

a. D_1 Rs. 3.00 (1.07) = Rs.3.21

D_2 3.21 (1.07) = Rs.3.435

D_3 3.435 (1.07) = Rs.3.675

D_4 3.675 (1.07) = Rs.3.932

b.

	Dividends	PV (14%)	PV of Dividends
D_1	Rs.3.21	.877	Rs. 2.815
D_2	3.435	.769	2.642
D_3	3.675	.675	2.481
D_4	3.932	.592	2.328
			Rs.10.266

c. $P_4 = \frac{D_5}{K_e - g}$ $\quad D_5 = 3.932\ (1.07) = Rs.4.207$

$= \frac{Rs.4.207}{.07} = Rs.60.10$

d. PV of P_4 for n=4, i=14%

Rs. 60.10 × .592 = 35.579

e. Answer to part b (PV of dividends) 10.266

Answer to part d (PV of P_4) 35.579

Current value of the stock Rs.45.845

f. $P_0 = \frac{D_1}{K_e - g} = \frac{Rs.3.21}{.14 - .07} = \frac{Rs.3.21}{.07} = Rs.45.857$

g. Price = P/E × EPS

P/E = 8 × 1.1 = 8.8

Price = 8.8 × Rs.5.32 = Rs.46.816

h. Part g Rs.46.816

Part f 45.857

.959

i. 1) D_1 increases, stock Price increases
2) K_e increases, stock Price decreases
3) G increases, stock Price increases

Stock valuation with a one year holding period

You expect that GK Corp stock will sell for Rs.25 one year from today. You expect to receive Rs.1.20 in dividends over the year you hold this stock. For a 15% required rate of return for this stock, how much should you pay for it? What is your projected capital gain?

Stock valuation with a two-year holding period

You expect to sell My Co for Rs.28 two years from today. You expect to receive Rs.1 dividend the first year, and Rs.1.10 dividend the second year. For a 16% discount rate, what is the maximum you should pay for this stock?

Stock valuation with a three-year holding period

What you be willing to pay for a stock which pays Rs.2 dividend the first year, a Rs.2.10 dividend the second year, and Rs.2.21 in the third year if you will sell the stock for Rs.40 after three years? Discount rate is 13%.

Example: According to the dividend discount or constant growth model, calculate the required rate of return for The Walt Disney Co. at a current price of Rs.35 per share, a projected dividend of 354 per share, projected dividend growth of 11% per year.

$$k = D_1/P_0 + g = \text{Rs.}0.35/\text{Rs.}35 + 11\% = 12\%.$$

Example: Wal-Mart Stores, Inc. (WMT) recently sold forRs.55 per share and paid aRs.0.93 dividend. If the dividend is expected to grow at 13% per year, use the constant growth model to calculate the expected rate of return.

From the constant growth model, the E(R) = 14.9% on WMT:

$$P_0 = D_0 (1 + g)/ (k - g)$$

$$\text{Rs.}55 = (\text{Rs.}0.93 \times 1.13)/ (k - 0.13)$$

Rearranging gives:

$$k - 0.13 = \$1.05/55$$

$$k = 1.9\% + 13\%$$

$$= 14.9\%$$

Example: Suppose a fast-growing company paid aRs.1 dividend per share this year that is expected to grow by 20% for three years. Afterwards, the dividend growth rate will be 7% per year indefinitely. If the required rate of is 9%, calculate the value of this stock.

$$P_0 = \frac{1.00(1+0.20)}{1+0.09} + \frac{1.00(1+0.20)^2}{(1+0.09)^2} + \frac{1.00(1+0.20)^3 + \dfrac{1.00(1+0.20)^3(1+0.07)}{0.09-0.07}}{(1+0.09)^3}$$

$$= \frac{1.20}{1.09} + \frac{1.44}{1.188} + \frac{1.728 + \dfrac{1.849}{0.02}}{1.295} = 1.101 + 1.212 + 72.724 = \$75.04$$

Example: According to Rama Finance, non-dividend paying Ranga recently had a book value per share of Rs.77.58 and was expected to earn Rs. 24.70 per share during the coming year. Calculate the company's retention rate, ROE, and the amount of sustainable growth.

Retention rate = 1 – Dividends/EPS

= 1 – Rs.0.00/Rs.24.70

= 100%

ROE = EPS/Book value

= Rs.24.70/Rs.77.58

= 31.8%

Sustainable growth = Retention rate H ROE

= 100% H 31.8%

= 31.8%

Vamsi Technologies (VT) earned Rs.4.27 in 2013. At that time, The Value Line Investment Survey projected five-year EPS growth of 13% and a typical P/E ratio of 16. Compute the stock price projected for VT in five years.

If VT grows EPS of Rs4.27 at an annual growth rate of 13%, the company will earn Rs.3.46 per share in five years and, at 16 times earnings, sell for 125.88:

$$\begin{aligned} P_5 &= EPS_5 \times P/E \\ &= EPS_0 \times (1+g)^5 \times P/E \\ &= Rs.4.27 \times (1.13)^5 \times 16 \\ &= Rs.125.88 \end{aligned}$$

Variable Growth Model Example

- Estimate the current value of Morris Industries' common stock, P_0
- Assume:
  - The most recent annual dividend payment of Morris Industries wasRs.4 per share.
  - Investors expect that these dividends will increase at an 8% annual rate over the next 3 years.
  - After three years, dividend growth will level out at 5%.
  - The firm's required return, is 12%.

For example, if ABC Company pays a 25 cent dividend every month and the required rate of return is 6% per year, then the expected value of the stock, using the dividend discount approach, would beRs.0.25/0.005 =Rs.50. The discount rate was divided by 12 to get 0.005, but you could also use the yearly dividend of (0.25*12) Rs.3 and divide it by the yearly discount rate of 0.06 to getRs.50. The point is that each issued dividend payment in the future needs to be discounted back to the present and each value is then added together.

$$V = \frac{D_1}{1+r} + \frac{D_2}{(1+r)^2} + \frac{D_3}{(1+r)^3} + \cdots + \frac{D_n}{(1+r)^n}$$

Where:

V = the value

D_1 = the dividend next period

r = the required rate of return

CONSIDERATIONS

Although the preferred shares give a dividend, which is usually guaranteed, the payment can be cut if there are not enough earnings to accommodate a distribution. This risk of a cut payment needs to be accounted for. This risk increases as the payout ratio (dividend payment compared to earnings) gets higher. Also, if the dividend has a chance of growing, the value of the shares will be higher than the result of the constant dividend calculation. Preferred shares usually lack the voting rights of common shares. This might be a valuable feature to individuals who own large amounts of shares, but for the average investor this voting right does not have much value. However, it still needs to be accounted for when evaluating the marketability of preferred shares.

Preferred shares have an implied value similar to a bond. This means the value will also move inversely with interest rates. When the interest rate goes up, the value of the preferred shares will go down, holding everything else constant. This is to account for other investment opportunities and is reflected in the discount rate used.

CALLABLE

If the preferred shares are callable, the company gains a benefit and the purchaser should pay less, compared to if there was no call provision. The call provision allows the company to basically take the shares off of the market at a predetermined price. A company might add to this if the current market interest rates are high (requiring a higher dividend payment) and the company expects the interest rates to go down. This is a benefit to the issuing company, because they can essentially issue new shares at a lower dividend payment. (Due to their lowered price, callable shares pose risk: read Bond Call Features: Don't Get Caught Off Guard.)

GROWING DIVIDEND

If the dividend has a history of predictable growth, or the company states a constant growth will occur, you need to account for this. The calculation is known as the Gordon Growth Model.

$$V = \frac{D}{(r - g)}$$

The added g is the growth of the payments. By subtracting the growth number, the cash flows are discounted by a lower number resulting in a higher value. Preferred shares are a type of equity investment, which provide a steady stream of income and potential appreciation. Both of these features need to be taken into account when attempting to determine value. Calculations using the dividend discount model are difficult because of the assumptions involved, such as the required rate of return and the growth or length of higher returns. The dividend payment is usually easy to find; the difficult part comes when this payment is changing or potentially could change in the future. Also, finding a proper discount rate is very difficult and if this figure is off, it could drastically change the calculated value of the shares. When it comes to classroom homework, these numbers will be simply given, but in the real world we are left to estimate the discount rate or pay a company to do the calculation.

Earnings per Share (EPS): EPS is the total net income of the company divided by the number of shares outstanding. They usually have a GAAP EPS number (which means that it is computed using all of mutually ssagreed upon accounting rules) and a Pro Forma EPS figure (which means that they have adjusted the income to exclude any one-time items as well as some non-cash items like amortization of goodwill or stock option expenses). The most important thing to look for in the EPS figure is the overall quality of earnings. Make sure the company is not trying to manipulate their EPS numbers to make it look like they are more profitable. Also, look at the growth in EPS over the past several quarters / years to understand how volatile their EPS is, and to see if they are an underachiever or an overachiever. In other words, have they consistently beaten expectations or are they constantly restating and lowering their forecasts?

The EPS number that most analysts use is the pro forma EPS. To compute this number, use the net income that excludes any one-time gains or losses and excludes any non-cash expenses like stock options or amortization of goodwill. Then divide this number by the number of fully diluted shares outstanding. You can easily find historical EPS figures and to see forecasts for the next 1–2 years by visiting free financial sites such as Yahoo Finance (enter the ticker and then click on "estimates").

By doing your fundamental investment research you'll be able to arrive at your own EPS forecasts, which you can then apply to the other valuation techniques below.

Price to Earnings (P/E): Now that you have several EPS figures (historical and forecasts), you'll be able to look at the most common valuation technique used by analysts, the price to earnings ratio, or P/E. To compute this figure, take the stock price and divide it by the annual EPS figure. For example, if the stock is trading at Rs.10 and the EPS is Rs.0.50, the P/E is 20 times. To get a good feeling of what P/E multiple a stock trades at, be sure to look at the historical and forward ratios.

Historical P/Es are computed by taking the current price divided by the sum of the EPS for the last four quarters, or for the previous year. You should also look at the historical trends of the P/E by viewing a chart of its historical P/E over the last several years (you can find on most finance sites like Yahoo Finance). Specifically, you want to find out what range the P/E has traded in so that you can determine if the current P/E is high or low versus its historical average.

Forward P/Es reflect the future growth of the company into the figure. Forward P/Es are computed by taking the current stock price divided by the sum of the EPS estimates for the next four quarters, or for the EPS estimate for next calendar of fiscal year or two.

P/Es change constantly. If there is a large price change in a stock you are watching, or if the earnings (EPS) estimates change, the ratio is recomputed.

Growth Rate. Valuations rely very heavily on the expected growth rate of a company. One must look at the historical growth rate of both sales and income to get a feeling for the type of future growth expected. However, companies are constantly changing, as well as the economy, so solely using historical growth rates to predict the future is not an acceptable form of valuation. Instead, they are used as guidelines for what future growth could look like if similar circumstances are encountered by the company. Calculating the future growth rate requires personal investment research. This may take form in listening to the company's quarterly conference call or reading press release or other company article that discusses the company's growth guidance. However, although companies are in the best position to forecast their own growth, they are far from accurate, and unforeseen events could cause rapid changes in the economy and in the company's industry.

And for any valuation technique, it's important to look at a range of forecast values. For example, if the company being valued has been growing earnings between 5 and 10% each year for the last 5 years, but believes that it will grow 15 - 20% this year, a more conservative growth rate of 10 - 15% would be appropriate in valuations. Another example would be for a company that has been going through restructuring. They may have been growing earnings at 10 - 15% over the past several quarters / years because of cost cutting, but their sales growth could be only 0 - 5%. This would signal that their earnings growth will probably slow when the cost cutting has fully taken effect. Therefore, forecasting an earnings growth closer to the 0 - 5% rate would be more appropriate rather than the 15 - 20%. Nonetheless, the growth rate method of valuations relies heavily on gut feel to make a forecast. This is why analysts often make inaccurate forecasts, and also why familiarity with a company is essential before making a forecast.

Example: In mid-2013, banking giant Citigroup, Inc. (C) sold for a market price of Rs.19.30 per share, had 2013expected earnings per share of Rs.2.70, and a projected dividend of Rs.1.28. Calculate Citigroup’s forward-looking P/E ratio and projected dividend yield

Forward P/E ratio= Stock price/Projected EPS
= Rs.19.30/Rs.2.70
= 7.14

Projected dividend yield = Projected dividend/Stock price
= Rs.1.28/Rs.19.30
= 6.63%

Price Earnings to Growth (PEG) Ratio: This valuation technique has really become popular over the past decade or so. It is better than just looking at a P/E because it takes three factors into account; the price, earnings, and earnings growth rates. To compute the PEG ratio, divide the Forward P/E by the expected earnings growth rate (you can also use historical P/E and historical growth rate to see where it's traded in the past). This will yield a ratio that is usually expressed as a percentage. The theory goes that as the percentage rises over 100% the stock becomes more and more overvalued, and as the PEG ratio falls below 100% the stock becomes more and more undervalued. The theory is based on a belief that P/E ratios should approximate the long-term growth rate of a company's earnings. Whether or not this is true will never be proven and the theory is therefore just a rule of thumb to use in the overall valuation process.

Here's an example of how to use the PEG ratio. Say you are comparing two stocks that you are thinking about buying. Stock A is trading at a forward P/E of 15 and expected to grow at 20%. Stock B is trading at a forward P/E of 30 and expected to grow at 25%. The

PEG ratio for Stock A is 75% (15/20) and for Stock B is 120% (30/25). According to the PEG ratio, Stock A is a better purchase because it has a lower PEG ratio, or in other words, you can purchase its future earnings growth for a lower relative price than that of Stock B.

Return on Invested Capital (ROIC): This valuation technique measures how much money the company makes each year per dollar of invested capital. Invested Capital is the amount of money invested in the company by both stockholders and debtors. The ratio is expressed as a percent and you should look for a percent that approximates the level of growth that you expect. In its simplest definition, this ratio measures the investment return that management is able to get for its capital. The higher the number, the better the return.

To compute the ratio, take the pro forma net income (same one used in the EPS figure mentioned above) and divide it by the invested capital. Invested capital can be estimated by adding together the stockholder's equity, the total long- and short-term debt and accounts payable, and then subtracting accounts receivable and cash (all of these numbers can be found on the company's latest quarterly balance sheet). This ratio is much more useful when you compare it to other companies that you are valuing.

Return on Assets (ROA): Similar to ROIC, ROA, expressed as a percent, measures the company's ability to make money from its assets. To measure the ROA, take the pro forma net income divided by the total assets. However, because of very common irregularities in balance sheets (due to things like Goodwill, write-offs, discontinuations, etc.) this ratio is not always a good indicator of the company's potential. If the ratio is higher or lower than you expected, be sure to look closely at the assets to see what could be over or understating the figure.

Price to Sales (P/S): This figure is useful because it compares the current stock price to the annual sales. In other words, it tells you how much the stock costs per dollar of sales earned. To compute it, take the current stock price divided by the annual sales per share. The annual sales per share should be calculated by taking the net sales for the last four quarters divided by the fully diluted shares outstanding (both of these figures can be found by looking at the press releases or quarterly reports). The price to sales ratio is useful, but it does not take into account any debt the company has. For example, if a company is heavily financed by debt instead of equity, then the sales per share will seem high (the P/S will be lower). All things equal, a lower P/S ratio is better. However, this ratio is best looked at when comparing more than one company.

Market Cap: Market Cap, which is short for Market Capitalization, is the value of all of the company's stock. To measure it, multiply the current stock price by the fully diluted shares outstanding. Remember, the market cap is only the value of the stock. To get a more complete picture, you'll want to look at the Enterprise Value.

Enterprise Value (EV): Enterprise Value is equal to the total value of the company, as it is trading for on the stock market. To compute it, add the market cap (see above) and the total net debt of the company. The total net debt is equal to total long- and short-term debt plus accounts payable, minus accounts receivable, minus cash. The Enterprise Value is the best approximation of what a company is worth at any point in time because it takes into account the actual stock price instead of balance sheet prices. When analysts say that a company is a "billion dollar" company, they are often referring to its total enterprise value. Enterprise Value fluctuates rapidly based on stock price changes.

EV to Sales: This ratio measures the total company value as compared to its annual sales. A high ratio means that the company's value is much more than its sales. To compute it, divide the EV by the net sales for the last four quarters. This ratio is especially useful when valuing companies that do not have earnings, or that are going through unusually rough times. For example, if a company is facing restructuring and it is currently losing money, then the P/E ratio would be irrelevant. However, by applying an EV to Sales ratio, you could compute what that company could trade for when its restructuring is over and its earnings are back to normal.

EBITDA: EBITDA stands for earnings before interest, taxes, depreciation and amortization. It is one of the best measures of a company's cash flow and is used for valuing both public and private companies. To compute EBITDA, use a company's income statement, take the net income and then add back interest, taxes, depreciation, amortization and any other non-cash or one-time charges. This leaves you with a number that approximates how much cash the company is producing. EBITDA is a very popular figure because it can easily be compared across companies, even if all of the companies are not profitable.

EV to EBITDA. This is perhaps one of the best measurements of whether or not a company is cheap or expensive. To compute, divide the EV by EBITDA (see above for calculations). The higher the number, the more expensive the company is. However, remember that more expensive companies are often valued higher because they are growing faster or because they are a higher quality company. With that said, the best way to use EV/EBITDA is to compare it to that of other similar companies.

APPROXIMATE VALUATION APPROACHES

Average growth approximation: Assuming that two stocks have the same earnings growth, the one with a lower P/E is a better value. The P/E method is perhaps the most commonly used valuation method in the stock brokerage industry. By using comparison firms, a target price/earnings (or P/E) ratio is selected for the company, and then the future earnings of the company are estimated. The valuation's fair price is simply estimated earnings times target P/E. This model is essentially the same model as Gordon's model, if k-g is estimated as the dividend payout ratio (D/E) divided by the target P/E ratio.

Constant growth approximation: The Gordon model or Gordon's growth model is the best known of a class of discounted dividend models. It assumes that dividends will increase at a constant growth rate (less than the discount rate) forever. The valuation is given by the formula:

$$P = D \cdot \sum_{i=1}^{\infty} \left(\frac{1+g}{1+k} \right)^i = D \cdot \frac{1+g}{k-g}.$$

And the following table defines each symbol:

Symbol	Meaning	Units
P	estimated stock price	Rs.
D	last dividend paid	Rs.
k	discount rate	%
g	the growth rate of the dividends	%

Limited high-growth period approximation: When a stock has a significantly higher growth rate than its peers, it is sometimes assumed that the earnings growth rate will be sustained for a short time (say, 5 years), and then the growth rate will revert to the mean. This is probably the most rigorous approximation that is practical. While these DCF models are commonly used, the uncertainty in these values is hardly ever discussed. Note that the models diverge for $k = g$ and hence are extremely sensitive to the difference of dividend growth to discount factor. One might argue that an analyst can justify any value (and that would usually be one close to the current price supporting his call) by fine-tuning the growth/discount assumptions.

IMPLIED GROWTH MODELS

One can use the Gordon model or the limited high-growth period approximation model to impute an implied growth estimate. To do this, one takes the average P/E and average growth for a comparison index, uses the current (or forward) P/E of the stock in question, and calculates what growth rate would be needed for the two valuation equations to be equal. This gives you an estimate of the "break-even" growth rate for the stock's current P/E ratio. (Note: we are using earnings not dividends here because dividend policies vary and may be influenced by many factors including tax treatment).

IMPUTED GROWTH ACCELERATION RATIO

Subsequently, one can divide this imputed growth estimate by recent historical growth rates. If the resulting ratio is greater than one, it implies that the stock would need to experience accelerated growth relative to its prior recent historical growth to justify its current P/E (higher values suggest potential overvaluation). If the resulting ratio is less than one, it implies that either the market expects growth to slow for this stock or that the stock could sustain its current P/E with lower than historical growth (lower values suggest potential undervaluation). Comparison of the IGAR across stocks in the same industry may give estimates of relative value. IGAR averages across an industry may give estimates of relative expected changes in industry growth (eg. the market's imputed expectation that an industry is about to "take-off" or stagnate). Naturally, any differences in IGAR between stocks in the same industry may be due to differences in fundamentals, and would require further specific analysis.

MARKET CRITERIA (POTENTIAL PRICE)

Some feel that if the stock is listed in a well-organized stock market, with a large volume of transactions, the listed price will be close to the estimated fair value. This is called the efficient market hypothesis. On the other hand, studies made in the field of behavioral finance tend to show that deviations from the fair price are rather common, and sometimes quite large. Thus, in addition to fundamental economic criteria, market criteria also have to be taken into account market-based valuation. Valuing a stock is not only to estimate its fair value, but also to determine its potential price range, taking into account market behavior aspects. One of the behavioral valuation tools is the stock image, a coefficient that bridges the theoretical fair value and the market price

DIVIDEND GROWTH MODEL

The common stock valuation formula used by this stock valuation calculator is based on the dividend growth model, which is just one of several stock valuation models used by investors to determine how much they should be willing to pay for various stocks.

The dividend growth model for common stock valuation assumes that dividends will be paid, and also assumes that dividends will grow at a constant pace for an indefinite period of time. Of course, neither of these assumptions rarely, if ever, occur in real life.

To Calculate the Value of Stocks

To determine the value of a common stock using the dividend growth model, you first determine the future dividend by multiplying the current dividend by the decimal equivalent of the growth percentage (dividend x (1 + growth rate)).

Lastly, the future dividend is divided by the difference between the decimal equivalent of expected rate of return and the decimal equivalent of the growth percentage (future dividend ÷ (expected rate of return - growth rate)).

What is Required Rate of Return?

Unlike bonds, where the risk of principal loss is minimal and dividends are paid on a fixed percentage, stocks come with an increased risk of losing your principal and stock dividends are never guaranteed and the dividend per share is not fixed. These added risks and uncertainties of investing in stocks explains why investors expect to earn a better return on investment on stocks than they do on bonds. In other words, more risk equates to a higher expected rate of return. This difference between a low-risk expected rate of return (such as the T-Bill rate), and the higher expected rate of return that comes from increased risk is often referred to as the risk premium.

Risk premium can be thought of as the percentage that would need to be added to a risk-free return on investment in order to entice an investor into investing in the risky investment being offered. Once this percentage is added, the result is referred to as the required rate of return.

With that, let's use the Stock Price Calculator to calculate the maximum price you could pay for a given stock and still earn your required rate of return.

MULTIPLE CHOICE QUESTIONS

1. The growth in book value per share shows the
   a. Rise in the share prices
   b. Increase in the physical assets of the firm.
   c. Increase in the net worth.
   d. Growth in reserves
2. A common stock pay-out ratio
   a. Is directly related to the company s growth rate.
   b. Can be zero for a growth firm
   c. Measures the earnings of shares as a percentage of its market price.
   d. Indicates the future cash dividends to be expected.
3. The price earnings ratio of a stock reflects
   a. The growth of the company
   b. The market mood for the company's stock
   c. The earnings retained and invested in the company
   d. The dividend paid ou for the company s stock
4. The market value of the scrip is determined by
   a. The dividend declared by the company.
   b. The present status of the stock market.
   c. The number of floating shares
   d. The interaction of demand and supply.
5. In the stock market psychology
   a. Investors forget the past b. History repeats itself
   c. More faith in future prediction d. A and B
6. Investors invest more in stocks during them
   a. Early career period.
   b. Mid-career level.
   c. Retirement stage with huge money.
   d. All the above-mentioned period
7. Many stock analysts assume that a mispriced stock will
   a. Immediately return to its intrinsic value.
   b. Gradually approach its intrinsic value over several years.
   c. Never return to its intrinsic value.
   d. Return to its intrinsic value within a few days.

8. Given the above information, what is the most you would pay today for Shoppers D-Mart's stock?
   a. Rs.60.40.
   b. Rs. 55.55.
   c. Rs. 53.13.
   d. Rs. 43.13.
   e. None of the above.

9. What is the expected dividend to be paid in three years if yesterday's dividend was $6.00, dividends are expected to grow at a constant 6% annual rate, and the firm has a 10% expected return.
   a. $6.75.
   b. $7.15.
   c. $7.80.
   d. $9.37.
   e. None of the above.

10. What dividend yield would be reported in the financial press for a stock that currently pays a Rs. 1 dividend per quarter and the most recent stock price was Rs.40?
    a. 2.5%.
    b. 4.0%.
    c. 10.0%.
    d. 15.0%.
    e. None of the above.

11. A stock will pay a dividend this year of Rs.2.40 per share. Its dividend yield is 8 percent. At what price is the stock selling?
    a. Rs.10.00.
    b. Rs.15.00.
    c. Rs.20.00.
    d. Rs.30.00.
    e. None of the above.

12. Which of the following might be interpreted as a signed that stock price is currently too high?
    a. An abnormally low dividend yield.
    b. A high E/P ratio.
    c. A low book value per share.
    d. A low P/E ratio.
    e. None of the above.

13. Hydro One is a regulated utility company that provides transmission and distribution of electricity in Ontario. Suppose Hydro One plans to pay Rs.2.30 per share in dividends in the coming year. If investors require a return of 7% and dividends are expected to grow by 2% per year in the future, calculate the market price of Hydro One's stock.
    a. 56.20%.
    b. 46.00%.
    c. 40.60%.
    d. 39.90%.
    e. None of the above.

14. Overland has just paid a dividend of Rs.2.25. These dividends are expected to grow at a rate of 5% in the foreseeable future. The risk of this company suggests that future cash how's should be discounted at a rate of 11%. What should be paid for Overland common stock?

    a. Rs. 49.32.
    b. Rs. 37.50.
    c. Rs. 21.48.
    d. Rs.39.37.
    e. None of the above.

15. Consider a company that is not currently paying dividends. You predict that in five years, the company will pay a dividend for the first time. The dividend will be Rs.0.50 per share. You expect this dividend to grow at 10 percent indefinitely. The required return on companies such as this one is 20 percent. What is the price of the stock today?

    a. Rs.3.54.
    b. Rs.2.41.
    c. Rs.4.25.
    d. Rs.6.23.
    e. None of the above.

A firm projects growth of 20 percent per year for 4 years. By then the sustainable growth rate will fall to 5 percent. The most recent annual dividend was *DI\o* = $1.00 per share.

16. Given the above information, what is the current stock price, if the discount rate is 10 percent?

    a. Rs.53.45.
    b. Rs.40.28.
    c. Rs.38.27.
    d. Rs.34.74.
    e. None of the above.

17. Given the above information, what is the dividend yield, $DIVi/P_0$?

    a. 13.45%.
    b. 10.28%.
    c. 8.27%.
    d. 3.45%.
    e. None of the above.

The following situation concerns questions 18-20.

A company is expected to pay a dividend of Rs.1.50 at the end of this year, Rs.2.00 dividend at the end of year 2, and Rs.2.30 dividend at the end of year 3. It is estimated that dividends will grow at a constant rate of 5 percent per year thereafter. Investors require a return of 10 percent.

18. Given the above information, what would be the dividend at the end of year

    a. Rs.5,405.
    b. Rs.4,554.
    c. Rs.3,130.
    d. Rs.2,415.
    e. None of the above.

19. Given the above information, what would be the expected price of this company's common stock at the end of year 3?

    a. Rs. 48.30. b. Rs. 45.54.
    c. Rs. 43.13. d. Rs. 0.45.
    e. None of the above.

20. Given the above information, what is the current market value of this company's common stock?

    a. 47.30. b. Rs.45.54.
    c. Rs.43.13. d. Rs. 41.03.
    e. None of the above.

21. Dividends that are expected to be paid far into the future have:

    a. Great impact on current stock price, due to their expected size.
    b. Equal impact on current stock price as near-term dividends.
    c. Lesser impact on current stock price due to discounting.
    d. No impact on current stock price because they are uncertain.
    e. None of the above.

22. A company's shares are selling for Rs.20 each in the market. The company's earnings per share (*EPS*\) is expected to be Rs.1.50 next year, and the required return on the shares is estimated to be 10 percent. What is the present value of growth opportunities (PVGO) per share?

    a. Rs.5. b. Rs.6.
    c. Rs.7. d. Rs.11.
    e. None of the above.

23. Suppose furniture manufacturer Herman Miller, Inc., has estimated earnings per share of Rs.1.38. If the average price-earnings (P/E) ratio of comparable furniture stocks is 21.3, estimate the value for Herman Miller stock.

    a. Rs.45.40. b. Rs. 38.55.
    c. Rs. 35.28. d. Rs. 29.39.
    e. None of the above.

24. A company pays out all of its earnings as dividends. It will pay its next Rs.4 per share dividend in a year. The discount rate is 12 percent. What is the price- earning (P/E) ratio of the company?

    a. 8.33. b. 5.12.
    c. 3.76. d. 11.30.
    e. None of the above.

25. Determine the required rate of return on preferred shares that provide a Rs.6 annual dividend if they are presently selling for Rs. 70.

    a. 4.57%. b. 5.98%.
    c. 6.45%. d. 8.57%.
    e. None of the above.

26. A company has issued preferred stock with a Rs.9 annual dividend that will be paid in perpetuity. What is the dividend yield on the stock if the discount rate is 10 percent?

    a. 10%. b. 13%.
    c. 14%. d. 16%.
    e. None of the above.

27. Preferred stock is:

    a. An example of a consol.
    b. Issued by corporations and usually pays a fixed dividend
    c. Issued by government agencies.
    d. Both (A) and (B).
    e. Both ((A) and (C).

The following information involves questions 28-29

You have Rs.10,000 to invest and are considering either a consol (a perpetual bond) or preferred shares of Canada Leasing. The consol has a Rs. 1,000 par value, an annual coupon rate of 4 percent, and never matures. The preferred share pays fixed dividends of $6 and is expected to continue indefinitely. Currently, the consol is selling for Rs,800 and the preferred share for Rs.120.

28. What is the expected rate of return on the consol?

    a. 9.43%. b. 8.59%.
    c. 7.00%. d. 5.00%.
    e. None of the above.

29. What is the expected rate of return on the preferred shares?

    a. 3.00%. b. 4.55%.
    c. 5.00%. d. 7.82%.
    e. None of the above.

30. If dividends on a common stock are expected to grow at a constant rate forever, and if you are told the most recent dividend paid, the dividend growth rate, and the appropriate discount rate today, you can calculate:

    I. the price of the stock today
    II. the dividend that is expected to be paid ten years from now

III. the appropriate discount rate ten years from now

a. I only
b. I and II only
c. I and III only
d. II and III only
e. I, II, and III

31. Which of the following statements is true?

I. The dividend growth model holds only if the dividend growth rate exceeds the stock's required return.

II. An increase in the dividend growth rate will increase a stock's market value, all else the same.

III. An increase in the required return on a stock will increase its market value, all else the same.

a. I only
b. II only
c. III only
d. I and III only
e. I, II, and III

32. Which of the following is false regarding the differences between debt and common stock?

a. Equity is ownership in a firm but debt is not.
b. Stockholders have voting power while creditors usually do not.
c. Periodic payments made to either class of security are tax deductible for the issuer.
d. Interest payments are legally binding while dividend payments generally are not.

33. Preferred stock is much like debt in that:

I. The payments on both are tax-deductible to the issuing firm.

II. Neither security is protected in the event of non-payment of promised cash flows.

III. Neither security participates in any unexpected profits the firm generates.

a. I only
b. II only
c. III only
d. I and II only
e. I and III only

34. What would you pay for a share of ABC Corporation stock today if the dividend one year from now will be Rs.3 per share and you can sell the stock (after you receive the dividend) for Rs.90 a year from today. Assume your required return is 15%.

a. Rs.78.26
b. Rs.80.87
c. Rs.82.56
d. Rs.90.00
e. Rs.98.12

35. The dividend on Simple Motors common stock will be Rs.3 in 1 year, Rs.4.25 in 2 years, and Rs.6.00 in 3 years. You can sell the stock, after you receive the dividend, for Rs.100 at the end of 3 years. If you require a 12% return on your investment, how much would you be willing to pay for a share of this stock today?

    a. Rs.75.45 b. Rs.77.24
    c. Rs.81.52 d. Rs.85.66

36. A stock that pays a constant dividend of Rs.1.50 forever currently sells for Rs.10.71. What is the required rate of return?

    a. 10% b. 12%
    c. 13% d. 14%

37. ABC Company's preferred stock is selling for Rs.30 a share. If the required return is 8%, what will the dividend be two years from now?

    a. Rs.2.00 b. Rs.2.20
    c. Rs.2.40 d. Rs.2.80

38. What would you pay today for a stock that is expected to make a Rs.2 dividend in one year if the expected dividend growth rate is 5% and you require a 12% return on your investment?

    a. Rs.28.57 b. Rs.29.33
    c. Rs.31.43 d. Rs.43.14
    e. Rs.54.30

39. The stock of MTY Golf World currently sells for Rs.90 per share. The firm has a constant dividend growth rate of 6% and just paid a dividend of Rs.5.09. You are unsure about the stock's required rate of return. What will the stock sell for one year from now?

    a. Rs.90.00 b. Rs.93.52
    c. Rs.95.40 d. Rs.99.80
    e. Rs.112.7

40. Llano's stock is currently selling for Rs.40.00. The expected dividend one year from now is Rs.2 and the required return is 13%. What is this firm's dividend growth rate assuming the constant dividend growth model is appropriate?

    a. 8% b. 9%
    c. 10% d. 11%

41. The current price of XYZ stock is Rs.80.00. Dividends are expected to grow at 5% Indefinitely and the most recent dividend was Rs.2.75. What is the required rate of return on XYZ stock?

    a. 7.3% b. 8.6%
    c. 9.5% d. 10.6%
    e. 11.2%

42. ABC Corporation's common stock dividend yield is 3.61%, it just paid a dividend of Rs.2.75, and is expected to pay a dividend of Rs.2.89 one year from now. Dividends are expected to grow at a constant rate indefinitely. What is the required rate of return on ABC stock?

    a. 7.3% b. 8.7%
    c. 9.5% d. 10.6%
    e. 11.2%

43. Suppose NoGro, Inc. has just issued a dividend of Rs.3.25 per share. Subsequent dividends will remain at Rs.3.25 indefinitely. Returns on the stock of firms like NoGro are currently running 10%. What is the value of one share of stock?

    a. Rs.22.50 b. Rs.27.25
    c. Rs.32.50 d. Rs.37.25
    e. Rs.39.75

44. Suppose Pale Hose, Inc. has just paid a dividend of Rs.1.80 per share. Sales and profits for Pale Hose are expected to grow at a rate of 8% per year. Its dividend is expected to grow by the same amount. If the required return is 14%, what is the value of a share of Pale Hose?

    a. Rs.18.00 b. Rs.25.20
    c. Rs.27.80 d. Rs.30.60
    e. Rs.32.40

SHORT ANSWER QUESTIONS

1. Define Common stock.
2. Define Undervalued.
3. Define Overvalued.
4. What is fair value of stock?
5. What are the methods of stock valuation?
6. What is intrinsic value of stock?
7. Define Dividend Discount Model.
8. Define Constant Dividend Growth Rate Model.
9. What is Discounted Cash Flow Model?
10. Define Comparable Method.
11. Define Preferred Stock Valuation.
12. Define Zero Growth Valuation Model.
13. Define Variable Growth Model Example.

14. Define Growing Dividend.
15. Define Earnings per Share (EPS).
16. Define Price to Earnings.
17. Define Price Earnings to Growth (PEG) Ratio.
18. Define Return on Assets.
19. What is Price to Sales?
20. What is Market Cap?
21. What is Enterprise Value?
22. Define Enterprise Value to sales?
23. Define EBITDA.
24. Define Imputed growth acceleration ratio.
25. Define potential price.
26. Define Dividend Growth Model.
27. What is Required Rate of Return?

ESSAY YPE QUESTIONS

1. What do you understand by common stock? Explain the various characteristics of common stock.
2. Critically examine the various approaches tp valuation of common stocks.
3. Describe various approaches that are used for the valuation of common stocks.
4. Write a detailed note regarding the dividend capitalization model for common stock valuation.
5. Explain about dividend capitalization model. State it Assumptions.
6. Write about constant growth model of dividend.
7. P/E ratios are used to estimate value of stocks rather than adopting discounting models. Elaborates.
8. Describe about the various determinants of P/E ratio.

EXERCISE PROBLEMS

1. What is the value of a stock that expects to pay aRs.5.00 dividend next year, and then increase the dividend at a rate of 8% per year, indefinitely? Assume a 11% expected return
2. Sultan & Company forecasts to pay a Rs.5.00 dividend next year, which represents 100% of its earnings. This will provide investors with a 10% expected return. Instead, we decide to plowback 50% of the earnings at the firm's current return on equity of 25%. What is the value of the stock before and after the plowback decision?

3. Required rate of return =19% Current dividend is 2.00 dividends are expected to grow at 14% for first 6 years then at 9%. Present value of First 5-Years' Dividends.
4. Vineeth's Corp. will pay Rs.5 dividend in two year. If investors expect that dividend to remain constant forever, and they require a 12% return on Vineeth's stock, what is the stock worth?
5. Suppose Walmart, just paid a dividend of Rs.55. It is expected to increase its dividend by 4% per year. If the market requires a return of 19% on assets of this risk level, how much the stock should be selling for.
6. Blue Print co. ltd issued preferred stock many years ago. It carries a fixed dividend of Rs. 10 per share. With the passage of time, yields have soared from the original 8 percent to 20 percent (yield is the same as required rate of return).
7. Venus Sportswear Corporation has preferred stock outstanding that pays an annual dividend of Rs. 16. It has a price of Rs.110. What is the required rate of return (yield) on the preferred stock?
8. Bose Technology has preferred stock outstanding that pays a Rs. 24 annual dividends. It has a price of Rs.92. What is the required rate of return (yield) on the preferred stock?
9. Madrick engineering will pay a common stock dividend of Rs.5.20 at the end of the year (D_1). The required return on common stock (K_e) is 19 percent. The firm has a constant growth rate (g) of 10 percent. Compute the current price of the stock (P_0).
10. Virat Steel Company will pay a dividend of Rs. 3.70 per share in the next 16 months (D_1). The required rate of return (K_e) is 12 percent and the constant growth rate is 5percent.
11. Compute P_0. (For parts b, c, and d in this problem all variables remain the same except the one specifically changed. Each question is independent of the others.)
12. Assume K_e, the required rate of return, goes up to 14 percent; what will be the new value of P_0?
13. Assume the growth rate (g) goes up to 9 percent; what will be the new value of P_0?
14. Assume D_1 is Rs. 5, what will be the new value of P_0?
15. Maxwell Communications paid a dividend of Rs. 5 last year. Over the next 18 months, the dividend is expected to grow at 8 percent, which is the constant growth rate for the firm (g). The new dividend after 10 months will represent D_1. The required rate of return (K_e) is 16 percent. Compute the price of the stock (P_0).
16. You expect that GK Corp stock will sell for Rs.45 one year from today. You expect to receive Rs.4.20 in dividends over the year you hold this stock. For a 25% required rate of return for this stock, how much should you pay for it? What is your projected capital gain?

17. Big Stores, recently sold forRs.75 per share and paid aRs.1.33 dividend. If the dividend is expected to grow at 15% per year, use the constant growth model to calculate the expected rate of return.

18. Suppose a fast-growing company paid aRs.3 dividend per share this year that is expected to grow by 25% for three years. Afterwards, the dividend growth rate will be 9% per year indefinitely. If the required rate of is 12%, calculate the value of this stock.

19. Shreya Technologies (ST) earned Rs.6.29 in 2013. At that time, The Value Line Investment Survey projected five-year EPS growth of 14% and a typical P/E ratio of 24. Compute the stock price projected for ST in five years.

MCQs Answers

1	2	3	4	5	6	7	8	9	10	11	12	13	14	15	16	17	18	19	20	21	22	23	24	25
d	b	b	d	d	a	b	e	b	c	d	a	b	d	b	d	d	d	a	d	c	a	d	a	d
26	27	28	29	30	31	32	33	34	35	36	37	38	39	40	41	42	43	44						
a	d	d	c	b	b	c	c	b	c	d	c	a	c	a	b	b	c	e						

CASE STUDIES

CASE STUDY 1

A naive investor wants to analyses the capital structure ABC Company. He has the following information.

ABC Company

	2012	2013	Rs. in million 2014
Long term debt (11%)	12.27	9.46	11.19
Preferred stock	0.13	0.13	0.12
Common stock (par Rs.10)	0.01	0.14	12.6
Capital surplus	5.67	6.35	6.19
Retained earnings	33.93	60.31	125.2
Dividend paid	3.005	3.684	10.8

The present price of ABC Company's share in Mumbai stock market is Rs. 450. There is a rumour in the market that the ABC Company may issue bonus shares shortly. The investors want the answers for the following:

(i) Is there any ground for such rumour?

(ii) Is the capital structure sound?

(iii) Is it proper to purchase the shares?

(iv) Analyze the given data and advise the naive investor.

CASE STUDY 2

Ragav is an Investment consultant with rich experience in equity research and portfolio management. He was requested by a client to give a presentation on equity valuation. You as an executive assistant prepare for him the following:

- Brief explanation of different types of Equity Valuation Models.
- How is Dividend Discount and Constant Growth Model valued?
- Calculation of required rate of return on the client firm's stock. Assume that the risk-free rate is 7% and the market premium is 6% and stock's beta is 1.2.
- Assume that the firm is a constant growth company which paid a dividend of Rs5 last year and the dividend is expected to grow at the rate of 10% forever. What is the expected value of the stock a year from now?
- If the stock is currently selling for Rs110, what is the expected rate of return on the stock?

CASE STUDY 3

Paint industry growth was at a rate of 12% during 1995-96. The industry as a whole will continue its grow at not less than 8-10% rate in the coming years. Asian Paints is the leader in decorative paints, controlling 45% of market segment of the total of Rs. 1,800 crore paints and varnishes industry. In industrial paints, it is the largest player with a market share of 14%.

With a low per capita consumption of paints in our country, it has good future prospects. The prospects for exports are good with an actual export of Rs. 16 crores in 1995-96. The users in industrial sector, namely, automobiles and its accessories, Household appliances and consumer durables etc. are showing prospects of rapid growth Thus, the potential for the industry both in the domestic and export sector is good.

Asian Paints that is a leader in this industry has an installed capacity of 1.08 lakh T.P.A. of Paints enamels and varnishes. Its gross block grew from Rs. 123 crores in 1993-94 to Rs. 187 crores in 1995-96, due to continuous expansion of capacity. The sales turnover recorded a compound growth rate of 13.5% p.a. during the last five years, while its net profit grew faster by 27.5 % during the same period. This company has many plus factors:

Good Collaborator namely, Chemische Werke Hals A.G. Germany for manufacture of Vinyl Pyrdine Latex and PPG Industries Inc. USA, for electro deposition coating on automobiles.

1. Product differentiation and brand image is secured by Asian Paints by spending only
2. 1.5% of revenue on advertisements to testing the quality, availability and dependability.
3. Plants well distributed geographically.
4. Six joint collaborations in foreign countries and good export growth

Asian Paints is one of the three winners of the ET - Harward Business School Association of India awards for its performance in 1994-95. The measures used by them are as follows:

Financial Ratios of the Company

Gross Profits / Total assets	21.36%
Retained Profits/Net worth	18.24%
Net Profit / Net Worth	25.96%

Growth in Market Cap / Growth in Net worth (over 5 years) 1.60 Cash flow to gross assets 20.64

Example of Company Analysis

It is necessary to analyze the financial data of the company in the background of the industry performance as shown below:

The data relates to 1996, but that may not matter as it is for illustration. Only selected companies are studied above. The debt-equity ratio representing leverage is good for NOCIL and Cochin Refineries. But PAT to NW is higher and the actual market price is covered by book value three times in the case of of Cochin Refineries As compared to the industry averages, although the gross profit margin is lower, capital efficiency is higher, and P/E ratio is lowest indicating that a multiple of 7 of price to earnings exhibits some potential for capital appreciation in the case of Cochin Refineries. Besides, examine the date of Gross Block, NW, Sales, Gross and Net Profits and their growth rates over a period of 5 years. Then assess whether the company's EPS and P/E ratios are better than the average industry performance and whether the scrip is underpriced or overpriced and buy only if it is underpriced with growth prospects or is fairly priced for its fundamentals. In the above example, Cochin Refineries is the best buy at its price.

How to Pick Up Growth Shares?

The growth companies are also called blue chip companies. The blue chips of yesteryears are not necessarily the blue chips of today. The investor has to review and assess the companies from time to tie to locate the blue chips, based on fundamental analysis, in order to enable one to identify these blue chips of tomorrow, one should know the nature and characteristics of these companies. A few guidelines in this regard are set out below.

Firstly, the management should be experienced and efficient; they should have the honesty, integrity and vision for expansion and growth. Such is the case with Ambani's, Tatas and Birlas.

Secondly, the market share of the company should be substantial and at least more than one- third. The larger the share, the better the prospects of controlling the market and profit margins and expanding the operations. Bajaj Auto has a share of two-thirds in the two-wheeler and three-wheeler market. So is the case with Asian Paints, Laxmi Machine Works etc.

Thirdly, the company must be well diversified into areas of growth potential. The growth potential changes from time to time. At present, industries with a growth potential are cement, paper, petrochemicals, etc. Thus, a company with a good diversification into such growth areas would does well in sales, profits, and earnings. Some of the consumer product industries producing soaps, cosmetics, toothpaste and powders etc. would generally record a consistent growth. A well-diversified company like L & T, Hindustan Lever, or Century Textiles is a good buy at any reasonable price.

Fourthly, the company's policy of expansion should be consistent and has a long-term perspective. Its assets growth should be reasonably good, reflecting its expansion goals. Growth helps the industry to stabilize its earnings from undue fluctuations and help the diversification process. The companies with a good asset growth are Reliance, L & T. GSFC etc.

Fifthly, the company should have a consistent and stable distribution policy with good profit margins. The company should distribute a reasonable proportion of its profits as dividends, bonus etc. Such companies like Ponds, Colgate, Glaxo etc., would be in good demand, as investors prefer regular dividend-paying companies.

Sixthly, such a company services the investors well with bonus or rights issue or convertible debentures, from time to time in addition to increasing dividend payments. The financial structure and utilization of capital are efficient. The profit margins are growing and the company is gaining in financial strength.

Lastly, the industry or industries in which the company is operating should have good growth prospects Pharmaceuticals, Biotech or multimedia. The products should be in continuous demand like food products, paper soaps, etc. or consumer non-durable goods. The future outlook of the company and prospects of the industry are interlinked. the prospects would depend also on the government policy and whether it is subject to price and distribution control or any restrictions or regulations. The prospects of the industry in which the company is operating should be assessed from all points of view. Thus, in the choice of blue chips, the investor has to examine the fundamentals of the companies through balance sheet analysis for a period of at least five years before finally selecting the shares. The time of purchase should be decided on the basis of technical analysis referred to later. But for a layman, the purchase time should be in the bearish phase of the market, when an all-round decline in prices is recorded. At such times, the companies with strong fundamentals should be picked up at low prices for long-term investment if they can be classified as blue chips as per the above guidelines.

Questions

- Explain the relationship between the price and the yield?
- How can we pick a higher return security?

CHAPTER 12

Bond/Debenture Valuation

DEFINITIONS AND CHARACTERISTICS OF BONDS/DEBENTURE

Bonds are securities that represent a loan. They can be issued by a company or by a State. These securities give rise to regular payment of coupons, which constitute the interest on the loan, and redemption of the security at maturity. The cash flow is therefore known in advance. Bonds represent an investment that is less risky than equities, but also less lucrative over the long term.

A bond/debenture is a long-term promissory note that promises to pay the bondholder a predetermined, fixed amount of interest each year until maturity. At maturity, the principal will be paid to the bondholder. In the case of a firm's insolvency, a bondholder has a priority of claim to the firm's assets before the preferred and common stockholders. Also, bondholders must be paid interest due them before dividends can be distributed to the stockholders. A bond's par value is the amount that will be repaid by the firm when the bond matures. The contractual agreement of the bond specifies a coupon interest rate that is expressed either as a percent of the par value or as a flat amount of interest which the borrowing firm promises to pay the bondholder each year. For example: A Rs. 1.00 par value bond specifying a coupon interest rate of 9 percent is equivalent to an annual interest payment of Rs. 9. The bond has a maturity date, at which time the borrowing firm is committed to repay the loan principal.

BONDS ARE SECURITIES WITH FOLLOWING BASIC CHARACTERISTICS

They are typically securities issued by a corporation or governmental body for specified term: bonds become due for payment at maturity, when the par value/ face value of bond is returned to the investors. Bonds usually pay fixed periodic interest installments, called coupon payments. Some bonds pay variable income. When investor buys bond, he or she becomes a creditor of the issuer. Buyer does not gain any kind of owner ship rights to the issuer, unlike in the case with equity securities.

The main advantages of bonds to the investor:

- They are good source of current income;
- Investment to bonds is relatively safe from large losses;
- In case of default bondholders receive their payments before shareholders can be compensated.

A major disadvantage of bonds is that potential profit from investment in bonds is limited. Currently in the financial markets there are a lot of various types of bonds and investor must understand their differences and features before deciding what bonds would be suitable for his/ her investment portfolio.

An indenture (or trust deed) is the legal agreement between the firm issuing the bonds and the bond trustee who represents the bondholders. It provides the specific terms of the bond agreement such as the rights and responsibilities of both parties. The current yield on a bond refers to the ratio of annual interest payment to the bond's market price.

In comparison to equities, bonds might, at first sight, appear much less glamorous and exciting, but bonds to have their subtleties and pitfalls for the unwary. In fact, in some ways bonds demand greater alertness and skill on the part of the investor. This is because, in general, there is less uncertainty about the cash flows accruing to the bond holder as compared to the shareholder: the emphasis is therefore, on more fine-tuned calculations and analysis. Typically, bond prices fluctuate less than equity prices, and the investor who desires superior performance has to be on the lookout for even small differentials in prices and returns.

Their risk is analysed in two ways:

1. The risk of non-redemption or credit risk, evaluated according to the quality of the issuer, which is measured by a rating system. The rating, which is made public, contributes to an efficient market and allows the return on the bond to be linked to its risk.
2. The market risk, or interest rate risk, which is analysed as a function of the opportunity cost represented by the difference between the return ensured by the bond and that of the market for an equivalent maturity. Bonds are grouped, consequently, into issuers or ratings and maturities.

Bonds classification by their key features:

By form of payment:

Nonintersecting bearing bonds - bonds issued at a discount. Throughout the bond's life its interest is not earned, however the bond is redeemed at maturity for face value.

Regular serial bonds - serial bonds in which all periodic installments of principal repayment are equal in amount.

Deferred -interest bonds -bonds paying interest at a later date;

Income bonds - bonds on which interest is paid when and only when earned by the issuing firm;

Indexed bonds - bonds where the values of principal and the payout rise with inflation or the value of the underlying commodity;

Optional payment bonds - bonds that give the holder the choice to receive payment on interest or principal or both in the currency of one or more foreign countries, as well as in domestic currency.

Coupon payment:

Coupon bonds - bonds with interest coupons attached;

Zero-coupon bonds - bonds sold at a deep discount from its face value and redeemed at maturity for full face value. The difference between the cost of the bond and its value when redeemed is the investor's return. These securities provide no interest payments to holders;

Full coupon bonds - bonds with a coupon rate near or above current market interest rate;

Floating-rate bonds - debt instruments issued by large corporations and financial organizations on which the interest rate is pegged to another rate, often the Treasury-bill rate, and adjusted periodically at a specified amount over that rate.

Collateral:

Secured bonds - bonds secured by the pledge of assets (plant or equipment), the title to which is transferred to bondholders in case of foreclosure;

Unsecured bonds - bonds backed up by the faith and credit of the issuer instead of the pledge of assets.

Debenture bonds - bonds for which there is no any specific security set aside or allocated for repayment of principal;

Mortgage bonds (or mortgage-backed securities) - bonds that have as an underlying security a mortgage on all properties of the issuing corporation;

Sinking fund bonds - bonds secured by the deposit of specified amounts. The issuing corporation makes these deposits to secure the principal of the bonds, and it is sometimes required that the funds be invested in other securities;

Asset-Backed Securities (ABS) - similar to mortgage bonds, but they are backed by a pool of bank loans, leases and other assets. The ABS are related with the new market terminology - **securitization** which understood as the process of transforming lending vehicles such as mortgages into marketable securities. The main features of ABS for investor: relatively high yield, shorter maturities (3-5 years) and monthly, rather than semiannual principal/ interest payments. From their introducing to the market they were ranked as high credit quality instruments. But the recent financial crises showed that these debt instruments could be extremely risky investment when banks loans portfolios as a guarantee of ABS become worthless causing banks' insolvency problems.

General obligation bonds - bonds, secured by the pledge of the issuer's full faith and credit, usually including unlimited tax-power;

Guaranteed bonds - bonds which principal or income or both are guaranteed by another corporation or parent company in case of default by the issuing corporation;

Participating bonds - bonds which, following the receipt of a fixed rate of periodic interest, also receive some of the profit generated by issuing business;

Revenue bonds - bonds whose principal and interest are to be paid solely from earnings.

Convertible bonds - bonds that give to its owner the privilege of exchanging them for other securities of the issuing corporation on a preferred basis at some future date or under certain conditions;

Interchangeable bonds - bonds in coupon form that can be converted to the other form or its original form at the request of the holder paying the service charge for this conversion.

Type of issuers:

Treasury (government) bonds - an obligation of the government. These bonds are of the highest quality in each domestic market because of their issuer - Government. This guarantee together with their liquidity makes them popular with both individual and institutional investors. The government bonds are dominant in the fixed-income market.

Municipal bonds - bonds issued by political subdivisions in the country (county, city, etc.);

Corporate bonds - a long-term obligation of the corporation;

Industrial bonds - bonds issued by corporations other than utilities, banks and railroads. This debt is used for expansion, working capital and retiring other debts;

Public utility bonds - high quality debt instruments issued by public utility firms.

Recall possibility:

Callable (redeemable) bonds - bonds issue, all or part of which may be redeemed by the issuing corporation under definite conditions, before the issue reaches maturity;

Non-callable (irredeemable) bonds - bonds issued which contains no provision for being "called" or redeemed prior to maturity date.

Place of circulation:

Internal bonds - bonds issued by a country payable in its own currency;

External bonds - bonds issued by government or firm for purchase outside the nation, usually denominated in the currency of the purchaser. The term **Eurobond** is often applied to these bonds that are offered outside the country of the borrower and outside the country in whose currency the securities are denominated. As the Eurobond market is neither regulated taxed, it offers substantial advantages for many issuers and investors in bonds.

Quality:

Gilt-edged bonds - high-grade bonds issued by a company that has demonstrated its ability to earn a comfortable profit over a period of years and to pay its bondholders their interest without interruption;

Junk bonds - bonds with low rating, also regarded as high yield bonds. These bonds are primarily issued by corporations and also by municipalities. They have a high risk of default because they are issued as unsecured and have a low claim on assets.

Other types of bonds:

Voting bonds - unlike regular bonds, these bonds give the holder some voice in corporation management;

Senior bonds - bonds which having prior claim to the assets of the debtor upon liquidation;

Junior bonds - bonds which is subordinated or secondary to senior bonds.

Basic Features of Bonds

In order to better understand more complicated topics, the CFA Institute requires CFA candidates to have the ability to describe the basic features of a bond. These features include

1. **Maturity**

   Maturity is the time at which the bond matures and the holder receives the final payment of principal and interest. The "term to maturity" is the amount of time until the bond actually matures. There are 3 basic classes of maturity:

   - A. Short-Term Maturity - One to five years in length
   - Intermediate-Term Maturity - Five to twelve years in length
   - C. Long-Term Maturity - Twelve years or more in length

   Maturity is important because:

   - It indicates the length of time in which an investor will receive interest as well as when he or she will receive principal payments.
   - It affects the yield on the bond; longer maturities tend to yield higher rates.
   - The price volatility of a bond is a function of its maturity. A longer maturity typically indicates higher volatility or, in Wall Street lingo, simply the "vole".

2. **Par Value**

   Par value is the dollar amount the holder will receive at the bond's maturity. It can be any amount but is typically Rs.1, 000 per bond. Par value is also known as principle, face, maturity or redemption value. Bond prices are quoted as a percentage of par.

   Example: 1

   Premiums and Discounts

   Imagine that par for ABC Corp. is Rs.1000, which would Rs.100. If the ABC Corp. bonds trade at 85 what would the dollar value of the bond be? What if ABC Corp. bonds at Rs102?

   Solution:

   At Rs.85, the ABC Corp. bonds would trade at a discount to par at Rs.850. If ABC Corp. bonds at Rs.102, the bonds would trade at a premium of Rs.1, 020.

3. **Coupon Rate**

   A coupon rate states the interest rate the bond will pay the holders each year. To find the coupon's dollar value, simply multiply the coupon rate by the par value. The rate is for one year and payments are usually made on a semi-annual basis. Some asset-backed securities pay monthly, while many international securities pay only annually. The coupon rate also affects a bond's price. Typically, the higher the rate, the less price sensitivity for the bond price because of interest rate movements.

4. **Redemption value**

   The value given on maturity is called redemption value. A bond/debenture may be redeemed at par or at premium (more than par value) or at discount (less than par value).

5. **Market value**

   This denotes the rate prevailing in a stock exchange. The price at which it is currently sold or brought is called the market value of the bond/debenture. Market value differs from par value or redemption value.

6. **Currency Denomination**

   Currency denomination indicates what currency the interest and principle will be paid in. There are two main types:

   - **Dollar Denominated -** refers to bonds with payment in USD.
   - **Non - dollar-Denominated** - denotes bonds in which the payments are in another currency besides USD.
   - Other currency denomination structures can use various types of currencies to make payments. Because the provisions for redeeming bonds and options that are granted to the issuer.

Bonds are of two types: (a) bonds with maturity and (b) perpetual bonds.

(a) **Bond with a maturity period:** A bond will be issued for a specified period of time. When a bond has definite maturity. We will have to consider the annual interest payments plus its terminal, or maturity value for determining its present value. Using the present value concept, the discounted value of these flows will be calculated. By comparing the present value of a bond with its current market value, it can be whether the bond is overvalued or undervalued.

(b) **Perpetual bonds:** These bonds will not be issued for some specific period. These bonds never mature. Hence, they are called perpetual bonds. Perpetual bonds or debentures are rarely found in practice, England issued these types of bonds long back to payoff many small issues. In case of the perpetual bonds, as there is no maturity, or terminal value, the value of the bonds would simply be discounted value of the infinite stream of interest flows.

For instance, supposing, a bond pays Rs. 70 interest annually into perpetuity, what would be its value if the current yield is 8 percent? The value of the bond is determined as follows: If the going interest rate is 7 percent, the value of the bond will be Rs. 1000 and if it is 9 percent the value will be Rs. 777.78. Thus, the value of the bond will decrease as the interest rate increases.

The following are the different concepts of value, used for different purposes.

1. **Book value**

   It is related to accounting concept. In this type, the assets are recorded at historical cost, and they are depreciated over years. Book value includes acquisition cost minus amortized value. The difference between the book values of assets and liabilities is equal to shareholders' funds or net worth. Book value per share is determined as net worth divided by the number of shares outstanding. Book value reflects historical cost, rather than value.

2. **Replacement value**

   This refers to the amount that a company would be required to spend if it were to replace its existing assets. It is difficult to find cost of assets currently being used by the company.

3. **Liquidation value**

   It refers to the amount that a company could realize if it sold its assets, after having terminated its business. It does not cover the value of intangibles since the operations of the company are assumed to cease. It is the minimum value which a company might accept if it sold its business.

4. **Going concerns value**

   It refers to the amount that a company could realize if it sold its business as an operating business. Generally, this value will be higher than the liquidation, the difference accounting for the usefulness of assets and value of intangible.

5. **Market value**

   It refers to the current price at which the assets or the security is being sold or bought in the market. This value per share is expected to be higher that the book value per share for profitable, growing firms. The market value per share will be affected by many factors and therefore, it shows wide fluctuations. In ideal situation, where the capital market is efficient and in equilibrium, market should be equal to present (or intrinsic) value of a share.

BASIC COUPON STRUCTURES

The various coupon rate structures that can be developed in the bond market.

Zero-Coupon Bonds - These instruments pay no interest to the holder and are issued at a deep discount. As the bond nears maturity, its price increases to reach par value. At maturity, the bondholder will receive the par price. The interest earned is the difference between the purchase price of the bond and what the holders receives at maturity.

- **Step-up Notes** - The interest rate of these bonds increases or "steps-ups" at a stated date(s). The rate may remain at this level until maturity and in this case would be considered a "single step-up note". Step-up notes can also have a series of rate increases and are then referred to as "multiple step-up notes".

- **Deferred Coupon Bonds** - A structure that essentially incorporates features of both a zero-coupon bond and a coupon paying bond. These bonds typical do not pay interest for the first couple of years. After this period the cash interest accrues at a stated rate and is usually paid semi-annually to the bondholders. The coupon rate is typically higher than other issues in order to entice investors to purchase these issues. Companies in the high yield arena typically issue these bonds to conserve their cash flows in the earlier years of their business life.
- **Floating-Rate Bonds** - These bonds have coupon rates that reset at predetermined times. The rate is usually based on an index or benchmark with some sort of spread added or subtracted to the benchmark.

STRUCTURE OF FLOATING-RATE BONDS

To find the coupon rate of floating rate bonds, all one has to find out is what the benchmark or reference rate is trading at and add or subtract the stated amount of basis points or other influencing variable. Let's take a closer look at the above example of the Federal Fund Floater:

Example: 2

Floating Rate Security: Federal Funds

Assume the coupon rate of a floating-rate bond is based on the Federal Funds rate plus 25 basis points at three-month intervals. If the Federal Funds are at 3%, what would the coupon rate for this bond be?

Coupon rate = Reference Rate + influencing variable.

Answer:

Coupon rate = 3% (Fed Funds) + 25 basis points.

Coupon rate = 3.25%

The coupon rate for this bond would be 3.25% until the next reset date. Floating- rate securities come in many forms.

BOND VALUATION

Bond valuation is the process of determining the fair price of a bond. As with any security, the fair value of a bond is the present value of the stream of cash flows it is expected to generate. Hence, the price or value of a bond is determined by discounting the bond's expected cash flows to the present using the appropriate discount rate.

Example: 3

Annuity valuation

Assume that the portfolio manager from the example above decides to invest in a bond with the following specifications:

Bond maturity	17
Yield to maturity	years
Price Coupon	14.49%
Par value	Rs. 100
Purchased	7% per coupon
	Rs. 9 0, 00,000

In order to see how much money he will have in seven years (assuming interest rates stay at 14.49%), first calculate the future value of the coupons, and second the value of the bond at maturity. During the seven years the portfolio manager will receive fourteen coupons, each valued at 7% x Rs.90, 00, 000 = Rs. 6, 30,000. Assuming that this money is placed on deposit at 14.49% each time it is received, the amount to which it will accumulate in the future must be calculated. The following formula can be utilized:

$$(1 + r)^n - 1$$

AF =R

Where:

AF = the future value of an annuity r = the half-yearly

interest rate n = the number of coupons.

Using the given figures, the annuity factor becomes:

$$(1 + 0.07)^{14} - 1 = 22.55$$

$$0.07$$

This means that if Rs. 6,30,000 is invested every six months for seven years, it will accumulate to Rs.6,30,000 x 22.55 = Rs.1,4 2,06, 807.

The value of the bond in the above case with ten years to maturity is:

$$(1 - (1 + 0.07)^{-20})$$

PAF = 10.594

$$0.07$$

And for a zero-coupon bond:

Rs.9 000 000 Rs.2 325

Z = 771

$$(1 + 0.07)^{20}$$

The present value of the bond with ten years to maturity is therefore 10.594 x 630 000 + Rs. 2 325 771 = Rs.9 000 000. The total value is Rs.9 000 000 + Rs.14 206 807 = Rs.23 206 807.

The above example is summarized as:

Bond maturity (in years)	14.49%
Yield to maturity Coupon p.a.	14%
Par value	Rs. 9 000 000.00
Purchased Value in 7 years	Rs.23 206 807.35

It can be seen from the above that the portfolio manager exactly meets his target when interest rates are 14.49%, but may fail to meet his target when interest rates change. The formula assumes that the coupons received are reinvested at the same rate as the yield. If the portfolio manager is only going to be able to reinvest the coupons at a lower rate, then the overall return generated by the bond will be lower than the yield.

GENERAL RELATIONSHIPS

The present value relationship: The fair price of a straight bond (a bond with no embedded option; is determined by discounting the expected cash flows:

- Cash flows: the periodic coupon payments C, each of which is made once every period; the par or face value P, which is payable at maturity of the bond after **T** periods.
- Discount rate: the required (annually compounded) yield or
- Rate of return **r**. o^r is the market interest rate for new bond issues with similar risk ratings

$$\text{Bond Price} = P_0 = \sum_{t=1}^{T} \frac{C}{(1+r_t)^t} + \frac{F}{(1+r_T)^T}.$$

Because the price is the present value of the cash flows, there is an inverse relationship between price and discount rate: the higher the discount rates the lower the value of the bond (and vice versa). A bond trading below its face value is *trading at a discount*; a bond trading above its face value is *at a premium*.

Coupon yield: The coupon yield is simply the coupon payment (C) as a percentage of the face value (F). Coupon yield = C / F Coupon yield is also called nominal yield.

Current yield: The current yield is simply the coupon payment (C) as a percentage of the bond price (P). Current yield = C / P_0.

Yield to Maturity: The yield to maturity, YTM, is the discount rate which returns the market price of the bond. It is thus the internal rate of return of an investment in the bond made at the observed price. YTM can also be used to price a bond, where it is used as the required return on the bond. Solve for YTM where

$$\text{Market Price} = \sum_{t=1}^{T} \frac{C}{(1+YTM)^t} + \frac{F}{(1+YTM)^T}.$$

To achieve a return equal to YTM, the bond owner must

1. Reinvest each coupon received at this rate
2. Redeem at Par
3. Hold until Maturity

BOND PRICING

Relative price approach

The bond will be priced relative to a benchmark, usually a government security. The discount rate used to value the bond is determined based on the bond's rating relative to a government security with similar maturity. The better the quality of the bond, the smaller the spread between its required return and the YTM of the benchmark. This required return is then used to discount the bond cash flows as above.

Arbitrage free pricing approach

In this approach, the bond price will reflect its arbitrage free price (arbitrage=practice of taking advantage of a state of imbalance between two or more markets). Here, each cash flow is priced separately and is discounted at the same rate as the corresponding government issues Zero coupon bond. (Some multiple of the bond (or the security) will produce an identical cash flow to the government security (or the bond in question).) Since each bond cash flow is known with certainty, the bond price today must be equal to the sum of each of its cash flows discounted at the corresponding risk-free rate- i.e. the corresponding government security. Were this not the case, arbitrage would be possible to see rational pricing. Here the discount rate per cash flow, r_{at}, must match that of the corresponding zero-coupon bond's rate.

$$\text{Bond Price} = P_0 = \sum_{t=1}^{T} \frac{C}{(1+r)^t} + \frac{P_T}{(1+r)^T}.$$

BOND INTRINSIC VALUES

As a final step in bond analysis, investors should examine the market position of bonds. They must investigate whether the market price of a bond is out of line with the similarly rated bonds by performing. An evaluation - calculating intrinsic values. Astute investors feel that value of bonds stems from the income stream these securities throw off. Thus, they feel that the value of a bond depends upon the present value of the aggregate interest payments plus the present value of the final maturity payment. But, this valuation technique presents investors with-a serious problem, namely, what is an appropriate discount rate?

The answer will depend upon the required rate of return the investor has in his mind. It will differ from person to person too. Generally, an Indian bond investor is aiming at a return of 15-18 percent per annum. The rate used to discount bond flows, thus, is a critical value judgment. The question can be answered through regression analysis marking returns with maturity dates so that a regression line can be determined. The investors can use their regression line to establish discount rates use with bond flows.

In addition, investors often average the yields supplied by investment services for various bonds retiring. This technique might be termed as the "quick method". Finally, the appraisal value is compared with the market price to indicate the degree of fairness present.

BOND MANAGEMENT STRATEGIES

Interest Rate Anticipation: Strategies which involve forecasting interest rates and altering a bond portfolio to take advantage of that forecast are called "interest rate anticipation" strategies. Interest rates are the most important factor in the pricing of bonds. The price of a bond is based on its interest rate or "yield" at any particular time and the most important influence on a bond's yield is the market interest rate structure. The market interest rate for any particular term of bond is generally agreed to be represented by the yields on government bonds, as these are viewed as highly liquid and of very low default risk.

Basic Interest rate Anticipation Strategy: Involves moving between long-term government bonds and very short-term treasury bills, based on a forecast of interest rates over a certain time horizon.

Yield Curve Strategies: Are more sophisticated interest rate anticipation strategies taking into account the differences in interest rates for different terms of bonds, called the "term structure" of interest rates? A chart of the interest rates for bonds of different terms is called the "yield curve". A *yield* curve strategy would position a bond portfolio to profit the most *from* an expected change in the yield curve, based on an economic or *market* forecast.

Sector Rotation in Bonds: A sector rotation strategy for bonds involves varying the weights of different types of bonds held within a portfolio. An investment manager will form an opinion on the valuation of a specific sector of the bond market, based on the credit fundamental factors for that sector and relative valuations compared to historical norms and technical factors, such as supply and demand, within that sector. A manager will usually compare her portfolio to the weightings of the benchmark index that she is being compared to on a performance basis.

Security Selection for Bonds: Security selection for bonds involves fundamental and credit analysis and quantitative valuation techniques at the individual security level. Fundamental analysis of a bond considers the nature of the security and the potential cash flows attached to it. Credit analysis evaluates the likelihood that the payments will be received as contemplated, or at all. Modern quantitative techniques use statistical analysis and advanced mathematical techniques to attach values to the cash flows and assess the probabilities inherent in their nature.

Yield to Maturity (YTM): Yield to maturity is the most popular measure of yield in the market. It is the rate that will make the present value of a bond's cash flows equal touts market price plus accrued interest. To find YTM, one has to develop the cash flows and then, through trial and error, find the interest rate that makes the present value of cash flow equal to the market price plus accrued interest. This is basically a special type of Internal Rate of Return (IRR).

Example: 4

Yield to Maturity: An example using the above IBM bond the cash flows will consist of 20 payments of Rs. 2.50 every six months and a payment, twenty six-month periods from now, of Rs.100. The present values, using various semi-annual discounts, are as follows:

Semi-annual interest Rate	Present Value
2.50%	100
2.60%	99.5
2.70%	99
2.80%	98.5
2.90%	98

When the rate of 2.9% is used the present value of the cash flows is equal to a price of Rs. 98.00. Hence the semi-annual yield to maturity is 2.9%. Now that we have found this we must make it into a market convention rate or the bond-equivalent yield. To get this yield, just double the semi-annual rate. In this example, it would be 5.8% yield to maturity.

Bond Price, Coupon Rate, Current Yield and Yield to Maturity

- For a bond selling at par: Coupon Rate = Current Yield = Yield to Maturity
- For a bond selling at a discount: Coupon Rate < Current Yield < Yield to Maturity.
- For a bond selling at a premium: Coupon Rate > Current Yield > Yield to Maturity.

The limitations of the yield to maturity measure are that it assumes that the coupon rate will be reinvested at an interest rate equal to the YTM. Besides that, it does take into consideration the coupon income and capital gains or loss as well as the timing of the cash flows.

1. **Yield to First Call:** Yield to first call is computed for a callable bond that is not currently callable. The actual calculation is the same as the Yield to Maturity with the only difference being that instead of using a par value and the stated maturity, the analyst will use the call price and the first call date in calculating the yield.
2. **Yield to First Par Call:** Again, yield to first par call is the same procedure as above, with the difference being that the maturity date that will be used instead of the stated maturity date is the first time the issuer can call the bonds at par value.
3. **Yield to Refunding:** Yield to refunding is used when the bonds are currently callable but there are certain restrictions on the source of funds used to buy back the debt when a call is exercised. The refunding date is the first date the bond can be called using a lower-cost debt. The calculation is the same as YTM.
4. **Yield to Put:** Yield to put is the yield to the first put date. It is calculated the same way as YTM but instead of the stated maturity of the bond, one uses the first put date.
5. **Yield to Worst:** Yield to worst is the yield occurs when one calculates every possible call and put date that has the lowest possible yield. For example, if you calculate all the call dates and the yield comes out as follows 5.6%, 7.6%, 8.2% and 7.5%, the yield to

worst would be 5.6%. This measure means little to the potential return; it is supposed to measures the worst possible return the investor will receive if the bond is called or put.

6. **Cash Flow Yield:** Cash flow yield deals with mortgage-backed and asset-backed securities. The cash flows of these securities are interest and principal payments. What makes this complicated is that the borrowers who make up the mortgage or asset pool can prepay their loans in whole or in part prior to the scheduled principal payment. Because of this, the cash flows have to be estimated and an assumption must be made as to when these principle prepayments may occur. The rate that exists when the prepayments occurs is called the prepayment rate or prepayment speed. Once this rate is estimated, a yield can be calculated. The yield is the interest rate that will make the present value of the estimated cash flows equal the price plus accrued interest.

Example: 5

Cash Flow Yield: Because cash flows for these securities are usually monthly, a bond-equivalent yield must be developed. The math here is a little different than in the above examples:

Step 1 - the effective semi-annual yield must be computed from the monthly yield by compounding it for six months.

Effective semi-annual yield = (1 + monthly yield) to the 6th power -1

Step 2 - Double the effective semi-annual yield to get the annual cash flow on a bond equivalent basis.

Cash flow yield = 2 x {(1 + monthly yield) to the sixth power-1}

Answer:

So if the monthly yield is .8% then:

Cash flow yield = 2*{1.008) to the sixth power -1}

= 2 x .04897 = 9.79%

Fixed Income Investments - Assumptions Underlying Traditional Yield Curve Measures.

The main underlying assumptions used to concern the traditional yield measures are:

1. the bond will be held to maturity.
2. Coupons can be reinvested at the yield to maturity

Limitations:

1. Current yield: Current yield only considers the coupon interest and no other sources for an investor's return. It does not take into consideration the capital gain when a bond is purchased at a discount or the capital loss when the bond is purchased at a premium. Also, reinvestment income is not taken into consideration.
2. Yield to Maturity: Yield to maturity measures assume that the coupon payments will be reinvested at the coupon rate.

3. Yield to Call: Yield to call assumes investor will hold the bond to the assumed call price and that the issuer will call the bond on that date which both are unrealistic. Also, the comparison of different yields to call with the YTM are meaningless because the cash flows stop once the issuer calls the bond.
4. Yield to put: This assumes that coupon payments will be reinvested at the calculated yield and that the bonds will be put on the first date.\
5. Yield to Worst: This measure does not identify the potential return over some time horizon and fails to take into account that the calculation for an YTW has different exposures to reinvestment risk.
6. Cash Flow Yield: Cash flow yield assumes that the coupons will be reinvested at the coupon rate and that the bond will be held to maturity. However, because cash flow yield tends to be used for MBSs or ABSs there is a risk that the bonds will be prepaid and the measure of cash flow yield will be thrown out the window.

Present Value of bond:

A bond is a long-term debt instrument. This bond is classified as bonds with maturity and perpetual bonds. The bond with maturity period is issued for a specific period of time. The present value of bond is identified with the help of annual interest payment and its terminal value by using present value concept.

The formula is as under,

$$P_0 = \frac{INT_1}{[1+kd_1]} + \frac{INT_2}{[1+kd]^2} + \dots\dots\dots\dots + \frac{INT_n + P_n}{[1+kd]^n}$$

P_0 = Present value of Bond/debt

INT_1 = Interest

Kid = Cost of debt

P_{an} = Maturity value

n = No of Years to Maturity

Example: 6

From the price data that follow compute holding period return

Time	Stock price
1	25
2	30
3	24
4	32

Solution:

Time	Stock price	Holding period return
1	25	
2	30	(30/25 -1) = 20%
3	24	(24/30 – 1) = -20%
4	32	(32/24 -1) = 33.3 %

Example: 7

An investor is considering the purchase of 5yr. Rs. 1000 for value gone. The rate of interest is 7% the required rate of return is 8% on maturity at the end of 5th year Rs. 1000 will be paid. What will be the value of bond?

Solution:

$$Po = \frac{INT_1}{[1+kd_1]} + \frac{INT_2}{[1+kd]^2} + \dots\dots\dots\dots\dots + \frac{INT_n + P_n}{[1+kd]^n}$$

P_o = Present Value of a Bond / Debentures

INT1 = Amount of Interest in Period t

Kid = Required Rate of Return on Bond %

Pan = Terminal or Maturity, Value in Period n

$$Po = \frac{70}{(1+0.08)^1} + \frac{70}{(1+0.08)^2} + \frac{70}{(1+0.08)^3} + \frac{70}{(1+0.08)^4} \frac{70}{(1+0.08)^5}$$

= 64.8+60.01+55.57+51.45 = 960.5

Example: 8

Mr. Mohan is considering invest in bonds which is currently selling for 8785. The bond has 4 years maturity face value is currently selling rate 8%. The approximate discount rate 10%. Calculate intrinsic value of bond. Should Mr. Mohan purchase the bond?

Solution:

$$Po = \frac{800}{(1+0.01)^1} + \frac{800}{(1+0.01)^2} + \frac{800}{(1+0.01)^3} + \frac{800+10,000}{(1+0.01)^4}$$

Po = (800x0.909) + (800x0.826) + (800x0.751) + 10,800x0.083

= 727.2 + 660.8 +600.8 + 896.4 + 2885.2

Perpetual Bond (Irredeemable)

$$Po = \frac{INT}{kd}$$

Example: 9

Rs. 100 perpetual bonds are currently selling at Rs. 95. The coupon rate of interest is 13.5%. The appropriate discount rate is 15%. Calculate the value of the bond. Should it be bought?

Solution:

$$\text{Value of bond} = \frac{13.5}{0.15} = \text{Rs. } 90/\text{-}$$

The limited present value of the bond is Rs. 90. But the market price is Rs.95. It is overpriced. It should not be bought at this price.

Example: 10

A limited company has 10-year debenture that pays Rs. 140 annual interest will be paid on maturity. What will be the value of the debenture if they require rate of return is 12%, 14% and 16%?

Solution:

(i) $$\frac{12\%}{140X5.650 + 1000X0.322}$$

$= 791\text{x}0.322$

$= 1113$

(ii) $$\frac{14\%}{140X5.216 + 1000X0.270}$$

$= 730.24\text{x}0.270$

$= 1000.24$

(ii) $$\frac{16\%}{140X4.833 + 1000X0.277}$$

$= 676.62 \text{ x } 0.227$

$= 903.62$

Example: 11

An investor is considering the purchase of a five-year Rs.1000 par value bond, bearing a nominal (coupon) rate of interest of 7%. The investor's required rate of return is 8% what would your wiling you to pay now to purchase the bond if it matures at par? The investor will receive cash Rs.70 as interest each year for 5 years and Rs.1000 on maturity (i.e., at the end of the fifth year)

Solution:

The present value of bond:

$$P_o = 70/\,(1.08)^1 + 70/\,(1.08)^2 + 70/\,(1.08)^3 + 70/\,(1.08)^4 + 70/\,(1.08)^5 + 70/\,(1.08)^6$$

$$P_o = 70 \text{ x } 3.993 + 1000 \text{ x } 0.681 = 279.51 + 681 = \text{Rs. } 960.51$$

This implies that Rs. 1000 bond is worth Rs. 960.51 today.

Example: 12

The government is proposing to sell a 5-year bond of Rs.1000 at 8% p.a. the bond amount will be amortized equally over its life. If an investor has a minimum required rate of return of 7%. What is the bond's present value for him?

Solution:

$$Po = \frac{80+200}{(1+0.07)^1} + \frac{64+200}{(1+0.07)^2} + \frac{48+200}{(1+0.07)^3} + \frac{70}{(1+0.07)^4}$$

$$Po = 280x0.935 + 264x0.873 + 248x0.816 + 232x0.763 + 216x0.713$$

$$= 261.8 + 230.47 + 202.37 + 177.02 + 154$$

$$Po = 1025.66$$

Note: each year they return Rs.200 and interest as balance.

Example: 13

A 10-year bond of Rs.1000 has annual rate of interest of 12 percent. The interest is paid half-yearly. If the required rate of return is 16%, what is the value of bond?

Solution:

$$P_o = \sum_{t=1}^{2n} \tfrac{1}{2}(Nit)/(1+Kd/2) + Ban/(1+Kd/2)^{2n}$$

$$P_o = \sum_{t=1}^{2 \times 10} \tfrac{1}{2}(120)/(1+0.16) + 1000/(1+0.16)^{2x10}$$

$$= \sum_{t=1}^{20} (60)/(1.08)^t + 1000/(1.08)^{20}$$

$$= \sum_{t=1}^{10} 120/(1.16)^1 + 1000/(1.16)^{10}$$

$$= 120x4.8333 + 0.227x1000$$

$$= 580 + 227$$

$$= Rs.\ 807$$

Yield of maturity bond (YTM)

Yield to maturity measure is most commonly used for bond. The YTM represents the yield will be earned on the bonds from the purchase date to the maturity date. It is the discount rate which equals the present value of the cash flow from a bond to the cost that is the market price.

Example: 14

Rs. 1000 par value bond carries coupon rate of 12% maturity period 8 years, interest rate semiannual, compute the value of bond if the required rate returns 14%.

Solution:

Fundamental analysis

$$Po = \sum_{t-1}^{Zn} \frac{1/2}{(1-kd/2)} + \frac{F}{(1+kd/2)^{2n}}$$

Po = value of bond

I/2 = Semiannual interest

Kid/2= discount rate applicable to a half period.

F= maturity period expressed in half year period.

$$Po = \frac{6}{(1.07)^{0.16}} + \frac{100}{(1.07)^{0.16}}$$

Po = 6x9.447 + 100x0.0388

= 95.5

Example: 15

Rs.100 perpetual bond is currently selling for Rs.95.the coupon rate of interest is 13.5% and the appropriate discount rate is 15%. Calculate the value of the bond. Should it be bought? What is its Yield to Maturity?

Solution:

$$\text{Yield of bond} = \frac{Interest}{kd}$$

= 13.5/0.15 = Rs. 90

The Bond is overvalued, it should not be bought.

Yield to maturity = interest / current value of bond

$$\text{Yield of maturity} = \frac{Interest}{Currentvalueofbond} = \frac{13.5}{90} x100 = 15\%$$

Example: 16

A company purchases to sell 10 years debenture of Rs. 10,000 each. The company would repay Rs. 1000 at the end of every year and will repay interest annually at 15% at on the outstanding amount. Determine the pressure value of debenture if the capital station rate is 16%.

	Interest	Installment	Total	Present value at 16%	Present value of interest and repayment
1	1500	1000	3500	0.862	2155.00
2	1350	1000	4350	0.743	1746.05
3	1200	1000	2200	0.641	1410.20
4	1050	1000	2050	0.552	1131.60
5	900	1000	1900	0.476	904.40
6	750	1000	1750	0.410	717.50
7	600	1000	1600	0.354	566.40
8	450	1000	1450	0.305	442.25
9	300	1000	1300	0.263	341.09
10	150	1000	1150	0.227	261.05
				Present value of debt.	9676.35

Example: 17

A market price of a bond Rs. 1000 par value coupon rate 14%. It matures after 5 year. The present value is 1050. What is yield to maturity?

Solution:

$$\text{YTM} = \frac{1+[F--p]/a}{0.4F+0.6P}$$

I = Int.

F = Fact value

P = Present value

N= number of years

$$\text{YTM} = \frac{100+[1000-1032.40]/5}{0.4X1000+0.6X1032.40} = 10.62$$

Example: 18

Mr. A. purchased a bond with Rs. 1000 face value 10% coupon rate and 4 years, maturity. The bond makes annual interest payment. The first should be received one year from today. He paid Rs. 1032.4 for the bond. What is the bond yield to maturity?

Solution:

$$\text{YTM} = \frac{100+[1000-1032.40]/4}{0.4X1000+0.6X1032.40}$$

$$= 9\%$$

Example: 19

Rs. 1000 par value bond carries coupon rate of 12% maturity period 8 years, interest rate semiannual, compute the value of bond if the required rate returns 14%.

Solution:

$$\text{Po} = \sum_{t-1}^{Zn} \frac{1/2}{(1-kd/2)} + \frac{F}{(1+kd/2)^{2n}}$$

Po = value of bond

I/2 = Semiannual interest

Kid/2 = discount rate applicable to a half period.

F = maturity period expressed in half year period.

$$\text{Po} = \frac{6}{(1.07)^{0.16}} + \frac{100}{(1.07)^{0.16}}$$

Po = 6x9.447 + 100x0.0388

= 95.5

Example: 20

Find out YTM from the following maturity value of the bond Rs. 1000. Interest rate of the bond 15% is maturity period is 5 years. Market price of the bond is Rs. 800.

Solution:

$$\text{Yield of maturity} = \frac{Interest}{Currentvalueofbond}$$

= (15/800) x 100 = 18.75%

Bond Valuation Theorem

Based on bond valuation model, several bound value theorems have been derived. They state that the following factors are considered for bond valuation.

1. The relations between the required rate of return and the coupon rate.
2. Number of maturities.

The following is the pertaining to the required rate of return and the theory pertaining to the required to the required rate of return and the coupon rate.

(i) When the required rate of return is equal to coupon rate, the value of bond is equal to face value.

(ii) When the required rate of return is greater than coupon rate the value of bond is less than face value.

(iii) When the require rate of return is less than coupon rate, the value is bond is more than face value. Theorem on numbers of year's maturity. The following theorems express the effect of number of years to maturity on bond values.

(iv) When the required rate of return is greater than coupon rate the discount on the bond declines as maturity approaches.

(v) When the required rate of return is less than the coupon rates the premium on bond declines as maturity approaches.

The longer the maturity of the bond the greater the price changes in response to given changes in the required of return

MACAULAY DURATION OF A BOND

Duration is a measure of a bond's sensitivity to interest rate changes. However, the sensitivity of a bond to movements in the interest rate is influenced by a number of different factors. For instance, bonds with a longer dated maturity will be more sensitive to changes in the interest rate than bonds with a shorter maturity. With regard to the coupon, the lower coupon bonds demonstrate the greatest degree of sensitivity to the yield. The lower coupon bonds have more of their value linked to the terminal value.

Which pays no coupons the entire value of the security is in the final payment, and if yields are high then the flows in the future are worth less and the sensitivity is diminished. It should be noted that the relationship between the coupon and maturity and the price is not symmetrical. This relationship is called convexity, and will be addressed below.

Thus, duration is a composite measure of risk and is effectively the weighted average length of time to the receipt of a bond's payments (coupon and principal). Duration values are stated in years. The weight associated with each cash flow is proportional to the present value of each cash flow. Where the triangle or point of balance represents the duration of the bond. In a bond portfolio there will be a number of different bonds, each with a distinctive cash flow structure and yield. Each of these bonds will have a mathematical duration which shows how sensitive the bond is to interest rate changes. Bond prices have an inverse relationship with interest rates. This means that as interest rates go up bond prices go down, and vice versa. The straight line indicates the duration estimate of the price change. The duration assumes that there is a linear relationship between interest rates and bond prices, while in reality there is a curved relationship

It means that the linear approximation will only be accurate if there are very small changes in the interest rate, and will be very inaccurate if the interest rates move by large amounts. The diagram also illustrates that when interest rates fall, bond prices will increase by an amount that is greater than that calculated by the duration. Conversely, when interest rates rise, the fall in the bond price will not be as great as that estimated by the duration. For this reason, bonds that have high convexity will be worth relatively more than bonds with low convexity when interest rates are very volatile. Convexity thus represents the curvature of the bond's price-yield curve, or the rate of change of the slope of the price-yield curve.

Calculating durationTo review, the present value of the future income flows generated by a bond is effectively what a buyer would be prepared to pay for the bond. This can be summarized in the formula. The duration is a measure of average life of an instrument, the duration of a bond is the weighted average time to full recovery of principal and interest payment. The formula is as under,

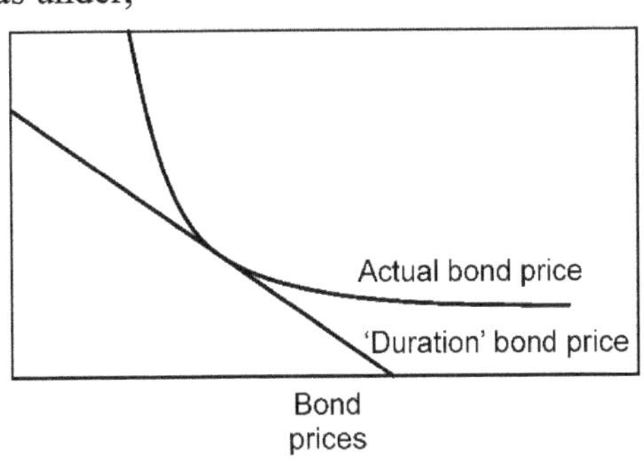

$$\text{Duration} = \sum_{t-1}^{Zn} [\ ciI\ ] \ / \ v$$

C1 = Interest and principal payment at time.

I = Length of time for payment... c
Kid = yield to maturity
v = value or market price of the
t = time value of money

Example: 21

Calculate the duration of the bond with the following particulars

Face value	100
Coupon rate	15%
Years to Maturity	6%
Current market price	89%
Yield to maturity	18%

$$D = \left[\frac{15x1}{(1.18)^1} + \frac{15x2}{(1.18)^2} + \frac{15x3}{(1.18)^3} + \frac{15x4}{(1.18)^4} + \frac{15x5}{(1.18)^5} + \frac{15x6}{(1.18)^6} + \frac{100}{(1.18)^6} /89.5\right]$$

D = 2.18 Years.

Calculate the value and duration for the following bonds:

Bonds	Year of maturity Annual interest	Maturity value
A Rs. 1000	10	Rs. 80
B Rs. 872	15	Rs. 65

Solution:

B and A Rs. 1000			B and B Rs. 872	
Year	CF	PV of into	Into	PV of into
1	80	74	65	60
2	80	137	65	111
3	80	191	65	155
4	80	235	65	191
5	80	272	65	221
6	80	302	65	246
7	80	327	65	265
8	80	346	65	281
9	80	360	65	293
10	1080	5002	65	301
11			65	307
12			65	310
13			65	311
14			65	310
15			1065	5036
Sum of PV of interest		Rs. 7,247		Rs. 8,398
Duration		7.25years		

Example: 22

The procedure for calculating the value of a bond here is to take the present value of the future income flows. A bond has a yearly coupon of Rs. 12, and has ten years to run before it matures. There are therefore ten separate cash flows and, because they will be received in the future, they must be discounted to their present value. The yield is 5%.

The figure of 687.5828 is obtained by taking the present value of the cash flow for that year, 68.75, and multiplying it by t (which in this case is 10).

Solution:

	Coupon Amount	*Discount using 5%*	*Present value*	*PV x No. of years*
1	12	0.9524	11.4286	11.4286
2	12	0.9070	10.8844	21.7687
3	12	0.8638	10.3661	31.0982
4	12	0.8227	9.8724	39.4897
5	12	0.7835	9.4023	47.0116
6	12	0.7462	8.9546	53.7275
7	12	0.7107	8.5282	59.6972
8	12	0.6768	8.1221	64.9766
9	12	0.6446	7.7353	69.6178
10	12	0.6139	68.7583	687.5828
Total			154.0521	1086.3986
Macaulay duration				7.0521
Modified duration				6.7163

Since what is required is calculation of the duration, the total of the adjusted cash flows is divided by the price of the bond: 1086/154 = 7.05 years. This calculation is also called Macaulay duration.

MODIFIED DURATION AND CONVEXITY

Whilst Macaulay duration looks at the sensitivity of a bond to changes in the interest rate, modified duration evaluates the impact of yield changes on the price. Modified duration can be utilized to approximate the change in a bond's price, given a small change in the required yield. The formula for modified duration is:

$$\text{Modified duration} = \frac{\text{Macaulay duration}}{1+y}$$

Where y = the yield.

Finally, as the formula suggests, the figure 7.0521 is divided by (1 + y) in order to obtain the modified duration:

$$\text{Modified duration} = \frac{7.0521}{1.05} = 6.7163$$

If the yield (y) were to increase to 5.1%, given the modified duration formula it is possible to calculate the approximate change in the bond's price. Using the following formula, the change in bond's price given a change in the yield can be calculated:

Approximate change in bond price = (- Modified duration) x (Ay) x (B) where: Ay = change in yield B = present value of the bond.

Using the example above, the calculation is:

Change in bond price = (-6.7163) x (0.001) x (Rs.154.0521) = Rs. -1.035

Therefore, if the yield increases from 5.0% to 5.1%, the price of the bond will fall by about Rs.1.04.

As mentioned above, the relationship between yield and price is convex - that is, non-linear. Convexity will cause the modified duration to be overstated when the bonds fall in price, and understated when the bonds rise in price. However, when yield changes are small in value the modified duration calculation will provide a good estimate. There may only be problems if the change in yield is of a substantive value.

Portfolio duration

The portfolio duration is simply the weighted average of the individual durations of the bonds within the portfolio. Often risk managers set targets for their portfolio, and from time to time they may need to decrease the inherent interest rate risk associated with the portfolios. This will depend on the priorities of the investors.

The immunization is the strategy of immunizing (protecting) a bond portfolio against interest rate risk (i.e., changes in the general level of interest rates). Applying this strategy, the investor attempts to keep the same duration of his portfolio.

Immunizing a portfolio: Immunization is a technique used by bond managers that allows them to meet a promised stream of cash outflows with a high degree of certainty. Immunization is achieved by calculating the duration of the promised outflow and then investing in a portfolio of bonds that has an identical duration. Provided the duration calculations are correct and there is no risk of a major convexity adjustment, the danger of not having sufficient cash to meet a future commitment is limited. The duration of a bond portfolio is simply calculated as the weighted average of the individual bonds within the portfolio.

As interest rates fluctuate, both the value of securities held in the portfolio and the rate at which those securities generate income fluctuates. Immunization, or the matching of assets on a duration basis, lets the portfolio meet its obligations despite interest rate movements. If yields rise, the portfolio's losses owing to the selling of a three-year bond in two years' time will be exactly offset by the gains from reinvesting the maturing one- year bond. Alternatively, if yields fall, the loss from being able to invest in a one-year bond will be exactly offset by being able to sell the three-year bond in two years at a premium. Therefore, the portfolio is immunized from the effect of any movement in interest rates.

PROBLEMS WITH IMMUNIZATION

One problem with immunization is that duration does not stay constant. With small changes in interest rates, duration will not change; however, when there is a significant change in interest rates, duration will change and the portfolio manager must therefore re-balance the portfolio with bonds of the new duration. The problem with this is that frequent rebalancing increases transactional costs and so the portfolio manager may have difficulty in achieving the re-balancing yield. Less frequent rebalancing will mean that the duration is allowed to change without sufficient attempts being made to track that change. The portfolio manager in these circumstances faces a trade-off.

Immunization strategies work best if the yield curve is flat. Where the yield curve is upward or downward sloping, problems can arise. Macaulay duration is calculated on the basis that there is a parallel change in the yield curve, but this is rarely the case in reality. Short-term interest rates tend to move faster than long-term interest rates, and so there is not always a high degree of correlation between them. Duration in these circumstances cannot be guaranteed.

STRATEGIES FOR INVESTING IN BONDS IMMUNIZATION

Two types of strategies investing in bonds:

- ➢ Passive management strategies;
- ➢ Active management strategies.

Passive bond management strategies are based on the proposition that bond prices are determined rationally, leaving risk as the portfolio variable to control. The main features of the passive management strategies:

- They are the expression of the little volatile in the investor's forecasts regarding interest rate and/ or bond price;
- Have a lower expected return and risk than do active strategies;
- The small transaction costs.

The passive bond management strategies include following two broad classes of strategies:

- Buy and hold strategies;
- Indexing strategies.

Buy and hold strategy is the most passive from all passive strategies. This is strategy for any investor interested in non-active investing and trading in the market. An important part of this strategy is to choose the most promising bonds that meet the investor's requirements. Simply because an investor is following a buy-and-hold strategy does not mean that the initial selection is unimportant. An investor forms the diversified portfolio of bonds and does not attempt to trade them in search for the higher return. Following this strategy, the investor has to make the investment decisions only in these cases:

- The bonds held by investor lost their rating, it decreases remarkably;
- The term to maturity ended;
- The bonds were recalled by issuer before term to maturity.

Using ***Indexing strategy,*** the investor forms such a bond portfolio which is identical to the well diversified bond market index. While indexing is a passive strategy, assuming that bonds are priced fairly, it is by no means a simply strategy. Each of the broad bond indexes contains thousands of individual bonds. The market indices are continually rebalanced as newly issued bonds are added to the index and existing bonds are dropped from the index as their maturity falls below the year. Information and transaction costs make it practically impossible to purchase each bond in proportion to the index. Rather than replicating the bond index exactly, indexing typically uses *a stratified sampling approach.* The bond market is stratified into several subcategories based on maturity, industry or credit quality. For every subcategory the percentage of bonds included in the market index that fall in that subcategory is computed. The investor then constructs a bond portfolio with the similar distribution across the subcategories.

There are various indexing methodologies developed to realize this passive strategy. But for all indexing strategies the specific feature is that the return on bond portfolio formed following this strategy is close to the average bond market return.

Active bond management strategies are based on the assumption that the bonds market is not efficient and, hence, the excess returns can be achieved by forecasting future interest rates and identifying over valuate bonds and under valuated bonds.

There are many different active bond management (speculative) strategies. *The* main classes of active bond management strategies *are:*

- The active reaction to the forecasted changes of interest rate;
- Bonds swaps;
- Immunization.

The essentiality of the active reaction to the anticipated changes of interest rate ***strategy:*** f the investor anticipates the decreasing in interest rates, he / she is attempting to prolong the maturity of the bond portfolio or duration, because long-term bonds' prices influenced by decrease in interest rates will increase more than short-term bonds' prices; if the increase in interest rates is anticipated, investor attempts to shorten the maturity of the bond portfolio or duration, by including more bonds with the shorter maturity of the portfolio.

The essentiality of bond swaps strategies is the replacement of the bond which is in the portfolio by the other bond which was not in the portfolio for the meantime. The aim of such replacement - to increase the return on the bond portfolio based on the assumptions about the tendencies of changes in interest rates. There are various types of swaps, but all are designed to improve the investor's portfolio position. The bond swaps can be:

- Substitution swap;
- Interest rate anticipation swap;
- Swaps when various bond market segments are used.

The essentiality of substitution swap: one bond in the portfolio is replaced *by* the other bond which fully suits the changing bond by coupon rate, term to maturity, credit rating, but suggests the higher return for the investor. The risk of substitution swap can be determined by the incorrect rating of the bonds and the exchange of the unequal bonds causing the loss of the investor.

Interest rate anticipation swap is based on one of the key features of the bond - the inverse relationship between the market price and the interest rate (this means that when the interest rates are growing, the bonds prices are decreasing and vice versa. The investor using this strategy bases on his steady belief about the anticipated changes of interest rates and attempts to change frequently the structure of his/ her bond portfolio seeking to receive the abnormal return from the changes in bonds' prices. This type of swaps is very risky because of the inexact and unsubstantiated forecasts about the changes in the interest rates.

Swaps when various bond market segments are used *are* based on the assessment of differences of yield for the bonds in the segregated bond market segments. The differences of the yields in the bond market are called *yield spreads* and their existence can be explained by differences between

- Quality of bonds credit (ratings);
- Types of issuers of the bonds (government, company, etc.);
- The terms to maturity of the bonds (2 years, 5 years, etc.).

This strategy is less risky than the other swaps' strategies; however, the return for such a portfolio is lower also.

Bond market factors (term of maturity, financial sector, bond quality, supply and demand for credit); the investor must understand which factors and conditions have the influence on the yield and the prices of the bonds. The main factors to be mentioned are:

Term to maturity. Generally, term to maturity and the interest rate (the yield) of the bond are directly related; thus, the bonds with the longer term to maturity have the higher yield than the bonds with shorter terms to maturity.

The sector in the economy which the issuer of the bonds represents. The yields of the bonds vary in various sectors of the economy; for example, generally the bonds issued by the utility sector firms generate higher yields to the investor than bonds in any other sector or government bonds.

The quality of the bonds. The higher the quality of the bond, the lower the yield. For the bonds with lower quality the yield is higher.

The level of inflation; the inflation decreases the purchasing power of the future income. Since the investors do not want to decrease their real yield generated from the bonds cash flows, they require the premium to the interest rate to compensate for their exposure related with the growing inflation. Thus, the yield of the bond increases (or decreases) with the changes in the level of inflation.

The supply and the demand for the credit; The interest rate on the price of borrowing money in the market depend on the supply and demand in the credit market; When the economy is growing the demand for the funds is increasing too and the interest rates generally are growing. Contrary, when the demand for the credits is low, in the period of economic crises, the interest rates are relatively low also.

Bond ratings. The ratings of the bonds sum up the majority of the factors which were examined before. A bond rating is the grade given to bonds that indicates their credit quality. Private independent rating services such as Standard & Poor's, Moody's and Fitch provide these evaluations of a bond issuer's financial strength, or it's the ability to pay a bond's principal and interest in a timely fashion. Thus, the role of the ratings of the bonds as the integrated indicator for the investor is important in the evaluation of yield and prices for the bonds. The rating of the bond and the yield of the bond are inversely related: the higher the rating, the lower the yield of the bond. Bond ratings are expressed as letters ranging from 'AAA', which is the highest grade, to 'C' ("junk"), which is the lowest grade. Different rating services use the same letter grades, but use various combinations of upper- and lower-case letters to differentiate themselves (see more information about the bond ratings in Annex 1 and the relevant websites of credit ratings agencies).

MARKET INTEREST RATES ANALYSIS

It's very important for the investor to the bonds to understand what causes the changes in the interest rates in the market in the different periods of time. We could observe frequent changes in the interest rates and the wide amplitude of its fluctuations during last decade, thus the interest rates became the crucial factor in managing fixed income securities portfolios as well as stock portfolios. The understanding of the macroeconomic processes and the causality of the various economic factors with the interest rates helps the investors to forecast the direction of the changes in interest rates. At the macroeconomic level the relationship between the interest rate and the level of savings and investments, changes in government spending, taxes, foreign trade balance is identified.

Macroeconomic factors with positive influence to the interest rates (from the investors in bonds position - increase in interest rates):

- Increase in investments;
- Decrease in savings level;
- Increase in export;
- Decrease in import;
- Increase in government spending;
- Decrease in Taxes.

Macroeconomic factors with negative influence to the interest rates (from the investors in bonds position - decrease in interest rates):

- Decrease in investments;
- Increase in savings level;

- Decrease in export;
- Increase in import;
- Decrease in government spending;
- Increase in Taxes.

By observing and examining macroeconomic indicators presented above the investors can assess the situation in the credit securities market and to revise his/ her portfolio

For interest rates forecasting purpose such tool as the term structure of interest rates is used. *Term structure of interest rates* is a yield curve displaying the relationship between spot rates of zero-coupon securities and their term to maturity. The resulting curve allows an interest rate pattern to be determined, which can then be used to explain the movements and to forecast interest rates. Unfortunately, most bonds carry coupons, so the term structure must be determined using the prices of these securities. Term structures are continuously changing, and though the resulting yield curve is usually normal, it can also be flat or inverted. Usually, longer term interest rates are higher than shorter term interest rates. This is called a *"normal yield curve"*. A small or negligible difference between short- and long-term interest rates is called a "flat" yield curve.

When the difference between long- and short-term interest rates is large, the yield curve is said to be "steep".

Three main factors influencing the yield curve

- Market forecasts and expectations about the direction of changes in interest rates;
- Presumable liquidity premium in the yield of the bond.
- Market inefficiency or the turn from the long-term (or short-term) cash flows to the short-term (or long-term cash flows.

On the bases of these key factors three **interest rates term structure theories** are developed to explain the shape of the yield curve.

The **Market expectations theory**, which states that since short term bonds can be combined for the same time period as a longer-term bond, the total interest earned should be equivalent, given the efficiency of the market and the chance for arbitrage (speculators using opportunities to make money). According to this theory, yield to maturity for the 5-year bond is simply the average of 1-year yield to maturity during next 5 years. Mathematically, the yield curve can then be used to predict interest rates at future dates.

The **Liquidity preference theory**, which states that the profile of yield curve depends upon the liquidity premiums. If the investor does not consider short-term and long-term bonds as the good substitutes for the investments he / she may require the different yields to the maturity, similar to the stocks with high and low Beta. Thus, Liquidity preference theory states that the yield curve of interest term structure depends not only upon the market expectations, but upon the spread of liquidity premiums between shorter-term and longer-term bonds.

The **Market segmentation theory** is based on the understanding of market inefficiency in defining the prices of the bonds. This theory states that each segment in the bonds 'market, identified on the basis of the yield to maturity of the bonds could be treated as independent segment from the others. These segments are represented by different groups of investors which are resolute about the necessity to invest in the bonds with this particular yield to maturity. These different groups of investors (for example - banks, insurance companies, non-financial firms, individuals, etc.) need to „employ "their funds for specific periods of time, hence a preference for long- or short-term bonds which is reflected in the shape of the yield curve. An inverted curve can then be seen to reflect a definite investor preference for longer term bonds. The profile of terms structure will depend not on the market expectations or risk Premium but most often because of the changes in the direction of cash flows.

Investors in bonds often use yield curves in making investment decisions. Analyzing the changes in yield curves over the time provides the investors with information about future interest rate movements and how they can affect price behavior and comparative returns. For example, if the yield curve begins to rise sharply, it usually means that inflation is growing or is expected to grow in the nearest future. In this case investors can expect that interest rates will rise also. Under these conditions, the active investors will turn to short or intermediate maturities, which provide reasonable returns and minimize exposure to capital loss then prices fall. Another example could be steep yield curves. They are generally viewed as a sign of bullish market. For aggressive investors in bonds this profile of the yield curve can be a signal to start moving into long-term bonds segment. Flatter yield curves, contrary, reduce the incentive for investing in long-term debt securities.

SUMMARY

1. The main advantages of bonds to the investor: they are good source of current income; investment to bonds is relatively safe from large losses; in case of default bondholders receive their payments before shareholders can be compensated. A major disadvantage of bonds is that potential profit from investment in bonds is limited.
2. Currently in the financial markets there are a lot of various types of bonds and investor must understand their differences and features before deciding what bonds would be suitable for his/ her investment portfolio. Bonds can be classified by such features as form of payment, coupon payment, collateral, type of circulation, recall possibility, issuers.
3. Investment in bonds decision making process: (1) selection of bond's type according to the investor's goals (expected income and risk); (2) bond analysis (quantitative and qualitative); (3) bond valuation; (4) Investment decision making.
4. The role of the bond ratings as the integrated indicator for the investor is important in the evaluation of yield and prices for the bonds. The bond rating and the yield of the bond are inversely related: the higher the rating, the lower the yield of the bond.

5. Macroeconomic factors, changes of which have an influence to the interest rates (increase or decrease), are: level of investment; savings level; export/ import; government spending; taxes.
6. Term structure of interest rates is a yield curve displaying the relationship between spot rates of zero-coupon securities and their term to maturity. The resulting curve allows an interest rate pattern to be determined, which can then be used to explain the movements and to forecast interest rates. The 3 main factors influencing the yield curve are identified: market forecasts and expectations about the direction of changes in interest rates; presumable liquidity premium in the yield of the bond; market inefficiency or the turn from the long-term (or short-term) cash flows to the short-term (or long-term cash flows.
7. In the bond market investment decisions are made more on the bond's yield than its price basis. There are three widely used measures of the yield: Current Yield; Yield-to-Maturity; Yield- to- Call. Current Yield indicates the amount of current income a bond provides relative to its market price. Yield- to- Maturity is the fully compounded rate of return earned by an investor in bond over the life of the security, including interest income and price appreciation. Yield- to- Maturity is the most important and widely used measure of the bonds returns and key measure in bond valuation process. Yield-to-Call measures the yield on the bond if the issue remains outstanding not to maturity, but rather until its specified call date.
8. The decision for investment in bond can be made on the bases of two alternative approaches: (1) using the comparison of yield-to-maturity and appropriate yield-to-maturity or (2) using the comparison of current market price and intrinsic value of the bond (similar to decisions when investing in stocks). Both approaches are based on the capitalization of income method of valuation.
9. Using yield-to-maturity approach, if yield-to-maturity is higher than appropriate yield-to-maturity, bond is under valuated and investor's decision should be to buy or to keep bond in the portfolio; if yield-to-maturity is lower than appropriate yield-to-maturity, bond is over valuated and investor's decision should be not to buy or to sell the bond; if yield-to-maturity is lower than appropriate yield-to- maturity, bond is valuated at the same range as in the market and its current market price shows the intrinsic value.
10. Two types of strategies investing in bonds: (1) passive management strategies; (2) active management strategies. Passive bond management strategies are based on the proposition that bond prices are determined rationally, leaving risk as the portfolio variable to control. Active bond management strategies are based on the assumption that the bonds market is not efficient and, hence, the excess returns can be achieved by forecasting future interest rates and identifying over valuate bonds and under valuated bonds.
11. The passive bond management strategies include two broad classes of strategies: "buy and hold" and indexing. "Buy and hold" is strategy for any investor interested in non-active investing and trading in the market. An important part of this strategy is to choose and to buy the most promising bonds that meet the investor's requirements. Using

Indexing strategy, the investor forms such a bond portfolio which is identical to the well diversified bond market index.

12. The active reaction to the anticipated changes of interest rate is based on the investor's decision making in his/ her portfolio as reaction to the anticipated changes in interest rates.
13. The essentiality of bond swaps strategies is the replacement of the bond which is in the portfolio by the other bond which was not in the portfolio for the meantime. The aim of such replacement - based on the assumptions about the tendencies of changes in interest rates to increase the return on the bond portfolio. The bond swaps can be: Substitution swaps; Interest rate anticipation swap; Swaps when various bond market segments are used.
14. The immunization is the strategy of immunizing (protecting) a bond portfolio against interest rate risk (i.e., changes in the general level of interest rates). Applying this strategy the investor attempts to keep the same duration of his/her portfolio.
15. Duration is the present value weighted average of the number of years over which investors receive cash flow from the bond and it measures the economic life or the effective maturity of a bond (or bond portfolio) rather than simply it's time to maturity.

FILL IN THE BLANKS & MCQS

1. Bonds and Debentures represent long term debt instruments.
2. The 8% taxable savings bonds are repayable after ________ years.
3. Debentures rated ________ are judged to offer sufficient safety of timely payment of interest and repayment of principal.
4. The ________% tax saving bonds of government of India have a tenure of 5 years.
5. The investor in bonds receives income from: - (Interest payments at coupon rates, Capital gain/loss arising out of the sale of the bond, Redemption of the bond of the issuer at a contracted value)
6. When a debenture is sold to the general public a ________ is appointed.
7. Debentures rated "BB" refers ________ of timely payment of interest and principal.
8. Current income Short term debt portfolio Fixed - income portfolio Stability of principal Fixed - income portfolio Short term debt portfolio Appreciation 75-100 % in equities 75-100 % in equities.
9. The firm issuing bonds operating sinking fund and repurchases bonds either: - (Calling in a certain number of bonds by lot, buying bonds in the open market Buying bonds issued to banks and fi the risk associated to get the required rate of return on the stock is measure by market beta.
10. The return to the bond investor can be measured in terms of: - Current yield, Yield to maturity, Realized yield

11. Gilt Edged Securities are :-(State Govt., Quasi-Got, Central Got
12. Features of PSU Bonds are: - No TDS, Transferable by endorsement, No stamp duty on transfer
13. Debt instruments that have a maturity period of more than one year are called as: - (Bonds)
14. The features of bond are: - (Collateral, Call provision, Sinking fund and protective covenants)
15. What are the features of post office monthly income scheme? (Investor earns bonus of 10% on completion of term, Rate of return is 8 %, Interest payable monthly)
16. The firm issuing bonds operating sinking fund and repurchases bonds either :(Calling in a certain number of bonds by lot, buying bonds in the open market, buying bonds issued to banks and financial institutions
17. The 8% taxable savings bonds are repayable after ________ years.
18. _______ Bonds are generally called for prepayment after interest rates have fallen, investors will not be able to find comparable investment avenues.
19. A GOI security with coupon of 11.68%, maturing on 6-Aug-2014, is to be settled on 1-Feb-13. What are the number of days from the previous coupon date?

    (a) 179 (b) 176

    (c) 178 (d) 175

    Answer: d.

    We use the coupon function in Excel and specify the following: Settlement date: February 1, 2013 Maturity Date: August 6, 2014 Frequency: 2 Basis: 4: The answer is: 175 days
20. What is the accrued interest on an 11.68% GOI security, maturing on 6-Aug-2014, trading on 1-Jun-2013 at an YTM of 7.7395%?

    (a) Rs. 3.6901 (b) Rs. 3.7311

    (c) Rs. 3.7105 (d) Rs. 3.7520

    Answer: b Accrued interest is computed as Coupon payment * (number of days from previous coupon/days in the coupon period) we use the coupon and coupon days functions to ascertain days from previous coupon and days in the coupon period. The amount of coupon is Rs. 11.68/2. Therefore, the accrued interest is = 5.84 * (115/180) = Rs. 3.7311
21. An 11.68% GOI security maturing on 6-Aug-2014, is being priced in the market on 11-Jul-013 at Rs. 104.34. The YTM of the bond is

    (a) 7.3728% (b) 7.3814%

    (c) 7.3940% (d) 7.3628%

We use the Yield function in Excel, specifying settlement (11 July 2013) and maturity dates (6 Aug 2014), coupon (0.1168), price of the security (104.34), redemption (100) frequency (2), basis (4). The answer obtained is 7.3728%.

Answer: a

22. On April 12, 2001, a dealer purchases an 11.68% GOI bond maturing on 6-Aug-2002 for Rs. 104.34. He holds the bond for 1 year, and sells it on April 11, 2002, for Rs. 100.90. If the coupons received during the holding period are re-invested at 8.2405% (1st coupon) and 6.7525% (2nd coupon), what is the realized yield on the investment?

    Answer: The components of realized yield are: Coupon income, re-investment of coupons and capital gains/losses.

    Coupon income: The number of coupons between the acquisition date and date of sale of the bond can be found with the coupon function. In this case there are two coupons. Therefore, the coupon received is: Rs. 11.68 Re-investment Income:

    We can find the first coupon date, by using the "coupon" function in Excel. The first coupon is due on August 6, 2013. Since the bond will be sold on April 11, 2014, the number of days for which the coupon will be re-invested will be 248 days. The interest rate applicable to this coupon, as given in the question, is 8.2405%. Therefore, the re-investment income can be computed as: = (11.68/2) * (248/365) * 0.082405 = 0.3270

    Similarly, the second coupon is due on 6th Feb 2014. It will be reinvested for 65 days, at 6.7525%. The reinvestment income will be = (11.68/2) * (64/365) * 0.067525 = 0. 0691
    Capital gain/loss: Rs. 100.90 - 104.34 = -3.44

    The total rupee returns from holding the bond for a year is 11.68 + 0.3270+ 0.0691 - 3.44 = 8.6361

    The released yield therefore is = (8.6361/104.34) *100 = 8.2

SHORT ANSWER QUESTIONS

1. Define Bond/Debenture
2. Define Active management strategies
3. Define Bond ratings
4. Define Bonds swaps
5. What is Buy and hold strategy?
6. Define Convertible bonds
7. Define Corporate bonds
8. Define Coupon bonds
9. Define Current Yield
10. Define Duration (Macaulay duration)

11. Define Full coupon bonds
12. Define Floating-rate bonds
13. Define External bonds
14. Define Eurobonds
15. Define General obligation bonds
16. Define Gilt edged bonds
17. Define Guaranteed bonds
18. Define Immunization Income bonds
19. Define Industrial bonds
20. Define Indexing Interchangeable bonds
21. Define Intrinsic value of the bond
22. Define Junior bonds Junk bonds
23. Define Liquidity preference theory
24. Define Passive management strategies
25. Define Participating bonds
26. Define Public utility bonds
27. Define Regular serial bonds
28. Define Revenue bonds
29. Define Quantitative indicators
30. Define Qualitative indicators
31. Define Secured bonds
32. Define Senior bonds
33. Define Sinking fund bonds
34. Define Term structure of interest rates
35. Define Treasury (government) bonds
36. Define Unsecured bonds
37. Define Voting bonds
38. Define Yield-to-Call
39. Define Yield-to-Maturity
40. Define Zero-coupon bonds

ESSAY TYPE QUESTIONS

1. What are the basic valuation models of bonds? How do you calculate 'yield' on bonds?
2. Is any mortgage bond or asset backed security necessarily a more secure investment than any debenture? Comment
3. What is debt instrument? Explain various types of debt instruments?
4. What are the factors that influences the value of debt instruments?
5. List out the differences between bonds and debentures.
6. What is bond yield? What are the various factors affecting bond yield? Illustrate with suitable examples.
7. Distinguish between current yield and yield to maturity. Illustrate the measurement of yield to maturity on bonds.
8. What sis bond valuation? Explain how the capitalization of income method is used in valuing bonds.
9. Explain the method for valuing debenture that is compulsorily convertible (partially or fully) into equity shares.
10. Explain how deep discount bonds can be valued.
11. What sis bond duration? How it can be calculated by Macaulay's duration method and modified Macaulay's duration?
12. Explain the concept of bond convexity.
13. Explain the important factors that are taken into account while managing the bond portfolio.
14. How the risk structure of interest rates has an impact on liquidity and taxes?
15. How can horizon analysis be used to manage a bond portfolio?
16. What is bond immunization? How immunization is accomplished? What are the factors influencing bond immunization?
17. Describe briefly about the active and passive bond portfolio management strategies
18. What are the different ways in which the return on coupon bond can be calculated? Illustrate with suitable examples.
19. What is the purpose of bond ratings? If the bonds ratings are so important to the investors why don 't common stock investors focus on quality ratings of the companies in making their investment decisions?
20. What is a key factor in analyzing bonds? Why?
21. Distinguish between yield-to-call and yield-to-maturity.
22. What is the difference between the market expectation theory and the liquidity preference theory?

EXERCISE PROBLEMS

1. Madan is considering investing in a bond currently selling in the market for Rs.875. The bond has four years to maturity, Rs.1000 face value and a 7% coupon rate. The next annual interest payment is due one year from today. The appropriate discount rate for the securities of similar risk is10%.
   (a) Estimate the intrinsic value of the bond. Based on the result of this estimation, should Ann purchase the bond? Explain.
   (b) Estimate the yield-to-maturity of the bond. Based on the result of this estimation, should Ann purchase the bond? Explain.
2. Using the resources available in your domestic investment environment select any 4 bonds issued by Government and corporations relevant to you.

   Determine the current yield and yield-to maturity for each bond.

   Assuming that you put an equal amount of money into each of 4 bonds selected, estimate the duration for the 4 bonds portfolio.

   What would happen to this bond portfolio if (1) market interest rates increase by 1%; (2) market interest rates decrease by 1%.
3. Find the present value of the bond when par value is Rs. 100, coupon rate is 15% and current market price is Rs. 90. The bond has a six-year maturity value and has a premium of 10%.
4. If a bond has a market price of Rs. 83 and a par value of Rs.100. It has an interest rate of 13% and matures after five years. What rate of return would an investor receive if he buys this bond and holds it till maturity?
5. Bond with face value of Rs.1000, 2 years' time to maturity and 10 % coupon rate, makes semiannual coupon payments and provides 8% yield-to-maturity.
   (a) Calculate the price of the bond.
   (b) If the yield-to-maturity would increase to 9%, what will be the price of the bond? How this change in the yield-to-maturity would influence bond price?
6. The callable bond has a par value of Rs.100, 8% coupon rate and five years to maturity. The bond makes annual interest payment. Investor purchased this bond for Rs.90 when it was issued in May 2014.
   (a) What is the yield-to-maturity of this bond?
   (b) What is the duration of this bond if currently its market price is Rs.95
   (c) If this bond would be called in May 2014 for Rs. 98, what would be the yield- to-call of this bond?
7. Investor plans his investments for the period of four years and selects for his portfolio two different bonds with the same face values: Bond A has 4 years' time to maturity, 8% coupon rate, and Rs.960 current market price. Bond B has 8 years' time to maturity, 12% coupon rate, and Rs.1085 current market price.

8. A limited company has 8-year debenture that pays Rs. 140 annual interest will be paid on maturity. What will be the value of the debenture if they require rate of return is 14%, 16% and 18%?
9. An investor is considering the purchase of a five-year Rs.1000 par value bond, bearing a nominal (coupon) rate of interest of 9%. The investor's required rate of return is 10% what would your wiling you to pay now to purchase the bond if it matures at par? The investor will receive cash Rs.90 as interest each year for 6 years and Rs.1000 on maturity (i.e., at the end of the fifth year)
10. The government is proposing to sell an 8-year bond of Rs.1000 at 7% p.a. the bond amount will be amortized equally over its life. If an investor has a minimum required rate of return of 9%. What is the bond's present value for him?
11. An 8-year bond of Rs.1100 has annual rate of interest of 12 percent. The interest is paid half-yearly. If the required rate of return is 16%, what is the value of bond?
12. Rs. 1000 par value bond carries coupon rate of 10% maturity period 8 years, interest rate semiannual, compute the value of bond if the required rate returns 14%.
13. Rs.100 perpetual bond is currently selling for Rs.90.the coupon rate of interest is 12.5% and the appropriate discount rate is 12%. Calculate the value of the bond. Should it be bought? What is its Yield to Maturity?
14. Mr. M. purchased a bond with Rs. 1200 face value 10% coupon rate and 4 years, maturity. The bond makes annual interest payment. The first should be received one year from today. He paid Rs. 1042.4 for the bond. What is the bond yield to maturity?
15. Rs. 1000 par value bond carries coupon rate of 14% maturity period 8 years, interest rate semiannual, compute the value of bond if the required rate returns 12%.
16. Find out YTM from the following maturity value of the bond Rs. 1000. Interest rate of the bond 16% is maturity period is 7 years. Market price of the bond is Rs. 900.
17. Calculate the duration of the bond with the following particulars

Face value	100
Coupon rate	10%
Years to Maturity	6%
Current market price	85
Yield to maturity	16%

CASE STUDIES

CASE STUDY 1

Using the resources available in your domestic investment environment select any 4 bonds issued by Government and corporations relevant to you.

- Determine the current yield and yield-to maturity for each bond.
- Assuming that you put an equal amount of money into each of 4 bonds selected, estimate the duration for the 4 bonds portfolio.
- What would happen to this bond portfolio if,

  Market interest rates increase by 1%;

  Market interest rates decrease by 1%.

CASE STUDY 2

MARKET RISK & TIME

While the stock and bond markets can be risky in the short run, time has a moderating effect on market risk. The longer you hold a stock or bond investment, the lower your chances of losing money, and the greater the odds of earning a return close to the long-term average. For example, a one-year investment in stocks has historically produced returns ranging from +53.9% to -43.3%. Over ten-year periods, however, returns have varied from -0.9% per year for the worst ten years to +20.1% per year for the best ten years.

Range Of Returns on Stocks: 1943 to 2014

Holding Period	Best Return		Worst Return	
1 Year	+53.9	%	-43.3	%
5 Years	+23.9	%	-12.5	%
10 Years	+20.1	%	- 0.9	%
15 Years	+18.2	%	+ 0.6	%
20 Years	+16.9	%	+ 3.1	%
25 Years	+14.7	%	+ 5.9	%

As you can see, risk can be substantial over short periods. But over longer horizons, the chance of losing money is substantially reduced. The same principle applies to bonds, though bonds are less risky than stocks. For long-term bonds, it takes ten years before returns are consistently positive; for shorter-maturity bonds, about three years. Of course, it should be noted that past performance in the stock and bond markets does not necessarily predict future performance.

QUESTIONS

1. Do you think that stocks become less risky, relative to bonds, as your time horizon is lengthened? If so, why? If not, why not?

2. What are the implications of this article for the measures of risk and risk premiums used in the risk and return models developed?

CASE STUDY 3

Mr. Bunny wants to make an investment in the security market. The securities available to him in the market are debentures issued by the corporate bodies, equities and bonds issued by the government bodies. The risk-free rate of interest is 5% and anticipated return on market is 14%. he wants to build portfolio of risk free and risky asset. His required rate of return is 13%.

Questions:

(a) He wants to find out whether the X, Y, Z companies with betas 1.2, 1.1 and 0.8 quality for purchase

(b) If he is a risk adverse investor which stock should he avoid? The market return variance is 100.

CHAPTER 13

Capital Asset Pricing Model (CAPM)

CAPITAL MARKET THEORY

Capital market theory is an extension of the portfolio theory of Markowitz. The portfolio theory explains how rational investors should build efficient portfolio based on their risk return preferences. Capital asset Pricing Model incorporates a relationship, explaining how assets should be prices in the capital market. Assumptions of capital market theory are:

- Investors are expected to make decisions based solely on risk return assessments (expected returns and standard deviation measures).
- The purchase and sale transactions can undertake in infinitely divisible units.
- Investors can sell any other of shares without limit.
- There is perfect competition and so single investor can influence prices with no transaction costs involved.
- Investors can borrow/lend, the desired amount at riskless rates.
- Personal income taxation is assumed to be zero.

CAPM was developed by W. F. Sharpe. CAPM simplified Markowitz 's Modern Portfolio theory, made it more practical. Markowitz showed that for a given level of expected return and for a given feasible set of securities, finding the optimal portfolio with the lowest total risk, measured as variance or standard deviation of portfolio returns, requires knowledge of the covariance or correlation between all possible security combinations. When forming the diversified portfolios consisting large number of securities investors found the calculation of the portfolio risk using standard deviation technically complicated.

Measuring Risk in CAPM is based on the identification of two key components of total risk (as measured by variance or standard deviation of return):

i. Systematic risk
ii. Unsystematic risk

UNSYSTEMATIC RISK

When all securities are combined into portfolios risk is reduced. Diversification reduce risk, when the returns of the securities do not exactly vary in the same direction. Risk has two parts.

A part of risk arises from the uncertainties, which are unique to individual securities, and which is diversifiable, if large number of securities all combined to form well diversified portfolio. The unique risk of individual securities in a portfolio cancel out each other. This part of the risk can be totally reduced through diversification, and it is called unsystematic or unique risk. The example of unsystematic risk is as fallows....

- Workers declare strike in a company.
- The R&D experts of the company leaves.
- A formidable competitor enters the market.
- A company loses a big contract in a bid.
- The government increases custom duty on the material used by a company.

SYSTEMATIC RISK

The second part of Risk which arises on account of the economy-wide uncertainties and the tendency of individual securities to more together, with changes in the market. This part of the Risk cannot be reduced through diversification and it is called systematic (or) Market Risk investors are exposed to market risk, even when they hold well diversified portfolios of securities. The examples of systematic risk are as follows:

- The corporate tax is increased.
- The inflation rate increased,
- The government change the interest rate policy.
- The RBI promulgates and restrictive Credit Policy.
- The Government resorts to massive deficit financing.

The total risk can be bifurcated into two parts i.e.

Total Risk = Systematic Risk + Unsystematic Risk

After careful study of the graph below, we can conclude that unsystematic risk can be reduced as more and more securities are added to a portfolio. Diversification is not able to reduce systematic risk. Diversification may be able to eliminate only half of the total risk i.e.... (Unsystematic risk). Systematic risk cannot be diversified and therefore an investor will expect a compensation for bearing this risk.

Diagram

The capital asset pricing model (CAPM) is used in finance to determine a theoretically appropriate rate of return of an asset, if that asset is to be added to an already well-diversified portfolio, given that asset's non-diversifiable risk. The CAPM formula considers the asset's sensitivity to non-diversifiable risk (also known as systematic risk or market risk), referred to as beta (β) in the financial industry, as well as the expected return of the market and the expected return of a theoretical risk-free asset.

The model was introduced by Jack Trey nor, William Sharpe, John Linter and Jan Mossing independently, building on the earlier work of Harry Markowitz on diversification and modern portfolio theory.

$$\beta_{im} = \frac{\mathrm{Cov}(R_i, R_m)}{\mathrm{Var}(R_m)}$$

Formula

$$E(R_i) = R_f + \beta_{im}(E(R_m) - R_f).$$

The CAPM is a model for pricing an individual security or a portfolio. The security market line (SML) and its relation to expected return and systematic risk (beta) show how the market must price individual securities in relation to their security risk class. It enables to calculate the reward-to-risk ratio for any security in relation to the overall markets. Therefore, when the expected rate of return for any security is deflated by its beta coefficient, the reward-to-risk ratio for any individual security in the market is equal to the market reward-to-risk ratio, thus:

Individual security's = Market's securities (portfolio)

Reward-to-risk ratio Reward-to-risk ratio

The market reward-to-risk ratio is effectively the market risk premium and by rearranging the above equation and solving for E (RI), the Capital Asset Pricing Model (CAPM) is obtained.

$$\frac{E(R_i) - R_f}{\beta_i} = E(R_m) - R_f$$

Where:

$E(R_m)$ E (RI) = is the expected return on the capital asset

Rf = is the risk-free rate of interest

β_{im} = (the beta *coefficient*) the sensitivity of the asset returns to

Is the expected return of the market?

is sometimes known as the *market premium* or risk premium (the difference between the expected market rate of return and the risk-free rate of return).

ASSET PRICING

Once the expected return, $E(R_I)$-, is calculated using CAPM, the future cash flows of the asset can be discounted to their present value using this rate ($E(R_I)$-), to establish the correct price for the asset. In theory, therefore, an asset is correctly priced when its observed price is the same as its value calculated using the CAPM derived discount rate. If the observed price is higher than the valuation, then the asset is overvalued

ASSET-SPECIFIC REQUIRED RETURN

The CAPM returns the asset-appropriate required return or discount rate - i.e. the rate at which future cash flows produced by the asset should be discounted given that asset's relative risk. Betas exceeding one signify more than average "risk"; betas below one indicates lower than average. Thus, a riskier stock will have a higher beta and will be discounted at a higher rate; fewer sensitive stocks will have lower betas and be discounted at a lower rate. The CAPM is consistent with intuition - investors (should) require a higher return for holding a riskier asset. Since beta reflects asset-specific sensitivity to non-diversifiable, i.e. market risk, the market as a whole, by definition, has a beta of one. Stock market indices are frequently used as local proxies for the market - and in that case (by definition) have a beta of one. An investor in a large, diversified portfolio (such as a mutual fund) therefore expects performance in line with the market.

RISK AND DIVERSIFICATION

The risk of a portfolio comprises systematic risk and specific risk. Systematic risk refers to the risk common to all securities - i.e. market risk. Specific risk is the risk associated with individual assets. Specific risk can be diversified away (specific risks "average out"); systematic risk (within one market) cannot. Depending on the market, a portfolio of approximately 15 (or more) well selected shares might be sufficiently diversified to leave the portfolio exposed to systematic risk only.

A rational investor should take only non-diversifiable risks, which are rewarded. Therefore, the return that compensates for risk taken must be linked to its riskiness in a portfolio context - i.e. its contribution to overall portfolio risk - as opposed to its "stand alone risk." In the CAPM context, portfolio risk is represented by higher variance i.e. less predictability.

THE EFFICIENT (MARKOWITZ) FRONTIER

The CAPM assumes that the risk-return profile of a portfolio can be optimized - an optimal portfolio displays the lowest possible level of risk for its level of return. Additionally, since each additional asset introduced into a portfolio further diversifies the portfolio, the optimal portfolio must comprise every asset, (assuming no trading costs) with each asset value-weighted to Since beta reflects asset-specific sensitivity to non-diversifiable, i.e. market risk, the market as a whole, by definition, has a beta of one. Stock market indices are frequently used as local proxies for the market - and in that case (by definition) have a beta of one. An investor in a large, diversified portfolio (such as a mutual fund) therefore expects performance in line with the market.

THE EFFICIENT (MARKOWITZ) FRONTIER

The CAPM assumes that the risk-return profile of a portfolio can be optimized - an optimal portfolio displays the lowest possible level of risk for its level of return. Additionally, since each additional asset introduced into a portfolio further diversifies the portfolio, the optimal portfolio must comprise every asset, (assuming no trading costs) with each asset value-weighted to achieve the above (assuming that any asset is infinitely divisible). All such optimal portfolios, i.e., one for each level of return, comprise the efficient (Markowitz) frontier. Because the unsystematic risk is diversifiable, the total risk of a portfolio can be viewed as beta...

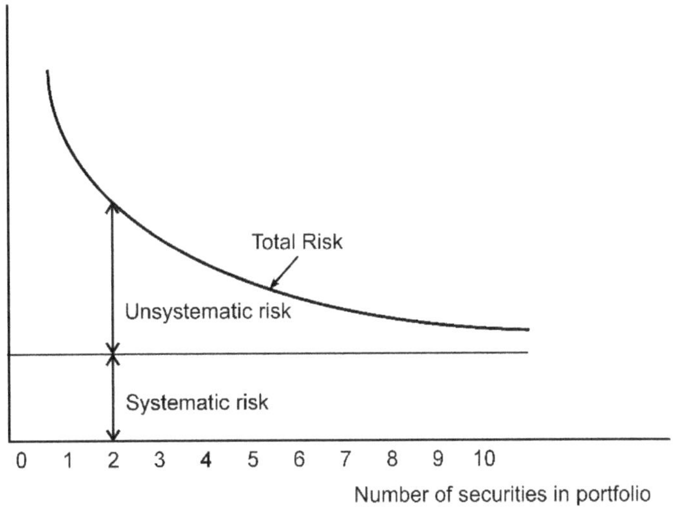

The essence of the CAPM: the more systematic risk the investor carry, the greater is his / her expected return.

RISK - FREE ASSET

According to the assumptions of capital market theory, investor have a lot of chance to borrow or lend the money at a risk-free rate of return. Determination of the free rate is one of the most important steps in the development of portfolio and CMT theories. Risk free asset is defined as the asset whose return is certain with a zero variance of return. The concept of risk-free asset is an extension of Markowitz's approach of investment. According to the theory of risk-free asset, the investors used to invest some part of their investment in risk free assets where the remaining is invested in risky portfolios or assets. Risk free rate of Markowitz approach helps an investor to borrow or lend the money at a risk-free rate. This may result in changing the concept of efficient frontier paving the path for the development of a general theory for pricing the assets under uncertain market conditions.

As, the risk-free asset is the characterized by the zero-standard deviation of the return, then there will not be uncertainties associated with the return on the investment. Thus, the variation is also equal to zero. Similarly, the covariance between the return on both the risk-free asset and risk assets becomes equal to zero. Practically, the product of correlation coefficient of asset and standard deviations is given by;

$\sigma ij = \Upsilon ij\ \sigma i \sigma j$

$\sigma i\ \sigma j$ are standard deviations for assets I and j i, j are the assets

Υij = is the correlation coefficient of two assets

As standard deviation of asset 'i' σi is 0 the covariance also becomes zero.

$\Sigma ij = \Upsilon ij . 0 . \sigma j = \sigma ij = 0$

The treasury bills which have a maturity period of far more or less than the investor's holding period does not quality as risk free assets as they involve some amount of risk. Such as interest rate and reinvestment rate-risk. Whereas the treasury bills with a maturity period equal to the investor's holding period can be treated as risk free assets. The risk-free assets are a type of fixed income securities that don't involve any risk and should only by federal government but not by any corporation.

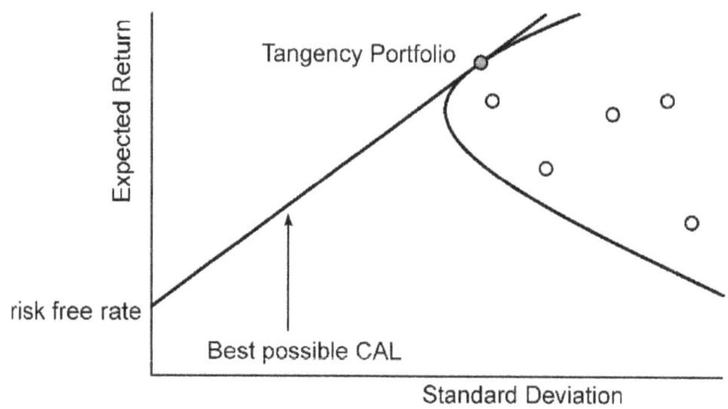

THE MARKET PORTFOLIO

An investor might choose to invest a proportion of his or her wealth in a portfolio of risky assets with the remainder in cash - earning interest at the risk-free rate Here, the ratio of risky assets to risk free asset determines overall return - this relationship is clearly linear. It is thus possible to achieve a particular return in one of two ways: By investing all of one's wealth in a risky portfolio, or by investing a proportion in a risky portfolio and the remainder in cash (either borrowed or invested).

For a given level of return, however, only one of these portfolios will be optimal (in the sense of lowest risk). Since the risk-free asset is, by definition, uncorrelated with any other asset, option 2) will generally have the lower variance and hence be the more efficient of the two. This relationship also holds for portfolios along the efficient frontier: a higher return portfolio plus cash is more efficient than a lower return portfolio alone for that lower level of return. For a given risk free rate, there is only one optimal portfolio which can be combined with cash to achieve the lowest level of risk for any possible return. This is the market portfolio.

- All investors have rational expectations.
- There are no arbitrage opportunities.
- Returns are distributed normally.
- Fixed quantity of assets.

- Perfect capital markets.
- Separation of financial and production sectors.
- Thus, production plans are fixed.
- Risk-free rates exist with limitless borrowing capacity and universal access.
- No inflation and no change in the level of interest rate exists

The model assumes that asset returns are normally distributed random variables. It is however frequently observed that returns in equity and other markets are not normally distributed. As a result, large swings occur in the market more frequently than the normal distribution assumption would expect. The model assumes that the variance of returns is an adequate measurement of risk. This might be justified under the assumption of normally distributed returns, but for general return distributions other risk measures will likely reflect the investors' preferences more adequately. The model does not appear to adequately explain the variation in stock returns. Empirical studies show that low beta stocks may offer higher returns than the model would predict. The model assumes that given a certain expected return investor will prefer lower risk to higher risk and conversely given a certain level of risk will prefer higher returns to lower ones. It does not allow for investors who will accept lower returns for higher risk. Casino gamblers clearly pay for risk, and it is possible that some stock traders will pay for risk as well.

The model assumes that all investors have access to the same information and agree about the risk and expected return of all assets. The model assumes that there are no taxes or transaction costs, although this assumption may be relaxed with more complicated versions of the model. The market portfolio consists of all assets in all markets, where each asset is weighted by its market capitalization. This assumes no preference between markets and assets for individual investors, and that investors choose assets solely as a function of their risk-return profile. It also assumes that all assets are infinitely divisible as to the amount which may be held or transacted.

The market portfolio should in theory include all types of assets that are held by anyone as an investment. In practice, such a market portfolio is unobservable and people usually substitute a stock index as a proxy for the true market portfolio. Unfortunately, it has been shown that this substitution is not innocuous and can lead to false inferences as to the validity of the CAPM, and it has been said that due to the inoperability of the true market portfolio, the CAPM might not be empirically testable.

PRESENT VALIDITY OF CAPM

The CAPM is greatly appealing at an intellectual level, logical and rational. The basic assumptions on which the model is built raise, some doubts in the minds of the investors. Yet, investment analysis has been more creative in adapting CAPM for their uses.

1. The CAPM focuses on the market risk, makes the investors to think about the risky ness of the assets in general CAPM provides basic concept, which is truly fundamental values.

2. The CAPM has been useful in the selection of securities and portfolio. Securities with higher returns are considered to be undervalued and attractive for buy. The below normal excepted return yielding securities are considered to be overvalued and suitable for sale.
3. In the CAPM, it has been assumed that investors consider only the market risk. Given the estimate of the risk-free rate, the beta of the firm, stock and the required market rate of return, one can find out the expected returns for a firm's security. This expected return could be used as an estimate of the cost of retained earnings.
4. Even through CAPM has been regarded as useful tools to financial analysis; it has it won critics too. They point out, when the model is ex-ante; the inputs also should be ex-ante, i.e. based on the expecat5ions of the f8re. Empirical test and analysis have used ex-post i. Past data only:

The historical data regarding the market return, risk free rate of return and betas vary differently for different periods. The various methods used to estimate these inputs also affect the beta value. Since the inputs cannot be estimated precisely, the expected return found out through the CAPM model is also subjected to criticism.

The risk-return implications of holding risky securities and the construction of the portfolio opportunity set. But we have not discussed about the question i.e.....

"What happens to the choices of investors in the market, if they could combine risky free security with risky security?"

CAPM provides answer to this question. Before giving answer to this question, CAPM assumes certain factors these assumptions are as fallows....

Assumptions of CAPM

1. **Market Efficiency:** The capital markets are efficient. The capital market efficiency implies that share prices reflect all available information.
2. **Risk Aversion:** Investors are risk averse. They evaluate a security's return and risk in terms of the expected return and variance or standard deviation respectively. They prefer the highest expected returns for a given level of risk.
3. **Homogeneous Expectations:** All investors have the same expectations about the expected return and risk of securities.
4. **Single Time Period**: All investor's decisions are based on single time period.
5. **Risk Free Rate**: All investors can lend and barrow @ a risk-free rate of returns.

A risk-free security is one which has zero variance or standard deviation, as result of which co variance between the risk-free security and risky security will be zero. The risk-free security will have the same return unless all possible economic conditions. Portfolio return and risk can be given by the following formula.

Portfolio under CAPM = Risk Free Security + Risky Security

Expected Returns on Portfolio: -

$$R_P = XR_M + (1\text{-}X)\ RF$$

Where RP = expected return on portfolio

X = percentage of funds invested in risky portfolio

(1-X) = percentage of funds invested in risk free asset

RM= expected returns on risky portfolio

RF= expected returns on risk free asset

STANDARD DEVIATION (OR) RISK OF PORTFOLIO

Since risk free security has a zero-standard deviation, the risk of a portfolio can be given by the fallowing formula

$$\sigma_p = X\ am$$

Where

σ_p = Expected standard deviation of the portfolio.

σ_M = Expected standard deviation on Risky Portfolio.

X_i = Percentage of funds invested in risky portfolio.

An investor can invest in the portfolio in three different combinations. They are as follows→

- Investment in Risky Security =100%
- Investment in Risky Security < 100%
- Investment in Risky Security > 100%

This aspect of security combinations can be explained with the help of the following example. Risk Return Analysis of a Risky and a Risk-Free Securities

Rm	Rf	Rp	σp
120	-20	17	7.2
100	0	15	6
80	20	13	4.8
60	40	11	3.6
40	60	9	2.4
20	80	7	1.2
0	100	5	0

Given →

Rf =0.05, Rm. = 0.15, σm= 0.06.

Diagram

Following Figure convey the following information: -

I. Point B represents 100% investment in the risky security expressed to yield 15% returns and 6% standard deviation. Investor can barrow @ risk free rate of 5% and invest in risky security to earn 15% return.

II. Point C represent 120% investment in the risky security after barrowing @ risk free rate of invest of 5% to earn a return of 17% and risk of 7.2%

III. Point A represent 60% investment in the risky security and 40% in risk free security. An investment lends this 40% a risk-free rate of interest and earns @ a return of 11% and risk of 3.6%

IV. A conservative investor will invest 100% in risk free security and here the point R_C represents this point.

V. R_d. represents the portfolio opportunity set for the possible combinations of risk-free security and risky security.

As we know that risk averse investment or investors prefer highest return for a given level of risk. So therefore, they will choose portfolios along the line F_M since they offer highest return for a given level of risk than choosing portfolios along any other line. So therefore, in an equilibrium situation, all investors will select portfolio consisting of risk-free security and the risky portfolio M. the line F_M is called as Capital Market Line (CML). This is so called because it shows the risk return trade off in the market equilibrium.

- Portfolio M is the market portfolio of risky securities where each security is held in portion of its market value. Portfolio M is called as the best portfolio, since it dominates the all other portfolios.
- An investor can investment structure according to his preferences i.e. he can have two separate investments 1) a risk-free asset 2) a portfolio of risky securities.
- This is known as the Separation Theorem.

In this figure R_C is termed as the intercept of the CML and its slope is given by the following formula

$$\textbf{Slope of CML} = \frac{[E(Rm) - R_f]}{\sigma_m}$$

Slope of CML describes the best price of a given level of risk in equilibrium. CML can also be defined by the fallowing equation.

$$E\,(R_{ap}) = R_f + \left[\frac{[E(Rm) - R_f]}{\sigma_m}\right] x\ \sigma_p$$

$$R_i - R_f = \frac{R_m - R_f}{\sigma_m} CovV_{im} / \sigma_m$$

Where $E(R_{ap})$ = expected return for portfolios along the CML

R_C = risk free rate of return (borrowing/ lending)

$E(M_{r.})$ = expected market portfolio M return.

σ_m= market portfolio standard deviation

σ_p= standard deviation of portfolio along the CML.

SECURITY MARKET LINE (SML)

Risk of an individual security can be divided into two parts. The first part is called as systematic risk and the second part is called as unsystematic risk. Unsystematic risk can be eliminated totally through diversification but systematic risk cannot be eliminated. Market will pay premium for systematic risk, since it is non-diversifiable. Now a question arises i.e.

How to measure the systematic risk of an individual security? And their risk adjusted rates of return?

To answer this question CAPM provides framework for measuring the systematic risk of an individual security and relate it to the systematic risk of a well-diversified portfolio. The risk of an individual security is measured by β. Beta is a measure of security's risk relative to the market portfolio. Since diversifiable risk does not matter, beta is thus a measure of the systematic risk of a security.

The equation of a straight line is as fallows

$$R_i = \alpha + b\,\beta_i \qquad \text{.... (1)}$$

On applying the two conditions to the equation we get when the first point on the line is the risk-free asset with β=0, then

$$R_f = \alpha + b\,(0)$$

$$R_f = \alpha \qquad \text{.... (2)}$$

Secondly, the point the line is the market portfolio with β=1, then

$$R_m = \alpha + b\,(1)$$

$$R_m - \alpha = b$$

$$R_m - R_f = b \qquad \text{.... (3)}$$

On combing equations 2 & 3 we get

$$R_i = R_f + (R_m - R_f)\beta_i$$

Where R_i= expected return on the security i

R_f = risk free rate of interest

R_m = exected return on the market portfolio

β_i = undiversifiable risk of security

β can be measured by the following formula i.e....

$$\beta_i = \frac{cov(R_i, R_m)}{var(R_m)} = \frac{cor_{im}\sigma_i\sigma_m}{\sigma_m^2} = \frac{cor_{im}\sigma_i}{\sigma_m}$$

The graphic representation of CAPM is called as SML. When security is perfectly correlated with market portfolio, the CML totally coincide with SML. Risk premium directly varies with systematic risk measured by beta (β). SML can be illustrated with the help of a diagram. i.e....

FIGURE

If β=1→ indicates security is having average rate of systematic risk.

B>1→securities return fluctuates more than the market returns.

B<1→ securities returns are less sensitive to the changes in the market returns.

Arbitrage Pricing Model (APM): The CAPM is not always able to account for the difference in assets return using their betas. This paved a way for the development of an alternative approach, called the arbitrage Pricing Model (APM), for estimating the assets expected returns. It is on the notion that, investors are rewarded for assuming no diversifiable (systematic risk). In APM there may be one or more macroeconomic factors that may measure the systematic risk of an asset. The fundamental logic in APM is that investors always indulge in arbitrage whenever they find differences in the returns of assets with similar risk characteristic.

FACTORS AFFECTING THE RETURN

The specification of the factors is carried out by much financial analysis, Chen, Roll and Ross have taken four Marco economic variable and tested them. According to them the factor is inflation, the term structure of interest rates, risk premiums and industrial production. Inflation affects the discount rate or the required rate of return and the size of the future cash flows. The short-term inflation is measured by monthly percentage changes in the consumer price index. The interest rate on long-term bonds and short-term bonds differ. This difference affects the value of payments in future relative to short-term payment. The difference between the return on the high-grade bonds and low grade (riskier) bonds indicates the market's reaction to risk. The industrial production represents the business cycle. Changes in the industrial production have an impact on the expectations and opportunities of the investor. The real value of the cash flow is also affected by it.

Burmeister and McElroy have estimated the sensitive with some other factors. They are given bellow: -

- Default risk
- Time premium
- Deflation
- Change in expected sales
- The market returns not due to the first four variables.

The default risk is measured by the difference between the return on long term government bonds and the return on long term bonds issued by corporate plus one-half of one percent. Time premium is measure by the return on long term government bonds minus one moth Treasury bill rate one month ahead. Deflation is measured by expected inflation at the beginning of the month minus actual inflation during the month. According to them, the first four factors accounted 25% of the variation in the standard and poor composite index and all the four co-efficient were significant.

Salmon Brothers identification five factors in their fundamental factor model Inflation is the only common factor identified by others. The other factors are given below: -

- Growth rate in gross nation a product
- Rate of interest
- Rate of change in oil prices

Rate of change in defense spending

Concept of Return Under APM: -

In APM, the return on asset is assumed to have two Components.

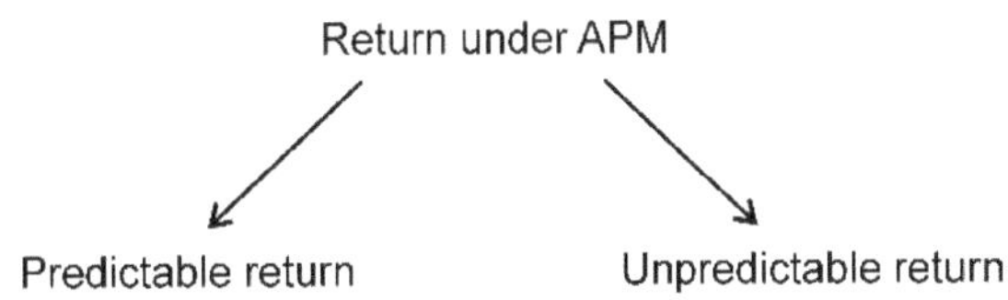

The return on an asset (I) is given by the fallowing equation

$$E\ (R_I) = F_o ur$$

Where R_C = predictable return (risk free return with β=0

UR = unpredictable return

These are two sources of unpredictable return on an asset

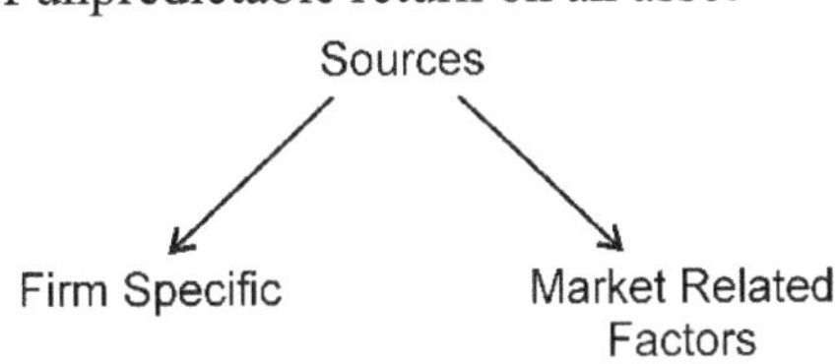

Firm Specific: The firm specific factors are special to the firm and affect only the firm

Market Related: these factors affect all assets and they comprise macro-economic factors. Depending on the above factors we can rewrite the equation (1) in the way

$$E\ (R_I) = R_{F+}UR_s+UR_m$$

Where

UR_s = unexpected return arising from the specific factors related to the firm.

Ru_{mp} =unexpected return arising from the economy wide market related factors.

Concept of Risk under APM: -

APM assumes that, market risk can be caused by economic factors such as changes in domestic product, price level, the structure of interest rates etc…. the sensitivity of the assets return to each factor is estimated. Thus, there will be as many betas as the number of factors. This equation also fallows

$$E\ (R_I) = R_C + (B1F1 + B2F2 + \ldots + B_N I_{NE})$$

Like CAPM, in APM also there is no compensation for the risk arising from the firm specific factor (UR_S). Portfolio will weight arrange of expect returns and market related unexpected returns.

$$E\ (R_I) = R_C + B1R1 + B2R2 + \ldots + B_N A_N$$

$$E\ (R_I) = R_C + \sum B_I R_E$$

Where $E\ (R_I)$ = expected returns on a risk-free asset

$E\ (R_{aj})$ = Expected return on asset (I)

BI = Sensitivity of asset (j) to factor (I)

Rig = Risk premium for factor (i)

APT AND CAPM

The simplest form of APT model is consistent with the simple form of the CAPM model, when only one factor is taken into consideration, the APT can be stated as.

$$R_i - \lambda_0 + b_i\lambda_I$$

It is similar to the capital market line equation:

$$R_i = R_f\beta_i + (R_m - R_F)$$, Which is similar to CAPM model

APT is more general and less restrictive than CAPM, in APT, the investor has no need to hold the market portfolio because it does not make use of the market portfolio concept. The portfolios are constructed on the basis of the factors eliminate arbitraged profits. APT is based on the law of one price to hold for all possible portfolio combinations.

The APT model takes on to account of the impact of numerous factors on the security. The |Macro economic factors are taken into consideration and it is closer to reality then CAPM.

The market portfolio is well defined conceptually. In APT model, factors are not well specified. Hence, the investor finds it difficult to establish equilibrium relationship. The well-defined market portfolio is a significant advantage of the CAPM leading to the wide usage of the model in the stock market.

The factors that have impact on one group of securities may not affect other group securities. There is a lack of constituency in the measurement of the APT model. Further, the influences of the factors are not independent of each other. It may be difficult to identify the influence corresponds exactly to each factor. Apart from this, not all variable that exerts influence on factor measurable.

PROBLEMS AND SOLUTIONS

1. **From the following compute the (β) of security j?**

   σ_j = 12%, σ_m = 9 %, cor_{jm}= +0.72

Solution: (β) of security j can be calculated by the following formula

$$\beta_j = \frac{corjm\ \sigma j\ \sigma m}{\sigma m\ 2}$$

$$= \frac{corjm\ \sigma j}{\sigma m}$$

On substituting the given values, we get

$$\beta_j = \frac{12 * 0.72}{9}$$

=0.96

2. **Calculate the expected rate of return for security i from the following information.**

   R_f = 10%, Rm=18% β_j=1.35

Solution:

Return on security can be given by the following formula

$R_i = R_F + (Rm - R_F)\beta_j$

=10+ (18-10) 1.35

=10+ 8*1.35

=20.8%

3. **P limited has an expected return of 22% and standard deviation of 40%. Q limited has an expected return of 24% and standard deviation of 38%. P has a (β) of 0.86 and Q has (β) of 1.84. The correlation between the returns of P and Q is 0.72. The standard deviation of market is 20%. Calculate R_F, R_m and β_p (70:30)?**

Solution: R_P= 22% R_Q=24%

σ_P = 40% σ_Q=38%

β_P= 0.86 β_Q=1.24

cor_{PQ}=0.72

σ_M=20%

Basic equation is as follows

$R_i = R_F + (Rm - R_F)\beta_j$

Here R_P= 22% = R_F + (Rm-R_F) *0.86------i

R_Q=24%= R_F + (Rm-R_F) *1.24--------ii

On subtracting i from ii we get

$2=(Rm-R_F) *[1.24-0.86]$

$2=(Rm-R_F) *0.38$

So therefore $R_m-R_F = 2/0.38 = 5.263\%$----iii

On substituting iii in i we get

$22= R_F + (5.26) *0.86$

$22= R_F +4.52$

$R_F=17.476\%$-----------------iv

On substituting iv in i we get

$R_m-R_F =5.26$

$R_m-17.5=5.26$

$R_m = 17.5+5.26$

$=22.76\%$

(b) $\beta_{PQ}= \beta_P W_P + \beta_Q W_Q$

$\beta_{PQ}= (0.86*0.70) +(1.24*0.30)$

$=0.602+0.372$

$=0.974$

4. You expect the stock of firm X to sell for Rs.70, a year from now and to play a Rs.4.00 dividend. If the stocks correlation with portfolio M is -0.3, σ_x= 40.0% σ_m=20.0%, R_F=5%, R_m=10%

Solution: Dividend = Rs40, σ_x= 40.0%

Selling P= Rs 70, σ_m= 20.0%

cor_{jm}=0.3 R_f= 5% R_m=10%

$$\beta_x= \frac{corjm\ \sigma x}{\sigma m}$$

$\beta_x = 40*(-0.3)/20$

$= -0.60$

Expected return E(R) =5% + (-0.60) *(5%)

=2%

Stock would be selling for

P_0 =[Rs70+Rs4.00]/1.02

=Rs72.55

5. Mr. Antony's Portfolio consists of two securities 'x' and 'Y'. Both the securities are equally weighted the following information is also given

E(R)=0.12 COV (RX, R_M) = 0.0375

R_F = 0.05 COV (RY, R_M) = 0.0225

σ_m^2=0.01 β_x=3.75 β_Y=2.25

σ_x=0.25 σ_Y=0.30

Solution:

Calculation of Expected rate of Return according to CAPM for i) security 'x', ii) security 'y', iii) for an equally weighted portfolio of securities 'x' and 'y'.

(i) $E(R_X) = R_f + [\frac{RM-RF}{\sqrt{\sigma m}} * corxm * \sigma x]$

(ii) $E(R_x) = 0.05 + [\frac{0.12-0.05}{\sqrt{0.01}} * 0.3 * 0.30] = 0.1375$

(iii) $E(R_y) = 0.05 + [\frac{0.12-0.05}{\sqrt{0.01}} * 0.5 * 0.25] = 0.1130$

(iv) $E(R_p) = 0.05 *(0.1375) + 0.5*(0.1130) = 0.1253$

6. Mrs.Rmani owns a diversified portfolio security, which she estimates to have a standard deviation of 0.37. The return on short term I-bills is 0.09 and she estimates the expected market return to be 0.14, Market Standard Deviation to be 0.28. What is the expected return on Mrs. Ramani's portfolio according to CML?

Solution: Given E (R_m)=0.14 R_F=0.09

σ_m = 028 σ_P= 0.37

$E(R_P) = R_f + [\frac{RM-RF}{\sigma m} * \sigma P]$

$=0.09 + [\frac{0.14-0.09}{0.28} * 0.37]$

=0.09+0.066

=0.15607

=15.607%

7. Rajesh babu's Auto Ltd has a β of 0.865. If the expected Market Return is 17.50 and the Risk-free rate of return is 8.50%. What is the approximate required rate of return of Rajesh Babu's Auto Ltd?

Solution: β= 0.865 R_F=8.50% R_M = 17.5%

Required rate of return = $R_f + (R_M - R_F)\ \beta$

= 8.50+ (17.5-8.50) *0.865

=8.50 + 7.785

=16.285%

8. The return on the market portfolio is 14% and the return on zero (β) portfolio is 8%. The Markets Standard Deviation is 40%. Assume the CAPM with Risk free lending but Risk-free borrowing. Complete the following table

Stock	E(R)	σ	β	Residual variance
A	0.20	-	-	0.0475
B	0.26	-	-	0.0650

Solution: Given $R_m = 14\%$ $\sigma_M = 40\%$

$R_F = 8\%$

$$\beta_A = \frac{(E(R_A) - R_f)}{R_m - R_f} = (0.20\text{-}0.08)/\ (0.14\text{-}0.08) = 20$$

$$\beta_B = \frac{(E(R_B) - R_f)}{R_M - R_f} = (0.26\text{-}0.08)/\ (0.14\text{-}0.08) = 30$$

After calculating the respective β for both stocks. We proceed with calculation of (σ).

$\sigma_A{}^2 = \beta_A{}^2\ \sigma_M{}^2 + e^2$

$\sigma_A{}^2 = (20)^2 * (0.40)^2 + 0.0475$

$= 0.6875$

So therefore $\sigma_A = \sqrt{0.6875} = 0.83$

$\sigma_B{}^2 = (30)^2 * (0.40)^2 + 0.0650$

$= 1.5050$

$\sigma_B = \sqrt{1.3450} = 1023$

Note: $\boldsymbol{\beta_P = W\ \beta_A + (1\text{-}W)\ \beta_B}$

$\boldsymbol{\beta_P = (0.5*2) + (0.5*30)}$

=25

Standard deviation of portfolio with equal amounts in stocks A & B.

i.e., $\sigma_p{}^2 = (2.5)^2(0.40)^{2+}(0.5)^2(0.0475) + (0.5)^2(0.0650)$

$= 100 + 0.011875 + 0.016250$

$= 1.028125$

So therefore $\sigma_p = \sqrt{1.028125}$

$= 1.0139$

9. Complete the blanks in the following, assuming the relevant equilibrium model to be CAPM with unlimited borrowing and lending @ the risk less Rate of Interest

Security	E(R)	Standard Variance	Residual	β
1	0.24	--	0.10	2.5
2	--	0.30	0.06	0.50
3	0.18	--	0.17	1.00

Solution: Equations for E(R)'s of securities (1) and (3) are as follow

$R_1 = R_F + (R_M - R_F)\ \beta_1$ .... (i)

Similarly, $3_1 = R_F + (R_M - R_F)\ \beta_3$ .... (ii)

Subtracting (ii) from (i) we get

$R_1 - R_3 = (R_M - R_F)\ \beta_1 - \beta_3$

So therefore $(R_M - R_F) = (R_1 - R_3)/\ (\beta_1 - \beta_3)$

$= (0.24-0.18)/\ (2.5-1.0)$

$=0.04$

Using the value of $(R_M - R_F)$, we we can calculate the R_f by using equation (i)

$R_1 = R_F + (R_M - R_F)\ \beta_1$

$0.24 = R_F + (0.04*2.5)$

Therefore $R_F = 0.24-0.1$

$=0.14$

14%

Expected rate of return for security (2) is as follows

$E(R_2) = R_F + (R_M - R_F)\ \beta_2$: $R_M - R_F = 0$

$=0.14 + (0.04) * 0.50$

$=0.16$

$=16\%$

The formula for calculating variance of security (2) is as follows

$\sigma_A^2 = \beta_A^2\ \sigma_M^2 + \sigma_e^2$

$(0.3)0^2 = (0.50)^2\ \sigma_M^2 + (0.06)^2$

$\sigma_M^2 = [(0.30)^2 - (0.06)]/\ (0.50)^2$

$=0.12$

Standard deviation of security (1) and (3) is as follows

$\sigma_1^2 = \beta_1^2\ \sigma_M^2 + \sigma_e^2$

$= (2.5)^2 * 0.12 + 0.10$

$= 0.85$

So therefore $\sigma_1 = \sqrt{0.85}$

$=0.92$

$\sigma_3^2 = \beta_3^2\ \sigma_M^2 + \sigma_e^2$

$= (1.0)^2 * 0.12 + 0.17$

$=0.29$

$\sigma_3 = \sqrt{0.29}$

$=0.5385$

10. Given the following data:

security (i)	r_{im}	σ_i
ABC	0.5	0.25
BCD	0.3	0.30

$E(R_M)=0.12$, $R_f=0.05$ $\sigma^2=0.01$

Calculate:

β's for securities ABC and BCD and a portfolio of equally weighted securities ABC/BCD.

(II) E(R) for the securities ABC and BCD and the portfolio i.e., (ABC + BCD).

Solution: (i) $\beta_{ABC} = \frac{(corABC,M)*(\sigma ABC)}{(\sigma M)}$

$\beta_{ABC} = (0.5*0.25)/0.1 = 1.25$

$\beta_{BCD} = \frac{(corBCD,M)*(\sigma BCD)}{(\sigma M)}$

$\beta_{BCD} = (0.3*0.30)/0.1 = 0.90$

$\beta_P = W\ \beta_{ABC} + (1-W)\ \beta_{BCD}$

$\beta_P = (0.5*1.25) + (0.5*0.90)$

$=0.625 + 0.45$

$=1.075$

(ii) $E(R_{ABC}) = R_F + [\frac{RM-RF}{\sigma M} * COR_{ABC,M} * \sigma ABC]$

$= 0.05 + [\frac{0.12-0.05}{0.1} * 0.3 * 0.30]$

$= 0.1130$

$E(R_P) = (0.5*0.1375) + (0.5*0.1130)$

$= 0.12525$

11. An investor is considering to make an investment in the share of Divine Home Company. The following are the attributes of five economic forces that influence the return of Divines share.

Factor	β	E(R)	Actual value
GNP	1.95	6.0%	6.5%
Inflation	0.85	5.0%	5.75%
Interest Rate	1.20	7.0%	8.0%
Stock Market I	2.50	9.5%	11.5%
Industrial Product	2.20	2.0%	10.0%

Risk Free (Anticipated Rate of Return) on the Divine's share is 9%. How much is the total return on the share?

$E(R_j) = R_f + \Sigma\beta_i r_i$

$E(R_j) = g + [(6.5-6.0)1.95+(5.75-5.0)0.85+(8-7)1.20+(11.5-9.5)2.50+(10-9)2.20]$

$= 9+10$

$= 19\%$

12. The investor is seeking an efficient portfolio in the corr. Of 0.7 between the portfolio and the market and the S.D. is 2.5. Market S.D. is 1.4%. Market rate of return is 16%. The risk-free rate of return is 8%. What is the required rate of return?

Solution:

$R_f + \{[R(m) - R_f]\} / (\sigma_m \sigma_p)$

$= 0.008 + (0.16 - 0.08) / (0.014 \times 0.025) = 22.13$

13. Calculate the expected rate of return on CAPM.

Risk free rate of return 18%

Market rate of return 12%

Solution:

β 0.75

$E(R_p) = R_f + (R_m - R_f)\ \beta_j$

$= 8 + (8\text{-}12)0.75$

$= 11\%$

14. From the following information calculate expected rate of return of a portfolio.

Risk free rate = 12%

Market return of portfolio = 18%

Std. dev. Of asset = 2.8%

Market S.D. = 2.3%

Solution:

Corr. Coeff. Between portfolio and market = 0.8

$\beta_j = (\sigma_j \text{ cor}_j \text{ m}) / \sigma_m$

$= [2.8(0.8)]/2.3 = 2.24/2.30 = 0.97$

$E(R_p) = 12 + (0.8\text{-}12)0.97$

$= 12 + 6\text{x } 0.97 = 17.82\%$

15. Following data regarding 6 securities.

Security	Return	Risk (s.d.)
	%	%
A	8	4
B	8	5
C	12	12
D	4	4
E	9	5
F	8	6

1. Which of the securities will be selected?
2. Assuming perfect corr. analyses whether it is preferable to invest 17% with security A and 25% in C.

Solution:

Security selection based on risk analysis.

Assuming the perfect correlation between A and C weightage of 3:1. The return and risk is as under

A & C = 3:1

Wtd. Avg. return = 8x (3/4) + 12 x (1/4) = 9%

Wtd. Risk avg. = 4 x (3/4) + 12 x (1/4) = 6

Based on the wtd. Average between A & C the risk is 6% and return is 9%.

16. An investor is seeking the price to pay for a security whose SD is 3%. The corr. coeff. Of the security in the market is 0.8. The market SD 2.2%. The return from

Government securities 5.2%. The return from market portfolio is 9.8%. What is the required rate of return?

Solution:

$\beta_j = (\sigma_j \text{ cor}_j \text{ m}) / \sigma_m$

$= [3(0.8)] / 2.2 = 2.4/2.2 = 1.09$

$E(R_p) = R_f + (R_m - R_f)\ \beta_j$

$ER_p = 5.2 + (9.8 - 5.2)1.09$

$= 10.22\%$

17. **Calculate market sensitivity index(B) and expected return and portfolio from the following data.**
    1. **S.D. of asset = 2.5%**
    2. **Market S.D = 2%**
    3. **Risk free rate of return = 13%**
    4. **Expected rate of return on market portfolio = 15%**
    5. **Corr. coeff. between portfolio and market = 0.8**
    6. **What will be the expected rate of return on portfolio if β is 0.5 and risk-free return is 10%?**

Solution:

$E(R_p) = R_f + (R_m - R_f)\ \beta_j$

$ERp = 13 + (15-13)1$

$= 15$

$\beta_j = (\sigma_j \text{ cor}_j \text{ m})/\sigma_m$

$= [2.5(0.8)]/2 = 1$

$ERp = 10 + [(15-10)0.5]$

$= 12.5$

18. **An investment manager provides the following data:**

Investment equity share	Initial price	Dividend	Market price	β
Cement Ltd.	25	Rs. 2	50	0.8
Steam Ltd.	35	Rs. 2	60	0.7
Liquor Ltd.	45	Rs. 2	135	0.5
Govt. bond	1000	Rs. 4	1005	0.99

Solution:

Risk free return is 14%. Calculate expected rate of return of portfolio of CAPM and based on which calculate average rate of return.

Expected return on market portfolio

$$R = \frac{P_1 - P_0}{P_0} + \frac{D_0}{P_0} \times 100$$

Particulars	Initial price	Dividend	Capital gain (M_p - I_p)
Cement Ltd	25	Rs. 2	50 – 25 = 25
Steam Ltd.	35	Rs. 2	60 – 35 = 25
Liquor Ltd.	45	Rs. 2	135 – 45 = 90
Govt. bond	1000	Rs. 140	1005 – 1000 = 5
Total			145

Return on market portfolio

R_m = [(146+145)/1105] x 100 = 26.35%

$ER_p = R_f + (R_m - R_f)\ \beta_j$

Cement = 14 + [(26.33-14)0.8]

= 23.86%

Steel = 14 + [(26.33-14)0.7]

= 22.63%

Liquor = 14 + [(26.33-4)0.5]

= 20.17

Bond = 14 + [(26.33-14)0.99]

= 26.21

Avg. rate of return = (23.86 + 22.63 + 20.17 + 26.21) / 4

= 23.22

19. From the following data compute B for security X and security Y and based on which calculated expected rate of return under CAPM.

Security	Co-eff corr.	S. D
X	0.5	0.25
Y	0.3	0.3

R_m = 12%

R_f = 5%

$\sigma^2 = 0.01$

$\sigma_m = 0.1$

$\beta_j = (\sigma_j\ cor_j\ m) / \sigma_m$

= [0.25(0.05)]/0.1 = 1.25

$ER_x = R_f + (R_m - R_f)\ \beta_j$

= 5 + (12- 5)1.25

= 13.75

By = [0.3(0.3)] / 0.1

= 0.9

ERy = 5 + (12 – 5)0.9

= 11.3

$ER(P) = R_f + (R_m - R_f)\ \beta_j$

ER(P) when β is 1.25

= 5 + (12-5) (1.25)

= 5 + 8.75

= 13

ER(P) when β is 0.9

= 5 + (12-5) (0.9)

= 5 + 6.3

= 11.3

20. Calculate the expected return on portfolio A with following data:

(i) risk free rate of return 8%

(ii) expected return on market portfolio 12%

(iii) market sensitivity index 0.75

Solution:

the expected rate of return on portfolio 'A' is calculated with the application of the following formula:

$E(Rj) = Rf + B_j\ [E(Rm) – Rf]$

= 8 + 7.5 (12 – 8) = 11%

21. From the following information, calculate the expected rate of return of a portfolio:

Risk free rate of interest	12%
Expected return of market	18%
Standard deviation of an assets	2.8%
Market standard deviation	2.3%
Correlation coefficient of portfolio with market	0.8%

Solution:

Since B is missed in the problem given, B is calculated by applying the following formula:

B_i = (6j 6m cor j m)/ 6^2m (or) (6j cor j m)/6m

= (0.80 x 0.028)/0.023 = 0.97

Now, we can calculate the expected rate of return of a portfolio by applying CAPM
$E(Rj) = Rf + B_j [E(Rm) - Rf]$

E (Rj) = 12 + .97 (18 – 12) = 17.82%

22. **Calculate the market sensitivity index and the expected return on the portfolio from the following data:**

Standard deviation of an assets	2.5%
Market standard deviation	2.0%
Risk free rate of return	13.0%
Expected return on market portfolio	15.0%
Correlation co-efficient of portfolio with market	0.8%

Solution:

ii) What will be expected return on the portfolio beta is 0.5 and risk-free return is 10%.

B_j = (6j cor j m)/6m = (0.8 x 0.025)/.02 = 1

$E(Rj) = Rf + B_j [E(Rm) - Rf]$

E(Rj) = 13% + 1 (15% - 13%) = 15%

iii) E(Rj) = 10% + .5 (15% - 10%) = 12.5%

Capital Market Instruments

23. **Jai Ltd. has an asset beta of 0.80 and debt ratio of 0.50. Expected market return is 25%, while the risk-free return is 10%. Assuming a tax rate of 40% compute the cost of equity under CAPM model.**

Solution:

Under CAPM cost of equity $Ke = R_f + \beta_{equity}(R_m - R_f)$

Also, we know that $\beta_{equity} = \frac{\beta_{assets}(1-RT)}{(1-R)}$

Where R is the debt ratio $\frac{D}{(D+E)}$ and T is the tax rate

$$Ke = R_f + \beta_{assets}\frac{(1-RT)}{(1-R)}(R_m - R_f)$$

$$K_e = 0.1 + \frac{0.80(1-0.5*0.4)}{(1-0.5)}[0.25-0.10]$$

$$= 0.10 + 1.28(0.15) = 0.292 = \boxed{29.2\%}$$

24. If alpha is 3%, riskless rate is 8%. Beta is 2 and the expected market return is 10%, then find out. The expected risk premiums on the portfolio under the CAPM model and Market model.

Solution:

We know that under Market Model risk premium is given by:

$$R_p - R_f = \alpha_p^* + \beta(Rm - Rf)$$

$$(R_p - R_f) = \alpha_p - R_f(1-\beta) + \beta(Rm - Rf),$$

Where $(R_p - R_f)$ Risk Premium

$$R_p - R_f = 3 - 8(1-2) + 2(10-8) = 3 + 8 + 4 = \boxed{15\%}$$

Under CAPM, risk premium is given by

$$R_p - R_f = \beta(Rm - Rf)$$

$$R_p - R_f = 2(10-8) = \boxed{4\%}$$

R_p =Return on portfolio,

R_f = Risk free rate of interest rate

β= Sensitivity of portfolio's return to market return,

α_p = Y intercept of characteristic line,

Rm = Expected market return.

25. The following date is available in respect of JK Ltd.

Return (%)	Probability
-10	0.1
10	0.3
15	0.4
20	0.2

Solution:

Find expected return and S.D

$$(-10)(0.1) + (10)(0.3) + (15)(0.4) + (20)(0.2) = -1 + 3 + 6 + 4 = \boxed{12\%}$$

$$(\sigma^2) = (-10-12)^2(0.1) + (10-12)^2(0.3) + (15-12)^2(0.4) + (20-12)^2(0.20)$$

$$= 48.4 + 1.2 + 3.6 + 12.8 = 66$$

$$\text{Standard devation } (\sigma) = \sqrt{\sigma^2} - \sqrt{66} - \boxed{8.12\%}$$

26. A portfolio consists of three securities A, B and C with the following relevant information.

	A	B	C
Expected return (%)	27	24	24
Standard deviation	33	28	26
Correlation Coefficient between			
		AB	0.2
		BC	0.4
		AC	0.5

If the weight of securities is equal find out the risk and expected return of the portfolio.

Expected Return of portfolio

$$= (27*1/3) + (24*1/3) + (22*1/3) = 9 + 8 + 7.33 = 24.33\%$$

$$\sigma_p^2 = (33)^2(1/3)^2 + (28)^2(1/3)^2 + (26)^2(1/3)^2 + 2(1/3)(1/3)(0.2)(33)(28) + 2(1/3)(1/3)(-0.4)(28)(26)$$

$$+ 2((1/3)(1/3)(0.5)(33)(26)$$

=121+87.11+75.11+41.07+64.71+95.33

=354.91

$$\sigma p = \sqrt{\sigma_p^2} = \sqrt{354.91} = \boxed{18.84\%}$$

27. The following information is available regarding the returns on the shares of x ltd. And on the shares of Y Ltd.

	X (Rx)	Condition probability	Y (Ry)
A	12%	0.2	16%
B	18%	0.4	15%
C	20%	0.4	25%

The current risk-free interest rate is 9%

Required: Calculate the coefficient of correlation between the returns on X ltd. And returns on Y ltd.

Solution:

The coefficient of correlation between the returns on X ltd. And returns on Y ltd is given by:

$$\text{Cor x, y} = \frac{COV(X,Y)}{\sigma_X * \sigma_y}$$

$$\text{cov}(X,Y) = \sum p(Rx - \overline{Rx})*(Ry - \overline{Ry})$$

The expected return on the C ltd., R_x, and the market portfolio, R_y are as follows:

$$\overline{Rx} = (0.2*16\%) + (0.4*15\%) + (0.4*25\%) = 19.2\%$$

$$\overline{Ry} = (0.2*12\%) + (0.4*18\%) + (0.4*20\%) = 17.6\%$$

Calculation of SD and the correlation coefficient

Probability	$(Rx - \overline{Rx})$	$(Ry - \overline{Ry})$	$(Rx - \overline{Rx})^2$	$(Ry - \overline{Ry})^2$	P (1)(2)
(p)	-1	-2			
0.2	(16-19.2) = -3.2	(12-17.6) = -5.6	2.05	6.27	3.58
0.4	(15-19.2) = -4.2	(18-17.6) = 0.4	7.06	0.06	0.67
0.4	(25-19.2) =5.8	(20-17.6) = 2.4	13.46	2.30	5.57
			22.57	8.63	8.48

Therefore, the SD of the security X

$$\sigma_X = \sqrt{22.57} = \boxed{4.75}$$

And, the SD of the security Y,

$$\sigma_y = \sqrt{8.63} = \boxed{2.94}$$

$$COV(X,Y) = \boxed{8.48}$$

$$COR(X,Y) = \frac{8.48}{4.75 * 2.94} = \boxed{0.61}$$

28. P ltd and Q ltd. Have correlation coefficient of +0.6 their respective return and risk is as under:

R_p=12%

R_q=17%

$\sigma_p = 22\%$

$\sigma_q = 27\%$

Solution:

Compute the portfolio of P&Q in order to minimize risk.

Let proportion of investment (or weight of securities) in P Ltd. And Q Ltd. Be W_p and W_q respectively. Then, in order to minimize risk, we have:

$$W_p = \frac{\sigma_Q^2 - r_{PQ}\,\sigma_p \sigma_Q}{\sigma_p^2 + \sigma_Q^2 - (2\,r_{PQ}\,\sigma_p \sigma_q)}$$

$$= \frac{(0.27)^2 - 0.6 * 0.22 * 0.27}{(0.22)^2 + (0.27)^2 - 2 * 0.6 * 0.22 * 0.27}$$

$$= \frac{0.073 - 0.036}{0.048 + 0.073 - 0.071}$$

$$= \frac{0.037}{0.05} = \boxed{0.074}$$

$$W_Q = 1 - 0.7 = 0.26 = \boxed{26\%}$$

SUMMARY

1. Essentiality of the Markowitz portfolio theory is the problem of optimal portfolio selection. The Markowitz approach included portfolio formation by considering the expected rate of return and risk of individual stocks measured as standard deviation, and their interrelationship as measured by correlation. The diversification plays a key role in the modern portfolio theory.
2. Indifference curves represent an investor's preferences for risk and return. These curves should be drawn, putting the investment return on the vertical axis and the risk on the horizontal axis.
3. Two important fundamental assumptions than applying indifference curves to Markowitz portfolio theory. An assumption of no satiation assumes that the investors prefer higher levels of return to lower levels of return, because the higher levels of return allow the investor to spend more on consumption at the end of the investment period. An assumption of risk aversion assumes that the investor when given the choice, will choose the investment or investment portfolio with the smaller risk, i.e. the investors are risk averse.
4. Efficient set theorem states that an investor will choose his/ her optimal portfolio from the set of the portfolios that (1) offer maximum expected return for varying level of risk, and (2) offer minimum risk for varying levels of expected return.
5. Efficient set of portfolios involves the portfolios that the investor will find optimal ones. These portfolios are lying on the "northwest boundary" of the feasible set and is called an efficient frontier. The efficient frontier can be described by the curve in the risk-return space with the highest expected rates of return for each level of risk. Feasible set is opportunity set, from which the efficient set of portfolios can be identified. The feasibility set represents all portfolios that could be formed from the number of securities and lie either or within the boundary of the feasible set.
6. Capital Market Line (CML) shows the trade off-between expected rate of return and risk for the efficient portfolios under determined risk-free return.

7. The expected rate of return on the portfolio is the weighted average of the expected returns on its component securities.
8. The calculation of standard deviation for the portfolio can 't simply uses the weighted average approach. The reason is that the relationship between the securities in the same portfolio measured by coefficient of correlation must be taken into account. When forming the diversified portfolios consisting large number of securities investors found the calculation of the portfolio risk using standard deviation technically complicated.
9. Measuring Risk in Capital asset Pricing Model (CAPM) is based on the identification of two key components of total risk: systematic risk and unsystematic risk. Systematic risk is that associated with the market. Unsystematic risk is unique to an individual asset and can be diversified away by holding many different assets in the portfolio. In CAPM investors are compensated for taking only systematic risk.
10. The essence of the CAPM: CAPM predicts what an expected rate of return for the investor should be, given other statistics about the expected rate of return in the market, risk free rate of return and market risk (systematic risk).
11. Each security has its individual systematic - undiversified risk, measured using coefficient Beta. Coefficient Beta (P) indicates how the price of security/ return on security depends upon the market forces. The Beta of the portfolio is simply a Weighted average of the Betas of its component securities, where the proportions invested in the securities are the respective weights.
12. Security Market Line (SML) demonstrates the relationship between the expected return and Beta. Each security can be described by its specific security market line, they differ because their Betas are different and reflect different levels of market risk for these securities.
13. Arbitrage Pricing Theory (APT) states, that the expected rate of return of security is the linear function from the complex economic factors common to all securities. There could presumably be an infinitive number of factors. The examples of possible macroeconomic factors which could be included in using APT model are GDP growth; an interest rate; an exchange rate; a default spread on corporate bonds, etc.

FILL IN THE BLANKS

1. In a perfectly efficient market all securities are correctly priced means there are no :- (Underpriced and overpriced securities)
2. A security is said to be ________ if its current market price is over its intrinsic value. (Overpriced)
3. What is sector specific funds? (Scheme which invest in certain sectors)
4. Formula for calculation of portfolio variance requires: - (Expected return on portfolio, expected return on assets, Weight of asset in the portfolio)
5. The security market is the market for: - (Correct Answer Equity, Debt, Derivatives)

6. In a typical stock market cycle which are the types of trends? (Trends upward, Trend downward, Sideway trend)
7. A market that is trading at a Price earnings ratio that is much higher than its historical norms is considered to be: - (Overvalued)
8. Under ________ EMH investors cannot earn abnormal/superior profits on securities on a consistent basis. (Semi-strong form)
9. When an investor invests in stock, expects to get the dividends and an expected price for the period the stock is held is the rule of: - (The General model).
10. Which market is affected with the improving and higher growth rate in economy? (Stock market)
11. If rupee weakens against the dollar, it has favorable impact for the importers. (False)
12. What is the objective of Portfolio management? (To Minimize risk and maximize return)
13. An asset which have certain expected return and variance of return is zero .... (Risk free asset)
14. ------------ is used to reflect the risk factor sensitivities can also be considered to arrive at the expected returns. (Beta coefficient)
15. ----------------is a portfolio selection approach developed by William Sharpe. (single index model)
16. By skillful balancing of the investment proportions in different securities, the portfolio risk can be minimized to zero, this portfolio is termed as............... (Minimum Variance Portfolio)
17. The relationship between an asset return and its systematic risk is expressed by.................. (CAPM)
18. The linear relationship between the required rates of return for efficient portfolio and their deviations is represented by......... (Capital market line)
19. .... states that two identical goods should be sold at the same price. (Law of One Price)
20. A professional who manages investment portfolios with the objectives of profitability, growth and risk minimizations............... (Portfolio Manager)

SHORT ANSWER QUESTIONS

1. Risk free Asset
2. Unsystematic Risk
3. Systematic Risk
4. Capital Asset Pricing Model
5. Asset pricing

6. Asset-specific required return
7. Risk and diversification
8. The efficient (Markowitz) frontier
9. Assumptions of CAPM
10. Security Market Line (SML)
11. Factors affecting the Return:
12. Concept of Risk under APM
13. Efficient Frontier.
14. Active Portfolio Strategy.
15. Capital Market Line.
16. Arbitrage Pricing.
17. Passive Portfolio strategy.
18. Inputs for Markowitz Model.
19. Portfolio Strategy.
20. Single Index.
21. Optimal portfolio.
22. Separation theorem.
23. Arbitrage portfolio.

ESSAY TYPE QUESTIONS

1. What is capital market theory of Portfolio?
2. Define risk free Asset. Discuss in brief regarding allowing for risk free lending and allowing for risk free borrowing.
3. Explain the concept of Capital Market Line.
4. What is separation theorem?
5. What is CAPM? Discuss its assumptions?
6. Explain the concept of Security Market Line.
7. How to identify over-priced and underpriced securities?
8. What is efficient frontier? How does the efficient frontier change when there are borrowings and lending portfolios?
9. What are the assumptions of CAPM and APT? Examine the similarities and dissimilarities between them.
10. What are the similarities and differences between CAPM and APT?

11. What is meant by an efficient market? What are the benefits to the economy from an efficient market?
12. If the efficient market hypothesis is true, what are the implications for the investors?
13. What are the conditions for an efficient market? Discuss if are they met in the reality.
14. How does Markowitz Theory help in planning an investor's portfolio?
15. Define Markowitz diversification. Explain the statistical method used by to obtain the risk reducing benefit?
16. What are the strength and weaknesses of the Markowitz approach?
17. Explain how the efficient frontier is determined using the Markowitz approach. Use a two-security approach.
18. Explain why most investors prefer to hold a diversified portfolio of securities as opposed to placing all of their wealth in a single asset.
19. In terms of the Markowitz portfolio model, explain, how an investor identifies his / her optimal portfolio. What specific information does an investor need to identify optimal portfolio?
20. How many portfolios are on an efficient frontier? How is an investor's risk aversion indicated in an indifference curve?
21. Describe the key assumptions underlying CAPM.
22. Many of underlying assumptions of the CAPM are violated in some degree in "real world". Does that fact invalidate model's calculations? Explain.

EXERCISE PROBLEMS

1. When we make risk return analysis of different securities from A to F we can observe that security A gives return of 8% and risk of 4% simultaneously securities B-F gives a return of 8% and risk of 5%, security D gives 4% return, 45 risk, C provides 12% return and 12% risk. Hence security A dominates B, D, F. in case of security C and e both provides high return high risk based on this arises, it can be observed that A provides high return low risk and C provides high return high risk.
2. Given the following data draw the SML. Plot each stock on your graph

Security	E(R)	β	S. D
Ram's Int	0.32	1.70	0.50
Jeans Ltd	0.30	1.40	0.35
Grow & Co	0.25	1.10	0.40
Needs Ltd	0.22	0.95	0.24

3. Assume there are two stocks, A and B, with ft $A = 1.4$ *and* ft B = *.8.* Assume also that the CAPM model applies. If the mean return on the market portfolio is 10% and the risk-free rate of return is 5%, calculate the mean return of the portfolios consisting of:

   75% of stock A and 25% of stock B,

   50% of stock A and 50% of stock B,

   25% of stock A and 75% of stock B.

   If the idiosyncratic variations of the stocks are *O€A = 4, <7eB = 2* and the variance of the market portfolio is $<J^2{}_M = 12,$ calculate the variance of the portfolios in (a), (b), (c). What are the mean return and variance of the portfolios if they are 50% financed by borrowing?

4. Assume there are just two risky securities in the market portfolio. Security A, which constitutes 40% of this portfolio, has an expected return of 10% and a standard deviation of 20%. Security B has an expected return of 15% and a standard deviation of 28%. If the correlation between the assets is 0.3 and the risk-free rate 5%, calculate the capital market line.

5. The market portfolio is composed of four securities. Given the following data, calculate the market portfolio's standard deviation.

Security	Covariance with market	Proportion
A	242	0.2
B	360	0.3
C	155	0.2
D	210	0.3

6. Consider an economy with just two assets. The details of these are given below.

Exercise 69 Consider an economy with just two assets. The details of these are given below.	Number of Shares	Price	Expected Return	Standard Deviation
A	100	1.5	15	15
B	150	2	12	9

7. Given the following data, calculate the security market line and the betas of the two securities.

	Expected return	Correlation with market portfolio	Standard deviation
Security 1	15.5	0.9	2
Security 2	9.2	0.8	9
Market portfolio	12	1	12
Risk free asset	5	0	0

The Correlation coefficient between the returns on the two assets if 1/3 and there is also a risk-free asset. Assume the CAPM model is satisfied.

(i) What is the expected rate of return on the market portfolio?

(ii) What is the standard deviation of the market portfolio?

(iii) What is the beta of stock A?

(iv) What is the risk-free rate of return

(v) Construct the capital market line and the security market line

8. Consider an economy with three risky assets. The details of these are given below

	No. of Shares	Price	Expected Return	Standard Deviation
A	100	4	8	10
B	300	6	12	14
C	100	5	10	12

The correlation coefficient between the returns on any pair of assets is 1/2 and there is also a risk-free asset. Assume the CAPM model is satisfied.

(i) Calculate the expected rate of return and standard deviation of the market portfolio.

(ii) Calculate the betas of the three assets.

(iii) Use solution to (ii) to find the beta of the market portfolio.

(iv) What is the risk-free rate of return implied by these returns?

(v) Describe how this model could be used to price a new asset, D.

9. Consider an asset with expected future price of 10 and a beta of 1.2. If rf = *0.05* and r_M = *0.1,* what is the fair market price of the asset today? If the equilibrium price today is? what is the expected price next year?

10. Given the following information:

- Expected return for stock A = 18%
- Expected return for stock B = 25%
- Standard deviation of stock A = 12%
- Standard deviation of stock B = 20%
- Correlation coefficient = 1,0.

11. Choose the investment below that represents the minimum risk portfolio:

100% invest in stock A;

100% invest in stock B;

50% in stock A and 50% in stock B;

20% invest in stock A and 80% in stock B

60% invest in stock A and 40% in stock B.

Portfolio	Expected rate of return, %	Standard deviation
A	12	15
B	10	8
C	10	9

The following investment portfolios are evaluated by investments. Using Markowitz portfolio theory explain the choice for investor between portfolios A, B and C.

12. Investor owns the portfolio composed of three stocks. The Betas of these stocks and their proportions in portfolio are shown in the table. What is the Beta of the investor's portfolio?

Stock	Beta	Proportion in portfolio, %
A	0,8	30
B	1,2	40
C	-0,9	30

13. Comment on the risk of the stocks presented below. Which of them are more /less risky and why?

Stock	Beta
A	0,92
B	2,20
C	0,97
D	-1.12
E	1.18
F	0,51

14. Investor ownes a portfolio of four securities. The characteristics of the securities and their proportions in the portfolio are presented in the table.

Security	Coefficient Beta	Proportion, %	Expected rate of return, %
A	1,40	30	13
B	0,90	30	18
C	1,00	20	10
D	-1,30	20	12

(a) What is the expected rate of return of this portfolio?

(b) What is the risk of the portfolio?

(c) If the investor wants to reduce risk in his portfolio how he could restructure his portfolio?

15. The following table presents the three-stock portfolio.

Stocks	Portfolio Weight	Coefficient Beta	Expected return	Standard deviation
A	0,25	0,50	0,40	0,07
B	0,25	0,50	0,25	0,05
C	0,50	1,00	0,21	0,07

Variance of the market returns is 0,06.

(a) What is the Beta coefficient of the portfolio?

(b) What is the expected rate of return on the portfolio?

(c) What is an actual variance of the portfolio, if the following actual covariance between the stock's returns is given: Cov (r**A**, r**B**) = 0.020 Cov (r**A**, r**C**) = 0.035 Cov (r**B**, r**C**) = 0,035

16. The rate of return of securities of ABC Ltd. and XYZ Ltd. in different market conditions is as follows:

Market Condition	*Probability*	*Rate of Return*	
		ABC Ltd.	XYZ *Ltd.*
Bearish'	0.30	15%	20%
Normal	0.30	20%	30%
Bullish	0.40	30%	40%

Find out the expected return and risk (O') for the securities of two companies, if an investor invests Rs. 3,00,000 in ABC Ltd. and Rs. 2,00,000 in XYZ Ltd., what will be the expected return of the investor?

17. Mr. Gupta makes an Investment at Rs. 50. The year end price of this investment under different market conditions with equal probabilities is as follows:

Condition	Year end Price (Rs.)
Bullish	75
Normal	60
Bearish	45

Find out the expected value of return for one year period and risk (O') of the return. Also calculate inflation adjusted return if rate of inflation during the year is 8%

18. In a portfolio of the company Rs, 2,00,000 have been invested in asset X which has an expected return of 8.5%, Rs, 2,80,000 in asset Y which has an expected return of 10.2% and Rs. 3,20,000 in asset Z which has expected return of 12%. What is the expected return for the portfolio? (9) [2009]

19. Mr. A has a portfolio of five securities whose expected return and amount invested are as follows. (9) [2009]

	I	II	III	IV	V
	(Rs.)	(Rs.)	(Rs.)	(Rs.)	(Rs.)
Amount	1,50,000	2,50,000	3,00,000	1,00,000	2,00,000
Expected Return	12%	9%	15%	18%	14%

Find out the % expected return of the portfolio.

20. The return on security 'X' and security 'Y' under different situations is given below.

Find its risk and return:

Probability	Security X	Security Y	Security
0	3	10	12
0	4	12	13
0	3	15	14

21. Mr. X considering investment in securities P and Q whose details are given below:

	P	Q
Expected return	13%	16%
Risk (standard deviation)	4%	7%

If a portfolio of 30% of P and 70% of Q is formed, find the:

(i) Expected return of the portfolio

(ii) Minimum risk of the portfolio

(iii) Maximum risk of the portfolio.

22. The following information is available from Z in respect of his portfolio:

Security	Weight	Expected Return	Standard Deviation
A	50%	20%	24%
B	50%	12%	16%

Find out the correlation between the return if the standard deviation of the portfolio is 20% or 18%.

Find out the standard deviation of the portfolio comprising A and B in the ratio of 25% and 75% respectively.

23. Two securities A and B have a variance of 13 and 12 and expected returns of 15% and 12% respectively. The covariance between the returns is 3. Find out the risk and return of the following portfolios:

	A	B
(0)	0.2	0.8
00	0.7	0.3
(Hi)	0.5	0.5

CASE STUDIES

CASE STUDY 1

Indian capital market has witnessed a phenomenal growth in the last two decades. Describe the salient features of capital market development in India and highlight the new financial instruments available for investment.

CHAPTER 14

Performance Evaluation of Portfolio's

MUTUAL FUNDS

Like most developed and developing countries the mutual fund culture has been catching on in India. There are various reasons for this. Mutual funds make it easy and less costly for investors to satisfy their need for capital growth, income and/or income preservation. And in addition to this a mutual fund brings the benefits of diversification and money management to the individual investor, providing an opportunity for financial success that was once available only to a select few.

A Mutual Fund is a trust that pools the savings of a number of investors who share a common financial goal. The money thus collected is then invested in capital market instruments such as shares, debentures and other securities. The income earned through these investments and the capital appreciations realized are shared by its unit holders in proportion to the number of units owned by them. Thus, a Mutual Fund is the most suitable investment for the common man as it offers an opportunity to invest in a diversified, -professionally managed basket of securities at a relatively low cost. The flow chart below describes broadly the working of a mutual fund:

MUTUAL FUND OPERATION FLOW CHART

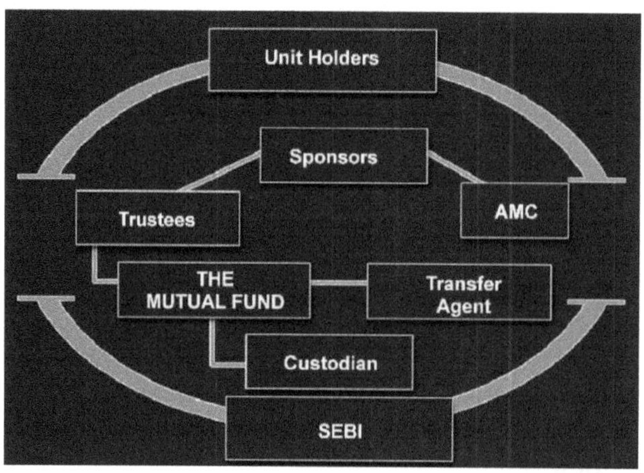

ORGANIZATION OF A MUTUAL

BENEFITS OF MUTUAL FUNDS

Investing in mutual has various benefits which makes it an ideal investment avenue. Following are some of the primary benefits.

PROFESSIONAL INVESTMENT MANAGEMENT

One of the primary benefits of mutual funds is that an investor has access to professional management. A good investment manager is certainly worth the fees you will pay. Good mutual fund managers with an excellent research team can do a better job of monitoring the companies they have chosen to invest in than you can, unless you have time to spend on researching the companies you select for your portfolio. That is because Mutual funds hire full-time, high-level investment professionals. Funds can afford to do so as they manage large pools of money. The managers have real-time access to crucial market information and are able to execute trades on the largest and most cost-effective scale. When you buy a mutual fund, the primary asset you are buying is the manager, who will be controlling which assets are chosen to meet the funds' stated investment objectives.

DIVERSIFICATION

'Do not put all of eggs in one basket" Diversification is the idea of not putting all of your money in one spot. It means holding many types of assets. For example, owning shares in many companies or owning some stocks and some bonds. Diversification lowers risk since when some assets are up in value, others are down in value.

A crucial element in investing is asset allocation. It plays a very big part in the success of any portfolio. However, small investors do not have enough money to properly allocate their assets. By pooling your funds with others, you can quickly benefit from greater diversification. Mutual funds invest in a broad range of securities. This limits investment risk by reducing the effect of a possible decline in the value of any one security. Mutual fund unit-holders can benefit from diversification techniques usually available only to investors wealthy enough to buy significant positions in a wide variety of securities.

Diversification, however, can drive up transaction costs for small investors. Mutual Funds are a solution to this problem. Investors pool their money and the fund then invests in many different assets. By spreading out trading costs over a larger investment, the percentage transaction costs are often lower. Additionally, each investor need not do the research which further saves expenses.

LOW COST

A mutual fund lets you participate in a diversified portfolio for as little as Rs.5,000, and sometimes less. And with a no-load fund, you pay little or no sales charges to own them.

CONVENIENCE AND FLEXIBILITY

Investing in mutual funds has its own convenience. While you own just one security rather than many, you still enjoy the benefits of a diversified portfolio and a wide range of services. Fund managers decide what securities to trade, collect the interest payments and see that your dividends on portfolio securities are received and your rights exercised. It also uses the services of a high-quality custodian and registrar. Another big advantage is that you can move your funds easily from one fund to another within a mutual fund family. This allows you to easily rebalance your portfolio to respond to significant fund management or economic changes.

LIQUIDITY

In open-ended schemes, you can get your money back promptly at net asset value related prices from the mutual fund itself.

TRANSPARENCY

Regulations for mutual funds have made the industry very transparent. You can track the investments that have been made on your behalf and the specific investments made by the mutual fund scheme to see where your money is going. In addition to this, you get regular information on the value of your investment.

VARIETY

There is no shortage of variety when investing in mutual funds. You can find a mutual fund that matches just about any investing strategy you select. There are funds that focus on blue-chip stocks, technology stocks, bonds or a mix of stocks and bonds. The greatest challenge can be sorting through the variety and picking the best for you.

TYPE OF INVESTMENT

An alternative way of classifying mutual funds is by the types of assets the fund buys. Some of the more popular are:

Money Markets

Stock Mutual Funds

Bond Funds

Funds that try to diversify across asset classes as well as within a given asset class are called balanced funds. A specific type of this is called a life cycle fund. A life cycle fund tries to invest in assets that are appropriate for the average investor in the fund. For example, a life cycle fund that targeted young investors would have riskier growth stocks whereas a fund that targeted retirees would likely have more invested in government bonds.

Within these broad categories there can be further stratification. For example: stock fund that invest only in internet firms, or stock funds that invest only in dividend paying firms.

Funds that specialize within a certain industry are often called sector funds. These are quite risky as they have not diversified away the industry specific risks.

LOCATION OF HOLDINGS

Yet another way of classifying funds is where the assets are located. For example, you can have Domestic or International funds. Some of the categories here include specific country funds (example the Mexico Fund) or region funds (example Latin America) or even by type of market (Emerging Market).

One important reason for locational municipal bond funds is for tax purposes. Interest earned on municipal bonds is tax-free in the state of the municipality. Thus, an investor in Nebraska that buys a muni-bond issued by the Omaha City government need not pay state or federal tax on the interest. The interest on the bond would however be taxable for an investor in New York.

MISCELLANEOUS

Hedge Funds-not a true "mutual fund" but in many ways quite similar. Funds that take very large bets on various types of investments. DO NOT assume that a HEDGE fund is low risk (the word Hedge is not correctly used here). Very low liquidity. Money is generally tied up for at least a year. Naked Funds- Mutual fund that allows investors to track every trade the fund manager makes. Interval Funds-In an effort to remain fully invested, certain mutual funds only allow withdrawals at certain times.

TYPES OF MUTUAL FUNDS

Getting a handle on what's under the hood helps you become a better investor and put together a more successful portfolio. To do this one must know the different types of funds that cater to investor needs, whatever the age, financial position, risk tolerance and return expectations. The mutual fund schemes can be classified according to both their investment objective (like income, growth, tax saving) as well as the number of units (if these are unlimited then the fund is an open-ended one while if there are limited units then the fund is close-ended).

This section provides descriptions of the characteristics -- such as investment objective and potential for volatility of your investment -- of various categories of funds. The type of securities purchased by each fund organizes these descriptions: equities, fixed-income, money market instruments, or some combination of these.

OPEN-ENDED SCHEMES

Open-ended schemes do not have a fixed maturity period. Investors can buy or sell units at NAV-related prices from and to the mutual fund on any business day. These schemes have unlimited capitalization, open-ended schemes do not have a fixed maturity, there is no cap on the amount you can buy from the fund and the unit capital can keep growing. These funds are not generally listed on any exchange.

Open-ended schemes are preferred for their liquidity. Such funds can issue and redeem units any time during the life of a scheme. Hence, unit capital of open-ended funds can fluctuate on a daily basis. The advantages of open-ended funds over close-ended are as follows:

Any time exit option. The issuing company directly takes the responsibility of providing an entry and an exit. This provides ready liquidity to the investors and avoids reliance on transfer deeds, signature verifications and bad deliveries. Any time entry option, an open-ended fund allows one to enter the fund at any time and even to invest at regular intervals.

CLOSE-ENDED SCHEMES

Close-ended schemes have fixed maturity periods. Investors can buy into these funds during the period when these funds are open in the initial issue. After that such schemes can not issue new units except in case of bonus or rights issue. However, after the initial issue, you can buy or sell units of the scheme on the stock exchanges where they are listed. The market price of the units could vary from the NAV of the scheme due to demand and supply factors, investors' expectations and other market factors

CLASSIFICATION ACCORDING TO INVESTMENT OBJECTIVES

Mutual funds can be further classified based on their specific investment objective such as growth of capital, safety of principal, current income or tax-exempt income.

In general, mutual funds fall into three general categories:

- Equity Funds are those that invest in shares or equity of companies.
- Fixed-Income Funds invest in government or corporate securities that offer fixed rates of return are
- While funds that invest in a combination of both stocks and bonds are called Balanced Funds.

EQUITY FUNDS

Equity funds primarily invest in common stock of companies. Equity funds can be growth funds or income funds. Growth funds focus on growth stocks, i.e., companies with strong growth potential, with capital appreciation being the major driver, while income funds focus on companies that have high dividend yields. Income funds focus on dividend income or coupon payments from bonds (if they are not pure equity). Equity funds may also be sector-specific wherein the investment is restricted to stocks from a specific industry. For example, in India we have many funds focusing on companies in power sector and infrastructure sector. Bond funds invest primarily in various bonds that were described in the earlier segment. They have a stable income stream and relatively lower risk. They could potentially invest in corporate bonds, Government. bonds, or both.

INDEX FUNDS

Index funds have a passive investment strategy and they try to replicate a broad market index. A scheme from such a fund invests in components of a particular index proportionate to their representation in the benchmark. It is possible that a scheme tracks more than one index (in some pre-specified ratio), in either equity, or across asset classes.

MONEY MARKET FUNDS

Money market mutual funds invest in money market instruments, which are short-term securities issued by banks, non-bank corporations and Governments. The various money market instruments have already been discussed earlier.

FUND OF FUNDS

Fund of funds add another layer of diversification between the investor and securities in the market. Instead of individual stocks, or bonds, these mutual funds invest in units of other mutual funds, with the fund managers' mandate being the optimal choice across mutual fund schemes given extant market conditions.

Other Investment Companies

In addition to the broad categories mentioned here, there are many other kinds of funds, depending on market opportunities, and investor appetite. Total return funds look at a combination of capital appreciation and dividend income. Hybrid funds invest in a combination of equity, bonds, convertibles, and derivative instruments. These funds could be further distributed as 'asset allocation', 'balanced', or 'flexible portfolio' funds, based on the breadth of their investment in different asset classes, and the frequency of modifying the allocation.

Global, regional, or emerging market funds recognize investment opportunities across the world, and accordingly base their investment focus. Such funds could again comprise either, or a combination of equity, debt, or hybrid instruments. We mention some other, specific

UNIT INVESTMENT TRUSTS (UIT)

Similar to mutual funds, UITs also pool money from investors and have a fixed portfolio of assets, which are not changed during the life of the fund. Although the portfolio composition is actively decided by the sponsor of the fund, once established the portfolio composition is not changed (hence called unmanaged fund.

The way an UIT is established is different from that of other mutual funds. UITs are usually created by sponsors, who first make investment in the portfolio of securities. The entire portfolio is then transferred to a trust and the trustees issue trust certificates to the public, which is similar to shares. The trustees distribute the incomes from the investment and the maturity (capital) amount to the shareholders on maturity of the scheme.

REITS (REAL ESTATE INVESTMENT TRUSTS)

REITS are also similar to mutual funds, but they invest primarily in real estates or loans secured by real estate. REIT can be of three types - equity, mortgage or hybrid trusts. Equity trusts invest in real estate assets, mortgage trusts invest in loans backed by mortgage and hybrid trusts invest in either.

Hedge Funds

Hedge funds are generally created by a limited number of wealthy investors who agree to pool their funds and hire experienced professionals (fund managers) to manage their portfolio. Hedge funds are private agreements and generally have little or no regulations governing them. This gives a lot of freedom to the fund managers. For example, hedge funds can go short (borrow) funds and can invest in derivatives instruments which mutual funds cannot do.

Hedge funds generally have higher management fees than mutual funds as well as performance-based fees. The management fee (paid to the fund managers), in the case of hedge funds is dependent on the assets under management (generally 2 - 4%) and the fund performance (generally 20% of the excess returns over the market return generated by the fund).

GROWTH FUNDS

Growth funds primarily look for growth of capital with secondary emphasis on dividend. Such funds invest in shares with a potential for growth and capital appreciation. They invest in well-established companies where the company itself and the industry in which it operates are thought to have good long-term growth potential, and hence growth funds provide low current income. Growth funds generally incur higher risks than income funds in an effort to secure more pronounced growth.

Some growth funds concentrate on one or more industry sectors and also invest in a broad range of industries. Growth funds are suitable for investors who can afford to assume the risk of potential loss in value of their investment in the hope of achieving substantial and rapid gains. They are not suitable for investors who must conserve their principal or who must maximize current income.

GROWTH AND INCOME FUNDS

Growth and income funds seek long-term growth of capital as well as current income. The investment strategies used to reach these goals vary among funds. Some invest in a dual portfolio consisting of growth stocks and income stocks, or a combination of growth stocks, stocks paying high dividends, preferred stocks, convertible securities or fixed-income securities such as corporate bonds and money market instruments. Others may invest in growth stocks and earn current income by selling covered call options on their portfolio stocks.

Growth and income funds have low to moderate stability of principal and moderate potential for current income and growth. They are suitable for investors who can assume some risk to achieve growth of capital but who also want to maintain a moderate level of current income.

FIXED-INCOME FUNDS

Fixed income funds primarily look to provide current income consistent with the preservation of capital. These funds invest in corporate bonds or government-backed mortgage securities that have a fixed rate of return. Within the fixed-income category, funds vary greatly in their stability of principal and in their dividend yields. High-yield funds, which seek to maximize yield by investing in lower-rated bonds of longer maturities, entail less stability of principal than fixed-income funds that invest in higher-rated but lower-yielding securities.

Some fixed-income funds seek to minimize risk by investing exclusively in securities whose timely payment of interest and principal is backed by the full faith and credit of the Indian Government. Fixed-income funds are suitable for investors who want to maximize current income and who can assume a degree of capital risk in order to do so.

BALANCED

The Balanced fund aims to provide both growth and income. These funds invest in both shares and fixed income securities in the proportion indicated in their offer documents. Ideal for investors who are looking for a combination of income and moderate growth.

MONEY MARKET FUNDS/LIQUID FUNDS

For the cautious investor, these funds provide a very high stability of principal while seeking a moderate to high current income. They invest in highly liquid, virtually risk-free, short-term debt securities of agencies of the Indian Government, banks and corporations and Treasury Bills. Because of their short-term investments, money market mutual funds are able to keep a virtually constant unit price; only the yield fluctuates.

Therefore, they are an attractive alternative to bank accounts. With yields that are generally competitive with - and usually higher than -- yields on bank savings account, they offer several advantages. Money can be withdrawn any time without penalty. Although not insured, money market funds invest only in highly liquid, short-term, top-rated money market instruments. Money market funds are suitable for investors who want high stability of principal and current income with immediate liquidity.

SPECIALTY/SECTOR FUNDS

These funds invest in securities of a specific industry or sector of the economy such as health care, technology, leisure, utilities or precious metals. The funds enable investors to diversify holdings among many companies within an industry, a more conservative approach than investing directly in one particular company.

Sector funds offer the opportunity for sharp capital gains in cases where the fund's industry is "in favor" but also entail the risk of capital losses when the industry is out of favor. While sector funds restrict holdings to a particular industry, other specialty funds such as index funds give investors a broadly diversified portfolio and attempt to mirror the performance of various market averages.

Index funds generally buy shares in all the companies composing the BSE Sensex or NSE Nifty or other broad stock market indices. They are not suitable for investors who must conserve their principal or maximize current income.

RISK VS REWARD

Having understood the basics of mutual funds the next step is to build a successful investment portfolio. Before you can begin to build a portfolio, one should understand some other elements of mutual fund investing and how they can affect the potential value of your investments over the years. The first thing that has to be kept in mind is that when you invest in mutual funds, there is no guarantee that you will end up with more money when you withdraw your investment than what you started out with. That is the potential of loss is always there. The loss of value in your investment is what is considered risk in investing. Even so, the opportunity for investment growth that is possible through investments in mutual funds far exceeds that concern for most investors. Here's why at the cornerstone of investing is the basic principal that the greater the risk you take, the greater the potential reward. Or stated in another way, you get what you pay for and you get paid a higher return only when you're willing to accept more volatility.

Risk then, refers to the volatility -- the up and down activity in the markets and individual issues that occurs constantly over time. This volatility can be caused by a number of factors -- interest rate changes, inflation or general economic conditions. It is this variability, uncertainty and potential for loss, that causes investors to worry. We all fear the possibility that a stock we invest in will fall substantially. But it is this very volatility that is the exact reason that you can expect to earn a higher long-term return from these investments than from a savings account.

Different types of mutual funds have different levels of volatility or potential price change, and those with the greater chance of losing value are also the funds that can produce the greater returns for you over time. So, risk has two sides: it causes the value of your investments to fluctuate, but it is precisely the reason you can expect to earn higher returns. You might find it helpful to remember that all financial investments will fluctuate. There are very few perfectly safe havens and those simply don't pay enough to beat inflation over the long run.

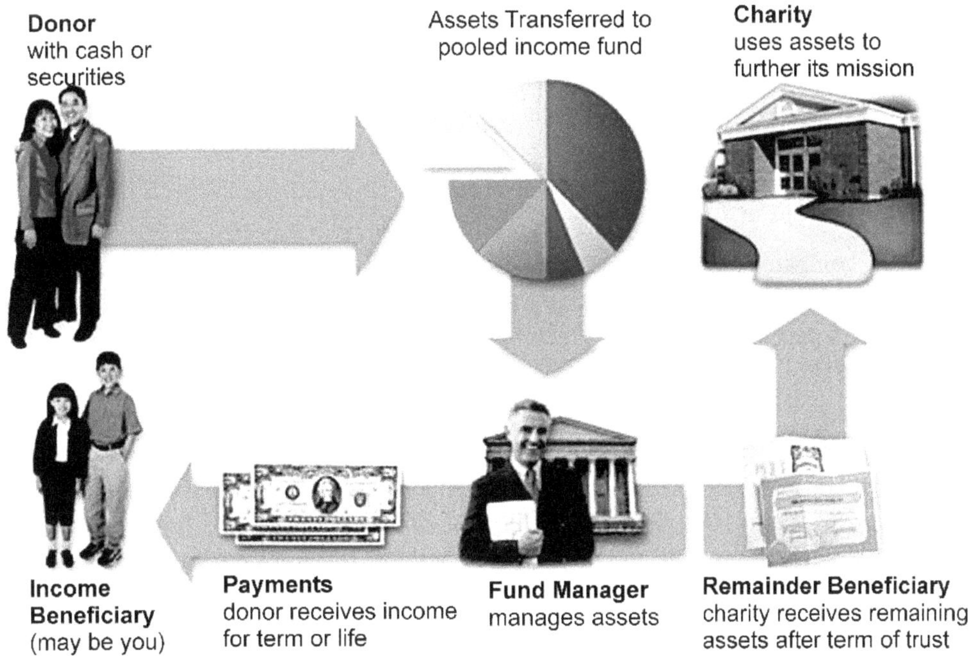

TYPES OF RISKS

All investments involve some form of risk. Consider these common types of risk and evaluate them against potential rewards when you select an investment.

MARKET RISK

At times the prices or yields of all the securities in a particular market rise or fall due to broad outside influences. When this happens, the stock prices of both an outstanding, highly profitable company and a fledgling corporation may be affected. This change in price is due to "market risk". Also known as systematic risk.

INFLATION RISK

Sometimes referred to as "loss of purchasing power." Whenever inflation rises forward faster than the earnings on your investment, you run the risk that you'll actually be able to buy less, not more. Inflation risk also occurs when prices rise faster than your returns.

CREDIT RISK

In short, how stable is the company or entity to which you lend your money when you invest? How certain are you that it will be able to pay the interest you are promised, or repay your principal when the investment matures?

INTEREST RATE RISK

Changing interest rates affect both equities and bonds in many ways. Investors are reminded that "predicting" which way rates will go is rarely successful. A diversified portfolio can help in offsetting these changes.

EXCHANGE RISK

A number of companies generate revenues in foreign currencies and may have investments or expenses also denominated in foreign currencies. Changes in exchange rates may, therefore, have a positive or negative impact on companies which in turn would have an effect on the investment of the fund.

INVESTMENT RISKS

The sectoral fund schemes, investments will be predominantly in equities of select companies in the particular sectors. Accordingly, the NAV of the schemes are linked to the equity performance of such companies and may be more volatile than a more diversified portfolio of equities.

CALL RISKS

Call risk is associated with bonds have and embedded call option in them. This option gives the issuer the right to call back the bonds prior to maturity. Then investor however is exposed to some risks here. The price of the callable bond many not rise much above the price at which the issuer may call the bond.

CHANGES IN THE GOVERNMENT POLICY

Changes in Government policy especially in regard to the tax benefits may impact the business prospects of the companies leading to an impact on the investments made by the fund. Effect of loss of key professionals and inability to adapt business to the rapid technological change. An industries' key asset is often the personnel who run the business i.e. intellectual properties of the key employees of the respective companies. Given the ever-changing complexion of few industries and the high obsolescence levels, availability of qualified, trained and motivated personnel is very critical for the success of industries in few sectors. It is, therefore, necessary to attract key personnel and also to retain them to meet the changing environment and challenges the sector offers. Failure or inability to attract/retain such qualified key personnel may impact the prospects of the companies in the particular sector.

INVESTMENT CYCLE IN MUTUAL FUNDS

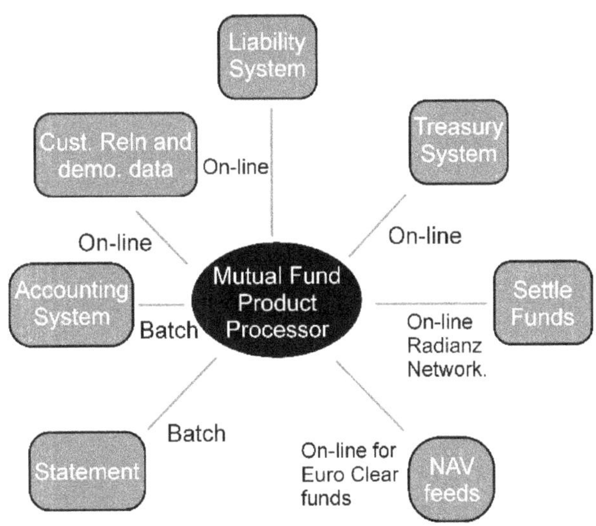

TYPES OF MUTUAL FUNDS

Mutual Fund Trust

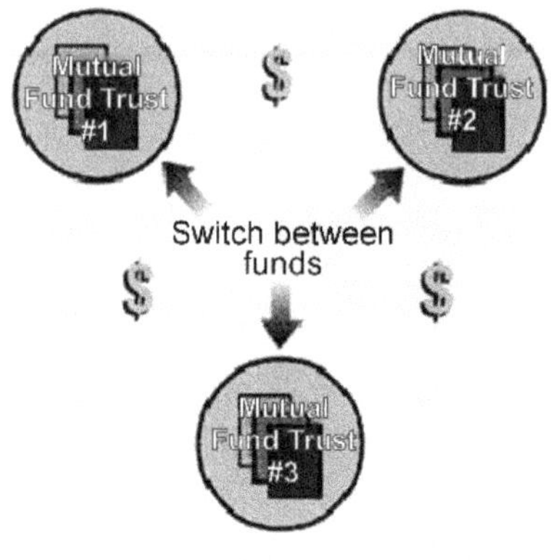

Capital Gains are triggered when moving to different funds

Corporate Class Funds

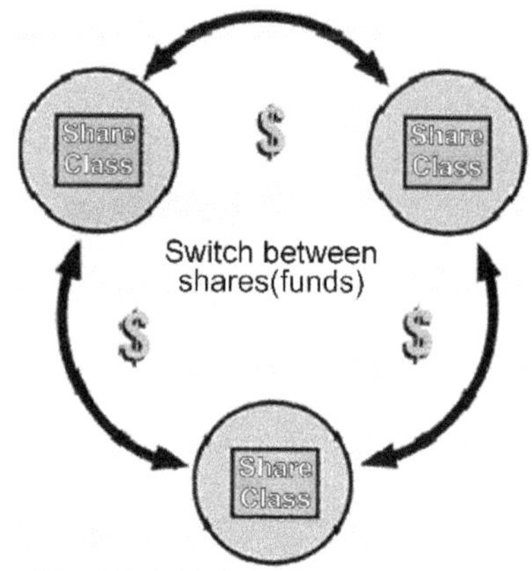

No Capital Gains are triggered when switching to different funds

History of the Indian Mutual Fund Industry

The mutual fund industry in India started in 1963 with the formation of Unit. Trust of India, at the initiative of the Government of India and Reserve Bank the. The history of mutual funds in India can be broadly divided into four distinct phases

First Phase – 1964-87(UTI MONOPOLY)

An Act of Parliament established Unit Trust of India (UTI) on 1963. It was set up by the Reserve Bank of India and functioned under the Regulatory and administrative control of the Reserve Bank of India. In 1978 UTI was de-linked from the RBI and the Industrial Development Bank of India (IDBI) took over the regulatory and administrative control in place of RBI. The first scheme launched by UTI was Unit Scheme 1964. At the end of 1988 UTI had Rs.6, 700 crores of assets under management.

Second Phase – 1987-1993 (Entry of Public Sector Funds)

1987 marked the entry of non- UTI, public sector mutual funds set up by public sector banks and Life Insurance Corporation of India (LIC) and General Insurance Corporation of India (GIC). SBI Mutual Fund was the first non- UTI Mutual Fund established in June 1987 followed by Can bank Mutual Fund (Dec 87), Punjab National Bank Mutual Fund (Aug 89), Indian Bank Mutual Fund (Nov 89), Bank of India (Jun 90), Bank of Baroda Mutual Fund (Oct 92). LIC established its mutual fund in June 1989 while GIC had set up its mutual fund in December 1990. At the end of 1993, the mutual fund industry had assets under management of Rs.47, 004 cores.

Third Phase – 1993-2003 (Entry of Private Sector Funds)

With the entry of private sector funds in 1993, a new era started in the Indian mutual fund industry, giving the Indian investors a wider choice of fund families. Also, 1993 was the year in which the first Mutual Fund Regulations came into being, under which all mutual funds, except UTI were to be registered and governed. The erstwhile Kothari Pioneer (now merged with Franklin Templeton) was the first private sector mutual fund registered in July 1993.

The 1993 SEBI (Mutual Fund) Regulations were substituted by a more comprehensive and revised Mutual Fund Regulations in 1996. The industry now functions under the SEBI (Mutual Fund) Regulations 1996.

The number of mutual fund houses went on increasing, with many foreign mutual funds setting up funds in India and also the industry has witnessed several mergers and acquisitions. As at the end of January 2003, there were 33 mutual funds with total assets of Rs. 1, 21,805 crores.

Fourth Phase – since February 2003

In February 2003, following the repeal of the Unit Trust of India Act 1963 UTI was bifurcated into two separate entities. One is the Specified Undertaking of the Unit Trust of India with assets under management of Rs.29, 835 crores as at the end of January 2003, representing broadly, the assets of US 64 scheme, assured return and certain other schemes. The Specified Undertaking of Unit Trust of India, functioning under an administrator and under the rules framed by Government of India and does not come under the purview of the Mutual Fund Regulations.

The second is the UTI Mutual Fund Ltd, sponsored by SBI, PNB, BOB and LIC. It is registered with SEBI and functions under the Mutual Fund Regulations. With the bifurcation of the erstwhile UTI which had in March 2000 more than Rs.76,000 crores of assets under management and with the setting up of a UTI Mutual Fund, conforming to the SEBI Mutual Fund Regulations, and with recent mergers taking place among different private sector funds, the mutual fund industry has entered its current phase of consolidation and growth. As at the end of June 30, 2003, there were 31 funds, which manage assets of Rs.104762 crores under 376 schemes.

GROWTH IN ASSETS UNDER MANAGEMENT

India is at the first stage of a revolution that has already peaked in the U.S. The U.S. boasts of an Asset base that is much higher than its bank deposits. In India, mutual fund assets are not even 10% of the bank deposits, but this trend is beginning to change. Recent figures indicate that in the first quarter of the current fiscal year.

The formation and operations of mutual funds in India is solely guided by SEBI (Mutual Fund) Regulations, 1993, which came into force on 20 January 1993. The regulations have since been replaced by the Securities and Exchange Board of India (Mutual Funds) Regulations, 1996, through a notification on 9 December 1996.

A mutual fund comprises four separate entities, namely sponsor, mutual fund trust, AMC and custodian. They are of course assisted by other independent administrative entities like banks, registrars and transfer agents. We may discuss in brief the formation of different entities, their functions and obligations.

The sponsor for a mutual fund can by any person who, acting alone or in combination with another body corporate establishes the mutual fund and gets it registered with SEBI. The sponsor is required to contribute at least 40 per cent of the minimum net worth (Rs 10 crore) of the asset management company. The sponsor must have a sound track record and general reputation of fairness and integrity in all his business transactions.

As per SEBI Regulation, 1996, a mutual fund is to be formed by the sponsor and registered with SEBI. A mutual fund shall be constituted in the form of a trust and the instrument of trust shall be in the form of a deed, duly registered under the provisions of the Indian Registration Act, 1908, executed by the sponsor in favor of trustees named in such an instrument.

The board of trustees manages the mutual fund and the sponsor executes the trust deeds in favor of the trustees. The mutual fund raises money through sale of units under one or more schemes for investing in securities in accordance with SEBI guidelines. It is the job of the mutual fund trustees to see that the schemes floated and managed by the AMC appointed by the trustees, are in accordance with the trust deeds and SEBI guidelines. It is also the responsibilities of the trustees to control the capital property of mutual funds schemes.

The trustees have the right to obtain relevant information from the AMC, as well as a quarterly report on its activities. They can also dismiss the AMC under specific condition as per SEBI regulations.

At least half the trustees should be independent persons. The AMC or its employees cannot act as a trustee. No person who is appointed as a trustee of a mutual fund can be appointed as a trustee of any other mutual fund unless he is an independent trustee and prior permission is obtained from the mutual fund in which he is a trustee.

The trustees are required to submit half-yearly reports to SEBI on the activities of the mutual fund. The trustees appoint a custodian and supervise their activities. The trustees can be removed only with prior approval of SEBI. As per SEBI guidelines, an asset management company is appointed by the trustees to float the schemes for the mutual fund and manage the funds raised by selling units under a scheme. The AMC must act as per SEBI guidelines, trust deeds and management agreement between trustee & the AMC.

THE IMPORTANCE OF ACCOUNTING KNOWLEDGE

Mutual funds in India are required to follow the accounting policies laid down in SEBI (Mutual Fund) Regulations, 1996 and the amendments in 1998. This section of the workbook summarizes the important Regulations, and periodical budgets.

NET ASSET VALUE (NAV)

A mutual fund is a common investment vehicle where the assets of the fund belong directly to the investors. The fund does not account for investors' subscriptions as liabilities or deposits but as Unit Capital. On the other hand, the investments made on behalf of the investors are reflected on the assets side and are the main constituents of the balance sheet. There are, however, liabilities of a strictly short-term nature that may be part of the balance sheet. The fund's Net Assets are therefore defined as the assets minus the liabilities. As there are many investors in a fund, it is common practice for mutual funds to compute the share of each investor on the basis of the value of Net Assets per Share/Unit, commonly known as the Net Asset Value (NAV).

The following are the regulatory requirements and accounting definitions lay down by SEBI.

NAV = Net Assets of the scheme / Number of Units Outstanding, i.e. Market value of investments + Receivables + Other Accrued Income + Other Assets

Accrued Expenses-Other Payables-Other Liabilities

No. Of Units Outstanding as at the NAV date

A fund's NAV is affected by four sets of factors:

- Purchase and sale of investment securities
- Valuation of all investment securities held
- Other assets and liabilities, and
- Units sold or redeemed

(Or)

The net asset value NAV is the most important and widely followed metric of a fund's performance. It is calculated per share using the following formula:

Market Value of Assets - Market Value of liabilities

$$\text{NAV (per share)} = \frac{\text{Market Value of Assets - Market Value of Liabilities}}{\text{Number of shares outs tan dign}}$$

Net asset value (NAV) is a term used to describe the per unit value of the fund's net assets (assets less the value of its liabilities). Hence the NAV for a fund is

Fund NAV = (Market Value of the fund portfolio - Fund Expenses) / Fund Shares Outstanding

Just like the share price of a common stock, the NAV of a fund would rise with the value of the fund portfolio, and is instantly reflective of the value of investment

1. A mutual fund that had a net asset value of Rs. 20 mat the beginning of month made income and capital gain distribution of Re. 0.03745 and Re. 0.03 per share respectively during the month, and then ended the month with a net asset value of Rs. 20.06. Calculate monthly return.

ANSWER:

Calculation of monthly return on the mutual funds:

$$r=\left(\frac{(NAV_t-NAV_{t-1}+I_t+G_t}{NAV_{t-1}}\right)$$

$$r=\left(\frac{(Rs.20.06-Rs.20.00)+(\text{Re}.0.0375+\text{Re}.0.03)}{20}\right)$$

$$=\frac{0.1275}{20}=0.006375$$

$$r=0.6375\%p.m$$

$$r=\boxed{6.375\%}$$

Where

r = Return on the mutual fund

NAV_t = Net assets value at time period t

NAV_{t-1}= Net assets value at time period t-1

I_t = Income at time period t

G_t = Capital gain distribution at time period t

2. Mr. A can earn a return of 16 per cent by investing in equity shares on his own. Now he is considering a recently announced equity based mutual fund scheme in which initial expenses are 5.5% and annual recurring expenses are 1.5%. How much should the mutual fund earn to provide Mr. A a return of 16%?

ANSWER:

Let the Personal earnings of Mr. A = E_p

Let the Mutual Fund earnings = E_m

$$E_m=\frac{1}{1-Initial\text{ expenses(\%)}}E_p+\text{ Recurring expenses (\%)}$$

$$=\left(\frac{1}{1-0.055}*16\%\right)+1.5\%$$

$$=\left(\frac{0.16}{0.945}\right)+0.015=0.1843$$

$$=\boxed{18.43\%}$$

Required Mutual Fund earnings = 18.43%.

A has invested in three Mutual Funds Schemes as per detailed below:

		MF A	MF B	MF C
Date of investment	01/12/2003 50000	01/01/2004 100000	01/03/2004A 50000	Amount of investment
Dividend received up to	31/03 Rs.950	Rs.1500	nil	
Net Asset value at entry date	10.5	10	10	
NAV as at 31.03.2004	10.4	10.1	9.8	

Required:

What is the effective yield on per annum basis in respect of each of the three schemes to Mr. A up to 31.03.2004?

ANSWER:

Scheme	Investment	Unit Nos	Unit NAV 31.03.3004	Total NAV 31.03.2004
	Rs		Rs	Rs.
MFA	50000	4761905	10.4	49523.812
MFB	100000	10000	10.10	101000
MFC	50000	5000	9.8	49000

Scheme	NAV (+)/ (-)	Dividend Received	Total Yield	Number Of days	Effective Yield (% P.A)
	Rs.	Rs.	Rs.		
MFA	(-)476.188	950	473.812	122	2.835%
MFB	(+)1000	1500	2500	91	10.027%
MFC	(-)1000	NIL	(-)1000	31	(-)24%

4. Sun Moon Mutual Fund (Approved Mutual Fund) sponsored open-ended equity-oriented scheme "Chanakya Opportunity Fund". There were three plans viz. "A"-Dividend Re-investment plan, 'B'-Bonus Plan &; 'C'-Growth Plan.

   At the time of Initial public offer on 1-4-1995, Mr Anand, Mr. Bacchan & Mrs. Charu, three investors invested Rs. 100000 each & chosen 'B', 'C' & 'A' plan respectively.

   The History of the Fund is as follows:

DATE	DIVIDEND%	BONUS RATIO	NET ASSET VALUE PER UNIT (F.V Rs. 10)			
			Plan A	Plan B	Plan C	
28-07-1999	20	-	30.7	31.4		33.42
31-03-200	70	5:4	58.42	31.05	70.05	
31-10-2003	40	-	42.18	25.02	56.15	
15-03-2004	25	-	46.45	29.1		64.28
31-03-2004	-	1:3	42.18	20.05	60.12	
24-03-2005	40	1:4	48.10	19.95	72.40	
31-07-2005	-	-	53.75	22.98	82.07	

On 31 st July all three investors redeemed all the balance units.

Calculate annual rate of return to each of the investors.

Consider:

1. Long-term Capital Gain is exempt from Income tax.
2. Short-term Capital Gain is subject to 10% Income tax.
3. Security Transaction Tax 0.2 % only on sale/redemption of units.
4. Ignore Education Cess.

ANSWER:

Mrs. Charu — Plan A Dividend Reinvestment

(Amount in Rs.)

Date	Investment	Rate	Units	Balance
01.04.1995	100000	10.00	10000.00	10000.00
28.07.1999	200000	30.70	651.47	10651.47
31.03.2000	74560.29	58.42	1276.28	11927.75
31.10.2003	47711	42.18	1131.13	13058.88
15.03.2004	32647	46.45	702.85	13761.73
31.03.2004	NA	N. A	N. A	13761.73
24.03.2005	55046.92	48.10	1144.43	14906.16

Redemption value 14906.16 * 53.7599
801206.10

(-) Security Transaction Tax (S.T.T) is 2%		1602.41
Net amount received		799603.69
(-) Short term capital gain tax @ 10%		
1144343 (53.64-48.10)	6340	634
i.e. 53.75-S.T.T.2%		798969.69 Net of tax
(-) Investment		100000.00
	698969.69	

Annual average return (%) **698969/100000*12/124*100**=67.64

Mr. Anand — Plan B- Bonus

Date	Units	Balance	NAV per unit
01.04.1995	10000	10000	10
31.03.2000	12500	22500	31.05
31.03.2004	7500	30000	20.05
24.03.2005	7500	37500	19.95

Redemption value 37500* 22.98	861750.00
(-) Security Transaction Tax (S.T.T) is 2%	1723.50
Net amount received	860026.50
(-) Short term capital gain tax @ 10%	
7500*(22.93-19.95) 22.350	
i.e. 2298 –S.T.T. 2%	2235.00
Net of tax	857791.50
(-) Investment	100000.00
Net gain	757791.50

Annual average return (%) **719058/100000*12*124*100 = 73.33**

Mr Bacchan	**Plan C- Growth**
Redemption value 10000*82.07	820700.00
(-) Security Transaction Tax (S.T.T.) is 2%	1641.40
Net amount received	819058.60
(-) Short term capital gain tax @ 10%	0.00
Net of tax	819058.60
(-) Investment	100000.00
Net gain	719058.60

Annual average return (%) **719058/100000*12/124*100=69.59**

5. A Mutual Fund having 300 units has shown Is NAV of Rs.8.75 and Rs. 9.45 at the beginning and at the end of the year respectively. The Mutual Fund has given two options:
   (i) Pay Rs. 0.75 per unit as dividend and Rs. 0.60 per unit as a capital gain, or
   (ii) These distributions are to be reinvested at an average NAV of Rs 8.65 per unit.

What difference it would make in terms of return available and which option is preferable?

ANSWER:

(i) Returns for the year	(per unit)
Change in price (Rs. 9.45-Rs8.75)	Re.0.70

Dividends received:		Re.0.75
Capital gains distribution	Re.0.60	
Total reward		Rs. 2.05

Holding period reward $r = \left(\frac{(NAV_t - NAV_{t-1} + I_t + G_t}{NAV_{t-1}} \right)$

Where

r = Return on the mutual fund

NAV_t =Net assets value at time period t (here Rs. 9.45)

NAV_{t-1}=Net assets value at time period t-1(here Rs. 8.75)

I_t = Income at time period t (here Re. 0.75)

G_t= Capital gain distribution at time period t (here Re. 0.60)

Holding period reward Rs2.05/Rs. 8.75 = 23.43%

(ii) When all dividends and capital gains distribution are re-invested into additional units of the fund @ (Rs. 8.65/unit)

- Dividend + Capital Gains per unit

  = Re. 0.75 + Re. 0.60 = Rs. 1.35

- Total Dividend & Capital Gains received from 300 units

  = Rs. 1.35 * 300 = Rs. 405/-

- Additional units that can be acquired

  = Rs 405/Rs. 8.65 = 46.82 units

- Total No. of Units after acquisition = 300 units + 46.82 units

  = 346.82 units

- Value of 346.82 units at the end of the year

  = 346.82 units * Rs. 9.45 = Rs. 3277.45

- Price paid for 300 units at the beginning of the year

  = 300 units * Rs. 8.75 = Rs. 2625.00

- Holding period reward

  Rs. (3277.45-2625.00) = Rs. 652.45

- % age of holding period reward

  Rs. 652.45*100/Rs. 2625.00 = 24.85%

Conclusion: Option 2 is preferred since the holding period reward is more in terms of percentage in option- two.

6. Mr. X on 1.7.2000 during the initial offer of some Mutual Fund invested in 10000 units having face value of Rs. 10 for each unit. On 31.3.2001 the dividend operated by the M.F. was 10% and Mr. X found that his annualized yield was 153.33%. On 31.12.2002, 20% dividend was given. On 31.3.2003 Mr. X redeemed all his balance of 11296. 11 units when his annualized yield was 73.52%. What is the NAV as on 31.3.2001, 31.12.2002 and 31.3.2003?

ANSWER:

Yield for 9 months = (153.33*9/12)	= 115%
Amount receivable as on 31.03.2001	= 100000 + (100000*115%)
	= Rs. 215,000
Therefore, NAV as on 31.03.2001	= (215000-10000)/10000
	= Rs.20.50
Therefore, units as on 31.03.2001	= 10487.80 i.e. (215000/20.50)
Dividend as on 31.03.2002	= 10487.8*10*0.2
	= Rs. 20975.60
Therefore, NAV as on 31.03.2002	= 20795.6/ (11296.11-10487.80)
	= Rs. 25.95

NAN as on 31.03.2003

=100000 + (100000*73.52%*33/12)/11296.11= Rs. 26.75

7. A mutual fund that had a net asset value of Rs.10 at the beginning of month made income and capital gain distribution of Rs. 0.05 and Rs. 0.04 per share respectively during the month, and then ended the month with a net asset value of Rs. 10.03. Calculate monthly return.

ANSWER:

Return on the mutual fund is given by:

$$r = \left(\frac{(NAV_t - NAV_{t-1} + I_t + G_t}{NAV_{t-1}} \right)$$

r = Return on the mutual fund

NAV_t = Net assets value at time period t

NAV_{t-1} = Net assets value at time period t-1

I_t = Income at time period t

G_t = Capital gain distribution at time period t

$$r = \left(\frac{(Rs.10.03 - Rs.10.00) + (Re.0.05 + Re.0.04)}{Rs.10} \right)$$

$$= 0.012$$

$$= 1.20\% \text{ P.M}$$

PRICING OF UNITS

Although NAV per share defines the value of the investor's holding in the fund, the fund may not repurchase the investor's units at the same price as NAV. However, SEBI requires that the fund must ensure that repurchase price is not lower than 93% of NAV (95% in the case of a closed end fund). On the other side, a fund may sell new units at a price that is different from the NAV, but the sale price cannot be higher than 107% of NAV. Also, the difference the repurchase price and the sale price of the unit is not permitted to exceed 7% of the sale price.

FEES AND EXPENSES

An AMC may incur many expenses specifically for given schemes, and other common expenses. In any case, all expenses should be clearly Unidentified and allocated to the individual schemes. The AMC may charge the scheme with investment management and advisory fees that are fully disclosed in the offer document subject to the following limits:

- @ 1.25% of the first Rs. 100 crore of weekly average net assets outstanding in the accounting year, and @ 1% of weekly average net assets in excess of Rs. 100 crores.
- For no load schemes, the AMC may charge an additional management fee up to 1% of weekly average net assets outstanding in the accounting year.

Investment management and advisory fees are subject to the overall ceiling for expenses.

A. Initial expenses of launching schemes (not to exceed 6% of initial resources raised under the scheme); and

B. Recurring expenses including:

(i) Marketing and selling expenses including agents' commission

(ii) Brokerage and transaction costs

(iii) Registrar services for transfer of units sold or redeemed

(iv) Fees and expenses of trustees

(v) Audit fees

(vi) Custodian fees

(vii) Costs related to investor communication

(viii) Costs of fund transfers from location to location

(ix) Costs of providing account statements and dividend / redemption cheques and warrants

(x) Insurance premium paid by the fund

(xi) Winding up costs for terminating a fund or a scheme

(xii) Other costs as approved by SEBI

The total expenses charged by the AMC to a scheme, excluding issue or redemption expenses but including investment management and advisory fees are subject to the following limits on the first Rs. 100 Crores of average weekly net assets-2.5%

- On the next Rs. 300 Crores of average weekly net assets -2.0%
- On the balance of average weekly net assets-1.75%
- For bond funds, the above percentages are required to be lower by 0.25%

INITIAL ISSUE EXPENSES

When a scheme is first launched, the AMC will incur significant expenses, whose benefit will accrue over many years. All expenses cannot, therefore, be charged to a scheme in the first year itself. SEBI permits "amortization" of initial expenses as follows:

- For a closed-end scheme floated on a 'load' basis, the initial issue expenses shall be amortized on a weekly basis over the period of scheme. For example, a 5-year (i.e. 260 week) closed-end scheme with initial issue expenses of Rs. 5 lakhs must charge Rs.1923 (5 lakhs / 260 weeks) every week to the fund. It cannot charge the entire amount of Rs. 5 lakhs at the time of issue.
- For an open-end scheme floated on a 'load' basis, initial issue expenses may be amortized over a period not exceeding five years. For example, if an open-end scheme has initial issue expenses of Rs. 10 lakhs, it need not charge this entire amount to the fund in the year of issue. Instead, it may charge Rs. 2 lakhs (10 lakhs / 5 years) per year to the fund, thereby spreading the charge of initial issue expenses over a maximum of 5 years. Issue expenses incurred during the life of an open-end scheme cannot be amortized.
- Un amortized portion of initial issue expenses shall be included for NAV calculation, considered as "other asset". The investment advisory fee cannot be claimed on this asset. Hence, they have to be excluded while determining the chargeable investment management / advisory fees. While calculating the maximum amount of chargeable expenses, the un amortized portion of the initial issue expenses will not be included as part of the average weekly net assets figure.

ACCOUNTING POLICIES

- Investments are required to be marked to market using market prices. Any unrealized appreciation cannot be distributed, and provision must be made for the same.
- Dividend received by the fund on a share should be recognized, not on the date of declaration, but on the date the share is quoted on ex-dividend basis. For example, if a fund owns shares on which dividend is declared on April 5, and the shares are quoted on ex-

dividend basis on April 20, the dividend income will be included by the fund for distribution/NAV computation only April 20.

- In determining gain or loss on sale of investments, the average cost method must be followed to determine the cost of purchase. This will be applied by security.
- Purchase / sale of investments should be recognized on the trade date and not settlement date
- Bonus / rights shares should be recognized only when the original shares are traded on the stock exchange on an ex-bonus /ex-rights basis
- Income receivable on investments, which is accrued, but not received for 12 months beyond due date, should be provided for, and no further accrual should be made for such investment
- An investment shall be regarded as non-performing if it has provided no returns through dividend/interest for more than 2years at the end of the accounting year
- Investments owned by mutual funds are marked to market. Therefore, the value of investments appreciates or depreciates based on market fluctuations, which is reflected in the balance sheet. However, this change in value constitutes unrealized gain/loss. When any investments are actually sold, the proportion of the unrealized gain / loss that pertains to such investments becomes realized gain/loss. Therefore, at any given time, the NAV includes realized and unrealized gain/loss on investments. While SEBI prohibits the distribution of unrealized appreciation on investments, realized gain in available for distribution.

An open-end scheme sells and repurchases units on the basis of NAV. SEBI therefore prescribes the use of an equalization account, to ensure that creation / redemption of units does not change the percentage of income distributed. This involves the following steps:

Computation of distributable reserves:

Income + Realized Gain on Investments- Expenses-Unrealized Losses (unrealized gains are excluded)

- If distributable reserves are positive, the following percentage is computed:
- Distributable Reserve / Units Outstanding
- The above percentage is multiplied with the number of new units sold, and the equalization account is credited by this amount, if units are sold above par; if the units are sold below par, the equalization account is debited by this amount. The same percentage is multiplying with the number of units repurchased, and the equalization account is debited by this amount if the units are repurchased above par; if the units are repurchased below par, the equalization account is credited.
- The net balance in the equalization account is transferred to the profit and loss account. It is only an adjustment to the distributable surplus and does not affect the net income for the period.

VALUATION

Mutual funds value their investments on a 'mark-to-market' basis with reference to the date on which they are valued i.e., the valuation date.

VALUATION OF TRADED SECURITIES

- Where a security is traded on a stock exchange, it is valued at the last quoted closing price on the stock exchange where it is "principally traded".
- If a security is not traded on any stock exchange on a particular valuation day, the value at which it was traded on the selected/other stock exchange on the
- Earliest previous day may be used, provided such date is not more than 60 days prior to the valuation date.
- Valuation of traded securities, once the market price is obtained as above, is quite simple. The fund will multiply its current holding in number of shares or bonds by the applicable market price to get the "mark to market" value.

VALUATION OF NON-TRADED SECURITIES

- When a security is not traded on any stock exchange for 60 days prior to the valuation date, it must be treated as non-traded' scrip.
- Non-traded securities shall be valued 'in good faith' by the AMC on the basis of appropriate valuation methods, which shall be periodically reviewed by the trustees and reported by the auditors as fair and reasonable. The following principles are to be applied for the valuation of non-traded securities:
- Equity instruments: are to be valued on the basis of capitalization of earnings solely or in combination with its balance sheet Net Asset Value. For this purpose, capitalization rate will be determined by reference to the price or earning rations of comparable traded securities with an appropriate discount for lower liquidity to be used.

Debt instruments: are to be valued on a yield to maturity basis, the capitalization factor being determined for comparable traded securities with an appropriate discount for lower liquidity.

- **Call money, bills purchased:** under rediscounting and short-term deposits with banks are to be valued at cost + accrual: other money market instruments at yield at which they are currently traded; non-traded instruments (not traded for 7 days) will be valued at cost plus interest accrued till the beginning of the valuation day plus the difference between redemption value and cost, spread uniformly over the remaining maturity of the instruments
- **Government Securities:** are to be valued at yield to maturity based on prevailing market rate
- **Convertible debentures and bonds:** non-convertible component is to be valued as a debt instrument, and convertible as any equity instrument. If after Conversion, the resultant equity instrument would be traded pari passu with an existing instrument, which is traded, the value of the latter instrument can be adopted after an appropriate discount for the non-tradability of the instrument.

Risk involved in mutual funds industry

Mutual funds are not free from risk. It is so because basically the mutual funds also invest their funds in stock markets on shares, which are volatile in nature and are not risk free, the following risk are inherent in their dealing.

INHERENT RISK FACTORS

Market Risks: In general, there are certain risks associated with every kind of investment on shares. They are called market risks. These market risks can be reduced, but cannot be completely eliminated even by a good investment.

Scheme Risks: There are certain risks inherent in the scheme itself. It all depends upon the nature of the scheme. For instance, in a pure growth scheme, risks are greater.

Investment Risks: Whether the mutual fund makes money in shares or loses depends upon the investment expertise of the Asset Management Company. If the investment advice goes wrong, the fund has to suffer a lot.

Business Risks: The corpus of a mutual fund might have been invested in a company's shares. If the business of that company suffers any set back, it cannot declare any dividend. It may even go to the extent of winding up its business.

Political Risks

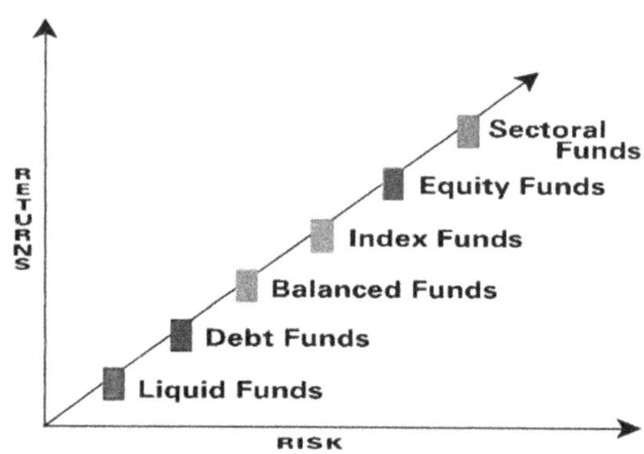

Successive Governments bring with them fancy new economic ideologies and policies. It is often said that many economic decisions are politically motivated.

PARAMETERS DESCRIPTION

THE FOLLOWING PARAMETERS WERE CONSIDERED FOR ANALYSIS:

- Beta
- Alpha
- Correlation coefficient

- Treynor's Ratio
- Sharpe's Ratio
- Jensen's Ratio

Beta: Beta is a measure of volatility, or systematic risk, of a security or portfolio in comparison to the market as a whole. Beta measures a stock's volatility, the degree to which a stock price fluctuates in relation to the overall market. Investment analysts use the Greek letter beta, β. It is calculated using regression analysis. A beta of 1 indicates that the security's price will move with the market. A beta greater than 1 indicates that the security's price will be more volatile than the market, and a beta less than 1 means that it will be less volatile than the market. While standard deviation determines the volatility of a fund according to the disparity of its returns over a period of time, beta, another useful statistical measure, determines the volatility, or risk, of a fund in comparison to that of its index.

Investors expecting the market to be bullish may choose funds exhibiting high betas, which increase investors' chances of beating the market. If an investor expects the market to be bearish in the near future, the funds that have betas less than 1 are a good choice because they would be expected to decline less in value than the index. For example, if a fund had a beta of 0.5 and the S&P 500 declined 6%, the fund would be expected to decline only 3%. Be aware of the fact that beta by itself is limited and can be skewed due to factors of other than the market risk affecting the fund's volatility. Here is a basic guide to various betas:

Negative beta - A beta less than 0 is possible but highly unlikely. People used to think that gold and gold stocks should have negative betas because they tended to do better when the stock market declined, but this hasn't been true overall.

Beta = 0 - Basically this is cash (assuming no inflation).

Beta between 0 and 1 - Low-volatility investments, such as utilities, are usually in this range

Beta = 1 - This is the same as an index, such as the S&P 500 or some other index fund.

Beta greater than 1 - This denotes anything more volatile than the broad-based index, like a sector fund.

Beta greater than 100 - This is impossible because the stock would be expected go to zero on any decline in the stock market. The beta never gets higher than two to three.

The beta value for an index itself is taken as one. Equity funds can have beta values, which can be above one, less than one or equal to one. By multiplying the beta value of a fund with the expected percentage movement of an index, the expected movement in the fund can be determined. Thus, if a fund has a beta of 1.2 and the market is expected to move up by ten per cent, the fund should move by 12 per cent Similarly if the market loses ten per cent, the fund should lose 12 per cent.

This shows that a fund with a beta of more than one will rise more than the market and also fall more than market. Clearly, if you'd like to beat the market on the upside, it is best to invest in a high-beta fund. But you must keep in mind that such a fund will also fall more than the market on the way down. So, over an entire cycle, returns may not be much higher than the market.

Similarly, a low-beta fund will rise less than the market on the way up and lose less on the way down. When safety of investment is important, a fund with a beta of less than one is a better option. Such a fund may not gain much more than the market on the upside; it will protect returns better when market falls.

ALPHA

A measure of risk, used for mutual funds with regards to their relation and the market. A positive alpha is the extra return awarded to the investor for taking a risk, instead of accepting the market return

The formula for alpha is:

Alpha = [(sum of y) - ((b) (sum of x))] / n

n = number of observations (36 mos.)

b = beta of the fund

x = rate of return for the market

y = rate of return for the fund

Alpha measures how much if any of this extra risk helped the fund outperform its corresponding benchmark. Using beta, alpha's computation compares the fund's performance to that of the benchmark's risk-adjusted returns and establishes if the fund's returns outperformed the market's, given the same amount of risk.

For example, if a fund has an alpha of 1, it means that the fund outperformed the benchmark by 1%. Negative alphas are bad in that they indicate that the fund under performed for the amount of extra, fund-specific risk that the fund's investors undertook. Standard Deviation.

Standard deviation is probably used more than any other measure to describe the risk of a security (or portfolio of securities). If you read an academic study on investment performance, chances are that standard deviation will be used to gauge risk. It's not just a financial tool, though. Standard deviation is one of the most commonly used statistical tools in the sciences and social sciences. It provides a precise measure of the amount of variation in any group of numbers--the returns of a mutual fund.

Measure of the dispersion of a set of data from its mean. The more spread apart the data is, the higher the deviation. Standard deviation is applied to the annual rate of return of an investment to measure the investment's volatility (risk).

A volatile stock would have a high standard deviation. In mutual funds, the standard deviation tells us how much the return on the fund is deviating from the expected normal returns. Standard deviation is a statistical measure of the range of a fund's performance. When a fund has a high standard deviation, its range of performance has been very wide, indicating that there is a greater potential for volatility.

Technically speaking, standard deviation provides a quantification of the variance of the returns of the security, not its risk. After all, a fund with a high standard deviation of returns is not necessarily "riskier" than one with a low-standard deviation of returns.

CORRELATION

Correlation is a useful tool for determining if relationships exist between securities. A correlation coefficient is the result of a mathematical comparison of how closely related two variables are. The relationship between two variables is said to be highly correlated if a movement in one variable result or takes place at the same time as a similar movement in another variable. A useful feature of correlation analysis is the potential to predict the movement in one security when another security moves. Sometimes, there are securities that lead other securities. In other words, a change in price in one result in a later change in price of the other. A high negative correlation means that when a securities price changes, the other security or indicator or otherwise financial vehicle, will often move in the opposite direction.

Correlation analysis is a measure of the degree to which a change in the independent variable will result in a change in the dependent variable. A low correlation coefficient (e.g., ±0.1) suggests that the relationship between the two variables is weak or non-existent. A high correlation coefficient (e.g., ±0.80) indicates that the dependent variable will most likely change when the Independent variable changes. Correlation can also be used for a study between an indicator and a stock or index to help determine the predictive abilities of changes in the indicator. Correlation is not static. In other words, the correlation between two things in the markets does change over time and so a careful understanding that what has happened in the past may not predict what will happen in the future should be part of any basis in trading financial instruments in the market.

So far, we have seen how to calculate the return and risk on the portfolio of the investor's choice, but we never thought of rating our portfolio with other alternative portfolios. I.e. how well is our portfolio functioning?

Investors are vitally interested in how-well they have fared both absolutely and relatively to the alternative; investments they might have made portfolio builder accept a certain risk levels and try to achieve the highest return compatible with that level. They cannot know, whether they are heading towards this objective unless they measure their portfolio performance periodically. However, in conducting such on evaluation, a means for determining the appropriate standard or benchmark must be established. Two major factors should be considered.

(i) The ability to derive above average returns for given risk

(ii) The ability to eliminate all unsystematic risk from portfolio.

In order to determine the risk-adjusted returns of investment portfolios, several eminent authors have worked since 1960s to develop composite performance indices to evaluate a portfolio by comparing alternative portfolios within a particular risk class. The standards which take risk and return into consideration are referred to as risk-adjusted measures of performance. The most important and widely used measures of performance are:

- The Sharpe's Measure
- The Tenor's Measure
- Jenson's Model
- Fame's Model

1. **Sharpe's Performance Measure for Portfolio:** William Sharpe has propounded a measure of portfolio performance. The measure properly adjusts the performance for Risk. Sharpe ratio or 'excess return to variability' measures the portfolio excess return over the sample period by the standard deviation of returns over that period. This ratio measures the effectiveness of a manager in diversifying the total risk (a). This measure is appropriate if one is evaluating the total portfolio of an investor or a fund, in which case the Sharpe ratio of the portfolio can be compared with that of the market. The Sharpe Index is given by

$$\text{Sharpe's Index} = \frac{\text{(Average return on portfolio - Risk less rate of interest)}}{\text{(Deviation of returns on portfolio)}}$$

$$S_t = \frac{(R_p - R_f)}{\sigma_i}$$

Where

St = Sharpe Index

Rp = average return on portfolio (t)

Rf = riskless rate of interest

σi = standard deviation of the returns of portfolio (t).

- Sharpe Index measures the risk premium of the portfolio relative to the total amount of risk in the portfolio. It can be explained with the help of a graphical presentation.

This will be compared to the Shape ratio of the market portfolio. A higher ratio is preferable since it implies that the fund manager is able to generate more return per unit of total risks. However, managers who are operating specific portfolios like a value tilted or a style tilted portfolio generally takes a higher risk, and therefore may not be willing to be evaluated based on this measure.

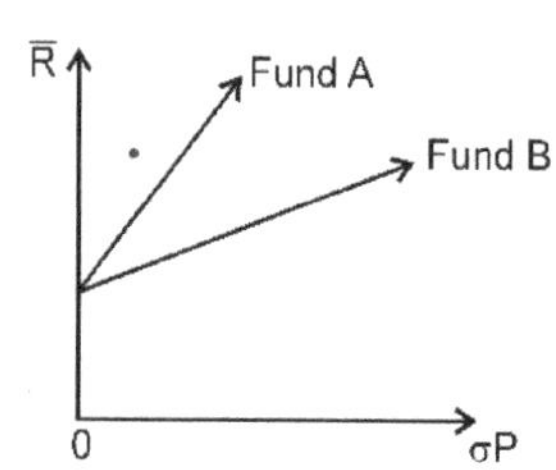

Index St, measures the scope of the line emanating from the riskless rate outward to the portfolio in the graph. Thus, the Sharpe index summarizes the risk & return of a portfolio in a single measure that categorize the performance of the fund on a risk-adjusted basis. Graphically the index measures the slope of the line emanating from the risk less rate outward to the portfolio in question. Thus, the Sharpe Index summarizes the risk and return of a portfolio in a single measure that categorizes the performance of the fund on a risk-adjusted basis. The larger the value of Sharpe Index the better the portfolio has performed.

Criterion for evaluation: Larger the (St); the better the Portfolio Performed.

2. **Treynor's Performance Measure for Portfolios:** Treynor's performance measure for a portfolio is associated with a characteristic line. When the market portfolio earns low or negative returns, the ideal portfolio still earns a positive return and when market portfolio earns a positive return, the ideal fund earns an even higher return. This line relates the market return to a specific portfolio return without any direct adjustment for risk.

   Slope of characteristic line is the beta coefficient a measure of the portfolio's systematic risk. By comparing the slopes of characteristic lines. The investors get an indication of the fund's volatility. The Steeper the line, the mere systematic risk or volatility the funds possesses. Treynor has proposed incorporating these various concepts into a single index to measure the portfolio performance more accurately. It is given by following formula:

   Treynor's ratio is given as

$$\text{Treynor Index} = \frac{\text{(Average return of portfolio-Risk less rate of interest)}}{\text{Beta coefficient of portfolio}}$$

$$T_n = \frac{\left(R_p - R_f\right)}{\beta}$$

   Where,

   T_n = Treynor Index

   R_p= average return on portfolio (n)

   R_f= riskless rate of interest

   β = beta coefficient of portfolio (n)

   Treynor's Index can be illustrated with the help of a graph

   Diagram

   Treynor Index measures the risk premium, which is related to the systematic risk assumed in the portfolio. Graphically, the index measures the scope of the line emanating outward from the riskless rate of the portfolio under consideration.

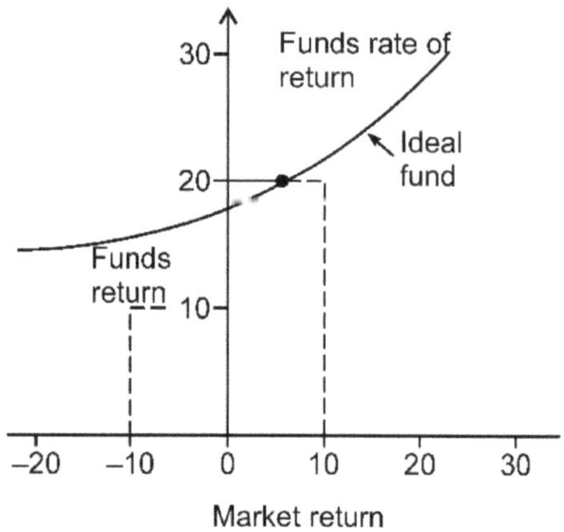

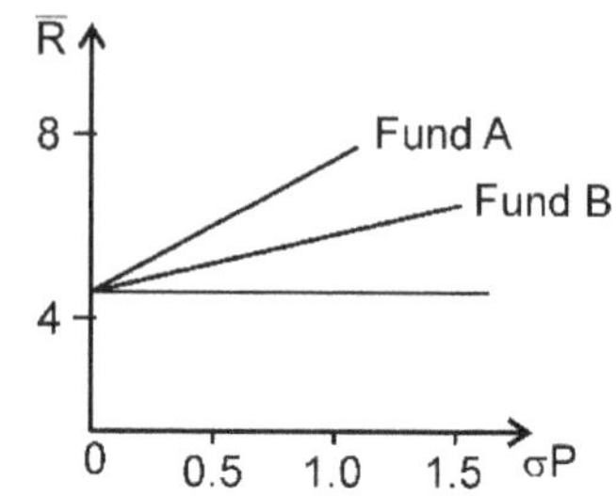

Comparison of Sharpe and Treynor

Sharpe and Treynor measures are similar in a way, since they both divide the risk premium by a numerical risk measure. The total risk is appropriate when we are evaluating the risk return relationship for well-diversified portfolios. On the other hand, the systematic risk is the relevant measure of risk when we are evaluating less than fully diversified portfolios or individual stocks. For a well- diversified portfolio, the total risk is equal to systematic risk. Rankings based on total risk (Sharpe measure) and systematic risk (Trey nor measure) should be identical for a well-diversified portfolio, as the total risk is reduced to systematic risk. Therefore, a poorly diversified fund that ranks higher on Trey nor measure, compared with another fund that is highly diversified, will rank lower on Sharpe Measure.

3. **Jenson's Performance Measure for Portfolio:** Jensen has constructed a measure of absolute performance on risk-adjusted basis, i.e. a definite standard against which performance of various funds can be measured. It refers the actual return earned in portfolio and return expected out of portfolio given its level of risk. CAPM – is used to calculate the expected return. The difference between the expected return and act retain can be said the return earned out of the mandatory of systematic risk. This excess return refers the manager's predictive ability and managerial skills.

   The returns predicted from the CAPM model is taken as the benchmark returns and is indicated by the formula within the brackets. The excess return is attributed to the ability of the managers for market timing or stock picking or both. This measure investigates the performance of funds and especially the ability of the managers in stock selection in terms of these contributing aspects. This measure is widely used in evaluating mutual fund performance. If a_P is positive and significant, it implies that the fund managers are able to identify stocks with high potential for excess returns. Market timing would refer to the adjustment in the beta of the portfolio in tandem with market movements. Specifically, timing skills call for increasing the beta when the market is rising and reducing the beta, when the market declines, for example through futures position. If the fund manager has poor market timing ability, then the beta of the portfolio would not have been significantly different during a market decline compared to that during a market increase.

In this process he has given a formula. i.e.

$$\bar{R_i} - R_f = \alpha + \beta\left(R_m - R_f\right)$$

Where,

$\bar{R_i}$ = average return on portfolio (j)

R_f= riskless rate of interest

α = intercept that measure the forecasting ability of the portfolio manager

β = a measure of systematic risk

R_m = average return on market portfolio (m)

Jensen's measure can be illustrated with the help of a diagram

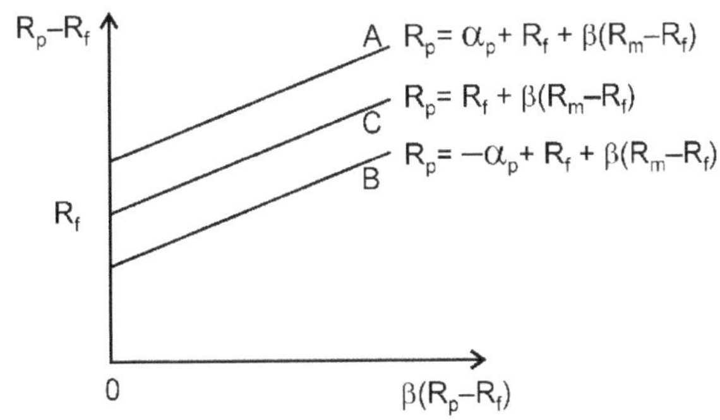

Fig: Graphical presentation of Jensen's measure of management ability

In Jensen's model intercept can be @ any point including the origin. Interpretation of graph is as follows. If α = positive, then, average superior extra return occurring to that particular portfolio because of superior management talent.

If α = o, then, Neutral performance by the management

If α = –v, then indicates inferior management performance. This arises due to insufficiency of portfolio returns to offset the expenses incurred in the selection and managing process.

4. **Fame Model Measure for Portfolio:** The Eugene Fame model is an extension of Jenson model. This model compares the performance, measured in terms of returns, of a fund with the required return commensurate with the total risk associated with it.

   The difference between these two is taken as a measure of the performance of the fund and is called net selectivity. The net selectivity represents the stock selection skill of the fund manager, as it is the excess return over and above the return required to compensate for the total risk taken by the fund manager. Higher value of which indicates that fund manager has earned returns well above the return commensurate with the level of risk taken by him.

Required return can be calculated as: **Ri = Rf + бi/бm*(Rm - Rf)**

Where, **Sm** is standard deviation of market returns. The net selectivity is then calculated by subtracting this required return from the actual return of the fund. Among the above performance measures, two models namely, Trey nor measure and Jenson model use systematic risk based on the premise that the unsystematic risk is diversifiable. These models are suitable for large investors like institutional investors with high risk-taking capacities as they do not face paucity of funds and can invest in a number of options to dilute some risks. For them, a portfolio can be spread across a number of stocks and sectors. However, Sharpe measure and Fame model that consider the entire risk associated with fund are suitable for small investors, as the ordinary investor lacks the necessary skill and resources to diversified. Moreover, the selection of the fund on the basis of superior stock selection ability of the fund manager will also help in safeguarding the money invested to a great extent. The investment in funds that have generated big returns at higher levels of risks leaves the money all the more prone to risks of all kinds that may exceed the individual investors' risk appetite.

1. **Venue's firm is trying to decide between two investments funds. From fast performance they will able to calculate the following average returns and standard deviations for these funds**

Average returns(R) %	ABC fund	XYZ fund
Stander deviation%	20%	15%
Average return(R) %	18%	16%

Risk-Free rate(R) = 8.0%

Calculate the sharps performance measure?

Sol: Sharps performance measure can be calculated by the following measure

$$S_t = \frac{r_t - r^*}{\sigma_t}$$

$$S_{ABC} = \left[\frac{0.18 - 0.08}{0.20}\right] = 0.5$$

$$S_{XYZ} = \left[\frac{0.16 - 0.08}{0.15}\right] = 0.5333$$

Result: It is that 'XYZ' fund has a slightly better performance and would be better alternative of the two

2. **XYZ and ABC are two mutual funds. XYZ has a sample mean of success 0.13 and fund ABC has a sample mean of success 0.18, with risker fund ABC having the**

double the beta @2.0 fund XYZ. If repetitive standard deviation is 15% of ABC and 19% of XYZ. The mean return for market index is 0.12. While the risk-free rate is 8%.

(a) Compute the Sharpe index for the funds and the markets

(b) Compute the Tenor's Index for the funds

(c) Compute the Jensen's index for each of the funds

Sol: Given

	ABC	XYZ	Market
Mean (%)	0.18	0.13	0.12
Σ	0.15	0.19	

$R_f = 8\%$

(a) Calculation of shapes index is as follows:

$$S_t = \frac{\bar{r}_t - r^*}{\sigma_t}$$

$$S_{ABC} = \left[\frac{18\% - 8\%}{15\%}\right] = \frac{10\%}{15\%} = 0.666\%$$

$$S_{XYZ} = \left[\frac{13\% - 8\%}{19\%}\right] = \frac{5\%}{19\%} = 0.26315\%$$

$$S_{MARKET} = \left[\frac{12\% - 8\%}{8\%}\right] = \frac{4\%}{8\%} = 0.5\%$$

(b) Calculation of Tenors index is as follows

$$T_n = \frac{\left(\bar{R}_n - R^*\right)}{\beta_n}$$

Fund	AV. Return	Standard Deviation	Beta
A	0.15	.25	1.25
B	0.12	.30	.75
C	0.10	.20	1
R*m*	0.12	.25	1
Rf	= 7%		

$$S_t = \frac{\bar{r}_t - r^*}{\sigma_t}$$

$$S_A = \left[\frac{.15-.07}{.25}\right] = .32$$

$$S_B = \left[\frac{.12-.07}{.30}\right] = .167$$

$$S_C = \left[\frac{.10-.07}{.20}\right] = .15$$

$$T_n = \frac{\left(\bar{R}_n - R^*\right)}{\beta_t}$$

$$T_A = \left[\frac{.15-.07}{1.25}\right] = .064$$

$$T_B = \left[\frac{.12-.07}{.75}\right] = .067$$

$$T_C = \left[\frac{.10-.07}{1.0}\right] = .03$$

Jenson's performance measure

$$\alpha = \left(R - R_f\right) - \beta_i\left(R_m - R_f\right)$$

$$\alpha_A = (.15-.07) - 1.25(.12-.07) = .0175$$

$$\alpha_B = (.12-.07) - .75(.12-.07) = .0125$$

$$\alpha_C = (.10-.07) - 1.00(.12-.07) = .0200$$

3. An example would illustrate the Sharpe's and Trener's Model:

Sharpe Index	Return	Std. Deviation	Riskless rate of return	n
A	20%	4%	10%	0.5
B	24%	8%	10%	1.5

Solution:

$$S_t = \frac{R_p - R_f}{\sigma}$$

St = Std. deviation at time period 't'

Rp = Average return of portfolio

Rf = Riskless rate of return

A = .20 - .10/.04 = .10/.04 = 2.5

B = .24 - .10/.08 = .14/.08 = 1.75

A ranked as better portfolio because the index is higher. 2.5 > 1.75 although portfolio B has a higher return 24 > 20.

4. **Extended Example = Average Return – Required Return / Standard deviation**

Sharpe's Model

Solution:

R_p = Average return of best portfolio

R_m = Average return on market portfolio

S. Dt = Standard deviation of returns on best portfolio

S_m = Standard deviation of returns on market portfolio

Alpha = 2.55

Average beta on managed portfolio	= 2.85
Beta on best portfolio	= 1.00
Standard deviation on best portfolio	= 15.24
Standard deviation of returns on managed portfolio	= 4.92
Riskless rate	= 3.00%
Return on best portfolio	= 6%
Average return on managed portfolio	= 3.30
Difference between best portfolio and average return	= 6.00 – 3.30 = 2.70
St = 6.00 -3.00/15.24 = 3.00/15.24	= .19
Sm = 3.30 – 3.00/4.92 = 0.30/4.92	= .06

Superior

Best portfolio out marks market portfolio

Treynor's Model

Average Return on portfolio – Riskless Rate of Return/Bn = $T_n = \frac{R_p - R_f}{\beta_i}$

Tn = Rp – Rf/Bn = 6.00 – 3.00/1 = 3.00/.1 = 3.00

Tm = 3.30 -3.00/2.85 = 3.00/2.85 = 1

The best portfolio outranks market portfolio.

Jenson's Model

(Rp – Rf) = 2.55 + 2.85 (Rm – Rf)

Alpha coefficient is the most important.

It measures bonus performance owing to superior portfolio management.

$R_p = R_f + \beta_i (R_m - R_f)$

Rp = 3.00 + 2.85 (3.00 – 2.85) = 5.85 (O.45) =2.63

Expected return from portfolio

The actual return on best portfolio was 6.00. The excess earned is 6.00 – 2.63 = 3.37 gives risk free rate portfolio and return on the market portfolio.

5. Calculate the portfolio evaluation under Sharpe and Treynor.

Fund	Return of Portfolio	Risk free rate of return	Standard deviation
1	20%	10%	8%
2	30%	10%	15%

Solution:

Sharpe

Fund 1 = 20 – 10/8 = 1.25

Fund 2 = 30 – 10/15 = 1.33

Treynor

Fund 1 = 20 – 10/.8 = 12.5

Fund 2 = 30 - 10/1.1 = 18.18

6. Rank the funds under Treynor's Performance Index.

Fund	Beta	Rp	Rf
X	1.15	15%	7%
Y	1.25	13%	7%

Solution:

$$\text{Treynor} = \frac{\left(R_p - R_f\right)}{\beta_i}$$

X = 15 -7/1.15 = 6.95

Y = 13 – 7/1.25 = 4.88

Rank 1 = Fund X

Rank 2 = Fund Y

7. Rank the following fund based on Sharpe & Treynor.

Solution:

Sharpe

Fund	Return	S. D	Beta	RF
T	15%	16%	1.15	7%
P	13%	18 %	1.25	7%
F	12%	11%	0.90	7%

T = 15 – 7/16 = 0.5

P = 13 – 7/1.25 = 4.8

F = 12 – 7/.90 = 5.55

8. From the following details, calculate the portfolio manager's efficiency by using Jensen's Model.

Solution:

Fund	**RF**	**RP**	**RM**	**Beta**
A	5%	12%	15%	.5
B	5%	20%	15%	1
C	5%	14%	15%	1.1

Jensen

Fund A = 12 – 5 = a + .5 (15-5)

7 = a + .5 (10)

7 = a + 5

a = 2

Fund B = 20 – 5 = a + 1(15-5)

15 = a + 10

a = 5

Fund C = 14 – 5 = a + 1.1 (15-5)

9 = a + 11

a = -2

Since the efficiency level of portfolio is high in Fund B, Fund B is relatively better than two.

9. A firm is to decide between two investment funds from the past performance, they were able to calculate the following average return and standard deviation for these funds, the current risk-free rate is 8%. The firm will use this as measure of risk-free rate.

Solution:

Particulars	ABC Fund	XYZ Fund
Average return (Rp)	18%	16%
Standard Deviation	20%	15%

The firm can decide investment fund by using Sharp model which are worked as under.

ABC Fund

Sp = 18 – 8/20% = 10/20 = 0.5

XYZ Fund

Sp = 16 – 8/15% = 8/15 = 0.53

10. With a risk-free rate of 10% and with the market portfolio having an expected return of 20% with a standard deviation of 8%, what is Sharpe Index for portfolio X, with a mean of 14% and a standard deviation of 18%? For portfolio Y, having a return of 20% and a standard deviation of 16%? Would you rather be in the market portfolio or one of the other two portfolios?

K = Market value of common stock/ Market value of total portfolio

Solution:

Portfolio X = Sharpe Index = $S_t = \frac{R_p - R_f}{\sigma}$ = 14 – 10/18 = 0.222

Portfolio Y = Sharp Index = 20 – 10/16 = 10/16 = 0.625

Market portfolio = 20 – 10/8 = 10/8 = 1.25

Market portfolio is superior to X and Y.

11. Consider the following data for a particular sample period.

Solution:

	Portfolio P	Market M
Average return	0.35	0.28
Beta	1.2	1.0
Standard deviation	0.42	0.30
Non – systematic risk	0.18	0

Calculate the following performance measure for Portfolio P and the market: Sharpe, Jenson, Treynor, Appraisal Ratio. The risk-free rate during the period was 0.06. By which measures did portfolio P outperform the market?

Sharpe

Sharpe for portfolio P = 0.35 – 0.06/0.42 = 0.69

Sharpe for portfolio M = 0.28 – 0.06/0.30 = 0.733

Treynor

Portfolio P = 0.35 – 0.06/1.2 = 0.242

Market M = 0.28 – 0.06/1.0 = 0.22

Jenseon

Portfolio P = 0.35 – [0.06 + 1.2(0.28 – 0.06)]

= 0.026

Market M = 0

Appraisal

Portfolio P = Tenson p/SD = 0.026/0.18 = 0.144

Market M = 0

12. With a risk-free rate of 5 % and with a market portfolio having an unexpected return of 10% and with a market portfolio having an expected return of 10% with a standard deviation of 5 percent, what is the Sharpe index for portfolio A, with a return of 8 percent and a standard deviation of 10 percent? For portfolio B, having a return of 12% and a standard deviation of 8%? Would you rather be in the market portfolio or one of the other two portfolios?

Solution:

Portfolio A = 8 – 5/10 = 3/10 = .3

Portfolio B = 12 – 5/8 = 7/8 = .875

Market = 10 – 5/5 = 5/5 = 1

Thus, the market is superior to both A and B.

13. Suppose a manager is holding 3 stocks with 25% invested in stock Y and 50% invested in stock Z, at the end of the next quarter, the manager's weights are 30% and 50% respectively. In the quarter after that, the stock produce returns of 15%, 5%, and 30% respectively. What is the manager PCM?

Solution:

The PCM is computed as follows:

0.5 = 15% (30% - 25%) + 5% (20% - 15%) + 30% (5o% - %50%)

= 15% (5%) + 5% (5 %) + 30% (0%)

= 25% + 25% = 50%

14. Here are Five Mutual Funds

Solution:

Funds	Return	Standard Deviation	Beta
ABC	16	8	1.50
WER	12	6	0.90
QWA	14	5	1.40
RDS	18	10	0.75
YTR	15	7	1.25

What is the reward to variability ratio and ranking if the risk-free rate is 7%

Sharpe

ABC = 16 – 7/8 = 9/8 = 1.125

WER = 12 – 7/6 =5/6 = 0.833

QWA = 14 – 7/5 = 7/5 = 1.4

RDS = 18 – 7/10 = 11/10 = 1.1

YTR = 15 – 7/7 = 8/7 = 1.142

Rank 1 = QWA

2 = YTR

3 = ABC

4 = RDC

5 = WER

Treynor

ABC = 16 – 7/1.50 = 9/1.50 = 6

WER = 12 – 7/0.90 = 5/0.90 = 5.55

QWA = 14 – 7/1.40 = 7/1.40 = 5

RDS = 18 – 7/0.75 = 11/0.75 = 14.66

YTR = 15 – 7/1.25 = 8/1.25 = 6.4

Rank 1 = RDS

2 = YTR

3 = ABC

4 = WER

5 = QWA

15. The following parameters are available for five mutual funds.

Fund	A	B	C	D	E
Expected Return (%)	15	18	17	16	20
Beta	0.5	0.8	0.7	0.6	1.0

Solution:

(a) Calculate Treynor's Performance Index and rank the funds on the assumptions that RF is 8% and alternatively 5%.

(b) What should be the RF such that the funds A&B will have same Treynor's performance?

When RF = 8%

Treynor's Performance

Fund A = 15 – 8/0.5 = 7/0.5 = 14

B = 18 – 8/0.8 = 10/0.8 = 12.5

C = 17 – 8/0.7 = 9/0.7 = 12.8

D = 16 – 8/0.6 = 8/0.6 = 13.33

E = 20 – 8/1.0 = 12/01.0 = 12

Rank 1 = Fund A

2 = D

3 = C

4 = B

5 = E

When RF = 5%

Fund A = 15 – 5/0.5 = 10/0.5 = 20

Fund B = 18 – 5/0.8 = 13/0.8 = 16.25

C = 17 – 5/0.7 = 12/0.7 = 17.14

D = 16 – 5/0.6 = 11/0.6 = 18.33

E = 20 – 5/1.0 = 15/1.0 = 15

Rank 1 = Fund A

2 = D

3 = C

4 = B

5 = E

(a) The risk-free ratio should be 6.5% so that both A and B funds will have the same performance index.

16. The data relating to market portfolio and an investor 'P' portfolio is as under:

	Investor P's Portfolio	Market Portfolio (M)
Average Return	**28%**	**18%**
Beta (b)	**1.4**	**1**
Standard Deviation (a)	**30%**	**20%**

Solution:

Assuming that the risk-free rate for the market is 8%, calculate (a) Sharpe Ratio Treynor Ratio and (c) Jensen Alpha for the investor P and the market.

Answer:

	Investor P Portfolio	Market Portfolio (M)
Sharpe Ratio = $(r_p - r_f) / a_p$	(28% - 8%)/30% = 0.67	(18% - 8%)/20% = 0.5
Treynor Ratio = $(r_p - r_f) / b_p$	(28% - 8%)/1.4 = 5	(18% - 8%)/1 = 10
Jensen Alpha	28% - [8% + 1.4*(18% - 8%)]	18% - [8% + 1
$(ap) = rp - [rf + bp\ (r_M - rf)]$	= 28% - 22% = 6%	(18% - 8%)] = 0

17. Portfolio P has a return of 14% and beta 0.5 if the market return is 14% and risk-free return 10% find Jensen's alpha.

Solution:

Jensen's alpha = Portfolio return- Expected Return

Expected return

= Risk free return + Beta (Market Return – Risk free return)

Expected return of P = 0.1 + 0.5 (0.14-0.10) = 0.12

Jensen's alpha = 0.14 – 0.12 = 0.02= **2%**

18. If during one year period an index fund earned @ 10%, risk free rate of return on investment is 8% and the standard deviation of the index fund was 20% find sharpe Ratio.

Solution:

Sharpe ratio

$$S_t = \frac{R_p - R_f}{\sigma}$$

$$= \frac{\text{Portfolio return - Risk free return on investment}}{s \tan dard \text{ deviation of portfolio}}$$

$$= \frac{10 - 8}{0.20} = \boxed{10\%}$$

19. The return of 2 portfolios x and y is given by r_x=10%, r_y= 12% and their beta is β_x= 0.5, β_y= 0.9; If risk free rate of return is 8% compute the Treynor ratio and the absolute risk adjusted return.

Solution:

$$Treynor\text{ ratio (T)} = \frac{\text{Portfolio return - Risk free return on investment}}{\text{portfolio beta}}$$

$$T_n = \frac{R_p - R_f}{\beta_i}$$

$$Tx = \frac{0.12 - 0.08}{0.9} = 0.04$$

$$Ty = \frac{0.12 - 0.08}{0.9} = 0.044$$

Risk adjusted return= Treynor ratio + Risk free rate of return

Risk adjusted return

For X = 0.04 + 0.08 = 0.12 = **12%**

Risk adjusted return

For Y= 0.044 + 0.08 = 0.124 = **12.4%**

MULTIPLE CHOICE QUESTIONS

1. Which of the following is NOT a reason for evaluating and understanding the performance of investments?
   a. The individual investor needs to know if handling his own investments is cost-effect in terms of time and effort.
   b. Owners of mutual funds need to know if their professional managers are performing effectively.
   c. Individual investors need to brag to their friends when discussing investments.
   d. Mutual funds companies need to report their result to current and prospective customers.
2. Which of the following is NOT a factor in evaluating and assessing portfolio performance?
   a. Performance measurement issues
   b. Composite measures of performance
   c. Performance attribution
   d. The investor's risk preference

3. What is the question which should be asked when evaluating the performance of a portfolio?
   a. Does the investor have enough money to buy what he wants?
   b. Has the portfolio returned more than comparable portfolios?
   c. Is the return, net of expenses, sufficient to compensate for the risk?
   d. Did the portfolio take any unnecessary risks?
4. Which of the following is NOT one of the three questions to answer in measuring portfolio performance?
   a. Was the return on the portfolio, after expenses, adequate?
   b. How much risk did the investor take in holding the portfolio?
   c. How much money did the investor get?
   d. What return could have been earned, if a similarly risky investment had been chosen instead?
5. Sam has invested in a mutual fund that invests in smaller, high tech companies. Which of the following indexes is most appropriate for which to Sam to use as a benchmark?
   a. The Dow Jones Average
   b. The Standard & Poor 500 Index
   c. The Nasdaq Composite Index
   d. The Lehman Bond Index
6. Which time period of reported returns should individual investors compare when comparing mutual funds?
   a. Latest one year return, ending the most recent Dec 31.
   b. Latest one year return, ending the most recent month end.
   c. Latest five-year return, ending the most recent Dec 31.
   d. No specific time period is necessarily better than any other.
7. Sam has made several investments to his mutual fund throughout the year. He now wants to calculate the return of the fund for the year. Which of the following measures should he use?
   a. Simple percentage return (Vt – Vb) / Vb
   b. Dollar weighted return, finding an IRR equating the discounted value of all flows, including the ending value as an outflow.
   c. Time weighted returns, using the geometric mean return of all subperids.
   d. None of these calculations is always correct.
8. Sam wants to compare the performance of several mutual fund managers, including the one in which he currently has his funds. He now wants to calculate the return of the funds for the year. Which of the following measures should he use?

a. Simple percentage return (Vt – Vb) / Vb
b. Dollar weighted return, finding an IRR equating the discounted value of all flows, including the ending value as an outflow.
c. Time weighted returns, using the geometric mean return of all sub-periods.
d. None of these calculations is always correct.

9. Which of the following is NOT an appropriate measure of risk?
   a. Total risk, as measured by standard deviation
   b. Systematic risk, as measure by beta
   c. Characteristic line, as measured by the coefficient of determination R^2
   d. The market return, as measured by S&P 500 index.

10. Which of the following is NOT an appropriate yardstick against which to measure the performance of a specific portfolio?
    a. A universe of similarly managed portfolios
    b. A benchmark such as a published index
    c. The desires of the investors
    d. Major, well-known index funds

11. Which of the following performance measures is more appropriate to measure the risk and return of a mutual fund which invests only in the health care industry?
    a. The Sharpe measure RVAR
    b. The Treynor measure RVOR
    c. Jensen's alpha
    d. All three will produce the same ranking of funds

12. Consider the Sharpe measure RVAR = (TRp – RF) / SDp. What is measured by the numerator?
    a. The total return of the portfolio
    b. The excess return of the portfolio
    c. The standard deviation of the portfolio
    d. The risk-adjusted return of the portfolio

13. Consider Figure 22-1. Which of the following best describes the interpretation of this information?
    a. The best choice for most investors is those funds lying on the CML
    b. The best choice for most investors is those funds lying above the CML
    c. The best choice for most investors is those funds lying below the CML
    d. The figure shows that most major funds are pretty much the same.

14. Which of the following best describes the difference between the Sharpe RVAR and the Treynor RVOL measures of portfolio return?
    a. Sharpe divides by beta, while Treynor divides by standard deviation.
    b. Sharpe divides by standard deviation, while Treynor divides by beta.
    c. Sharpe assume the portfolio is fully diversified, Treynor does not make this assumption.
    d. Sharpe and Treynor are expressing the same concept using different words.

15. Let's assume that the XYZ Fund ranks high on the Sharpe RVAR, but not so high on the Treynor RVOL. Which of the following is the best conclusion?
    a. The managers of the XYZ fund have performed well because they concentrated in sectors or stocks that performed well.
    b. The XYZ is fully diversified, similar to the S&P 500.
    c. In the interest of conservatism, the investor should choose to follow the lower Tryenor measure.
    d. Because it better justifies his choice, the investor should follow the higher Sharpe measure.

16. Consider the Jensen Differential Return Measure. Which variable measures how well the fund manager has performed?
    a. RF_t b. $\square_p$
    c. R_{pt} d. $\square_p$

17. Which of the following indexes is NOT used as a performance benchmarks for U.S. equities?
    a. S&P 500 b. Wilshire 5000
    c. Russell 2000 d. MSCI EAFE

18. The M2 measure of portfolio performance will produce the same results as which other measure?
    a. Sharpe b. Treynor
    c. Jensen d. All measures produce different rankings

19. Sharpe developed a returns-based based on many asset classes, but which asset class is NOT included?
    a. Treasury bills b. Bonds
    c. Stocks d. Gold

20. Performance attribution examines all but which of the following characteristics?
    a. Portfolio weights b. Industry selection
    c. Security selection d. Bogey selection

TRUE OR FALSE

1. Individual investors should choose funds based on which fund shows the highest returns.
   (False)
2. The time weighted returns are a better measure of return, because it considers the inflows and outflows the investor makes.
   (False)
3. Standard deviation is a more appropriate measure of risk than beta.
   (False)
4. Beta measures the total risk of an asset or portfolio.
   (False)
5. Morningstar publishes on the internet a wide variety of information investors can use to compare the risk and returns of mutual funds.
   (True)
6. Sharpe's RVAR uses standard deviation in the denominator, while Treynor's RVOL use beta in the denominator.
   (True)
7. Jensen's alpha measures how much better the portfolio has performed, compared to the performance predicated by the CAPM. We can assume this favorable performance is attributable to the skill of the fund manager.
   (True)
8. The Sharpe and Treynor measures can be used to rank portfolio performance and indicate the relative positions of the portfolios being evaluated.
   (True)
9. The Dow Jones Industrial Average is a widely-used benchmark portfolio used by institutional money managers.
   (False)
10. AIMR set up performance presentation standards to reduce misrepresentation of performance results.
    (True)

SHORT ANSWER QUESTIONS

1. Define Mutual Fund
2. What is Diversification?

3. What are the types of Mutual Funds?
4. Define Open-Ended Schemes
5. Define Close-Ended Schemes
6. Define Equity funds
7. Define Index funds
8. Define Money market funds
9. Define Unit Investment Trusts
10. What are the Benefits of Mutual Funds?
11. Define Hedge Funds
12. Define Growth and Income Funds
13. Define Fixed-Income Funds
14. Define Money Market Funds/Liquid Funds
15. Define Risk Vs. Reward
16. Define Net Asset Value (NAV)
17. Define Beta.
18. Define Alpha
19. Define Asset classes
20. Define Asset allocation
21. Define Sharpe's ratio
22. Define Treynor's ratio
23. Define Jensen's Alpha
24. What is mean by Fama Model?
25. Define Benchmark portfolios
26. Define Tracking error
27. Define Strategic asset allocation
28. Define Tactical asset allocation

ESSAY TYPE QUESTIONS

1. What are mutual funds? Explain the importance and benefits of Mutual Funds.
2. "Do not put all of eggs in one basket" Explain.
3. What is the classification of mutual funds is by the types of assets the funds buy? Explain
4. Briefly explain the types of Mutual funds.
5. Discuss the various types of risks.
6. Explain the history of the Indian Mutual Fund Industry.

7. What is NAV? How to measure the value of NAV?
8. How to valuation of traded securities and non-trading securities.
9. What is the debt explain instruments? Briefly.
10. Beta is a measure of volatility of stock market and explain the various Betas.
11. Alpha is measure of risk. Explain.
12. Why benchmark portfolios are important in investment portfolio management?
13. Briefly describe each of the portfolio performance measures and explain how they are used:

    Sharpe's ratio; Treynor's ratio; Jensen's Alpha.
14. Discuss fully the Sharpe, Treynor and the Jensen measures of portfolio returns.
15. Assume that you plan to construct a portfolio aimed at achieving your stated objectives. The portfolio can be constructed by allocating your money to the following asset classes: common stock, bonds, and short-term securities.
    (a) Identify state and comment your investment objectives.
    (b) Determine an asset allocation to these three classes of assets considering your stated investment objectives. Explain your decision.
    (c) What reasons could cause you to make changes in your asset allocations?
16. An investor's portfolio consists of 50000 EURO in stocks and 5000 EURO in cash. the Beta of the portfolio is 1,10. How the investor could reduce Beta of the portfolio to 0,95? Show and explain.
17. Select four stocks which were actively traded in the local stock exchange last calendar year, find the information about their prices at the beginning and at the end of the year, number of dividends paid on each stock for this year and stock Beta at the end of the year. Also find a risk-free rate of return and the market return for the given year. Assume that these four stocks were put to the portfolio in equal proportions (25% in each stock). Assume that the standard deviation for this portfolio is 16, 75% and that standard deviation for the market portfolio is 13, 50%.
    (a) Find the portfolio return for the given year (see chapter 3.1.2, formula 3.1).
    (b) Calculate Sharpe's, Treynor's ratios and Jensen's Alpha.
    (c) Compare and comment the results of measuring portfolio performance with different measures.

EXERCISE PROBLEMS

1. RAM and SRIRAM are two mutual funds. RAM has a sample mean of success 0.15 and fund ABC has a sample mean of success 0.2, with risker fund ABC having the double the beta @4.0 fund RAM. If repetitive standard deviation is 20% of SRIRAM and 16% of RAM. The mean return for market index is 0.10. While the risk-free rate is 10%.

(a) Compute the Sharpe index for the funds and the markets

(b) Compute the Tenor's Index for the funds

(c) Compute the Jensen's index for each of the funds

Calculate Sharpe's, Trenor's and Jensen's measure of performance.

Fund	AV. Return	Standard Deviation	Beta
A	0.16	.20	1.35
B	0.14	.35	.70
C	0.12	.25	1cA
R_m	0.14	.30	1
R_f	= 9%		

2. Calculate the portfolio evaluation under Sharpe and Treynor.

Fund	Return of Portfolio	Risk free rate of return	Standard deviation
1	30%	15%	10%
	40%	15%	12%

3. Rank the funds under Treynor's Performance Index.

Fund	Beta	Rp	Rf
X	1.25	18%	9%
Y	1.35	15%	9%

4. Rank the following fund based on Sharpe & Treynor.

Fund	Return	S. D	Beta	RF
T	15%	16%	1.15	7%
P	13%	18 %	1.25	7%
F	12%	11%	0.90	7%

5. A firm is to decide between two investment funds from the past performance, they were able to calculate the following average return and standard deviation for these funds, the current risk-free rate is 10%. The firm will use this as measure of risk-free rate.

Particulars	IPIP Fund	CDST Fund
Average return (Rp)	19%	26%
Standard Deviation	24%	19%

The firm can decide investment fund by using Sharp model which are worked as under.

6. With a risk-free rate of 9% and with the market portfolio having an expected return of 24% with a standard deviation of 12%, what is Sharpe Index for portfolio X, with a mean of 14% and a standard deviation of 16%? For portfolio Y, having a return of 28% and a standard deviation of 19%? Would you rather be in the market portfolio or one of the other two portfolios?

7. With a risk-free rate of 6% and with a market portfolio having an unexpected return of 14% and with a market portfolio having an expected return of 14% with a standard

deviation of 7 percent, what is the Sharpe index for portfolio A, with a return of 8 percent and a standard deviation of 16 percent? For portfolio B, having a return of 16% and a standard deviation of 9%? Would you rather be in the market portfolio or one of the other two portfolios?

8. Suppose a manager is holding 3 stocks with 40% invested in stock Y and 55% invested in stock Z, at the end of the next quarter, the manager's weights are 38% and 60% respectively. In the quarter after that, the stock produce returns of 18%, 9%, and 38% respectively. What is the manager PCM?

9. **Here are Five Mutual Funds**

Funds	Return	Standard Deviation	Beta
1	18	10	2.50
2	14	9	1.0
3	16	8	1.80
4	20	13	1.75
5	18	9	1.45

10. The following parameters are available for five mutual funds.

Fund	A	B	C	D	E
Expected Return (%)	16	20	20	18	24
Beta	0.8	1.8	1.0	.8	1.0

(a) Calculate Treynor's Performance Index and rank the funds on the assumptions that RF is 9% and alternatively 7%.

(b) What should be the RF such that the funds A&B will have same Treynor's performance?

11. Portfolio A has a return of 18% and beta 0.9 if the market return is 19% and risk-free return 9% find Jensen's alpha.

12. The return of 2 portfolios A and Bis given by r_x=12%, r_y= 14% and their beta is β_x= 0.7, β_y=0.8; If risk free rate of return is 9% compute the Treynor ratio and the absolute risk adjusted return.

13. A mutual fund that had a net asset value of Rs. 24 mat the beginning of month made income and capital gain distribution of Re. 0.02755 and Re. 0.05 per share respectively during the month, and then ended the month with a net asset value of Rs. 25.06. Calculate monthly return.

14. Mr. X can earn a return of 20 per cent by investing in equity shares on his own. Now he is considering a recentXy announced equity based mutual fund scheme in which initial expenses are 5.8% and annual recurring expenses are 1.7%. How much should the mutual fund earn to provide Mr. X a return of 20%?

15. X Mutual Fund having 350 units has shown Is NAV of Rs.8.95 and Rs. 10.45 at the beginning and at the end of the year respectively. The Mutual Fund has given two options:
    (i) Pay Rs. 0.95 per unit as dividend and Rs. 0.75 per unit as a capital gain, or
    (ii) These distributions are to be reinvested at an average NAV of Rs 9.50 per unit. What difference it would make in terms of return available and which option is preferable?
16. A mutual fund that had a net asset value of Rs.15 at the beginning of month made income and capital gain distribution of Re. 0.15 and Re. 0.08 per share respectively during the month, and then ended the month with a net asset value of Rs. 12.23. Calculate monthly return.

MCQs Answers

1	2	3	4	5	6	7	8	9	10	11	12	13	14	15	16	17	18	19	20
c	d	c	c	c	d	b	b	d	c	a	b	b	b	a	d	d	a	d	d

CASE STUDIES

CASE STUDY 1

Select four stocks which were actively traded in the local stock exchange last calendar year, find the information about their prices at the beginning and at the end of the year, number of dividends paid on each stock for this year and stock Beta at the end of the year. Also find a risk-free rate of return and the market return for the given year. Assume that these four stocks were put to the portfolio in equal proportions (25% in each stock). Assume that the standard deviation for this portfolio is 16, 75% and that standard deviation for the market portfolio is 13, 50%.

(a) Find the portfolio return for the given year.

(b) Calculate Sharpe's, Treynor's ratios and Jensen's Alpha.

Compare and comment the results of measuring portfolio performance with different measures.

CASE STUDY 2

An aggressive Mutual Fund promises an expected rate of rectum of 18% with a standard deviation of 22%. On the other hand, a conservative mutual fund promises an expected rate of return of 16% and fluctuations of 13%.

- In which of the funds would you like to invest?
- Would you like io invest in both the funds?

If you can borrow money from your provident fund at an opportunity cost of 15%, in which fund would you invest your money?

CASE STUDY 3

A Mutual Fund has 200 shares of XYZ Co., currently trading at Rs. 14 and 200 shares of ABC 10, currently trading at Rs. 140. The fund has issued 150 shares.

(i) What is the NAV of the fund?

(ii) If investors expect the price of the XYZ Co's shares to increase to Rs. 18 and price of ABC Co., to decline Rs. 110 by the end of the year, what is the expected Rs. 110 by the end of the year.

(iii) What is the maximum that the price of ABC Co., can decline to maintain the NAV as estimated in (i)?

CASE STUDY 4

Many people advocate mutual funds for small investors. They suggest that the best strategy for small investors is to shares in good mutual fund and put them away. What do you think is preferable? Why?

CASE STUDY 5

Many people advocate mutual funds for small investors. They suggest that the best strategy for small investors is to shares in good mutual fund and put them away. What do you think is preferable? Why?

CASE STUDY 6

Closed-end funds generally invest in securities and financial instruments that are relatively illiquid. Whereas most mutual funds invest in widely traded stocks and bonds. Explain the differences between closed-end and open-end funds and why this liquidity distinction matters?

CASE STUDY 7

Following parameters are available for the five mutual funds. Fund A B C D E Expected return % 15 18 17 16 20 Beta 0.5 0.8 0.7 0.6 1.0. Calculate Treynor's performance index and rank the funds on the assumption that risk free rate (T) is 8% and alternatively that T = 5%. What should be the risk-free rate (T) such that funds A & B will have the same Treynor's performance index?

CHAPTER 15

Portfolio Revision

INTRODUCTION

Portfolio management would be an incomplete exercise without a periodic review. The portfolio, which is once selected, has to be continuously reviewed over a period of time and if necessary revised depending on the objectives of investor. Thus, portfolio revision means changing the asset allocation of a portfolio. However, the frequency of review depends upon the size of the portfolio, the sum involved, the kind of securities held and the time available to the investor. The review should include a careful examination of investment objectives, targets for portfolio performance, actual results obtained and analysis of reason for variations. The review should be followed by suitable and timely action.

Meaning

The art of changing the mix of securities in a portfolio is called as portfolio revision.

The process of addition of more assets in an existing portfolio or changing the ratio of funds invested is called as portfolio revision. The sale and purchase of assets in an existing portfolio over a certain period of time to maximize returns and minimize risk is called as Portfolio revision.

Techniques of portfolio revision: - Investors buy stock according to their objectives and return-risk framework. These fluctuations may be related to economic activity or due to other factors. Ideally investors should buy when prices are low and sell when prices rise to levels higher than their normal fluctuations. The investor should decide how often the portfolio should be revised. If revision occurs too often, transaction and analysis costs may be high. The important factor to take into consideration is, thus, timing for revision of portfolio. Passive Management It is a process of holding a well-diversified portfolio for long term with the buy and hold approach. It also refers to the investor's attempt to construct a portfolio that resembles the overall market returns. For e.g- If Reliance Industry's stock constitutes 5% of the index, the fund also invests of 5% of its money in Reliance Industry Stock. Active Management It is holding securities based on the forecast about the future. The portfolio managers vary their cash position or beta of the equity portion of the portfolio based on the market forecast. For e.g.- IT or FMCG industry stocks may be given more weights than their respective weights in the NSE-50.

NEED FOR PORTFOLIO REVISION

- An individual at certain point of time **might feel the need to invest more**. The need for portfolio revision arises when an individual has some additional money to invest.
- **Change in investment goal** also gives rise to revision in portfolio. Depending on the cash flow, an individual can modify his financial goal, eventually giving rise to changes in the portfolio i.e. portfolio revision.
- Financial market is subject to risks and uncertainty. An individual might sell off some of his assets owing to fluctuations in the financial market.

MONITORING AND REVISION OF THE PORTFOLIO

Portfolio revision is the process of selling certain issues in portfolio and purchasing new ones to replace them. ***The main reasons for the necessity of the investment portfolio revision:***

- ➢ As the economy evolves, certain industries and companies become either less or more attractive as investments;
- ➢ The investor over the time may change his/her investment objectives and in this way his/ her portfolio isn't longer optimal;
- ➢ The constant need for diversification of the portfolio. Individual securities in the portfolio often change in risk-return characteristics and their diversification effect may be lessened.

Three areas to monitor when implementing investor's portfolio monitoring:

1. Changes in market conditions;
2. Changes in investor's circumstances;
3. Asset mix in the portfolio.

The need to monitor changes in the market is obvious. Investment decisions are made in dynamic investment environment, where changes occur permanently. The key macroeconomic indicators (such as GDP growth, inflation rate, interest rates, others), as well as the new information about industries and companies should be observed by investor on the regular basis, because these changes can influence the returns and risk of the investments in the portfolio. Investor can monitor these changes using various sources of information, especially specialized websites (most frequently used are presented in relevant websites). It is important to identify he major changes in the investment environment and to assess whether these changes should negatively influence investor's currently held portfolio. If it so investor must take an action to rebalance his/ her portfolio.

When monitoring the changes in the investor's circumstances, following aspects must be taken into account:

- Change in wealth
- Change in time horizon

- Change in liquidity requirements
- Change in tax circumstances
- Change in legal considerations
- Change in other circumstances and investor's needs.

Any changes identified must be assessed very carefully before usually they generally are related with the noticeable changes in investor's portfolio.

Rebalancing a portfolio is the process of periodically adjusting it to maintain certain original conditions. Rebalancing reduces the risks of losses - in general, a rebalanced portfolio is less volatile than one that is not rebalanced. Several methods of rebalancing portfolios are used:

- ➢ Constant proportion portfolio;
- ➢ Constant Beta portfolio;
- ➢ Indexing.

Constant proportion portfolio. A constant proportion portfolio is one in which adjustments are made so as to maintain the relative weighting of the portfolio components as their prices change. Investors should concentrate on keeping their chosen asset allocation percentage (especially those following the requirements for strategic asset allocation). There is no one correct formula for when to rebalance. One rule may be to rebalance portfolio when asset allocations vary by 10% or more. But many investors find it bizarre that constant proportion rebalancing requires the purchase of securities that have performed poorly and the sale of those that have performed the best. This is very difficult to do for the investor psychologically (see Chapter 6). But the investor should always consider this method of rebalancing as one choice, but not necessarily the best one.

Constant Beta portfolio. The base for the rebalancing portfolio using this alternative is the target portfolio Beta. Over time the values of the portfolio components and their Betas will change and this can cause the portfolio Beta to shift. For example, if the target portfolio Beta is 1,10 and it had risen over the monitored period of time to 1,25, the portfolio Beta could be brought back to the target (1,10) in the following ways:

- ➢ ***Put additional money into the stock portfolio and hold cash.*** Diluting the stocks in portfolio with the cash will reduce portfolio Beta, because cash has Beta of 0. But in this case cash should be only a temporary component in the portfolio rather than a long-term;
- ➢ ***Put additional money into the stock portfolio and buy stocks with a Beta lower than the target Beta figure.*** But the investor may be is not able to invest additional money and this way for rebalancing the portfolio can be complicated.
- ➢ ***Sell high Beta stocks in portfolio and hold cash.*** As with the first alternative, this way reduces the equity holdings in the investor's portfolio which may be not appropriate.
- ➢ ***Sell high Beta stocks and buy low Beta stocks.*** The stocks bought could be new additions to the portfolio, or the investor could add to existing positions.

Indexing. This alternatives for rebalancing the portfolio are more frequently used by institutional investors (often mutual funds), because their portfolios tend to be large and the strategy of matching a market index are best applicable for them. Managing index based portfolio investor (or portfolio manager) eliminates concern about outperforming the market, because by design, it seeks to behave just like the market averages. Investor attempts to maintain some predetermined characteristics of the portfolio, such as Beta of 1,0. The extent to which such a portfolio deviates from its intended behaviors called *tracking error.*

Revising a portfolio is not without costs for an individual investor. These costs can be direct costs - ***trading fees and commissions*** for the brokers who can trade securities on the exchange. With the developing of alternative trading systems (ATS) these costs can be decreased. It is important also, that the selling the securities may have income tax implications which differ from country to country.

PORTFOLIO REVISION STRATEGIES

There are two types of Portfolio Revision Strategies.

1. **Active Revision Strategy:** Active Revision Strategy involves **frequent changes** in an existing portfolio over a certain period of time for maximum returns and minimum risks. Active Revision Strategy helps a portfolio manager to sell and purchase securities on a regular basis for portfolio revision.
2. **Passive Revision Strategy:** Passive Revision Strategy involves rare changes in portfolio only under certain predetermined rules. These predefined rules are known as formula plans.

WHY FORMULA PLANS?

- Formula plans help an investor to make the best possible use of fluctuations in the financial market. One can purchase shares when the prices are less and sell off when market prices are higher.
- With the help of Formula plans an investor can divide his funds into aggressive and defensive portfolio and easily transfer funds from one portfolio to other.

AGGRESSIVE PORTFOLIO

Aggressive Portfolio consists of funds that appreciate quickly and guarantee maximum returns to the investor.

DEFENSIVE PORTFOLIO

Defensive portfolio consists of securities that do not fluctuate much and remain constant over a period of time. Formula plans facilitate an investor to transfer funds from aggressive to defensive portfolio and vice a versa. According to passive revision strategy a portfolio manager can bring changes in the portfolio as per the formula plans only.

The Formula Plans The formula plans provide the basic rules and regulations for the purchase & sale of securities. These predetermined rules call for specified actions when there are changes in the securities market. In this, the investor divides his investment funds into 2 portfolios i.e. one aggressive (portfolio consists of equity shares) & other conservative or defensive (bonds & debentures)

BASIC RULES OF FORMULA REVISION

Basic Rules of Formula Revision Formula plans require the investor to divide his investment funds in two portfolios i.e. aggressive & Conservative (defensive) 1. The volatility of aggressive portfolio must be greater than that of conservative portfolio, the larger the difference between the two, the greater the profits the formula plan can yield. 2. The conservative (defensive) portfolio must include high- grade bonds having a high degree of safety and stability of the returns.

The conservative portfolio tends to decline during periods of prosperity, owing to falling interest rates. While the stock prices are rising, therefore, the aggressive portfolio also rises. 1. The basic premise of formula plans is that stock and bond prices of the portfolios move in opposite direction. If they move in same direction then this phenomenon certainly impairs profitability of the formula plans. 2. The formula plans do not deal with the selection of stocks or bonds.

DIFFERENT TYPES OF FORMULA PLANS ARE

- Rupee Cost Averaging
- Constant Rupee Plan
- Constant Ratio Plan
- Variable Ratio Plan

Once an optimal portfolio has been constructed, it becomes necessary for the investor to constantly monitor the portfolio to ensure that it does not lose it optimality. Since the economy and financial markets are dynamic in nature, changes take place in these variables almost on a daily basis and securities which were once attractive may cease to be so with the passage of time. New securities with expectations of high returns and low risk may emerge. In light of these developments in the market, the investor now has to revise his portfolio. This revision leads to addition (purchase) of some new securities and deletion (sale) of some of the existing securities from the portfolio. The nature of securities and their proportion in the portfolio changes as a result of the revision.

This portfolio revision may also be necessitated by some investor-related changes such as availability of additional funds for investment, change in risk appetite, need of cash for other alternative use, etc.

Portfolio revision is not a casual process to be taken lightly and needs to be carried out with care, scientifically and objectively so as to ensure the optimality of the revised portfolio. The entire process of portfolio management, portfolio revision is as important as portfolio analysis and selection.

CONSTANT RATIO PLAN

This ratio plan is slightly different from the constant rupee value plan. This plan is a method of identifying the ratio of value in the aggressive portfolio to the value of the conservative portfolio. The aggressive portfolio is divided by the market value of the total portfolio should be held constant.

K = Market value of common stock/Market value of total portfolio

METHODOLOGY

1. According to this method the stock should be sold when value rises to make it constant with the value of the conservative portfolio. The investor should transfer funds to common stock when the stock value falls. In this way he should also change from conservative to aggressive value.
2. Under this plan the aggressive value to be kept by the investor constant of the portfolio's total value. The investor will according to the rule, have to shift from the conservative to the aggressive value if the prices of the stock fall.
3. The formula plan based on constant ratio does not require the investor to make forecasts of the lower levels at which the price fluctuates.
4. The constant ratio plan differs from the constant rupee value plan. While the constant rupee value plan was opted on the principle of constant aggressiveness in the transfer to and from the stock portfolio, the constant ratio plan draws a relationship which results in the purchasing of stock, in a less aggressiveness, manner as the prices fall down because constant ratio plan is applicable in the case of a total fund which is decreasing in value.
5. The constant ratio plan operates in a less aggressive manner when the stock prices move up and in rising price level also it consists of sales which are less aggressive in nature. The reason for being less aggressive in nature is that under the constant ratio the value of the total fund increases in a manner to allow large rupee value in the stock portfolio.
6. The middle range of fluctuations is, deciding factors for the sales and purchase of aggressive stock in the constant ratio plan. When the fluctuations are just above the middle range of the sales that take place, it is identified as the most aggressive point.
7. Similarly, when the fluctuations are just below the middle range it is considered to be the most aggressive. The most optimum formula plan is when the stock is prices are sold aggressively as their prices fluctuates above the middle range of fluctuations and by purchasing aggressively when the prices move below the middle range of fluctuations.
8. In the constant ratio plan if the fluctuations of stock take a long time to move in a direction which is either upward or downward then their plan does not work at its optimum value. This formula plan will work originally and with the maximum utility if it is forecasted carefully. But if an investor begins to forecast then it goes against the constant ratio plan which is to rest on the fact that there is no requirement for forecasting.

9. In the constant ratio plan, the investor will get high profits if there is a continuous sustained rise or fall in prices. These profits would be higher under this plan rather that under the constant rupee value plan or the variable ratio plan. This large profits due to sustained rise or fall of prices under this formula is due to the fact that the ratio under this formula itself leaves the investor into a more optimum position as there is a larger investment during boom and lower investment in depression periods under this formula plan.
10. Taking into consideration the full cycle of fluctuation it has been found that the constant ratio plan does not work with full efficiency when it has been noticed under the full cycle of fluctuations or movements both upward and downwards. The reason for this inefficiency is that the plan does not have aggressive purchase and sale during the turning points. These aggressive movements are made during the middle level of fluctuations.

The methodology adopted in this plan to reach the fluctuations because the range is small and many transactions will take place. On the contrary a few transactions will take place when the range of fluctuation is large. Experts are of the opinion that the fluctuations should be neither too small nor too large. If it is small then the adjustment action will not have enough time.

VARIABLE RATIO PLAN

The variable ratio plan is considered by the investor under the following methodology adopted for its study.

METHODOLOGY

- The investor should sell stock when price of stock rises and bond should be purchased when stock prices fall they should be bought and the bonus should be sold.
- The methodology of the formula plan should have a predetermined set of rules and consist of different proportions of stock prices.

EXAMPLE OF CONSTANT RATIO PLAN

month	Investment In fixed income securities conservative	Equity stock aggressive	K = market value of stock.		
			Total portfolio	Actual K	Common stock strategy
1	5000	5000	10,000	0.50	Bye sells
2	5000	7000	12,000	0.58	Bye neither
3	6000	8000	14,000	0.57	Bye neither
4	7000	7000	14,000	0.50	Bye sells
5	7000	5000	12,000	0.42	Sell neither
6	6000	4000	10,000	0.40	Sell neither

It is desired to maintain K at 0.50.

VARIABLE RATIO PLAN

Month	Market index direction	Ratio desired	Actual ratio (calculated from portfolio)	Strategy for purchase or sell of common stock
1	Moderate prices upwards	0.70	0.95	Buy
2	High prices upwards	0.50	0.75	Buy
3	Very high price downwards	0.00	0.60	Buy
4	Moderate price downward	0.30	0.00	Sell
5	Moderate price upward	0.70	0.25	Sell
6	High prices upward	0.50	0.80	Buy

Date Prices of Previous 5 Months

1. If stock prices more upward it would be good to hold 30% of stocks in equity and10%in fixed income securities.
2. When prices more downward and prices as shown in (4) then 50% of the portfolio should consist of equity and 50% in fixed income securities.
3. In variable ratio can be adjusted to suit every investor.
4. Under this plan the ratio of value of aggressive portfolio, the value of conservative portfolio decreases when the aggressive portfolio rise in the value. Similarly, the ratio increases when aggressive portfolio value decreases.
5. The aggressive portfolio consists of the total amount which the investor is able to risk in investing in common stock taking a median round which the fluctuations will move.
6. The complete program of investment will be drawn by the investor from the median.
7. The investor under this formula plan will have to make forecast in the range of fluctuations which move both side and below the median to find out the different ratios at different level of stocks.
8. The most important tool of the variable ratio plan may be said to be forecasting.
9. Under this plan the ratio has to be varied if purchases and sales have to make more aggressive the varying ratio would lead to movement of prices in different directions which are either upwards or downwards and are away from median.
10. This plan is most profitable or an investor when there is change in the economic or market index. The most important factor after forecasting is that this plan takes into consideration change. Whenever he is faced with the risk of change the very fact the formula is the dependency in forecast and so on.

SHORT ANSWER QUESTIONS

1. What are Formula Plans?
2. What is Rupee Cost Averaging
3. Why Formula Plans?
4. Briefly explain Variable ratio plan.
5. What are the basic rules of Formula revision
6. Define Constant proportion portfolio method
7. Define Constant Beta portfolio method
8. Define Indexing method
9. Define Rebalancing a portfolio
10. Define Portfolio monitoring
11. Define Portfolio revision

ESSAY TYPE QUESTIONS

1. Explain the role of revision in the process of managing a portfolio.
2. Why is portfolio revision not free of cost?
3. What is Portfolio Revision? Briefly explain.
4. What is the need of the portfolio revision? Explain Strategies of Portfolio revision.
5. Briefly explain Constant Ratio Plan with methodology.

CHAPTER 16

Derivatives Market

INTRODUCTION

The concept of risk is at the heart of investment management. Financial analysts and portfolio managers continually identify, measure, and manage risk. In a simple world where only stocks and bonds exist, the only risks are the fluctuations associated with market values and the potential for a creditor to default. Measuring risk often takes the form of standard deviations, betas, and probabilities of default. In the above simple setting, managing risk is limited to engaging in stock and bond transactions that reduce or increase risk. For example, a portfolio manager may hold a combination of a risky stock portfolio and a risk-free bond, with the relative allocations determined by the investor's tolerance for risk. If for some reason the manager desires a lower level of risk, the only transactions available to adjust the risk downward are to reduce the allocation to the risky stock portfolio and increase the allocation to the risk-free bond.

The financial markets have created their own way of offering insurance against financial loss in the form of contracts called derivatives. *A derivative is a financial instrument that offers a return based on the return of some other underlying asset.* In this sense, its return is *derived* from another instrument—hence, the name.

As the definition states, a derivative's performance is based on the performance of an underlying asset. This underlying asset is often referred to simply as the underlying.[1] It trades in a market in which buyers and sellers meet and decide on a price; the seller then delivers the asset to the buyer and receives payment. The price for immediate purchase of the underlying asset is called the cash price or spot price.

The emergence of the market for derivative products, most notably forwards, futures and options, can be traced back to the willingness of risk-averse economic agents to guard themselves against uncertainties arising out of fluctuations in asset prices. By their very nature, the financial markets are marked by a very high degree of volatility. Through the use of derivative products, it is possible to partially or fully transfer price risks by locking-in asset prices. As instruments of risk management, these generally do not influence the fluctuations in the underlying asset prices. However, by locking in asset prices, derivative products minimize the impact of fluctuations in asset prices on the profitability and cash flow situation of risk-averse investors.

Derivatives are risk management instruments, which derive their value from an underlying asset. The underlying asset can be bullion, index, share, bonds, currency, interest, etc. Banks, Securities firms, companies and investors to hedge risks, to gain to cheaper money and to make profit, se derivatives. Derivatives are likely to grow even at a faster rate in future.

One of the most significant events in the securities markets has been the development and expansion of financial derivatives. The term "derivatives" is used to refer to financial instruments which derive their value from some underlying assets. The underlying assets could be equities (shares), debt (bonds, T-bills, and notes), currencies, and even indices of these various assets, such as the Nifty 50 Index. Derivatives derive their names from their respective underlying asset. Thus, if a derivative's underlying asset is equity, it is called equity derivative and so on. Derivatives can be traded either on a regulated exchange, such as the NSE or off the exchanges, i.e., directly between the different parties, which is called "over-the-counter" (OTC) trading. (In India only exchange traded equity derivatives are permitted under the law.) The basic purpose of derivatives is to transfer the price risk (inherent in fluctuations of the asset prices) from one party to another; they facilitate the allocation of risk to those who are willing to take it. In so doing, derivatives help mitigate the risk arising from the future uncertainty of prices. The price of this derivative is driven by the spot price of price which is the "underlying".

A security whose price is dependent upon or derived from one or more underlying assets. The derivative itself is merely a contract between two or more parties. Its value is determined by fluctuations in the underlying asset. The most common underlying assets include stocks, bonds, commodities, currencies, interest rates and market indexes. Most derivatives are characterized by high leverage. Futures contracts, forward contracts, options and swaps are the most common types of derivatives.

Derivatives are contracts and can be used as an underlying asset. There are even derivatives based on weather data, such as the amount of rain or the number of sunny days in a particular region. **Derivatives** are generally used as an instrument to hedge risk, but can also be used for speculative purposes. For example, a European investor purchasing shares of an American company off of an American exchange would be exposed to exchange-rate risk while holding that stock. To hedge this risk, the investor could purchase currency futures to lock in a specified exchange rate for the future stock sale and currency conversion back into Euros.

A **derivative** is a financial contract with a value that is derived from an underlying asset. Derivatives have no direct value in and of themselves -- their value is based on the expected future price movements of their underlying asset. A derivative is a contract between two parties which derives its value/price from an underlying asset.

A derivative is a contract between two parties which derives its value/price from an underlying asset. The most common types of derivatives are futures, options, forwards and swaps. It is a financial instrument which derives its value/price from the underlying assets. Originally, underlying corpus is first created which can consist of one security or a combination of different securities. The value of the underlying asset is bound to change as the value of the underlying assets keep changing continuously. Generally, stocks, bonds, currency, commodities and interest rates form the underlying asset.

Derivatives are often used as an instrument to hedge risk for one party of a contract, while offering the potential for high returns for the other party. Derivatives have been created to mitigate a remarkable number of risks: fluctuations in stock, bond, commodity, and index prices; changes in foreign exchange rates; changes in interest rates; and weather events, to name a few.

In finance, a security whose price is dependent on or derived from one or more underlyin g assetThe derivative itself ismerely a contract between two or more parties, with a value det ermined by fluctuations in the underlying asset, which could bestocks, bonds, commodities, currencies, interest rates, and market indexes. Most derivatives are characterized by high leverage

ONE OF THE MOST COMMONLY USED DERIVATIVES IS THE OPTION

Example: Say Company XYZ is involved in the production of pre-packaged foods. They are a large consumer of flour and other commodities, which are subject to volatile price movements. In order for the company to assure any kind of consistency with their product and meet their bottom-line objectives, they need to be able to purchase commodities at a predictable and market-friendly rate. In order to do this, company XYZ would enter into an options contract with farmers or wheat producers to buy a certain amount of their crop at a certain price during an agreed upon period of time. If the price of wheat, for whatever reason, goes above the threshold, then Company XYZ can exercise the option and purchase the asset at the strike price. Company XYZ pays a premium for this privilege, but receives protection in return for one of their most important input costs. If XYZ decides not to exercise its option, the producer is free to sell the asset at market value to any buyer. In the end, the partnership acts as a win-win for both parties: Company XYZ is guaranteed a competitive price for the commodity, while the producer is assured of a fair value for its goods.

In this example, the value of the option is "derived" from an underlying asset; in this case, a certain number of bushels of wheat. Other common derivatives include futures, forwards and swaps. As often is the case in trading, the more risk you undertake the more reward you stand to gain. Derivatives can be used on both sides of the equation, to either reduce risk or assume risk with the possibility of a commensurate reward.

This is where derivatives have received such notoriety as of late: in the dark art of speculating through derivatives. Speculators who enter into a derivative contract are essentially betting that the future price of the asset will be substantially different from the expected price held by the other member of the contract. They operate under the assumption that the party seeking insurance has it wrong in regard to the future market price, and look to profit from the error. Contrary to popular opinion, though, derivatives are not inherently bad. In fact, they are a necessity for many companies to ensure profits in volatile markets or provide mitigated risk for everyday investors looking for investment insurance.

Derivatives are financial products, such as futures contracts, options, and mortgage-backed securities. Most of derivatives'value is based on the value of an underlying security,

Commodity, or another financial instrument.
For example, the changing value of a crude oil futures contract depends primarily on the up ward or downward movement of oil prices.
An equity option's value is determined by the relationship between its strike price and the va lue of the underlying stock, thetime until expiration, and the stock's volatility.
Certain investors, called hedgers, are interested in the underlying instrument. For example, a baking company might buywheat futures to help estimate the cost of producing its bread in t he months to come.

Derivatives are defined as financial instruments whose value derived from the prices of one or more other assets such as equity securities, fixed-income securities, foreign currencies, or commodities. Derivative is also a kind of contract between two counter parties to exchange payments linked to the prices of underlying assets.

In the Indian context the Securities Contracts (Regulation) Act, 1956 (SC(R) A) defines "**derivative**" to include-

1. A security derived from a debt instrument, share, loan whether secured or unsecured, risk instrument or contract for differences or any other from of security.
2. A contract which derives its value from the prices, or index or prices, of underlying securities
3. The above definition conveys that

Derivatives are financial products and derive its value from the underlying assets.

Derivatives are derived from a matter financial contract called the underlying.

DIFFERENCE BETWEEN DERIVATIVES AND SHARES:

The subtle, but crucial, difference is that while shares are assets, derivatives are usually contracts (the major exception to this are warrants and convertible bonds, which are similar to shares in that they are assets).

INVESTING IN DERIVATIVES

If one is interested in getting directly involved with futures or options, then the idea "to incest" is inappropriate they are traded. This implies that one monitors the price more closely, and uses more sophisticated trading techniques (for example, the use if stop orders). There are a number of brokers that specialize in private client futures/options trading, list of these can usually be requested from futures exchanges.

USAGE OF DERIVATIVES

Any person who has funds invested, (e.g. an insurance policy or a pension fund), are mostly exposed to derivatives in some or other way. Due to its great flexibility, derivatives are used by many different types of investors. From this stand point, derivatives will allow the modern investor the full range of investment strategy: speculation, hedging, arbitrage and all of the possible combinations thereof.

MEASURES OF DERIVATIVES

The value of a derivatives contract equals the difference between the value of the underlying asset and the cost of financing a purchase of the asset, Further the value also depends on the price of the underlying asset and the level of interest rates.

APPLICATIONS OF DERIVATIVES

In this chapter, we look at the participants in the derivatives markets and how they use derivatives contracts.

FACTORS AFFECTING GROWTH OF DERIVATIVE

Growth of derivative is affected by a number of factors, some of the important factors are started below.

- Increased volatility in asset prices in financial markets.
- Increased integration of national financial markets with the international markets.
- Marked improvement in communication facilities and sharp decline in their costs.
- Development of more sophisticated risk management tools, providing economic agents, a wider choice of risk management strategies.
- Innovation in the derivative markets, which optimally combine the risk and returns.
- Reduced risk as well as transaction costs as compared to individual financial assets.

PARTICIPANTS IN THE DERIVATIVES MARKET

As equity markets developed, different categories of investors started participating in the market. In India, equity market participants currently include retail investors, corporate investors, mutual funds, banks, foreign institutional investors etc. Each of these investor categories uses the derivatives market to as a part of risk management, investment strategy or speculation.

Based on the applications that derivatives are put to, these investors can be broadly classified into three groups:

- Hedgers
- Speculators, and
- Arbitrageurs

We shall now look at each of these categories in detail.

HEDGERS

These investors have a position (i.e., have bought stocks) in the underlying market but are worried about a potential loss arising out of a change in the asset price in the future. Hedgers participate in the derivatives market to lock the prices at which they will be able to transact in the future. Thus, they try to avoid price risk through holding a position in the derivatives market. Different hedgers take different positions in the derivatives market based on their exposure in the underlying market. A hedger normally takes an opposite position in the derivatives market to what he has in the underlying market. Hedging in futures market can be done through two positions, viz. short hedge and long hedge.

SHORT HEDGE

A short hedge involves taking a short position in the futures market. Short hedge position is taken by someone who already owns the underlying asset or is expecting a future receipt of the underlying asset.

For example, an investor holding Reliance shares may be worried about adverse future price movements and may want to hedge the price risk. He can do so by holding a short position in the derivatives market. The investor can go short in Reliance futures at the NSE. This protects him from price movements in Reliance stock. In case the price of Reliance shares falls, the investor will lose money in the shares but will make up for this loss by the gain made in Reliance Futures. Note that a short position holder in a futures contract makes a profit if the price of the underlying asset falls in the future. In this way, futures contract allows an investor to manage his price risk.

Similarly, a sugar manufacturing company could hedge against any probable loss in the future due to a fall in the prices of sugar by holding a short position in the futures/ forwards market. If the prices of sugar fall, the company may bse on the sugar sale but the loss will be offset by profit made in the futures contract.

LONG HEDGE

A long hedge involves holding a long position in the futures market. A Long position holder agrees to buy the underlying asset at the expiry date by paying the agreed futures/ forward price. This strategy is used by those who will need to acquire the underlying asset in the future.

For example, a chocolate manufacturer who needs to acquire sugar in the future will be worried about any loss that may arise if the price of sugar increases in the future. To hedge against this risk, the chocolate manufacturer can hold a long position in the sugar futures. If the price of sugar rises, the chocolate manufacture may have to pay more to acquire sugar in the normal market, but he will be compensated against this loss through a profit that will arise in the futures market. Note that a long position holder in a futures contract makes a profit if the price of the underlying asset increases in the future.

Long hedge strategy can also be used by those investors who desire to purchase the underlying asset at a future date (that is, when he acquires the cash to purchase the asset) but wants to lock the prevailing price in the market. This may be because he thinks that the prevailing price is very low.

For example, suppose the current spot price of Wipro Ltd. is Rs. 250 per stock. An investor is expecting to have Rs. 250 at the end of the month. The investor feels that Wipro Ltd. is at a very attractive level and he may miss the opportunity to buy the stock if he waits till the end of the month. In such a case, he can buy Wipro Ltd. in the futures market. By doing so, he can lock in the price of the stock. Assuming that he buys Wipro Ltd. in the futures market at Rs. 250 (this becomes his locked-in price), there can be three probable scenarios:

Scenario I: Price of Wipro Ltd. in the cash market on expiry date is Rs. 300.

As futures price is equal to the spot price on the expiry day, the futures price of Wipro would be at Rs. 300 on expiry day. The investor can sell Wipro Ltd in the futures market at Rs. 300. By doing this, he has made a profit of 300 - 250 = Rs. 50 in the futures trade. He can now buy Wipro Ltd in the spot market at Rs. 300. Therefore, his total investment cost for buying one share of Wipro Ltd equals Rs.300 (price in spot market) - 50 (profit in futures market) = Rs.250. This is the amount of money he was expecting to have at the end of the month. If the investor had not bought Wipro Ltd futures, he would have had only Rs. 250 and would have been unable to buy Wipro Ltd shares in the cash market. The futures contract helped him to lock in a price for the shares at Rs. 250.

Scenario II: Price of Wipro Ltd in the cash market on expiry day is Rs. 250.

As futures price tracks spot price, futures price would also be at Rs. 250 on expiry day. The investor will sell Wipro Ltd in the futures market at Rs.250. By doing this, he has made Rs. 0 in the futures trade. He can buy Wipro Ltd in the spot market at Rs. 250. His total investment cost for buying one share of Wipro will be = Rs. 250 (price in spot market) + 0 (loss in futures market) = Rs. 250.

Scenario III: Price of Wipro Ltd in the cash market on expiry day is Rs. 200.

As futures price tracks spot price, futures price would also be at Rs. 200 on expiry day. The investor will sell Wipro Ltd in the futures market at Rs. 200. By doing this, he has made a loss of 200 - 250 = Rs. 50 in the futures trade. He can buy Wipro in the spot market at Rs. 200. Therefore, his total investment cost for buying one share of Wipro Ltd will be = 200 (price in spot market) + 50 (loss in futures market) = Rs. 250. Thus, in all the three scenarios, he has to pay only Rs. 250. This is an example of a Long Hedge.

SPECULATORS

A Speculator is one who bets on the derivatives market based on his views on the potential movement of the underlying stock price. Speculators take large, calculated risks as they trade based on anticipated future price movements. They hope to make quick, large gains; but may not always be successful. They normally have shorter holding time for their positions as compared to hedgers. If the price of the underlying moves as per their expectation they can make large profits. However, if the price moves in the opposite direction of their assessment, the losses can also be enormous.

Illustration: Currently ICICI Bank Ltd (ICICI) is trading at, say, Rs. 500 in the cash market and also at Rs. 500 in the futures market (assumed values for the example only). A speculator feels that post the RBI's policy announcement, the share price of ICICI will go up. The speculator can buy the stock in the spot market or in the derivatives market. If the derivatives contract size of ICICI is 1000 and if the speculator buys one futures contract of ICICI, he is buying ICICI futures worth Rs 500 X 1000 = Rs. 5,00,000. For this he will have to pay a margin of say 20% of the contract value to the exchange. The margin that the speculator needs to pay to the exchange is 20% of Rs. 5,00,000 = Rs. 1,00,000. This Rs. 1,00,000 is his total investment for the futures contract. If the speculator would have invested Rs. 1,00,000 in the spot market, he could purchase only 1,00,000 / 500 = 200 shares.

Let us assume that post RBI announcement price of ICICI share moves to Rs. 520. With one lakh investment each in the futures and the cash market, the profits would be:

- 500) X 1,000 = Rs. 20,000 in case of futures market and

(520 - 500) X 200 = Rs. 4000 in the case of cash market.

It should be noted that the opposite will result in case of adverse movement in stock prices, wherein the speculator will be losing more in the futures market than in the spot market. This is because the speculator can hold a larger position in the futures market where he has to pay only the margin money.

ARBITRAGEURS

Arbitrageurs attempt to profit from pricing inefficiencies in the market by making simultaneous trades that offset each other and capture a risk-free profit. An arbitrageur may also seek to make profit in case there is price discrepancy between the stock price in the cash and the derivatives markets.

For example, if on 1st August, 2009 the SBI share is trading at Rs. 1780 in the cash market and the futures contract of SBI is trading at Rs. 1790, the arbitrageur would buy the SBI shares (i.e. make an investment of Rs. 1780) in the spot market and sell the same number of SBI futures contracts. On expiry day (say 24 August, 2009), the price of SBI futures contracts will close at the price at which SBI closes in the spot market. In other words, the settlement of the futures contract will happen at the closing price of the SBI shares and that is why the futures and spot prices are said to converge on the expiry day. On expiry day, the arbitrageur will sell the SBI stock in the spot market and buy the futures contract, both of which will happen at the closing price of SBI in the spot market. Since the arbitrageur has entered into off-setting positions, he will be able to earn Rs. 10 irrespective of the prevailing market price on the expiry date.

There are three possible price scenarios at which SBI can close on expiry day. Let us calculate the profit/ loss of the arbitrageur in each of the scenarios where he had initially (1 August) purchased SBI shares in the spot market at Rs 1780 and sold the futures contract of SBI at Rs. 1790:

Scenario I: SBI shares closes at a price greater than 1780 (say Rs. 2000) in the spot market on expiry day (24 August 2009): SBI futures will close at the same price as SBI in spot market on the expiry day i.e., SBI futures will also close at Rs. 2000. The arbitrageur reverses his previous transaction entered into on 1 August 2009.

Profit/ Loss (-) in spot market = 2000 - 1780 = Rs. 220

Profit/ Loss (-) in futures market = 1 790 - 2000 = Rs. (-) 210

Net profit/ Loss (-) on both transactions combined = 220 - 210 = Rs. 10 profit.

Scenario II: SBI shares close at Rs 1780 in the spot market on expiry day (24 August 2009): SBI futures will close at the same price as SBI in spot mar ket on expiry day i.e., SBI futures will also close at Rs 1780. The arbitrageur reverses his previous transaction entered into on 1 August 2009.

Profit/ Loss (-) in spot market = 1780 - 1780 = Rs 0

Profit/ Loss (-) in futures market = 1790 - 1780 = Rs. 10

Net profit/ Loss (-) on both transactions combined = 0 + 10 = Rs. 10 profit.

Scenario III: SBI shares close at Rs. 1500 in the spot market on expiry day (24 August 2009)

Here also, SBI futures will close at Rs. 1500. The arbitrageur reverses his previous transaction entered into on 1 August 2009.

Profit/ Loss (-) in spot market = 1500 - 1780 = Rs. (-) 280 Profit/ Loss (-) in futures market = 1790 - 1500 = Rs. 290

Net profit/ Loss (-) on both transactions combined = (-) 280 + 290 = Rs. 10 profit.

Thus, in all three scenarios, the arbitrageur will make a profit of Rs. 10, which was the difference between the spot price of SBI and futures price of SBI, when the transaction was entered into. This is called a "risk less profit" since once the transaction is entered into on 1 August, 2009 (due to the price difference between spot and futures), the profit is locked.

Irrespective of where the underlying share price closes on the expiry date of the contract, a profit of Rs. 10 is assured. The investment made by the arbitrageur is Rs. 1780 (when he buys SBI in the spot market). He makes this investment on 1 August 2009 and gets a return of Rs. 10 on this investment in 23 days (24 August). This means a return of 0.56% in 23 days. If we annualize this, it is a return of nearly 9% per annum. One should also note that this opportunity to make a risk-less return of 9% per annum will not always remain. The difference between the spot and futures price arose due to some inefficiency (in the market), which was exploited by the arbitrageur by buying shares in spot and selling futures. As more and more such arbitrage trades take place, the difference between spot and futures prices would narrow thereby reducing the attractiveness of further arbitrage.

USES OF DERIVATIVES

Risk management

The most important purpose of the derivatives market is risk management. Risk management for an investor comprises of the following three processes:

- Identifying the desired level of risk that the investor is willing to take on his investments;
- Identifying and measuring the actual level of risk that the investor is carrying; and
- Making arrangements which may include trading (buying/selling) of derivatives contracts that allow him to match the actual and desired levels of risk.

The example of hedging discussed above illustrates the process of risk management through futures.

MARKET EFFICIENCY

Efficient markets are fair and competitive and do not allow an investor to make risk free profits. Derivatives assist in improving the efficiency of the markets, by providing a self-correcting mechanism. Arbitrageurs are one section of market participants who trade whenever there is an opportunity to make risk free profits till the opportunity ceases to exist. Risk free profits are not easy to make in more efficient markets. When trading occurs, there is a possibility that some amount of mispricing might occur in the markets. The arbitrageur's step in to take advantage of this mispricing by buying from the cheaper market and selling in the higher market. Their actions quickly narrow the prices and thereby reducing the inefficiencies.

PRICE DISCOVERY

One of the primary functions of derivatives markets is price discovery. They provide valuable information about the prices and expected price fluctuations of the underlying assets in two ways:

- First, many of these assets are traded in markets in different geographical locations. Because of this, assets may be traded at different prices in different markets. In derivatives markets, the price of the contract often serves as a proxy for the price of the underlying asset. For example, gold may trade at different prices in Mumbai and Delhi but a derivatives contract on gold would have one value and so traders in Mumbai and Delhi can validate the prices of spot markets in their respective location to see if it is cheap or expensive and trade accordingly.
- Second, the prices of the futures contracts serve as prices that can be used to get a sense of the market expectation of future prices. For example, say there is a company that produces sugar and expects that the production of sugar will take two months from today. As sugar prices fluctuate daily, the company does not know if after two months the price of sugar will be higher or lower than it is today. How does it predict where the price of sugar will be in future? It can do this by monitoring prices of derivatives contract on sugar (say a Sugar Forward contract). If the forward price of sugar is trading higher than the spot price that means that the market is expecting the sugar spot price to go up in future. If there were no derivatives price, it would have to wait for two months before knowing the market price of sugar on that day. Based on derivatives price the management of the sugar company can make strategic and tactical decisions of how much sugar to produce and when

Types of derivatives: The following are the most common types of derivatives. They are

Forwards: A forward contract is a customized contract between two entities, where settlement takes place on a specific date in the future at today's pre-agreed price.

Futures: A futures contract is an agreement between two parties to buy or sell an asset at a certain time in the future at a certain price. Futures contracts are special types of forward contracts in the sense that the former are standardized exchange-traded contracts. These are one of the most popular and widely used derivative instruments.

OPTIONS

Options are of two types – calls and puts.

- **Calls** give the buyer the right but not the obligation to buy a given quantity of the underlying asset, at a given price on or before a given future date.
- **Puts** give the buyer the right, but not the obligation to sell a given quantity of the underlying asset at a given price on or before a given date.

Warrants: Options generally have lives of up to one year, the majority of options traded on options exchanges having a maximum maturity of nine months. Longer-dated options are called warrants and are generally traded over-the-counter.

Leaps: The acronym LEAPS means Long-Term Equity Anticipation Securities. These are options having a maturity of up to three years.

Baskets: Basket options are options on portfolios of underlying assets. The underlying asset is usually a moving average of a basket of assets. Equity index options are a form of basket options.

Swaps: Swaps are private agreements between two parties to exchange cash flows in the future according to a prearranged formula. They can be regarded as portfolios of forward contracts. The two commonly used swaps are:

Interest Rate Swaps: These entail swapping only the interest related cash flows between the parties in the swap currency.

Currency Swaps: These entail swapping both principal and interest between the parties, with the cash flows in one direction being in a different currency than those in the opposite direction.

Swaptions: Swaptions are options to buy or sell a swap that will become operative at the expiry of the options. Thus, a swaption is an option on a forward swap. Rather than have calls and puts, the swaptions market has receiver swaptions and payer swaptions. A receiver swaption is an option to receive fixed and pay floating. A payer swaption is an option to pay fixed and receive floating.

DERIVATIVES MARKETS

Derivatives markets are markets that are based upon another market, which is known as the underlying market. Derivatives markets can be based upon almost any underlying market, including individual stock markets (e.g. the stock of company XYZ), stock indices (e.g. the Nasdaq 100 stock index), and currency markets (i.e. the forex markets).

TRADING DERIVATIVES MARKETS

Of the above types of derivatives markets, futures markets and contract for difference markets are traded in the same manner as their underlying markets, but options markets and warrants markets are traded differently from their underlying markets. For example, futures markets are traded by making a long trade when the market is expected to move upwards, and a short trade when the market is expected to move downwards, whereas options markets can be traded by making either a long trade or a short trade when the market is expected to move upwards. Spread betting is different from both groups of derivatives markets because it is classified as gambling rather than trading, and therefore can be traded in several different forms.

DIFFERENCES BETWEEN DERIVATIVES MARKETS

A single underlying market usually has several different derivatives markets, which provides several choices for trading a particular market. For example, the FTSE 100 stock index can be traded via futures markets, options market, warrants markets, contract for difference markets, and spread betting markets. The different derivatives markets for a single underlying market usually have different tick sizes, tick values, and margin requirements, which allows a single underlying market to be traded using a variety of different trading configurations (e.g. different amounts of risk, different amounts of trading capital, etc.).

TYPES OF DERIVATIVES MARKETS

Derivatives markets take many different forms, some of which are traded in the usual manner.

A **collateralized debt obligation (CDO)** is a type of structured asset-backed security (ABS). Originally developed for the corporate debt markets, over time CDOs evolved to encompass the mortgage and mortgage-backed security (MBS) markets. Like other private-label securities backed by assets, a CDO can be thought of as a promise to pay investors in a prescribed sequence, based on the cash flow the CDO collects from the pool of bonds or other assets it owns. The CDO is "sliced" into "tranches", which "catch" the cash flow of interest and principal payments in sequence based on seniority. If some loans default and the cash collected by the CDO is insufficient to pay all of its investors, those in the lowest, most "junior" tranches suffer losses first. The last to lose payment from default are the safest, most senior tranches. Consequently, coupon payments (and interest rates) vary by tranche with the safest/most senior tranches paying the lowest and the lowest tranches paying the highest rates to compensate for higher default risk. As an example, a CDO might issue the following tranches in order of safeness: Senior AAA (sometimes known as "super senior"); Junior AAA; AA; A; BBB; Residual.

A **credit default swap (CDS)** is a financial swap agreement that the seller of the CDS will compensate the buyer (the creditor of the reference loan) in the event of a loan default (by the debtor) or other credit event. The buyer of the CDS makes a series of payments (the CDS "fee" or "spread") to the seller and, in exchange, receives a payoff if the loan defaults.

FORWARDS

In finance, a **forward contract** or simply a **forward** is a non-standardized contract between two parties to buy or to sell an asset at a specified future time at a price agreed upon today, making it a type of derivative instrument. This is in contrast to a spot contract, which is an agreement to buy or sell an asset on its spot date, which may vary depending on the instrument, for example most of the FX contracts have Spot Date two business days from today. The party agreeing to buy the underlying asset in the future assumes a long position, and the party agreeing to sell the asset in the future assumes a short position. The price agreed upon is called the delivery price, which is equal to the forward price at the time the contract is entered into. The price of the underlying instrument, in whatever form, is paid before control of the instrument changes. This is one of the many forms of buy/sell orders where the time and date of trade is not the same as the value date where the securities themselves are exchanged.

The forward price of such a contract is commonly contrasted with the spot price, which is the price at which the asset changes hands on the spot date. The difference between the spot and the forward price is the forward premium or forward discount, generally considered in the form of a profit, or loss, by the purchasing party. Forwards, like other derivative securities, can be used to hedge risk (typically currency or exchange rate risk), as a means of speculation, or to allow a party to take advantage of a quality of the underlying instrument which is time-sensitive.

A closely related contract is a futures contract; they differ in certain respects. Forward contracts are very similar to futures contracts, except they are not exchange-traded, or defined on standardized assets. Forwards also typically have no interim partial settlements or "true-ups" in margin requirements like futures—such that the parties do not exchange additional property securing the party at gain and the entire unrealized gain or loss builds up while the contract is open. However, being traded over the counter, forward contracts specification can be customized and may include mark-to-market and daily margin calls. Hence, a forward contract arrangement might call for the loss party to pledge collateral or additional collateral to better secure the party at gain. In other words, the terms of the forward contract will determine the collateral calls based upon certain "trigger" events relevant to a particular counterparty such as among other things, credit ratings, value of assets under management or redemptions over a specific time frame.

FUTURES

In finance, a **futures contract** (more colloquially, **futures**) is a standardized contract between two parties to buy or sell a specified asset of standardized quantity and quality for a price agreed upon today (the *futures price*) with delivery and payment occurring at a specified future date, the *delivery date*, making it a derivative product (i.e. a financial product that is derived from an underlying asset). The contracts are negotiated at a futures exchange, which acts as an intermediary between buyer and seller. The party agreeing to buy the underlying asset in the future, the "buyer" of the contract, is said to be "long", and the party agreeing to sell the asset in the future, the "seller" of the contract, is said to be "short".

While the futures contract specifies a trade taking place in the future, the purpose of the futures exchange is to act as intermediary and mitigate the risk of default by either party in the intervening period. For this reason, the futures exchange requires both parties to put up an initial amount of cash (performance bond), the margin. Margins, sometimes set as a percentage of the value of the futures contract, need to be proportionally maintained at all times during the life of the contract to underpin this mitigation because the price of the contract will vary in keeping with supply and demand and will change daily and thus one party or the other will theoretically be making or losing money. To mitigate risk and the possibility of default by either party, the product is marked to market on a daily basis whereby the difference between the prior agreed-upon price and the actual daily futures price is settled on a daily basis. This is sometimes known as the variation margin where the futures exchange will draw money out of the losing party's margin account and put it into the other party's thus ensuring that the correct daily loss or profit is reflected in the respective account. If the margin account goes below a certain value set by the Exchange, then a margin call is made and the account owner must replenish the margin account. This process is known as "marking to market". Thus on the delivery date, the amount exchanged is not the specified price on the contract but the spot value (i.e., the original value agreed upon, since any gain or loss has already been previously settled by marking to market). Upon marketing the strike price is often reached and creates lots of income for the "caller".

A closely related contract is a forward contract. A forward is like a future in that it specifies the exchange of goods for a specified price at a specified future date. However, a forward is not traded on an exchange and thus does not have the interim partial payments due to marking to market. Nor is the contract standardized, as on the exchange. Unlike an option, both parties of a futures contract must fulfil the contract on the delivery date. The seller delivers the underlying asset to the buyer, or, if it is a cash-settled futures contract, then cash is transferred from the futures trader who sustained a loss to the one who made a profit. To exit the commitment prior to the settlement date, the holder of a futures position can close out its contract obligations by taking the opposite position on another futures contract on the same asset and settlement date. The difference in futures prices is then a profit or loss.

A MORTGAGE-BACKED SECURITIES

A **mortgage-backed security (MBS)** is a asset-backed security that is secured by a mortgage, or more commonly a collection ("pool") of sometimes hundreds of mortgages. The mortgages are sold to a group of individuals (a government agency or investment bank) that "securitizes", or packages, the loans together into a security that can be sold to investors. The mortgages of an MBS may be residential or commercial, depending on whether it is an Agency MBS or a Non-Agency MBS; in the United States they may be issued by structures set up by government-sponsored enterprises like Fannie Mae or Freddie Mac, or they can be "private-label", issued by structures set up by investment banks. The structure of the MBS may be known as "pass-through", where the interest and principal payments from the borrower or homebuyer pass through it to the MBS holder, or it may be more complex, made up of a pool of other MBSs. Other types of MBS include collateralized mortgage obligations.

The shares of subprime MBSs issued by various structures, such as CMOs, are not identical but rather issued as tranches, each with a different level of priority in the debt repayment stream, giving them different levels of risk and reward. Tranches—especially the lower-priority, higher-interest tranches—of an MBS are/were often further repackaged and resold as collaterized debt obligations The total face value of an MBS decreases over time, because like mortgages, and unlike bonds, and most other fixed-income securities, the principal in an MBS is not paid back as a single payment to the bond holder at maturity but rather is paid along with the interest in each periodic payment (monthly, quarterly, etc.). This decrease in face value is measured by the MBS's "factor", the percentage of the original "face" that remains to be repaid.

OPTION

In finance, an **option** is a contract which gives the *buyer* (the owner) the right, but not the obligation, to buy or sell an underlying asset or instrument at a specified strike on or before a specified date. The *seller* has the corresponding obligation to fulfil the transaction—that is to sell or buy—if the buyer (owner) "exercises" the option. The buyer pays a premium to the seller for this right. An option that conveys to the owner the right to buy something at a certain price is a "call option"; an option that conveys the right of the owner to sell something at a certain price is a "put option". Both are commonly traded, but for clarity, the call option is more frequently discussed. Options valuation is a topic of ongoing research in academic and practical finance. In basic terms, the value of an option is commonly decomposed into two parts:

- The first part is the "intrinsic value", defined as the difference between the market value of the underlying and the strike price of the given option.
- The second part is the "time value", which depends on a set of other factors which, through a multivariable, non-linear interrelationship, reflect the discounted expected of that difference at expiration.

Although options valuation has been studied since the 19th century, the contemporary approach is based on the Black–Scholes model, which was first published in 1973.

Options contracts have been known for many centuries, however both trading activity and academic interest increased when, as from 1973, options were issued with standardized terms and traded through a guaranteed clearing house at the Chicago Board Options Exchange. Today many options are created in a standardized form and traded through clearing houses on regulated options exchanges, while other over-the-counter options are written as bilateral, customized contracts between a single buyer and seller, one or both of which may be a dealer or market-maker. Options are part of a larger class of financial instruments known as derivative products or simply derivatives.

SWAPS

A **swap** is a derivative in which two counterparties exchange cash flows of one party's financial instrument for those of the other party's financial instrument. The benefits in question depend on the type of financial instruments involved. For example, in the case of a swap involving two bonds, the benefits in question can be the periodic interest (coupon) payments associated with such bonds. Specifically, two counterparties agree to exchange one stream of cash flows against another stream. These streams are called the swap's "legs". The swap agreement defines the dates when the cash flows are to be paid and the way they are accrued and calculated. Usually at the time when the contract is initiated, at least one of these series of cash flows is determined by an uncertain variable such as a floating interest rate, foreign exchange rate, equity price, or commodity price.

The cash flows are calculated over a notional principal amount. Contrary to a future, a forward or an option, the notional amount is usually not exchanged between counterparties. Consequently, swaps can be in cash or collateral. Swaps can be used to hedge certain risks such as interest rate risk, or to speculate on changes in the expected direction of underlying prices.

FUNCTIONS OF DERIVATIVE MARKET

The following are the various functions that are performed by the derivatives markets. They are:

- Price in an organized derivatives market reflects the perception of market participations about the futures and let the prices of underlying to the perceived future level.
- Derivatives market helps to transfer risks from those who have them but may not like them to those who have an appetite for them.
- Derivative trading acts as a catalyst for new entrepreneurial activity.
- Derivatives markets help increase savings and investment in the long run.

DERIVATIVE MARKET IN INDIA

DATE	PARTICULARS
14 DEC 1996	NSE asked SEBI for permission to trade Index Futures.
18 NOV 1996	Formed L.C.Gupta Committee to design framework for Index Futures.
7 JULY 1999	RBI gave permission of OTC Forward Rate Agreements and Interest Rate Swaps.
24 MAY 2000	SIMEX chose NIFTY for trading futures and options on India Index.
25 MAY 2000	SEBI gave permission to NSE to do Index Futures trading.
9 JUN 2000	Trading of BSE Futures.
22 JUN 2000	Trading of NSE Futures and Index Options market.
JULY 2001	Stock Options introduced.
NOV 2001	Stock Futures.
3 OCT 2003	Commodity Futures.

REGULATORY FRAMEWORK

The trading of derivatives is governed by the provisions contained in the SC (R) A, the SEBI Act and the regulations framed there under the rules and byelaws of stock exchanges.

REGULATIONS FOR DERIVATIVES TRADING

SEBI set up a 24-member committed under Chairmanship of Dr. L. C. Gupta develop the appropriate regulatory frame work for derivative trading in India. The committee submitted its report in March 1998. On May 11, 1998 SEBI accepted the recommendations of the committee and approved the phased introduction of Derivatives trading in India beginning with Stock Index Futures. SEBI also approved he 'Suggestive bye-laws' recommended by the committee for regulation and control of trading and settlement of Derivatives contracts. The provision in the SC (R) A governs the trading in the securities. The amendment of the SC(R) A to include 'DERIVATIVES' within the ambit of 'Securities' in the SC (R) A Made trading in Derivatives possible within the frame work of the Act.

- Eligibility criteria as prescribed in the L.C. Gupta committee report may apply to SEBI for grant of recognition under Section 4 of the SC(R)A 1956 to start Derivatives Trading. The derivatives exchange/segment should have a separate governing council and representation of trading/ clearing members shall be limited to maximum of 40% of the total members of the governing council. The exchange shall regulate the sales practices of its members and will obtain approval of SEBI before start of Trading in any derivative contract.
- The exchange shall have minimum 50 members.
- The members of an existing segment of the exchange will not automatically become the members of the derivative segment. The members of the derivative segment need to fulfill the eligibility conditions as lay down by the L. C. Gupta Committee.
- The clearing and settlement of derivates trades shall be through a SEBI approved Clearing Corporation / Clearing house. Clearing Corporation / Clearing House complying with the eligibility conditions as lay down By the committee have to apply to SEBI for grant of approval.
- Derivatives broker / dealers and Clearing members are required to seek registration from SEBI.
- The minimum contract value shall not be less than Rs.2Lakh. Exchanges should also submit details of the futures contract they purpose to introduce.
- The trading members are required to have qualified approved user and sales person who have passed a certification programme approved by SEBI.

THE ECONOMIC ROLE OF DERIVATIVES

Derivative markets provide three essential economic functions:

- Risk management
- Price discovery
- Transactional efficiency

- **Risk management:** The principal benefit of the Derivative market is that it provides the opportunity for risk management through Hedging.
- **Risks involved in derivatives:** Risk can be defined as "The possibility or probability of loss". Derivatives are used to separate risks from traditional instruments and transfer these risks. The fundamental risks involved in derivatives business includes following:
- **Credit risk:** This is the risk of a counterpart to perform its obligations as per the contract. Also known as default or counterpart risk, it differs with different instruments.
- **Market risk:** Market risk is a risk of financial loss as a result of adverse movements of prices of the underlying asset.
- **Liquidity risk:** The inability of a firm to arrange a transaction at prevailing market prices is termed as liquidity risk. Related to liquidity of separate products. Related to the funding of activities of the firm including derivatives.
- **Legal risk:** Derivatives cut a cross judicial boundaries therefore the legal aspects Associated with the deal should be looked into carefully.
- **Risk management/Hedging** strategies can be broadly grouped into three categories:
    - **(i)** ***Inventory hedging*** to protect the value of existing portfolio of assets.
    - **(ii)** ***Anticipatory hedging*** to sell/buy derivatives especially forwards and futures instead of the anticipated inflows (assets)/ outflows (liabilities). A classic example is that of exporters and importers who sells/buys currency futures/options.
    - **(iii)** ***Return enhancement*** hedge using derivatives to create synthetic securities, which mimic cash assets

Price discovery: The second major function of derivative market is price discovery. This is a process of providing equilibrium prices that reflect current and prospective demands on current and prospective supplies, and making these prices visible to all.

Transactional efficiency: Derivative markets allow institution to transact more efficiently than otherwise. They reduce the direct cost of transacting in cash/financial markets are also provided, through clearing houses, an efficient mechanism to deal with counter party risk.

DERIVATIVES IN INDIA

In India, derivatives markets have been functioning since the nineteenth century, with organized trading in cotton through the establishment of the Cotton Trade Association in 1875. Derivatives, as exchange traded financial instruments were introduced in India in June 2000. The National Stock Exchange (NSE) is the largest exchange in India in derivatives, trading in various derivatives contracts. The first contract to be launched on NSE was the Nifty 50 index futures contract. In a span of one and a half years after the introduction of index futures, index options, stock options and stock futures were also introduced in the derivatives segment for trading. NSE's equity derivatives segment is called the Futures &

Options Segment or F&O Segment. NSE also trades in Currency and Interest Rate Futures contracts under a separate segment.

A series of reforms in the financial markets paved way for the development of exchange-traded equity derivatives markets in India. In 1993, the NSE was established as an electronic, national exchange and it started operations in 1994. It improved the efficiency and transparency of the stock markets by offering a fully automated screen-based trading system with real-time price dissemination. A report on exchange traded derivatives, by the L.C. Gupta Committee, set up by the Securities and Exchange Board of India (SEBI), recommended a phased introduction of derivatives instruments with bi-level regulation (i.e., self-regulation by exchanges, with SEBI providing the overall regulatory and supervisory role). Another report, by the J.R. Varma Committee in 1998, worked out the various operational details such as margining and risk management systems for these instruments. In 1999, the Securities Contracts (Regulation) Act of 1956, or SC(R)A, was amended so that derivatives could be declared as "securities". This allowed the regulatory framework for trading securities, to be extended to derivatives. The Act considers derivatives on equities to be legal and valid, but only if they are traded on exchanges.

The Securities Contracts (Regulation) Act, 1956 defines "derivatives" to include:

1. A security derived from a debt instrument, share, loan whether secured or unsecured, risk instrument, or contract for differences or any other form of security.
2. A contract which derives its value from the prices, or index of prices, of underlying securities.
3. At present, the equity derivatives market is the most active derivatives market in India. Trading volumes in equity derivatives are, on an average, more than three and a half times the trading volumes in the cash equity markets.

SUMMARY

- A derivative contract is a financial instrument with a return that is obtained from or “derived” from the return of another underlying financial instrument.
- Exchange-traded derivatives are created, authorized, and traded on a derivatives exchange, an organized facility for trading derivatives. Exchange-traded derivatives are standardized instruments with respect to certain terms and conditions of the contract. They trade in accordance with rules and specifications prescribed by the derivatives exchange and are usually subject to governmental regulation. Exchange-traded derivatives are guaranteed by the exchange against loss resulting from the default of one of the parties. Over-the-counter derivatives are transactions created by any two parties off of a derivatives exchange. The parties set all of their own terms and conditions, and each assumes the credit risk of the other party.
- A forward commitment is an agreement between two parties in which one party agrees to buy and the other agrees to sell an asset at a future date at a price agreed on today. The three types of forward commitments are forward contracts, futures contracts, and swaps.

- A forward contract is a forward commitment created in the over-the-counter market. A futures contract is a forward commitment created and traded on a futures exchange. A swap is an over-the-counter transaction consisting of a series of forward commitments.
- A contingent claim is a derivative contract with a payoff dependent on the occurrence of a future event. The primary types of contingent claims are options, but other types involve variations of options, often combined with other financial instruments or derivatives.
- An option is a derivative contract giving one party the right to buy or sell an underlying asset at a fixed price over a period of time or at a specific point in time. The party obtaining the right pays a premium (the option price) at the start and receives the right to buy or sell, as prescribed by the contract. The two types of options are a call (the right to buy) and a put (the right to sell).
- The size of the global derivatives market can be measured by notional principal, which is the amount of the underlying on which a derivative is based, and by market value, which is the economic worth of the derivative.
- Derivative markets serve many useful purposes such as providing price discovery, facilitating risk management, making markets more efficient, and lowering transaction costs. Derivatives are often criticized as being excessively dangerous for unknowledgeable investors and have been inappropriately likened to gambling.
- Arbitrage is a process through which an investor can buy an asset or combination of assets at one price and concurrently sell at a higher price, thereby earning a profit without investing any money or being exposed to any risk. The combined actions of many investors engaging in arbitrage results in rapid price adjustments that eliminate these opportunities, thereby bringing prices back in line and making markets more efficient.

MULTIPLE CHOICE QUESTIONS

1. An investor is long 2 contracts of Nifty futures purchased at Rs. 5035 each. The next morning a scam is disclosed of a large company because of which markets sell off and Nifty futures goes down to Rs. 4855. What is the mark to market for the investor? (1 Nifty contract is 50 shares).

   a. Rs. -18000 b. Rs. 18000

   c. Rs. -9000 d. Rs. 9000

2. If SBI is trading at Rs. Rs 2200 a share in the spot market and an investor wants to buy 200 SBI shares then he has to make a payment of

   a. Depends on the initial margin of SBI

   b. Rs. 2200

   c. Rs. 4400

   d. Rs. 440000

3. An investor buys 4 lots of TATASTEEL futures at Rs. 545 each and sells it at Rs. 447 each. If one contract is 764 shares what is the Profit/ Loss in the transaction?
   a. Profit Rs. 74872
   b. Loss 74872
   c. Loss Rs. 299488
   d. Profit Rs. 299488
4. What are the types of settlement (s) in forward contracts?
   a. Physical and Cash
   b. Cash
   c. Physical
   d. There are no settlements for forward contracts
5. An investor sells 3 lots of Nifty futures at Rs. 5231 each. On that day Nifty closes at Rs. 5310 in the futures market. What is the mark to market for the investor if any? One lot of Nifty is 50 shares.
   a. Profit of Rs. 11000
   b. Loss of Rs. 11850
   c. Loss of Rs. 10000
   d. Profit of Rs. 13000
6. In a business daily to get information about the top gainers in the futures market, one has to look in the heading:
   a. Contract details
   b. Positive trend
   c. Open Interest
   d. Negative trend
7. An investor bought a put option on a stock with a strike price Rs. 2000 for Rs. 200. The option will be in the money when .
   a. The stock price is less than Rs. 2000
   b. The stock price is greater than Rs. 2200
   c. The stock price is greater than Rs. 2000
   d. The stock price is less than Rs. 1800
8. All Stock Options are American in nature.
   a. TRUE
   b. FALSE
9. On 3rd August, NTPC is trading at Rs. 200 and 200 strike call option for one month is trading at Rs. 7.50. An investor who is bearish on NTPC sells the call option. NTPC on that month's expiry closes at Rs. 207.5. What is the investor's Profit / Loss in the trade? 1 lot of NTPC is 1625 shares.
   a. Rs. -12187
   b. Rs. 10000
   c. Rs. 12187
   d. No Profit no Loss
10. In futures trading initial margin is paid by :
   a. buyer only
   b. clearing member
   c. Seller only.
   d. buyer and seller

11. An investor has Unitech shares in her portfolio. RBI is increasing interest rates which is negative for the stock. She wants to protect the downside in the stock as she feels RBI will decide on increasing interest rates in the next 3 months. What should she do?
    a. Buy 3-month call option of Unitech
    b. Buy 2 month put option of Unitech
    c. Buy 1 month put option of Unitech
    d. Buy 3 month put option of Unitech
12. In India, all Options traded on a stock are :
    a. Continental Options b. Asian Options
    c. European options d. American options
13. SBI is trading at Rs. 1800 in the cash market. What would be the price of SBI futures expiring three months from today? Risk free rate = 8% p.a.
    a. 1844 b. 1895
    c. 1814 d. 1836
14. Stock Futures contracts traded on NSE will expire on :
    a. Last Thursday of December 2009
    b. Exchanges decides on expiry day and will update the investors on 1st December 2009
    c. Last Friday of December 2009
    d. 3rd Thursday of December 2009
15. In India, all Options traded on Nifty are :
    a. Asian Options b. American options
    c. Continental Options d. European options
16. Nifty futures is trading at Rs. 3325 and an investor buys a 3400 call for current month for Rs. 100. What should be the closing price of Nifty only above which the investor starts to make Profits if he holds his long option position? 1 lot of Nifty = 50 shares
    a. 3425 b. 3400
    c. 3325 d. 3500
17. Which of the following is an exchange traded contract?
    a. Futures on Nifty b. Forward contract on oil
    c. An interest rate swap d. A 10 year loan
18. As more and more trades take place, the difference between spot and futures prices would narrow.
    a. Hedge b. Delta
    c. Arbitrage d. Speculative

19. Nifty is at 5200. A put option at 5000 strike price is trading at Rs. 150. What is the intrinsic value of the option?
    a. 200 b. 0
    c. 350 d. 150

20. Nifty is currently at 5100. An investor feels Nifty will not go beyond 4500 in next three months. He sells two lots of 5100 strike call on Nifty for Rs. 200 a lot. Because of good industrial production data, Nifty rallies to 5200 on the option's expiry day. What is the Profit/ Loss to the investor? (1 lot = 50 shares)
    a. Rs. 10000 b. Rs. -10000
    c. Rs. 20000 d. Rs. -20000

21. On 1st November, SBI is trading at Rs. 2300. An investor is bearish on the company because of the earnings of last quarter and sells a SBI futures at Rs. 2325. He buys back SBI futures at Rs. 2300. What is the Profit / Loss for the investor if 1 lot of SBI is 250 shares?
    a. Rs. 6250 b. Rs.0
    c. Rs. -6250 d. Rs. -10000

22. Which of the following is NOT a hedge for a long position in an underlying stock?
    a. Sell call option b. Sell futures
    c. Sell put option d. Buy Put option

23. When the strike price is lower than the spot price of the underlying, a call option will be.
    a. At the money b. In the money
    c. Out of the money d. American Type

24. On 1st January, SBI is trading at Rs. 2310. An investor is bullish on the company because of the earnings of last quarter and buys a SBI futures at Rs. 2310. He sells SBI futures at Rs. 2335. What is the Profit / Loss for the investor if 1 lot of SBI is 250 shares?
    a. Rs. -10000 b. Rs. -6250
    c. Rs. 6250 d. Rs.0

25. An investor buys TCS for Rs. 575 in the futures market. At the end of the day TCS futures closes at Rs. 500 in the futures market. What is the mark to market the investor is making/ losing ? (1 lot of TCS = 1000 shares)
    a. Rs. 500000 b. Rs. 575000
    c. Rs. -75000 d. Rs. 75000

26. An investor buys a 4 lots of Nifty at Rs. 5100 each. He sells 2 lots at Rs. 5050 and carries 2 lots for next day. On that day Nifty futures closes at Rs. 5000. What is his total Loss including mark to market Loss? One lot of Nifty is 50 shares.
    a. Loss of Rs. 5000 b. Profit of Rs. 5000
    c. Profit of Rs. 2000 d. No. Loss, no Profit

27. Infosys is trading at Rs. 1500 in the cash market. What should be the fair price of Infosys futures expiring 90 days from today. Risk free rate is 8% p.a.

    a. 1550 b. 1515
    c. 1530 d. 1540

28. An investor buys a 1 lot of Nifty futures at Rs. 4927 and sells it at Rs. 4567 If one contract is 50 shares what is the Profit/ Loss in the transaction?

    a. Loss Rs. 22000 b. Profit Rs. 22000
    c. Loss Rs. 18000 d. Profit Rs. 18000

29. Which of the following positions has a limited downside .

    a. Sell futures b. Buy Call Option
    c. Sell stock d. Sell Call option

30. Reliance is trading at Rs. 1520 in the cash market. What should be the fair price of Reliance futures expiring 90 days from today. Risk free rate is 8% p.a.

    a. 1529 b. 1537
    c. 1551 d. 1563

31. Like Futures contracts there is daily settlement of options contracts.

    a. TRUE b. depends on the expiry
    c. FALSE d. depends if the option is call or put

32. TCS is trading at Rs. 420 in the spot market and Rs. 435 in the futures market. Is there an arbitrage opportunity? The Futures contract is settling today.

    a. No b. Depends on Market Sentiment
    c. Yes

33. Reliance Capital is trading at Rs. 1000 in cash market. What should be the price of Reliance capital futures expiring 60 days from today. Risk free rate is 8% p.a.

    a. 1087 b. 1013
    c. 1081 d. 1121

34. An investor buys 2 contracts of TCS futures for Rs. 570 each. He sells of one contract at Rs. 585. TCS futures closes the day at Rs. 550. What is the net payment the investor has to pay/ receive from his broker? 1 TCS contract = 1000 shares

    a. Pay Rs. 20000 to the broker
    b. Pay Rs. 5000 to the broker
    c. Receive Rs. 5000 from the broker
    d. Receive Rs. 15000 from the broker

35. The value of a put option is positively related to all of the following EXCEPT:

    a. exercise price b. risk-free rate
    c. time to maturity

36. If a farmer expects to sell his wheat in three months' time in anticipation of a harvest. He wants to hedge his risk, he needs to:

a. buy wheat futures now
b. buy wheat now
c. sell wheat now
d. sell wheat futures now

37. DLF is trading at Rs. 380 in the spot market and Rs. 395 in the futures market. Is there an arbitrage opportunity? The Futures contract is settling today.

a. Depends on Market Sentiment
b. Yes
c. No

38. Security descriptor for stock Futures contract is :

a. FUTSTK
b. OPTIDX
c. OPTSTK
d. FUTIDX

39. Derivatives help in .

a. Risk Management
b. Price Discovery of the underlying
c. Improving Market Efficiency
d. All of the above

40 Nifty is at 3900. What should be the fair price of Nifty futures expiring 180 days from today. Risk free rate is 8% p.a.

a. 4027
b. 4083
c. 4031
d. 4059

41. The maximum expiry for individual stock options contract is :

a. 2 months
b. 6 months
c. 1 months
d. 3 months

42. The parties for the Futures contract have the flexibility of closing out the contract prior to the maturity by squaring off the transactions in the market. State true or false.

a. TRUE
b. FALSE

43. Nifty is at 3375. What should be the fair price of Nifty futures expiring 30 days from today. Risk free rate is 8% p.a.

a. 3367
b. 3377
c. 3398
d. 3352

44. Nifty futures is trading at Rs. 4955. An investor feels the market will not go beyond 5100. He can

a. Sell 5000 Nifty call
b. Sell 5100 Nifty put
c. Sell 5000 Nifty put
d. Sell 5100 Nifty Call

45. Arbitrage is a ______.
    a. Risk free Strategy
    b. High Risk Strategy

46. If an option is out of the money and the strike price of the option is lower than the spot price of the underlying, then we are referring to ______.
    a. A Put Option
    b. A European Option
    c. A Call option
    d. An American option

47. Nifty is at 5000. An investor buys a 5000-strike price put option for Rs. 170. The option is currently.
    a. Out of the money
    b. American Type
    c. At the money
    d. In the money

48. Nifty futures is trading at Rs. 3975 and an investor buys a 4000 call for current month for Rs. 100. What should be the closing price of Nifty only above which the investor starts to make Profits if he holds his long option position? 1 lot of Nifty = 50 shares.
    a. 3975
    b. 4000
    c. 4075
    d. 4100

49. Price that is agreed upon at the date of the contract for the delivery of an asset at a specific futures date is called
    a. Spot Price
    b. Discount Price
    c. Cash market price
    d. Futures Price

50. Price of an option expiring three months from today will be higher than price of an option expiring in two months from today.
    a. Incomplete data
    b. Depends if it is call or put option
    c. TRUE
    d. FALSE

SHORT ANSWER QUESTIONS

1. What do you mean by Derivatives?
2. "Derivatives are financial products" explain.
3. "Difference between derivatives and shares" Explain.
4. What are the Measures of derivatives?
5. Which Factors affecting growth of Derivative?
6. Who are the Participants in the Derivatives Market
7. Who are Hedgers?
8. Define Speculators.
9. Define Arbitrageurs.

10. Define Short Hedge and Long Hedge.
11. What are the three processes of Risk management features?
12. Define Options.
13. Define Futures.
14. Define warrants.
15. Define Swaps.
16. Define Call and put Options.
17. Define currency swaps.
18. What sis Derivative markets?
19. What is mean by trading derivatives markets?
20. Define mortgage-backed security (MBS).
21. Define Risk Management.
22. Define Credit risk.
23. Define Market Risk.
24. Define Liquidity Risk.
25. Define Legal Risk.

ESSAY TYPE QUESTIONS

1. What do you mean by Derivatives? Explain the Measures of derivatives?
2. Which Factors affecting growth and Participants in the Derivatives Market?
3. What is mean by trading derivatives markets?
4. Briefly explain the uses of Derivatives.
5. What are the common types of Derivatives? Explain briefly.
6. Define Derivatives Markets and explain trading of Derivatives market.
7. Explain the types and functions of Derivatives Markets.
8. Explain the role and economic functions derivative market.
9. Explain the Regulatory frame work for derivatives trading in Indi

MCQs Answers

1	2	3	4	5	6	7	8	9	10	11	12	13	14	15	16	17	18	19	20	21	22	23	24	25
a	d	c	a	b	b	a	b	d	d	d	c	d	a	d	d	a	c	b	a	a	c	b	c	c
26	27	28	29	30	31	32	33	34	35	36	37	38	39	40	41	42	43	44	45	46	47	48	49	50
a	c	c	b	c	c	c	b	b	b	d	b	a	d	d	d	a	c	d	a	a	c	d	d	c

CHAPTER 17

Futures and Options

The objectives of this unit are to help one understand, in general

- The general frame work of Futures and Options as financial derivatives.
- Importance and working of Futures and Options in the financial market.

INTRODUCTION

TRADING in stock index futures contracts was introduced by the Kansas City Board of Trade on February 24, 1982.In April 1982, the Chicago Mercantile Exchange (CME) began trading in futures contract based on the Standard and Poor's Index of 500 common stocks. The introduction of both contracts was successful, especially the S&P 500 futures contract, adopted by most institutional investors.

BSE created history on June 9the, 2000 by launching the first Exchange traded Index Derivative Contract i.e. futures on the capital market benchmark index - the BSE Sensex. The inauguration of trading was done by Prof. J.R. Varna, member of SEBI and chairman of the committee responsible for formulation of risk containment measures for the Derivatives market. The first historical trade of 5 contracts of June series was done on June 9, 2000 at 9:55:03 a.m. between M/s Kanji & Malik Securities Pvt. Ltd. and M/s Elkay Share & stock Brokers Ltd. at the rate of 4755. In the sequence of product innovation, the exchange commenced trading in Index Options on Sensex on June 1, 2001. Stock options were introduced on 31 stocks on July 9, 2001 and single stock futures were launched on November 9the 2002. September 13, 2004 marked another milestone in the history of Indian Capital Markets, the day on which the Bombay Stock Exchange launched Weekly Options, a unique product unparallel in derivatives markets, both domestic and international. BSE permitted trading in weekly contracts in options in the shares of four leading companies namely Reliance, Satyam, State Bank of India, and Tesco in addition to the flagship index-Sensex.

An option is a contract whereby one party (the holder or buyer) has the right, but not the obligation, to exercise the contract (the option) on or before a future date (the exercise date or expiry). The other party (the writer or seller) has the obligation to honor the specified feature of the contract. Since the option gives the buyer a right and the seller an obligation, the buyer has received something of value. The amount the buyer pays the seller for the option is called the option premium. Because this is a security whose value is determined by an underlying asset, it is classified as a derivative. The idea behind an option is present in everyday situations. For example, you discover a house that you'd love to purchase. Unfortunately, you won't have the cash to buy it for another three months. You talk to the owner and negotiate a deal that gives you an option to buy the house in three months for a price of Rs.200, 000. The owner agrees, but for this option, you pay a price of Rs.3, 000.

Now, consider two theoretical situations that might arise it's discovered that the house is actually the true birthplace of a great man. As a result, the market value of the house skyrockets to Rs.1 core. Because the owner sold you the option, he is obligated to sell you the house for Rs.200, 000. In the end, you stand to make a profit of Rs.97, 97,000 (Rs.1 Core – Rs.200, 000 – Rs.3, 000). While touring the house, you discover not only that the walls are chock-full of asbestos, but also that a ghost haunts the master bedroom; furthermore, a family of super-intelligent rats have built a fortress in the basement. Though you originally thought you had found the house of your dreams, you now consider it worthless. On the upside, because you bought an option, you are under no obligation to go through with the sale. Of course, you still lose the Rs.3, 000 price of the option. This example demonstrates two very important points. First, when you buy an option, you have a right but not an obligation to do something. You can always let the expiration date go by, at which point the option becomes worthless. If this happens, you lose 100% of your investment, which is the money you used to pay for the option. Second, an option is merely a contract that deals with an underlying asset. For this reason, options are called derivatives, which mean an option derives its value from something else. In our example, the house is the underlying asset. Most of the time, the underlying asset is a stock or an Index.

REASON FOR USING OPTIONS.

Two main reasons why an investor would use options are:

SPECULATION

Speculation is the betting on the movement of a security. The advantage of options is that one isn't limited to making a profit only when the market goes up. Because of the versatility of options, one can also make money when the market goes down or even sideways. Speculation is the territory in which the big money is made - and lost. The use of options for making big money or less is the reason why they have the reputation of being risky. This is because when one buys an option; one has to be correct in determining not only the direction of the stock's movement, but also the magnitude and the timing of this movement. To succeed, one must correctly predict whether a stock will go up or down, and has to be right about how much the price will change as well as the time frame it will take for all this to happen commissions must also be taken into account.

HEDGING

The other function of options is hedging. Think of this as an insurance policy. Just as one insures one's house or car, options can be used to insure the investments against a downturn. By using options, one would be able to restrict one's downslide while enjoying the full upside in a cost-effective way.

WORKING OF OPTIONS

In order to understand the working of options, an assumed firm by the name Justus Company, is taken Let's say that on May 1, the stock price of Justus Co. was Rs.75 and the premium (cost) was Rs.3.15 for a July 78 Call, which indicated that the expiration was the third Friday of July and the strike price was Rs.78. The total price of the contract was Rs.3.15 x 100 = Rs.315. In reality, you'd also have to take commissions into account, but we'll ignore them for this example. Remember, a stock option contract is the option to buy 100 shares; that's why you must multiply the contract by 100 to get the total price. The strike price of Rs. 78 means that the stock price must rise above Rs.78 before the call option is worth anything; furthermore, because the contract is Rs.3.70 per share, the break-even price would beRs.81. When the stock price is Rs.67, it's less than the Rs.70 strike price, so the option is worthless. But don't forget that you've paid Rs.315 for the option, so you are currently down by this amount.

Three weeks later the stock price is Rs.84. The options contract has increased along with the stock price and is now worth Rs.6 x 100 = Rs.600. Subtract what you paid for the contract, and your profit is (Rs.3) x 100 = Rs.300. You almost doubled the money in just three weeks! You could sell your options, which are called "closing your position," and take your profits- unless, of course, you think the stock price will continue to rise. For the sake of this example, let's say we let it ride. By the expiration date, the price drops to Rs.60. Because this is less than our Rs.78 strike price and there is no time left, the option contract is worthless. We are now down to the original investment of Rs.300. Putting it in the form of a table: here is what happened to our option investment.

Date	May 1	May,21	Expiry Date
Stock Price	Rs.78	Rs.84	Rs.60
Option Price	Rs.3	Rs.6	worthless
Contract Value	Rs.300	Rs.600	Rs.0
Paper Gain/Loss	Rs.0	Rs.300	-Rs.300

The price swing for the length of this contract from high to low was Rs.600, which would have given us over double our original investment. This is leverage in action.

OPTION FRAMEWORKS

The buyer pays the price (premium) to the seller (writer). The buyer assumes a long position and the writer a corresponding short position. Thus, the writer of a call option is "short a call" and has the obligation to sell to the holder, who is "long of a call option" and who has the right to buy. The writer of a put option is "on the short side of the position", and has the obligation to buy from the taker of the put option, who is "long a put". The option style determines when the buyer may exercise the option which will affect the valuation. Generally, the contract will either be American style - which allows exercise up to the expiry date - or European style -where exercise is only allowed on the expiry date - or Bermudian style - where exercise is allowed on several, specific dates up to the expiry date. European contracts are easier to value.

Buyers and sellers of exchange-traded options do not usually interact directly - the futures and options exchange acts as intermediary. The seller guarantees the exchange to fulfill his obligation if the buyer chooses to execute. The risk for the option holder is limited: he cannot lose more than the premium paid as he can “abandon the option". His potential gain with a call option is theoretically unlimited; the maximum loss for the writer of a put option is equal to the strike price. In general, the risk for the writer of a call option is unlimited. However, an option writer who owns the underlying instrument has created a covered position; he can always meet his obligations by using the actual underlying. Where the seller does not own the underlying on which he has written the option, he is called a "naked writer", and has created a "naked position".

Options can be in-the-money, at-the-money or out-of-the-money. The "in- the-money" option has a positive intrinsic value, options in "at-the-money” or “out-of-the-money” have an intrinsic value of zero. Additional to the intrinsic value an option has a time value, which decreases when the option is closer to its expiry date.

TYPES OF OPTIONS

There are two main types of options:

American options can be exercised at any time between the date of purchase and the expiration date.

European options can only be exercised at the end of their lives.

Long-Term Options are options with holding times of one, two or multiple years, which may be more appealing for long-term investors, which are called long-term equity anticipation securities (LEAPS). By providing opportunities to control and manage risk or even to speculate, LEAPS are virtually identical to regular options. LEAPS, however, provide these opportunities for much longer periods of time. Although they are not available on all stocks, LEAPS are available on most widely held issues.

Real option is a choice that an investor has when investing in the real economy - in the production of goods or services, rather than in financial contracts – which may be something as simple as the opportunity to expand production, or to change production inputs. They are an increasingly influential tool in corporate finance with typically difficult or impossible to trade.

Traded options (also called "Exchange-Traded Options” or "Listed Options”) are Exchange traded derivatives which have: standardized contracts; quick systematic pricing; and are settled through a clearing house (ensuring fulfillment.) These include: stock options; bond options; interest rate options; and station.

Vanilla options are 'simple', well understood and traded options, whereas an exotic option is more complex, or less easily understood and non-standard in nature. Asian options, look back options, barrier options are considered to be exotic, especially if the underlying instrument is more complex than simple equity or debt.

Employee stock options are issued by a company to its employees as compensation.

PRICING OF OPTIONS

Factors affecting the Option premium: Options are used as risk management tools and the valuation or pricing of the instruments is a careful balance of market factors. There are four major factors affecting the Option premium:

Price of Underlying

Time to Expiry

Exercise Price Time to Maturity

Volatility of the Underlying

And two less important factors:

Short – Term Interest Rates

Dividends

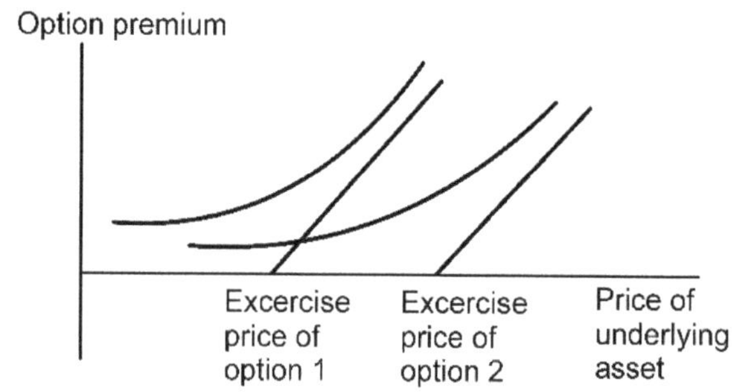

The Intrinsic Value of an Option

The intrinsic value of an option is defined as the amount by which an option is in-the immediate exercise value of the option when the underlying position is marked-to-market.

For a call option: Intrinsic Value = Spot Price – Strike Price

For a put option: Intrinsic Value = Strike Price – Spot Price

The intrinsic value of an option must be positive or zero. It cannot be negative. For a call option, the strike price must be less than the price of the underlying asset for the call to have an intrinsic value greater than 0. For a put option, the strike price must be greater than the underlying asset price for it to have intrinsic value. Comparing two calls with the same underlying asset; the higher the exercise price of a call, the lower its premium.

Call

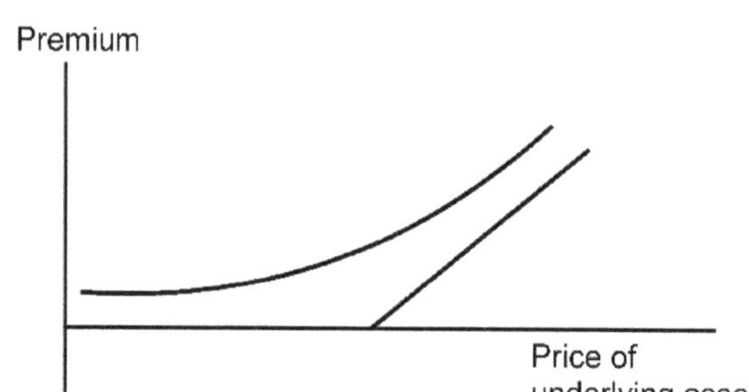

Put

Comparing two puts with the same underlying asset; the higher the exercise price of a put, the higher its premium.

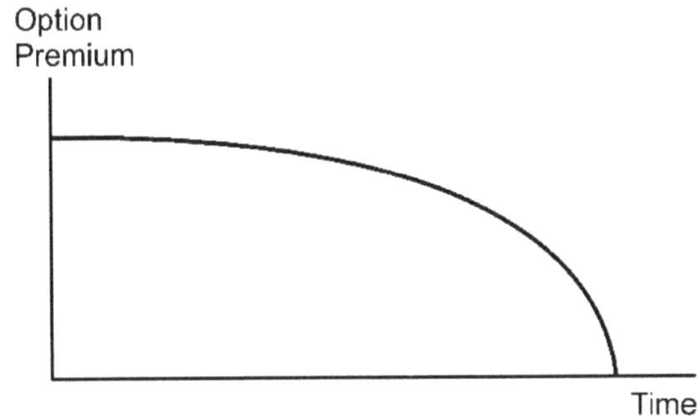

Price of Underlying

The premium is affected by the price movements in the underlying instrument. For Call options the right to buy the underlying at a fixed strike price – as the underlying price raises so does its premium. As the underlying price falls so does the cost of the option premium. For put options – the right to sell the underlying at a fixed strike price as the underlying price rises, the premium falls; as the underlying price decreases the premium cost raises. Call options become more valuable as the stock price increases and less valuable as the strike price increases. For a put option, the payoff on exercise is the amount by which the strike price exceeds the stock price. Put options, therefore, behave in the opposite way to call options. They become less valuable as the stock price increases and more valuable as the strike price increases.

The price of underlying asset

The option premium will be higher when the price of the underlying asset is higher.

Call

The option premium will be lower when the price of the underlying asset is lower.

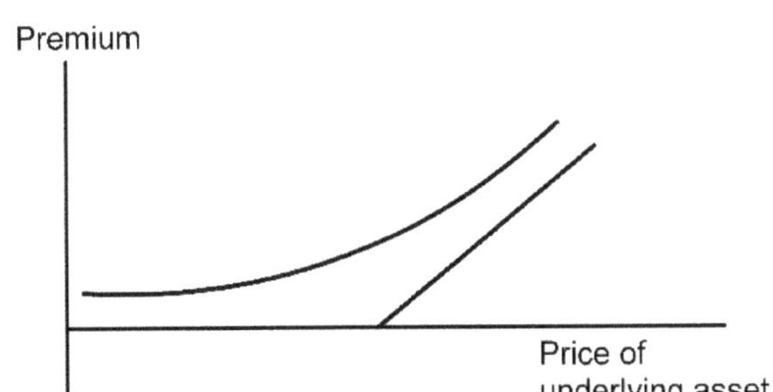

Put

The more the options are in-the-money or out-of-the-money, the lower is its time value; i.e. the option premium is close to the intrinsic value of the option.

The Time Value of an Option

Generally, the longer the time remaining until an options expiration, the higher will be its premium, because the longer an option's lifetimes, greater is the possibility that the underlying share price might move so as to make the option in-the-money. All other factors affecting an option's price remaining the same, the time value portion of an option's premium will decrease with the passage of time. Both put and call American options become more valuable as the time to expiration increases. To see this, consider two options that differ only with respect to the expiration date. The owner of the long-life option has all the exercise opportunities open to that of the owner of the short-life on- and more.

The long-life option must, therefore, always be worth at least as much as the short-life option. European put and call options do not necessarily become more valuable as the time to expiration increases. This is because the owner of a long-life European option does not have all the exercise opportunities open to the owner of a short-life European option. The owner of the long-life. European option can exercise only at the maturity of that option. Consider two European call options on a stock, one with an expiration date in one month and the other with an expiration date in two months. Suppose that a very large dividend is expected in six weeks. The dividend will cause the stock price to decline. It is possible that this will lead to the short-life option being worth more than the long-life option. The value of an option will be lower at the near closer of the expiration date, when all other factors remaining equal. The loss of time value is faster as the expiration date approaches.

Volatility

Volatility is the tendency of the underlying security's market price to fluctuate either up or down. It reflects a price change's magnitude; it does not imply a bias towards price movement in one direction or the other. Thus, it is a major factor in determining an option's premium. The higher the volatility of the underlying stock, the higher the premium because there is a greater possibility that the option will move in-the-money. Generally, as the volatility of an under-lying stock increases, the premiums of both calls and puts overlying that stock increase, and vice versa.

Higher volatility = Higher premium

Lower volatility = Lower premium

The volatility of a stock price, σ is defined so that $\Delta\sigma/\Delta$ is the Standard deviation of the return on the stock in a short length of time t. It is a measure of how uncertain we are about future stock price movements. As volatility increases, the chance that, the stock will do very well or very poorly increases. For the owner of a stock. These two outcomes tend to offset each other. However, this is not so for the owner of a call or put. The owner of a call benefits from price increases but bas limited downside risk in the event of price decreases because the most that the owner can lose is the price of the option. Similarly, the owner of a put benefits from price decreases but has limited downside risk in the event of price increases. The value of both calls and puts, therefore, increases a volatility increase. The higher the price volatility of the underlying asset, the higher the likelihood that the option will end up in-the-money; therefore, the higher the premium.

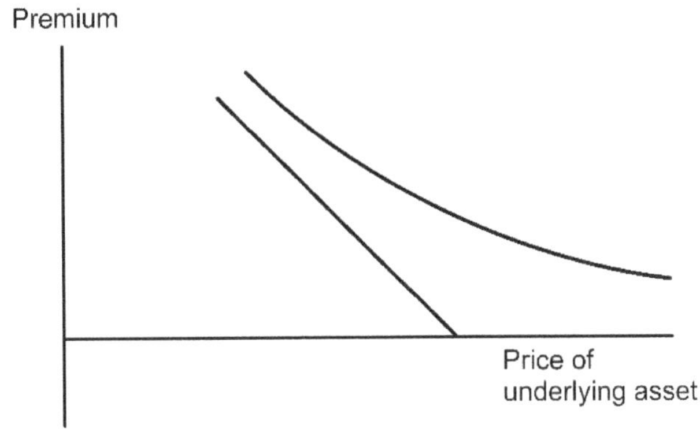

Call

The higher the price volatility of the underlying asset, the higher the likelihood that the option will end up out-of-the-money; therefore, the lower the premium.

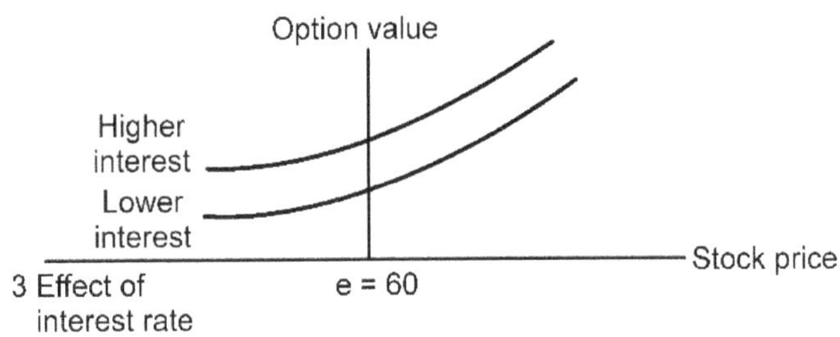

Put

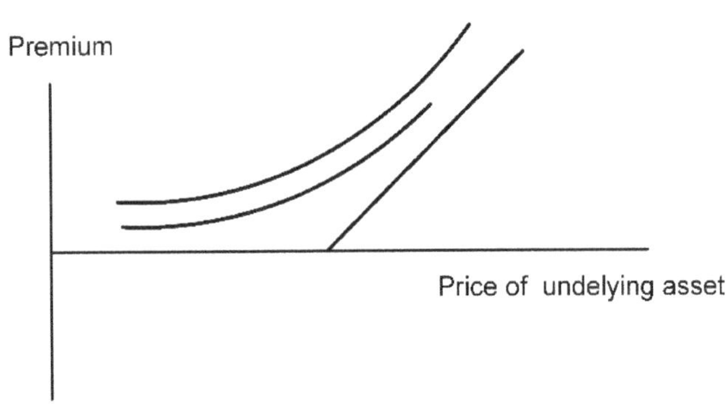

Interest rates

In general interest rates have the least influence on options and equate approximately to the cost of carry of a futures contract. If the size of the options contract is very large, then this factor may take on some importance. All other factors being equal as interest rates rise, premium costs fall and vice versa. The relationship can be thought of as an opportunity cost. In order to buy an option, the buyer must either borrow funds or use funds on deposit. Either way the buyer incurs an interest rate cost. If interest rates are rising, then the opportunity cost of buying options increases and to compensate the buyer premium costs fall. Why should the buyer be compensated? Because the option writer receiving the premium can place the funds on deposit and receive more interest than was previously anticipated. The situation is reversed when interest rates fall -premiums rise.

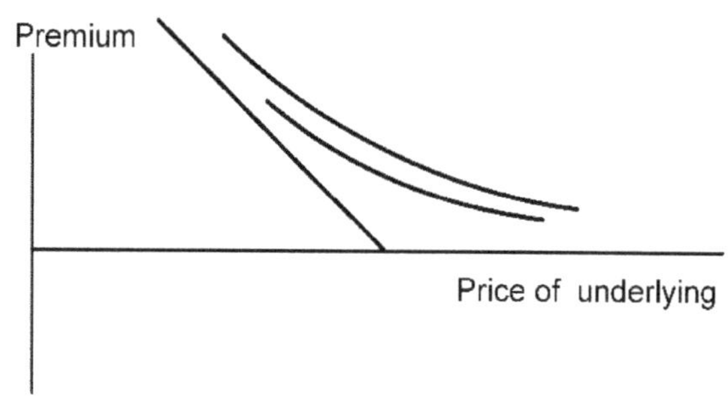

This time it is the writer who needs to be compensated. As interest rates in the economy increases, the expected growth rate of the stock price tends to increase and the present value of any future cash flows received by the holder of the option decreases. These two effects tend to decrease the value of a put option and hence, put option prices decline as the risk-free interest rate increases. In the case of calls, the first effect tends to increase the price and the second effect tends to decrease it. It can be shown that the first effect always dominates the second effect; that the price of a call always increases as the risk-free interest rate increases. The higher the "riskless interest rate", the higher the call premium. The higher the "riskless interest rate", the lower the put premium.

Dividends

Dividends have the effect of reducing the stock price on the ex-dividend date. The value of a call option is negatively related to the size of any anticipated dividend and the value of a put option is positively related to the size of any anticipated dividend.

Option zones

The value of the stock option has three different zones, as shown below:

- **Out of the Money:** Where the stock price is below the exercise price.
- **At the Money:** Where it is close to or at the exercise price.
- **In the Money:** Where the stock price is above the exercise price. These zones are depicted in the chart below:

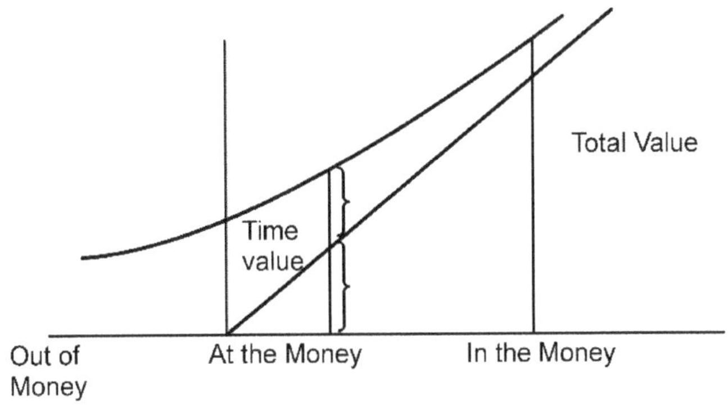

Say the exercise price is Rs.60. If the stock price is below 60, there is no economic value. There is only time value; if stock price starts above Rs.60 it will have been economic value and time value. As seen from the chart time value is maximum, when the exercise price and stock price are the same but is lower below the exercise price or above it. If the actual price is lower than the exercise price there is less change of profit on the call. If the actual price is above the exercise price, then there is a chance of profit, and there is less reason to pay a premium over the economic value (intrinsic value)

Assumptions and Notation

Some relationships have been derived between option price that do not require any assumptions about volatility and the probabilistic behavior of stock prices for this purpose it is, therefore, reasonable to assume that there are no arbitrage opportunities. The following notations have been used:

So: current stock price

ST: stock price at time T

X: strike price of option

T: time of expiration of option

R: risk-free rate of interest for maturity T (continuously compounded)

C: value of American call option to buy one share

P: value of American put option to sell one share

C: value of European all option to buy one share

P: value of European put option to sell one share

It should be noted that r is the nominal rate of interest, not the real rate of interest and assumed that r > O. Otherwise, a risk-free investment would provide no advantages over cash.

Upper and Lower Bounds for Option Prices

If the option price is above the upper bound or below the lower bound, there are profitable opportunities for arbitrageurs.

Upper Bounds

An American or European call option gives the holder the right to buy one share of a stock for a certain price. No matter what happens, the option can never be worth more than the stock. Hence, the stock price is an upper bound to the option price:

$$c < So \text{ and } C < So$$

If these relationships do not hold, an arbitrageur can easily make a risk less profit by buying the stock and selling the call option.

An American or European put option gives the holder the right to sell one share of a stock for X. No matter how low the stock price becomes, the option can never be worth more than X. Hence

$$P < X \text{ and } P < X$$

For European put options, we know that at time at the option will not be worthmore than X. It follows that its value today cannot be more than the

Present value of X: P < Axe- rat

If this were not true, an arbitrageur could make a risk less profit by selling the option and investing proceeds of the sale at the risk-free Interest rate.

Lower Bound for European Calls on Non-Dividend-Paying Stocks

A lower bound for the price of a European call option on a non-dividend-paying stock is

So-X- rat

First illustrated with a numerical example and then with a more formal argument.

Suppose that So = Rs20, X = Rs18, r = 10% per annum, and T = 1 year. In this case,

So -Axe- rat = 20 -18e-0-i = 3.71 or Rs3.71.

Consider the situation where the European call price is Rs. 3.00, which is less than the theoretical minimum of Rs. 3.71. An arbitrageur can buy the call and short the stock. This provides a cash inflow of Rs. 20.00 Rs. 3.00 = Rs. 17.00. If invested for one year at 10% per annum, the Rs. 17.00 grows to Rs18.79. At the end of the year, the option expires. If the stock price is greater than Rs.18, the arbitrageur exercises the option, closes out the short position, and makes a profit of Rs.18.79 -Rs.18.00 = Rs.0.79

If the stock price is less than Rs18, the stock is bought in the. market and the short (X) position is closed out. The arbitrageur then makes an even greater profit. For example, if the stock price is Rs.17, the arbitrageur's profit is Rs.18.79 -Rs.17.00 = l. 79 For a more formal argument, we consider the following two portfolios: Portfolio A: one European call option plus an amount of cash equal to Axe- rat (Portfolio B: one share)

In portfolio A, if the cash is invested at the risk-free interest rate, it will grow to X at time T. If ST > X, the call option is exercised at time T and portfolio A is worth ST. If ST < X, the call option expires worthless and the portfolio is worth X. Hence, at time T portfolio A is worth max (ST, X)

Portfolio B is worth ST at time T. Hence, portfolio A is always worth at least as much and is sometimes worth more than, portfolio B at time T. It follows that it must be, worth at least as much as portfolio B today. Hence, C + X e-rat> so

Or

C > So-Axe-rat.

Because the worst that can happen to a call option is that it expires worthless, its value must be positive. This means that c > 0 and, therefore,

C+ Exerts > So

Or

C > max (So - Axe-rat, 0)

Lower Bound for European Puts on Non-Dividend-Paying Stocks

For a European put option on a non-dividend-paying stock, a lower bound for the price is

Axe –rat - So

Suppose that So = Rs37, X = Rs40, r = 5% per annum, and T = 0.5 year. In this case

Axe-rat-So = 40e-o. osxo. s -37 = 2.01

Rs2.01. Consider the situation where the European put price is Rs1.00, which is less in the theoretical minimum of Rs2.01. An arbitrageur can borrow Rs38.00 for six months to buy both the put and the stock. At the end of the six months, the arbitrageur will be required to repay 38-o. osxo. s= Rs38.96. If the stock price is below Rs40. 00, arbitrageur exercises the option to sell the stock for Rs40.00, repays the loan, and makes a profit of Rs.40.00 –Rs.38.96 = Rs1.04

If the stock price is greater than Rs40.00, the arbitrageur discards the option, sells and repays the loan for an even greater profit. For example, if the stock price is. 2.00, the arbitrageur's profit is

Rs.42.00 –Rs.38.9.6 = Rs3.04

For a more formal argument, we consider the following two portfolios:

Portfolio C: one European put option plus one share

Portfolio D: an amount of cash equal to Axe-rat

If ST < X, the option in portfolio C is exercised at time T, and the portfolio becomes worth X. If ST > X, the put option expires worthless, and the portfolio is worth ST at time T. Hence portfolio C is worth max (ST. X) at time T. Assuming that the cash is invested at the risk-free interest rate, portfolio D is worth X at time T. Hence, portfolio C is always worth as much as, and is sometimes worth more than, portfolio D at time T. It follows that in the absence of arbitrage opportunities. Portfolio C must be worth at least as much as portfolio D today. Hence

p + so > Axe-rat

Or p > Axe-rat-So

Because the worst that can happen to a put option is that it expires worthless, value must be non-negative. This means that p > max (Axe-rat-So. 0).

Summary - Factors affecting the option premium

Factors	Call Premium	Put Premium
Longer time to expiration	+	+
Higher price of underlying	+	-
Higher volatility of underlying	+	+
Higher exercise price	-	+
Higher interest rate	+	-
Dividend	-	+

The more sophisticated tools used to measure the potential variations of options premiums are as follows:

- Delta
- Gamma
- Vega
- Rho
- Delta

Delta

Delta is the measure of an option's sensitivity to changes in the price of the underlying asset. Therefore, it is the degree to which an option price will move given a change in the underlying stock or index price, all else being equal.

Delta = Change in option premium / Change in underlying price

For example, an option with a delta of 0.5 will move Rc 5 for every change of Rc 10 in the underlying stock or index.

Illustration:

A trader is considering buying a Call option on a futures contract, which has a price of as 19. The premium for the Call option with a strike price of as 19 is 0.80. The delta for this option is +0.5. This means that if the price of the underlying futures contract rises to as 20 -a rise of Rs.1 -then the premium will increase by 0.5 x 1.00 = 0.50. The new option premium will be 0.80 + 0.50 = As 1.30.

Far out-of-the-money calls will have a delta very close to zero, as the change in underlying price is not likely to make them valuable or cheap. At-the- money call would have a delta of 0.5 and a deeply in-the-money call would have a delta close to 1. While Call deltas are positive, put deltas are negative, reflecting the fact that the put option price and the underlying stock price are inversely related. This is because if one buys a put his view is bearish and expects the stock price to go down. However, if the stock price moves up it is contrary to his view therefore, the value of the option decreases. The put delta equals the call delta minus 1. It may be noted that if delta of one's position is positive, he desires the underlying asset to rise in price. On the contrary, if delta is negative, he wants the underlying asset's price to fall.

Uses: The knowledge of delta is of vital importance for option traders because this parameter is heavily used in margining and risk management strategies. The delta is often called the hedge ratio. e.g. if you have a portfolio of 'n' shares of a stock then 'n' divided by the delta gives you the number of calls you would need to be short (i.e. need to write) to create a riskless hedge -i.e. a portfolio which would be worth the same whether the stock price rose by a very small amount or fell by a very small amount. In such a "delta neutral" portfolio any gain in the value of the shares held due to a rise in the share price would be exactly offset by a loss on the value of the calls written, and vice versa. Note that as the delta changes with the stock price and time to expiration the number of shares would need to be continually adjusted to maintain the hedge. How quickly the delta changes with the stock price is given by gamma, which we shall learn subsequently.

Gamma

This is the rate at which the delta value of an option increases or decreases as a result of a move in the price of the underlying instrument.

Gamma = Change in an option delta / Change in underlying price

For example, if a Call option has a delta of 0.50 and a gamma of 0.05, then a rise of +/- 1 in the underlying means the delta will move to 0.55 for a price rise and 0.45 for a price fall. Gamma is rather like the rate of change in the speed of a car -its acceleration -in moving from a standstill, up to its cruising speed, and braking back to a standstill. Gamma is greatest for an A TM (at-the- money) option (cruising) and falls to zero as an option moves deeply ITM (in-the-money) and OTM (out-of-the-money) (standstill).

If you are hedging a portfolio using the delta-hedge technique described under "Delta", then you will want to keep gamma as small as possible as the smaller it is the less often you will have to adjust the hedge to maintain a delta neutral position. If gamma is too large a small change in stock price could wreck your hedge. Adjusting gamma, however, can be tricky and is generally done using options --unlike delta, it can't be done by buying or selling the underlying asset as the gamma of the underlying asset is, by definition, always zero so more or less of it won't affect the gamma of the total portfolio.

Theta

It is a measure of an option's sensitivity to time decay. Theta is the change in option price given a one-day decrease in time to expiration. It is a measure of time decay (or time shrunk). Theta is generally used to gain an idea of how time decay is affecting your portfolio.

Theta = Change in an option premium / Change in time to expiry

Theta is usually negative for an option as with a decrease in time, the option value decreases. This is due to the fact that the uncertainty element in the price decreases. Assume an option has a premium of 3 and a theta of 0.06. After one day it will decline to 2.94, the second day to 2.88 and so on. Naturally other factors, such as changes in value of the underlying stock will alter the premium. Theta is only concerned with the time value. Unfortunately, we cannot predict with accuracy the changes in stock market's value, but we can measure exactly the time remaining until expiration.

Vega This is a measure of the sensitivity of an option price to changes in market volatility. It is the change of an option premium for a given change - typically 1 % -in the underlying volatility.

Vega = Change in an option premium / Change in volatility. If for example, XYZ stock has a volatility factor of 30% and the current premium is 3, a Vega of .08 would indicate that the premium would increase to 3.08 if the volatility factor increased by 1 % to 31 %. As the stock becomes more volatile the changes in premium will increase in the same proportion. Vega measures the sensitivity of the premium to these changes in volatility.

What practical use is the Vega to a trader? If a trader maintains a delta neutral position, then it is possible to trade options purely in terms of volatility -the trader is not exposed to changes in underlying prices. "

Rho

Rho measures the change in an option's price per unit increase - typically 1 % -in the cost of funding the underlying.

Rho = Change in an option premium / Change in cost of funding underlying

Example:

Assume the value of Rho is 14.10. If the risk-free interest rates go up by 1 % the price of the option will move by Rs 0.14109. To put this in another way: if the risk-free interest rate changes by a small amount, then the option value should change by 14.10 times that amount.

For example, if the risk-free interest rate increased by 0.01 (from 10% to 11 %), the option value would change by 14.10*0.01 = 0.14. For a put option, inverse relationship exists. If the interest rate goes up the option value decreases and therefore, Rho for a put option is negative. In general Rho tends to be small except for long-dated options.

Trading Strategies

Bull Market Strategies

Call in a Bullish Strategy:

An investor with a bullish market outlook should buy call option. It one expects the market price of the underlying asset to rise, then, he would rather have the right to purchases at a specified price and sell later at a higher price than have the obligation to deliver later at a higher price.

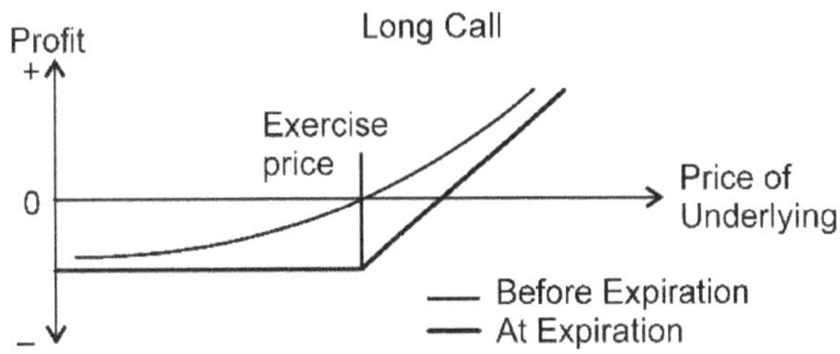

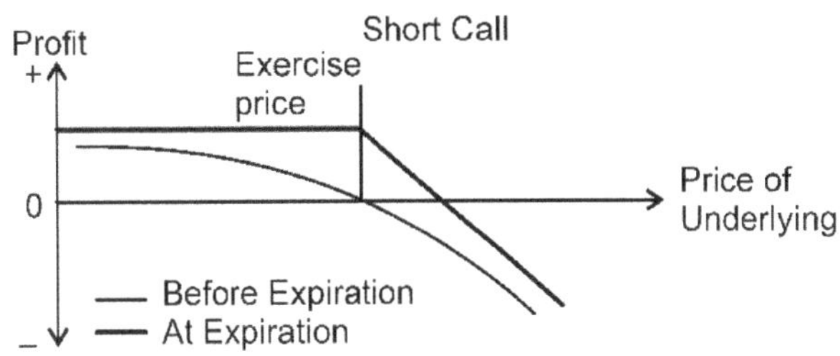

The investor's profit potential on buying a call option is unlimited. His profit is the market price less the exercise price less the premium. The increase in price of the underlying increases the investor's profit. The investor's potential loss is limited. Even if the market takes a drastic decline in price levels, the holder of a call is under no obligation to exercise the option and let the option expire worthless. The investor breaks even when the market price equals the exercise price plus the premium. An increase in volatility will increase the value of call and thereby increases the return. Because of the increased likelihood that the option will become in- the-money, an increase in the underlying volatility (before expiration), will increase the value of a long options position.

PUTS IN A BULLISH STRATEGY

An investor with a bullish market outlook can also go short on a Put option. Basically, an investor anticipating a bull market could write put options. If the market price increases and puts become out-of-the-money, investors with long put positions will let their options expire worthless. By writing Puts, profit potential is limited. A Put writer profits when the price of the underlying asset increases and the option expires worthless. The maximum profit is limited to the premium received.

However, the potential loss is unlimited. Because a short put position holder has an obligation to purchase if exercised. He will be exposed to potentially large losses if the market moves against his position and declines. The break-even point occurs when the market price equals the exercise price: minus the premium.

At any price less than the exercise price minus the premium, the investor loses money on the transaction. At higher prices, his option is profitable. An increase in volatility will increase the value of your put and decrease your return. As an option writer, the higher price you will be forced to pay in order to buy back the option at a later date, lower is the return. Bullish Call Spread Strategies

A vertical call spread is the simultaneous purchase and sale of identical call options but with different exercise prices. To "buy a call spread" is to purchase a call with a lower exercise price and to write a call with a higher exercise price. The trader pays a net premium for the position.

To "sell a call spread" is the opposite, here the trader buys a call with a higher exercise price and writes a call with a lower exercise price, receiving a net premium for the position. An investor with a bullish market outlook should buy a call spread. The "Bull Call Spread" allows the investor to participate to a limited extent in a bull market, while at the same time limiting risk exposure.

To put on a bull spread, the trader needs to buy the lower strike call and sell the higher strike call. The combination of these two options will result in a bought spread. The cost of Putting on this position will be the difference between the premium paid for the low strike call and the premium received for the high strike call.

The investor's profit potential is limited. When both calls are in-the- money, both will be exercised and the maximum profit will be realized. The investor delivers on his short call and receives a higher price than he is paid for receiving delivery on his long call. The investor's potential loss is limited. At the most, the investor can lose is the net premium. He pays a higher premium for the lower exercise price call than he receives for writing the higher exercise price call than he receives for writing the higher exercise price call.

The investor breaks even when the market price equals the lower exercise price plus the net premium. At the most, an investor can lose is the net premium paid. To recover the premium, the market price must be as great as the lower exercise price plus the net premium.

An example of a Bullish call spread:

Let's assume that the cash price of a scrip is Rs. 100 and one bought a November call option with a strike price of Rs. 90 and paid a premium of RS. 14. At the same time he sold another November call option on a scrip with a strike price of Rs.110 and received a premium of Rs.4. Here, he is buying a lower strike price option and selling a higher strike price option. This would result in a net outflow of Rs.10 at the time of establishing the spread.

Now let us look at the fundamental reason for this position. Since this is a bullish strategy, the first position established in the spread is the long lower strike price call option with unlimited profit potential. At the same time to reduce the cost of purchase of the long position a short position at a higher call strike price is established. While this not only reduces the outflow in terms of premium but also his profit potential and at the sometime the risk is limited. Based on the above figures the maximum profit, maximum loss and breakeven point of this spread would be as follows:

Maximum profit = Higher strike price - Lower strike price - Net premium paid = 110 – 90 - 10 = 10

Maximum Loss = Lower strike premium -Higher strike premium = 14-4 = 10

Breakeven Price = Lower strike price + Net premium paid = 90 + 10 = 100

Bullish Put Spread Strategies. A vertical Put spread is the simultaneous purchase and sale of identical. Put options but with different exercise prices. To "buy a put spread" is to purchase a Put with a higher exercise price and to write a Put with a lower exercise price. The trader pays a net premium for the position. To "sell a put spread" is the opposite: the trader buys a Put with a lower exercise price and writes a put with a higher exercise price, receiving a net premium for the position. An investor with a bullish market outlook should sell a Put spread.

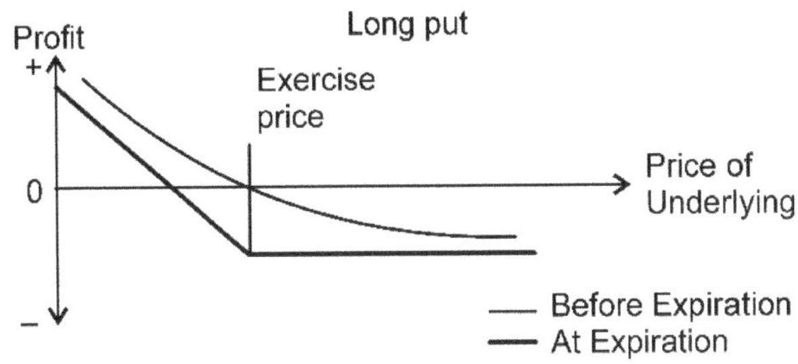

Vertical Bull Put Spread

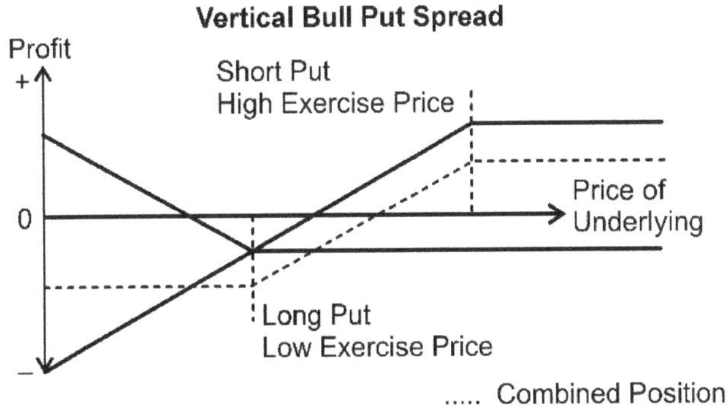

The "vertical bull put spread" allows the investor to participate to a limited extent in a bull market, while at the same time limiting risk exposure. To put on a bull spread can be created by buying the lower strike and selling the higher strike of either calls or put. The difference between the premiums paid and received makes up one leg of the spread.

The investor's profit potential is limited. When the market price reaches or exceeds the higher exercise price, both options will be out-of-the-money and will expire worthless. The trader will realize his maximum profit, the net premium. The investor's potential loss is also limited. If the market falls, the options will be in-the-money. The puts will offset one another, but at different exercise prices. The investor breaks-even when the market price equals the lower exercise price less the n premium. The investor achieves maximum profit i.e. the premium received; when the mark price moves up beyond the higher exercise price (both puts are then worthless).

An example of a bullish put spread.

Lets us assume that the cash price of the scrip is Rs.100. One now buys a November put option scrip with a strike price of Rs.90 at a premium of Rs.5 and sells a put option with a strike price Rs.110 at a premium of Rs.15. The first position is a short put at a higher strike price. This has resulted in some inflow in terms of premium. But here the trader is worried about risk and so caps his risk by buying another put option at the lower strike price. As such, a part of the premium received goes off and the ultimate position has limited risk and limited profit potential. Based on the above figures the maximum profit, maximum loss and breakeven point of this spread would be as follows:

Maximum profit = Net option premium income or net credit = 15-5= 10

Maximum loss = Higher strike price -Lower strike price -Net premium received

= 110-90-10= 10

Breakeven Price = Higher Strike price -Net premium income

= 110-10= 100

BEAR MARKET STRATEGIES

Puts in a Bearish Strategy When one purchases a put he is long and wants the market to fall. A put option is a bearish position which will increase in value if the market falls. By purchasing put options, the trader has the right to choose whether to sell the underlying asset at the exercise price. In a falling market, this choice is preferable to being obligated to buy the underlying at a price higher.

An investor's profit potential is practically unlimited. The higher the fall in price of the underlying asset, higher the profits.

The investor's potential loss is limited. If the price of the underlying asset rises instead of falling as' the investor has anticipated, he may let the option expire worthless. At the most, he may lose the premium for the option. The trader's breakeven point is the exercise price minus the premium. To profit, the market price must be below the exercise price. Since the trader has paid a premium he must recover the premium he paid for the option.

An increase in volatility will increase the value of the put and increases the return. An increase in volatility will make it more likely that the price of the underlying instrument will move, increasing the value of the option.

Calls in a Bearish Strategy

Another option for a bearish investor is to go short on a call with the intent to purchase it back in the future. By selling a call, you have a net short position and needs to be bought back before expiration and cancel out your position.

For this an Investor needs to write a call option. If the market price falls, long call holders will let their out-of-the-money options expire worthless, because they could purchase the underlying asset at the lower market price.

The investor's profit potential is limited because the trader's maximum profit is limited to the premium received for writing the option. Here the loss potential is unlimited because a short call position holder has an obligation to sell if exercised; he will be exposed to potentially large Losses if the market rises against his position.

The investor breaks even when the market price equals the exercise price: plus, the premium. At any price greater than the exercise price plus the premium, the trader is losing money. When the market price equals the exercise price plus the premium, the trader breaks even. An increase in volatility will increase the value of call and decreases its return. When the option writer has to buy back the option in order to cancel out his position, he will be forced to pay a higher price due to the increased value of the calls.

BEARISH PUT SPREAD STRATEGIES

A vertical put spread is the simultaneous purchase and sale of identical put options but with different exercise prices. To "buy a put spread" is to purchase a put with a higher exercise price and to write a put with a lower exercise price. The trader pays a net premium for the position. To "sell a put spread" is the opposite. The trader buys a put with a lower exercise price and writes put with a higher exercise price, receiving a net premium for the position. To put on a bear put spread buy the higher strike put and sell the lower strike put. Sell the lower strike and buy the higher strike of either calls or puts to set up a bear spread.

An investor with a bearish market outlook should: buy a put spread. The "Bear Put Spread" allows the investor to participate to a limited extent in a bear market, while at the same time limiting risk exposure. The investor's profit potential is limited. When the market price falls to or below the lower exercise price, both options will be in-the-money and the trader will realize his maximum profit when he recovers the net premium paid for the options. The investor's potential loss is limited. The trader has offsetting positions at different exercise prices. If the market rises rather than falls, the options will be out-of-the-money and expire worthless. Since the trader has paid a net premium.

The investor breaks even when the market price equals the higher exercise price less the net premium. For the strategy to be profitable, the market price must fall. When the market price falls to the high exercise price less the net premium, the trader breaks even. When the market falls beyond this point, the trader profits.

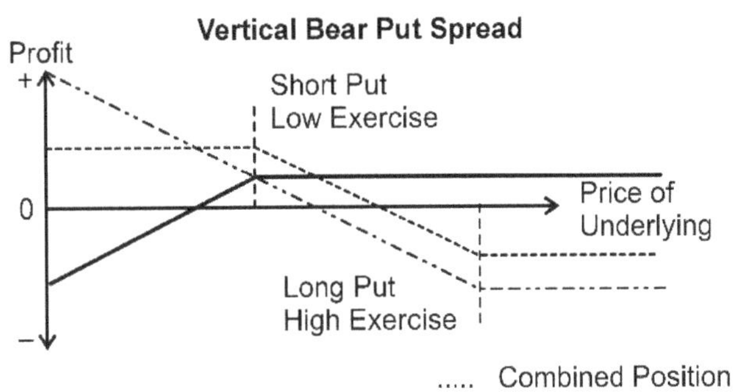

An example of a bearish put spread.

Let's assume that the cash price of the scrip is Rs 100. One buys a November put option on a scrip with a strike price of Rs 110 at a premium of Rc 15 and sell a put option with a strike price of Rs 90 at a premium of Rs 5. In this bearish position the put is taken as long on a higher strike price put with the outgo of some premium. This position has huge profit potential on downslide. The trader may recover a part of the premium paid by him by writing a lower strike price put option. The resulting position is a mildly bearish position with limited risk and limited profit profile. Though the trader has reduced the cost of taking a bearish position, he has also capped the profit potential as well. The maximum profit, maximum loss and breakeven point of this spread would be as follows:

Maximum profit = Higher strike price option -Lower strike price option -Net premium paid

= 110-90-10= 10

Maximum loss = Net premium paid = 15-5= 10

Breakeven Price = Higher strike price -Net premium paid = 110-10= 100

Bearish Call Spread Strategies A vertical call spread is the simultaneous purchase and sale of identical call options but with different exercise prices. To "buy a cal' spread" is to purchase a call with a lower exercise price and to write a call with a higher exercise price. The trader pays a net premium for the position. To "sell a call spread" is the opposite: the trader buys a call with a higher exercise price and writes a call with a lower exercise price, receiving a net premium for the position. To put on a bear ca" spread you sell the lower strike call and buy the higher strike call. An investor sells the lower strike and buys the higher strike of either calls or puts to put on a bear spread. An investor with a bearish market outlook should: sell a call spread. The "Bear Call Spread" allows f the investor to participate to a limited extent in a bear market, while at the same time limiting risk exposure.

The investor's profit potential is limited. When the market price falls to the lower exercise price, both out-of-the-money options will expire worthless. The maximum profit that the trader can realize is the net premium: The premium he receives for the call at the higher exercise price. Here the investor's potential loss is limited. If the market rises, the options will offset the investor's profit potential is limited.

When the market price falls to the lower exercise price, both out-of-the-money options will expire worthless. The maximum profit that the trader can realize is the net premium: The premium he receives for the call at the higher exercise price. Here the investor's potential loss is limited. If the market rises, the options will offset one another, At any price greater than the high exercise price, the maximum loss will equal high exercise price minus low exercise price minus net premium one another, At any price greater than the high exercise price, the maximum loss will equal high exercise price minus low exercise price minus net premium. The investor breaks even when the market price equals the lower exercise price plus the net premium. The strategy becomes profitable as the market price declines. Since the trader is receiving a net premium, the market price does not have to fall as low as the lower exercise price to breakeven.

An example of a bearish call spread

Let us assume that the cash price of the scrip is Rs.100. One now buys a November call option on a scrip with a strike price of Rs.110 at a premium of Rs.5 and sell a call option with a strike price of Rs.90 at a premium of Rs.15.

In this spread he has to buy a higher strike price call option and sell a lower strike price option. As the low strike price option is more expensive than the higher strike price option, it is a net credit strategy. The final position is left with limited risk and limited profit. The maximum profit, maximum loss and breakeven point of this spread would be as follows:

Maximum profit = Net premium received = 15-5= 10

Maximum loss = Higher strike price option -Lower strike price option -Net premium received = 110-90-10= 10

Breakeven Price = Lower strike price + Net premium paid= 90 + 10 = 100

VOLATILE MARKET STRATEGIES

STRADDLES IN A VOLATILE MARKET OUTLOOK

Volatile market trading strategies are appropriate when the trader believes the market will move but does not have an opinion on the direction of movement of the market. As long as there is significant movement upwards or downwards, these strategies offer profit opportunities. A trader need not be bullish or bearish. He must simply be of the opinion that the market is volatile.

- A straddle is the simultaneous purchase (or sale) of two identical options, one a call and the other a put.
- To "buy a straddle" is to purchase a call and a put with the same exercise price and expiration date.
- To "sell a straddle" is the opposite: the trader sells a call and a put with the same exercise price and expiration date.

A trader, viewing a market as volatile, should buy option straddles. A "straddle purchase" allows the trader to profit from either a bull market or from a bear market.

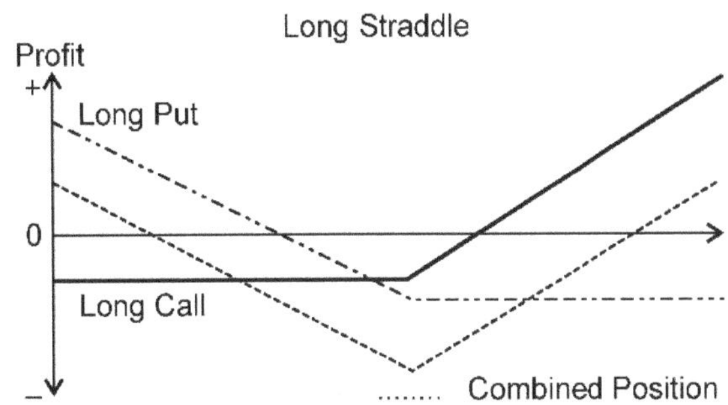

Here the investor's profit potential is unlimited. If the market is volatile, the trader can profit from an up- or downward movement by exercising the appropriate option while letting the other option expire worthless. (Bull market, exercise the call; bear market, the put.) If the price of the underlying asset remains stable instead of either rising or fallin. As the trader anticipated, the maximum he will lose is the premium he paid for the options. In this case the trader has long two positions and thus, two breakeven points. One is for the call which is exercise price plus the premiums paid, and the other for the put, which is exercise price minus the premiums paid.

STRANGLES IN A VOLATILE MARKET OUTLOOK

A strangle is similar to a straddle, except that the call and the put have different exercise price

Usually, both the call and the put are out-of-the-money. To "buy a strangle" is to purchase a call and a put with the same expiration date, but differ exercise prices. To "sell a strangle" is to write a call and a put with the same expiration date, but different exercise prices. A trader, viewing a market as volatile, should buy strangles. A "strangle purchase" allows the trader to profit from either a bull or bear market. Because the options are typically out-of-the money, the market must move to a greater degree than a straddle purchase to be profitable.

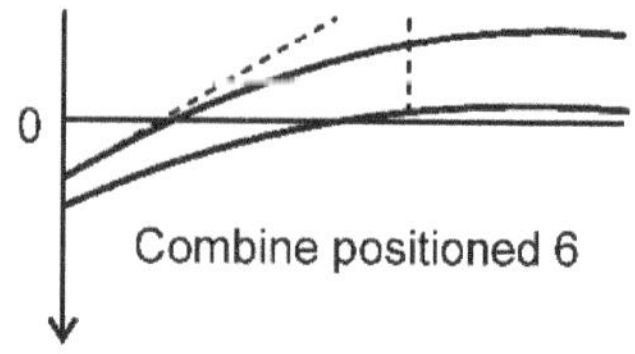

The trader's profit potential is unlimited. If the market is volatile, the trader can profit from up or downward movement by exercising the appropriate option, and letting the other expire worthless. (In a bull market, exercise the call; in a bear market exercise the put). The investor's potential loss is limited. Should the price of the underlying remain stable, the most the trader would lose is the premium he paid for the options. Here the loss potential is also very minimal because, the more the options are out-of-the-money, the lesser the premiums. Here the trader has two long positions and thus, two breakeven points. One for the call, which breakevens when the market price equals the high exercise price plus the premium paid, and the put, when the market price equals the low exercise price minus the premium paid.

The Short Butterfly Call Spread:

Like the volatility positions, the Short Butterfly position will realize a profit if the market makes a substantial move. It also uses a combination of puts and calls to achieve its profit/loss profile -but combines them in such a manner that the maximum profit is limited. The profit loss profile of a short butterfly spread looks like two short options coming together at the center Calls. One's potential gains or losses are: limited on both the upside and the downside.

The Call Ratio Back spread

The call ratio back spread is similar in contraction to the short butterfly call spread. The only difference is that one omits one of the components (or legs) used to build the short butterfly when constructing a call ratio back spread. When putting on a call ratio back spread, one is neutral but want the market to move in either direction. The call ratio back spread will lose money if the market sits. The market outlook one would have in putting on this position would be for a volatile market, with greater probability that the market will rally.

To put on a call ratio back spread, one sells one of the lower strikes and buy two or more of the higher strike. By selling an expensive lower strike option and buying two less expensive high strike options, one receives an initial credit for this position. The maximum loss is then equal to the high strike price minus the low strike price minus the initial net premium received.

The profit on the downside is limited to the initial net premium received when setting up the spread. The upside profit is unlimited. An increase in implied volatility will make the spread more profitable. Increased volatility increases a long option position's value. The greater number of long options will cause this spread to become more profitable when volatility increases.

The Put Ratio Back spread

In combination positions (e.g. bull spreads, butterflies, ratio spreads), one can use calls or puts to achieve similar, if not identical, profit profiles. Like its call counterpart, the put ratio back spread combines options to create a spread which has limited loss potential and a mixed profit potential.

It is created by combining long and short puts in a ratio of 2: 1 or 3: 1. In a 3: 1 spread, one would buy three puts at a low exercise price and write one put at a high exercise price. While one may, of course, extend this position out to six long and two short or nine long and three shorts, it is important that one respect the (in this case) 3: 1 ratio in order to maintain the put ratio back spread profitless profile. When put on a put ratio back spread one is neutral but wants the market to move in either direction.

One's market expectations here would be for a volatile market with a greater probability that the market will fall than rally. Unlimited profit would be realized on the downside. The two long puts offset the short. Put and result in practically unlimited profit on the bearish side of the market. The cost of the long puts is offset by the premium received for the (more expensive) short put, resulting in a net premium received. To put on a put ratio back spread, one buy two or more of the lower strike and sell one of the higher strikes.

One sells the more expensive put and buy two or more of the cheaper put. One usually receives an initial net premium for putting on this spread. The Maximum loss is equal to: High strike price -Low strike price -Initial net premium received.

STABLE MARKET STRATEGIES

STRADDLES IN A STABLE MARKET OUTLOOK

- A straddle is the simultaneous purchase (or sale) of two identical options, one a call and the other a put.
- To "buy a straddle" is to purchase a call and a put with the same exercise price and expiration date.
- To "sell a straddle" is the opposite: the trader sells a call and a put with the same exercise price and expiration date.

A trader, viewing a market as stable, should: write option straddles. A "straddle sale" allows the trader to profit from writing calls and puts in a stable market environment. The investor's profit potential is limited. If the market remains stable, traders long out-of-the-money calls or puts will let their options expire worthless. Writers of these options will not be called to deliver and will profit from the sum of the premiums received. The investor's potential loss is unlimited. Should the price of the underlying rise or fall, the writer of a call or put would have to deliver, exposing himself to unlimited loss if he has to deliver on the call and practically unlimited loss if on the put. The breakeven points occur when the market price at expiration equals the exercise price plus the premium and minus the premium. The trader is short two positions and thus, two breakeven points; One for the call (common exercise price plus the premiums paid), and one for the put (common exercise price minus the premiums paid). **Strangles in a Stable Market Outlook** A strangle is similar to a straddle, except that the call and the put have different exercise prices. Usually, both the call and the put are out-of-the-money. To "buy a strangle" is to purchase a call and a put with the same expiration date, but different exercise prices. Usually the call strike price is higher than the put strike price.

To "sell a strangle" is to write a call and a put with the same expiration date, but different exercise prices. A trader, viewing a market as stable, should: write strangles. A "strangle sale" allows the trader to profit from a stable market. The investor's profit potential is: limited. If the market remains stable, investors having out-of-the-money long put or long call positions will let their options expire worthless and seller of the options will have limited Profit and will be equal to the premium received. The investor's potential loss is: unlimited.

If the price of the underlying interest rises or falls instead of remaining stable as anticipated, he will have to deliver on the call or the put. The breakeven points occur when market price at expiration equals the high exercise price the premium and the low exercise price minus the premium. The trader is short two positions and thus, two breakeven points. One for the call (high exercise price plus the premiums paid), and one for the put (low exercise price minus the premiums paid).

The risk is lower with a strangle. Although the seller gives up a substantial amount of potential profit by selling a strangle rather than a straddle, he also holds less risk. Notice that the strangle requires more of a price move in both directions before it begins to lose money.

Long Butterfly Call Spread Strategy: The long butterfly call spread is a combination of a bull spread and a bear spread, utilizing calls and three different exercise prices. A long butterfly call spread involves:

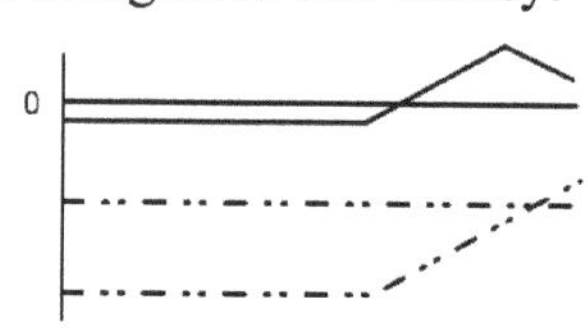

- Buying a call with a low exercise price,
- Writing two calls with a mid-range exercise price,
- Buying a call with a high exercise price.

This spread is put on by purchasing one each of the outside strikes selling two of the inside strike. To put on a short butterfly, you do just the opposite.

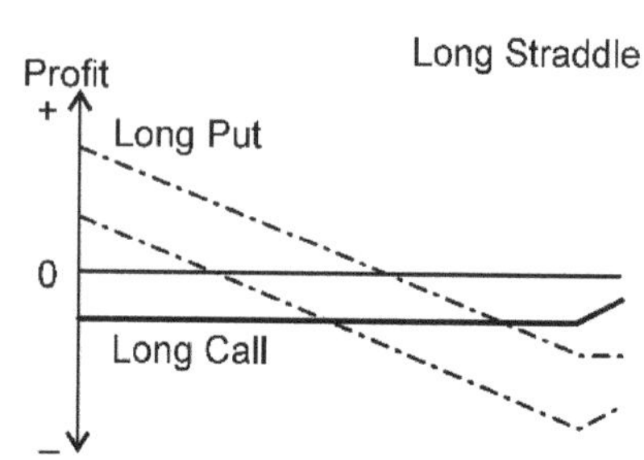

The investor's profit potential is limited.

Maximum profit is attained when the market price of the underlying interest equals the mid-range exercise price (if the exercise prices are symmetrical).

The investor's potential loss is limited.

The maximum loss is limited to the net premium paid and is realized when the market price underlying asset is higher than the high exercise price or lower than the low exercise price.

The investor's potential loss is limited.

The maximum loss is limited to the net premium paid and is realized when the market price underlying asset is higher than the high exercise price or lower than the low exercise price. The breakeven points occur when the market price at expiration equals the high exercise minus the premium and the low exercise price plus the premium. The strategy is profitable when the market price is between the low exercise price plus the net premium and the high exercise price minus the net premium.

Calendar Spreads

A calendar spread can be created by selling a call option with a certain strike price and buying a longer-maturity call option with the same strike price. The longer the maturity of an option the more experience its. A calendar spread, therefore required an initial investment. The following figure shows the: profit from a calendar spread at the time when the short-maturity option expires. (It is assumed that the long-maturity option is sold at this time.) The trader makes a profit if the stock price at the expiration of the short-maturity option is close to the strike price of the short-maturity option. However, a loss is incurred if the stock price is significantly above or significantly below this strike price.

To understand the profit pattern from a calendar spread, first consider what happens if the stock price is very low when the short-maturity option expires. The short-maturity option is worthless, and the value of the long- maturity option is close to zero. The trader, therefore, incurs a loss that is only a little less than the cost of setting up the spread initially. Consider next what happens if the stock prices, is very high when the short-maturity option expires. The short-maturity option costs the trader ST -' X, I and the long- maturity option is worth a little more than ST -Xl where Xl is the strike price of die options. Again, the trader has a net loss that is a little less than the cost of setting up the spread initially. If ST is close to X, the short-maturity option costs the trader either a small amount or nothing at all. However, the long-maturity option is still quite valuable. In this case, a significant net profit is made.

Calendar Spread created using two calls.

In a *neutral calendar spread* a strike price close to the current stock price is chosen. A bullish calendar spread involves a higher strike price, whereas a bearish calendar spread, involves a lower strike price.

Calendar Spread Created using two calls.

In a *neutral calendar spread* a strike price close to the current stock price is chosen. A bullish calendar spread involves a higher strike price, whereas a bearish calendar spread, involves a lower strike price.

Calendar spread created using two puts.

Calendar spreads can be created with put options as well as call options. The trader buys long maturity put option and sells a short-maturity put option. As shown in the above figure, the profit pattern is similar to that obtained from using calls.

A *reverse calendar spreads* the opposite trading strategy where the trader buys a short-maturity option and sells a long-maturity option. A small profit arises if the stock price at the expiration of the short-maturity option is well above or well below the strike price of the short-maturity option. However, a significant loss results if it is close to the strike price.

Diagonal Spreads

Bull, bear, and calendar spreads can all be created from a long position in one call (put) and a short position in another call (put). In the case of bull and rear spreads, the calls (puts) have different strike prices and the same expiration date. In the case of calendar spreads, the calls (puts) have the same strike price and different expiration dates. In its diagonal spread both the expiration dates and the strike prices of the call (puts) are different. There are several types of diagonal spreads. Their profit pattern are generally variations on the profit patterns from the corresponding bull or spreads.

COMBINATIONS

A combination is an option trading strategy that involves taking a position in both calls and puts on the same stock. We will consider straddles, strips, straps, and strangles.

STRADDLE

One popular combination is a straddle, which involves buying a call and a put with the same strike price and expiration date. The profit pattern is shown in Figure 8.10. The strike price is denoted by X. If the stock price is close to this strike price at expiration of the options, the straddle leads to a loss. However, if there is a sufficiently large move in either direction, a significant profit will result the payoff from a straddle is calculated in Table 8.4. straddle is appropriate when a trader is expecting a large move in a stock price but does not know in which direction the move will be. Consider a trader who feels that the price of a certain stock, currently valued at Rs69 by the market. Will move significantly in the next three months. The trader could create astraddle by buying both a put and a call with a strike price of Rs70 and an expiration date in three months. Suppose that the call costs Rs4 and the put costs Rs3. If the stock price stays at Rs69, it is easy to see that the strategy costs the trader Rs6.

(An up- Straddle front investment of Rs7 is required, the call expires worthless, and the put expires worth Rs1.) If the stock price moves to Rs70, a loss of Rs7 is experienced- (This is the worst that can happen.)

Range of Stock Price	Pay off from call	Pay off from Put	Total Pay off
ST <X ST SX	0ST– X	X-ST 0	X – ST ST – X

However, if the stock price jumps to Rs90, a profit ofRs13 is made; if the stock moves down to Rs55, a profit of 'I; 8 is made; and so on. A straddle seems like a natural trading strategy when a big jump in the price of a company's stock is expected for example, when there is a takeover bid for the company or when the outcome of a major lawsuit is expected to be announced soon. However, this is not necessarily the case. If the general view of the market is that there will be a big jump in the stock price soon, that view will be reflected in the prices of. Options. A trader will find options on the stock to be significantly more expensive I than options on a similar stock. For which no jump is expected. For a straddle to be an t effective strategy, the trader must believe that there are likely to be big movements in the stock price, and this belief must be different from those of most other market participants.

The straddle in Figure 8.10 is sometimes referred to as a bottom straddle or straddle purchase. A top straddle or straddle write is the reverse position. It is created by selling a call and a put with the same exercise price and expiration date. It is a highly risky strategy. If the stock price on the expiration date is close to the strike price, a significant profit result. However, the loss arising from a large move in either direction is unlimited.

Strips and Strops

A strip consists of a long position in one call and two puts with the same strike price and one put with the same price and expiration data. A strap consists of a long position in two calls and one put with the same strike price and expiration data. The profit patterns from strips and straps are show in Figure 8.11. In a strip the trader is betting that there will be a big stock price move and considers a decrease in the stock price to be more likely than an increase. In a strap the trader is also betting that there will be a big stock price move. However, in a strap the trader is also betting that there will be a big stock price move. However, in this case, an increase in the stock price is considered to be more likely than a decrease.

Option strategies – in brief

Combining any of the four basic kinds of option trades (possibly with different exercise prices) and the two basic kinds of stock trades (long and short) allows a variety of options strategies. Simple strategies usually combine only a few trades, while more complicated strategies can combine several.

Covered call — Long the stock, short a call. This has essentially the same payoff as a short put.

Straddle — Long a call and long a put with the same exercise prices (a long straddle), or short a call and short a put with the same exercise prices (a short straddle).

Strangle — Long a call and long a put with different exercise prices (a long strangle), or short a call and short a put with different exercise prices (a short strangle).

Bull spread — Long a call with a low exercise price and short a call with a higher exercise price, or long a put with a low exercise price and short a put with a higher exercise price.

Bear spread — Short a call with a low exercise price and long a call with a higher exercise price, or short a put with a low exercise price and long a put with a higher exercise price.

Butterfly — Butterflies require trading options with 3 different exercise prices. Assume exercise prices X1 < X2 < X3 and that (X1 + X3) /2 = X

Long butterfly — long 1 call with exercise price X1, short 2 calls with exercise price X2, and long 1 call with exercise price X3. Alternatively, long 1 put with exercise price X1, short 2 puts with exercise price X2, and long 1 put with exercise price X3.

Short butterfly — short 1 call with exercise price X1, long 2 calls with exercise price X2, and short 1 call with exercise price X3. Alternatively, short 1 put with exercise price X1, long 2 puts with exercise price X2, and short 1 put with exercise price X3.

Box spreads — any combination of options that has a constant payoff at expiry. For example, combining a long butterfly made with calls, with a short butterfly made with puts will have a constant payoff of zero, and in equilibrium will cost zero. In practice any profit from these spreads will be eaten up by commissions (hence the name "alligator spreads").

FUTURES CONTRACT-MEANING

A futures contract is a type of derivative instrument, or financial contract, in which two parties agree to transact a set of financial instruments or physical commodities for future delivery at a particular price. If one buys a futures contract, he is basically agreeing to buy something that a seller has not yet produced for a set price. But participating in the futures market does not necessarily mean that he will be responsible for receiving or delivering large inventories of physical commodities, instead, buyers and sellers in the futures market primarily enter into futures contracts to hedge risk or speculate rather than to exchange physical goods (which is the primary activity of the cash/spot market). That is why futures are used as financial instruments by not only producers and consumers but also speculators.

The consensus in the investment world is that the futures market is a major financial hub, providing an outlet for intense competition among buyers and sellers and, more importantly, providing a center to manage price risks. The futures market is extremely liquid, risky and complex by nature, but can be understood

FUTURESCHARA CHARACTERISTICS

MARGINS

In the futures market, margin has a definition distinct from its definition in the stock market, where margin is the use of borrowed money to purchase securities. In the futures market, margin refers to the initial deposit of "good faith" made into an account in order to enter into a futures contract. This margin is referred to as good faith because it is this money that is used to debit any day-to-day losses.

When one opens a futures contract, the futures exchange will state a minimum amount of money that one must deposit into one's account which is called the initial margin. When the contract is liquidated, the initial margin plus or minus any gains or losses that occur over the span of the futures contract will be refunded. The minimum-level margin is determined by the futures exchange and is usually 5% to 10% of the futures contract. These predetermined initial margin amounts are continuously under review: at times of high market volatility, initial margin requirements can be raised.

The initial margin is the minimum amount required to enter into a new futures contract, but the maintenance margin is the lowest amount an account can reach before needing to be replenished. For example, if your margin account drops to a certain level because of a series of daily losses, brokers are required to make a margin call and request that you make an additional deposit into your account to bring the margin back up to the initial amount. When a margin call is made, the funds usually have to be delivered immediately. If they are not, the brokerage can have the right to liquidate your position completely in order to make up for any losses it may have incurred on your behalf.

Leverage

In the futures market, leverage refers to having control over large cash amounts of commodities with comparatively small levels of capital. In other words, with a relatively small amount of cash, you can enter into a futures contract that is worth much more than you initially have to pay (deposit into your margin account). It is said that in the futures market, more than any other form of investment, price changes are highly leveraged, meaning a small change in a futures price can translate into a huge gain or loss. Futures positions are highly leveraged because the initial margins that are set by the exchanges are relatively small compared to the cash value of the contracts in question (which is part of the reason why the futures market is useful but also very risky). The smaller the margin in relation to the cash value of the futures contract, the higher the leverage.

As a result of leverage, if the price of the futures contract moves up even slightly, the profit gain will be large in comparison to the initial margin. However, if the price just inches downwards, that same high leverage will yield huge losses in comparison to the initial margin deposit.

Pricing and Limits

Futures prices have a price change limit that determines the prices between which the contracts can trade on a daily basis. The price change limit is added to and subtracted from the previous day's close and the results remain the upper and lower price boundary for the day. The exchange can revise this price limit if it feels it's necessary. It's not uncommon for the exchange to abolish daily price limits in the month that the contract expires (delivery or "spot" month). This is because trading is often volatile during this month, as sellers and buyers try to obtain the best price possible before the expiration of the contract.

In order to avoid any unfair advantages, the futures exchanges impose limits on the total amount of contracts or units of a commodity in which any single person can invest. These are known as position limits and they ensure that no one person can control the market price for a particular commodity. Stock index futures are traded in terms of number of contracts. Each contract is to buy or sell a fixed value of the index. The value of the index is defined as the value of the index multiplied by the specified monetary amount. The monetary value is fixed by the exchange where the contract is traded. An index future is a future on the index i.e. the underlying is the index itself and no underlying security or a stock, which is to be delivered to fulfill the obligations. Index futures are cash settled. As other derivatives, the contract derives its value from the underlying index. The underlying indices in this case will be the various eligible indices and as permitted by the Regulator from time to time.

CONTRACT SPECIFICATION FOR INDEX FUTURES CONTRACTS

Contract Period	1, 2, 3 months
Tick size	0.05 index points index points
Price Quotation	: 30 a.m. to 3:30 p.m.
Trading Hours	Last Thursday of the contract month. If it is Holiday, the immediately preceding business day. Note: Business day is a day during which the
Last Trading/Expiration Day	Underlying stock market is open for trading.
Final Settlement	Cash Settlement. On the last trading day, the closing value of the underlying index would be the final settlement price of the expiring futures contract.

Sr. No.	Security Symbol	Underlying	Contract Multiplier
1	BSE	BSE SENSEX	25
2	TEK	BSE TECK INDEX	125
3	BNK	BSE BANKEX	50
4	OGX	BSE OIL & GAS INDEX	38
5	PSU	BSE PSU INDEX	50
6	MET	BSE METAL INDEX	25
7	FMC	BSE FMCG INDEX	175

Eligibility criteria for introducing Futures Option Contracts on Index

The Futures Options Contracts on an index can be issued only if 80% of the index constituents are individually eligible for derivatives trading. However, no single ineligible stock in the index shall have a weight age of more than 5% in the index. The index on which Futures and Options contracts are introduced shall be required to comply with the eligibility criteria on a monthly basis.

Discontinuance of Derivatives Contracts on index:

If the index fails to meet the above eligibility criteria for three months consecutively, then no fresh month contract shall be issued on that Index. However, the existing unexpired contracts shall be permitted to trade till expiry and new strike prices will continue to be introduced in the existing contracts.

IMPORTANCE OF INDEX FUTURES

Technical analysts thrive on their ability to predict the movement of the broad market indices. However, as they cannot trade the index, the normal practice is to try to capture a relation between the index and individual stocks. The introduction of the futures contract on stock indices gives them the opportunity to actually buy into the components of the index. The other important use of stock index futures is for hedging. Mutual funds and other institutional investors are the main beneficiaries. Hedging is a technique by which such institutions can protect their portfolios from market risks. There are three different views in the literature on the nature and purpose of hedging:

- Risk minimization.
- Profit maximization.

Reaching a satisfactory risk-return trade-off using a portfolio. Historically, stock index futures have supplemented, and often replaced, the secondary stock market as a stock price discovery mechanism. The futures market has heralded institutional participation in the market with increased velocity and concentration on stock-trading. Programmed-trading and index arbitrage are necessary for an efficient and thriving futures market. However, on the flip side, these strategies have increased the risks associated with stock specialists. The increased concentration, the velocity of futures trading, and the resultant increase in volatility in the stock market, may have a long-term impact on the participation of individual investors in the market. However, index futures provide investors an efficient and cost-effective means of hedging and significant improvements in market timing.

A SECURITY FUTURES

Contract is a legally binding agreement between two parties to buy or sell a specific quantity of shares of an individual stock or a narrow-based security index at a specified price, on a specified date in the future (known as the settlement or expiration date). If one buys a futures contract, he is entering into a contract to buy the underlying security and are said to be "long" the contract. Conversely, if one sells a futures contract, he is entering into a contract to sell the underlying security and are considered "short" the contract.

SECURITY FUTURES CONTRACT SPECIFICATIONS

Contract size - Typically, one single stock futures contract will represent 100 shares of the underlying stock. A narrow-based index futures contract will represent the value of the index times rupee amount set by the exchange.

Contract month - The month when the contract expires. There will be several different contract months available for trading at any one time, and the number of contract months may vary from exchange to exchange.

OFFSETTING TRANSACTIONS

Prior to expiration, one can realize the current gains or losses by executing an offsetting sale or purchase in the same contract (i.e., an equal and opposite transaction to the one that opened the position).

Example: Investor A is long one September ABC Corp. futures contract. To close out or offset the long position, Investor A would sell an identical September ABC Corp. contract. Investor B is short one October XYZ Corp. futures contract. To close out or offset the short position, Investor B would buy an identical October XYZ Corp. contract.

CONTRACT EXPIRATION AND DELIVERY

Any futures contract that hasn't been liquidated by an offsetting transaction before the contract's expiration date will be settled at that day's settlement price. The terms of the contract specify whether a contract will be settled by physical delivery - receiving or giving up the actual shares of stock - or by cash settlement. Where physical delivery is required, a holder of a short position must deliver the underlying security. Conversely, a holder of a long position must take delivery of the underlying shares. Where cash settlement is required, the underlying security is not delivered. Rather, any security futures contracts that are open are settled through a final cash payment based on the settlement price. Once this payment is made, neither party has any further obligations on the contract.

MARGIN & LEVERAGE

When a brokerage firm lends one part of the funds needed to purchase a security, such as common stock, the term "margin" refers to the amount of cash, or down payment, the customer is required to deposit. By contrast, a security futures contract is an obligation not an asset and has no value as collateral for a loan. When one enters into a security futures contract, he is required to make a payment referred to as a "margin payment" or "performance bond" to cover potential losses. For a relatively small amount of money (the margin requirement), a futures contract worth several times as much can be bought or sold. The smaller the margin requirement in relation to the underlying values of the futures contract, the greater the leverage. Because of this leverage, small changes in price can result in large gains and losses in a short period of time.

GAINS & LOSSES

Unlike stocks, gains and losses in security futures accounts are posted to the account every day, which are determined by the settlement price set by the exchange. If due to losses one's account falls below maintenance margin requirements, he will be required to place additional funds in the account to cover those losses.

TAX IMPLICATIONS

Sl. No.	Stock future market products	Product code
1.	ACC FUTURES	ACCFUT
2	ALLAHABAD BANK FUTURES	ALBKFUT
3	ALOK INDUSTRIES FUTURES	ALOKFUT
4	ARVIND MILLS FUTURES	ARVFUT
	ASHOK LEYLAND FUTURES	ASHFUT
5	BAJAJ AUTO FUTURES	BAJFUT
	BANK OF BARODA FUTURES	BOBFUT
6	BHARTI TELE FUTURES	BTLFUT
	BHEL FUTURES	BHEFUT
7	BOI FUTURES	BOIFUT
	BPCL FUTURES	BPCFUT
8	CANARA BANK FUTURES	CNBFUT
	CENTURY TEXTILES FUTURES	CENFUT
9	CIPLA FUTURES	CIPFUT
	DR. REDDY FUTURES	DRRFUT
10	GACL FUTURES	GACFUT
	GAIL FUTURES	GAILFUT
11	GESCO FUTURES	GESHFUT
12	GMR INFRASTRUCTURE FUTURES	GMRFUT
	GNFC FUTURES	GNFCFUT
13	GRASIM FUTURES	GRSFUT
	HCLTECH FUTURES	HCLTFUT
14	HDFC BANK FUTURES	HDBKFUT
	HDFC FUTURES	HDFFUT
15	HEROHONDA FUTURES	HEROFUT
	HINDALCO FUTURES	HNDFUT
16	HLL FUTURES	HLLFUT
	HPCL FUTURES	HPCFUT
17	ICICI BANK FUTURES	ICICFUT
	IDBI FUTURES	IDBIFUT
18	IDFC FUTURES	IDFCFUT
19	IFLEX FUTURES	IFLXFUT
	INDIA CEMENT FUTURES	INCMFUT
20	INDUSIND BANK FUTURES	INBKFUT
	INFOSYS FUTURES	INFFUT
21	IOCL FUTURES	IOCLFUT
	IPCL FUTURES	IPCLFUT
22	ITC FUTURES	ITCFUT
	JET AIRWAYS FUTURES	JETFUT
23	JHPL FUTURES	JHPFUT
24	JINDAL STEEL & POWER FUTURES	JNSTFUT
25	LIC HOUSING FINANCE FUTURES	LICHFUT
26	LNT FUTURES	LNTFUT
27	MAHINDRA & MAHINDRA FUTURES	MNMFUT
	MARUTI UDYOG FUTURES	MULFUT

Contd...

28	MTNL FUTURES	MTNFUT
29	NALCO FUTURES	NALCFUT
	NICHOLAS PIRAMAL FUTURES	NCPRFUT
30	NTPC FUTURES	NTPCFUT
	OBC FUTURES	OBCFUT
31	ONGC FUTURES	ONGCFUT
	ORCHID CHEMICALS FUTURES	ORCHFUT
32	PNB FUTURES	PNBFUT
	POLARIS FUTURES	POLAFUT
33	PUNJ LLYOD FUTURES	PNJFUT
	RANBAXY FUTURES	RBXFUT
34	RELENRG FUTURES	RENFUT
	RELIANCE CAPITAL FUTURES	RCAPFUT
35	RELIANCE COMMUNICATION Ltd Futures	RILFUT
36	RIL FUTURES 61 RPL FUTURES	RPLFUT
37	SAIL FUTURES	SAILFUT
38	SATYAM FUTURES	SATFUT
39	SBI FUTURES	SBIFUT
40	SCI FUTURES	SCIFUT
41	SIEMENS FUTURES	SIEMFUT
42	STERLITE INDS FUTURES	STERFUT
43	SUNTV FUTURES	SNTVFUT
	SUZLON FUTURES	SUZFUT
44	TATA CHEMICALS FUTURES	TCHMFUT
	TATA MOTORS FUTURES	TELFUT
45	TATA POWER FUTURES	TPWFUT
	TATA TEA FUTURES	TTEFUT
46	TCS FUTURES	TCSFUT
	TISCO FUTURES	TISFUT
47	UBI FUTURES	UBIFUT
	UTI BANK FUTURES	UTIBFUT
	VSNL FUTURES	VSNLFUT
	WIPRO FUTURES	WIPRFUT
	ZEE TELEFILMS LTD	ZEEFUT

The tax consequences of a security futures transaction may depend on the status of the taxpayer and the type of position (that is, long or short, covered or uncovered). For example, for most individual investors, security futures are not taxed as futures contracts. Short security futures contract positions are taxed at the short-term capital gains rate, regardless of how long the contract is held. Long security futures contracts may be taxed at either the long-term or short- term capital gains rate, depending on how long they are held. For dealers, however, security future contracts are taxed like other futures contracts at a blend of 60% long-term and 40% short-term capital gains rates. Depending on the type of trading strategy that is used, there can be additional or different tax consequences too.

VARIETY AND FUNGIBILITY OF SECURITY FUTURES CONTRACTS

Contract specifications may vary from contract to contract as well as from exchange to exchange. For instance, most security futures contracts require settling by making physical delivery of the underlying security, as opposed to making cash settlement. Carefully review the settlement and delivery conditions before entering into a security futures contract. At this time, security futures traded on one exchange are not "fungible" with security futures traded on another exchange. This means one will only be able to offset a position on the exchange where the original trade took place - even though a better price may be available for a comparable futures contract on the same underlying security or index on another exchange.

Contract Period	1, 2 & 3 months
Tick size	0.05 points i.e. 5 paisa
Price Quotation	Rupees per share.
Trading Hours	9:30 a.m. to 3:30 p.m.
Last Trading/Expiration Day	Last Thursday of the contract month. If it is holiday, then the immediately preceding business day. Note: Business day is a day during which the underlying Stock market is open for trading.
Final Settlement	Cash Settlement. On the last trading day, the closing value of the underlying stock is the final settlement price of the expiring futures contract.

ELIGIBILITY CRITERIA FOR INTRODUCING FUTURES OPTION CONTRACTS ON STOCKS

- The stocks would be chosen from amongst the top 500 stocks in terms of average daily market capitalization and average daily traded value in the previous six-month on a rolling basis.
- For a stock to be eligible, the median quarter-sigma order size over the last six months should not be less than Rs. 1 lac. For this purpose, a stock's quarter sigma order size shall mean the order size (in value terms) required to cause a change in the stock price equal to one-quarter of a standard deviation.
- The market wide position limit in the stock should not be less than Rs. 50 cores. Since, the market wide position limit in terms of number of shares is computed at the end of every month, the Exchange shall ensure that the stocks comply with this criterion before the introduction of new contracts. The market wide position limit in terms of number of shares shall be valued taking the closing prices of the stocks in the underlying cash market on the date of expiry of contract in the month.

Eligibility criteria for stocks on account of corporate restructuring:

All the following conditions should be met in the case of shares of a company undergoing restructuring through any means for eligibility to re- introduce derivative contracts on that company from the first day of listing of the post restructured company in the underlying market:

- The Futures and Options contracts on the stock of the original (pre-restructure) company were traded on any exchange prior to its restructuring. The pre restructured company had a market capitalization of at least Rs. 1000 cores prior to restructuring.
- The post restructure company would be treated like a new stock and if it is, in the opinion of the exchange, likely to be at least one third of the size of the pre structuring company in terms of revenues or assets or analyst valuations, and
- In the opinion of the exchange, the scheme of restructuring does not suggest that the post restructured company would have any characteristic that would render the company ineligible for derivatives trading.
- If the post restructured company comes out with an Initial Public Offering (IPO), then the same prescribed criteria as currently applicable for introduction of derivatives on a company coming out with an IPO is applied for introduction of derivatives on
- stocks of the post restructured company from its first day of listing.
- Discontinuance of Derivatives Contracts on stocks:
- No fresh month contracts shall be issued on the stocks under the following instances: If a stock does not conform to the above eligibility criteria for a consecutive period of three months, no fresh month contracts shall be issued on the same.
- If the stock remains in the banned position in the manner stated as per para 4 (I) (a), (b) (c) of the aforementioned SEBI circular, for a significant part of the month, consistently for three months, then no fresh month contracts shall be issued on those scraps. However, in both the above instances, the existing unexpired contracts shall continue to be available for trading till they expire on the last Thursdays of the respective months and new strike prices will continue to be introduced in the existing contracts.

DIFFERENCES BETWEEN SECURITY FUTURES AND STOCK OPTIONS

Although security futures share some characteristics in common with stock options, these products differ significantly. Most importantly, an option buyer may choose whether or not to exercise the option by the exercise date. Options purchasers who neither sell their options in the secondary market nor exercise them before they expire will lose the amount of the premium they paid for each option, but they cannot lose more than the amount of the premium. A security futures contract, on the other hand, is a binding agreement to buy or sell. Based upon movements in price of the underlying security, holders of a security futures contract can gain or lose many times their initial margin deposit.

TRADING SYSTEM

The futures market is a centralized marketplace for buyers and sellers from around the world who meet and enter into futures contracts. Pricing can be based on an open cry system, or bids and offers can be matched electronically. The futures contract will state the price that will be paid and the date of delivery. But don't worry, as we mentioned earlier, almost all futures contracts end without the actual physical delivery of the commodity.

The Players

The players in the futures market fall into two categories: hedgers and speculators.

Hedgers

Farmers, manufacturers, importers and exporters can all be hedgers. A hedger buys or sells in the futures market to secure the future price of a commodity intended to be sold at a later date in the cash market. This helps protect against price risks. The holders of the long position in futures contracts (the buyers of the commodity), are trying to secure as low a price as possible. The short holders of the contract (the sellers of the commodity) will want to secure as high a price as possible. The futures contract, however, provides a definite price certainty for both parties, which reduces the risks associated with price volatility. Hedging by means of futures contracts can also be used as a means to lock in an acceptable price margin between the cost of the raw material and the retail cost of the final product sold.

Speculators

Other market participants, however, do not aim to minimize risk but rather to benefit from the inherently risky nature of the futures market. These are the speculators, and they aim to profit from the very price change that hedgers are protecting themselves against. Hedgers want to minimize their risk no matter what they're investing in, while speculators want to increase their risk and therefore maximize their profits.

In the futures market, a speculator buying a contract low in order to sell high in the future would most likely be buying that contract from a hedge selling a contract low in anticipation of declining prices in the future. Unlike the hedger, the speculator does not actually seek to own the commodity in question. Rather, he or she will enter the market seeking profits by offsetting rising and declining prices through the buying and selling of contracts.

Trader	Short	Long
The Hedger	Secure a price now to protect against future declining prices	Secure a price now to protect against future rising prices
The Speculator	Secure a price now in anticipation of declining prices	Secure a price now in anticipation of rising prices

In a fast-paced market into which information is continuously being fed, speculators and hedgers bounce off of - and benefit from - each other. The closer it gets to the time of the contract's expiration, the more solid the information entering the market will be regarding the commodity in question. Thus, all can expect a more accurate reflection of supply and demand and the corresponding price. Futures contracts are traded on recognized exchanges. In India, both the NSE and the BSE introduced index futures in the S&P CNX Nifty and the BSE Sensex. The operations are similar to that of the stock market, the exception being that, in index futures, the marking-to-market principle is followed, and that is, the portfolios are adjusted to the market values on a daily basis. The Derivatives Trading at BSE takes place through a fully automated screen-based trading platform called as DTSS (Derivatives Trading and Settlement System). The DTSS is designed to allow trading on a real time basis. In addition to generating trades by matching opposite orders, the DTSS also generates various reports for the member participants.

ORDER MATCHING RULES

Order Matching will take place after order acceptance wherein the system searches for an opposite matching order. If a match is found, a trade will be generated. The order against which the trade has been generated will be removed from the system. In case the order is not exhausted further matching orders will be searched for and trades generated till the order gets exhausted or no more match-able orders are found. If the order is not entirely exhausted, the system will retain the order in the pending order book. Matching of the orders will be in the priority of price and timestamp. A unique trade-id will be generated for each trade and the entire information of the trade is sent to the members involved.

ORDER CONDITIONS

The derivatives market is order driven i.e. the traders can place only Orders in the system. Following are the Order types allowed for the derivative products. These order types have characteristics similar to ones in the cash market.

- Limit Order: An order for buying or selling at a limit price or better, if possible. Any unexecuted portion of the order remains as a pending order till it is matched or its duration expires.
- Market Order: An order for buying or selling at the best price
- prevailing in the market at the time of submission of the order.
- There are two types of Market orders:
  1. Partial fill rest Kill (PF): execute the available quantity and kill any unexecuted portion. Partial fill rest Convert (PC): execute the available quantity and convert any unexecuted portion into a limit order at the traded price.

Stop Loss: An order that becomes a limit order only when the market trades at a specified price.

- All orders shall have the following attributes:
- Order Type (Limit / Market PF/Market PC/ Stop Loss)
- The Asset Code, Product Type, Maturity, Call/Put and Strike Price.
- Buy/Sell Indicator
- Order Quantity
- Price
- Client Type (Own / Institutional / Normal) \
- Client Code
- Order Retention Type (GFD / GTD / GTC) Good for Day (GFD) The lifetime of the order is that trading session.
- Good Till Date (GTD) - The life of the order is till the number of days as specified by the Order Retention Period.

- Good Till Cancelled (GTC) - The order if not traded will remain in the system till it is cancelled or the series expires, whichever is earlier.
- Order Retention Period (in calendar days) this field is enabled only if the value of the previous attribute is GTD. It specifies the number of days the order is to be retained.
- Protection Points This is a field relevant in Market Orders and Stop Loss orders. The value enterable will be in absolute underlying points and specifies the band from the touchline price or the trigger price within which the market order or the stop loss order respectively can be traded.

Risk Reducing Orders (Y/N): When the member's collateral falls below 50 laces then he will be allowed to put only risk reducing orders and he will not be allowed to take any fresh positions. It is not essentially a type of order but a mode into which the member is put into when he violates his collateral limit. A member who has entered the risk-reducing mode will be allowed to put only

One risk reducing order at a time.

Session Timings

SESSION	FROM	TO
Beginning of the Day Session	8:00	9:00
Login Session	9:00	9:30
Trading Session	9:30	15:30
Position Transfer Session	15:30	15:50
Closing Session	15:50	16:05
Option Exercise Session	16:05	16:35
Margin Session	16:35	16:50
Query Session	16:50	17:35
End of Day Session	17:35	17:35

Price Bands

There are no maximum and minimum price ranges for Futures and Options Contracts. However, to avoid erroneous order entry, dummy price bands have been introduced in the Derivatives Segment. Further, no price bands are prescribed in the Cash Segment for stocks on which Futures & Options contracts are available for trading. Also, for those stocks which do not have Futures & Options Contracts available on them but are forming part of the index on which Futures & Options contracts are available, no price bands are attracted provided the daily average trading on such indices in the F & O Segment is not less than 20 contracts and traded on not less than 10 days in the preceding month.

Limited Trading Membership for Base Derivatives Segment

A Limited Trading Member (LTM) is a non-clearing trading participant having full trading rights and direct market access to the Derivatives Trading System of the Exchange.

- An LTM is provided with derivatives trading terminals for execution of trades either on his own account or on account of his clients.
- An LTM can issue contract notes to his clients in his own name.
- An LTM can exercise and perform trade and position management functions online and also check his payment obligations that may result from his trading activities.
- A LTM, however, cannot clear and settle trades executed by him directly with the Clearing House of the Exchange. For this purpose, we would need to enter into an arrangement with an existing Clearing Member of the Derivatives Segment of BSE. (A list of Clearing Members can be obtained from the Exchange.)

Advantages of becoming an LTM

1. Direct access to the on-line Derivatives Trading System of the Exchange
2. Trading in Option and Futures on Sensex, Single Stock Futures and options in eligible scraps and interest rate derivative instruments
3. Access to new products as and when they are introduced

Requirements for becoming an LTM

Individuals, firms, corporate and institutions, who are not members of the Cash Segment of BSE, can become LTM

- Minimum net worth of Rs. 25 lakhs
- A registration with SEBI
- One-time (non-refundable) contribution to Trade Guarantee Fund (TGF): Rs.1,00,000
  One-time (non-refundable) contribution to Investors Protection Fund (IPF): Rs.2,00,000
- Annual membership charges: Rs.25,000

LTM has to maintain a minimum-security deposit of Rs.7,50,000 with the Clearing Member and the same is available to him for the purpose of trading limits and initial margin requirements. The members are at present required to pay transaction charges at a Re. 0.25 per Rs.1, 00,000 of turnover which is appropriated towards TGF & IPF. Sub-brokers in the Cash Segment can become LTMs of the Derivatives Segment with minimum investment and significant advantages as mentioned above.

FUTURES STRATEGIES

Essentially, futures contracts try to predict what the value of an index of commodity will be at some date in the future. Speculators in the futures market can use different strategies to take advantage of rising and declining prices. The most common are known as going long, going short and spreads.

GOING LONG

When an investor goes long - that is, enters a contract by agreeing to buy and receive delivery of the underlying at a set price - it means that he or she is trying to profit from an anticipated future price increase.

GOING SHORT

A speculator who goes short - that is, enters into a futures contract by agreeing to sell and deliver the underlying at a set price - is looking to make a profit from declining price levels. By selling high now, the contract can be repurchased in the future at a lower price, thus generating a profit for the speculator.

SPREADS

Spreads involve taking advantage of the price difference between two different contracts of the same commodity. Spreading is considered to be one of the most conservative forms of trading in the futures market because it is much safer than the trading of long/short (naked) futures contracts. S There are many different types of spreads, including:

Calendar Spread - This involves the simultaneous purchase and sale of two futures of the same type, having the same price, but different delivery dates.

Aftermarket Spread - Here the investor, with contracts of the same month, goes long in one market and short in another market. For example, the investor may take Short June Wheat and Long June Pork Bellies.

Inter-Exchange Spread - This is any type of spread in which each position is created in different futures exchanges. For example, the investor may create a position in the Chicago Board of Trade (CBOT) and the London International Financial Futures and Options Exchange (LIFFE).

ADVANTAGE OF FUTURES INDEX

It is a risk hedge and caters to speculative instinct of investors. It is a more efficient method of controlling risk on a portfolio, as it reduces the" transactions trading costs and price pressure. Neither the buyer nor the seller pays the full value of the underlying asserts but deals only in differences, in cash without involving delivery of the assets. The futures smoothen the asset reallocation, provides hedge hedge inflows or outflows of cash and reduces the impact of bullish and bearish ling as futures do not involve full payment on receipt both the underlying assets is a dealing in differences.

OPERATION OF HEDGE OF RISK

To illustrate the coverage of risk, assume that you expect a future cash inflow of Rs.50, 000 a month hence, which you wish to invest in equities. But the market is bullish and prices are expected to rise. Then you buy an index future contract to be the expected rise in price. You can also sell short if the market is expected to fall in prices. Suppose, you have the securities in your portfolio and expect the market to fall then you can sell the futures, instead of the securities. If the actual fall lore than the expected price, you will receive the difference in cash. A bullish expectation makes you buy the futures contract and a bearish expectation makes you the futures contract. If your expectations are correctly realized, you can make they on the deals without actually buying and selling the underlying securities. s will enable you to trade on a smaller investment as the margins you have to p for trading in Futures is generally 6 to 10%, and the loss of interest money is expensive then the loss of interest on a bigger outlay involved in buying and mg for deliveries of underlying securities or shares or bonds.

FUTURES ON FIXED INCOME SECURITIES

Investment strategies of fixed income securities are fairly simple when compared to equity as they invest in government securities, corporate bonds, etc where the returns are fixed. Though fixed income securities have much lower risks than equities, they are not completely risk free either. The following are the various risks associated with them.

CREDIT RISK

Credit risk is the possibility of default in the repayment of principal and interest by a borrower. Among fixed income securities, corporate bonds carry the highest credit risk. If the issuing company falls into serious financial difficulties, there is every possibility that repayment will be delayed considerably and may never even be made. Funds reduce this risk by investing only in bonds issued by companies with good credit rating. However, a good credit rating is no guarantee that the company would continue to perform well in future and honor all its financial commitments.

Government securities carry no credit risk, as the issuer can never default, and are backed by the sovereign guarantee of the country and are called sovereign securities. However, they carry lower returns than other fixed income securities.

LIQUIDITY RISK

Liquidity in any market refers to the possibility for traders to enter and exit positions with relative ease in relation to volume and size of transactions. Highly liquid markets also reduce the impact costs of transactions which result from fluctuations in prices when large transactions are pushed through in a less liquid market. (The difference between the market price before the sale offer and the price at which the bonds are sold constitutes the impact cost for the seller). The market for government securities and short-term money markets are very liquid where the impact costs are almost negligible, but, the returns offered by these assets are much lower than the relatively illiquid corporate bonds.

PRICE RISKS

Corporate bonds will always be rated by a reputed rating agency for their creditworthiness which may be changed to reflect the changes in the economy, industry or the company in question. These rate changes can affect the market prices of the bonds. This exposes the fund investing in such bonds to a price risk.

INTEREST RATE RISKS

Market prices of all fixed income securities are largely dependent on the prevailing interest rate in the economy. If interest rates are expected to come down in future, bonds issued in the past would become more attractive and vice versa. Almost all investments made by fixed income funds are subject to interest rate risks. But, the securities with longer maturities are more volatile than shorter term securities.

OTHER RISKS

Indian mutual funds are allowed to invest in overseas fixed income securities denominated in a foreign currency. Such investments are subject to fluctuations in currency values. They are also exposed to various political and economic risks associated with the country in which the security was issued.

HEDGING BY FIXED INCOME FUNDS

Like equity funds, fixed income funds can also hedge their price risks by entering into derivative transactions. However, fixed income derivatives are not easily understood and they are not traded in an open market like stock futures. Two common derivatives used by fixed income funds are:

INTEREST RATE SWAPS

Interest rates are of two types, fixed interest rates and floating rates which vary according to changes in a standard benchmark interest rate. An investor holding a security which pays a floating interest rate is exposed to interest rate risk. The investor can manage this risk by entering into an interest rate swap. An interest rate swap is a financial agreement between two parties to swap or exchange interest obligations of varying nature for an agreed period. The contract will specify the interest rates, the benchmark rate to be followed, the notional principal amount for the transaction, etc. For example, take the case of a mutual fund which has invested Rs.50 core in a floating interest bond of one-year maturity. The interest payable by the issuer of the bond is not fixed and will vary with the changes in the benchmark interest rate specified.

The mutual fund can enter into an interest rate swap agreement with a counter party who will guarantee to pay interest at a fixed rate, say 10 per cent, on the notional amount of Rs.50 core for a period of one year. In return, the fund will guarantee to pay the counter party interest at the benchmark rate on Rs.50 core for one year. In other words, the fund will pass on the interest received on its investment in floating rate bond to the counter party and receive a fixed interest in return.

In practice, at the end of the contract period the total interest payable by each party is calculated and the net amount is settled in cash. If the benchmark rate, compounded daily for one year as it fluctuates on a daily basis, is lower than 10 per cent the mutual fund will receive the difference from the counter party. If it is the other way round the fund will pay the difference to the counter party. Either way, the fund is assured of an interest rate of 10 per cent whatever happens to the benchmark rate.

FORWARD RATE AGREEMENTS

A forward rate agreement, commonly known as FRA, is another form of interest rate swap. Under an FRA, the parties agree to pay and receive the difference between a fixed interest rate and the benchmark interest rate prevailing on a future date. As in the case of a swap, the interest rate, the benchmark rate and the notional amount will be mentioned in the contract. The difference is that unlike a swap in which the benchmark interest rate for a period is considered and is calculated on a daily compounding basis, an FRA considers the benchmark date only on a specified future date.

Funds having fixed income derivative positions are exposed to counter party risk. This is the risk of parties on the other side of the derivative transactions failing to honor their contractual commitments. Since fixed income derivatives are not traded on recognized stock exchanges like stock derivatives, counter party risk is higher in their case.

VALUATION OF INDEX FUTURES

If an investor invests in B.S.E. 30 index he will collect dividends on the scraps he holds and his principal value may go up or down depending on the index. In the case of the futures index, the investor will get the same outcome as if he invests all his money in riskless Treasury bills and enters into a futures contract for future delivery of the index. The futures then must sell at a price equal to today's price of the index plus a premium equal to risk free return plus dividend on the index shares. To show this symbolically let Fe be the price of the futures, Fs is today's price of futures, is current price of the Index and D is dividend on the index shares, and IE is the index price at the expiration date.

The Index price (that is Fad < I.) and (RF<D). Return to Index = Index price at Expiration – Current Index Price+ Dividend = IE- IB+D.

Return to Futures= Futures price at Expiration – Current futures price+ Interest on risk free asset= FE- FB+RF

The above equation means that the present price of futures, will equal present price of Index plus the "cost of carry", which equals (Rc - D), namely, the interest obtainable on risk-free asset (Rc) minus dividend on Index Shares (D). The cost of purchasing the Index Shares is substantially higher than the cost of buying the futures contract for the same index. The money used to buy the futures will involve interest cost and by not buying the shares, dividends are lost. Assume that the money used to purchase the index shares is invested in Treasury bills to give risk free return (RC). If RC is less than the dividends lost, the futures price will be below the Index price (that is Fad < I.) and (RF<D).

FUTURES ON BOND

While stock index future provides low cost and efficient method of insuring inst systematic risk of the portfolio, futures on bonds and Treasury bills provide risk coverage to interest rate risk, which is the largest source of systematic risk lading fixed income securities. In the case of index futures, delivery is in cash settlements only but in the case Futures on Treasury bills or bonds, delivery is in bills or bonds. In the U.S., Treasury note futures are more popular and easier to understand and operate. These contracts are available for delivery dates in March, June, Sept. and Dec. for delivery dates of up to two years from the current date. Yields are basic unit on which prices are determined.

Portfolio can have reduced duration by selling short in futures and increased duration by buying futures. If cash is expected and interest rates are likely to futures pushing up the prices of bonds, then investor can go tong in futures and when funds come in, the futures can be converted into cash purchase of bonds or the underlying security. The opposite stand can be taken (if an) outflow of cash is expected at a one specific time period in future.

Hedging Effect

Hedging in futures can be done to reduce the interest rate risk. A futures f position can be taken to offset the risk in the cash market. Thus, a ten-year bond is likely to suffer capital loss due to rise in yields and that is held in the portfolio of the investor. The risk can be hedged by an appropriate sale of that security -backed future. If the loss on the existing security is offset by the gain in the futures contract then it is called a perfect hedge. The difference between futures price and cash price is called the basis and the risk of variance of this basis is called basis risk. The above bond's risk is substantial when the cross hedging is one. Cross hedging is hedging in a bland future, which is not identical with the bland to be hedged and held in the portfolio. A hedged position thus creates a basis risk which can be reduced or eliminated by taking extreme caution and use of expertise in anticipation of the proper time and bond to be hedged.

YIELD ENHANCEMENT EFFECT

The futures on fixed income security, say a bond, can be used to improve yields also. What hedging has done is to reduce the risk on the portfolio by holding a long-term bond for a short maturity. As the price of the futures is fixed, the risk is nil on this period of the futures say 3 months, and the ten-year bond of 10 years, purch3Sed will have greater risk than a riskless bond of 3months in futures plus a 9-year 9-month bond in the portfolio. The holding of a riskless bond for short period... of time in the futures, reduces the risk. This process may, or may not increase the yield however.

To enhance the yields, the yield on the synthetic security should be higher than on the cash market security. This synthetic security is created by being short in a three months futures Treasury bill along with a long position in the cash market. If the yield on the three-month Treasury bill is higher say 6.6% as against the Treasury bill yield in cash market of 6.4%, then the portfolio will benefit, from higher yield of 0.2% on the synthetic security, in the futures market.

SECURITY FUTURES RISKS

All security futures contracts involve risk, and there is no trading strategy that can eliminate it. Strategies using combinations of positions, such as spreads may be as risky as outright long or short futures positions. The following specific risks involved when trading security futures contracts:

- Trading security futures contracts may result in potentially unlimited losses that are greater than the amount deposited with the broker. As with any high-risk financial product, one should not risk any money that one cannot afford to lose, such as: retirement savings, medical and other emergency funds, funds set aside for education or home ownership, or funds required meeting living expenses.
- Be cautious of claims that one can make large profits from trading security futures. Although the high degree of leverage in futures can result in large and immediate gains, it can also result in large and immediate losses. As with any financial product, there is no such thing as a "sure winner."
- Because of the leverage involved and the nature of futures transactions, one may feel the effects of his losses immediately. Unlike holdings in traditional securities, gains and losses in security futures are credited or debited to one's account on a daily basis at a minimum. Daily market moves may require one to have or make additional funds available. If one's account is under the minimum margin requirements set by the exchange or the firm, his position may be liquidated at a loss, and he will be liable for any deficit in his account.
- Under some market conditions, it may be difficult or impossible to hedge or liquidate a position. If one cannot hedge or liquidate his position, any existing losses may continue to mount. Even if one can hedge or liquidate his position, he may be forced to do so at a price that involves a large loss. This can occur, for example:

If trading is halted due to unusual trading activity in either the security futures contracts or the underlying security, if trading is halted due to recent news events involving the issuer of the underlying security, if computer systems failures occur on an exchange or at the firm carrying one's position, or If the market is illiquid and therefore doesn't have enough trading interest to get a good price.

Under some market conditions, the prices of security futures may not maintain their customary or anticipated relationships to the prices of the underlying security or index. This can occur, for example, when the market for the security futures contract is illiquid and lacks trading interest, when the primary market for the underlying security is closed, or when the reporting of transactions in the underlying security has been delayed. For index products, this could also occur when trading is delayed or halted in some or all of the securities that make up the index.

May experience losses due to computer systems failures. As with any financial transaction, one may experience losses if the orders cannot be executed normally due to systems failures on a regulated exchange or at the firm carrying the position and the losses may be greater if the brokerage firm does not have adequate back-up systems or procedures.

Placing contingent orders, if permitted, such as "stop-loss" or "stop-limit" orders, will not necessarily limit your losses to the intended amount. Market conditions may make it impossible to execute the order or to get the stop price.

Day trading strategies involving security futures pose special risks. As with any financial product, seeking to profit from intra-day price movements poses a number of risks, including increased trading costs, greater exposure to leverage, and heightened competition with professional traders.

SOME TECHNICAL TERMS

Futures contract - a futures contract is (1) an agreement to purchase or sell a commodity for delivery in the future; (2) at a price determined at initiation of the contract; (3) that obligates each party to the contract to fulfill it at the specified price; (4) that is used to assume or shift risk; and (5) that may be satisfied by delivery or offset.

Narrow-based security index - In general, an index that has any one of the following four characteristics: (1) it has nine or fewer component securities; (2) any one of its component securities make up more than 30% of its weighting; (3) the five highest weighted component securities together make up more than 60% of its weighting; or (4) the lowest weighted component securities making up, in the aggregate, 25% of the index's weighting have an aggregate dollar value of average daily trading volume of less than $50 million (or in the case of an index with 15 or more component securities, $30 million).

Nominal value - The face value of the futures contract, obtained by multiplying the contract price by the number of shares or units per contract. If XYZ stock index futures are trading at $.50.25 and the contract is for 100 shares of XYZ stock, the nominal value of the futures contract would be $5,025.

Settlement price - 1) The daily price that the clearing organization uses to mark open positions to market for determining profit and loss and margin calls and for invoicing deliveries in physical delivery contracts, 2) The price at which open cash settlement contracts are settled on the last trading day and open physical delivery contracts are invoiced for delivery.

Spread - 1) Holding a long position in one futures contract and a short position in a related futures contract or contract month in order to profit from an anticipated change in the price relationship between the two, 2) The price difference between two contracts or contract months.

MULTIPLE CHOICE QUESTIONS AND FILL IN THE BLANKS

1. The underlying asset of a derivative contract can be ______.
   a. Only equity
   b. Only interest rate
   c. Only commodities
   d. all of the above

2. The losses of option buyer are ______.
   a. Unlimited
   b. Limited to the extent of premium paid
   c. Generally larger than the premium paid
   d. None of the above.
3. In the F&O trading system, execution priority of orders stored in the oder book is based on:
   a. Time price priority (i.e. first priority is given to the time of the order entry)
   b. Price time priority (i.e. first priority is given to the price of the order Entry)
   c. Both price and time is given equal priority
   d. The first order which comes to the system will get executed first
4. The minimum tick for an index options contract is:
   a. 0.01 Paisa
   b. 0.05 Paisa
   c. 0.10 Paisa
   d. 0.50 Paisa
5. The stock options contracts traded at NSE are of ______.
   a. American Style
   b. Asian Style
   c. Indian Style
   d. European Style
6. The trading cycle for Index futures contracts may be described as:
   a. The contracts with a maximum of three-month trading cycle-the near month (one), the next month (two) and the far month (Three).
   b. The contracts with a maturity period of one year with three months continuous contracts for the first three months and fixed quarterly contracts for the entire year
   c. The contracts with a maturity period of one year, with fixed quarterly contracts only.
   d. None of the above.
7. Which of the following is false regarding the eligibility of a stock to be traded in the F&O segment?
   a. The stock shall be chosen from amongst the top 500 stock in terms of average daily market capitalisation and average daily traded value in the previous six month on a rolling basis.
   b. For a security to be added in the F&O segment that stock's median quarter-sigma order size over the last six months shall be at least Rs.1 lakh.
   c. Once a security is introduced for trading in the derivatives segment, it will continue to be eligible for trading in derivatives segment, even if the median quarter-sigma order size of the Security is less than Rs.5 lakh continuously.

d. For unlisted companies coming out with initial public offering, if the net public offer is Rs.500 core or more, then the exchanges may consider introducing stock options and stock futures on such stocks at the time of its listing in the cash market.

8. According to the Standard Pricing Models, what are the factors that affect value of an option at a given point in time?
   a. Underlying Market Price
   b. Volatility (variability) of underlying instrument
   c. Time to Expiration
   d. All of the above

9. For which of the following derivative products/instruments trading facilities on the F&O segment of NSE are not provided currently?
   a. Index options
   b. Individual stock futures
   c. Interest rate futures
   d. Currency Swaps.

10. Which of the following order type/condition is not available in the F&O trading system at NSE?
    a. Market If Touched (MIT)
    b. Day order
    c. Immediate or Cancel (IOC)
    d. Stop-Loss orders.

11. Mar. Paul has placed a stop–loss buy order for the security XYZ Ltd, in the F&O trading system. The following are the details of the order: The trigger price is kept at Rs.1027.00 and the limit price is kept at Rs.1030.00. This order will be released into the system in which of the following scenarios:
    a. The market price of the security reaches or exceeds Rs.1027.00
    b. Only if the market price of the security reaches or exceeds Rs.1030.00
    c. Only if the market price of the security falls below Rs.1027.00
    d. The market price of the security reaches or exceeds Rs.1024.00

12. Revenue securities Ltd., a trading member in F&O segment has executed a client trade in options segment. Given the following details of the trade, what is the maximum brokerage the trading member can charge from the client for the above trade? The Strike price of the contract is 250, Traded premium is 10 and the traded quantity is 800.
    a. Rs.520 b. Rs.200
    c. Rs.5000 d. Rs.5200

13. Spot value of Nifty is 1240. An investor buys a one-month Nifty 1255 Call option for a premium of Rs. 7. The option is said to be _________.

    a. in-the-money b. at-the-money

    c. out-of-the-money d. above-the money Correct answer: (c)

14. ....is a type of contract between 2 persons where one person grants the other person the right to buy or to sell a specific asset at a specific price within a specific time period. The most often options are used in the trading of securities. (Option)
15. Two main types of option contracts: .... (call option and put option).
16. .... (Call option) gives the buyer the right to buy (to call away) a specific number of shares of a specific company from the option writer at a specific purchase price at any time up to including a .... (specific date).
17. .... (Put option) gives the buyer the right to sell (to put away) a specific number of shares of a specific company to the option writer at a specific selling price at any time up to including a specific date.
18. The most important characteristics of option contract are exercise price or.......... (strike price) and expiration date. Exercise price is the purchase or selling price for the underlying shares. Expiration date defines the time than the option contract expires.
19. The value of .... (put or call options) is closely related with the market value/ price of the security that underlies the option.
20. .... (Intrinsic value) for call option will be 0, if the underlying stock price at the end of expiration period is less than the exercise price, intrinsic value of call option will be.................. (positive), if the underlying stock price at the end of expiration period is higher than the exercise price, because the investor will use call option to buy the underlying stock at exercise price as this price is more.............. (favourable) (lower) than price in the market.
21. ....(Intrinsic value) for put option will be 0, if the underlying stock price at the end of expiration period is higher than the exercise price, intrinsic value of put option will be positive, if the underlying stock price at the end of expiration period is lower than the exercise price, because the investor will use put option to sell the underlying stock at exercise price as this price is more ....((favourable (higher)) than price in the market.
22. .... (In the money) "is a situation in which strike price of the option is below the market price of underlying stock for a call, or the strike price is above the market price of the underlying stock for a put.
23. .... (Out of money) "is a situation in which strike price of the option is above the market price of underlying stock for a call, or the strike price is below the market price of the underlying stock for a put.
24. .... (At the money) "is used to denote an option (put or call) whose strike price is at or near the price of underlying stock.

25. .... (Option premium) is the quoted price the investor pays to buy put or call option. Option premium is used to describe the market price of option.

26. .... (The time value) reflects the option's potential appreciation and can be calculated as the difference between the option price (premium) and intrinsic value.

27. The profit or loss of using options is defined as difference between the............ (intrinsic value of the option and option premium).

28. .... (Option strategy) known as straddle involves buying (or writing) both a call and put options on the same stock, with the options having the same exercise price and expiration date.

29. .... (Hedging) with options is especially attractive because they can give protection against loss or the stock protects the option against loss. Hedging reduces the dispersion of possible outcomes to the investor. There is a floor below which losses cannot be increased, while the size of the loss would be limited to the option premium paid.

30. .... (Index option) is based on stock index instead of an underlying stock. When index option is exercised, settlement is made by cash payment, not delivery of shares.

31. Using..................... (hedging strategies) very important characteristic is the hedge ratio of the portfolio. Hedge ratio is a number of stocks to buy or sell with options such that the future portfolio value is risk-free.

32 .... (Riskless (perfect) hedge) is such a hedge which allows in each moment given to compensate the decrease in prices of the stocks by increase in value of option.

MULTIPLE CHOICE QUESTIONS

1. Which of the following is a contract where both parties are committed?

   a. Forward b. Future

   c. Both the above d. Option

2. Swaps can be based on

   a. Interest b. Principal and Interest

   c. Equity d. Any of the above

3. An option to buy an underlying is called

   a. Forward b. Call

   c. Put d. None of the above

4. If the security is priced at Rs. 300, what will be the price in 1 month, taking continuous compounding rate of 7%?

   a. Rs. 321 b. Rs. 301.75

   c. Rs. 301.76 d. Rs. 301.74

5. Which of the following is exercisable before expiry?
   a. Forward b. Future
   c. American call d. European put
6. Normal distribution is denoted by the following symbol
   a. ND b. A
   c. O d. n
7. Mean ± 2 Standard Deviation covers ______ % of the area under the curve.
   a. 95.45 b. 68.27
   c. 99.73 d. 62.50%
8. Normal distribution is a suitable assumption to capture the behaviour of stock prices.
   a. True b. False
9. The value of 'e' is
   a. 2.81728 b. 2.71282
   c. 2.71828 d. 2.82718
10. Volatility is of little practical relevance in estimation the value of options.
    a. True b. False
11. Binomial model assumes that over a short period of time, a stock can take either of two prices, which may be higher or lower than the current price.
    a. True b. False
12. Which of the following is true?
    a. Delta of a call option is positive b. Delta of a put option is negative
    c. Both the above d. None of the above
13. Delta hedging can be costly because:
    a. Option premia are higher for delta hedges as compared to regular trading
    b. Exchange imposes additional margins for delta hedges
    c. Risk-free rate to be used is higher
    d. Delta hedge entails buying shares in a rising market, and selling them in a falling market
14. On maturity, there is no difference in valuation of European and American options.
    a. True b. False
15. Binomial model of option pricing can be used in which of the following cases
    a. European Call b. European Put
    c. American Call d. All the above

16. Suppose a stock, trading at Rs. 60, has volatility of 25% p.a. A 1-month option on that stock has exercise price of Rs. 58. Risk-free rate is 6% p.a. What would be its price if it is a European Call?

    a. Rs. 3.08 b. Rs. 3.03
    c. Rs. 2.97 d. Rs. 2.93

17. Suppose a stock, trading at Rs. 60, has volatility of 25% p.a. A 1-month option on that stock has exercise price of Rs. 58. Risk-free rate is 6% p.a. What would be its price if it is a European Put?

    a. Rs. 0.79 b. Rs. 0.83
    c. Rs. 1.02 d. Rs. 0.93

18. Suppose a stock, trading at Rs. 60, has volatility of 25% p.a. A 1-month option on that stock has exercise price of Rs. 58. Risk-free rate is 6% p.a. The continuous dividend yield on the stock is 3%. What would be its price if it is a European Call?

    a. Rs. 3.08 b. Rs. 3.03
    c. Rs. 2.97 d. Rs. 2.93

19. Suppose a stock, trading at Rs. 60, has volatility of 25% p.a. A 1-month option on that stock has exercise price of Rs. 58. Risk-free rate is 6% p.a. The continuous dividend yield on the stock is 3%. What would be its price if it is a European Put?

    a. Rs. 0.79 b. Rs. 0.83
    c. Rs. 1.02 d. Rs. 0.93

20. is a measure of sensitivity of the value of an option to its stock price.

    a. Delta b. Theta
    c. Gamma d. Rho

21. As the call option goes deeper in the money, its delta gets closer to

    a. 0 > -1 > 1 b. Infinity

22. Other things remaining the same, Gamma is the same for both call and put contracts

    a. True b. False

23. Call on a dividend paying stock can have a positive theta.

    a. True b. False

24. Other things remaining the same, Vega is the same for both call and put contracts

    a. True b. False

25. is a measure of sensitivity of the value of an option to risk-free rate.

    a. Delta b. Theta
    c. Gamma d. Rho

26. Annual volatility is calculated by multiplying the standard deviation by
    a. 252
    b. V252
    c. 2522
    d. Depends on frequency of data
27. ARCH Models are characterised by
    a. Equal importance to all data
    b. More importance to more recent data
    c. More importance to data relating to stable market conditions
    d. None of the above
28. EWMA stands for
    a. Excess Weighted Moving Average
    b. Exponentially Weighted Moving Average
    c. Exponentially Weighted Market Average
    d. Excess Weighted Markovitz Average
29. Historic volatility depends on
    a. Periodicity of data
    b. Period covered by the data
    c. Model used
    d. All the above
30. Which of the following is true?
    a. Option premia in market depend on historical volatility
    b. Theoretic valuation of option depends on implied volatility
    c. Both the above
    d. None of the above
31. In which of the following is the loss unlimited?
    a. Long call
    b. Long put
    c. Short call
    d. Short put and Short call
32. In a long call, maximum loss is
    a. Premium paid
    b. Exercise price plus premium
    c. Exercise price minus premium
    d. Market price minus exercise price
33. In a short call, profit is
    a. Unlimited
    b. Limited to premium
    c. Premium plus Market price minus exercise price
    d. Premium minus exercise price
34. The pay-off in which of the following is asymmetric?
    a. Stock
    b. Options
    c. Both the above
    d. None of the above

35. A long-put position break even at
    a. The premium
    b. The exercise price
    c. Exercise price minus premium
    d. Exercise price plus premium
36. All options on the same underlying
    a. Are traded in the same exchange
    b. Belong to the same class
    c. Belong to the same series
    d. Are settled by the same settlement house.
37. Protective put is same as
    a. Synthetic long put
    b. Synthetic long call
    c. Covered put
    d. Covered call
38. Pay-off in a covered call is similar to
    a. Long call
    b. Long stock
    c. Short put
    d. Short call
39. In a bull spread, the investor makes profits if market goes
    a. Up
    b. Down
    c. Sideways
    d. None of the above
40. Butter fly entails strikes
    a. 1 > 2
    b. 3
    c. 4
41. In a reverse calendar spread, the option bought is of a shorter maturity than the option sold.
    a. True
    b. False
42. In a diagonal spread, which of the following remains constant?
    a. Underlying
    b. Underlying & Strike
    c. Underlying & Maturity
    d. Underlying, Strike & Maturity
43. In option, the pay-off depends on the average price of the underlying during the tenor of the contract.
    a. American
    b. European
    c. Asian
    d. Dutch
44. Which of the following is true of compound options?
    a. Based on calls or puts
    b. Two strike prices
    c. Two strike dates
    d. All the above
45. Which of the following is a binary option?
    a. Cash or nothing
    b. Stock or nothing
    c. Both the above
    d. None of the above

46. Asset or nothing Put options are valued at

    a. S0e-qTN(-d1)
    b. Soe-qTN(d1)
    c. Soe-qTN(-d2)
    d. Soe-qTN(d2)

47. Knock in option is a type of barrier option

    a. True
    b. False

48. A shout option is one which is traded through open cry system in the trading floor.

    a. True
    b. False

49. Put-Call ratio is used as a lead indicater of market swings.

    a. True
    b. False

50. Higher put-call ratio is indicative that the market expects in the market / stock.

    a. Increase
    b. Decrease
    c. Sideways movement
    d. None of the above

51. Increase in put-call ratio in a bullish market is an indication of trend reversal.

    a. True
    b. False

52. In general, an uptrend in prices, together with rise in trading volumes and open interest is a signal.

    a. Bearish
    b. Bullish
    c. Mixed
    d. Weak

53. A large percentage of roll overs indicates that the market participants expect the trend to continue.

    a. True
    b. False

54. The near month, middle month and far month open positions are 100, 200 and 300. What is the roll-over?

    a. One-third
    b. One-half
    c. One-fourth
    d. Two-third

SHORT ANSWER QUESTIONS

1. Define Options
2. Reasons for using Options.
3. Define Working of options.
4. What are the types of Options?
5. Define Pricing of Options
6. What are the Factors affecting the Option premium
7. Define Option zones

8. Explain Assumptions and Notations
9. Define Upper and Lower boundaries for option prices
10. Define Greeks
11. Define Trading Strategies
12. Define Bull Market Strategies
13. Define Bear Market Strategies
14. What are Volatile Market Strategies?
15. What are Stable Market Strategies?
16. Futures Contract - Meaning
17. What are the Characteristics Futures
18. Contract specification for Index futures contracts.
19. Eligibility Criteria for introducing futures option contracts on Index.
20. Importance of index futures.
21. Define Security Futures
22. Define Cataract specifications for single stock futures.
23. Eligibility criteria for introducing futures option contracts on stocks.
24. Security Futures Vs stock options.
25. Define Trading system.
26. Define the players
27. Define Order matching rules.
28. Define Order conditions
29. Define Session timings
30. Define Price bands.
31. Limited trading membership
32. What are Futures strategies?
33. Advantages of Future Index
34. Future on fixed income securities.
35. Hedging by fixed income funds.
36. Valuations of index futures.
37. Define Futures of bonds.
38. Define Security futures risks.

ESSAY TYPE QUESTIONS

1. Distinguish between a put and a call.
2. What does it mean to say „an option buyer has a right but not an obligation?
3. Explain the following terms used with the options:
   (a) „In the money "
   (b) „Out of money "
   (c) „At the money "
4. What is the difference between option premium and option price?
5. What is the relationship between option prices and their intrinsic value?
6. Why is the call or put writer 's position considerably different from the buyer 's position?
7. What is an index option? What are the main differences between index option and stock option?
8. How can a put used to protect a particular investors position?
9. What is the maximum amount the buyer of an option can loses?
10. Draw the profit/ loss graph for the following option strategies:
    (a) Buy a put with Rs.3 premium and Rs.70 exercise price;
    (b) Write a call with Rs. 2 premium and Rs. 50 exercise prices.
11. Robert has only one day left to decide whether to exercise a call option on the Company X stock, which he purchased six months ago for Rs.300. (Rs. 3 per share). The call option exercise price is Rs.54.
    (a) For what range of stock price should Robert exercise the call on the last day of the call life?
    (b) For what range of stock price would Robert realize a loss (including the premium paid for the call option)?

MCQs Answers

1	2	3	4	5	6	7	8	9	10	11	12	13	14	15	16	17	18	19	20	21	22	23	24	25
c	d	b	c	c	c	a	b	c	b	b	c	d	a	d	a	a	c	b	a	c	a	a	a	d
26	27	28	29	30	31	32	33	34	35	36	37	38	39	40	41	42	43	44	45	46	47	48	49	50
d	b	c	b	d	a	c	a	b	b	c	b	b	c	a	c	a	a	c	d	c	a	a	b	a
51	52	53	54																					
b	a	b	a																					

CASE STUDIES

CASE STUDY 1

1. Robert has only one day left to decide whether to exercise a call option on the Company X stock, which he purchased six months ago for Rs.300 (Rs.3 per share). The call option exercise price is Rs. 54.
   (a) For what range of stock price should Robert exercise the call on the last day of the call life?
   (b) For what range of stock price would Robert realize a loss (including the premium paid for the call option)?
2. Using information about several call and put options in the table below, identify, which of these options are „in the money ", „at the money "or „out of money "and fulfil the last column in the table.

Type of option	Exercise price Rs.	Premium Rs.	Current price of underlying stock Rs.	Your evaluation
Call	18	0.25	19.50	
Put	30	0.50	31.20	
Call	24	0.25	21.40	
Call	45	0.30	46.10	
Put	60	1.25	56.25	
Call	20	0.25	20.00	
Put	35	1.00	37.80	
Put	20	0.80	17.60	
Call	65	050	65.50	

3. Assume you hold a well-diversified portfolio of common stocks. Under what conditions might you want to hedge it using a stock index option?
   (a) Explain how these options can be used for hedging.
   (b) What happens with your hedged portfolio if the stock market will fall?
   (c) What happens with your hedged portfolio if the stock market will grow?

Appendix

Future value interest factor of `1 per period at i% for n periods, FVIF(i,n).
(The Compound Sum of One Rupee)

Period	1%	2%	3%	4%	5%	6%	7%	8%	9%	10%
1	1.010	1.020	1.030	1.040	1.050	1.060	1.070	1.080	1.090	1.100
2	1.020	1.040	1.061	1.082	1.103	1.124	1.145	1.166	1.188	1.210
3	1.030	1.061	1.093	1.125	1.158	1.191	1.225	1.260	1.295	1.331
4	1.041	1.082	1.126	1.170	1.216	1.262	1.311	1.360	1.412	1.464
5	1.051	1.104	1.159	1.217	1.276	1.338	1.403	1.469	1.539	1.611
6	1.062	1.126	1.194	1.265	1.340	1.419	1.501	1.587	1.677	1.772
7	1.072	1.149	1.230	1.316	1.407	1.504	1.606	1.714	1.828	1.949
8	1.083	1.172	1.267	1.369	1.477	1.594	1.718	1.851	1.993	2.144
9	1.094	1.195	1.305	1.423	1.551	1.689	1.838	1.999	2.172	2.358
10	1.105	1.219	1.344	1.480	1.629	1.791	1.967	2.159	2.367	2.594
11	1.116	1.243	1.384	1.539	1.710	1.898	2.105	2.332	2.580	2.853
12	1.127	1.268	1.426	1.601	1.796	2.012	2.252	2.518	2.813	3.138
13	1.138	1.294	1.469	1.665	1.886	2.133	2.410	2.720	3.066	3.452
14	1.149	1.319	1.513	1.732	1.980	2.261	2.579	2.937	3.342	3.797
15	1.161	1.346	1.558	1.801	2.079	2.397	2.759	3.172	3.642	4.177
16	1.173	1.373	1.605	1.873	2.183	2.540	2.952	3.426	3.970	4.595
17	1.184	1.400	1.653	1.948	2.292	2.693	3.159	3.700	4.328	5.054
18	1.196	1.428	1.702	2.026	2.407	2.854	3.380	3.996	4.717	5.560
19	1.208	1.457	1.754	2.107	2.527	3.026	3.617	4.316	5.142	6.116
20	1.220	1.486	1.806	2.191	2.653	3.207	3.870	4.661	5.604	6.727
25	1.282	1.641	2.094	2.666	3.386	4.292	5.427	6.848	8.623	10.835
30	1.348	1.811	2.427	3.243	4.322	5.743	7.612	10.063	13.268	17.449
35	1.417	2.000	2.814	3.946	5.516	7.686	10.677	14.785	20.414	28.102
40	1.489	2.208	3.262	4.801	7.040	10.286	14.974	21.725	31.409	45.259
50	1.645	2.692	4.384	7.107	11.467	18.420	29.457	46.902	74.358	117.391

Contd.......

Period	11%	12%	13%	14%	15%	16%	17%	18%	19%	20%
1	1.110	1.120	1.130	1.140	1.150	1.160	1.170	1.180	1.190	1.200
2	1.232	1.254	1.277	1.300	1.323	1.346	1.369	1.392	1.416	1.440
3	1.368	1.405	1.443	1.482	1.521	1.561	1.602	1.643	1.685	1.728
4	1.518	1.574	1.630	1.689	1.749	1.811	1.874	1.939	2.005	2.074
5	1.685	1.762	1.842	1.925	2.011	2.100	2.192	2.288	2.386	2.488
6	1.870	1.974	2.082	2.195	2.313	2.436	2.565	2.700	2.840	2.986
7	2.076	2.211	2.353	2.502	2.660	2.826	3.001	3.185	3.379	3.583
8	2.305	2.476	2.658	2.853	3.059	3.278	3.511	3.759	4.021	4.300
9	2.558	2.773	3.004	3.252	3.518	3.803	4.108	4.435	4.785	5.160
10	2.839	3.106	3.395	3.707	4.046	4.411	4.807	5.234	5.695	6.192
11	3.152	3.479	3.836	4.226	4.652	5.117	5.624	6.176	6.777	7.430
12	3.498	3.896	4.335	4.818	5.350	5.936	6.580	7.288	8.064	8.916
13	3.883	4.363	4.898	5.492	6.153	6.886	7.699	8.599	9.596	10.699
14	4.310	4.887	5.535	6.261	7.076	7.988	9.007	10.147	11.420	12.839
15	4.785	5.474	6.254	7.138	8.137	9.266	10.539	11.974	13.590	15.407
16	5.311	6.130	7.067	8.137	9.358	10.748	12.330	14.129	16.172	18.488
17	5.895	6.866	7.986	9.276	10.761	12.468	14.426	16.672	19.244	22.186
18	6.544	7.690	9.024	10.575	12.375	14.463	16.879	19.673	22.901	26.623
19	7.263	8.613	10.197	12.056	14.232	16.777	19.748	23.214	27.252	31.948
20	8.062	9.646	11.523	13.743	16.367	19.461	23.106	27.393	32.429	38.338
25	13.585	17.000	21.23	26.462	32.919	40.874	50.658	62.669	77.388	95.396
30	22.892	29.960	39.116	50.950	66.212	85.850	111.065	143.371	184.675	237.376
35	38.575	52.800	72.069	98.100	133.176	180.314	243.503	327.997	440.701	590.668
40	65.001	93.051	132.782	188.884	267.864	378.721	533.869	750.378	1,051.668	1,469.772
50	184.565	289.002	450.736	700.233	1,083.657	1,670.704	2,566.215	3,927.357	5,988.914	9,100.438

Present value interest factor of Re 1 per period at i% for n periods, PVIF(i,n).

Period	1%	2%	3%	4%	5%	6%	7%	8%	9%	10%
1	0.990	0.980	0.971	0.962	0.952	0.943	0.935	0.926	0.917	0.909
2	0.980	0.961	0.943	0.925	0.907	0.890	0.873	0.857	0.842	0.826
3	0.971	0.942	0.915	0.889	0.864	0.840	0.816	0.794	0.772	0.751
4	0.961	0.924	0.888	0.855	0.823	0.792	0.763	0.735	0.708	0.683
5	0.951	0.906	0.863	0.822	0.784	0.747	0.713	0.681	0.650	0.621
6	0.942	0.888	0.837	0.790	0.746	0.705	0.666	0.630	0.596	0.564
7	0.933	0.871	0.813	0.760	0.711	0.665	0.623	0.583	0.547	0.513
8	0.923	0.853	0.789	0.731	0.677	0.627	0.582	0.540	0.502	0.467
9	0.914	0.837	0.766	0.703	0.645	0.592	0.544	0.500	0.460	0.424
10	0.905	0.820	0.744	0.676	0.614	0.558	0.508	0.463	0.422	0.386
11	0.896	0.804	0.722	0.650	0.585	0.527	0.475	0.429	0.388	0.350
12	0.887	0.788	0.701	0.625	0.557	0.497	0.444	0.397	0.356	0.319
13	0.879	0.773	0.681	0.601	0.530	0.469	0.415	0.368	0.326	0.290
14	0.870	0.758	0.661	0.577	0.505	0.442	0.388	0.340	0.299	0.263
15	0.861	0.743	0.642	0.555	0.481	0.417	0.362	0.315	0.275	0.239
16	0.853	0.728	0.623	0.534	0.458	0.394	0.339	0.292	0.252	0.218
17	0.844	0.714	0.605	0.513	0.436	0.371	0.317	0.270	0.231	0.198
18	0.836	0.700	0.587	0.494	0.416	0.350	0.296	0.250	0.212	0.180
19	0.828	0.686	0.570	0.475	0.396	0.331	0.277	0.232	0.194	0.164
20	0.820	0.673	0.554	0.456	0.377	0.312	0.258	0.215	0.178	0.149
25	0.780	0.610	0.478	0.375	0.295	0.233	0.184	0.146	0.116	0.092
30	0.742	0.552	0.412	0.308	0.231	0.174	0.131	0.099	0.075	0.057
35	0.706	0.500	0.355	0.253	0.181	0.130	0.094	0.068	0.049	0.036
40	0.672	0.453	0.307	0.208	0.142	0.097	0.067	0.046	0.032	0.022
50	0.608	0.372	0.228	0.141	0.087	0.054	0.034	0.021	0.013	0.009

Contd....

Period	11%	12%	13%	14%	15%	16%	17%	18%	19%	20%
1	0.901	0.893	0.885	0.877	0.870	0.862	0.855	0.847	0.840	0.833
2	0.812	0.797	0.783	0.769	0.756	0.743	0.731	0.718	0.706	0.694
3	0.731	0.712	0.693	0.675	0.658	0.641	0.624	0.609	0.593	0.579
4	0.659	0.636	0.613	0.592	0.572	0.552	0.534	0.516	0.499	0.482
5	0.593	0.567	0.543	0.519	0.497	0.476	0.456	0.437	0.419	0.402
6	0.535	0.507	0.480	0.456	0.432	0.410	0.390	0.370	0.352	0.335
7	0.482	0.452	0.425	0.400	0.376	0.354	0.333	0.314	0.296	0.279
8	0.434	0.404	0.376	0.351	0.327	0.305	0.285	0.266	0.249	0.233
9	0.391	0.361	0.333	0.308	0.284	0.263	0.243	0.225	0.209	0.194
10	0.352	0.322	0.295	0.270	0.247	0.227	0.208	0.191	0.176	0.162
11	0.317	0.287	0.261	0.237	0.215	0.195	0.178	0.162	0.148	0.135
12	0.286	0.257	0.231	0.208	0.187	0.168	0.152	0.137	0.124	0.112
13	0.258	0.229	0.204	0.182	0.163	0.145	0.130	0.116	0.104	0.093
14	0.232	0.205	0.181	0.160	0.141	0.125	0.111	0.099	0.088	0.078
15	0.209	0.183	0.160	0.140	0.123	0.108	0.095	0.084	0.074	0.065
16	0.188	0.163	0.141	0.123	0.107	0.093	0.081	0.071	0.062	0.054
17	0.170	0.146	0.125	0.108	0.093	0.080	0.069	0.060	0.052	0.045
18	0.153	0.130	0.111	0.095	0.081	0.069	0.059	0.051	0.044	0.038
19	0.138	0.116	0.098	0.083	0.070	0.060	0.051	0.043	0.037	0.031
20	0.124	0.104	0.087	0.073	0.061	0.051	0.043	0.037	0.031	0.026
25	0.074	0.059	0.047	0.038	0.030	0.024	0.020	0.016	0.013	0.010
30	0.044	0.033	0.026	0.020	0.015	0.012	0.009	0.007	0.005	0.004
35	0.026	0.019	0.014	0.010	0.008	0.006	0.004	0.003	0.002	0.002
40	0.015	0.011	0.008	0.005	0.004	0.003	0.002	0.001	0.001	0.001
50	0.005	0.003	0.002	0.001	0.001	0.001	0.000	0.000	0.000	0.000

Future value interest factor of an ordinary annuity of Re 1 per period at i% for n periods, FVIFA(i,n). (The Compound Value of an Annuity of One Rupee)

Period	1%	2%	3%	4%	5%	6%	7%	8%	9%	10%
1	1.000	1.000	1.000	1.000	1.000	1.000	1.000	1.000	1.000	1.000
2	2.010	2.020	2.030	2.040	2.050	2.060	2.070	2.080	2.090	2.100
3	3.030	3.060	3.091	3.122	3.153	3.184	3.215	3.246	3.278	3.310
4	4.060	4.122	4.184	4.246	4.310	4.375	4.440	4.506	4.573	4.641
5	5.101	5.204	5.309	5.416	5.526	5.637	5.751	5.867	5.985	6.105
6	6.152	6.308	6.468	6.633	6.802	6.975	7.153	7.336	7.523	7.716
7	7.214	7.434	7.662	7.898	8.142	8.394	8.654	8.923	9.200	9.487
8	8.286	8.583	8.892	9.214	9.549	9.897	10.260	10.637	11.028	11.436
9	9.369	9.755	10.159	10.583	11.027	11.491	11.978	12.488	13.021	13.579
10	10.462	10.950	11.464	12.006	12.578	13.181	13.816	14.487	15.193	15.937
11	11.567	12.169	12.808	13.486	14.207	14.972	15.784	16.645	17.560	18.531
12	12.683	13.412	14.192	15.026	15.917	16.870	17.888	18.977	20.141	21.384
13	13.809	14.680	15.618	16.627	17.713	18.882	20.141	21.495	22.953	24.523
14	14.947	15.974	17.086	18.292	19.599	21.015	22.550	24.215	26.019	27.975
15	16.097	17.293	18.599	20.024	21.579	23.276	25.129	27.152	29.361	31.772
16	17.258	18.639	20.157	21.825	23.657	25.673	27.888	30.324	33.003	35.950
17	18.430	20.012	21.762	23.698	25.840	28.213	30.840	33.750	36.974	40.545
18	19.615	21.412	23.414	25.645	28.132	30.906	33.999	37.450	41.301	45.599
19	20.811	22.841	25.117	27.671	30.539	33.760	37.379	41.446	46.018	51.159
20	22.019	24.297	26.870	29.778	33.066	36.786	40.995	45.762	51.160	57.275
25	28.243	32.030	36.459	41.646	47.727	54.865	63.249	73.106	84.701	98.347
30	34.785	40.568	47.575	56.085	66.439	79.058	94.461	113.28	136.31	164.49
35	41.660	49.994	60.462	73.652	90.320	111.43	138.24	172.32	215.71	271.02
40	48.886	60.402	75.401	95.026	120.80	154.76	199.64	259.06	337.88	442.59
50	64.463	84.579	112.80	152.67	209.35	290.34	406.53	573.77	815.08	1,163.9

Contd....

Period	11%	12%	13%	14%	15%	16%	17%	18%	19%	20%
1	1.000	1.000	1.000	1.000	1.000	1.000	1.000	1.000	1.000	1.000
2	2.110	2.120	2.130	2.140	2.150	2.160	2.170	2.180	2.190	2.200
3	3.342	3.374	3.407	3.440	3.473	3.506	3.539	3.572	3.606	3.640
4	4.710	4.779	4.850	4.921	4.993	5.066	5.141	5.215	5.291	5.368
5	6.228	6.353	6.480	6.610	6.742	6.877	7.014	7.154	7.297	7.442
6	7.913	8.115	8.323	8.536	8.754	8.977	9.207	9.442	9.683	9.930
7	9.783	10.089	10.405	10.730	11.067	11.414	11.772	12.142	12.523	12.916
8	11.859	12.300	12.757	13.233	13.727	14.240	14.773	15.327	15.902	16.499
9	14.164	14.776	15.416	16.085	16.786	17.519	18.285	19.086	19.923	20.799
10	16.722	17.549	18.420	19.337	20.304	21.321	22.393	23.521	24.709	25.959
11	19.561	20.655	21.814	23.045	24.349	25.733	27.200	28.755	30.404	32.150
12	22.713	24.133	25.650	27.271	29.002	30.850	32.824	34.931	37.180	39.581
13	26.212	28.029	29.985	32.089	34.352	36.786	39.404	42.219	45.244	48.497
14	30.095	32.393	34.883	37.581	40.505	43.672	47.103	50.818	54.841	59.196
15	34.405	37.280	40.417	43.842	47.580	51.660	56.110	60.965	66.261	72.035
16	39.190	42.753	46.672	50.980	55.717	60.925	66.649	72.939	79.850	87.442
17	44.501	48.884	53.739	59.118	65.075	71.673	78.979	87.068	96.022	105.93
18	50.396	55.750	61.725	68.394	75.836	84.141	93.406	103.74	115.27	128.12
19	56.939	63.440	70.749	78.969	88.212	98.603	110.28	123.41	138.17	154.74
20	64.203	72.052	80.947	91.025	102.44	115.38	130.03	146.63	165.42	186.69
25	114.41	133.33	155.62	181.87	212.79	249.21	292.10	342.60	402.04	471.98
30	199.02	241.33	293.20	356.79	434.75	530.31	647.44	790.95	966.71	1,181.9
35	341.59	431.66	546.68	693.57	881.17	1,120.7	1,426.5	1,816.7	2,314.2	2,948.3
40	581.83	767.09	1,013.7	1,342.0	1,779.1	2,360.8	3,134.5	4,163.2	5,529.8	7,343.9
50	1,668.8	2,400.0	3,459.5	4,994.5	7,217.7	10,436	15,090	21,813	31,515	45,497

Present value interest factor of an (ordinary) annuity of Re 1 per period at i% for n periods, PVIFA(i,n).

Period	1%	2%	3%	4%	5%	6%	7%	8%	9%	10%
1	0.990	0.980	0.971	0.962	0.952	0.943	0.935	0.926	0.917	0.909
2	1.970	1.942	1.913	1.886	1.859	1.833	1.808	1.783	1.759	1.736
3	2.941	2.884	2.829	2.775	2.723	2.673	2.624	2.577	2.531	2.487
4	3.902	3.808	3.717	3.630	3.546	3.465	3.387	3.312	3.240	3.170
5	4.853	4.713	4.580	4.452	4.329	4.212	4.100	3.993	3.890	3.791
6	5.795	5.601	5.417	5.242	5.076	4.917	4.767	4.623	4.486	4.355
7	6.728	6.472	6.230	6.002	5.786	5.582	5.389	5.206	5.033	4.868
8	7.652	7.325	7.020	6.733	6.463	6.210	5.971	5.747	5.535	5.335
9	8.566	8.162	7.786	7.435	7.108	6.802	6.515	6.247	5.995	5.759
10	9.471	8.983	8.530	8.111	7.722	7.360	7.024	6.710	6.418	6.145
11	10.368	9.787	9.253	8.760	8.306	7.887	7.499	7.139	6.805	6.495
12	11.255	10.575	9.954	9.385	8.863	8.384	7.943	7.536	7.161	6.814
13	12.134	11.348	10.635	9.986	9.394	8.853	8.358	7.904	7.487	7.103
14	13.004	12.106	11.296	10.563	9.899	9.295	8.745	8.244	7.786	7.367
15	13.865	12.849	11.938	11.118	10.380	9.712	9.108	8.559	8.061	7.606
16	14.718	13.578	12.561	11.652	10.838	10.106	9.447	8.851	8.313	7.824
17	15.562	14.292	13.166	12.166	11.274	10.477	9.763	9.122	8.544	8.022
18	16.398	14.992	13.754	12.659	11.690	10.828	10.059	9.372	8.756	8.201
19	17.226	15.678	14.324	13.134	12.085	11.158	10.336	9.604	8.950	8.365
20	18.046	16.351	14.877	13.590	12.462	11.470	10.594	9.818	9.129	8.514
25	22.023	19.523	17.413	15.622	14.094	12.783	11.654	10.675	9.823	9.077
30	25.808	22.396	19.600	17.292	15.372	13.765	12.409	11.258	10.274	9.427
35	29.409	24.999	21.487	18.665	16.374	14.498	12.948	11.655	10.567	9.644
40	32.835	27.355	23.115	19.793	17.159	15.046	13.332	11.925	10.757	9.779
50	39.196	31.424	25.730	21.482	18.256	15.762	13.801	12.233	10.962	9.915

Contd....

Period	11%	12%	13%	14%	15%	16%	17%	18%	19%	20%
1	0.901	0.893	0.885	0.877	0.870	0.862	0.855	0.847	0.840	0.833
2	1.713	1.690	1.668	1.647	1.626	1.605	1.585	1.566	1.547	1.528
3	2.444	2.402	2.361	2.322	2.283	2.246	2.210	2.174	2.140	2.106
4	3.102	3.037	2.974	2.914	2.855	2.798	2.743	2.690	2.639	2.589
5	3.696	3.605	3.517	3.433	3.352	3.274	3.199	3.127	3.058	2.991
6	4.231	4.111	3.998	3.889	3.784	3.685	3.589	3.498	3.410	3.326
7	4.712	4.564	4.423	4.288	4.160	4.039	3.922	3.812	3.706	3.605
8	5.146	4.968	4.799	4.639	4.487	4.344	4.207	4.078	3.954	3.837
9	5.537	5.328	5.132	4.946	4.772	4.607	4.451	4.303	4.163	4.031
10	5.889	5.650	5.426	5.216	5.019	4.833	4.659	4.494	4.339	4.192
11	6.207	5.938	5.687	5.453	5.234	5.029	4.836	4.656	4.486	4.327
12	6.492	6.194	5.918	5.660	5.421	5.197	4.988	4.793	4.611	4.439
13	6.750	6.424	6.122	5.842	5.583	5.342	5.118	4.910	4.715	4.533
14	6.982	6.628	6.302	6.002	5.724	5.468	5.229	5.008	4.802	4.611
15	7.191	6.811	6.462	6.142	5.847	5.575	5.324	5.092	4.876	4.675
16	7.379	6.974	6.604	6.265	5.954	5.668	5.405	5.162	4.938	4.730
17	7.549	7.120	6.729	6.373	6.047	5.749	5.475	5.222	4.990	4.775
18	7.702	7.250	6.840	6.467	6.128	5.818	5.534	5.273	5.033	4.812
19	7.839	7.366	6.938	6.550	6.198	5.877	5.584	5.316	5.070	4.843
20	7.963	7.469	7.025	6.623	6.259	5.929	5.628	5.353	5.101	4.870
25	8.422	7.843	7.330	6.873	6.464	6.097	5.766	5.467	5.195	4.948
30	8.694	8.055	7.496	7.003	6.566	6.177	5.829	5.517	5.235	4.979
35	8.855	8.176	7.586	7.070	6.617	6.215	5.858	5.539	5.251	4.992
40	8.951	8.244	7.634	7.105	6.642	6.233	5.871	5.548	5.258	4.997
50	9.042	8.304	7.675	7.133	6.661	6.246	5.880	5.554	5.262	4.999

www.ingramcontent.com/pod-product-compliance
Lightning Source LLC
Chambersburg PA
CBHW080935240926
51849CB00004BA/462
* 9 7 8 9 3 4 9 5 6 2 5 7 8 *